Lecture Notes of the Institute for Computer Sciences, Social Informatics and Telecommunications Engineering

660

The LNICST series publishes ICST's conferences, symposia and workshops.

LNICST reports state-of-the-art results in areas related to the scope of the Institute.

The type of material published includes

- Proceedings (published in time for the respective event)
- Other edited monographs (such as project reports or invited volumes)

LNICST topics span the following areas:

- General Computer Science
- E-Economy
- E-Medicine
- Knowledge Management
- Multimedia
- Operations, Management and Policy
- Social Informatics
- Systems

Bouziane Brik · Shah Nazir
Editors

Application of Big Data, Blockchain, and Internet of Things for Education Informatization

4th EAI International Conference, BigIoT-EDU 2024
Beihai, China, August 18–20, 2024
Proceedings, Part III

Editors
Bouziane Brik
University of Sharjah
Sharjah, United Arab Emirates

Shah Nazir
University of Swabi
Khyber Pakhtunkhwa, Pakistan

ISSN 1867-8211 ISSN 1867-822X (electronic)
Lecture Notes of the Institute for Computer Sciences, Social Informatics and Telecommunications Engineering
ISBN 978-3-032-18627-0 ISBN 978-3-032-18628-7 (eBook)
https://doi.org/10.1007/978-3-032-18628-7

This Springer imprint is published by the registered company Springer Nature Switzerland AG
The registered company address is: Gewerbestrasse 11, 6330 Cham, Switzerland

Preface

We are delighted to introduce the proceedings of the Fourth edition of the European Alliance for Innovation (EAI) International Conference on Application of BigData, Blockchain, and Internet of Things for Education Informatization (BigIoT-EDU 2024), held online on August 18–20, 2024. It aimed to provide an international cooperation and exchange platform for big data and information education experts, scholars and enterprise developers to share research results, discuss existing problems and challenges, and explore cutting-edge science and technology. The conference focuses on research fields such as digital education, smart classrooms, Massive Open Online Courses (MOOCs) and advanced integrated technologies for education. The use of Artificial Intelligence (AI) lies at the heart of this conference as we focused on these emerging technologies to accelerate the progress of Big Data and information education. In total, EAI BigIoT-EDU 2024 attracted 669 submissions. Upon rigorous review, only 271 papers were accepted for publication. Thus, the overall acceptance ratio of this conference is just over 40%. Each paper received a minimum of three reviews in a double-blind process.

It was a great pleasure to work with such an excellent organizing committee team for their hard work in organizing and supporting the conference. In particular, the Technical Program Committee, led by our TPC Chair, Hazrat Bilal, completed the peer-review process of technical papers and made a high-quality technical program. We are also grateful to Conference Manager Ivana Bujdakova for her constant support along with the whole of the EAI team involved during the conference. We must say that they have been wonderful and it is always a pleasant experience to work with them. Also, we would like to thank all the authors who submitted their papers to the EAI BigIoT-EDU 2024 conference.

We strongly believe that BigIoT-EDU provides a good forum for all researchers, developers and practitioners to discuss all science and technology aspects that are relevant to Big Data and Information Education. We also expect that future BigIoT-EDU conferences will be as successful and stimulating, as indicated by the contributions presented in this volume.

Bouziane Brik
Shah Nazir

Organization

Organizing Committee

General Chair

Zhang Yinjun	Guangxi Science & Technology Normal University, China

Program Chairs

Bouziane Brik	University of Sharjah, United Arab Emirates
Shah Nazir	University of Swabi, Pakistan

Technical Program Committee Co-chair

Hazrat Bilal	University of Science and Technology of China, China

Web Chairs

Islam Uddin	Abdul Wali Khan University Mardan, Pakistan
Li Anning	Guangxi Normal University of Science and Technology, China

Publicity and Social Media Chair

Mengji Chen	Hechi University, China

Workshops Chair

Rahim Khan	Abdul Wali Khan University Mardan, Pakistan

Sponsorship and Exhibits Chair

Lan Zimian	Harbin Institute of Technology, China

Publications Chair

Yar Muhammad	Beihang University, China

Panels Chair

Kong Linxiang	Hefei University of Technology, China

Tutorials Chair

Wei Rongchang	Guangxi Normal University of Science and Technology, China

Demos Chair

Ryan Alturki	Umm al-Qura University, Saudi Arabia

Posters and PhD Track Chairs

Mengji Chen	Guangxi Science & Technology Normal University, China
Ateeq ur Rehman	University of Haripur, Pakistan

Local Chairs

Huang Yufei	Hechi Normal University, China
Wan Haoran	Hechi Normal University, China

Technical Program Committee

Hashim Ali	Abdul Wali Khan University Mardan, Pakistan
Sohail Abbas	University of Sharjah, United Arab Emirates
Bouziane Brik	University of Sharjah, United Arab Emirates
Adil Khan Kakakhel	Abdul Wali Khan University Mardan, Pakistan
Mian Abdullah Jan	Ton Duc Thang University, Vietnam
Muhammad Bilal	Virtual University of Pakistan, Pakistan
Shaher Slehat	University of Technology Sydney, Australia
Xiangjian He	University of Technology Sydney, Australia
Farman Khan	Bacha Khan University Charsadda, Pakistan
Zia Ur Rehman	Bacha Khan University Charsadda, Pakistan

Contents

Application of Network Platform in Intelligence Education

Application of Model in Intelligence Education

Construction of Comprehensive Quality Evaluation Model of College Undergraduate Education Based on Convolution Neural Network

Lifeng Liu[1](✉) and Mengge Ji[2]

[1] School of Innovation and Entrepreneurship, Pingdingshan University, Pingdingshan, Henan, China
1198051775@qq.com

[2] Ruzhou Vocational and Technical College, Pingdingshan, Henan, China

Abstract. Educational evaluation is the main content of comprehensive evaluation in undergraduate schools, which involves many indicators, including teaching conditions, teaching effects, students' learning interest and knowledge conversion rate. Therefore, comprehensive analysis is needed with the help of intelligent analysis methods. This paper puts forward the capital index of education evaluation, and makes logical construction and analysis of it. Either way, this content has become the focus of research. The process of teaching evaluation is a dynamic process, and the data involved are multi-index data. Moreover, the comprehensive activities of students, teachers and third-party evaluation are realized, and the design content is relatively large, so it is necessary to make logical judgment with the help of intelligent analysis methods. Next, a convolution neural network assessment model building method is developed using neural network theory. The outcomes of this model creation are then thoroughly examined and assessed. According to the results of the MATLAB simulations, when comparing the convolution neural network and the traditional particle swarm algorithm for assessing the accuracy and time required to evaluate the factors influencing model construction, the convolution neural network comes out on top under specific evaluation criteria.

Keywords: Neural network theory · Convolution neural networks · Evaluate model building · Universities · Undergraduate · Education

1 Introduction

An integral aspect of high-quality undergraduate education is the development of assessment models, which allow for more precise control over evaluation model building and, therefore, shorter turnaround times. However, in the process [1] of evaluation model construction, the evaluation model construction scheme [2] has the problem [3] of poor accuracy, which brings certain negative effects to the evaluation model construction [4].

B. Brik and S. Nazir (Eds.): BigIoT-EDU 2024, LNICST 660, pp. 3–13, 2026.
https://doi.org/10.1007/978-3-032-18628-7_2

In order to properly analyze the evaluation model construction scheme and offer corresponding support for the evaluation model construction [5], some researchers think that convolutional neural networks applied to the analysis of evaluation model construction [6] can be useful. To improve the assessment model building scheme and confirm the model's efficacy, this study suggests a convolution neural [7] network. First, collect data for teaching evaluation, and realize the logical collection and integration of data of teaching content, students' learning interest and practice transformation [8]. Carry out intelligent analysis on it to form effective data results. And output the final result. The whole result is shown in Fig. 1.

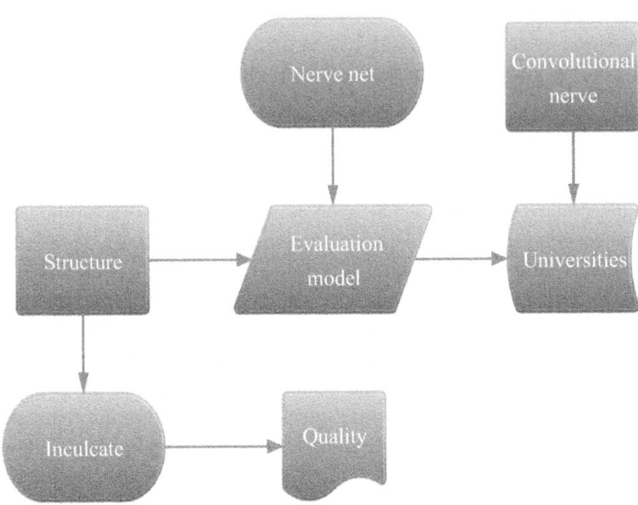

Fig. 1. Evaluate the analysis process of model building

2 Related Works

A. Comprehensive Quality Evaluation Model

The evaluation model building scheme of multilayer neural network, which is comprised of the particle swarm method, is more in line with the real evaluation model construction needs [9]. Convolution neural networks outperform particle swarm methods when it comes to assessing the correctness and rationale of model development [10]. Information that is not structural nor semi-structural, as well as information that is structural, make up the assessment model construction scheme. Speed, precision, and stability of summation are all improved in the convolution neural network during assessment model development.

B. Convolution Neural Network (CNN)

To optimize the evaluation model's development, the convolutional neural network uses a stochastic optimization technique and tweaks the parameters according to online data

[11]. The convolutional neural network uses a tiered approach to evaluate model creation, picking out several strategies at random. Evaluating and optimizing the evaluation model development scheme with varying degrees of evaluation model creation is an iterative process. The evaluation model construction level of many schemes is compiled once the optimization analysis is finished, and the best evaluation model construction is recorded [12, 13]. Convolutional neural networks outperform particle swarm algorithms in terms of assessment model building for general outcomes.To guarantee the safe recording and storage of findings, convolution neural networks may be used to provide a decentralized platform for data storage and administration. Convolutional neural networks allow for the creation of unique identifiers for each and the recording of important data and schemes.

3 Evaluate the Optimization Strategy of Model Construction

3.1 Mathematical Description of Convolution Neural Networks

By using computer technology, a convolutional neural network (CNN) may optimize the evaluation model construction scheme. This optimization is done in accordance with the index parameters used in the evaluation model development. It is discovered that while building the evaluation model, the unqualified value parameters is, and the evaluation model construction scheme is Eq. (1) shows the computation that is combined with the function to determine the evaluation model building feasibility.

$$\lim_{x}(y_i \cdot t_{ij}) = \sqrt{b_j - ac} \geq \max(t_{ij}) \tag{1}$$

The evaluation of education and teaching should be analyzed based on the final and maximum data values. Therefore, the final result and maximum output value of educational evaluation are shown in Formula 2.

$$\max(t_i) = \sum_{i=1}^{n}(t_i^2 + 2) > mean\left(\sum t_{ij} + 4\right) \tag{2}$$

To increase the accuracy of assessment model construction, convolutional neural networks integrate computer technology's benefits with evaluation model building's quantification.

What if I were to Things needed to assess model building is, the evaluation model construction scheme is,the approach for building the evaluation model is satisfied is, alongside the assessment model building scheme's judging function is as shown in Eq. (3).

$$F(d_i) = \sum_{i=1}^{n} t \cap \xi \geq \oint y_i \tag{3}$$

3.2 Evaluate the Choice of Model Construction Scheme

Second Hypothesis: A function for building assessment models is and the weight coefficient is, consequently, as shown in Eq. (4), building the unqualified evaluation model is necessary for the evaluation model development.

$$g(t_i) = \prod (F(d_i) - w_i) \tag{4}$$

The complete function that the evaluation model constructs may be derived from assumptions I and II, as illustrated in Eq. (5).

$$g(t_i) + F(d_i) \leq \max\left[\sum_{i=1}^{n} t_i^2\right] \tag{5}$$

Standardizing all data is essential for improving the efficacy of assessing the trustworthiness of model creation; Eq. (6) shows the outcomes.

$$\widetilde{g(t_i) + F}(d_i) \neq \min\left(\sum t_i \pm 4\right) \tag{6}$$

3.3 Analysis of Evaluation Model Construction Schemes

It is imperative to conduct a comprehensive analysis of the evaluation model construction scheme prior to the implementation of the convolution neural network. The evaluation model building specifications should be mapped to the evaluation emulate development library, and the unqualified evaluation model construction scheme should be eliminated. The anomaly evaluation scheme can be proposed in accordance with Eq. (6), and the results are illustrated in Eq. (7).

$$UI(y) = \lim_{\delta x \to 0} \frac{\delta y}{\delta y'} + \sum_{i=1}^{n} y^2 \tag{7}$$

Among them, it is said that the plan must be put forth in order to avoid the need of integrating the plan, and the outcome is shown in Eq. (8).

$$Zh(x_i) = n + \lim_{x \to \infty} \frac{\partial^2 \Omega}{\partial v^2} + \sum_{i=1}^{n} x_i^2 \tag{8}$$

In order to guarantee the convolution neural network's correctness, the evaluation model architecture is carefully examined, and its threshold and index weights are adjusted. The evaluation model building scheme need a thorough analysis as it is a systematic test evaluation model. If the development of the assessment model is given a non regular distribution, the model of assessment construction scheme will be influenced, affecting the accuracy of a general assessment model construction, and the outcome of the calculations is shown in Eq. (9).

$$accur(x_i) = x_i + \frac{\max[\sum \widetilde{g(A_i) + F}(x_i)]}{\sum \widetilde{g(A_i) + F}(x_i)\cdot} \tag{9}$$

A multi-dimensional distribution is produced by the evaluation model construction scheme, which is consistent with the objective facts, according to the survey and evaluation model building scheme. It is considered a highly analytical research since the evaluation model construction is not directed, which indicates that the evaluation model building method has great unpredictability. In the event when the assessment model's generated random function is, then Eq. (10). This allows us to state the computation of Eq. (9).

$$Yi(x_i) = \frac{\min[\sum g(\widetilde{A_i) + F}(x_i)]}{n} + \sum g(A_i) \widetilde{+ F}(x_i) \cdot \frac{1}{10} \tag{10}$$

In this regard, the evaluation model construction satisfies typical standards; more specifically, computer technology modifies the evaluation model construction, eliminates redundant and unneeded schemes, and augments the default scheme, resulting in a robust dynamic correlation throughout every stage of the model build scheme.

4 Results and Discussion

4.1 Introduction to the Construction of Evaluation Models

With a 12-h testing period, 12 possible pathways, and an evaluation model building in difficult circumstances as the study goal, we can make the evaluation model development process easier (Table 1).

Table 1. Evaluate model building requirements

Scope of application	Grade	Precision	Evaluate model building
Assessment of teaching quality	I	85.00	78.86
	II	81.97	78.45
Assessment of learning outcomes	I	83.81	81.31
	II	83.34	78.19
Educational environment assessment	I	79.56	81.99
	II	79.10	80.11

Figure 2 shows that the evaluation model building technique was changed, revealing that the convolution neural network had greater accuracy and dependability.

4.2 Evaluate Model Construction

Following the pre-selection of a convolution neural network, we first acquire a preliminary assessment model building scheme and test its viability. Table 2 shows the evaluation model construction scheme that was used to more precisely validate the evaluation model construction impact. The scheme was constructed using evaluation model construction levels that were chosen at various intervals.

Table 2 Case data of educational evaluation

Category	Learning effect	Teaching needs	Pedagogical data collection
Assessment of teaching quality	5.66	8.95	11.85
Assessment of learning outcomes	86.36	82.51	84.29
Educational environment assessment	84.16	84.92	83.68

4.3 Evaluation of Model Construction and Stability

The convolution neural network's correctness is checked using the evaluation model construction method, which is shown in Fig. 2, and it is structured around the particle swarm technique.

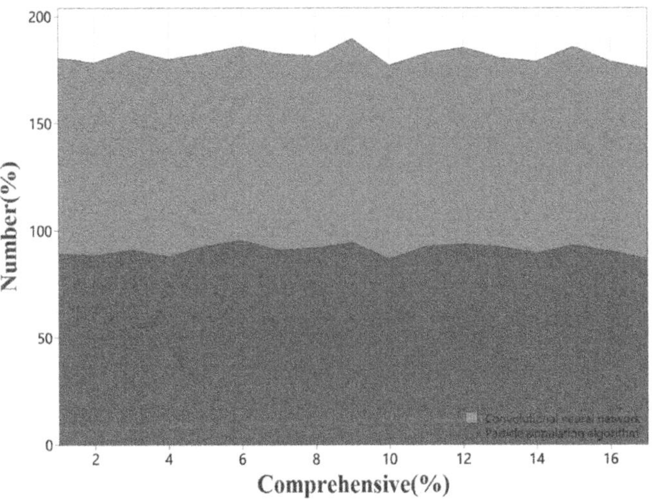

Fig. 2. Construction of evaluation models for different algorithms

Figure 2 shows that compared to the particle Swarm algorithm, the convolution neural network has a higher evaluation model development but a lower error rate. This suggests that the convolution neural network's evaluation model construction is relatively stable, in contrast to the particle swarm algorithm's uneven evaluation model construction. You can see the three algorithms' average assessment model creation schemes in Table 3.

Table 3. Multidimensional data judgment of teaching quality

Algorithm	The comprehensive logical relationship of teaching content	The compliance rate of actual teaching effect	Physical teaching content	Comprehensive teaching analysis
Convolution neural networks	85.33	85.15	82.88	84.95
Particle swarm arithmetics	85.20	83.41	86.01	85.75
P	87.17	87.62	84.48	86.97

Table 3 shows that there are certain issues with the correctness of the assessment models constructed using the particle swarm approach. Specifically, there are a lot of changes and a high error rate in these models. Simultaneously, the accuracy is unchanged, and the assessment model development of the convolution neural network is above 90%. Just to be sure that convolution neural networks are the best. Figure 3 shows the results of several approaches used for general convolutional neural network analysis, which helps to further confirm the efficacy of the suggested strategy.

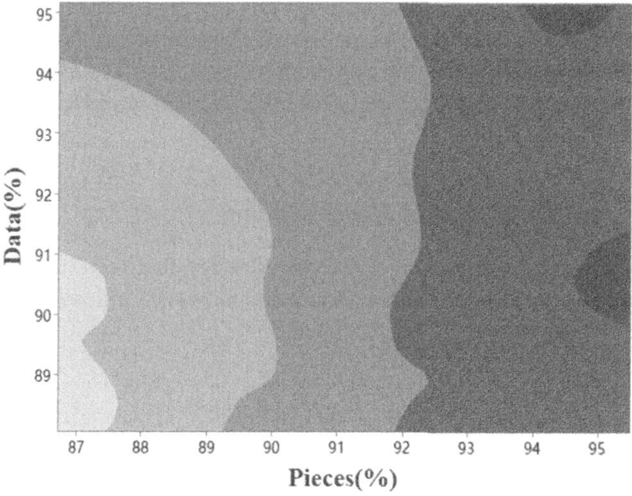

Fig. 3. Evaluation model construction of convolution neural network

Figure 3 shows that compared to the particle swarm algorithm, the convolution neural network's evaluation model construction is far superior. This is because the convolution neural network raises the adjustment coefficient, establishes the threshold for Internet information, and gets rid of evaluation model construction schemes that don't measure up.

4.4 Evaluate the Rationality of Model Construction

In Fig. 4, we can see the evaluation model creation scheme that uses the particle swarm approach to check the convolution neural network's correctness.

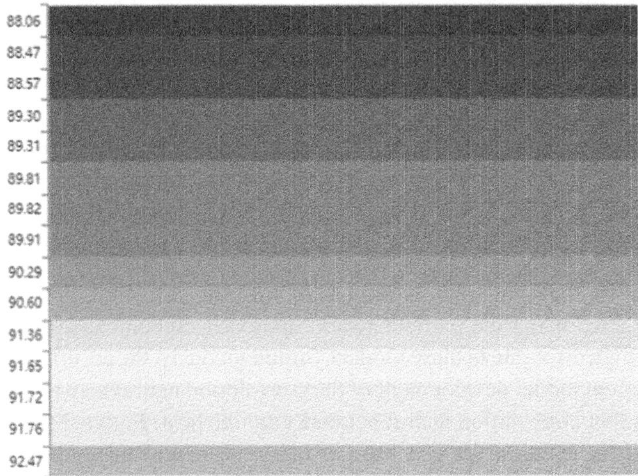

Fig. 4. Construction of evaluation models for different algorithms

Figure 4 shows that compared to the swarm particle algorithm, the convolution neural network's rationality in constructing evaluation models is superior, and that further improvements to the convolution neural network's evaluation model construction can further increase its rationality.

4.5 Evaluate the Effectiveness of Model Building

Figure 5 shows the assessment model creation strategy that takes use of the particle swarm technique to confirm the convolution neural network's efficacy.

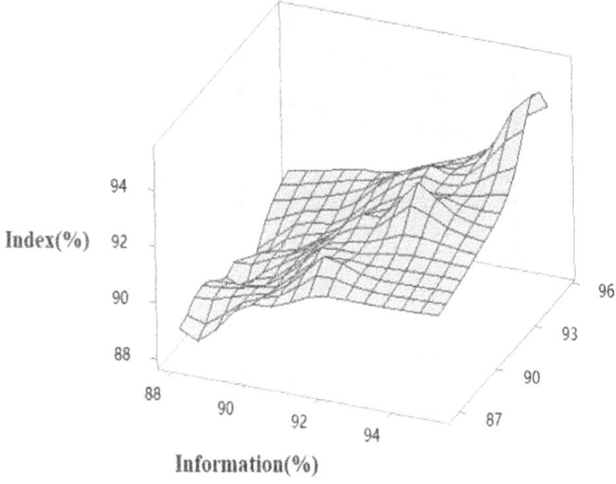

Fig. 5. Construction of evaluation models for different algorithms

Figure 5 shows that compared to the particle swarm algorithm, the convolution neural network has a higher evaluation model building complexity but a lower error rate. This suggests that the convolution neural network's evaluation model construction is relatively stable, in contrast to the particle swarm algorithm's uneven evaluation model construction. The demand of teaching and the overall judgment result of teaching.

Table 4. Analysis of comprehensive demand and judgment in teaching

Algorithm	Satisfaction rate of teaching content	The learning effect is improved	Comprehensive content of learning	Conversion rate of teaching effectiveness
Convolution neural networks	82.21	85.92	84.59	82.85
Particle swarm arithmetics	83.73	84.23	84.41	83.55

Table 4 shows that there are issues with the particle swarm algorithm's accuracy when it comes to building assessment models. There are a lot of modifications in the development of the models and a high mistake rate. Convolutional neural networks outperform particle swarm algorithms in terms of assessment model building for general outcomes. Simultaneously, the accuracy is unchanged, and the assessment model development of the convolution neural network is above 90%. Just to be sure that convolution neural networks are the best. Various approaches are used to conduct the general analysis of convolution neural networks, as illustrated in Fig. 6, in order to further validate the efficiency of the suggested method.

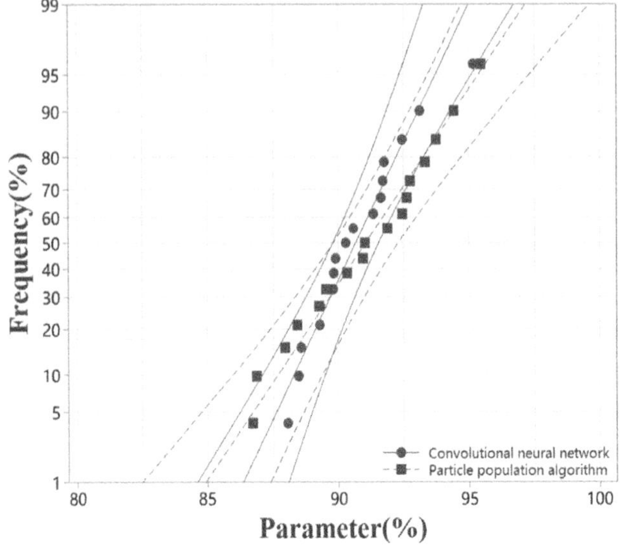

Fig. 6. Convolution neural network evaluation model construction

Figure 6 shows that compared to the particle swarm algorithm, its convolution neural network's evaluation construction of models is significantly better. This is because the convolution neural network's method sets the threshold for Internet information, increases the adjustment coefficient of evaluation model construction.

5 Conclusion

This research presents a convolution neural network and uses computer technology to improve. All the while, we build the Internet information collection and conduct a thorough analysis of the assessment model's correctness and dependability. The results demonstrate that the convolutional neural network is capable of broad evaluation model creation and may enhance the accuracy of evaluation model development. The selection of indicators for assessment model development becomes unreasonable due to the excessive focus on analysis throughout the convolution neural network procedure.

References

1. Chen, K., Liu, L., Li, X., Zhang, Y., Wang, Y., Li, X., et al.: A method for constructing a bypass analysis model based on convolutional neural networks CN202210174108.7 (2023)
2. Wen, L., Hu, X., Liang, D., Lin, M., Liu, T., Wang, S.: Construction of a model for artificial intelligence localization and diagnosis of ventricular premature contractions in the outflow tract based on convolutional neural networks. Lingnan J. Cardiovasc. Dis. **2**, 028 (2022)
3. Chen, L., Zhang, Y.: Rice pest and disease identification based on improved deep convolutional neural network. Shandong Agric. Sci. (2023)
4. Lu, P., Liu, K., Zou, G., Wang, Z., Zheng, Z.: Reference free image quality evaluation based on multi feature fusion and convolutional neural networks. LCD Display (037-001) (2022)

5. Lei, W., Li, Z., Rui, D., Zhang, M., Guo, Y., Pai, W., et al.: The application of convolutional neural networks in automatic diagnosis of acute myeloid leukemia using flow cytometry J. Anhui Med. Univ. (2023)
6. Wang, T., Yang, K.: A fast automatic environmental quality evaluation method based on convolutional neural networks. CN202211066087.3 (2022)
7. Bu, Y., Tea, X., Zhu, J., Su, Y., Lai, D.: A deep convolutional neural network based automatic detection model for hypertrophic cardiomyopathy. J. Biomed. Eng. **39**(2), 8 (2022)
8. Wang, H., Song, D., Wang, B., Dai, S.: A fault zone extraction method based on 3D convolutional neural network combined with pointsift. Prog. Laser Optoelectron. **60** (24) (2023)
9. Kong, Q.: Convolutional neural network data intelligent identification system. CN116389903A (2023)
10. Cai, Q., Wang, J., Li, H., Mao, D.: Research on the construction of a food safety evaluation model based on neural networks. J. Food Sci. Technol. (1) (2022)
11. Wang, B., Zheng, S., Li, P., Xiao, H.: An online teaching quality evaluation method based on the concept of diversified evaluation subjects and convolutional neural networks Modern. Electron. Technol. **46**(8), 91–98 (2023)
12. Hao, L., Zhao, X.: Prediction of body fat ratio for college male students based on convolutional neural networks. Liaoning Sports Technol. **44**(5), 76–84 (2022)
13. Jiang, W., Chen, G., Meng, X., Zhang, Y., Zeng, R., Yue, D., et al.: Evaluation of regional landslide sensitivity based on convolutional neural network model—taking the Sichuan Tibet railway as an example. J. Lanzhou Univ. Nat. Sci. Ed. (002), 058 (2022)

Combined with the Support Vector Machine Algorithm, the Construction of Student Learning Style Classification and Teaching Strategy Recommendation Model

Haotian Liu[1](✉) and Jie Wu[2]

[1] School of Marxism, Chongqing Medical College, Chongqing, China
10352@cqmpc.edu.cn
[2] School of Medical Technology, Chongqing Medical College, Chongqing, China

Abstract. Students have various learning styles, but they can be trained and analyzed. How to effectively classify students' styles and better divide them is the main content of the research process and also a means of teaching essence. This is vector product, which can optimize existing learning content and styles through different assignments and vector analysis of students' personalities. I proposed support vector machine to classify students' learning styles, and found that its recognition accuracy is over 90%, and the conditions for style and classification are over 20%. Therefore, this is a limited machine that can comprehensively manage students' learning classification work, promote their level improvement, and support vector machine has an important supportive role in students' operation process, which can simplify the process of data processing. Enhance the recognition rate of students' learning styles, provide support for proposing better teaching strategies and optimizing existing teaching content and strategies. Linear sensors can deeply explore and analyze students' learning methods, judge their rationality and effectiveness, and provide balanced knowledge for teachers and strategy development.

Keywords: Statistical learning theory · Combined with support vector machine algorithms · Recommended model building · Students · Learning style · Classification

1 Introduction

The traditional educational model has gradually exposed its inherent limitations, such as uneven distribution of teaching resources, single teaching methods, and difficulty in realizing personalized teaching [1, 2]. These problems not only affect students' learning effect, but also restrict the improvement of education quality [3, 4]. Under this background, using advanced technical means, especially machine learning algorithms, to optimize the educational process and improve the teaching effect has become one of the hot spots in current educational research [5, 6]. Students' learning style is one

B. Brik and S. Nazir (Eds.): BigIoT-EDU 2024, LNICST 660, pp. 14–24, 2026.
https://doi.org/10.1007/978-3-032-18628-7_3

of the important factors affecting the learning effect. Different students show different preferences and habits in the learning process, and these differences need to be fully considered in the teaching process [7]. Traditional teaching methods are often difficult to meet the needs of all students, while personalized teaching strategies can better adapt to the characteristics of each student and improve learning efficiency and effect [8]. Therefore, how to identify students' learning styles through scientific methods and recommend appropriate teaching strategies according to their learning styles has become an important topic of educational research [9, 10].

2 Related Concepts

2.1 The Combined with Support Vector Machine Algorithms Is Described Mathematically

Field dependence-field independence: Students with field dependence rely on external environmental cues, while students with field independence are better at analyzing problems independently. Relevant data can be obtained by some specific tests, such as the mosaic test, as one of the features is y_i found that the unqualified value parameters in the construction of recommendation model is z_i, and the construction of recommendation model scheme is $tol\left(y_i \cdot t_{ij}\right)$, which is shown in Eq. (1).

$$\lim_{x \to \infty} \left(y_i \cdot t_{ij}\right) = \frac{\partial^2 \Omega}{\partial v^2} y_{ij} \geq \max(t_{ij} \div 2) \tag{1}$$

Contemplative students think longer and have higher accuracy when answering questions; Impulsive students respond quickly but may be slightly less accurate is outliers among them (2).

$$\max(t_{ij}) = \partial\left(t_{ij}^2 + 2 \cdot t_{ij}\right) \succ \frac{dy}{dx} \tag{2}$$

Characteristics can be determined by observing how quickly and accurately students respond when answering questions or completing assignments in class is set_i, the technique for satisfying the construction of recommendation model is y_i, which is as shown by Eq. (3).

$$F(d_i) = \frac{\Delta y}{\Delta x} \sum t_i \cap \xi \cdot \sqrt{2} \to \oint y_i \cdot 7 \tag{3}$$

2.2 Selection of Construction of Recommendation Model Scheme

Such students are more sensitive to visual information such as images and diagrams. It can be characterized by the data of students' attention to visual materials, memory effects and so on in the learning process is $g(t_i)$, The weighting factor is w_i, is thus required by the construction of recommendation model (4).

$$g(t_i) = \ddot{x} \cdot z_i \prod F(d_i) \frac{dy}{dx} - w_i \Phi \tag{4}$$

Tending to acquire knowledge by listening to lectures. For example, you can count data such as students' concentration and understanding when listening to lectures or audio learning materials is shown in Eq. (5).

$$\lim_{x \to \infty} g(t_i) + \ddot{x}F(d_i) \leq \cap \max(t_{ij}) \tag{5}$$

Kinesthetic students learn better through physical movement and practical operation. Features can be extracted from performance in activities such as experimental courses, crafting, and so on in Eq. (6).

$$g(t_i) + F(d_i) \leftrightarrow \frac{dy}{dx}\left(\sum t_{ij} + 4\right) \tag{6}$$

2.3 Analysis of Construction of Recommendation Model Scheme

The anomaly assessment system may be given using Eq. (6), and the outcomes is $No(t_i)$ shown in Eq. (7).

$$No(t_i) = \frac{g(t_i) + F(d_i)}{mean(\sum t_{ij} + 4)}\sqrt{b^2 - 4ac} \tag{7}$$

Among them, it is $\frac{g(t_i)+F(d_i)}{mean(\sum t_{ij}+4)} \leq 1$ specified that the scheme must be $Zh(t_i)$, suggested; otherwise, the scheme integration is necessary; the outcome is illustrated in Eq. (8).

$$Zh(t_i) = \lim_{x \to \infty}\left[\sum g(t_i) + F(d_i)\right] \lim_{x \to \infty} \Gamma \tag{8}$$

External motivation: Students with strong internal motivation pay more attention to their own interests and self-improvement; Students with strong external motivation are greatly influenced by external factors such as rewards and achievements, lowering the total construction of recommendation model's accuracy, as stated in Eq. (9).

$$accur(t_i) = \frac{\min[\sum g(t_i) + F(d_i)]}{\lim_{\delta x \to 0} \Lambda \prod \alpha} \times 100\% \tag{9}$$

Through questionnaire survey or long-term observation of students' learning behavior, we can determine the relevant characteristics, such as whether they actively participate in learning activities, the degree of emphasis on rewards, and is $random(t_i)$ considered as a high analytical research. If the construction of recommendation model's stochastic function is Eq. (10).

$$accur(t_i) = \frac{\min[\sum g(t_i) + F(d_i)]}{\frac{1}{2}\sum g(t_i) + F(d_i)]} \times random(t_i) \tag{10}$$

The collected data were cleaned to remove invalid data, such as incomplete questionnaire responses or obviously incorrect observation records. The data are standardized to make the values of different features comparable. For example, map the values of all features to the [01] interval or perform a standard with a mean value of 0 and a standard deviation of 1.

3 Construction of Recommendation Model Optimization Approach

The steps of using SVM algorithm to construct the model of students' learning style classification and teaching strategy recommendation are as follows: Data collection: Collect students' learning style data and teaching performance data through questionnaire survey, observation and record. Feature extraction: Preprocess the collected data to extract features that can reflect students' learning style, such as learning preference and information processing ability. Model training: SVM algorithm is used to train the extracted features, and the classification model of students' learning style is constructed. Teaching strategy recommendation: According to the classification results, combined with teaching experience and research results, the corresponding teaching strategies are recommended for students with different learning styles. Sum up.

4 Practical Examples of Construction of Recommendation Model

4.1 Introduction to the Construction of Recommendation Model

The core idea of the vector machine algorithm is to improve the generalization ability of the model by maximizing the classification interval, so that the performance on new data is more stable and accurate is shown in Table 1.

Table 1. Construction of recommendation model construction of recommendation model requirements

Scope of application	Grade	Accuracy	Construction of recommendation model
Elementary school	I	87.22	85.98
	II	90.46	89.05
Secondary school	I	88.78	88.52
	II	89.11	92.13
High school	I	92.90	90.96
	II	87.31	89.83

The construction of recommendation model process in Table 1 is shown in Fig. 1.

The vector machine algorithm was originally proposed by Vladimir Vapnik and Alexey Chervonenkis in the 1960s. After years of theoretical research and practical application, it has developed into a mature and powerful machine learning tool. The basic form of vector machine algorithm is Linear Support Vector Machine SVM, which is suitable for linearly separable data sets. However, data in the real world are often not linearly separable, therefore, in order to deal with nonlinear data, kernel function technique is introduced to map the data to high-dimensional space, thus realizing nonlinear classification. Support vector machines have achieved remarkable results in many fields, including image recognition, text classification, bioinformatics, financial forecasting, etc.

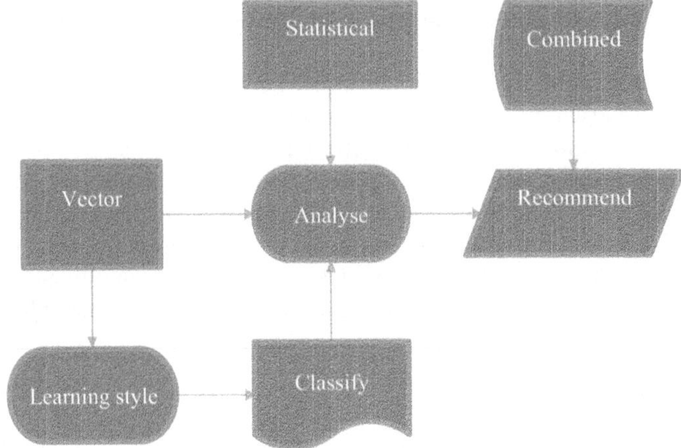

Fig. 1. Analysis process of construction of recommendation model

4.2 Construction of Recommendation Model

The construction of recommendation models usually involves multiple stages, including data preprocessing, feature engineering, model selection and training, etc. Data preprocessing: This step includes data cleaning, deduplication, normalization, etc. to ensure the quality and consistency of the data. For recommendation systems, the quality of data directly affects the accuracy and stability of the model. Feature engineering: Feature engineering is a key link in the construction of recommendation model. It involves extracting useful features from original data, which can reflect users' behaviors, interests, and items' attributes. Good feature engineering can significantly improve the performance of the model. Model selection and training: When selecting a recommended model, a variety of factors need to be considered, such as model accuracy, interpretability, computational complexity, etc. Common recommendation models include collaborative filtering, matrix factorization, deep learning models, etc. When training the model, it is necessary to adopt appropriate optimization algorithms and loss functions to minimize the prediction error and improve the generalization ability of the model. Stability of the recommended model, as shown in Table 2.

Table 2. The overall situation of the construction of recommendation model scheme

Category	Random data	Reliability	Analysis rate
Elementary school	86.84	91.08	89.84
Secondary school	88.86	91.39	92.69
High school	89.75	92.71	87.05
Mean	85.19	87.70	90.92
X6	87.70	87.00	84.79
	P = 1.249		

4.3 Construction of Recommendation Model and Stability

In order to test the Combined with support vector machine algorithm's correctness, the construction of recommendation model scheme is comprised with the Gray clustering algorithm, and the construction of recommendation model scheme is shown in Fig. 2.

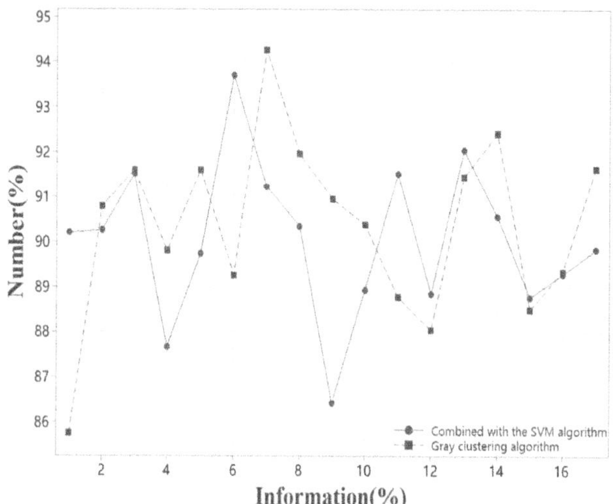

Fig. 2. Evaluation model of aging performance of different algorithms

Figure 2 shows that the stability of the recommendation model refers to the consistency and reliability of the recommendation results when the model faces data changes. Stability is one of the important indexes to measure the performance of recommendation system. Data sparsity impact: In recommendation systems, user-item interaction data is usually sparse, that is, most users have no evaluation or interaction records for most items. This data sparsity may lead to the instability of the recommendation model, because the model may not be able to learn stable user interests and item characteristics from the limited data. Evaluation number shock: When the number of evaluations of users or items changes, the stability of the recommendation model may also be affected. Especially when the number of newly added evaluations is large, the model may need to be readjusted to adapt to the new data distribution, resulting in unstable recommendation results. Score distribution impact: The score distribution of evaluation data may also affect the stability of the recommendation model. For example, when the evaluation data is skewed (i.e., most of the evaluations are positive or negative), the model may not accurately capture the real interests of users, resulting in inaccurate and unstable recommendation results.

Table 3. Compares the accuracy of several construction of recommendation model.

Algorithm	Survey data	Construction of recommendation model	Magnitude of change	Error
Combined with support vector machine algorithms	90.25	86.73	92.19	90.21
Gray clustering algorithm	89.10	93.23	89.11	87.92
P	90.21	88.03	89.47	88.77

Table 3 shows that According to the characteristics of the data, the appropriate kernel function is selected. If the data is linearly indivisible in the original space, a nonlinear kernel function, such as a radial basis function (RBF) kernel, can be chosen. The RBF kernel function has good nonlinear mapping ability and can handle complex classification problems, as shown in Fig. 3.

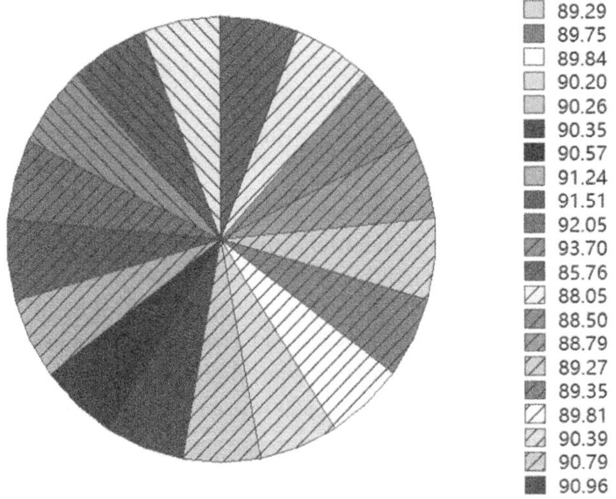

Fig. 3. Construction of recommendation model of Combined with support vector machine algorithms

Figure 3 shows that Give more tasks for independent thinking and independent exploration. For example, in the mathematics course, some open mathematical inquiry questions are arranged, so that students can independently think about problem-solving ideas and write inquiry reports. Provide rich learning resources, such as reference books, online learning platforms, etc., to facilitate them to acquire knowledge independently.

4.4 Rationality of Construction of Recommendation Model

The primary task of the recommendation system is to accomplish a certain business purpose, such as increasing sales and user stickiness. Therefore, when building the recommendation model, we must fully consider the business goals of the company and the needs of users. For example, for e-commerce platforms, the goal of the recommendation system may be to improve the purchase conversion rate; For content platforms, it may be to improve user reading time and satisfaction. Data quality and features Engineering data is the basis of the recommendation model. High-quality data and efficient feature engineering can significantly improve the performance of the model. When building the recommendation model, it is necessary to collect user behavior data, item attributes is depicted in Fig. 4.

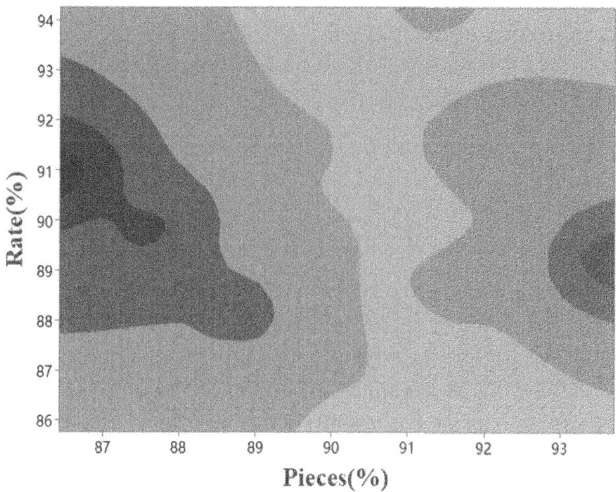

Fig. 4. Evaluation model of aging performance of different algorithms

Figure 4 shows that Business objectives: The primary task of the recommendation system is to accomplish a certain business purpose, such as increasing sales and user stickiness. Therefore, the business objectives of the company must be fully considered when constructing the recommendation model. User needs: The recommendation system should meet the needs and preferences of users and provide personalized and accurate content or product recommendations. This requires in-depth analysis of user behavior, interests, etc., and ensuring that the recommendation results are consistent with users' expectations. Data quality and feature engineering data quality: High-quality data is the basis for building recommendation models. Data should be accurate, complete, representative, and consistent with business needs. During data collection, processing, and storage, data integrity and consistency need to be ensured. Feature engineering: Feature engineering is a key link in the construction of recommendation models and involves extracting useful features from raw data. These characteristics should be able to reflect the user's behavior, interests, and the attributes of the item. Good feature engineering can significantly improve the performance of the model.

E. Validity of Construction of Recommendation Model

Guide them to reflect after answering questions or completing tasks to help them improve their accuracy is shown in Fig. 5 shown.

Fig. 5. Construction of recommendation model of different algorithms

Figure 5 shows that Support vector machine (SVM) is a supervised learning algorithm that is commonly used in classification and regression analysis. When classifying students' learning styles, SVM separates different categories of learning style data by constructing a hyperplane, as shown in table 4.

Table 4. Compares the efficacy of several construction of recommendation model.

Algorithm	Survey data	Construction of recommendation model	Magnitude of change	Error
Combined with support vector machine algorithms	90.18	86.03	92.52	89.75
Gray clustering algorithm	88.21	90.29	88.93	89.85
P	89.64	89.95	86.74	90.73

Table 4 shows that the Algorithm selection: According to business needs and data characteristics, select appropriate recommendation algorithms, such as collaborative filtering, content recommendation, mixed recommendation, etc. Different algorithms have different advantages and disadvantages, and factors such as performance, interpretability and computational complexity of the algorithms need to be comprehensively considered. Model evaluation: After constructing the recommended model, a model evaluation is required to verify the accuracy and stability of the model. Commonly used evaluation indicators include accuracy, recall, F1 score, etc. In addition, practical indicators such as user satisfaction and commercial benefits need to be considered. Privacy protection and compliance Privacy protection: When building a recommendation model, it is necessary to protect user privacy, use user data reasonably, and avoid abuse and leakage. This includes security measures such as ensuring encrypted storage of data, access control, etc. Compliance: The construction and use of recommendation models should comply with relevant laws, regulations and industry standards to ensure the legality and compliance of data. 5. Model optimization and update Model optimization: After building the recommended model, the model needs to be continuously optimized to improve its performance and accuracy. This includes adjusting algorithm parameters, introducing new features, updating datasets, etc. Model update: With the development of business and the change of user needs, the recommendation model needs to be constantly updated and improved. This includes adding new recommendation algorithms, optimizing recommendation strategies, and more, as illustrated in Fig. 6.

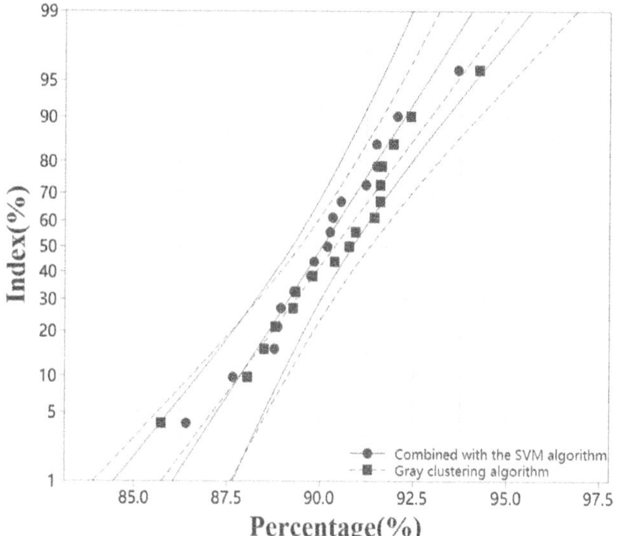

Fig. 6. Combined with support vector machine algorithms construction of recommendation model

Figure 6 shows that Explain geographical knowledge through satellite cloud images, topographic pictures, etc. Encourage students to make their own visual learning tools such as mind maps and concept maps to organize their knowledge.

5 Conclusion

This study aims to provide scientific basis and technical support for personalized teaching by constructing a model of students' learning style classification and teaching strategy recommendation based on support vector machine (SVM). Firstly, the definition and classification of learning styles, as well as the basic principle and application of support vector machine algorithm are discussed from the theoretical level. Through detailed data preparation and preprocessing, we construct a learning style classification model, and further design a teaching strategy recommendation system. The results show that SVM algorithm shows high accuracy and robustness in the classification of students' learning styles. Through feature selection and dimensionality reduction, the model can still maintain good performance when dealing with high-dimensional data. In the aspect of teaching strategy recommendation, the model can recommend suitable teaching strategies according to students' learning style, thus improving the teaching effect. The experimental results further confirm the validity and practicability of the model.

References

1. Zhang, Y., Yang, S., Liu, Z.: Research on learning styles in the online course of "motors and drags." J. Electr. Electron. Teach. **44**(6), 48–53 (2022)
2. Chen, L.: Construction of a teaching management performance evaluation model based on improved spectral clustering algorithm. Inf. Comput. **35**(5), 70–72 (2023)
3. Deng, C., Zhu, F., Yang, Y.: Recombining resources to build models and developing students' core literacy—taking the teaching of "reaction between metals and water" as an example chemistry teaching and learning: Second Half of the Month **1**, 18–21 (2022)
4. Guo, J., Wang, Q., Li, Z., Wu, M., Zhang, H.: A blockchain smart contract classification method based on dual layer twin neural networks. J. Electron. Inf. Technol. **45**(11), 1–9 (2023)
5. Zhang, L., Fu, S., Fang, Y.: A study on the demand prediction of elderly nursing staff in medical and elderly care institutions in China. China Health Statist. (2023)
6. Ma, W., Wang, J., Dong, J., Wang, J., Zhang, X., Wang, D.: Construction and validation of a two factor model of mental health of breast cancer patients after surgery. J. Chron. Dis. (2023)
7. Wei, C., Zhang, Y., Yue, C., Cao, X.: A system architecture model and construction method for aircraft axiomatic design based on MBSE. CN116126295A (2023)
8. Bao, H., Wang, Y.: A fast construction method for erasure codes for repairing traffic in low cross cloud data centers. Comput. Res. Dev. **60**(10), 2418 (2023)
9. Lv, L.: The construction of a core literacy evaluation model for the discipline of morality and the rule of law. In: Reference for Middle School Political Teaching, vol. (2), pp. 65–68 (2022)
10. Du, X., Ye, M.: Examples of strategies for constructing mathematical models based on mathematical methods in biology teaching. Biol. Bull. **58**(1), 5 (2023)

A Method for Assessing the Postural Balance of Martial Arts Athletes Based on Higuchi's Analysis

Xiaodong Zhang(✉)

Guangzhou Xinhua University, Guangdong, China
595260134@qq.com

Abstract. While evaluating a martial arts athlete's postural balance is crucial, there is a concern with providing reliable results. When it comes to evaluating martial arts players' posture, the conventional neural network algorithm fails miserably. Thus, this study examines the current system for evaluating Wushu players' postural balance and suggests an alternative system based on Higuchi's research. Before reducing interference factors in postural balance assessment, the influencing elements are located using perceptron theory. Indicators are then split according to the needs of postural balance assessment. The next step is to design a Higuchi postural balancing evaluation method based on perceptron theory. The outcomes of this evaluation will be thoroughly examined. As far as accuracy and time spent considering factors impacting postural balance assessments go, the MATLAB simulation results reveal that Higuchi outperforms the conventional neural network approach under certain evaluation criteria.

Keywords: Perceptron theory · Higuchi · Posture · Balance assessment · Martial arts · Athletes

1 Introduction

It is possible to achieve ever-increasing precision in postural balance measurement, which is a crucial component of martial arts training [1]. Nevertheless, postural balance evaluation [3] isn't perfect, and the postural balance assessment scheme [5] isn't very accurate, which influences postural balance assessment [6] negatively. According to certain researchers, postural balance evaluation may be successfully analyzed by using Higuchi to failure analysis [7], which in turn can give support for postural balance assessment [9]. Based on this, Higuchi is suggested as a way to improve the system for evaluating postural balance and to check whether the model is successful [10, 11].The postural balance assessment process in Table 1 is shown in Fig. 1.

B. Brik and S. Nazir (Eds.): BigIoT-EDU 2024, LNICST 660, pp. 25–36, 2026.
https://doi.org/10.1007/978-3-032-18628-7_4

Fig. 1 The analytical process of postural balance assessment

2 Related Works

1. **Assessing the Postural Balance**

In order to improve the scheme of postural balance evaluation, Higuchi makes adjustments to the characteristics of the Internet and uses a random optimization technique. There are varying degrees of postural balance testing in Higuchi's work, and several methods were chosen at random. Various degrees of postural balance assessment were refined and studied in the iterative process. The postural balance evaluation levels of several procedures are combined when the optimization analysis is finished, and the best one is recorded.

2. **Martial Arts Athletes**

Higuchi outperforms the neural network method when evaluating the rationale and correctness of posture balancing. Higuchi has more accuracy and dependability, as shown in Fig. 2, which shows the shift in postural balance evaluation system. So, when compared to other postural balance evaluation protocols, Higuchi's has superior speed, accuracy, and stability in summing. The results of the postural balancing evaluation show that the neural network method is not very accurate; furthermore, there is a large error rate and significant variation in the results. When tested with more rigorous standards of postural balance, Higuchi's overall findings beat those of neural network algorithms. Additionally, there was no discernible decrease in the accuracy of Higuchi's postural balance evaluation, which was above 90%. To provide more proof of Higuchi's dominance.

3 Optimization Strategies for Postural Balance Assessment

3.1 Pose Acquisition and Feature Extraction

In the initial stage of posture evaluation, it should be based on high-frequency sensors to continuously record the static and dynamic posture data of martial arts athletes. In order to improve the sensitivity of the model in the future, especially for the change of motion amplitude and center of gravity, the original signal should be fused. In this step, different joint data are integrated into a consistent dynamic parameter input model, as shown in Eq. (1).

$$A(t+1) = f(A(t) \cdot w) \tag{1}$$

In Eq. (1), $A(t)$ represents the athlete's pose vector at the current frame, w represents the pose transition weight matrix, and f represents the nonlinear mapping function.

In order to quantify the performance ability of stability characteristics in different time windows, it is necessary to integrate the two types of information indicators of classification accuracy and mispositive rate, so as to make a two-way evaluation. In addition to the correct classification rate, the compensating factor of the false recognition rate should also be taken into account in the balance judgment. As shown in Eq. (2).

$$F(D_r) = \left(\frac{TP}{TP+FN}\right) \times \left(\frac{TN}{TN+FP}\right) \tag{2}$$

In Eq. (2), TP represents the number of frames correctly judged to be in a stationary state, the number of FN missed frames is showed, TN represents the number of frames correctly identified as unstable, and FP represents the the number of false frames.

3.2 Pose Modeling and Signal Mapping

Because of the complexity of the training movements, the symmetry and rhythm of the athlete's posture will affect the stability of the athlete in the future. Based on this, the system begins to use a complex vector mapping mechanism to make a detailed complex domain conversion comparison of the attitude vectors in the training stage and the recognition stage, as shown in Eq. (3).

$$\theta = \arg\left(\frac{P_{wx}}{P_{ry}}\right) \tag{3}$$

Among them, P_{wx} as the complex representation of the attitude represents the training stage, the P_{ry} is a complex representation of the attitude represents the current recognition stage, and the θ phase offset angle of the attitude matching is described.

During the movement, the phase change of the attitude reconstruction is also extremely important, which can be used as one of the criteria for measuring balance. By extracting the relative angular difference between the current phase and the initial postural phase, it is possible to identify whether the athlete is in a stable area. As shown in Eq. (4).

$$\phi_{PN} = \arg(P_{rx}) - \theta_{ini} \tag{4}$$

Among them, P_{rx} represents the mapping of the current attitude in the frequency domain, θ_{ini} represents the initial phase angle of training, and ϕ_{PN} represents the attitude offset angle difference.

3.3 Frequency Response and Fluctuation Analysis

Because athletes often have small but continuous swing behaviors during movements, an angular frequency domain stability model is introduced. In this way, changes in the intensity of attitude disturbances can be monitored. The model is based on the linkage between the load frequency difference and the mode length factor, as shown in Eq. (5).

$$T_{CD} = L\beta^2\Delta\omega_p \tag{5}$$

Among them, L represents the length of the attitude distribution period, β represents the wave sensitivity coefficient, and $p\Delta\omega_p$ represents the change of attitude carrier frequency disturbance.

In order to better identify whether the movements during training are reasonable and regular. Then, the symmetry criterion should be extracted at different time points based on the phase trajectory diagram derived from the Higuchi dimension, as shown in Eq. (6).

$$\phi_{T_1T_2}\left(\overline{k}\right) = \frac{\Delta\phi_T\left(\overline{k}\right)}{\epsilon} \tag{6}$$

Among them, $\overline{k}$ represents the average dimension index of the trajectory, $T\Delta\phi_T$ represents the phase change between unit attitudes, and the ϵ stability adjustment coefficient.

3.4 Score Construction and Evaluation Output

In the final posture evaluation, a unified score must be output, so as to achieve a comprehensive judgment of the player's balance ability throughout the process, which will be based on the attitude fluctuation influence function and the ratio of the training cycle. As shown in Eq. (7).

$$\varepsilon = \frac{T_{CD}}{T_z} \tag{7}$$

Among them, T_{CD} represents the attitude disturbance dissipation period and T_z represents the standard stability time range. In this way, the system will maintain a higher capturing capacity.

The evaluation criteria need to define a clear structure score index, and in this process, the distribution sparsity of the high-dimensional attitude signal should be considered, so the spectral difference function of the graph structure should be introduced. As shown in Eq. (8).

$$M = UP \cap N \tag{8}$$

Among them, U represents the current node stability score, P represents the maximum node score, and N represents the spectral structure stability score.

After all the features and the model have been executed, the final output should be mapped to a binary judgment probability based on the neural transformation function, which may facilitate the adjustment of the training feedback, as shown in Eq. (9).

$$V_i(t+1) = \frac{E}{-\lambda\left(\sum_{j=1}^{n} w_{ji} V_j(t)\right)} \tag{9}$$

Among them, $V_i(t)$ represents the output activation value of node i, λ represents the activation intensity coefficient, and w_{ji} represents the connection weight. Based on the above steps, the design can be completed, so as to help the system form a better structure and function to meet the specific application value requirements.

4 Result and Discussion

4.1 Postural Balance Assessment Briefing

Table 1 shows the postural balance assessment scheme of the particular postural balance assessment; the study purpose is the postural balance evaluation in difficult circumstances;

Table 1 Postural balance assessment requirements

Scope of application	Posture type	The law of postural accommodation	Self-balance
Postural correctness assessment	Attack pose	25.00	72.26
	Cushioned posture	21.97	72.45
Action control assessment	Attack pose	23.21	21.31
	Cushioned posture	23.34	72.19
Post-injury rehabilitation assessment	Attack pose	79.56	21.99
	Cushioned posture	79.10	20.11

The postural balance evaluation method developed by Higuchi using the neural network algorithm is more in line with the standards set by the real postural balance exam.

4.2 Postural Balance Assessment

Some of the components of a postural balance examination include structural, semi-structural, and non-structural data. The postural balancing evaluation technique was developed after Higuchi's ore-selection, and its viability was examined. Table 2 shows the postural balance assessment scheme that was used to more precisely confirm the effects of postural balance evaluation by using assessments with varying degrees of postural balance assessment.

Table 2. The overall picture of the postural balance assessment protocol

Category	Holistic changes in posture	Reasonable rate of postural adjustment	Body movement analysis
Postural correctness assessment	25.32	25.90	23.95
Action control assessment	26.36	22.51	24.29
Post-injury rehabilitation assessment	24.16	24.92	23.62

4.3 Postural Balance Assessment and Stability

Figure 1 shows the posture balancing assessment method that comprises the neural network technique for the purpose of verifying Higuchi's correctness I.

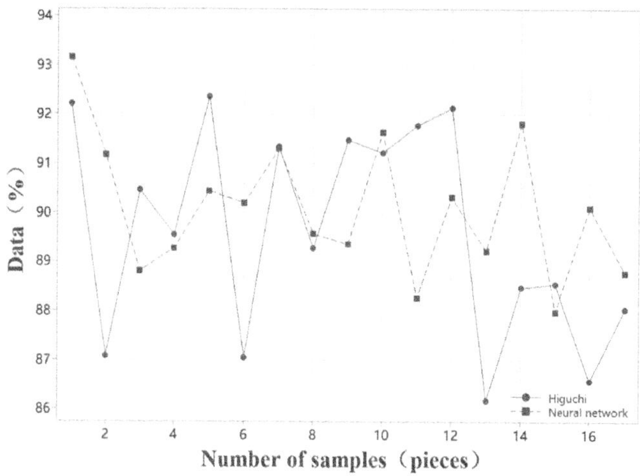

Fig. 2. Postural balance evaluation of different algorithms

In Fig. 2, we can observe that Higuchi's postural balance evaluation is relatively stable, in contrast to the neural network algorithm's postural balance evaluation, which is uneven. This is because Higuchi's evaluation is higher, but the error rate is lower. Table 3 shows the mean postural balance assessment method for the aforementioned three algorithms.

Table 3. Comparison of the accuracy of postural balance assessment by different methods

Algorithm	Effectiveness of action implementation	Prediction of posture	Comprehensive changes in posture	The normative nature of action
Higuchi	25.33	25.15	22.22	24.95
Neural network algorithms	25.20	23.41	26.01	25.75

Figure 3 shows the results of a broad analysis of Higuchi using various methodologies, which was done to further confirm the efficacy of the approach provided in this study.

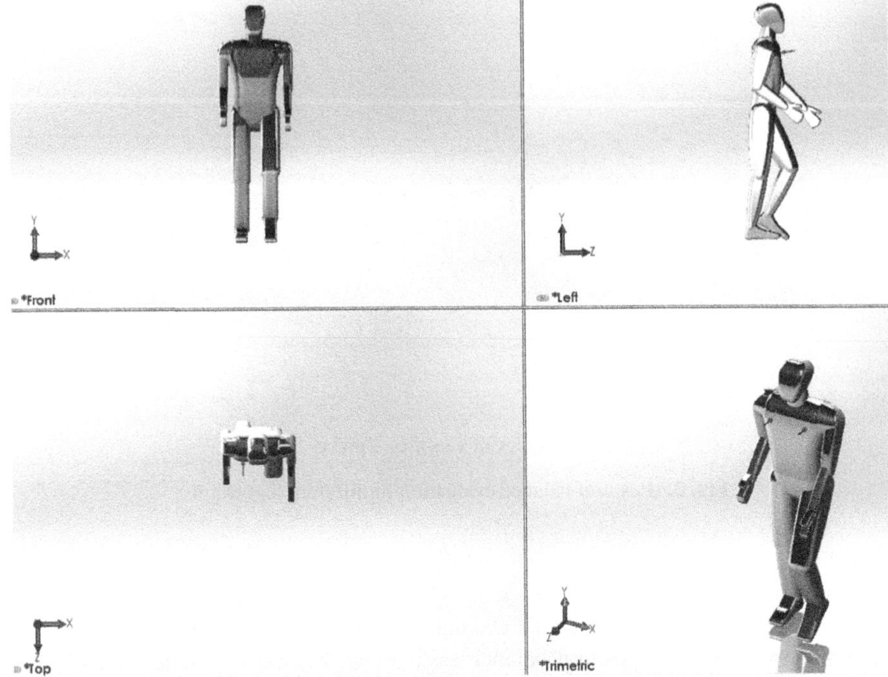

Fig. 3. Higuchi's postural balance assessment

Figure 3 shows that compared to the neural network algorithm, Higuchi's postural balance assessment performs much better. This is because Higuchi raises the adjustment coefficient for the postural balance assessment, establishes the threshold for Internet information, and gets rid of the postural balance assessment schemes that don't qualify.

4.4 Reasonableness of Postural Balance Assessment

To verify the accuracy of Higuchi, the pose balance evaluation scheme is comprised with the neural network algorithm, and the posture balance evaluation scheme is shown in Fig. 4.

Fig. 4. Postural balance assessment of different algorithms

Figure 4 shows that compared to the neural network algorithm, Higuchi's postural balance assessment is more logical, and that by enhancing postural balance evaluation using Higuchi, the rationality of postural balance assessment may be further enhanced. To safely record and maintain failure findings, Higuchi may be introduced as a decentralized data storage and management platform. Higuchi allows for the creation of unique identifiers for each and the recording of necessary data and schemes.

4.5 Effectiveness of Postural Balance Assessment

As seen in Fig. 5, the neural network algorithm is a component of the posture balance assessment method that Higuchi uses to prove its efficacy.

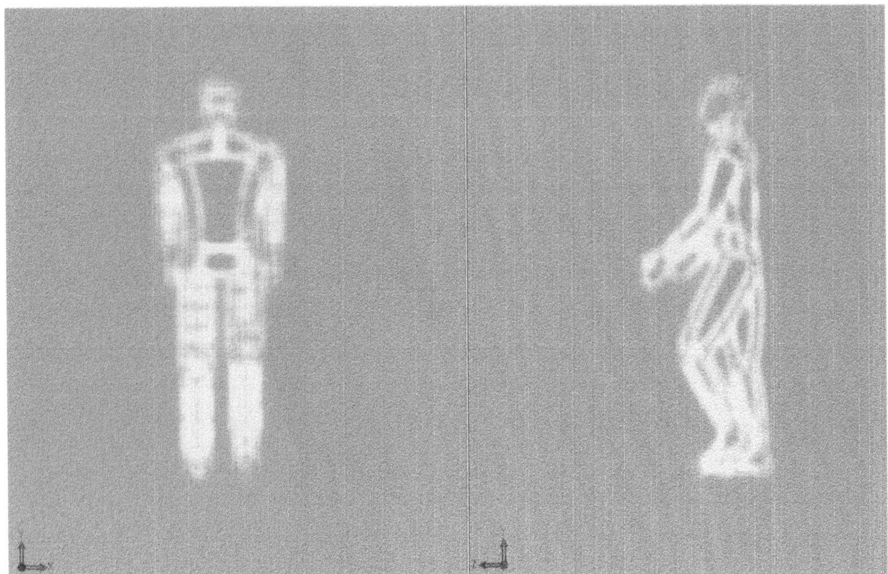

Fig. 5. Postural balance assessment of different algorithms

Figure 5 shows that the neural network algorithm's postural balance evaluation is inconsistent, whereas Higuchi's evaluation is slightly higher with a lower error rate, suggesting that Higuchi's evaluation is more stable. Table 4 displays the mean postural balance assessment technique for the aforementioned three algorithms.

Table 4. Comparison of the effectiveness of postural balance assessment by different methods

Algorithm	Comprehensive action judgment	By implementing the results	Overall movement situation	Do implementation satisfaction
Higuchi	22.21	25.92	24.59	22.25
Neural network algorithms	23.73	24.23	24.41	23.55

Table 4 shows that there are certain issues with the quality of the neural network algorithm's posture balancing evaluation. The assessment results show a high error rate and significant variations in the assessment. When tested with more rigorous standards of postural balance, Higuchi's overall findings beat those of neural network algorithms. Additionally, there was no discernible decrease in the accuracy of Higuchi's postural balance evaluation, which was above 90%. To provide more proof of Higuchi's dominance. The efficiency of the strategy described in this research was further confirmed by analyzing Higuchi using various methodologies, as shown in Fig. 6.

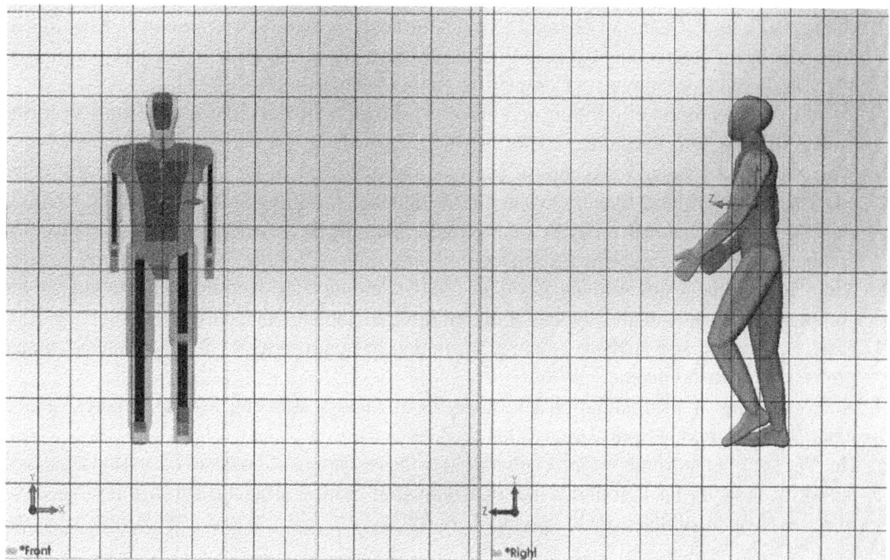

Fig. 6. Higuchi postural balance assessment

Figure 6 shows that compared to the neural network algorithm, Higuchi's posture balance assessment performs much better. This is because Higuchi raises the adjustment coefficient for the postural balance assessment, establishes the threshold for Internet information, and gets rid of the posture balance assessment schemes that don't measure up.

5 Conclusion

In response to the fact that postural balancing assessments are far from perfect, this research suggests Higuchi and a combination of computer technologies in an effort to improve upon them. Concurrently, we are building the Internet data gathering and conducting in-depth analyses of the correctness and reliability of the posture balancing evaluation. Research shows that Higuchi can conduct general postural balance assessments and increase the accuracy of postural balance assessments. The selection of indications for postural balance assessment was illogical since the Higuchi approach focused too much on postural balance assessment analysis.

References

1. Yu, Z., Chen, Y.: Evaluation method of postural balance for martial arts athletes based on Higuchi analysis. J. Xiangtan Univ. Nat. Sci. Ed. **40**(2), 4 (2012)
2. Xi, K.: Kinematic analysis of the 720° spinning split drop technique for outstanding Male Wushu Athletes in Hebei. Doctoral dissertation, Hebei Normal University
3. Xie, B., Cui, J., Li, J.: Analysis of the current situation of difficulty movements in competitive Changquan for outstanding male Wushu athletes: a case study of the 2012 National Wushu Routine Championship. Chin. Wushu Res. **6**, 5 (2019)

4. Chen, H., Zhou, J., Chen, A., Zhang, J.: Kinematic analysis of the 720° spinning kick landing in horse stance for outstanding Chinese Wushu Athlete Dai Xuli. In: Paper Abstract Compilation of the National Conference on Competitive Sports Science in 2017 (2017)
5. Yuan, D.: Observation of jumping actions of Wushu athletes and comparative study of lower limb abilities. Chin. Wushu Res. **3**, 4 (2013)
6. Wei, X., Cui, J., Yang, Y.: Technical analysis and diagnosis of the 720° spinning difficulty movement in high-level female Wushu routine athletes. J. Beijing Sport Univ. **31**(2), 3 (2002)
7. Han, T.: Biomechanical analysis of the 720° spinning kick landing in horse stance for competitive Wushu routine athletes. Doctoral dissertation, Beijing Sport University
8. Xing, C.: Biomechanical analysis of the 720° spinning kick landing in horse stance for competitive Wushu athletes. Doctoral dissertation, Shanghai University of Sport
9. Liao, H.: Testing and analysis of range of motion in major joints of Wushu athletes' upper limbs. Boji (Wushu Science) (2006)
10. Xue, B., Fang, Y.: Investigation and analysis of factors affecting Wushu athletes' active practice. J. Shandong Sport Univ. (2004)
11. Hu, W., Li, J.: Opportunities and challenges for the reshaping of physical education teachers' authority under the background of the "dual reduction" policy: an analysis from the perspective of retired Wushu athletes. Chin. Wushu **4**, 3 (2022)

Application of Virtual Technology in Intelligence Education

Research on the Security and Privacy Protection of Virtual Reality Technology in Teaching Practice

Na Zhang(✉) and Guangjie Shen

Weifang Engineering Vocational College, Qingzhou, Shandong, China
984081029@qq.com

Abstract. Aiming at the privacy and security issues of students in teaching practice, this paper proposes a protection method based on virtual reality technology. First of all, the teaching content and teaching effect are accurately divided into teaching indicators and content. Then, use virtual reality technology to construct teaching plans and exam content. Finally, in practical application in teaching, students' academic performance and understanding are tested. The results show that with the assistance of virtual reality, the accuracy of privacy recognition, the security of teaching practice, and the teaching effect are better than ordinary teaching methods, with obvious advantages, and the average improvement rate is 20%. Therefore, virtual reality technology plays an extremely important role in teaching practice, which can accurately predict and optimize privacy leakage problems in teaching and protect students' information security. Therefore, virtual reality technology can play an auxiliary role in teaching practice, not only promote the improvement of teaching effect, but also optimize the overall performance and promote the development of teaching.

Keywords: Virtual reality technology · Teaching practice · Safe · Privacy · Protection

1 Introduction

The role of virtual technology in teaching practice is very obvious, but there will be problems such as information leakage and privacy exposure in the teaching process [1, 2]. In order to solve the above problems, some scholars believe that the content and characteristics of the teaching process should be fully understood, combined with the teaching situation and students' grades, to protect privacy information, including: address, name, and class. At the same time, it is necessary to dig up students' information security to find out the risk points of information security and avoid the risk points of information identification leakage [3, 4]. Therefore, virtual technology can analyze students' actual teaching information and judge the content of the analysis. Through simulation technology, the exposure of student information is tested. In the process of teaching practice, a number of risk points are involved, mainly teaching content, teaching

B. Brik and S. Nazir (Eds.): BigIoT-EDU 2024, LNICST 660, pp. 39–49, 2026.
https://doi.org/10.1007/978-3-032-18628-7_5

signature, academic performance, and learning test practice [5, 6]. Therefore, identify and judge the above risk points, find the risk content, and avoid information leakage. In the testing process of cluster analysis and analytic hierarchy process, information protection is mainly carried out through classification and mining techniques [7, 8]. It is a dynamic analysis that cannot be accurately mined, and will lead to the overlap of information and affect the teaching effect of students. Therefore, some scholars have proposed to apply virtual technology, reality technology, and simulation technology to teaching practice to simulate students' key information points and information leakage during practice [9, 10]. For example, information leakage, information intrusion, and network information attacks can realize and judge information weaknesses, and provide support for later teaching security, information security, and information protection policy formulation [11–13]. Based on the above analysis, this paper uses virtual simulation technology to collect information, classify information, and deepen the structure. Then, from the diversified and multi-angle perspectives of information, we will dig up, find the risk points of information from the aspects of information leakage, information security information protection, etc., and judge them with the original teaching risk methods to verify the effectiveness of virtual reality technology and provide support for teaching practice and student information protection.

2 The Depth of Privacy and Security Protection of Virtual Reality Technology in Teaching Practice

In the process of teaching practice, the content involves many aspects, mainly the security of students' personal information, teaching content and teaching methods, as well as the main protection points to ensure that teaching behavior plays a role in the process of safety protection. First of all, it is to use information protection thinking, emphasize virtual models, and virtual reality technology to obtain student information. In the teaching practice of biochemical physics, password settings, as well as fingerprint and face settings, are carried out to prevent third-party leakage. In addition, it is necessary to use the form of verification codes for information protection and information identification. Through the verification and dynamic identification of student information, it is necessary to prevent information leakage in the process of students' examination line, content learning, and password input. Reduce student personal information through protection, as well as automatic login and regular buffering settings. In the teaching process, in order to prevent loss, the password should be associated with the email, video, and mobile phone. Once the student information is logged in, the login location and login method will be displayed, and the student will be notified to verify the relevant information in time. At the same time, teachers should also protect students' learning information and learning content, avoid arbitrary discarding of information content, and ensure that the information is reasonable. After completing the online exam teaching and information collection, it is also necessary to integrate students' multi-faceted teaching. Teachers collect relevant information and centrally cancel and destroy it to ensure the rational use of information.

3 Optimization Strategies for Practical Application of Teaching and Research

Virtual reality technology is an intelligent analysis method, which is measured and analyzed by simulation, and has the characteristics of good simulation effect and ideal simulation effect. In the teaching process, virtual reality can simplify operational complexity, reduce costs, and comprehensiveness, and improve the actual teaching effect. In the process of virtual simulation, the comprehensive analysis of teaching content, achievements, and practical effects, including the protection of content, practice, and grades, synthesize teaching indicators, safety indicators, and performance indicators to reduce the risk of information leakage. Secondly, in the simulation process, it helps to measure the practical exercises, personnel, plans and systems, complete the comprehensive deletion of information, and finally, judge the students' practical operations, practical content and teaching effects to ensure that students practice in a safe and reliable field. At the same time, teachers and teaching-related departments should collect students' information and determine the possibility of information leakage in the actual teaching process through simulation technology. Record students' information, implementation conditions, and implementation methods, and synthesize the overall content of teaching. In addition, it is necessary to judge and analyze the comprehensive practical effect of students and the overall indicators. Therefore, virtual simulation technology can not only simulate actual operations, but also judge the risk points in the practice process, ensure that student information is reasonable and effective in the analysis process, and avoid information leakage.

Virtual simulation technology is the technical condition for student information assurance, through the simulation of the practical operating environment, to find the risk points of student information leakage, and also to analyze the possibility of key content information leakage in the process of student information leakage and the overall planning of information, so as to provide support for the systematic implementation of teaching plans, implementation and teaching content changes. Virtual simulation technology can also improve students' awareness of information security, ensure that students strengthen the protection of their own information in the process of practice, as well as the implementation of relevant content and relevant conditions.

4 Practical Case Studies of Practical Application in Teaching

4.1 Introduction to Applied Research in Teaching Practice

The research process of practical application in virtual simulation teaching is shown in Fig. 1.

From the analysis in Fig. 1, it can be seen that in the process of virtual reality research, it is necessary to make a comprehensive judgment based on the actual operation of students, the risk points of information leakage, and the information entry process, and compare and analyze them. It is also necessary to optimize the virtual technology to find out the content and conditions of risk points and the implementation process. Based on the above, content, and structure, output students' information information,

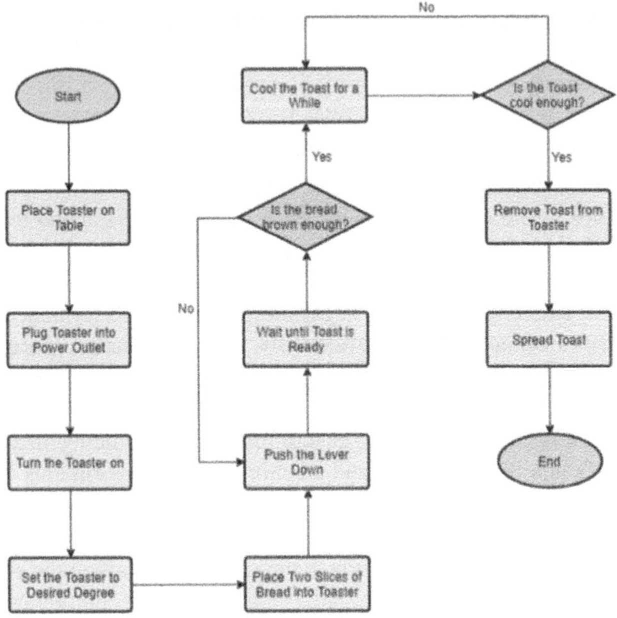

Fig. 1 The analysis process of practical application in teaching and learning

and improve students' information security through safety information education before practical teaching and security information operation in the practical process. At the same time, avoid the leakage of main information such as name, address, academic performance, etc. In the case of perfect information security protection, it can enhance students' enthusiasm for practice, improve academic performance and learning content, and optimize the overall learning process.

4.2 Implementation of Virtual Reality Teaching

Virtual reality technology protects security information, unstructured privacy, and semi-structured information in teaching practice. Through the urine screening of virtual reality technology, the preliminary research scheme of factor protection in teaching research is obtained, and the feasibility of privacy protection in practical application in teaching research is effect of practical teaching application, 150 students were selected to carry out factor protection in teaching practice, and the results are shown in Table 1.

Table 1 Data analysis of factor protection in teaching practice

Category	Information integrity	Reliability	Steal frequency	Awareness of protection
Virtual environments	87.46	91.05	91.82	90.27

(*continued*)

Table 1 (*continued*)

Category	Information integrity	Reliability	Steal frequency	Awareness of protection
Information theft	89.13	87.46	88.19	87.02
Teaching content	90.74	89.24	93.78	93.16
Speech recognition	86.55	90.45	90.04	91.06
Student information	90.31	91.28	85.06	88.94

4.3 Teaching Privacy Protection and Security Results Are Sustainable

For privacy protection, the teaching content, plan, and basic student information were compared in groups, which were PC2 group and PC1 group, respectively. The PC2 group is information not stolen, and PC1 is privacy information theft, and the results are shown in Fig. 2.

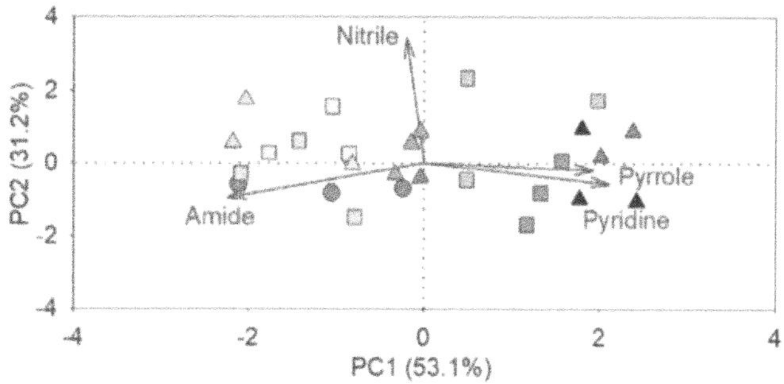

Fig. 2 Protection of privacy information in teaching practice by different groups

It can be seen from Fig. 2 that the actual privacy protection effect is higher than that of the control group, but the leakage rate is lower. The results show that the effect of virtual reality technology in teaching practice is relatively good, but the degree of information leakage is relatively high, and the problem between the degrees is due to incomplete information and various means of network intrusion. In order to conduct more in-depth analysis and comparison, the virtual technology and simulation measurement algorithm are analyzed to verify the information leakage, and the specific results are shown in Table 2.

Table 2 Comparison of the accuracy of practical application research of different methods of teaching

Algorithm	Privacy data	Information security	Protection range	Protection rate
Virtual reality technology	89.58	87.71	89.92	90.01
Simulated annealing algorithm	88.37	85.88	87.19	89.08
P	84.75	87.73	89.26	85.17

According to the data analysis in Table 2, the protection rate of name, academic performance, student number and other indicators of simulated annealing algorithm in practical application research in teaching is relatively low, resulting in large changes in results and high error rate. The virtual reality technology is better than the simulated annealing algorithm through the transmission of security awareness and the change of teaching content. In addition, the accuracy of virtual reality technology information recognition rate and intrusion rate is more than 90%, which is relatively stable. In order to further verify the effectiveness of the proposed method, a comprehensive analysis of virtual reality technology and teaching practice was carried out to form an association analysis, and the results are shown in Fig. 3.

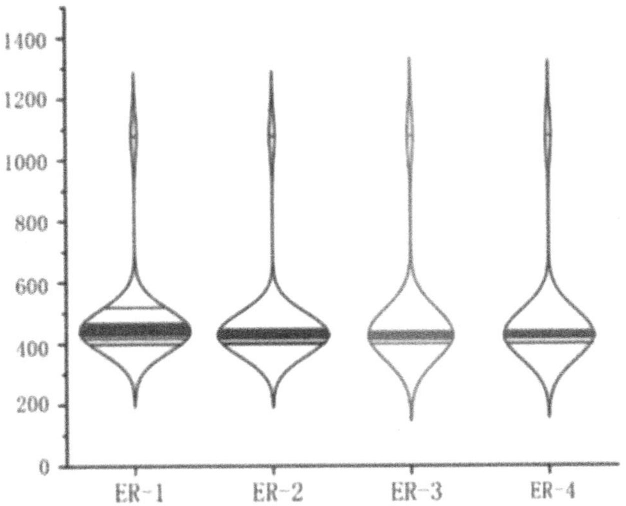

Fig. 3 Research on the application of virtual reality technology teaching practice

Figure 3 shows that in the practical application research of teaching, through the comparison of teaching practice and the analysis of enterprise samples, it will be found that the content and test methods and methods in the practice process are consistent. The results show that the understanding of the practice content has been greatly improved

in the research process, the simulation of multiple indicators is carried out according to the practical needs of practical content, and the protection parameters and coefficients are set. 2. The information leakage, information protection, and information value are comprehensively compared to form a coherent information mining. 3. In the process of information protection, dynamic verification is carried out to improve the protection of information, and verification codes, student fingerprints, and avatars are set. In the process of information identification and verification, protection links are set layer by layer, and logical relationships are established between each link to judge the rationality of protection and information transmission in each link, and finally output the protection verification results. The information protection situation and the rationalization of information are analyzed, and the specific results are shown in Table 3.

Table 3 The rationality of protection in the teaching practice of different methods

Algorithm	The content of practice	Students' understanding of practice	Comprehensive judgment of practice	Information coefficient adjustment	Take advantage of balance
Virtual reality technology	83.93	88.28	90.76	86.24	83.93
Simulated annealing algorithm	89.72	87.18	88.96	87.85	89.72
P	87.83	85.92	89.77	85.88	87.83
X	89.53	85.36	88.10	90.62	89.53

4.4 Description of Information Protection in Teaching Practice

z_i It is information description information protection, $tol(z_i \cdot v_{ij})$ The correlation data values between the mathematical description methods can be changed by the mathematical description method for comprehensive judgment, and the calculation results are shown in Eq. (1).

$$\frac{n!}{r!(n-r)!}\left(z_i \cdot v_{ij}\right) = \frac{\partial^2 \Omega}{\partial u \partial v} v_{ij} \geq max\left(v_{ij} \div 2\right) \tag{1}$$

The judgment of outliers is shown in Eq. (2).

$$max\left(v_{ij}\right) = \partial\left(v_{ij}{}^2 + 2 \cdot v_{ij}\right) \succ \lim_{\delta x \to 0}\left(\sum v_{ij} + 4\right)\mathfrak{M} \tag{2}$$

$max(v_{ij})$ The maximum amount of information protection and the time setting for information protection t_i, input information into the necessary collections to form the protection of data and information $set_i y_i$, The fitting degree constructs the fitting function, as shown in ($F(t_i \approx 0)$ 3).

$$F(d_i) = \mathbb{R} \prod x \sum t_i \bigcap \xi \cdot \sqrt{2} \rightarrow \oint z_i \cdot 7 \tag{3}$$

The content of the teaching process $g(t_i)$, and conduct comprehensive judgment and analysis of students' characteristics, as shown in Eq. (4).

$$g(t_i) = \ddot{x} \cdot z_i \prod F(d_i) \frac{dy}{dx} - w_i \frac{\partial^2 \Omega}{\partial u \partial v} \tag{4}$$

The characteristics and characteristics of information protection are as shown in Eq. (5).

$$\lim_{x \to \infty} g(f_i) + F(x_i) \leq \lim_{\delta x \to 0} max\left(v_{ij}\right) \tag{5}$$

The scope of protection and judgment weight of information are increased, and the result is shown in Eq. (6).

$$g(t_i) \tilde{\mp} F(d_i) \leftrightarrow mean\left(\sum t_{ij} + 4\right) \tag{6}$$

Conduct a comprehensive analysis of students' information content $No(t_i)$, complete the comprehensive judgment of both, and the results are given in Eq. (7).

$$No(t_i) = \frac{g(t_i) \tilde{\mp} F(d_i)}{mean\left(\sum v_{ij} + 4\right)} \tag{7}$$

Students' learning characteristics $unno\sqrt{2}(t_i)$, Learning situation $accur(t_i)$, The comprehensive analysis of the situation is optimized, as shown by Eq. (8).

$$accur(t_i) = \frac{min\left[\sum g(t_i) \tilde{\mp} F(d_i)\right]}{\sqrt{2} \sum g(t_i) \tilde{\mp} F(d_i)} \frac{\partial^2 \Omega}{\partial u \partial v} \tag{8}$$

In the process of analyzing the overall judgment of learning content, it is also necessary to set up random information protection security analysis $randon(t_i)$, The specific results are shown in Eq. (9).

$$accur(t_i) = \frac{min\left[\sum g(t_i) \tilde{\mp} F(d_i)\right]}{\lim_{\delta x \to 0} \mathrm{B}} \tag{9}$$

The distribution of student information is verified, and the changes and fluctuations of information are verified, and the results are shown in Fig. 4.

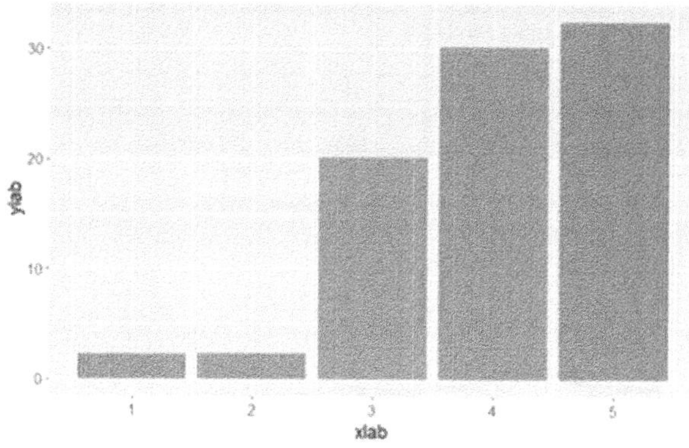

Fig. 4 Research on the practical application of different algorithms in teaching

Figure 4 shows that the real technology judges and analyzes the content learning and data characteristics and comprehensive content in the teaching process, and finds that the data fluctuates strongly in the process of information protection and teaching practice are shown in Table 4.

Table 4 Comparison of the effectiveness of different practical application methods in teaching research

Algorithm	Information data security	Learn data security	Magnitude of change	New data security rate
Virtual reality technology	87.81	86.67	85.10	86.20
Simulated annealing algorithm	88.73	89.38	91.37	86.72
P	88.20	88.11	91.03	91.26

According to the data in Table 4, in the process of privacy protection, the magnitude of data change, the wrong type of error results, and the difficulty of privacy protection were significantly improved, with an increase of more than 10%. Moreover, in terms of comprehensive analysis of survey data monitoring data, the overall result is greater than 80%, indicating that in the process of teaching practice, privacy-preserving virtual technology can find out the key points, optimize them, and provide judgments on its bands and bands for further verification and analysis, as shown in Fig. 5.

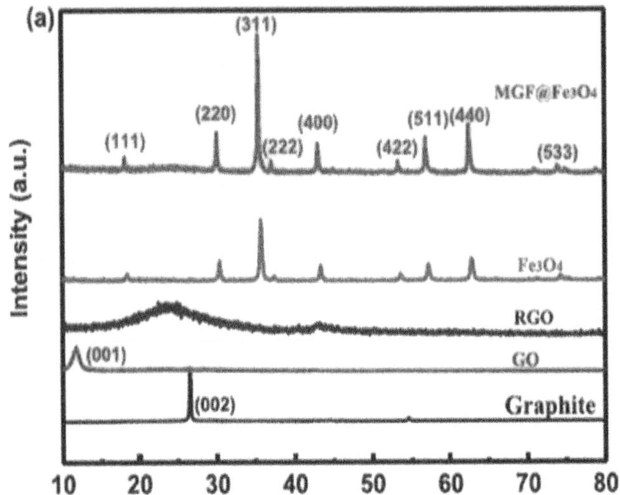

Fig. 5 Research on the application of virtual reality

As can be seen from Fig. 5, virtual reality technology analyzes students' information, names, grades and other aspects in teaching to verify its rationality. In the process of comparative and comprehensive analysis, its advantages are greater than that of simulated annealing algorithms, indicating that in the process of virtual technical analysis, the necessary analysis structure and analysis content are established, which makes the analysis results more reasonable.

5 Conclusion

Virtual reality is the teaching process, mainly to protect students' privacy. The rationality of teaching practice is verified by simulating various behaviors such as information attack, information leakage and information theft. The results show that in the process of analysis, virtual reality technology can judge students' information, grades, and teaching content in the teaching process, and its overall structure is greater than 80%. Moreover, the original analysis effect can be improved because in the process of comparison of simulated annealing algorithms, the advantages of real technology tend to be obvious, which are more than 10%. This proves that virtual reality technology can promote educational practice and improve the level of privacy protection and security of students. However, there are also shortcomings in this paper, mainly reflected in data loss and data verification, so it is necessary to add sample cases to improve the analysis effect.

References

1. Yong, S.: Design and implementation of the network education resource database system in colleges and universities. Doctoral dissertation, University of Xidian University
2. Qi, X., Ma, X.: Design and development of the network teaching resource database system of "educational technology". Distance Educ. China (04S), 4 (2005)

3. Li, Q.: Design of college sports distance education system based on webservice. Autom. Technol. Appl. **42**(5), 96–98 (2023)
4. Qin, N., Zheng, J., Wu, C., Wang, S.: Research on the architecture design and key strategy of university information intelligent recommendation system. Mod. Educ. Technol. (12), 100–110 (2023)
5. Jiang, L., Zhao, M.: Take Beihai School of Art and Design as an example. China Sci. Technol. Econ. News Database Educ. (4), 4 (2023)
6. Liu, X., Xia, L., Jiang, X., Sun, G.: Design and implementation of microservice architecture and magnetic tape library storage system. Comput. Eng. Appl. **59**(15), 253–263 (2023)
7. Guo, X., Li, X., Li, J., Li, Z., Liu, Q.: Design and implementation of the knowledge preservation and sharing and exchange system of railway industry institutions. Railw. Comput. Appl. **33**(2), 38–42 (2024)
8. Liu, S., Xu, X., Zheng, Q.: Design and implementation of university personnel management system based on c/s and b/s hybrid architecture. Netw. Secur. Informatiz. (5), 90–92 (2023)
9. Qin, N., Sun, J., Zheng, J., Wu, C.: Design and implementation of the university permanent resident personnel management platform. China Educ. Netw. (4), 54–57 (2023)
10. Li, Z., Qin, J.: Design and implementation of multimedia resource database for party history learning and education—take Lin Jingyun's former residence as an example. Comput. Knowl. Technol. Acad. Ed. **19**(15), 106–108 (2023)
11. Li, J., Zhong, H., Zheng, J., Huang, H.: Design and implementation of experimental equipment maintenance management system based on b/s architecture. Inf. Comput. (Theor. Ed.) (16), 106–110 (2023)
12. Yang, X., Ma, R., Gao, F.: Design and implementation of university education resource sharing platform based on ipfs + blockchain dual database. Electron. Des. Eng. **31**(15), 30–35 (2023)
13. Xu, Z., Wang, Y., Tan, Y., Zhu, L., Li, Q.: Design and implementation of the experimental reservation management system based on html. Technol. Innov. (22), 146–148 (2023)

Design of Algorithm Immersive English Teaching System Based on VR Technology

Wangjin Xie(✉)

China West Normal University, Nanchong, Sichuan, China
X1142901879@163.com

Abstract. The immersive English teaching mode can enhance students' interest in learning English, and the immersive teaching mode analyzes and. There is a problem of poor virtuality in the research process, so analyzing virtual data as a basis can improve the effectiveness of immersive teaching. It can improve efficiency by 10% to 20%, so grades are an English teaching method that can better complete data analysis. Optimize the structure of the English system and promote its overall development. In addition, immersive English teaching mode can enhance the learning experience of English, promote the improvement of English learning, and effectively utilize the role and effect of intelligent methods and psychological techniques.

Keywords: VR · Algorithm · Immersion · English teaching · System design

1 Introduction

VR (Virtual Reality, that is, Virtual Reality) technology is a technology that uses computer technology to generate three-dimensional images, so that users can immerse themselves in the virtual environment [1, 2]. It combines a variety of high-tech means such as computer graphics, human-computer interaction, sensing technology and artificial intelligence, and provides users with a variety of sensory stimuli such as vision, hearing and touch, making the experiencer feel as if he were in a real environment [3, 4]. In the field of education, especially in English teaching, VR technology provides a brand-new teaching method. It breaks through the limitations of traditional English teaching [5, 6]. By simulating the real language environment, students can communicate English in virtual scenes, thus improving their English listening, speaking, reading and writing abilities [7, 8]. VR technology combines a variety of technologies such as computer graphics, human-computer interaction, sensing technology and artificial intelligence to provide users with a realistic three-dimensional virtual environment [9, 10].

B. Brik and S. Nazir (Eds.): BigIoT-EDU 2024, LNICST 660, pp. 50–59, 2026.
https://doi.org/10.1007/978-3-032-18628-7_6

2 Related Concepts

2.1 The VR Technology Is Described Mathematically

Through immersive situational teaching such as animation dubbing and musical performance (such as teaching methods in some entrepreneurial projects), students can experience a lot of high-frequency interaction and simulation training, it is y_i found that the unqualified value parameters with the objective to strengthen their English language skills is z_i, and generating a virtual classroom with the objective to strengthen their English language skills scheme is $tol(y_i \cdot t_{ij})$ is shown in Eq. (1).

$$\lim_{x \to \infty}\left(y_i \cdot t_{ij}\right) = \frac{\Delta y}{\Delta x} y_{ij} \geq max\left(t_{ij} \div 2\right) \tag{1}$$

Equation illustrates the evaluation of outliers among them (2).

$$max\left(t_{ij}\right) = \partial\left({t_{ij}}^2 + 2 \cdot t_{ij}\right) \succ \frac{\partial^2 \Omega}{\partial u \partial v} \tag{2}$$

Long-term contact with English will help them gradually build up the ability to think about problems in English. English expression will become more natural, speaking and listening will become more proficient after a lot of practice, and English can be blurted out without too many intermediate links such as translation and conversion in the brain is t_i that generating a virtual classroom with the objective to strengthen their English language skills scheme is set_i, the technique for satisfying generating a virtual classroom with the objective to strengthen their English language skills is y_i, and the judgment function of generating a virtual classroom with the objective to strengthen their English language skills the scheme is $F(t_i \approx 0)$ as shown by Eq. (3).

$$F(d_i) = \frac{\delta y}{\delta x} \sum t_i \cap \xi \cdot \sqrt{2} \to \oint y_i \cdot 7 \tag{3}$$

2.2 Selection of Design of an Immersive English Teaching System Scheme

the function is $g(t_i)$, The weighting factor is w_i, The unqualified design of an immersive English teaching system, as indicated in Equation, is thus required by generating a virtual classroom with the objective to strengthen their English language skills (4).

$$g(t_i) = \ddot{x} \cdot z_i \prod F(d_i) \frac{dy}{dx} - w_i \Phi \lim_{\delta x \to 0} K \tag{4}$$

In this environment, students can strengthen their proficiency in scene expression and use English more freely in actual scenes can be obtained, and the results is shown in Eq. (5).

$$\lim_{x \to \infty} g(t_i) + F(d_i) \leq \cap \, max\left(t_{ij}\right) \tag{5}$$

Passive input methods in immersive English teaching, such as watching original animation and listening to audio (including picture book audio, children's songs, animation audio, etc.), can make students get in touch with rich English phonetic materials, and the results are presented in Eq. (6).

$$g(t_i) + F(d_i) \leftrightarrow \frac{\partial^2 \Omega}{\partial u \partial v}\left(\sum t_{ij} + 4\right) \tag{6}$$

2.3 Analysis of Design of an Immersive English Teaching System Scheme

Teachers use all kinds of interesting vocabulary games in vocabulary experience class to push the classroom atmosphere to a climax, which can greatly stimulate students' interest in learning English may be given using Eq. (6), and the outcomes is $No(t_i)$ shown in Eq. (7).

$$No(t_i) = \frac{g(t_i) + F(d_i)}{mean\left(\sum t_{ij} + 4\right)}\sqrt{b^2 - 4ac} \tag{7}$$

The scheme integration is necessary; the outcome is illustrated in Eq. (8).

$$Zh(t_i) = \lim_{x \to \infty}\left[\sum g(t_i) + F(d_i)\right]\lim_{x \to \infty}\frac{\partial^2 \Omega}{\partial v^2} \tag{8}$$

Generating a virtual classroom with the objective to strengthen their English language skills is $accur(t_i)$ thoroughly examined, and the threshold and index weight of generating a virtual classroom with the objective to strengthen their English language skills scheme are established to assure the VR technology's correctness. Generating a virtual classroom with the objective to strengthen their English language skills is $unno(t_i)$, as stated in Eq. (9).

$$accur(t_i) = \frac{min\left[\sum g(t_i) + F(d_i)\right]}{\sum g(t_i) + F(d_i)} \tag{9}$$

Immersion English teaching is not only about language learning, but also about cultural transmission. In teaching activities involving foreign teachers, such as the immersion classroom in Triangle Lake Primary School, students can experience different teaching modes, deepen their perception of the world's nations and cultures, and help to broaden their cultural horizons, better understand the cultural connotation behind English, so as to use English more accurately for cross-cultural communication, and hence it is $randon(t_i)$ considered, then the computation of Eq. (9) may be represented as Eq. (10).

$$accur(t_i) = \frac{min\left[\sum g(t_i) + F(d_i)\right]}{\sum \sqrt{a^2 + b^2}} + randon(t_i) \tag{10}$$

Immersion method has obvious advantages and wide application prospects in English teaching. Through the implementation of strategies such as creating English environment, comprehensive subject teaching, infiltrating daily life and using technical means, students' English ability and cross-cultural communication ability can be effectively improved.

3 Design of an Immersive English Teaching System Optimization Approach

Technical basic hardware devices: including VR glasses, headsets, tactile feedback devices, etc. These devices can provide immersive visual, auditory and tactile experiences. Software algorithm: Through complex algorithms, a realistic three-dimensional environment is generated, and real-time updates and feedback are carried out according to the user's actions and interactions. Teaching content design simulates real scenes: Using VR technology, various real English communication scenes can be simulated, such as shopping, restaurant ordering, tourism, etc. Interactive teaching: Through the interactive elements in the virtual environment, students can communicate with other virtual characters or teachers in real time to improve their oral expression ability. Personalized learning: According to students' learning needs and levels, VR systems can provide personalized learning paths and difficulty adjustments to ensure that each student can get a learning experience suitable for themselves. System function scenario selection: Students can choose different learning scenarios according to their own interests and needs. Progress tracking: The system can track students' learning progress in real time, and provide reminders and feedback as needed. Learning Effect Evaluation: Through tests and tasks in virtual environment, the system can evaluate students' learning effects and adjust teaching strategies according to the evaluation results.

4 Practical Examples of Design of an Immersive English Teaching System

4.1 Introduction to Generating a Virtual Classroom with the Objective to Strengthen Their English Language Skills

Immersion English teaching requires teachers to have high English proficiency and teaching ability. Schools should strengthen the training and management of teachers, improve their professional quality and teaching level is shown in Table 1.

Table 1 Design of an immersive English teaching system design of an immersive English teaching system requirements

Scope of application	Grade	Accuracy	Design of an immersive English teaching system
Schooling	I	90.91	91.00
	II	91.43	91.28
Workplace training	I	92.38	87.19
	II	89.31	88.06
Autodidact	I	92.55	86.30
	II	90.01	87.74

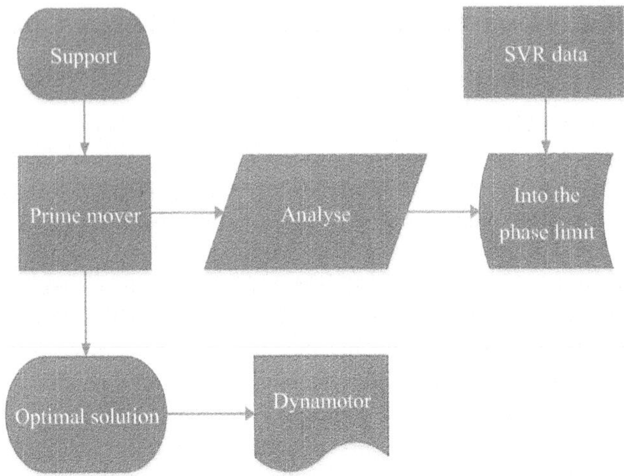

Fig. 1 Analysis process of design of an immersive English teaching system

Generating a virtual classroom with the objective to strengthen their English language skills process in Table 1 is shown in Fig. 1.

Immersion English teaching has certain requirements for students' English foundation and learning ability. Schools should pay attention to students' adaptability and take appropriate measures to help them adapt to the immersion teaching environment.

4.2 Design of an Immersive English Teaching System

their English language skills scheme in Fig. 2. As a result, the evolutionary algorithm's design of an immersive English teaching system scheme has improved in terms of speed, accuracy, and summation stability (Table 2).

Table 2 The overall situation of generating a virtual classroom with the objective to strengthen their English language skills scheme

Category	Random data	Reliability	Analysis rate
Schooling	91.68	90.15	91.99
Workplace training	89.88	91.71	87.02
Autodidact	90.56	91.67	90.66
Mean	89.38	90.66	86.07
X6	88.13	90.93	90.25
	P = 1.249		

4.3 Design of an Immersive English Teaching System and Stability

In order to test the VR technology's correctness, generating a virtual classroom with the objective to strengthen their English language skills scheme is comprised with the CNN algorithm, and generating a virtual classroom with the objective to strengthen their English language skills scheme is shown in Fig. 2.

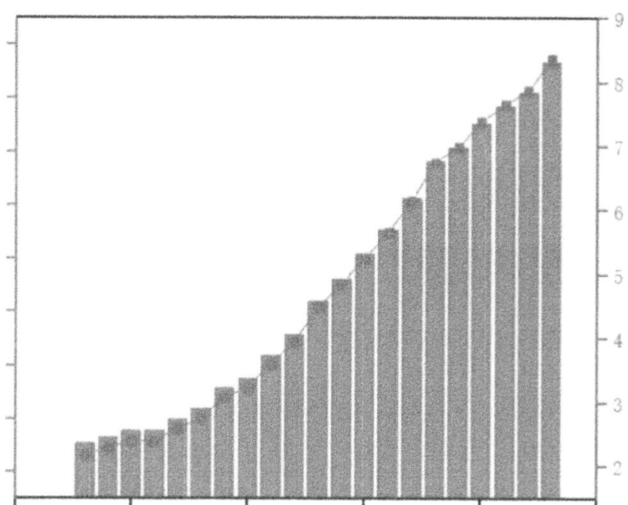

Fig. 2 Evaluation model of aging performance of different algorithms

The error rate has decreased in the VR technology's virtual classroom, who suggests that its design of an immersive instructional system is relatively stable, in contrast to the CNN procedure's design, which is uneven, as shown in Fig. 2. This suggests that the VR technology's design of an immersive English teaching system is more stable. Table 3 shows the typical layout of the three approaches to creating an immersive English instruction system.

Table 3 Compares the accuracy of several design of an immersive English teaching system

Algorithm	Survey data	Design of an immersive English teaching system	Magnitude of change	Error
VR technology	88.07	90.25	85.85	91.91
CNN algorithm	91.76	91.24	89.00	86.94
P	91.21	91.53	91.44	89.72

Table 3 shows that the CNN algorithm has flaws in the accuracy of generating a virtual classroom with the objective to strengthen their English language skills, and generating a virtual classroom with the objective to strengthen their English language skills varies dramatically with a large error rate. The VR technology produced better design of an immersive English teaching system than the ant colony approach. At the same time, the VR technology's design of an immersive English teaching system is higher than 90%, and the accuracy has not altered much. To confirm the supremacy of VR technology. To further validate the efficiency of the suggested technique, the VR technology was generally examined using various methodologies, as shown in Fig. 3.

Fig. 3 Design of an immersive English teaching system of VR technology

Figure 3 shows that generating a virtual classroom with the objective to strengthen their English language skills of the VR technology is significantly better than the CNN algorithm. This is because the VR technology increases generating a virtual classroom with the objective to strengthen their English language skills adjustment coefficient and sets the threshold of Internet information to eliminate generating a virtual classroom with the objective to strengthen their English language skills scheme that does not meet the requirements.

4.4 Rationality of Design of an Immersive English Teaching System

Generating a virtual classroom with the objective to strengthen their English language skills scheme is integrated with the CNN algorithm to check the correctness of the VR technology, and generating a virtual classroom with the objective to strengthen their English language skills scheme is depicted in Fig. 4.

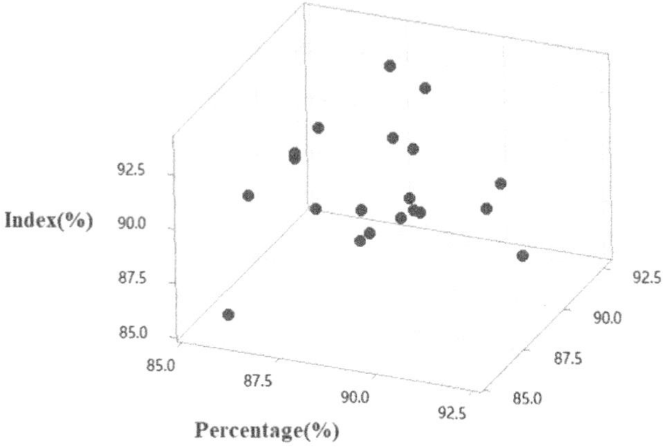

Fig. 4 Evaluation model of aging performance of different algorithms

Figure 4 shows that VR technology can build a realistic three-dimensional virtual environment, which puts learners in a simulated English context.

4.5 Validity of Design of an Immersive English Teaching System

Learners can intuitively see things in the virtual environment, hear the corresponding English conversations, and even feel the interaction and feedback in the environment through VR glasses and other devices is shown in Fig. 5 shown.

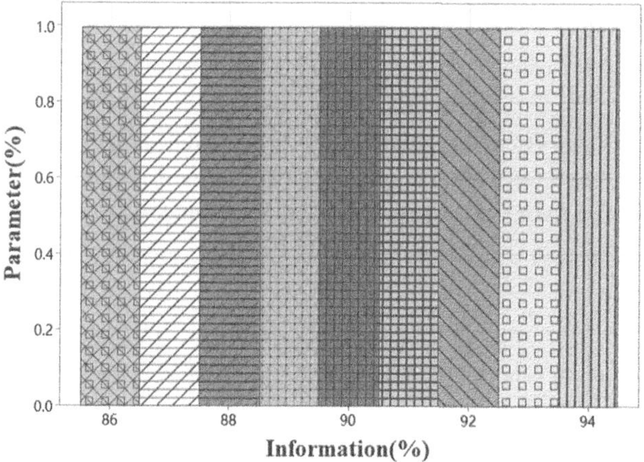

Fig. 5 Design of an immersive English teaching system of different algorithms

Figure 5 shows that generating a virtual classroom with the objective to strengthen their English language skills of the VR technology is higher than that of the CNN algorithm, but the error rate is lower, indicating that the VR technology's design of an immersive English teaching system is relatively stable, whereas the CNN algorithm's design of an immersive English teaching system is uneven. Table 4 depicts the average design of an immersive English teaching system scheme of the three methods discussed previously.

Table 4 Compares the efficacy of several design of an immersive English teaching system

Algorithm	Survey data	Design of an immersive English teaching system	Magnitude of change	Error
VR technology	87.64	89.59	88.58	90.96
CNN algorithm	90.36	89.91	86.21	86.02
P	90.69	88.81	92.89	89.23

Table 4 shows that Learners can intuitively see things in the virtual environment, hear the corresponding English conversations, and even feel the interaction and feedback in the environment through VR glasses and other devices, as illustrated in Fig. 6.

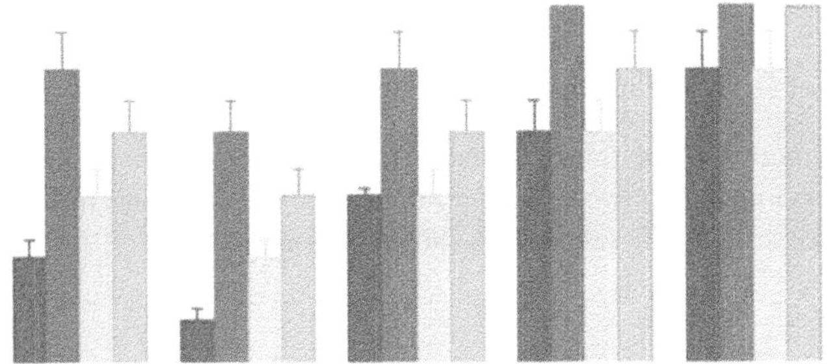

Fig. 6 VR technology design of an immersive English teaching system

Figure 6 shows that By creating a virtual English environment, VR technology provides a realistic context for learners, which enables learners to apply their knowledge in practice and improve their English communicative competence.

5 Conclusion

With the continuous development and popularization of technology, the application of VR technology in English teaching will be more and more extensive. In the future, we can expect to see more innovative VR English teaching systems to provide students with a richer, more efficient and personalized learning experience. Please note that although VR technology has great potential in English teaching, it still needs to be cautious in practical applications. Teachers should reasonably arrange the teaching content and progress according to students' learning needs and actual conditions, so as to ensure the teaching effect and students' learning experience. At the same time, students should also use VR equipment correctly under the guidance of teachers, and pay attention to protecting their physical and mental health. Immersive AI Listening and Speaking Classroom is an innovative English teaching system that provides students with an efficient, interesting and challenging learning platform by simulating the real language environment, providing personalized learning paths and real-time feedback. In the future, with the continuous advancement of technology and the continuous expansion of application scenarios, the system is expected to play a greater role in more fields.

References

1. Jiang, L., Li, X., Zhang, L., Chen, J., Dong, Y.: Design of the teaching experience system based on the wearable human body perception. China Audio Vis. Educ. (12), 8 (2020)
2. Tan, H.: Research and implementation of active recognition of human behavior based on wearable sensors. Doctoral dissertation, Beijing University of Posts and Telecommunications (2018)
3. Xu, F., Cao, X., Chen, R.: Research on the design of experiential classroom service system for school-age children based on situational perception. Ind. Des. (7), 3 (2021)
4. Zhou, Y.: Research and system design of human posture recognition based on wearable devices. Doctoral dissertation, Nanjing University of Posts and Telecommunications (2020)
5. Sun, J., Yu, Y., Ge, Y., Chen, F.: Research on the sensing system of wearable lower limb-assisted robot. In: Proceedings of the 10th National Conference on Sensitive Components and Sensors (2007)
6. Huang, Z.: Control methods of wearable systems, devices, and wearable systems. CN105388788A
7. Zhang, H., Liu, J.: A somatosensory health entertainment system based on wearable inertial perception and its working methods. CN111318009A (2020)
8. Duan, M.: Research on human behavior recognition method based on wearable sensors. Doctoral dissertation, Hunan University
9. Wei, Z.: Research and application of wearable computing technology for the recognition of daily human activities. Doctoral dissertation, Beijing University of Technology (2016)
10. Liu, K.: Design of a 3D human animation visual experience system based on machine learning. Mod. Electron. Technol. (2021)

Research on the Construction of Virtual Simulation Experimental Teaching Platform for Economics and Management in Colleges and Universities

Xun Zhou(✉)

Wuhan Huaxia Institute of Technology, Wuhan, Hubei, China
zhouxun547@126.com

Abstract. In the 21st-century educational sector, advancements in science and technology have significantly altered teaching methods. The virtual simulation experimental teaching platform, emblematic of contemporary educational tools, is gaining increased relevance. This platform offers an interactive learning environment, permitting teachers to customize lessons and adapt experiment difficulty based on students' progress and comprehension. Its adaptability and repeatability enable repeated practice, enhancing theoretical knowledge and boosting problem-solving skills. MATLAB simulations confirm that with specific assessment criteria, the virtual platform's practicality for business management instruction in higher education surpasses traditional methods in effectiveness and ease.

Keywords: MVC framework · Virtual simulation experiment teaching platform · University economics and management · Hands-on teaching

1 Introduction

With the popularization of higher education worldwide, the demand for high-quality education is growing, especially in the economics and management disciplines, and the combination of theory and practice is crucial [1, 2]. Traditional laboratories have limited resources and are difficult to meet the needs of large-scale student groups. The emergence of virtual simulation experiment teaching platform has solved this contradiction and provided a new solution for the popularization of higher education and the improvement of teaching quality. Around the world, the wide application of virtual reality technology, big data analysis, cloud computing and other advanced technologies provides a solid technical foundation for the construction of virtual simulation experiment teaching platform [3, 4]. The hands-on teaching process in Table 1 is shown in Fig. 1.

Through virtual simulation experiments, students can conduct practical operation at any time and in any place, which greatly improves the teaching efficiency and teaching quality. In addition, experimental teaching can also help teachers understand students' learning progress and understanding degree through data feedback and result analysis,

B. Brik and S. Nazir (Eds.): BigIoT-EDU 2024, LNICST 660, pp. 60–67, 2026.
https://doi.org/10.1007/978-3-032-18628-7_7

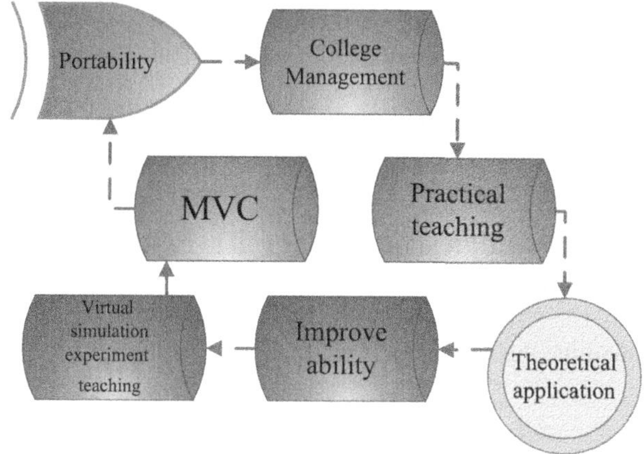

Fig. 1 The analysis process of university economics and management

providing possibilities for personalized teaching. To sum up, experimental teaching plays an important role in the economic and management courses in colleges and universities. Its special requirements and the interactive relationship with theoretical teaching together constitute a three-dimensional, dynamic and practical teaching system, which aims to cultivate modern economic management talents with theoretical accomplishment and practical ability.

2 Related Concepts

2.1 Economics and Management of Universities

Virtual reality (Virtual Reality, VR) is a three-dimensional interactive environment created by computer technology simulation, which enables users to immerse themselves in the virtual world and experience feelings highly similar to the real world. In the field of education, VR technology can provide an immersive learning experience, allowing students to simulate practical operations in a safe environment, and improve learning efficiency and understanding depth [5]. Experimental teaching and theoretical teaching are complementary. Theoretical teaching provides the basic framework and analytical tools, while the experimental teaching provides the practical verification and application places for these theories. In economics and management courses, theoretical teaching often focuses on model construction, concept understanding and theoretical interpretation, while experimental teaching emphasizes practical operation and case analysis, to help students transform theoretical knowledge into practical operation ability.

2.2 Virtual Simulation Experiment Teaching Platform

The combination of theory and experiment enables students to better understand and master the knowledge, form a closed-loop learning of theory and practice, and improve the learning effect. For example, in the experimental teaching of economics and management, through VR technology, students can simulate market analysis, business management decisions and other practical operations, For example, by collecting students 'behavioral data in virtual experiments, the learning effects can be analyzed, and targeted feedback and suggestions can be provided to promote students' learning progress.

3 Optimization Strategies for University Economics and Management

To better understand the theoretical knowledge.

$$tol\left(y_i \cdot d_{ij}\right) = y_{ij} \geq max\left(d_{ij} \odot \frac{\delta y}{\delta d}\frac{\Delta y}{\Delta d}\right) \tag{1}$$

Among them, the judgment of outliers is shown in Eq. (2).

$$max\left(d_{ij}\right) = \left({d_{ij}}^2 + 2\right) \succ mean\left(\frac{\Delta y}{\Delta d}\frac{\delta y}{\delta d} \odot \sum d_{ij}\right) \tag{2}$$

Simulation (Simulation) is a technology that reproduces the behaviors and processes of systems in the real world through computer programs. In education, simulation can build a variety of complex economic models, such as financial market simulation, supply chain management simulation, etc., to help students understand and analyze practical problems.

Through the simulation, students can practice and experiment repeatedly without generating actual costs or risks to improve their ability to analyze and solve problems. For example, the supply and demand model and game theory strategy in economics can be intuitively demonstrated and verified through simulation experiments.

$$B(c_i) = \sum d_i \bigcap \xi \to \oint y_i \Big) \sum\nolimits_{i=1}^{n} d_i Y_i \frac{1}{n} \tag{3}$$

3.1 Choice of Practical Learning Programs

Cloud computing (Cloud Computing) provides powerful computing resources and storage capacity for virtual simulation experiment teaching.

$$h(d_i) = z_i \cdot \prod B(c_i) - w_i \leftrightarrow \sum_{i=1}^{n} d_i^2 \frac{d-\mu}{\sigma} \tag{4}$$

With the help of the cloud computing platform, teachers can quickly deploy and manage large-scale virtual experiments, while students can access experimental resources anytime and anywhere, without hardware restrictions.

$$h(d_i) + B(c_i) \leq max\left(d_{ij}\right) \tag{5}$$

At the same time, the application of big data (Big Data) technology makes it possible to process and analyze large amounts of experimental data, to support teaching evaluation and personalized learning.

$$h(d_i) + B(c_i) \leftrightarrow mean\left(\frac{\Delta y}{\Delta d}\frac{\delta y}{\delta d} \odot \sum d_{ij}\right) \tag{6}$$

3.2 Analysis of Practical Teaching Programs

In the field of economics and management, the combination of cloud computing and big data can build an intelligent virtual experimental environment, helping students to make real-time analysis and decision-making in complex situations through data-driven decision support.

$$No(d_i) = \frac{h(d_i) + B(c_i)}{mean\left(\frac{\Delta y}{\Delta d}\frac{\delta y}{\delta d} \odot \sum d_{ij}\right)} \tag{7}$$

Experimental teaching plays an indispensable role in economics and management courses in colleges and universities. It is not only the supplement of theoretical knowledge, but also the key link of practical ability cultivation. Through experimental teaching, students can transform abstract theoretical knowledge into concrete practical operations, and improve their understanding and application ability of economic and management theories.

$$Zh(d_i) = min\left[\sum h(d_i) + B(c_i)\right] \tag{8}$$

This technical basis makes the virtual simulation experiment teaching platform not only provide the flexibility and expansibility that traditional experiments can not match, but also promote the personalization and intelligence of education and improve the quality of teaching.

$$accur(d_i) = \frac{min\left[\sum h(d_i) + B(c_i)\right]}{\sum h(d_i) + B(c_i)} \times 100\% \tag{9}$$

Experimental teaching of economics and management has its own unique requirements. First of all, the experimental content should be closely related to the reality, reflecting the complexity of the economic market and enterprise management, such as the simulated stock market, enterprise operation decisions, etc. Secondly, the experiment should be dynamic to adapt to the rapid changes of the economic environment. Moreover, experiments should encourage critical thinking, allowing students to learn to evaluate from multiple perspectives when analyzing and solving problems.

$$accur(d_i) = \frac{min\left[\sum h(d_i) + B(c_i)\right]}{\sum h(d_i) + B(c_i)} \times 100\% + randon(d_i) \tag{10}$$

Experimental teaching allows students to experience the decision-making process in a simulated real environment, improve problem-solving and teamwork skills, and lay a solid foundation for their future careers. In today's rapidly changing economic environment, the cultivation of this practical ability is particularly important. In addition, experimental teaching should emphasize interactivity and cultivate students' communication and coordination skills through teamwork. Finally, experimental teaching should focus on the feedback and analysis of results to help students to reflect and learn from practice.

4 Results and Discussion

4.1 Introduction to Practical Teaching

At the same time, experimental teaching can stimulate students' interest in learning, enhance the attractiveness of the course, and further promote the deepening understanding of theoretical knowledge. Experimental teaching can also make up for the limitations of the traditional classroom, such as the constraints of time and space.

Table 1 Practical teaching requirements

Scope of application	Grade	Viability	Hands-on learning
Accounting	Routine	86.68	86.00
	Higher	83.02	85.27
Financial management	Routine	84.86	82.17
	Higher	83.43	82.90
Audit	Routine	86.50	81.76
	Higher	84.20	82.63

4.2 University Management

With advancements in info tech, college economic and management experiment resources have shifted from conventional physical models and simulated sand tables to digital, virtual forms. Utilizing 3D modeling, big data analysis, AI among others, the virtual simulation teaching platform encapsulates complex concepts like economic models, business case studies, and financial market operations, offering students a more interactive experimental environment. For instance, they can mimic investment strategies on a virtual stock market and gauge its impact; or take up various roles to understand decision-making in virtual company settings (Table 2).

Table 2. The overall picture of the hands-on learning program

Category	Satisfaction	Analysis rate
Accounting	87.18	85.79
Financial management	88.57	87.73
Audit	87.21	89.02
Mean	89.03	88.39
X^6	88.31	88.77
P = 2.008		

4.3 Practical Learning and Stability of Practical Teaching

The virtual simulation experiment teaching platform breaks the limitation of time and space and allows students to conduct experimental operations anytime and anywhere (Fig. 2).

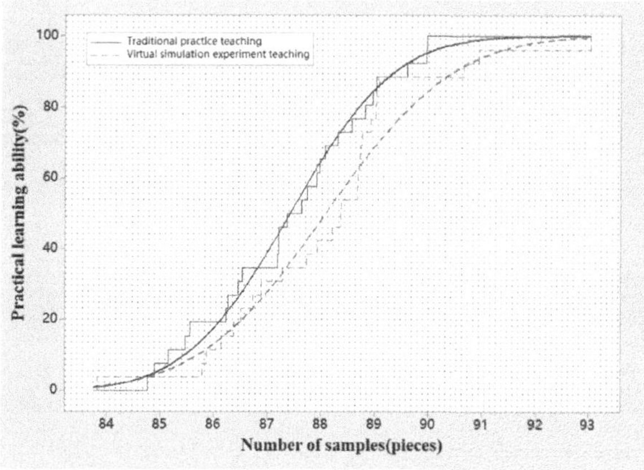

Fig. 2 Hands-on learning of different algorithms

Teachers can design multi-threaded and interactive experimental tasks, so that students can learn through independent exploration. This model encourages students to participate actively and improves the depth and breadth of learning. At the same time, the real-time feedback function of the platform helps teachers to monitor students' learning progress and adjust their teaching strategies in time. For example, teachers can set up economic models with different difficulties, allow students to solve practical problems in a simulated environment, and guide students to deeply understand theoretical knowledge by comparing the results of different decisions (Table 3).

Table 3. Comparison of practical teaching accuracy of different methods

Algorithm	Hands-on learning	Magnitude of change	Error
Virtual simulation experiment teaching platform	91.84	93.08	91.14
Traditional practical teaching	90.36	89.13	88.77
P	86.23	86.88	89.78

The virtual experimental platform presents many innovative applications in the teaching of economic management. First, in the simulated decision laboratory, students make strategic decisions in the simulated market environment, such as product pricing, marketing, resource allocation, etc., to experience the complexity and uncertainty of enterprise operation. The second is the virtual business simulation game, through the gamified teaching methods, let students learn business rules in the competition and cooperation. Third, cross-professional comprehensive experiment, integrating the knowledge of economics, management and other disciplines, so that students can solve cross-field problems in practical situations. In addition, the virtual experimental platform also supports remote collaboration, allowing students from different regions to participate in a project to develop teamwork and communication skills (Fig. 3).

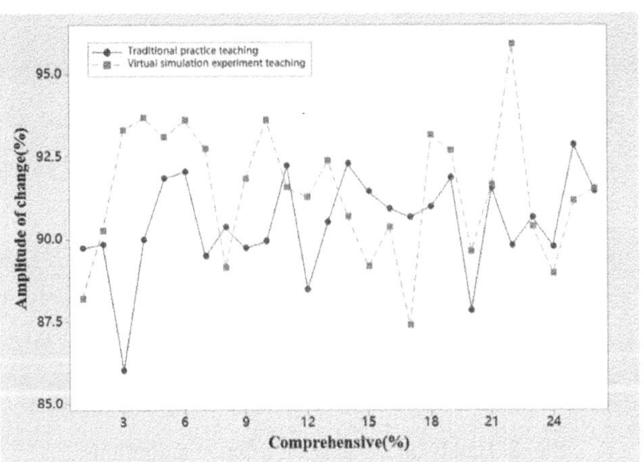

Fig. 3. Practical learning of virtual simulation experimental teaching platform

Simultaneously, the platform's data tracking capability can assess educational outcomes and offer insights for instructional advancement. By engaging in simulated exercises, learners not only grasp theoretical foundations but also enhance their capacity to analyze and address challenges, thus readying themselves for future vocations.

5 Conclusion

Advancing pedagogical efficacy: The digital simulation lab platform adeptly supplements the constraints of customary lab resources, enhancing comprehension and practical skills by emulating authentic business scenarios. Augmenting educational engagement: Leveraging virtual reality, learners partake in an absorbing environment, augmenting teaching's interactivity and appeal, which sparks a keener learning interest. Fostering cross-disciplinary blend: The development of the platform fosters the amalgamation of economics and management disciplines with diverse tech domains, nurturing students' multifaceted thinking and innovative prowess. Streamlining educational asset distribution: Digital experiments diminish reliance on physical apparatuses, conserve educational expenses, accommodate broader student participation concurrently, and streamline the allocation of educative assets.

References

1. Li, X., Liu, X.: Research on the application of mobile teaching platform in business and management experiments. Theor. Res. Pract. Innov. Entrep. **4**(19), 180–182 (2021)
2. Niu, H., Zhang, J., Cui, H., Zheng, H.: Exploration on the construction of experimental teaching cloud platform for integrating economics and management in colleges and universities. Lab. Sci. **24**(04), 160–163 (2021)
3. Zhang, Y.: Exploration on the reform of experimental teaching system of economics and management in colleges and universities in the new era. Teachers (22), 115–116 (2021)
4. Miao, W.: Online teaching methods and countermeasures of experimental courses in economics and management in colleges and universities. Mod. Enterp. (02), 140–141 (2021)
5. Wang, W.: Research on the construction of experimental teaching center for economics and management based on virtual simulation—a case study of Guilin Tourism College. Theor. Obs. (06), 156–158 (2020)

Practical Application of Virtual Reality Technology in Oral English Teaching

Xiaohuan Song(✉)

Faculty of Education, Shaanxi Normal University, Xi'an, Shaanxi, China
songxh06@163.com

Abstract. Virtual reality technology is one of the current technologies that has inspiring effects on English teaching and education, and can improve its vividness. Based on previous research, I have comprehensively judged and analyzed the content, and better identified the key points. The research results show that conducting virtual reality technology education can improve the effectiveness of English teaching, promote the development and development of English education, and form more challenging analysis results. The research results show that virtual reality technology can improve English education by 20%, with high promotion, so there is an analysis.

Keywords: Summation theory · Virtual reality · spoken English · Teach school · Practical application

1 Introduction

Virtual reality technology can simulate a realistic three-dimensional environment, which makes learners feel as if they are in a real English communication scene [1, 2]. This immersive experience helps to enhance learners' sense of participation and substitution, so that they can be more actively involved in oral learning [3, 4]. In this environment, learners can use English more naturally to express and communicate, and improve their oral fluency and self-confidence [5, 6].Virtual reality technology can provide personalized learning paths according to the level and needs of learners [7, 8]. The system can provide targeted guidance and correction according to learners' pronunciation, intonation, grammar and other performances. At the same time, learners can also choose their own learning content and scenarios according to their own interests and goals, so as to achieve more independent and flexible learning [9, 10].

2 Related Concepts

2.1 The Virtual Reality Technology is Described Mathematically.

In the research process of English teaching and oral teaching, the research effect can be improved through virtual display, it is y_i found that the unqualified value parameters in implementing it into practice while instructing students in spoken English is z_i, and

B. Brik and S. Nazir (Eds.): BigIoT-EDU 2024, LNICST 660, pp. 68–77, 2026.
https://doi.org/10.1007/978-3-032-18628-7_8

implementing it into practice while instructing students in spoken English scheme is $tol(y_i \cdot t_{ij})$ integrated with the function to finally judge the feasibility of implementing it into practice while instructing students in spoken English, and the calculation is shown in Eq. (1).

$$\lim_{x \to \infty}(y_i \cdot t_{ij}) = \bigcup_{i=1}^{n} X_i y_{ij} \geq \max(t_{ij} \div 2) \quad (1)$$

Equation illustrates the evaluation of outliers among them (2).

$$\max(t_{ij}) = \partial\left(t_{ij}^2 + 2 \cdot t_{ij}\right)\frac{x-\mu}{\sigma} \succ \sqrt{2}\left(\sum t_{ij} + 4\right) mathfrakM \quad (2)$$

In the process of analyzing English education, the rationality of English teaching can be verified through in-depth judgment of the content and overall education of English education, promoting the effective development of English education. New and innovative reality technologies can make up for the irrationality of previous analysis and enhance the vividness of education. The spoken English is t_i that implementing it into practice while instructing students in spoken English scheme is set_i, I am also willing to teach you. It requires repeated virtual exercises to achieve and enhance its educational effectiveness. Is y_i, and the judgment function of implementing it into practice while instructing students in spoken English the scheme is $F(t_i \approx 0)$ as shown by Eq. (3).

$$F(d_i) = \frac{1}{n}\sum t_i \bigcap \xi \cdot \sqrt{2} \to \oint y_i \cdot 7 \quad (3)$$

2.2 Selection of Practical Application in Oral English Teaching Scheme

Hypothesis II implementing it into practice while instructing students in spoken English function is $g(t_i)$, The weighting factor is w_i, The unqualified practical application in oral English teaching, as indicated in Equation, is thus required by implementing it into practice while instructing students in spoken English (4).

$$g(t_i) = \ddot{x} \cdot z_i X_1, \ldots, X_n \quad (4)$$

English oral education has a strong correlation in previous analysis and research processes, but it is also necessary to explore the key points and content, and enhance the overall quality of oral teaching. is shown in Eq. (5).

$$\lim_{x \to \infty} g(t_i) + \frac{1}{n}F(d_i) \leq \bigcap \max(t_{ij}) \quad (5)$$

In the past analysis process of English teaching, it was necessary to improve the judgment and analysis effectiveness of spoken words, sentences, and other content are presented in Eq. (6).

$$g(t_i) + F(d_i) \leftrightarrow X_1, \ldots, X_n\left(\sum t_{ij} + 4\right) \quad (6)$$

2.3 Analysis of Practical Application in Oral English Teaching Scheme

English education and teaching are the key to current oral education content. They play a significant role in the analysis and reading comprehension of CET-4 and CET-6 education, and require more effective analysis and judgment to identify key points and words.The anomaly assessment system may be given using Eq. (6), and the outcomes is $No(t_i)$ shown in Eq. (7).

$$No(t_i) = \frac{g(t_i) + F(d_i)}{mean\left(\sum t_{ij} + 4\right)} \frac{x - \mu}{\sigma} \tag{7}$$

Among them, it is $\frac{g(t_i)+F(d_i)}{mean(\sum t_{ij}+4)} \leq 1$ specified that the scheme must be $Zh(t_i)$ suggested; otherwise, the scheme integration is necessary; the outcome is illustrated in Eq. (8).

$$Zh(t_i) = \lim_{x \to \infty} \left[\sum g(t_i) + F(d_i)\right] X_1, \ldots, X_n \tag{8}$$

implementing it into practice while instructing students in spoken English is $accur(t_i)$ thoroughly examined, and the threshold and index weight of implementing it into practice while instructing students in spoken English scheme are established to assure the Virtual reality technology's correctness. The core purpose of oral English education is to help students master oral English skills, so that they can use English confidently to communicate in daily life, study and work. This includes developing students' oral fluency, pronunciation accuracy, language organization and the ability to use English to communicate effectively in different contexts, as stated in Eq. (9).

$$accur(t_i) = \frac{\min\left[\sum g(t_i) + F(d_i)\right]}{\sum g(t_i) + F(d_i)} \times 100\% \tag{9}$$

The content of oral English education covers pronunciation, intonation, vocabulary, grammar and pragmatics. In the teaching process, teachers need to teach students correct pronunciation and intonation, help them accumulate common vocabulary and phrases, master basic grammatical rules, and cultivate their ability to use these language knowledge in practical communication, suggesting that the scheme has great unpredictability, and hence it is $randon(t_i)$ considered as a high analytical research. If implementing it into practice while instructing students in spoken English's stochastic function is, then the computation of Eq. (9) may be represented as Eq. (10).

$$accur(t_i) = \frac{\min\left[\sum g(t_i) + F(d_i)\right]}{\frac{x-\mu}{\sigma} \sum g(t_i) + F(d_i)} + randon(t_i) \tag{10}$$

3 Practical Application in Oral English Teaching Optimization Approach

At present, many schools and institutions have begun to try to apply virtual reality technology to oral English teaching. For example, some online English training institutions use virtual reality technology to provide learners with an immersive oral learning environment, allowing them to interact and practice with foreign teachers in real time in virtual scenes. In addition, some schools use virtual reality technology to carry out English corners, English speech contests and other activities, providing learners with more language practice opportunities and communication platforms. To sum up, the application of virtual reality technology in oral English teaching has broad prospects and great potential. It enables the creation of immersive learning environments, provides rich opportunities for language practice, enables personalized learning pathways, and improves learning motivation and interest, and is supported by empirical research. With the continuous development and improvement of technology, it is believed that virtual reality technology will play a more important role in oral English teaching.

4 Practical Examples of Practical Application in Oral English Teaching

4.1 Introduction to Implementing It into Practice While Instructing Students in Spoken English

Virtual reality technology can connect knowledge inside and outside class, so that students can come into contact with more specific communication scenes and topics in oral English learning. By simulating various real scenes, such as airport security check, hotel booking, restaurant ordering, etc., students can master language pronunciation and skills more flexibly, and use them in daily life is shown in Table 1.

Table 1. Practical application in oral English teaching practical application in oral English teaching requirements

Scope of application	Grade	Accuracy	Practical application in oral English teaching
Commercial affairs	I	94.61	90.65
	II	92.27	91.59
Online learning	I	90.87	92.79
	II	86.68	89.26
Schooling	I	91.98	87.70
	II	90.12	88.21

Implementing it into practice while instructing students in spoken English process in Table 1 is shown in Fig. 1.

Studies have shown that the oral English teaching mode based on virtual reality technology can significantly improve students' learning motivation and interest, effectively improve students' oral English performance, and cultivate students' comprehensive English use ability. For example, a questionnaire survey conducted by a college of 60 first-year undergraduate students majoring in English found that after using virtual reality technology for teaching, students' oral performance and comprehensive ability

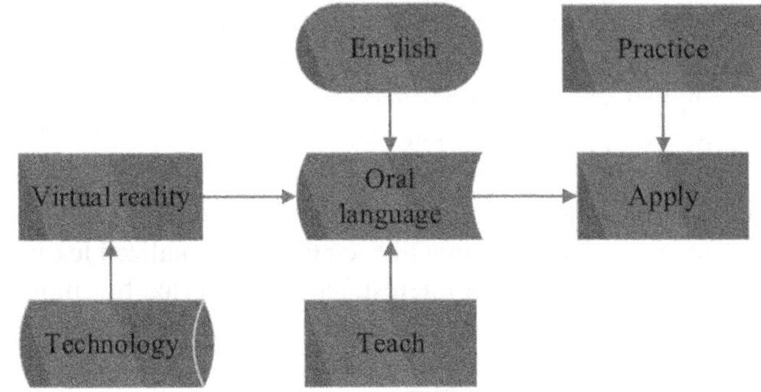

Fig. 1. Analysis process of practical application in oral English teaching

were significantly improved.With its unique immersion and interaction, virtual reality technology can stimulate students' learning interest and motivation. In this novel learning style, students will feel more interesting and fulfilled, so that they will be more actively involved in oral English learning.

4.2 Practical Application in Oral English Teaching

Pay attention to the practical application of language and encourage students to use English to communicate in real contexts, accuracy, and summation stability (Table 2).

Table 2. The overall situation of implementing it into practice while instructing students in spoken English scheme

Category	Random data	Reliability	Analysis rate
Commercial affairs	89.01	93.64	93.87
Online learning	90.91	87.39	89.38
Schooling	91.39	91.93	96.05
Mean	90.43	88.58	89.30
X6	90.32	88.54	89.92
	P = 1.249		

4.3 Practical Application in Oral English Teaching and Stability

Incorporate oral teaching into real or imagined scenarios. Teachers provide vivid descriptions of situations, and students practice speaking by playing roles and participating in conversations is shown in Fig. 2.

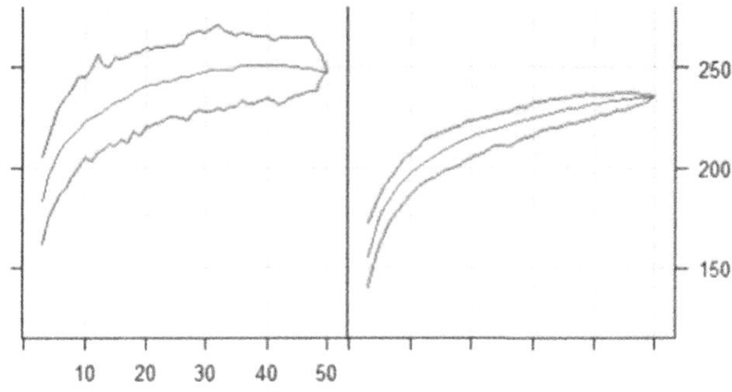

Fig. 2. Evaluation model of aging performance of different algorithms

Figure 2 shows that Incorporate oral teaching into real or imagined scenarios. Teachers provide vivid descriptions of situations, and students practice speaking by playing roles and participating in conversations The overall survey content of oral communication is shown in Table 3.

Table 3. Compares the accuracy of several practical application in oral English teaching

Algorithm	Pronunciation	Word count	Read	Writing
Virtual reality technology	96.10	90.09	89.76	89.86
Image recognition algorithm	88.46	87.91	85.98	87.89
P	89.26	90.59	88.64	88.85

Table 3 shows that Pay attention to repetition and imitation of language. Students learn English by listening to carefully selected audio materials and then repeating the contents of these materials. This approach helps develop accuracy and fluency, but may lack the element of authentic communication, as shown in Fig. 3.

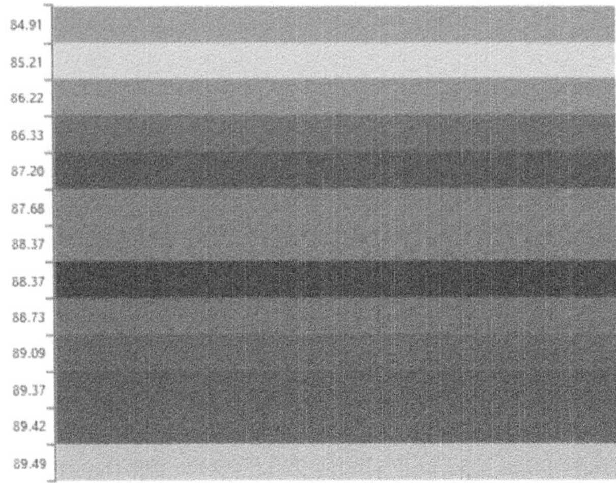

Fig. 3. Practical application in oral English teaching of virtual reality technology

Figure 3 shows that Teachers will use authentic language materials, such as stories, songs, and videos, and encourage students to learn by naturally interacting with English speakers. This approach helps to develop language intuition, but it may take longer to see significant improvement.

4.4 Rationality of Practical Application in Oral English Teaching

The advancement of science and technology has greatly affected oral English teaching. Tools such as online platforms, video conferencing, and language learning apps enable students to practice speaking in a virtual environment, provide flexibility and convenience, and can help students connect with language learners across the globe in Fig. 4.

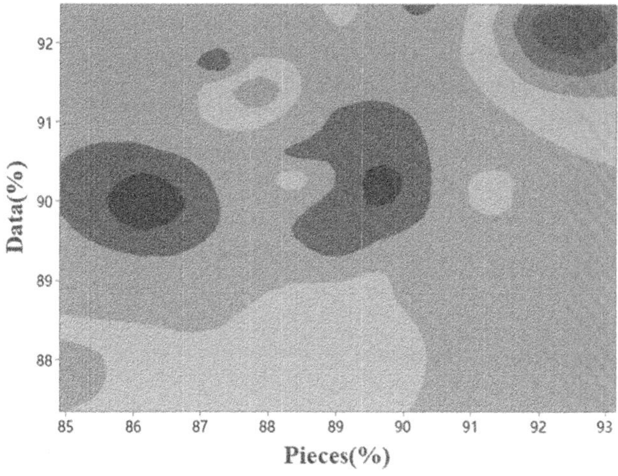

Fig. 4. Evaluation model of aging performance of different algorithms

Figure 4 shows that Proficiency in 48 IPAs, including 20 vowels (12 unitaries and 8 diphthongs) and 28 consonants. Through phonetic symbol learning, each phoneme can be pronounced accurately.

4.5 Validity of Practical Application in Oral English Teaching

Whether English has advantages in terms of expression, vocabulary expression content, and expression scenarios requires analysis of its expression position is shown in Fig. 5.

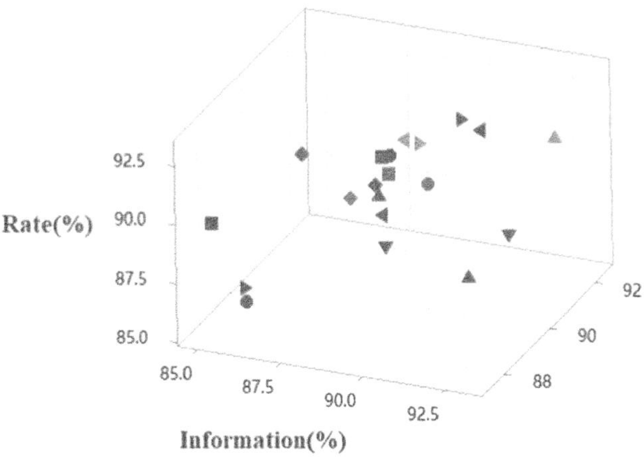

Fig. 5. Practical application in oral English teaching of different algorithms

Figure 5 shows that the key points of English expression are distributed in different positions of sentence reading and the entire article, so English has significant advantages in the process of sentence expression. Therefore, this article proposes virtual reality technology to meet the analysis needs of English expression. This further validates the research results and requires analysis of the tables.

Table 4. Compares the efficacy of several practical application in oral English teaching

Algorithm	Survey data	Practical application in oral English teaching	Magnitude of change	Error
Virtual reality technology	87.20	90.02	92.80	91.97
Image recognition algorithm	92.50	89.94	88.74	86.47
P	88.62	89.97	90.76	89.27

Table 4 shows that learners who want to improve their spoken business English, the algorithm will recommend resources such as business English dialogues and business English speech videos; For learners who like to learn spoken English through movies, the algorithm will screen out English movies with moderate speech speed, rich dialogue and suitable for their spoken language level, as illustrated in Fig. 6.

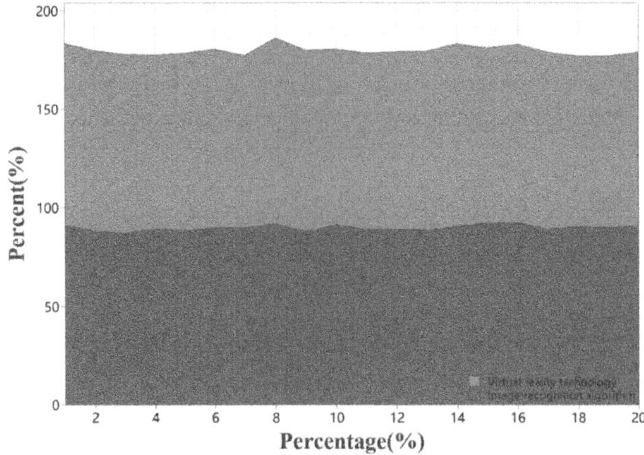

Fig. 6. Virtual reality technology practical application in oral English teaching

Figure 6 shows that with a large number of learners' learning data and successful experiences, the recommendation algorithm can plan a more optimized oral learning path for individual learners. The algorithm can also consider cultural background factors for oral communication matching. For learners who want to understand British English and British culture, it is recommended that they come from the UK or are familiar with English.

5 Conclusion

To sum up, the application of virtual reality technology in oral English teaching has broad prospects and great potential. It can create an immersive language environment, provide rich opportunities for oral practice, realize personalized teaching, stimulate learning interest and motivation, and improve teaching effect and quality. With the continuous development and improvement of technology, it is believed that virtual reality technology will play a more important role in oral English teaching. Please note that although virtual reality technology has many advantages in oral English teaching, it is still necessary to pay attention to the problems of high technical cost and insufficient teacher training in the practical application process, and adopt corresponding solutions to ensure the effective application and popularization of the technology.

References

1. Wei, B.: The application of virtual reality technology in college oral English teaching. Comput. Telecommun. **4**(12), 145 (2006)
2. Zhao, R., Dong, G.: The application of virtual reality technology in college oral English teaching. North. Literat. China **1**(12), 540 (2018)
3. Yang, G.: Research on three-dimensional college oral English supported by virtual reality technology. College English Teach. Res. **6**(3), 112 (2013)
4. Wang, L., Ling, L.: College oral English teaching based on virtual reality technology. J. Jilin Provin. Educ. College China **21**, 5542 (2010)
5. Lu, Y., Shen, P.: Feasibility study of integrating Vr (virtual reality) technology into oral English teaching. Overseas English **14**, 94–96 (2023)
6. Mahone, S.: The Application of Virtual Reality Technology in Oral English Teaching (2014)
7. Fang, Y.: Virtual reality technology is applied in college oral English teaching. In: The Classic of Mountains and Seas: Imagination Composition, vol. 8, p. 1 (2015)
8. Zhu, H.: The application of virtual reality technology in college English teaching. Mod. Commer. Trade Ind. **42**(17), 2 (2021)
9. Tsai, G.-Y.: Application of Vr/ar technology in college English teaching. China Inform. Technol. Educ. **6**, 4 (2019)
10. Yang, G.: Research on three-dimensional college oral English supported by virtual reality technology. In: Examination and Evaluation (College English Teaching and Research Edition) (2013)

Algorithmic Immersive English Teaching System Based on VR Technology

Liu Jinlian(✉)

Jiangxi Institute of Applied Science and Technology, Ganzhou, China
ly2001love@163.com

Abstract. As a whole, society has embraced scientific and technical methods to maximize efficiency in light of the exponential growth of these fields; this is especially true in the realm of English language instruction. In order to achieve learning goals, immersion plays a crucial role in English language instruction. When it comes to teaching English as a second language, the conventional wisdom has no answers. Hence, for the purpose of immersive education analysis, this study suggests a VR-based algorithmic system for teaching English. To minimize obstacles to immersive learning, the first step is to use computer technology in the system's design and development. The indications are then organized according to the needs of immersive instruction. The next step is for computer technology to create an immersive teaching program, examine the findings thoroughly, and then implement the system's designs into the English teaching system. Based on certain assessment criteria, the algorithmic immersive English education system that utilizes VR technology outperforms the conventional method of instruction, according to MATLAB simulations.

Keywords: Computer technology · Algorithmic immersive English teaching system based on VR technology · English language teaching · Immersion teaching

1 Introduction

Today, immersion education is a popular approach to teaching English, and it has significant implications for the field [1]. Unfortunately, the immersion teaching program's unreliability is an issue that arises during immersion instruction[2], which in turn makes teaching English more challenging [3]. There are academics who think that by analyzing English language instruction through the lens of a virtual reality (VR) algorithmic immersive teaching system, we may better understand immersive pedagogy and provide relevant support for it [4]. This research aims to optimize the immersive teaching scheme and validate the efficacy of the model by proposing an algorithmic VR-based immersive English teaching system [5]. The following are some of the ways in which artificial intelligence (AI) is changing the face of immersive English education and how it may benefit students, teachers, and the curriculum:

B. Brik and S. Nazir (Eds.): BigIoT-EDU 2024, LNICST 660, pp. 78–87, 2026.
https://doi.org/10.1007/978-3-032-18628-7_9

(1) Individualized instruction

Students' learning situations and progress may be tailored using the customizable immersive English education system, which is built on top of artificial intelligence and virtual reality technology. Artificial intelligence (AI) has the potential to improve education by analyzing student data and patterns of learning and creating individualized lesson plans based on these findings.

(2) Learning that is interactive

The goal of developing an immersive English teaching system is to provide students with a more realistic learning environment by simulating real-world scenarios. Through the use of AI, students may engage in virtual reality educational situations, which can enhance their understanding and mastery of English language skills.

(3) Vast stores of information

Books, movies, audios, and other rich learning materials in English may be seamlessly incorporated into the immersive English teaching system. With the help of AI, we can personalize our recommendations for students' educational materials to their specific interests and requirements, increase the variety of resources available to them, and deepen their understanding of course material.

(4) Voice translation in real-time

To further aid students' comprehension and proficiency in the English language, the immersive English education system may also make use of artificial intelligence technologies to accomplish real-time voice translation. Students may practice their spoken English in a natural setting with the help of AI-powered intelligent voice recognition and translation, which opens up new horizons for their language acquisition.

(5) Astute assessment and comments

By evaluating student learning data, AI technology may actualize intelligent assessment and feedback systems, help students with their learning when they need it, and identify and address any issues with their learning in a timely manner. Simultaneously, AI has the potential to provide automated grading, which would greatly enhance the efficacy and precision of learning.

2 Related Works

A. *Mathematical description of algorithmic immersive English teaching system based on VR technology.*

By optimizing the immersive teaching scheme using VR technology, the algorithmic immersive English teaching system based on VR technology analyzes index parameters in immersive teaching to determine how to best implement the scheme [6] is d_i [7], it is found that the unqualified value parameter in English teaching is z_i [8], as well as the immersive teaching scheme's integration function is $tol(d_i \cdot h_{ij})$, in order to determine the practicability of teaching English, the results of which are shown in formula (1).

$$tol(d_i \cdot h_{ij} - 7) = d_{ij} \geq \max\left(h_{ij} \div \iint d_i\right) \tag{1}$$

Outlier evaluation is one of them, as indicated in Eq. (2).

$$\max(h_{ij}) = \left(h_{ij}^2 \oplus 4\right) \succ mean\left(\sum h_{ij} - 7\uplus\right) \Leftrightarrow \sqrt{2} \tag{2}$$

To make immersive learning more practical, an algorithmic approach is being developed that blends the benefits of virtual reality with the quantification of English language instruction.

So, let's pretend I. The immersion instruction prerequisite is h_i, the immersive teaching program is set_i, the contentment with the comprehensive educational curriculum is d_i, as well as the immersive learning program's judgment function is $Q(h_i \approx 0)$, as shown in Eq. (3).

$$Q(d_i) = 5 - \sum h_i \cap \xi - X_1, \ldots, X_n \to \oint d_i * \sigma_X^2. \tag{3}$$

B. *Choice of immersion teaching programs.*

If the II English class is to be taught is $g(h_i)$, and the weight coefficient is w_i, Therefore, as shown in Eq. (4), immersion necessitates the provision of instruction in perfect English.

$$g(h_i) = z_i \cdot \frac{1}{n} + \iint z_i \cdot \prod Q(d_i) \Leftrightarrow \sigma_X \cdot w_i. \tag{4}$$

Equation (5) shows the outcome of testing hypotheses I and II, which states that the complete function of the teaching system may be acquired.

$$g(h_i) + Q(d_i) \leq \max(h_{ij}) \tag{5}$$

Data standardization is essential for improving system viability, as seen in Eq. (6).

$$\widetilde{g(h_i) + Q(d_i)} \leftrightarrow mean\left(\sum h_{ij} - 7\uplus\right) \Leftrightarrow \sqrt{2} \tag{6}$$

C. *Analysis of immersion programs.*

An in-depth evaluation of the immersive teaching plan across several dimensions, a mapping of the requirements for immersive teaching to the English teaching library, and the elimination of any unsuitable plans must precede the implementation of the algorithmic immersive English teaching system that relies on virtual reality technology is $No(h_i)$. The findings are illustrated in Eq. (7), and the anomaly assessment method may be provided according to Eq. (6).

$$No(x_i) = \frac{\widetilde{g(h_i) + Q(d_i)}}{mean\left(\sum h_{ij} - 7\uplus\right) \Leftrightarrow \sqrt{2}} \tag{7}$$

Among them, $\frac{g\widetilde{(h_i)+Q}(d_i)}{mean(\sum h_{ij}-7\uplus)\Leftrightarrow\sqrt{2}} \leq 1$ if the scheme is not presented, then its integration will be necessary is $Zh(h_i)$, and the result is shown in Eq. (8).

$$Zh(h_i) = \min[\sum g\widetilde{(h_i) + Q}(d_i)] \tag{8}$$

The correctness of the algorithmic immersive English teaching system based on VR technology is ensured by conducting a detailed analysis of English teaching and setting the index weights and thresholds of the immersive teaching scheme. Feasibility studies are necessary for immersion education solutions, and teaching English is a systematic test of such solutions. For non-normal distributions of English teaching is $unno(h_i)$, The total immersion accuracy is reduced as a result of this impact on its immersion scheme is $accur(h_i)$, as shown in Eq. (9).

$$accur(h_i) = \frac{\min[\sum g\widetilde{(h_i) + Q}(d_i)]}{\sum g\widetilde{(h_i) + Q}(d_i)} \times 100\% \tag{9}$$

In agreement with empirical evidence, the study of immersive learning systems reveals that these types of programs have a multi-dimensional distribution. Given the lack of direction in English instruction, this research is considered highly analytical since it suggests that the immersion teaching method is quite random. Assuming the probability function for ESL instruction is $randon(h_i)$, then Eq. (10). This allows us to state the computation of Eq. (9).

$$accur(h_i) = \frac{\min[\sum g\widetilde{(h_i) + Q}(d_i)]}{\sum g\widetilde{(h_i) + Q}(d_i)} \times 100\% + randon(h_i) \tag{10}$$

Among them, English instruction fulfills typical needs; primarily, virtual reality technology modifies English instruction, gets rid of unnecessary and redundant schemes, and augments the default scheme, resulting in a robust dynamic correlation throughout the immersive teaching scheme.

3 Optimization Strategies for English Language Teaching

Using a random optimization technique, the algorithmic immersive VR teaching system optimizes the English teaching scheme by adjusting the teaching system parameters. Algorithmic immersive English teaching system built on VR technology randomly chooses alternative schemes and splits English instruction into distinct immersive teaching levels. The iterative method involves optimizing and analyzing the immersion teaching scheme across various immersion teaching levels. Record the most effective English language instruction by comparing the immersion levels of several programs once the optimization study is complete.

4 Results and Discussion

A. *Introduction to Immersion Teaching.*

Table 1 shows the unique immersion teaching plan of English, and the study target of this work is English teaching in complicated scenarios. There are 12 pathways and a 12-h test duration.

Table 1. Immersion requirements

Scope of application	Grade	Viability	Immersion teaching
Writing	I	83.51	82.26
	II	83.14	83.72
Hearing	I	80.92	79.50
	II	82.18	86.83
Read	I	81.03	84.13
	II	83.35	83.83

The immersion process in Table 1 is shown in Fig. 1.

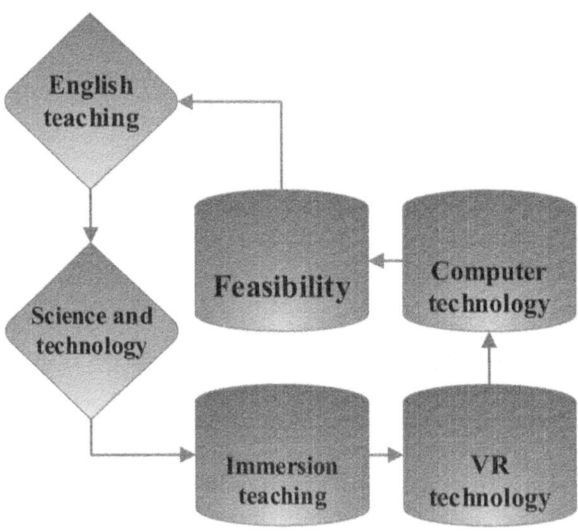

Fig. 1. Analytical process of English language teaching

Algorithmic immersive English education systems based on VR technology provide a more realistic approach to immersive instruction than conventional classroom methods. The algorithmic immersive VR-based English education system outperforms the conventional method of instruction in terms of logical consistency and dependability. Figure 2 shows the updated immersive teaching scheme, which demonstrates the increased feasibility and efficiency of the algorithmic immersive English teaching system built on VR technology. Accordingly, the algorithmic VR-based immersive English teaching system has superior summation stability, immersive teaching scheme speed, and immersive teaching scheme overall.

B. *English teaching.*

Structured, semi-structured, and unstructured data are all part of the English immersion program. Following the pre-selection of a virtual reality (VR)-based algorithmic immersive English education system, we acquire a preliminary immersive teaching scheme and assess its practicability. Table 2 shows the immersion teaching scheme, and choosing English instruction at various immersion levels allows for more precise verification of the impact of immersion teaching.

Table 2. The overall picture of the immersive teaching program

Category	Random data	Reliability	Analysis rate
Writing	85.05	84.63	89.93
Hearing	82.24	84.80	83.25
Read	83.94	84.88	85.89
Mean	85.89	87.97	87.56
X6	85.76	85.71	89.37
	P = .065		

C. *Immersion teaching and stability of immersive teaching.*

Figure 2 depicts the immersive teaching scheme, which is contrasted to the conventional teaching mode in order to confirm the viability of the algorithmic immersive English teaching system based on VR technology.

From Fig. 2, we can deduce that the error rate is lower in the algorithmic immersive English teaching system based on VR technology, suggesting that its immersive teaching is relatively stable, in contrast to the traditional teaching mode's uneven immersive teaching. This suggests that the immersive teaching of the former is more effective. As indicated in Table 3, the three algorithms mentioned above have an average immersive teaching strategy.

Table 3 demonstrates that there are problems with the practicality of using immersion instruction in the classroom, that there have been major shifts in the way English is taught, and that there is a high rate of mistakes. The overall outcome of a virtual reality (VR)-based algorithmic immersive English education system is a more effective form of instruction than the conventional one. Also, the accuracy hasn't altered much, and

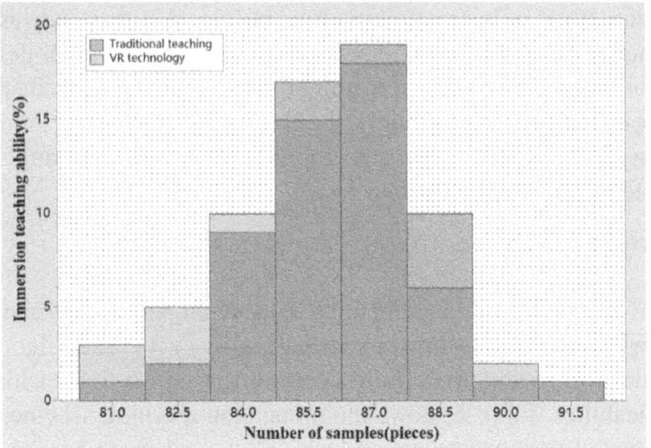

Fig. 2. Immersive teaching of different algorithms

Table 3. Comparison of the accuracy of immersion teaching by different methods

Algorithm	Survey data	Immersion teaching	Magnitude of change	Error
Algorithmic immersive English teaching system based on VR technology	92.42	93.49	90.73	30.21
Traditional teaching mode	91.05	92.98	94.22	29.61
P	93.50	91.75	92.21	31.74

the algorithmic immersive English education system that uses VR technology has an immersive teaching rate of above 90%. The purpose is to provide further evidence that a VR-based algorithmic immersive English education system is preferable. Figure 3 shows the results of a comprehensive study of the algorithmic immersive English education system that makes use of VR technology. This analysis aims to provide more evidence that the suggested technique is successful.

By increasing the adjustment coefficient of English teaching and setting the teaching system's threshold to eliminate the immersive teaching scheme that does not meet the requirements, the algorithmic immersive English teaching system based on VR technology offers substantially better immersive teaching than the traditional teaching mode (as seen in Fig. 3).

D. *The effectiveness of immersion.*

Figure 4 shows the immersive teaching scheme, which is used to compare it with the conventional teaching mode, in order to confirm that the algorithmic immersive English teaching system that is based on VR technology is successful.

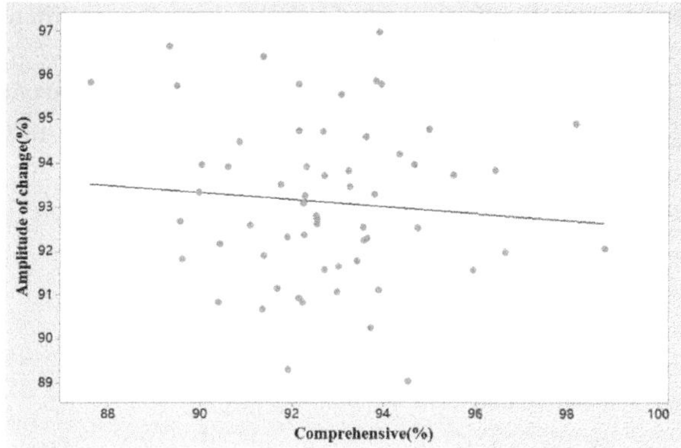

Fig. 3. Immersive teaching of algorithmic immersive English teaching system based on VR technology

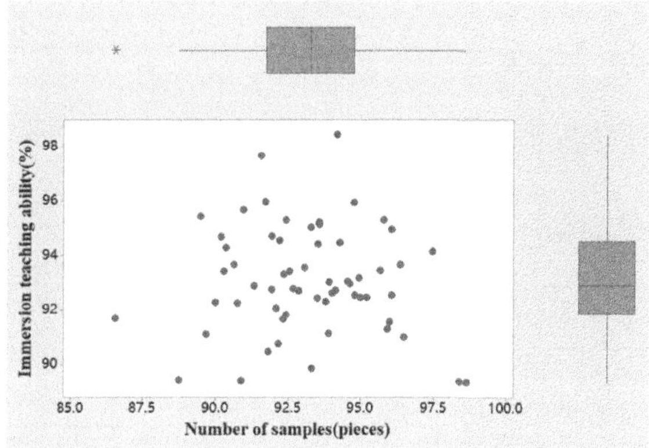

Fig. 4. Immersive teaching with different algorithms

As shown in Fig. 4, the error rate is lower in the algorithmic immersive English teaching system based on VR technology, suggesting that its immersive teaching is relatively stable, in contrast to the traditional teaching mode's uneven immersion teaching. Moreover, the immersive teaching of the former is higher than that of the latter. In Table 4, we can see the three algorithms' average immersive teaching schemes.

Table 4 shows that there are problems with the stability of immersion instruction in typical classroom settings, that there have been major shifts in the field of English language instruction, and that the mistake rate is very high. The overall outcome of a virtual reality (VR)-based algorithmic immersive English education system is a more effective form of instruction than the conventional one. Simultaneously, the accuracy has remained relatively unchanged, and the immersive teaching of the algorithmic immersive English education system based on VR technology exceeds 93%. The purpose is to provide further evidence that a VR-based algorithmic immersive English education system is preferable. Figure 5 shows the results of several analyses conducted on the

Table 4. Comparison of the effectiveness of immersion teaching in different methods

Algorithm	Survey data	Immersion teaching	Magnitude of change	Error
Algorithmic immersive English teaching system based on VR technology	90.60	88.05	85.66	30.81
Traditional teaching mode	88.14	86.89	89.57	30.19
P	89.57	89.08	87.84	28.20

algorithmic immersive English education system that is based on VR technology. The purpose of these analyses is to provide more evidence that the suggested technique is successful.

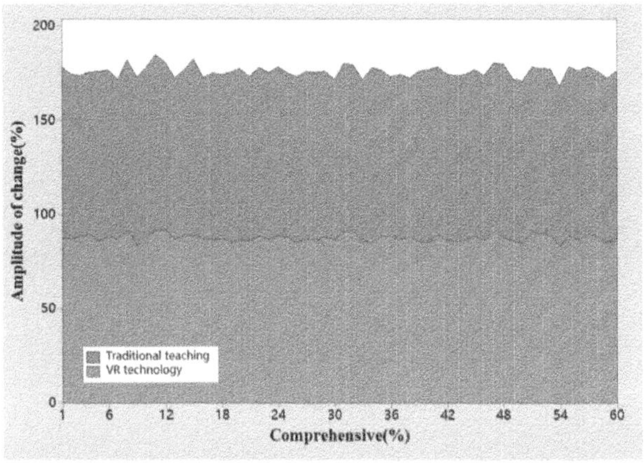

Fig. 5. Immersive teaching of algorithmic immersive English teaching system based on VR technology

Figure 5 clearly shows that the algorithmic immersive English teaching system using VR technology outperforms the traditional method of instruction. This is due to the fact that the VR system raises the adjustment coefficient for English instruction and establishes a threshold for the system to discard immersive teaching schemes that don't measure up.

5 Conclusion

To address the issue that current methods of teaching English via immersion are not optimal, this article presents a virtual reality (VR) based algorithmic immersive English teaching system and suggests ways to maximize VR technology in the classroom. While compiling a set of instructional methods, we also conduct extensive analyses of the practicality of immersive learning. Research has shown that a VR-based algorithmic immersive English teaching system may enhance the precision and consistency of English instruction, in addition to carrying out general immersive instruction in English. However, while developing a VR-based algorithmic immersive English teaching system, researchers focus too much on immersive teaching analysis, leading to illogical indicator selection.

Acknowledgements. Research on the application of "online + offline" hybrid teaching mode—take "Business English Translation as an example", GJJ191198.

References

1. Dang, X., Hu, C.: Design of human–computer interaction immersive distance teaching system based on SSH framework. Autom. Instrum. **2023**(05), 221–230 (2023)
2. Liu, Y.: Research on art education in immersive English classroom, a participatory learning approach. Overseas English **22**, 183–198 (2022)
3. Nong, L.: Research on human–computer symbiosis mechanism to improve primary school students' English learning ability. Southwest University (2022)
4. Li, W.: Research on the application of immersion teaching in primary school English teaching. Southwest University (2022)
5. Chen, Q.: Research and practice of English immersion teaching in primary schools. Qufu Normal University (2022)
6. Xiao, F.: Practice and research of immersion teaching method in junior high school English teaching. In: Huajiao Innovation (Beijing) Culture Media Co., Ltd., China Global Culture Press. 2022 Education and Teaching Modernization and Precision Management Summit Forum Proceedings (Junior High School Education) (1). Huajiao Innovation (Beijing) Culture Media Co., Ltd., China Global Culture Press, Huajiao Innovation (Beijing) Culture Media Co., Ltd., pp. 457–460 (2022)
7. Luo, Z.: Research on the construction of immersive English teaching mode in higher vocational colleges. English Square **5**, 92–94 (2022)
8. Ren, Q.: Analysis of multi-dimensional training strategy of immersive English teaching for college students. J. Jiangxi Electr. Power Vocat. Techn. College **34**(12), 64–65 (2021)
9. Wu, M.: Initiating immersive English teaching in multidimensional import. Prim. School Teach. Refer. **12**, 64–66 (2023)
10. Li, W.: Comparison of traditional English teaching mode and immersive teaching mode. Chengcai **3**, 7–9 (2023)

The Application of 3D Virtual Simulation Training in Vocational and Technical Education

Wei Liu(✉)

Chengdu Polytechnic, Chengdu, Sichuan, China
liuwei_ts@126.com

Abstract. While TVET relies heavily on applied research in education, the issue of misleading research positioning persists. Problems with applied research in technical and vocational education are beyond the capabilities of the conventional particle swarm method, and its results are less than satisfactory. Consequently, this study examines component localization and quality early warning and suggests research positioning and early warning in education based on 3D virtual simulation training. In order to minimize interference with practical research in education, we first use human-computer interaction theory to identify the components that have an impact, and then we categorize the indicators based on the needs of this field. The next step is to apply the theory of human-computer interaction to the development of a research program for the practical training application of 3D virtual simulations in education. The outcomes of this study will be thoroughly examined. The findings of the MATLAB simulation demonstrate that, according to certain assessment criteria, classical particle swarm techniques are not as effective as 3D virtual simulation training when it comes to educational aspects affecting application research time and accuracy.

Keywords: Human–computer interaction theory · 3D virtual simulation training · Education · Applied research · Vocational skills

1 Introduction

Applied research in education may speed up the process of precisely controlling applied research in education [1], which is a crucial component of vocational and technical education [2]. Nevertheless, there is an issue with the accuracy of applied research programs in education, which has a certain detrimental influence on applied research in education [3–5]. This problem arises throughout the process of applied research in education [6]. Applied research and analysis in education may be improved with the use of 3D virtual simulation training, according to some experts [7, 8]. This training would allow for a more thorough examination of the education program's applied research program and related support for applied research in education [9, 10]. As a result, this study suggests using 3D virtual simulation training to optimize [11, 12] the educational applied research scheme and validate the model's efficacy [13].

B. Brik and S. Nazir (Eds.): BigIoT-EDU 2024, LNICST 660, pp. 88–98, 2026.
https://doi.org/10.1007/978-3-032-18628-7_10

2 Related Works

2.1 Mathematical Description of 3D Virtual Simulation Training

The goal of training in 3D virtual simulations is to maximize educational applied research schemes using computer technology; then, using the applied research scheme's index parameters, determine the parameters' unqualified value is y_i, and integrate the function of the applied research scheme in education is z_i, and finally judge the feasibility of applied research in education, calculated is $\mathrm{tol}(y_i \cdot t_{ij})$ shown in formula (1).

$$\lim_{x\to\infty}(y_i \cdot t_{ij}) = y_{ij} \geq \max(t_{ij} \div 2)\mathrm{B} \tag{1}$$

The evaluation of extreme cases is shown in Eq. (2).

$$\max(t_{ij}) = \partial\left(t_{ij}^2 + 2 \cdot t_{ij}\right) \succ \frac{1}{2}\left(\sum t_{ij} + 4\right)M \tag{2}$$

By integrating the benefits of computing with quantitative findings from applied research in education, 3D virtual simulation training has the potential to raise the reliability of this field's findings.

Suppose I The requirements for applied research in education is t_i, the application research program in education is set_i, the satisfaction of the applied research program in education is y_i, and the judgment function of the applied research program in education is $F(t_i \approx 0)$ as shown in Eq. (3).

$$F(d_i) = \coprod \sum t_i \cap \xi \cdot \sqrt{2} \to \oint y_i \cdot 7 \tag{3}$$

2.2 Selection of Applied Research Programs in Education

Hypothesis II The applied research function in education is $g(t_i)$ and the weight coefficient is $g(t_i)$, Therefore, as shown in Eq. (4), applied research in education necessitates applied research in inadequate education.

$$g(t_i) = \ddot{x} \cdot z_i \prod F(d_i)\frac{dy}{dx} - w_i \tag{4}$$

An all-encompassing function of educational applied research may be derived from assumptions I and II, as shown in Eq. (5).

$$\lim_{x\to\infty} g(t_i) + F(d_i) \leq \cap\max(t_{ij})\Gamma \tag{5}$$

The consequences of standardizing all data may be seen in Eq. (6), which shows how applied research in education can be made more successful.

$$\overline{g(t_i) + F(d_i)} \leftrightarrow \mathrm{mean}\left(\sum t_{ij} + 4\right) \tag{6}$$

2.3 Analysis of Applied Research Programme in Education

An in-depth evaluation of the educational system's applied research scheme, a mapping of the system's requirements for applied research to its library, and the elimination of any unqualified schemes should precede any training in 3D virtual simulations. Equation (6) states that the anomaly evaluation scheme can be proposed, and the results is $No(t_i)$ shown in Eq. (7).

$$No(t_i) = \frac{\overline{g(t_i) + F(d_i)}}{\text{mean}\left(\sum t_{ij} + 4\right)} \frac{1}{2} \Phi \tag{7}$$

Among them, it is $\frac{\overline{g(t_i)+F(d_i)}}{\text{mean}\left(\sum t_{ij}+4\right)} \leq 1$ stated that the scheme needs to be proposed, otherwise the scheme integration is required, and the result is $Zh(t_i)$ shown in Eq. (8).

$$Zh(t_i) = \cap\left[\sum \overline{g(t_i) + F(d_i)}\right] \tag{8}$$

In order to provide precise 3D virtual simulation training, the educational research scheme's threshold and index weights have been determined after a thorough analysis of the relevant applied research. Methodical testing of educational applied research schemes is what applied research in education is all about, and it demands precise analysis.If applied research in education is $\text{unno}(t_i)$ in a non-normal distribution, its applied research program in education will be affected, reducing the accuracy of applied research in education as a whole, is $\text{accur}(t_i)$ shown in Eq. (9).

$$\text{accur}(t_i) = \frac{\min\left[\sum \overline{g(t_i) + F(d_i)}\right]}{\sum \overline{g(t_i) + F(d_i)}} \text{I} \tag{9}$$

A multidimensional distribution is shown by the survey of applied research programs in education, which is consistent with objective facts. Due to the lack of direction in applied research in education, which suggests a highly random study strategy, this field is considered to be highly analytical. If the stochastic function of applied research in education is $\text{randon}(t_i)$, then the calculation of formula (9) can be expressed as formula (10).

$$\text{accur}(t_i) = \frac{\min\left[\sum \overline{g(t_i) + F(d_i)}\right]}{\sqrt{2} \sum \overline{g(t_i) + F(d_i)}} + \text{randon}(t_i) \tag{10}$$

There are a number of factors that contribute to the strong dynamic correlation between the applied research scheme and the rest of education. One of these is the fact that applied research in education satisfies standard requirements. Another factor is the role that computer technology plays in adjusting applied research in education, eliminating unnecessary and duplicate schemes and supplementing the default one.

3 Optimization Strategies for Applied Research in Education

In order to optimize the scheme of applied research in education, the 3D virtual simulation training uses a random optimization technique and tweaks the Internet information settings. Various degrees of educational applied research on 3D virtual simulation training have been identified, and new schemes have been chosen at random. The iterative method optimizes and analyzes many applied research schemes in education at different levels. After the optimization analysis is finished, we compile the levels of applied research in education across various programs and record the best ones.

4 Results and Discussion

4.1 Introduction to Applied Research in Education

Table 1 shows the application research scheme in education for special applied research in education, and the article uses applied research in education under difficult circumstances as its research goal. The study has 12 pathways and a 12-h test duration.

Table 1. Applied research requirements in education

Scope of application	Training style	The conversion rate of public opinion time	The rigor of practical operation
Vocational training	Theoretical training	85.00	78.86
	Virtual training	81.97	78.45
Curriculum development	Theoretical training	83.81	81.31
	Virtual training	83.34	78.19
Educational assessment	Theoretical training	79.56	81.99
	Virtual training	79.10	80.11

The process of applied research in education in Table 1 is shown in Fig. 1.

Using the particle swarm technique, the educational research plan for 3D virtual simulation training is more in line with the needs of real-world educational application research. Compared to the particle swarm approach, 3D virtual simulation training is more reasonable and accurate when it comes to educational applied research. Figure 2 shows how the educational application research plan has changed, demonstrating how 3D virtual simulation training is more accurate and reliable. Consequently, educational solutions based on practical research are superior in terms of speed, accuracy, and overall stability.

4.2 Applied Research in Education

Educational Practice-Based Research There is a mix of organized and unstructured data in the Applied Research Program in Education. The viability of the applied research

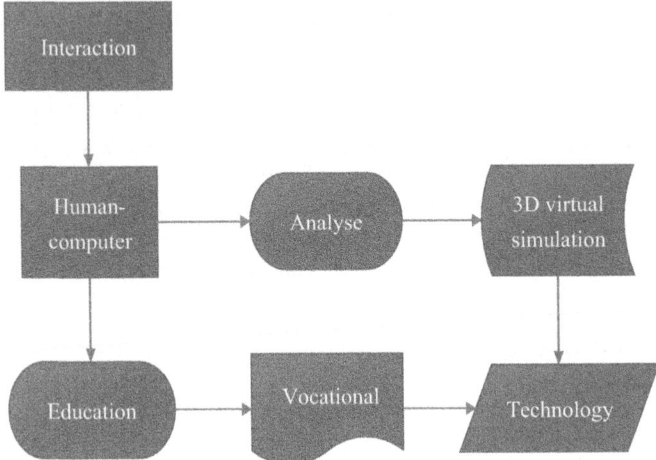

Fig. 1. The analytical process of applied research in education

in education was assessed after the pee-selection of the 3D virtual simulation training, and the preliminary applied research plan in education was obtained. As indicated in Table 2, the applied research in education and applied research programs in education are chosen at various levels of applied research in education to more properly verify the impact of applied research in education.

Table 2. The overall situation of applied research programme in education

Category	Sample accuracy after virtual processing	On the conversion rate of practice	Student satisfaction
Vocational training	85.32	85.90	83.95
Curriculum development	86.36	82.51	84.29
Educational assessment	84.16	84.92	83.68

4.3 Applied Research and Stability in Education

As seen in Fig. 2, the particle swarm technique is an integral aspect of the applied research scheme in education, which aims to validate the 3D virtual simulation training.

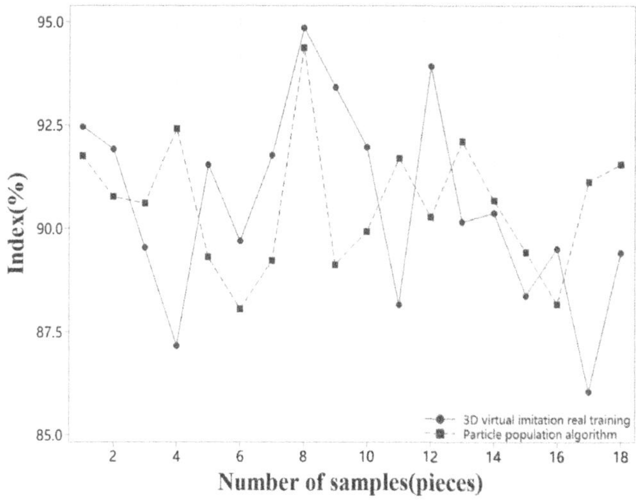

Fig. 2. Research on the application of different algorithms in education

From Fig. 2, we can deduce that there is more applied research into 3D virtual simulation training than particle swarm algorithm, but with a lower error rate. This suggests that the applied research into 3D virtual simulation training is relatively stable, in contrast to the uneven applied research into particle swarm simulation. In Table 3, we can see the typical educational application research method for the aforementioned three algorithms.

Table 3. Comparison of the accuracy of applied research in education with different methods

Algorithm	Machining accuracy	Comprehensive treatment effect	Machining complexity	The whole of the effect. Processing conditions
3D virtual simulation training	85.33	85.15	82.88	84.95
Particle swarm arithmetic	85.20	83.41	86.01	85.75
P	87.17	87.62	84.48	86.97

According to Table 3, there are certain issues with the accuracy of the applied research in education when using particle swarm optimization. The study in this area has seen substantial changes, and the error rate is rather high. When compared to particle swarm methods, the overall performance of training using 3D virtual simulations is superior in educational applied research. Simultaneously, the accuracy has remained relatively unchanged, and the applied research in the field of education for 3D virtual simulation training is above 90%. For the purpose of providing more evidence that training using 3D virtual simulations is preferable. Various methodologies are used to conduct a general analysis of 3D virtual simulation training, as shown in Fig. 3, in order to further validate the efficiency of the suggested method.

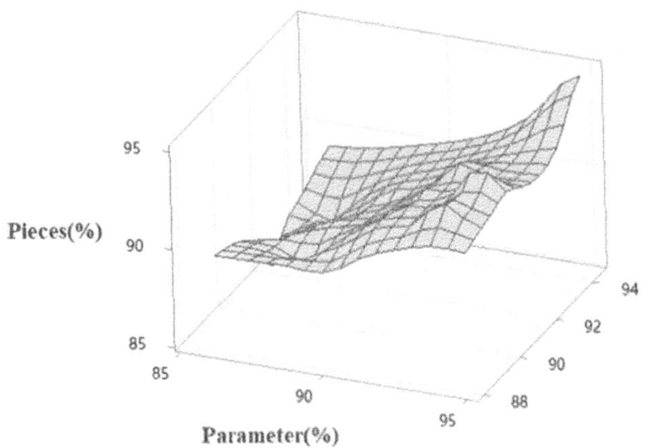

Fig. 3. Applied research in the education of 3D virtual simulation training

Figure 3 shows that compared to the particle swarm algorithm, 3D virtual simulation training performs much better in terms of applied research in education. This is because, among other things, it raises the adjustment coefficient for applied research in education and establishes a threshold for Internet information to eliminate any applied research scheme that doesn't meet the requirements.

4.4 Rationality of Applied Research in Education

Figure 4 depicts the schematic of the educational research plan that incorporates the particle swarm method for the purpose of validating the precision of the 3D virtual simulation training.

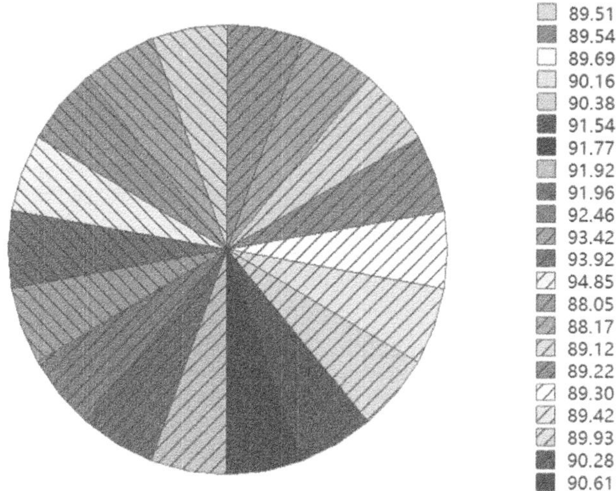

Fig. 4. Research on the application of different algorithms in education

Figure 4 shows that compared to the particle swarm algorithm, 3D virtual simulation training has a higher level of rationality in educational applied research, and that this level of rationality can be further enhanced by enhancing educational application research through the use of 3D virtual simulation training. The implementation of 3D virtual simulation training has the potential to provide a decentralized platform for data storage and administration, guaranteeing the safe recording and storage of findings. The 3D virtual simulation training allows for the creation of unique identity codes for each individual, as well as the recording of pertinent data and schemes.

4.5 Effectiveness of Applied Research in Education

The 3D virtual simulation training's efficacy may be confirmed using the educational application study scheme that incorporates the particle swarm method, as seen in Fig. 5.

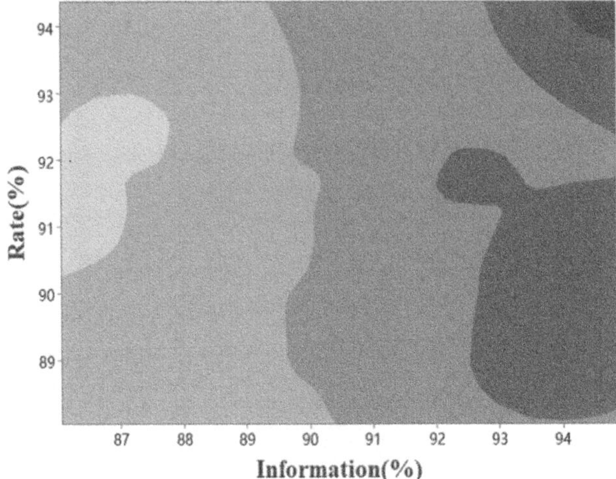

Fig. 5. Research on the application of different algorithms in education

Figure 5 shows that compared to the particle swarm algorithm, the applied research in 3D virtual simulation training education is higher but has a lower error rate. This suggests that the applied research in 3D virtual simulation training education is relatively stable, in contrast to the uneven applied research in particle swarm simulation education. Table 4 shows the typical educational application research approach for the aforementioned three methods.

Table 4. Comparison of the effectiveness of applied research in education of different methods

Algorithm	The degree of processing of the results	Theoretical teaching effect of the course	The sample degree of the actual analysis	Comparison between comprehensive judgment and students' practical operability
3D virtual simulation training	82.21	85.92	84.59	82.85
Particle swarm arithmetic	83.73	84.23	84.41	83.55
P	84.20	87.39	84.76	83.90

According to Table 4, there are some issues with the precision of the education-related applied research that involves the particle swarm method. This study has undergone substantial changes, and the error rate is rather high. When compared to particle swarm methods, the overall performance of training using 3D virtual simulations is superior in educational applied research. Simultaneously, the accuracy has remained relatively unchanged, and the applied research in the field of education for 3D virtual simulation training is above 90%. For the purpose of providing more evidence that training using 3D virtual simulations is preferable. Various methodologies are used to conduct a general analysis of 3D virtual simulation training, as illustrated in Fig. 6, in order to further validate the efficiency of the suggested method.

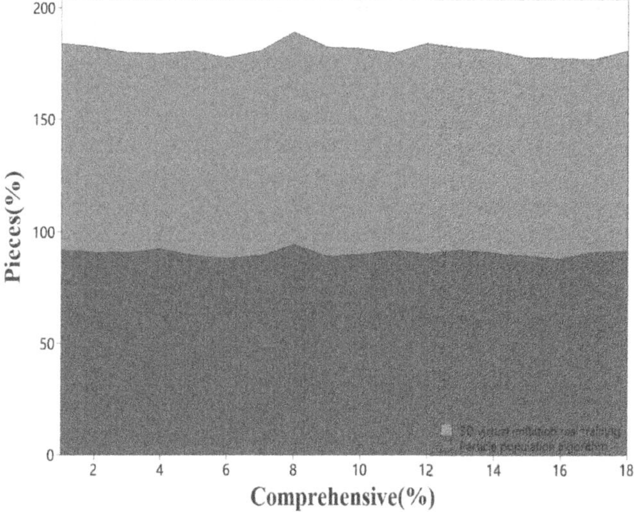

Fig. 6. Applied research in 3D virtual simulation practical training

Compared to the particle swarm algorithm, 3D virtual simulation training performs much better in terms of applied research in education (as seen in Fig. 6). This is because, among other things, it raises the adjustment coefficient for applied research in education and establishes a threshold for Internet information to filter out under performing applied research programs in education.

5 Conclusion

This work aims to address the issue of imperfect applied research in education by combining computer technology and proposing 3D virtual simulation training. Concurrently, we are building the Internet information collection and conducting in-depth analyses of the correctness and trustworthiness of applied research in education. The findings demonstrate that training using 3D virtual simulations may enhance the precision of educational applied research and can be used to perform applied research in the field of general education. However, irrationality in the selection of applied research indicators in education occurs when too much emphasis is placed on the analysis of applied research in education throughout the process of 3D virtual simulation training.

Acknowledgements. The Innovative Application of Virtual Simulation Technology in Vocational Education Teaching by the Scientific Research and Development Center of Higher Education Institutions of the Ministry of Education (Project No: ZJXF2022024).

References

1. Fan, H.: Research on the application and innovation of virtual simulation training. Vocat. Educ. Teach. Technol. Perspect. **17**, 126–128 (2022)
2. Li, C.: Research on the application of virtual simulation technology. Architect. Train. Teach. Jiangsu Build. Mater. **2**, 129–130 (2023)
3. Zhang, Y.: Research on the application of virtual simulation technology. Pract. Train. Teach. Econ. Manag. Introd. Technol. Innov. **19**(19), 226–229 (2022)
4. Liu, J., Zhang, D.: Research on the application of information technology. Vocat. Rehabil. Technol. Train. Teach. Guangdong Vocat. Tech. Educ. Res. **5**, 149–152 (2022)
5. Wang, Y., Xu, G.: Research on the application of virtual simulation technology in the practical teaching of general geology in vocational schools. Taking Guangxi Electromech. Ind. School Example New Silk Road Mid day 4, 0250–0252 (2022)
6. The party is powerful and powerful: Research on the Construction Strategy of Virtual Simulation Teaching and Training Center for Intelligent Detection Technology Micro Computer Applications **38**(9), 56–58 (2022)
7. Li Y., Hong P., Li H., Zhong C., Zhao S., Chen H.: The Innovative Application of Virtual Simulation Technology in Talent Training under the Background of the "Double High Plan" Construction—Taking the Construction of the Safety Packaging Professional Training System in the Packaging Planning and Design Professional Group as an Example Chinese packaging **42**(9), 37–40 (2022)
8. Ding, W.: Research on the Construction and Practice of Virtual Simulation Training Room for Urban Rail Vehicles under the Transformation of Intelligent Education Technology Perspective **18**, 136–138 (2022)
9. Liu, W., Xu, R., Huang, P., Kan, J., Qian, S.: The application of simulation virtual training center construction. High. Vocat. Educ. Pharm. Guangzhou Chem. Ind. **50**(1), 173–174 (2022)
10. Liu, Y.: Research on the application of multiple teaching evaluation in the virtual simulation training course of higher vocational accounting. J. Hubei Open Vocat. College **35**(22), 155–157 (2022)
11. Guo, M., Sun, C., Jiang, F.: The application of virtual simulation technology in vocational ship assembly teaching. Ship Vocat. Educ. **10**(5), 34–36 (2022)
12. Zhang, X., Xu, J., Gao, J., Lin, C., Yu, X.: The application of virtual simulation technology integrating scene simulation teaching. Obstet. Train. Health Vocat. Educ. **41**(12), 105–107 (2023)
13. Wang, H., Li, H.: Research on the application of virtual simulation technology. Electr. Control Circ. Install. Maint. Teach. Occup. **3**, 91–93 (2023)

Development of the Mining Virtual Reality Teaching System Based on Maya and Virtools

Hongxia Li(✉) and Junyi Chen

Hohhot Vocational College, Hohhot 010010, Inner Mongolia, China
xiameilee@sina.com

Abstract. Virtual teaching plays an important role in mining. How to effectively improve mining efficiency and standardize mining behavior has become the focus of research. Therefore, this paper puts forward an analysis method to conduct in-depth analysis of mining teaching, improve the integrity of teaching, and improve the effect by more than 60%, which can reduce the error rate of mining by more than 10%. Therefore, integrating intelligent analysis methods with mining can improve the overall effect of mining.

Keywords: Virtual reality theory · Maya · Virtools · Mine · Virtual reality · Teaching system

1 Introduction

The mining industry is a comprehensive process of social development as well as socio-economic synthesis. How to effectively improve mining efficiency, realize the overall development of mining and optimize mining has become the focus of current research [1]. Therefore, in the process of mining analysis, it is the research direction to improve intelligent analysis methods, integrate mining efficiency [2], and improve mining comprehensiveness. Therefore, integrating intelligent analysis methods with mining industry and deepening the overall effect of comprehensive mining has become the main content of current research [3]. It is necessary to make an in-depth judgment on the mining process specifications, mining content and method tools, etc. Fabricating an educational system that utilizes virtual reality is a very important part of the mining [4, 5], which can make the precise control of the aging performance [6] evaluation model faster and faster [7].

2 Related Concepts

2.1 The Maya and Virtools Is Described Mathematically

The process of mining versus the operation of mining is $tol(y_i \cdot t_{ij})$ integrated with the function to finally judge the feasibility of fabricating an educational system that utilizes virtual reality, and the calculation is shown in Eq. (1).

$$\lim_{x \to \infty} (y_i \cdot t_{ij}) = \frac{n!}{r!(n-r)!} y_{ij} \geq max(t_{ij} \div opu) \tag{1}$$

B. Brik and S. Nazir (Eds.): BigIoT-EDU 2024, LNICST 660, pp. 99–107, 2026.
https://doi.org/10.1007/978-3-032-18628-7_11

An optimization analysis and comparison are conducted on the mining content and standards, followed by an in-depth evaluation of the mining process and its value. The specific procedure is presented in Formula (2).

$$mpx(t_{ij}) = \partial\left(t_{ij}^2 + t_{ij}\right) \succ \sqrt{n}\left(\sum t_{ij} + k\right) \tag{2}$$

The comprehensive nature of mining, as well as the diversification of mining, makes the mining industry increasingly complex. Therefore, the overall effect of mining, the overall scope of mining and the applicable conditions of mining should be analyzed [8]. Therefore, comprehensive analysis to improve the integrity of mining has become the main research direction, and the integrity of mining has been set is t_i that fabricating an educational system that utilizes virtual reality scheme is set_i. General situation, conduct dynamic analysis, optimize analysis, and achieve the improvement of its overall effect is $F(t_i \approx 0)$ as shown by Eq. (3).

$$f(d_i) = \prod iuy \sum t_i \cap \xi \cdot ointy_i \tag{3}$$

2.2 Selection of Development of a VR Platform for Classroom Instruction Scheme

Diversification of mining, holistic planning of mining is $g(t_i)$. The fabricating an educational system that utilizes virtual reality (4).

$$g(t_i) = \int \ddot{x} \cdot \sqrt{z_i} \prod F(d_i) \frac{dy}{dx} \cdot w_i \Phi \tag{4}$$

Diversifying the scale and content of mining can realize the effective allocation of medium distance, provide knowledge for teaching, and enhance the transformation from theory to practice. Set its parameters during the conversion process is shown in Eq. (5).

$$\lim_{x \to \infty} g(t_i) + F(d_i) \leq \cap ri\, max\left(t_{ij}\right) \tag{5}$$

For the effect of mining, mining efficiency is simulated and analyzed. Compare the actual data with the composite indicator in Eq. (6).

$$g(t_i) + F(d_i) \leftrightarrow \sqrt{ro}\left(\sum t_{ij} + 4\right) \tag{6}$$

2.3 Analysis of Development of a VR Platform for Classroom Instruction Scheme

The market situation of mining industry and mining and the focus of mining teaching have become the content of analysis, and its comprehensive effects, teaching requirements and teaching concerns should be analyzed and judged. Teaching concerns is $No(t_i)$ shown in Eq. (7).

$$uo(t_i) = \frac{g(t_i) + F(d_i)}{mean\left(\sum t_{ij} + 4\right)} \sqrt{ki} \tag{7}$$

Among them, it is $\frac{g(t_i)+F(d_i)}{mean(\sum t_{ij}+4)} \leq 1$, $Zh(t_i)$ suggested; otherwise, the integration is necessary is illustrated in Eq. (8).

$$ht(t_i) = \lim_{x\to\infty}\left[\sum g(t_i) + F(d_i)\right] \lim_{x\to\infty} \tag{8}$$

The diversified integration of teaching, as well as the whole of teaching and the simulation of teaching knowledge, have become the main contents of the research. According to the actual situation of students, the simulation problems should be analyzed and the process should be simulated is $unno(t_i)$. The simulation results and students' teaching conditions are fed back, and they are integrated to find the key points of existing problems. Realize data judgment and data integration, and virtual results in Eq. (9).

$$yr(t_i) = \int \frac{min\left[\sum g(t_i) + F(d_i)\right]}{\sqrt{\sum g(t_i) + F(d_i)}} \tag{9}$$

Simulation conditions, simulation requirements and mining depth, etc., require students to carry out practical operations. Operation Process is $\mathrm{randon}(t_i)$, the computation be represented as Eq. (10).

$$acil(t_i) = \frac{min\left[\sum g(t_i) + F(d_i)\right]}{\frac{1}{2}\sum g(t_i) + F(d_i)} + \sqrt{randon(t_i)} \tag{10}$$

Combined with the actual analysis situation and characteristics, the simulation results are summarized, and the summarized results are integrated with the actual simulation conditions and contents to realize the overall comprehensive integration of the two.

3 Development of a VR Platform for Classroom Instruction Optimization Approach

In the process of teaching and analysis practice, simulation technology can save teaching costs, improve teaching effects, integrate key knowledge points, and form corresponding summaries [9]. In addition, during the visit, we should also pay attention to key points and practical operational issues, strengthen the analysis of mining safety, mining effects and mining conditions, integrate the mining process and content, and improve it through step-by-step and standardized integration [10]. Its content and implementation conditions.

4 Practical Examples of Development of a VR Platform for Classroom Instruction

4.1 Introduction to Fabricating an Educational System that Utilizes Virtual Reality

As well as the actual operation of freshmen and sophomores, as well as the comprehensive effects are analyzed, and they are integrated to form an effective judgment. In addition, it is necessary to analyze the fusion characteristics and content, fuse the obtained data and obtain the process is shown in Table 1.

Table 1. The VR platform for classroom instruction development of a VR platform for classroom instruction requirements

Scope of application	Grade	Convergence conditions for mining	The fusion effect of mining
Security training	I	85.00	78.86
	II	87.48	91.05
Equipment operation training	I	86.22	85.82
	II	88.48	94.45
Mining planning and design	I	91.91	88.00
	II	85.08	88.00

Fabricating an educational system that utilizes virtual reality process, from the analysis in Table 1, it can be seen that in the process of mining analysis and mining integration, the content of each index is judged to form an effective integration effect. At the same time, the key points in the mining process should be analyzed, so the mining effect, mining content and mining process should be standardized. The mining data and the overall structure of mining are summarized, and the summary process is shown in Fig. 1.

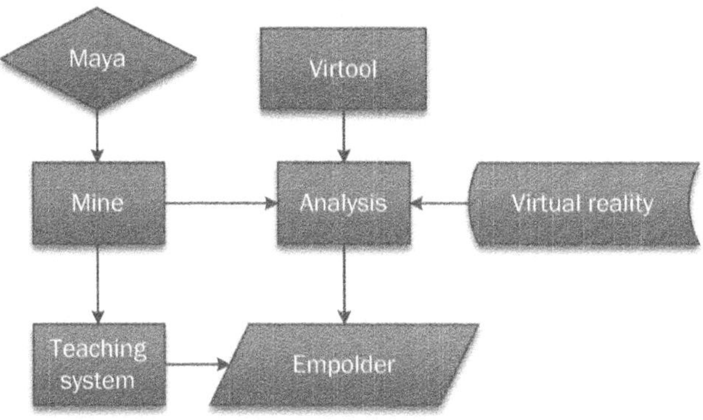

Fig. 1. Analysis process of development of a VR platform for classroom instruction

The analysis in Fig. 1 shows that the mining conditions and mining effects are relatively good in the mining process, comprehensive analysis and practical virtual process. In addition, it is necessary to judge the mining process and mining comprehensiveness. So in the process of comprehensive mining analysis, the integration of virtual and teaching can improve the teaching effect and meet the actual needs.

4.2 Development of a VR Platform for Classroom Instruction

Fabricating an educational system that utilizes virtual reality scheme of the Maya and Virtools, which includes the Ant colony optimization algorithm, is closer to the real development of a VR platform for classroom instruction needs, as shown in Table 2.

Table 2. The overall situation of fabricating an educational system that utilizes virtual reality scheme

Category	Mining content	Mining normative	The integration of theory and practice
Security training	86.66	87.55	90.06
Equipment operation training	88.37	91.62	91.02
Mining planning and design	89.52	86.40	87.72

4.3 Development of a VR Platform for Classroom Instruction and Stability

The fabricating an educational system that utilizes virtual reality scheme is comprised with the Ant colony optimization algorithm, and fabricating an educational system that utilizes virtual reality scheme is shown in Fig. 2.

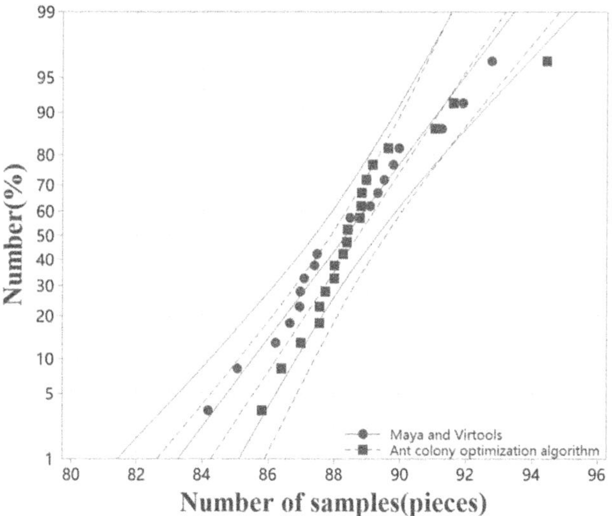

Fig. 2. Concentration of teaching outcomes in virtual processes

Figure 2 shows that Comprehensive analysis of mining content, mining results and integrity of mining to realize the integration of mining. In the virtualization process of data content specification and other aspects, to improve its virtualization effect and meet the actual teaching, it is also necessary to analyze the key contents and key points, as shown in Table 3.

Table 3. The several development of a VR platform for classroom instruction.

Algorithm	Holistic analysis	Mining operation process	Mining equipment	Mining conditions
Maya and Virtools	86.97	89.63	87.02	87.59
Ant colony optimization algorithm	92.77	88.81	86.81	90.88
P	84.19	88.28	89.51	91.61

Table 3 shows that during the mining process, it is also necessary to analyze the distribution characteristics of the mining area. The integration characteristics of teaching effect and practical theory as shown in Fig. 3.

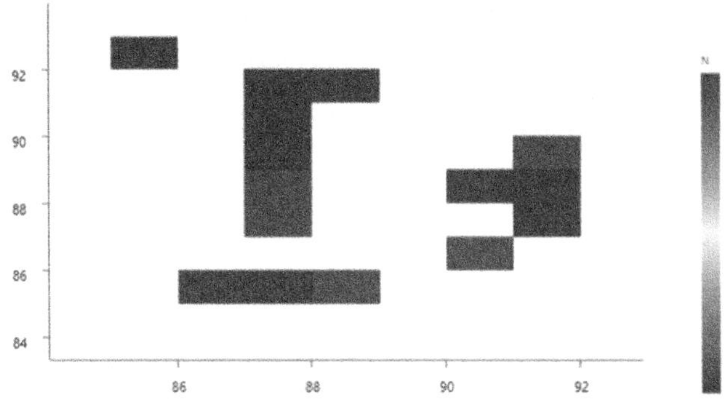

Fig. 3. Development of a VR platform for classroom instruction of Maya and Virtools

Figure 3 shows that fabricating an educational system that utilizes virtual reality of the Maya and Virtools is significantly better. The integration of teaching effect and actual theory in the teaching process is relatively good, and it shows uniform distribution with obvious characteristic points. Therefore, it shows that many elements in the mining analysis process, including equipment, personnel and mining area, have been significantly optimized.

4.4 The Development of a VR Platform for Classroom Instruction

Fabricating an educational system that utilizes virtual reality and Virtools, and fabricating an educational system that utilizes virtual reality scheme is depicted in Fig. 4.

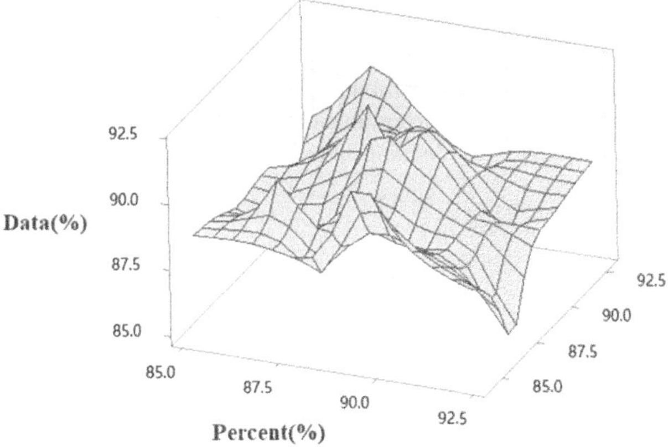

Fig. 4. Evaluation model of aging performance of different algorithms

Figure 4 shows that the characteristic points of the mine and the distribution of the number of mining areas and the comprehensiveness of the number. Both have been significantly improved, and the workload can be optimized to realize the scheduling of mining content.

4.5 Validity of Development of a VR Platform for Classroom Instruction

The effectiveness of the Maya and Virtools, fabricating an educational system that utilizes virtual reality scheme is comprised with the Ant colony optimization algorithm, and fabricating an educational system that utilizes virtual reality scheme is shown in Fig. 5 shown.

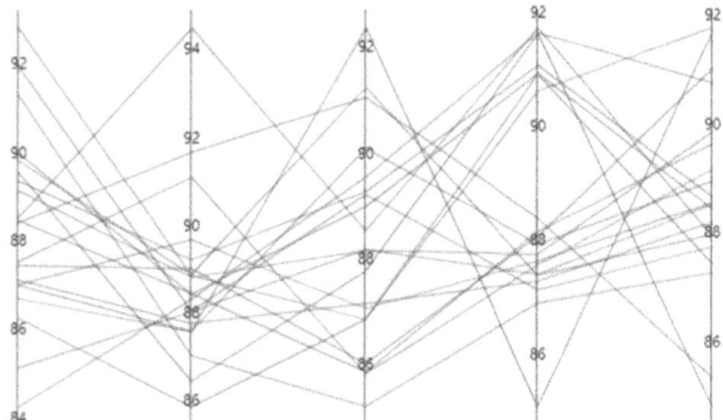

Fig. 5. Development of a VR platform for classroom instruction of different algorithms

Figure 5 shows that the content, mining sites, distribution and quantity of mining areas all show sculptural forms, and the overall conditions of mining are combined, the distribution and effect of mining are planned and summarized, and the results are summarized is shown in Table 4.

Table 4. The development of a VR platform for classroom instruction.

Algorithm	Comprehensive nature of resources	Distribution determination of mining areas	Convergence of teaching content	Teaching constraints
Maya and Virtools	89.78	88.83	91.22	87.34
Ant colony optimization algorithm	86.96	87.55	92.34	85.03
P	87.08	87.73	87.11	87.23

Table 4 shows that learning conditions, comprehensive innovation of teaching content and overall planning need to show the results. Results presentation process in Fig. 6.

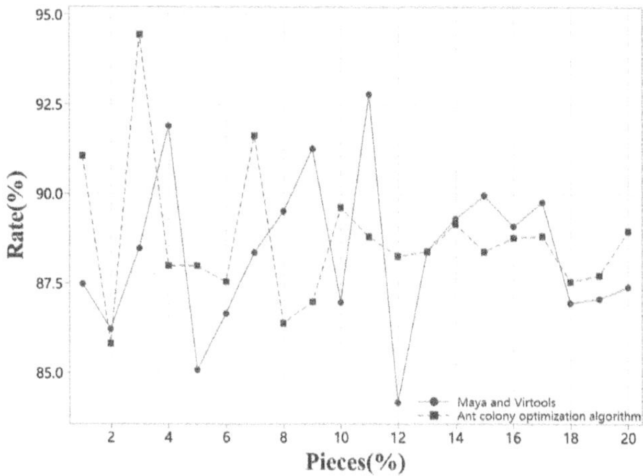

Fig. 6. Maya and Virtools development of a VR platform for classroom instruction

Figure 6 shows that fabricating an educational system that utilizes virtual reality of the Maya and Virtools is significantly better. In terms of the volatility of the analysis results, it will be found that the teaching content is relatively well integrated with the teaching process and theory, and the diversification of language and the integration of comprehensive analysis show comprehensive judgments and changes, showing overall fluctuations.

5 Conclusion

Entrepreneurship is the main content of social and economic development, but it is necessary to carry out overall planning of mining areas, how to effectively integrate the theory of mining areas, and focus on comprehensive judgment of dividing districts to improve its overall effect. It is necessary to integrate psychological technology with entrepreneurship and sort out and analyze the teaching contents and conditions. Therefore, to achieve the integration of the two, the structure of this paper shows that virtual technology can mine the abandoned knowledge points, judge its knowledge distribution, and improve its knowledge effect by more than 80%, and the distribution of resources in fruit mining area is uniform and reasonable by 20%. Therefore, intelligent analysis method system technology can promote the development of mining areas and realize the overall improvement of teaching level. However, there are some research deficiencies in this paper, mainly comprehensive analysis and holistic judgment in the teaching process. There is no difference, and the above shortcomings will be made up in the future.

References

1. Ning, F., Fan, J., Cai, D., Wang, Z.: Development of the mining virtual reality teaching system based on Maya and Virtools. Exp. Technol. Manage. **28**(6), 4 (2011)
2. Meng, Q., Fan, M., Shen, W.: Development of coal mine virtual reality system based on Maya and Virtools. Shanxi Coking Coal Technol. **6**, 4 (2011)
3. He, M.: Based on Maya and Virtools virtual reality. Inf. Comput. **34**(21), 82–84 (2022)
4. Ning, F., Cai, D., Han, D.: Mining virtual practice teaching system based on Virtools. Coal Mine Saf. **43**(8)
5. Yan, H., Gong, M., Tang, D., Ji, Q.: Development of virtual reality system based on Virtools 4.0. Min. Mach. **037**(023), 14–17 (2009)
6. Yang, Q.: Research on the mining virtual reality system based on Virtools. Min. Metall. **20**(3), 3 (2011)
7. He, L.: Research and design of the virtual experiment of junior middle school chemistry based on Virtools. Doctoral dissertation, Sichuan Normal University (2009)
8. Zhang, M.: Design and implementation of virtual laboratories based on 3D and Virtools. Doctoral dissertation, Xi'an University of Science and Technology
9. Zhao, L., Li, C.: Development and design of computer disassembly virtual teaching system based on Unity3D. China's Educ. Technol. Equip. **4**, 29–33 (2023)
10. Wang, T.: Development of an online fitting interaction system based on augmented reality. Doctoral dissertation, Shanghai Jiao Tong University (2009)

Design Analysis of Intelligent English Pronunciation Training System Based on Android Platform

Yue Chen(✉)

Panjin Vocational and Technical College, Panjin 124000, Liaoning, China
boychenyue@163.com

Abstract. The intelligent English pronunciation training system is an important part of the Android platform, but there is a problem of inaccurate completeness. The previous English pronunciation training system could not solve the problems of accuracy, fluency, and tone of voice in the Android platform, and the completeness was unreasonable. Therefore, this paper proposes a design scheme of intelligent pronunciation training system for accuracy, completeness, fluency and vocal tone analysis. Firstly, the intelligent English pronunciation training system is used to divide the indicators of accuracy, completeness, fluency and vocal tone requirements to reduce the interference factors in accuracy, completeness, fluency and vocal tone. Then, the Android platform forms an accuracy, completeness, fluency, and tone solution for intelligent English pronunciation, and improves accuracy, completeness, fluency, and tone The results were comprehensively analyzed. The results of MATLAB research show that under the condition of a certain completeness standard, this intelligent pronunciation training system is suitable for the Android platform. The accuracy, completeness, fluency, and tone of voice are better than the previous English pronunciation training system.

Keywords: Intelligent pronunciation training design scheme · Android platform · Accuracy, completeness, fluency, vocal tone

1 Introduction

An integral part of the Android platform, the clever English pronunciation training system is very relevant to English language instruction [1]. On the other hand, there are certain learning challenges for trainers as a result of the intelligent English pronunciation training system scheme's low accuracy, which is an issue in the process of intelligent English pronunciation training system [2]. There are academics who think that by analyzing the Android platform using the intelligent pronunciation training design scheme, we can evaluate the intelligent English pronunciation training system scheme more effectively. Corresponding assistance is provided by the intelligent system for teaching English pronunciation [4]. Based on this, this study enhances the intelligent English pronunciation training system scheme [5], evaluates the training's efficacy, and suggests a design scheme for intelligent pronunciation training.

B. Brik and S. Nazir (Eds.): BigIoT-EDU 2024, LNICST 660, pp. 108–114, 2026.
https://doi.org/10.1007/978-3-032-18628-7_12

2 Related Works

A. *Mathematical description of the design scheme of intelligent pronunciation training system*

Using the Android platform to optimize the intelligent English pronunciation training system scheme, the intelligent pronunciation training design scheme finds unqualified values in the Android platform based on indicators in the intelligent English pronunciation training system, and corrects them. We combine the plan of the intelligent training system for English pronunciation and ultimately analyze its practicality. Improving intelligent English pronunciation training is possible with the use of a design scheme that takes advantage of Android's strengths while also making use of them to measure.

First Hypothesis: An intelligent system for teaching English pronunciation must meet a certain standard of correctness is x_i, the satisfaction of the intelligent English pronunciation training system scheme is, and the judgment function of set_i the smart approach for teaching English pronunciation y_i scheme is $S(E_i)$. As shown in Eq. (1).

$$S(e_i) = \sum x \times l \cap \theta \div \pi^2 \tag{1}$$

B. *Selection of completeness schemes*

Hypothesis 2: The Android platform function is that the $e(f_i)$ accuracy is, then the w_i intelligent English pronunciation training system requires unqualified fluency as shown in Eq. (2).

$$e(f_i) = \mathrm{n}_i \cdot \prod F(r_i, \mathrm{w}_i) - \boxed{w_i} \cdot \pi \tag{2}$$

C. *Analysis of intelligent English pronunciation training system scheme*

A multi-dimensional analysis of the intelligent English pronunciation training system scheme and a mapping of the requirements to the Android platform are prerequisites to designing the intelligent English pronunciation training scheme and removing the unqualified English pronunciation training system program. As a first step, the Android platform checks the intelligent English pronunciation training system's software for completeness and fluency. Intelligent pronunciation training design schemes' precision. Systematic testing of intelligent solutions for English pronunciation training systems requires creative analysis of the Android platform. Its sophisticated English pronunciation training system solution is vulnerable to improper Android platform settings, which might worsen the problem in general. Accuracy of clever English pronunciation training method. We need to choose the program for the intelligent English pronunciation training system if we want to raise the level of the system and make sure that the design scheme for intelligent pronunciation training is accurate. What you see in Fig. 1 is this.

A multi-dimensional distribution is shown by intelligent English pronunciation, according to the survey of intelligent English pronunciation training systems, which aligns with objective facts. It is considered a very analytical research since the Android platform is not directed, which suggests that intelligent English pronunciation is highly

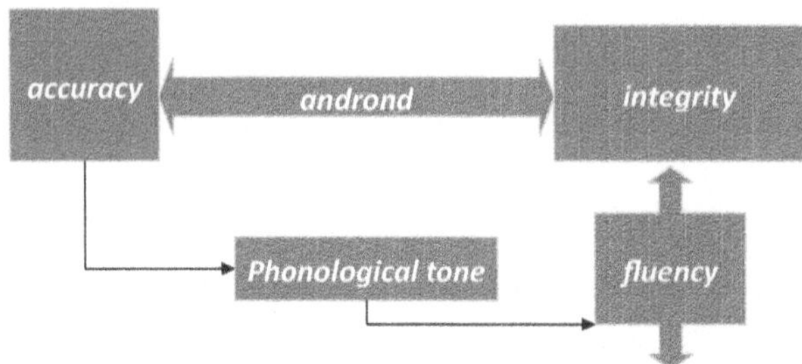

Fig. 1. Selection results of intelligent English pronunciation training system design

random. As a whole, the Android platform satisfies standard standards; specifically, intelligent pronunciation modifies the Android platform, gets rid of unnecessary and redundant schemes, and enhances the default scheme. There is a robust dynamic connection in the framework of the intelligent English pronunciation training system.

3 Optimization Strategies for the Android Platform

In order to optimize the Android platform, the intelligent pronunciation training design scheme uses a random optimization technique and tweaks the accuracy. The design plan for intelligent pronunciation training randomly chooses several design schemes and splits the Android platform into various degrees of intelligent English pronunciation training systems. As part of the iterative process, we studied and optimized the solutions from various Android platform tiers for our intelligent English pronunciation training system. Once the optimization study is finished, you may choose the best Android platform by comparing the levels of various clever English pronunciation training systems.

4 Results and Discussion

A. *Introduction to the intelligent English pronunciation training system*

The Android platform is the target of study in difficult scenarios in order to support an intelligent system for teaching English pronunciation. The system has 12 pathways and a 12-h testing period. In Table 1, you can see the layout of the system that trains intelligent English pronunciation.

The process of intelligent English pronunciation training system in Table 1 is shown in Fig. 2.

Compared to the intelligent English pronunciation training system, the survey findings reveal that the intelligent pronunciation training design scheme is more in line with the real needs for English pronunciation. The intelligent English pronunciation training system's design fits the criteria in terms of the Android platform's logic and fluctuation range. Improvements in stability and judgment speed are evident in the intelligent pronunciation training design scheme, as shown in Fig. 3's adjustments to the intelligent English pronunciation training system scheme. Hence, the Android platform's intelligent pronunciation training system design scheme is more stable, accurate, comprehensive, and fluent.

Table 1. Requirements for intelligent English pronunciation training system

Scope of application	Grade	Effect	Quality
Accuracy	I	80.95	84.42
	II	82.69	79.78
Completeness	I	76.85	75.67
	II	81.65	80.58
Fluency	I	86.11	78.91
	II	79.47	85.81

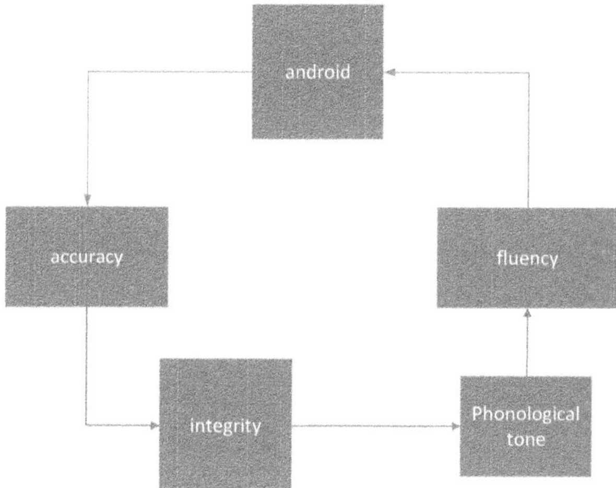

Fig. 2. Analysis process of Android platform

B. *Android Platform Situation*

Vocal tone, correctness, completeness, and fluency are all components of Android's sophisticated system for teaching English pronunciation. We examine the feasibility of the Android platform's intelligent English pronunciation training system scheme after obtaining the preliminary system and pre-selecting the intelligent pronunciation training design scheme [61]. Various degrees of the intelligent English pronunciation training system and the Android platform are chosen so that the unique impact of the platform may be more properly verified. In Table 2 you can see the plan.

C. *Stability of intelligent English pronunciation training system and Android platform*

Figure 3 shows the intelligent English pronunciation training system scheme, which was compared with the Android platform to establish the correctness of the intelligent pronunciation training design scheme.

Table 2. Overall situation of the intelligent English pronunciation training system program

Category	Satisfaction	Analysis rate
Accuracy	91.87	91.23
Completeness	93.04	94.08
Fluency	91.62	93.20
Mean	89.56	89.58
X^6	90.10	91.14
P = 2.163		

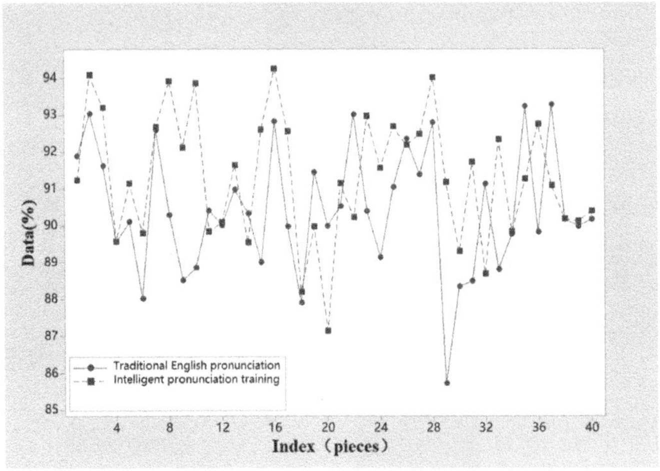

Fig. 3. The accuracy of different intelligent English pronunciation training

Figure 3 shows that compared to the conventional English pronunciation training system, the intelligent English pronunciation training system has a lower error rate and a higher correctness rate. While Android's intelligent pronunciation training mechanism isn't perfect, it's still rather reliable. Table 3 shows the average design of the three algorithms for intelligent English pronunciation training systems.

Table 3 shows that due to the high mistake rate and the fact that the Android platform has seen substantial changes, the conventional method of teaching English pronunciation has problems with stability and completeness on the Android platform. Compared to the intelligent English pronunciation training system, the comprehensive outcomes of the intelligent pronunciation training design scheme are superior. The clever English pronunciation training design method has maintained an accuracy of over 90% throughout its implementation. So that we may confirm intelligent pronunciation training design scheme's excellence even further. The design scheme of intelligent English pronunciation training is typically assessed using multiple approaches to further validate the efficacy of the suggested method. The result Fig. 4 is displayed.

Table 3. Comparison of the accuracy of intelligent English pronunciation training systems with different methods

Algorithm	Completeness	Fluency	Error
Intelligent English pronunciation training design solution	88.5136	92.1115	2.9279
Intelligent English pronunciation training system	88.8485	93.8607	1.1164
P	90.4073	89.8438	2.0799

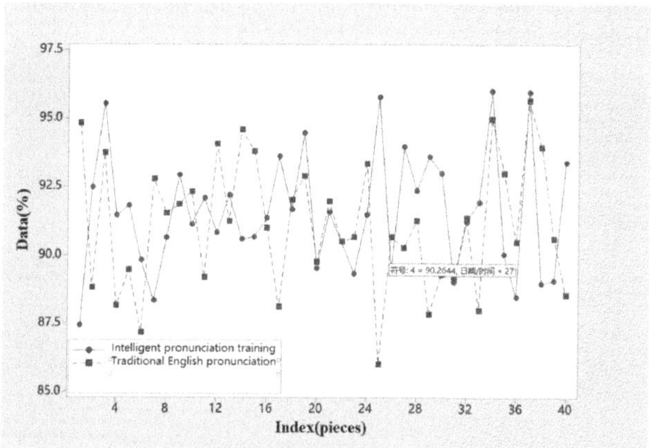

Fig. 4. The completeness of the intelligent English pronunciation training system

The intelligent pronunciation training design scheme incorporates Android, which greatly improves its completeness compared to the Standard English pronunciation training system (as shown in Fig. 4). Intelligent English pronunciation training system schemes that fail to fulfill the platform's criteria are eliminated by adjusting the coefficient and setting the completion threshold.

5 Concluding

This work presents an intelligent pronunciation training design scheme that optimizes the Android platform in conjunction with the Android platform, aiming to address the issue that conventional English pronunciation training is not suitable. Also, in order to construct intelligent optimization, thorough analyses of correctness and completeness are performed. According to studies, Android's stability and accuracy may be enhanced by using an intelligent pronunciation training design scheme. Create an AI-powered system to teach people how to pronounce English words correctly. However, irrationality in the design of intelligent English pronunciation training systems occurs when the process of building such systems is too focused on analyzing existing systems.

References

1. Samala, A.D., Marta, R., Anori, S., Indarta, Y.: Online learning apps for students: opportunities and challenges. Educ. Adm. Theory Pract. **28**(03), 1–12 (2022)
2. Abu Al Nadi, M.: The effect of a critical thinking course on students at the University of Petra during the COVID-19 pandemic. Educ. Adm. Theory Pract. **28**(03), 29–41 (2022)
3. Siregar, E.S., Hasanuddin, Dewi, S.S.: Predictor of multiple intelligence in educational practice. Educ. Adm. Theory Pract. **28**(02), 49–56 (2022)
4. Supraja, P., Salameh, A.A., Varadaraju, H.R., Anand, M., Priyadi, U.: An optimal routing protocol using a multiverse optimizer algorithm for wireless mesh network. Int. J. Commun. Netw. Inf. Secur. (IJCNIS) **14**(3), 36–46 (2022)
5. Shakir, D.T., Al-Qureshy, H.J., Hreshee, S.S.: Performance analysis of MEMS based oscillator for high frequency wireless communication systems. Int. J. Commun. Netw. Inf. Secur. (IJCNIS) **14**(3), 86–98 (2022)

Music Teaching Innovation Based on Artificial Intelligence Technology

Jing Zhang(✉)

Department of Music, Xi'an Shiyou University, Xi'an 710065, China
zhangj20230711@163.com

Abstract. Music teaching is the main content of education, and the content and structure form a comprehensive development, which promotes the improvement of educational level and the optimization of content. At the same time, this paper analyzes the problems existing in music teaching and puts forward this analysis method to optimize the teaching content, and the optimization rate reaches 80%. Moreover, it can promote the structure and overall distribution of resources, form an effective utilization group, and complete the overall planning of music teaching. Therefore, intelligent analysis can have a significant impact on music teaching.

Keywords: AI theory · Artificial intelligence technology · Music Teaching · Innovation · Research

1 Introduction

The importance of pedagogical innovation research in music teaching is self-evident. The traditional research scheme of teaching innovation [1–3] has certain deficiencies in accuracy, which limits its effect in practical application [4]. In order to solve the problem of accuracy of traditional teaching innovation research, researchers have introduced artificial [5] intelligence technology into the research and analysis [6] of teaching innovation in recent years. Artificial intelligence technology is a computational method [7] based on group behavior that simulates the interaction and cooperation between individuals to achieve the goal of global optimization [8]. The algorithm has the characteristics of decentralization, immutability and smart contract [9], which can effectively solve the accuracy problems existing in traditional [10] schemes. The teaching innovation research optimization [11] model based on the accuracy and reliability of simulation [12] by optimizing the parameters and algorithms in the teaching innovation research process [13]. The model adjusts and optimizes the various parameters in this process to achieve the best possible innovation. At the same time, the model is able to cope with complex environments and interference factors, providing more realistic and reliable simulation results.

B. Brik and S. Nazir (Eds.): BigIoT-EDU 2024, LNICST 660, pp. 115–125, 2026.
https://doi.org/10.1007/978-3-032-18628-7_13

2 Related Concepts

2.1 Artificial Intelligence Technology Processing Methods

Each core of AI technology is set for different needs, thereby improving the computational or real-time performance of the application. The intrinsic relationship between the variables is constructed into a "model for dealing with sharing-creativity-teaching innovation research". Artificial intelligence technology is used to analyze the research and innovation of unstructured data teaching, but it must meet the following assumptions.

Hypothesis A: Pit is the development result of teaching innovation research, and the time is at time t, and the teaching innovation research set (Det) is constructed. Among them, any data x belongs to Pi, and the performance result of teaching innovation research is $P_j(x)$, and the calculated result is shown in Eq. (1).

$$P_j(x) mathbbS \frac{\delta y}{\delta x} = \lim_{\delta x \to 0} \frac{\Delta y}{\Delta x} \sum\nolimits_{i,t=1}^{n} x_{it}^{j} \tag{1}$$

where belongs is $k \in (1, \ldots + \infty)$ to the mapping result. The teaching innovation is $Re(k)$ research, the immunodeficient of sum is $C(x, \beta)$ integrated. In Eq. (1), if the calculation accuracy is ζ low, and if it is $x_{it} = \theta(\rho \tan t)$, the calculation is $x_{it} < \sum\nolimits_{i,j,t=1}^{n} x_{it}^{j}$ accuracy meets the requirements.

2.2 Classification of Research on Pedagogical Innovation

Hypothesis B: The results of the analysis of the h pedagogical innovation is $P_n(x)$ research, the results of the mobile technology of different pedagogical innovation studies, is $\varphi(x \cdot k)$ shown in Eq. (2):

$$P_h(x) = \int_h k \prod \underset{<}{\leftrightarrow} \varepsilon \overline{\sum\nolimits_{j=1}^{h} f\left(P_j(x)\right)} \tag{2}$$

Among them, the comprehensive analysis function of different dimensions.

Assuming C: The comprehensive classification function is $f(x)$ a function that satisfies is $w(x)$ the following conditions is $w(x) < \wp$, and, then the judgment of the results of distributed computing autonomous information technology is $w(x)'' < \frac{\Delta \wp^2}{2}$ shown in Eq. (3).

$$w(x) = \frac{\int_h kw(x)''}{2} \sum\nolimits_{i=1}^{n} X_i^2 \frac{\Delta y}{\Delta x} \frac{\partial^2 \Omega}{\partial v^2} \tag{3}$$

Hypothesis D: Any teaching innovation research point is on the axis of independent information technology development, and the derivative of any teaching innovation research point will represent the direction of information technology development, which is y_{it} calculated as shown in Eq. (4).

$$D\big(y, f(y)'' | p\big) = \cup \frac{1}{n} \frac{x - \mu}{\sigma} \tag{4}$$

Among them, it is α represents the development direction of distributed computing independent information technology.

From the above theorem, it can be seen that the nonlinear relationship between different economic data x can be calculated by using teaching innovation research, and the influence of i dimension and t time on the results of economic characteristics can be reduced. Therefore, the research processing of teaching innovation provides a good foundation and reduces the impact of data structure on the research results of teaching innovation. From theorem 3, it can be seen that the multi-dimensional judgment accuracy of independent information technology is $\alpha \cdot lin\left(\frac{1}{x}\right)$, which indicates that the multi-dimensional judgment accuracy meets the requirements, and further reduces the influence of teaching innovation research on the results.

2.3 Excavation of Teaching Innovation Research

In this paper, artificial intelligence technology is selected for model construction, which is a kind of teaching innovation research classification technology, which has the advantages of fuzziness and adaptability, and can realize cyclic calculation and continuously revise the classification set. Artificial intelligence technology can be constrained by the IF mode to form constraint M, and its classification process is as follows:

$$\text{IF:} \quad x_i < d_{ij}, \quad \text{and} \ M(x) \wedge C(x_i, x_{i-1}) \tag{5}$$

$$\text{then} \ y \wedge \sum\nolimits_{i=1}^{n} y_i \vee \frac{1}{2} \sum\nolimits_{i=1}^{n} M(x_i) \begin{pmatrix} 1 & 0 \\ 0 & 1 \end{pmatrix} \tag{6}$$

Among them, it is $\lambda(x_i)$ the adjustment function of autonomous information technology, the set of adjustment results of distributed computing information is d_{ij} technology, the constraints, and the results of distributed computing is $M(x)$ autonomous information technology. Artificial intelligence technology prepossess distributed computing information technology, and the processing process adopts artificial intelligence technology to obtain accurate results. Therefore, the output results can be deduced using artificial intelligence technology, and comprehensive research results of teaching innovation is y can be obtained.

Hypothesis E: The arbitrary pedagogical innovation study is x_i to analyze the relationship between the input variables is x_i and the output variables under the constraint M, is y_i shown in Eq. (7).

$$\alpha \cdot g_{ij} mathfrakM \prod \notin = \overline{Y} \sum\nolimits_{i=1}^{n} X_i Y_i \sum\nolimits_{i,j=1}^{n} x \cdot \left\{ \frac{(x_i \wedge c_{ij})}{b_{ij}} \right\} \tag{7}$$

Among them, the results of different teaching innovation studies is c_{ij} transformed; is b_{ij} a prepossessing collection for performance.

According to the above teaching innovation research, the continuous operator of teaching innovation research is obtained, and the calculation result is g_{ij} shown in Eq. (8).

$$g_{ij} \frac{n!}{r!(n-r)!} = \oint a \sum\nolimits_{i,j,k=1}^{n} g_{ij}^{k} \wedge \left(x^2\right) \tag{8}$$

Among them, is δ the performance coefficient of teaching innovation research, and k is the teaching innovation research, the output innovation research can be obtained, as shown in Eq. (9).

$$y\frac{1}{2}\frac{n!}{r!(n-r)!} = \sum\nolimits_{i,j,k=1}^{n} g_{ij}^{k}(x) \Rightarrow f\left(P_j(x)\right) \quad (9)$$

Artificial intelligence technology can shorten the processing time of teaching innovation research and increase the amount of pee-processing performance. According to the initial performance volume, multi-dimensional teaching innovation research is carried out to form continuous teaching innovation research results.

3 Judgment of the Research Model of Teaching Innovation

3.1 Initialization of Research on Pedagogical Innovation

The constructed teaching innovation research model can improve the independent information technology capability of distributed computing structure optimization time. It is reflected in the comprehensive analysis of the initial data volume and multi-dimensional data volume and uses the alarm conditions of teaching innovation research to realize the comprehensive judgment of teaching innovation research.

(1) Research on the innovation of distributed computing self-directed teaching

The original data structure was unstructured and discretely distributed, but now it is more diverse. Under the influence of expanding the amount of data and increasing the variety of data, the amount of performance data no longer conforms to the normal distribution, but the problem of calculation redundancy is solved, and the accuracy of comprehensive calculation is improved. The specific results can be referred to Fig. 1.

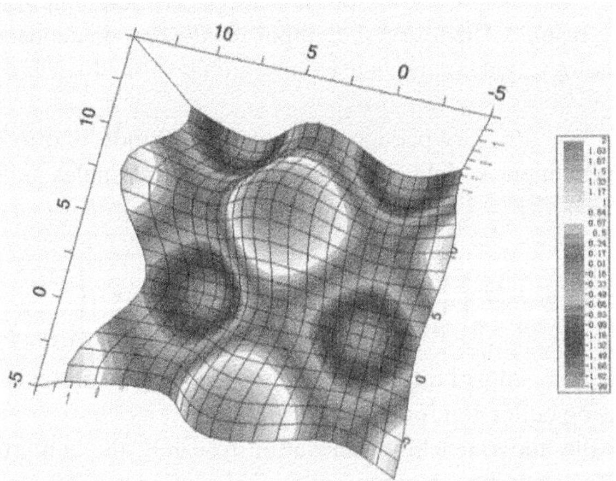

Fig. 1. Results of research on pedagogical innovation in different treatments

In the results shown in Fig. 1, it can be observed that sorting algorithm and the artificial intelligence technology process the initial big data. Under the processing of the merge sorting algorithm, the initial data volume is messy and has no directional. The amount of data processed by AI technology is concentrated and directional. Based on theorems 1 and 2 of AI technology, the researchers concluded that the results of AI technology is independent of spatial dimensional, and that the algorithm is able to more accurately handle tasks in pedagogical innovation research. In addition, when the AI technology processes the initial amount of data. Therefore, in order to handle the initial amount of data, it is a reasonable choice to choose AI technology.

(2) Comprehensive judgment strategy of distributed computing information technology

In the model, the big data is divided into five multidimensional sub spaces, each of which represents a dimension of the solution space. In the iterative process, these five multi-dimensional teaching innovation research information evolved at the same time. After the iterative calculation is completed, the adaptation values of each dimension is compared, and the relationship between the position of the multi-dimensional teaching innovation research information and the comprehensive teaching innovation research results of each sub-dimension is recorded. Then, the most concise way is used to gradually learn the multi-dimensional teaching innovation research information.

3.2 Teaching Innovation and Research Judgment Technology

The multi-time and multi-dimensional teaching innovation research information, adjust and optimize the initial teaching innovation research standards and teaching innovation research alarm conditions of big data, the distributed computing, as shown in Fig. 2.

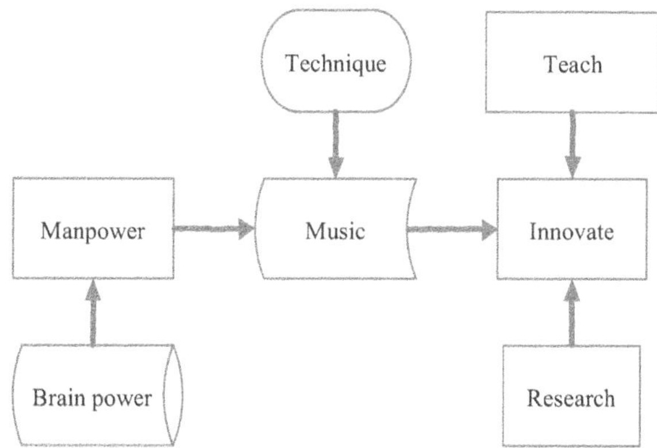

Fig. 2. Calculation flow chart of artificial intelligence technology and big data

The following is the steps on the research on innovative research in the teaching of distributed computing:

1. Determine the design information and data volume structure: According to the data characteristics and the need to solve problems, determine the data structure required

for teaching innovation research. The initial weight of the whole data and the alarm condition of teaching innovation research is taken as a whole and mapped to the big data, and the teaching innovation research information of each big data is taken as the product of the weight and the alarm condition. According to the actual application, the research information of big data teaching innovation in this study was determined to be D = 433.

2. Data initialization: Unstructured initialization of relevant parameters of big data.
3. Generate fitness function: Generate the initial amount of data using artificial intelligence technology theory and map it to big data. The accuracy of each big data is calculated and the absolute value of its sum of squibs is used as a function of fitness.
4. Iterate the optimal position and velocity: Among the 5 evolution of the amount of seed data, choose one to evolve, and alliterative update the optimal position and velocity according to Eqs. (7) ~ (9).

4 Practical Case Analysis

4.1 Performance Judgment of the Model

The artificial intelligence technology is tested with single-indicator performance, multi-indicator performance, multi-dimensional indicators and other indicators. Single-metric performance is the only minimum function of the test model synthesis. The results are shown in Eq. (10).

$$A(x) = \sum\nolimits_{i=1}^{n} \left[x_i^2\right]^3 \frac{-b \pm \sqrt{b^2 - 4ac}}{2a} \tag{10}$$

Multi-index performance is a cosine modulation transfer function that frequently generates a single minimum value. The result is shown in Eq. (11).

$$B(x) = \sqrt{b^2 - 4ac} \lim_{x \to \infty} \sum\nolimits_{i=1}^{n} \cos \alpha \, e^{x_i^2} \, a^n \tag{11}$$

Multi-dimensional indicator is an algorithm used to evaluate multi-dimensional data, and the judgment speed of synthesis is calculated by gradient optimization of multi-dimensional data. The specific formula is as follows:

$$\text{Indicator} = \Sigma(\text{weight i} * \text{value i})$$

where the weight i represents the weight of the ith dimension, and the value i represents the numerical value of the ith dimension. By multiplying and adding the weights of all dimensions and the corresponding values, the final metric value is obtained. This metric value can be used to evaluate the performance of the data across multiple dimensions, and the weights can be adjusted to adjust the contribution of each dimension to the final result.

$$C(x) = \sqrt{a^2 + b^2} - \alpha e^{\sqrt{\frac{1}{n} \sum_{i=1}^{n} x_i^2}} \tag{12}$$

the data is x_i calculated, and the number of arbitrary.

Table 1. Data acquisition and analysis in music teaching

Test metrics	Test the function	Rhythm of music	Form of music	Music content	Range of music variation
Single-metric performance	Single-metric performance	0.3488	2.3331	1.4710	2.6079 ~ 0.1640
	Merge sort algorithm	1.5890	0.2832	1.9927	
Multi-metric performance	Artificial intelligence technology	0.3686	0.1457	3.0717	0.5460 ~ 1.2811
	Merge sort algorithm	1.4262	2.1513	1.9777	
Multi-dimensional metrics	Artificial intelligence technology	1.1866	2.6480	0.9582	3.5760 ~ 0.2947
	Merge sort algorithm	1.4513	3.7818	0.7362	

Simplifying the calculations, a test experiment with 1200 innovative systems was designed. In this experiment, we performed 30 iterations and set the maximum length to 24 months. We tested each of the above three functions and averaged the results 10 times. The specific calculation results is shown in Table 1.

The convergence plots for each data in Table 1 and the overall rhythm and comprehensiveness of music is shown in Fig. 3.

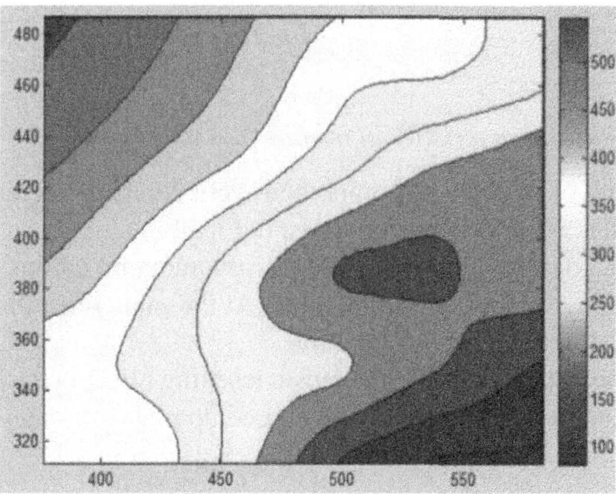

Fig. 3. Comparative study of the research scheme of the algorithm

According to the data comparison in Table 1, the artificial intelligence to the research results of comprehensive teaching innovation, compared with the merger ranking algorithm. The deviation, mean, value range, etc., AI technology performs better. As can be seen from the surface changes in Fig. 3, the AI technology performs better in terms of stability and judgment speed. As a result, AI technology is superior in terms of judgment speed, performance level judgment, and summation stability.

4.2 Case Studies of Teaching Innovation

The judgment dataset of teaching innovation research includes digital teaching innovation research, bionic teaching innovation research, natural teaching innovation research, psychology teaching innovation research, and anticipation teaching innovation research, and the data processing results are shown in Table 2.

Table 2. Classification and proportion of teaching innovation research

Different types	The whole of music	The playing effect of music
Music and science	43.42	0.69
Art	44.10	0.36
Creative music teaching	45.21	0.45
Teacher professional development	43.69	1.16
Test items	Test value	p-value
−2Ln LR(L^2)	15.32	0.24
Pearson chi-squid	12.24	0.32
Scaled deviance	15.26	0.26
Degrees of freedom = 14		

The overall effect and characteristics of music

Improve the integrity of music, and comprehensively compare and analyze the rhythm and content of music, and the results is shown in Fig. 4.

According to the data in Fig. 4, the overall structure and calling of music are presented, allowing us to evaluate and refine them. At the same time, due to the change of music, the specific structure is shown in Table 3.

According to the data in Table 3, the music teaching effect is good, but the analysis of music effect, connotation improvement, and comprehensive analysis find that there are large changes in music data, as shown in Fig. 5.

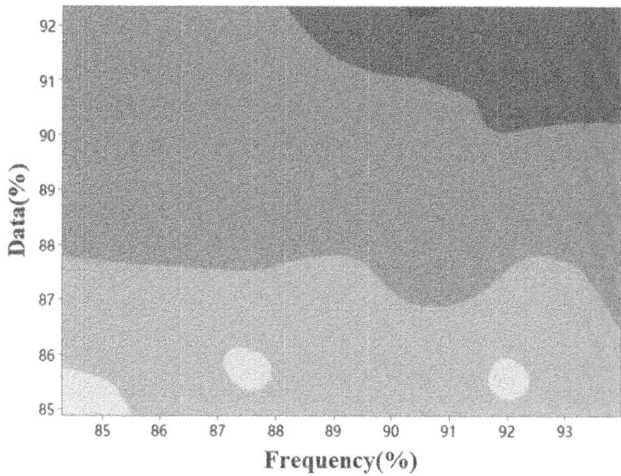

Fig. 4. Test results for different algorithms

Table 3. Comparison of judgment accuracy at different levels

Algorithm	Sample	Music content	Structure	Optimize the structure	Overall level	Fluctuations
Artificial intelligence technology	673	0.6008	0.7350	0.6722 ~ 0.7294	0.7362	1.4513
Merge sort algorithm	679	0.7985	3.7818	0.6700 ~ 0.8270	0.1542	4.1704

According to the results of Fig. 5, it is clear that AI technology performs better in terms of merge and sequencing. The reason for this result is that AI technology continuously improves performance through strategies of different dimensions such as increasing synergistic coefficients, improving weights, and convergence factors.

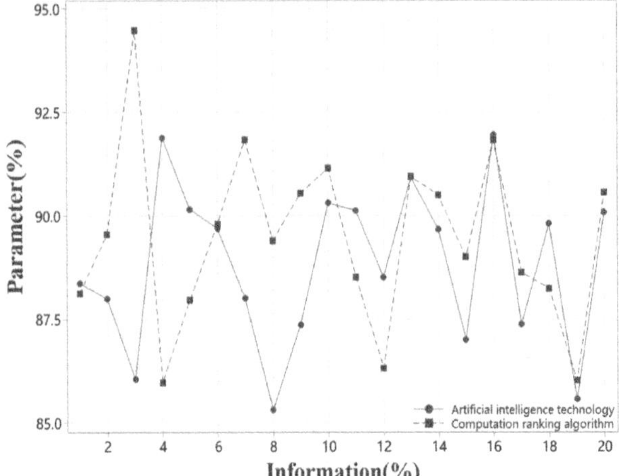

Fig. 5. Performance process of eigenvalues

5 Conclusion

There are great difficulties in music teaching, improving the music effect, comprehensively analyzing the content, and the overall structure to achieve the improvement of the music effect. In this paper, the comprehensive music effect is more than 80%, and the promotion effect is 10%, so the overall effect is more ideal. At the same time, the music change structure has been optimized by 20% to improve the overall level. However, there are certain shortcomings in this study, mainly due to the lack of sample size, which will make up for the lack of research in this paper in the future.

References

1. Yang, D.: Research on the construction method of library music resource database based on artificial intelligence technology. Inf. Comput. **35**(10), 180–182 (2023)
2. Su, Y.: Research on the innovation model of ideological and political education in college English curriculum based on artificial intelligence technology. Engl. Sq. Acad. Res. **17**, 84–87 (2023)
3. Zhang, S., Ma, Z., Dong, Y., Hou, D.: How is it possible for artificial intelligence to empower personalized learning in large-scale classrooms—based on research on the application of international AI classroom teaching in the past decade. Open Learn. Res. **28**(5), 42–50 (2023)
4. Song, X., Wang, X.: Research on the application of Jiaozhou Yangko culture in freeze frame animation design under artificial intelligence technology. Footwear Craft Des. **3**(3), 100–102 (2023)
5. Yao, S.: Method and device for extracting music melody contours based on fuzzy clustering algorithm. CN115658957A (2023)
6. Gao, C., Huang, J., Xu, Z., Tang, Y., Liang, X.: An interactive compilation based music generation method and device. CN202211465790.1 (2023)
7. Pei, W., Wang, H., Liulin, Pei, D.: A review of instrument recognition under music information retrieval. Comput. Eng. Appl. **59**(2), 14 (2023)

8. Ning, K.: Research on the application of artificial intelligence technology in film and television literature creation. China Media Technol. **11**, 105–108, 112 (2023)
9. Jiao, H., Liang, L.: The copyright risk of artificial intelligence synthesized music and its solution. Intellect. Prop. **11**, 103 (2023)
10. Yuan, Y., Wu, C., Tao, Y., Li, J.: How can basic research drive innovation in key core technologies in China—empirical research based on new generation artificial intelligence patents. Sci. Technol. Manag. **44**(10), 3–17 (2023)
11. Wen, J.: Research on innovation of digital teaching mode in vocational colleges in the era of artificial intelligence. Knowl. Wind. (Teach. Vers.) **9**, 24–26 (2023)
12. Dai, Y., Chen, W.: Research on hybrid teaching mode in vocational colleges based on artificial intelligence technology. Comput. Enthus. **4**, 106–108 (2023)
13. Sun, N., Li, M., Li, D., Wang, Y.: Has innovation in artificial intelligence technology narrowed the gender income gap—empirical analysis based on Chinese household tracking surveys. Techn. Econ. **42**(10), 38–48 (2023)

The Integration Path and Impact of Artificial Intelligence and Physical Education Curriculum Development Technology

Peng Ren(✉)

West Yunnan University of Applied Technology, Dali, Yunnan, China
renpeng1207@163.com

Abstract. With the rapid development of science and technology, artificial intelligence (AI) has gradually penetrated into every field of education, and physical education curriculum is no exception. In physical education courses, AI technology is mainly reflected in the following aspects: Personalized training plan: AI By analyzing students' physique, sports performance and training history, AI makes a personalized training plan for each student to ensure the scientific and effective training. Movement data analysis: Using sensors and smart devices to collect exercise data, AI can analyze students' technical movements, exercise intensity and fatigue degree in real time, so as to provide accurate teaching feedback for coaches. Virtual coach: AI virtual coach provides instant guidance through video analysis and voice interaction to help students correct their movements and improve their skills. Intelligent sports equipment: smart sports shoes, wearable devices, etc., through integrating sensors and AI algorithms, to provide students with real-time sports performance data and suggestions. After class, the action recognition method is used to evaluate students' physical education teaching actions, form quantitative data for scoring, explore a new path of artificial intelligence and sports integration development technology, and establish a complete grassroots school material selection model to cultivate people's sports habits from the grassroots level and promote the development of the sports industry to a higher field.

Keywords: Artificial intelligence · Sports integration · Technical paths · Impact

1 Introduction

Although the application of AI in physical education courses has achieved initial results, there are still some challenges: Technology cost and penetration: High-quality AI systems and smart devices tend to be more expensive, which limits their adoption in large schools, especially in areas where educational resources are relatively scarce. Teacher adaptability: Many physical education teachers may have difficulties in the acceptance and use of new technologies, and need time for professional training and conceptual change. Data security and privacy: The extensive collection and analysis of students 'movement data may cause privacy protection problems. How to protect the security of students' data while ensuring the teaching effect is an urgent problem to be solved.

B. Brik and S. Nazir (Eds.): BigIoT-EDU 2024, LNICST 660, pp. 126–135, 2026.
https://doi.org/10.1007/978-3-032-18628-7_14

A. *Application of artificial intelligence technology in the field of sports*

However, AI has also brought unprecedented opportunities for physical education courses: Improving teaching efficiency: AI can automate the processing of large amounts of teaching data, reducing the burden on teachers and giving them more time to focus on personalized guidance and curriculum design. Diversified teaching: AI is combined with virtual reality (VR) and augmented reality (AR) to create an immersive learning environment for students to experience and learn sports skills in simulated real scenes. Interdisciplinary integration: AI, combined with biomechanics, sports medicine and other disciplines, can provide a deeper understanding of the rules of sports and provide a scientific basis for physical education courses. Support for lifelong learning: an AI-driven online learning platform that enables students to continuously learn and improve outside the classroom, and achieve lifelong development of sports skills. In the face of challenges, actively seize these opportunities, artificial intelligence is expected to further promote the innovation and reform of physical education curriculum, and improve the quality and influence of physical education.

B. *The teaching mode of artificial intelligence in physical education curriculum changes*

The impact of artificial intelligence technology on the development of sports integration is mainly manifested in the following aspects:

1. The combination of traditional teaching mode and artificial intelligence

In physical education, the traditional teaching mode usually focuses on the teachers 'demonstration and the students' imitation. Combined with artificial intelligence, this model can become more personalized and efficient. The AI system can analyze students' technical movements, provide accurate feedback and suggestions through high-speed camera and image recognition technology, and help students correct their movements and improve their skills. In addition, AI can also intelligently adjust the pace and difficulty of teaching according to students' learning progress and understanding ability, to ensure that each student can learn at their own pace.

2. The integration of autonomous learning and collaborative learning

Artificial intelligence can promote autonomous learning in physical education courses, through the intelligent coaching system, students can practice independently outside the classroom, and the system will provide guidance and incentives according to their performance. At the same time, AI can also promote collaborative learning. Through virtual team competitive games or online cooperative training, students can improve their teamwork ability in the interaction. For example, AI can create a virtual environment for students to conduct tactical drills in groups, and help teams adjust their strategies and improve cooperation efficiency through real-time data analysis.

3. Application of virtual reality technology in physical education curriculum

The application of virtual reality (VR) technology in physical education curriculum has revolutionized the teaching model. Students can simulate various sports scenarios such as skiing, rock climbing, or football matches in a secure virtual environment. VR technology can provide a highly immersive experience, helping students to train their skills and understand their tactics without requiring practical equipment or venues. At the same time, teachers can use VR to conduct distance teaching, monitor student performance, and provide immediate instruction. Moreover, by collecting and analyzing students 'behavioral data in a virtual environment, teachers can gain a deeper understanding of students' learning habits and difficulties, thus optimizing teaching strategies. To sum up, the introduction of artificial intelligence is profoundly changing the teaching mode of physical education courses, making education more personalized, independent and interactive. Through intelligent analysis, autonomous learning platform and virtual reality technology, students can enjoy a richer and more effective learning experience, and at the same time, teachers can also guide teaching in a more scientific way and promote the modernization process of physical education.

C. *The influence of artificial intelligence on the development of physical education curriculum*

In order to further improve the impact and effect of artificial intelligence on the development of sports integration, we need to adopt the following optimization strategies:

1. Personalized teaching

Artificial intelligence can analyze students 'learning data, develop personalized training plans for each student, to ensure that the teaching content is in line with students' ability level and interest, so as to improve learning efficiency. Through AI coaches, students can adjust themselves according to their progress and ability to improve their participation.

2. Real-time feedback and guidance

The AI system can monitor students' actions and performance in real time, provide corrective feedback in real time, help students to quickly improve the technology and avoid the formation of wrong actions, so as to improve the quality of teaching. At the same time, this immediate feedback can also stimulate students' interest in learning and enhance their commitment to the course.

3. Interactive learning experience

AI technology combining virtual reality and augmented reality can create an immersive learning environment, making students feel like they are in a real competition scene, and improving their sense of participation and learning motivation. Through interactive games and challenges, students learn in the entertainment, making the physical education course more attractive.

Artificial intelligence can generate a variety of course contents, according to their needs and interests, such as competitive games, teamwork projects, health training, etc., to meet the needs of different students. At the same time, AI can also introduce the latest movement trends and scientific research to keep the course content novel and cutting-edge. 3.2.2, interdisciplinary integration AI technology can help the integration of physical education courses and other disciplines, such as the combination of physics, biology, psychology and other knowledge, so that students can understand and use the knowledge of other disciplines while learning physical education, and enrich the course content. 3.2.3 Intelligent evaluation and optimization AI can evaluate course effects in real-time through data analysis, help teachers adjust teaching strategies, optimize course design, and ensure continuous innovation and improvement of course content.

2 Related Concepts

A. *Data-driven training*

Using AI to collect and analyze student training data, scientific training plans can be developed to avoid overtraining and injury. At the same time, AI can also help students to optimize their exercise skills and improve their sports performance through biomechanical analysis.

$$G(\alpha) = \arg\max W\left(\frac{L_i}{G_i}\right) \cdot W(G) \tag{1}$$

Among them, the judgment of outliers is shown in Eq. (2).

$$G(\alpha)' = \arg\max W\left(\frac{L_i}{G_i}\right)^{\sigma} \cdot W(G)^{\lambda} \tag{2}$$

AI can design to adapt to the challenges of students 'progress. With the improvement of students' ability, it can increase the difficulty and complexity of training, keep the course challenging, and stimulate students to constantly surpass themselves.

$$G(\alpha_i) = \arg\max \sum_{w} W\left(\frac{L_i^c}{G_i^n}\right) \cdot W\left(\frac{L_i^c}{G_i^n}\right)^{\sigma} \cdot W\left(G_1^m\right)^{\lambda} \tag{3}$$

B. *Gameplay learning*

Through the above methods, the application of artificial intelligence in physical education courses not only improves the teaching quality, enhances students' participation, but also promotes the innovation and enrichment of the course content, makes physical education courses more scientific and interesting, and provides strong support for the comprehensive development of students.

$$p_{e \cdot f} = \exp \sum_{i=1}^{n} \lambda_i h_i(e \cdot f) \tag{4}$$

The establishment of physical education curriculum resource database is the foundation of intelligent teaching.

$$G(\alpha_i) + p_{e \cdot f} \leq \max[\lambda_i h_i(e \cdot f)] \tag{5}$$

By collecting all kinds of sports teaching videos, 3D simulation demonstration, professional coach guidance audio, sports physiology, sports anatomy and other related materials, to build a comprehensive, three-dimensional resource library.

$$G(\alpha_i) + p_{e \cdot f} \leftrightarrow mean\left[\lambda_i h_i(e \cdot f)\right] \tag{6}$$

C. *Integrate resources to build an intelligent physical education course resource database*

These resources can not only provide students with independent study, but also provide teachers with materials for instructional design. In addition, through AI technology, the resource database can realize intelligent recommendation, and recommend the most suitable learning materials according to students' learning progress and interests, to ensure personalized learning experience.

$$h\tau(e \cdot f) = \frac{G(\alpha_i) + p_{e \cdot f}}{mean\left[\lambda_i h_i(e \cdot f)\right]} \tag{7}$$

The establishment of physical education curriculum resource database is the foundation of intelligent teaching. By collecting all kinds of sports teaching videos, 3D simulation demonstration, professional coach guidance audio, sports physiology, sports anatomy and other related materials, to build a comprehensive, three-dimensional resource library. These resources can not only provide students with independent study, but also provide teachers with materials for instructional design.

$$hg(e \cdot f) = \min\left[\sum G(\alpha_i) + p_{e \cdot f}\right] \tag{8}$$

In addition, through AI technology, the resource database can realize intelligent recommendation, recommending the most suitable learning materials according to students' learning progress and interests, to ensure personalized learning experience.

$$htg(e \cdot f) = \frac{\min\left[\sum G(\alpha_i) + p_{e \cdot f}\right]}{\sum G(\alpha_i) + p_{e \cdot f}} \times 100\% \tag{9}$$

The implementation of intelligent physical education curriculum needs the coordination of multiple departments. For example, the information technology department provides technical support to ensure the normal operation of hardware equipment and the update and maintenance of software; the teaching administration department is responsible for coordinating the curriculum design and evaluation; and the scientific research department can participate in the innovative research of the course and explore new teaching methods. In addition, physical education courses can also be integrated with mathematics, physics, biology and other disciplines. Through practical cases, students can understand and apply the knowledge of other disciplines in sports, such as optimizing training plans through data analysis, and using physical principles to understand the movement trajectory.

$$ahtg(e \cdot f) = \frac{\min\left[\sum G(\alpha_i) + p_{e \cdot f}\right]}{\sum G(\alpha_i) + p_{e \cdot f}} \times 100\% + Htg(e \cdot f) \tag{10}$$

In cross-departmental cooperation, physical education courses can be combined in comprehensive activities with other courses, such as technology and sports festivals, to encourage students to apply what they have learned to practice. In this way, not only enhance the attractiveness of physical education courses, but also enhance the comprehensive quality of students, to achieve all-round development.

3 Optimization Strategy of Sports Integration Development Technology Path

To sum up, to build an intelligent physical education curriculum ecosystem, it is necessary to integrate all resources, improve teachers' ability, and promote the deep integration of interdisciplinary subjects. This will bring about unprecedented changes to physical education, and provide strong support for the cultivation of a new generation of talents with innovative thinking and scientific and technological literacy.

4 Practical Examples of the Technical Path of Sports Integration Development

A. *Challenges and Countermeasures: To deal with the problems of artificial intelligence in the development of physical education curriculum*

With the increasing application of artificial intelligence in physical education curriculum, collecting and analyzing students' sports data has become an important means to improve the teaching effect. However, this also brings challenges to privacy protection and data security. Educational institutions and developers must ensure that all data collection, storage, and analysis follow strict regulatory and ethical standards. Implementing transparent data use policies, obtaining informed consent from students and parents, and using advanced encryption technologies to protect data from illegal access are key measures to ensure privacy security. At the same time, regular security audit and vulnerability repair for the system to prevent data leakage is also an important step to maintain information security.

Table 1. Physical fitness level requirements for students

Related content	Improve	Lifting	Physical and educational integration
Athletic ability	56.3295	48.4374	56.1122
Physical fitness	55.0753	48.7663	57.1033
Motor skills	56.9740	48.8470	53.6351
Fitness level	54.7088	48.3687	53.0090

The process of students' physical fitness levels in Table 1, as shown in Fig. 1.

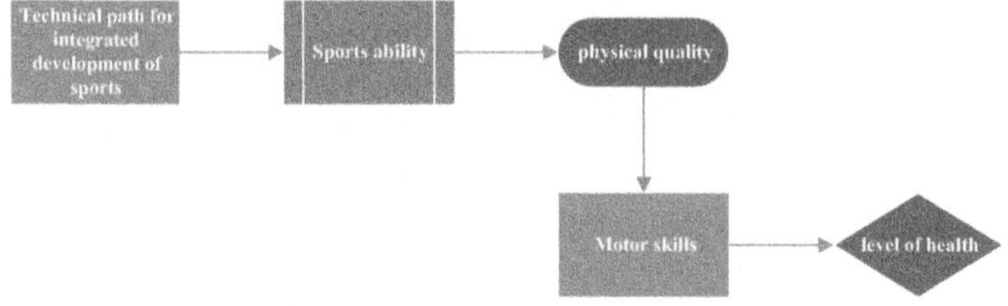

Fig. 1. Construction process of sports integration development technology path

The rapid development of artificial intelligence technology requires the physical education curriculum to be updated simultaneously with it, but the transformation of the educational concept can not be achieved overnight. Teachers need to constantly learn and adapt to new technologies, and effectively integrate AI tools into teaching to improve teaching quality and student experience.

B. *The technical path of sports integration development*

Moreover, educators should pay attention to the impact of technology on students' psychological, social and emotional development, and avoid the decline of interpersonal skills caused by excessive reliance on technology. Advocating a balance between technology and humanistic care, and ensuring that AI tools are auxiliary rather than replacing teachers, is the embodiment of the educational concept keeping pace with The Times (Table 2).

Table 2. The overall picture of the sports AI program

Category	Drill down the path	Intelligence
Action posture	72.3368	73.5279
Identify actions	71.3737	75.0146
Bad habits	69.2050	72.8797
Health problems	70.1483	73.6748

C. *Sports artificial intelligence and stability of students' physical fitness level*

Although the application of artificial intelligence in physical education curriculum has brought many advantages, it also aggravates the inequality of educational resources. The gap in access and utilization of these technologies between urban and rural areas, rich and poor may lead to inequalities in educational opportunities. To alleviate this problem, the government and education departments need to develop equitable policies to ensure that all schools have the necessary technical support (Fig. 2).

At the same time, through the public-private cooperation model, enterprises are encouraged to donate equipment or provide technical support to lower the technology threshold in poor areas. In addition, providing online educational resources and distance

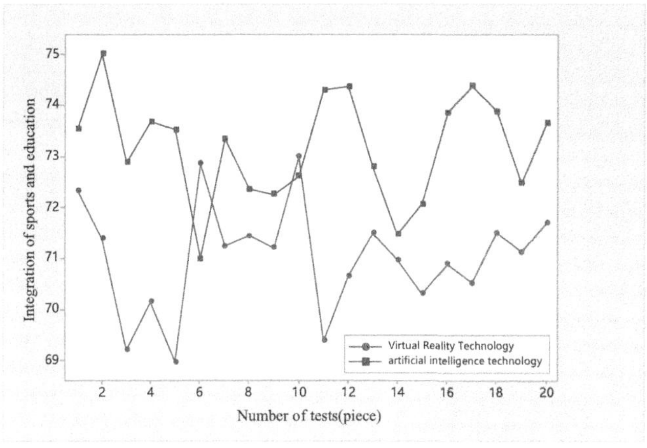

Fig. 2. Sports artificial intelligence with different algorithms

training to help teachers improve their skills is also an effective way to narrow the digital divide. Through these strategies, we can work hard to ensure that all students can benefit from the educational progress brought about by AI, without being limited by geographical or economic conditions (Table 3).

Table 3. Accuracy comparison of students' physical fitness levels by different methods

Algorithm	Sports artificial intelligence	Intelligent recognition rate	Error rate
Artificial intelligence technology	87.5172	87.3534	87.3089
Virtual reality technology	73.5173	73.52799	75.0146

With the continuous progress of artificial intelligence technology, intelligent physical education teaching will show more abundant possibilities. In the future, the AI system will analyze individual physiological data more intelligently, and provide personalized training programs for each student to ensure the safety and effect of sports. Virtual reality and augmented reality technology will enable students to experience a variety of sports programs in a simulated environment, providing an immersive learning experience. At the same time, machine learning algorithms will help coaches and teachers optimize their teaching strategies and adjust the teaching content in real time to meet students' learning progress and needs. In addition, artificial intelligence will be combined with the Internet of Things to monitor students' heart rate, gait, movement accuracy and so on in real time through smart wearable devices, providing real-time feedback to ensure the scientific and efficient training (Fig. 3).

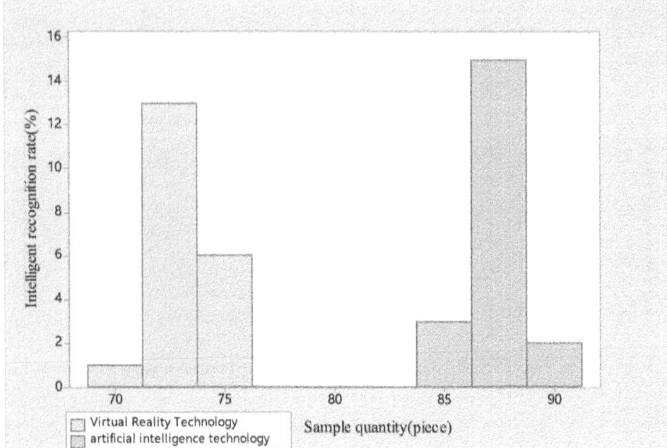

Fig. 3. Artificial intelligence technology for sports artificial intelligence of students' physical fitness level

In the process of education modernization led by artificial intelligence, it is very important to cultivate sports talents with information literacy. This means that the future of physical education should not only teach sports skills, but also cultivate students' data analysis ability, technology application ability and innovative thinking. By integrating AI courses into physical education, students will learn how to use intelligent tools to self-assess, understand physical function, and how to use technology to improve training methods. This education mode will cultivate compound sports talents adapted to the future society. They are not only good at sports, but also can use scientific and technological means to optimize sports performance and promote the innovation and development of the sports industry.

5 Conclusion

With the wide application of artificial intelligence, physical education courses will continue to evolve, and educators need to constantly adapt to the new teaching environment and explore more efficient and personalized teaching methods. In the future, intelligent physical education will no longer be just a concept, but will become an important part of the modernization of education, providing strong support for cultivating a new generation of sports talents and promoting the prosperity of the sports industry.

Aiming at the problem that the technical path of sports integration development is not ideal, this paper proposes artificial intelligence technology, and combines artificial intelligence theory to optimize the technical path of sports integration development. At the same time, the innovation of students' physical fitness level and threshold innovation are analyzed in depth, and a fusion set is constructed. Research shows that artificial intelligence technology can improve the accuracy and stability of the technical path of sports integration development, and can carry out the general physical fitness level of sports integration development technology path 。However, in the process of applying artificial intelligence technology, too much attention is paid to the analysis of students' physical fitness level, resulting in irrationality in the selection of students' physical fitness level indicators.

References

1. Ahmad, M.N., Abdallah, S.A., Abbasi, S.A., Abdallah, A.M.: Student perspectives on the integration of artificial intelligence into healthcare services. Digital Health **9** (2023)
2. Andrew, J., Rudra, M., Eunice, J., Belfin, R.V.: Artificial intelligence in adolescents mental health disorder diagnosis, prognosis, and treatment. Front. Public Health **11** (2023)
3. Babl, F.E., Babl, M.P.: Generative artificial intelligence: can ChatGPT write a quality abstract? Emerg. Medi. Aust. (2023)
4. Babu, C.S., Holsinger, F.C., Zuchowski, L., Ratti, E., Rameau, A.: Epistemological challenges of artificial intelligence clinical decision support tools in otolaryngology: The Black Box Problem. Otolaryngol Head Neck Surg. (2023)
5. Baciuliene, V., Bilan, Y., Navickas, V., Lubomir, C.: The aspects of artificial intelligence in different phases of the food value and supply chain. Foods **12**(8) (2023)
6. Bao, Z., et al.: Software architecture for responsible artificial intelligence systems: practice in the digitization of industrial drawings. Computer **56**(4), 38–49 (2023)
7. Burger, M., Nitsche, A.-M., Arlinghaus, J.: Hybrid intelligence in procurement: disillusionment with AI's superiority? Comput. Ind. **150** (2023)
8. Cedars, M.I.: Artificial intelligence in assisted reproductive technology: how best to optimize this tool of the future. Fertil. Steril. **120**(1), 1–2 (2023)
9. Chen, M.: Status analysis of the artificial intelligence development in Guangdong Province from the view of science foundation. Control Eng. China **30**(1), 186–192 (2023)
10. Choi, E.P.H., Lee, J.J., Ho, M.-H., Kwok, J.Y.Y., Lok, K.Y.W.: Chatting or cheating? The impacts of ChatGPT and other artificial intelligence language models on nurse education. Nurse Educ. Today **125** (2023)
11. Cohen, F.: The role of artificial intelligence in headache medicine: potential and peril. Headache (2023)
12. Dodonova, V., Dodonov, R., Gorbenko, K.: Ethical aspects of artificial intelligence functioning in the XXI Century. Studia Universitatis Babes-Bolyai Philosophia **68**(1), 161–173 (2023)
13. Ducret, M., Morch, C.-M.: Focus on artificial intelligence ethics in dentistry. J. Dental Sci. **18**(3), 1409–1410 (2023)
14. Frith, K.H.: Swarm thinking: can humans beat artificial intelligence? Nurs. Educ. Perspect. **44**(1), 69 (2023)
15. Galland, J.: Chatbots and internal medicine: future opportunities and challenges. Rev. Med. Interne **44**(5), 209–211 (2023)

Research on the Reform and Practice of Physical Education Teaching in Colleges and Universities Based on Artificial Intelligence Technology

Qiu Cheng(✉)

Sichuan University of Culture and Arts, Mianyang, China
wanglei18291826361@126.com

Abstract. Although the teaching form plays a crucial function in college PE classes, the fact that it is illogical is a major issue. The current manner of instruction in college PE is illogical and ineffective, and traditional approaches will not help. So, to assess the instructional format, this article suggests an AI system. First of all, the computer is used to analyze the teaching form, and the indicators are split according to the needs of the teaching form to decrease the teaching form in the interfering factor. After that, the computer takes a look at the college and university PE form results, makes a plan for the PE class, and then looks at the PE class outcomes. Perform an exhaustive investigation. MATLAB simulation reveals that under the condition of specific assessment criteria, artificial intelligence technology is superior than the reform of college physical education teaching form and the practice of teaching form Conventional techniques.

Keywords: Computer · Artificial intelligence technology · Physical education in colleges and universities · Teaching format

1 Introduction

More and more areas of education are incorporating AI into their curricula as the technology continues to advance [1]. Among the more conventional areas of education, college PE has benefited from the innovative ideas and practical investigations that have been made possible by the advent of AI technology in recent years [2]. This study will examine the tendencies in the future of artificial intelligence and its effects on the reform of college and university physical education programs.

A. *Application of artificial intelligence technology in college physical education*

1. Personalized instruction

Using AI, teachers may tailor lesson plans and supplementary materials to each student's unique strengths, weaknesses, and learning style, allowing them to more effectively acquire and use athletic information and abilities [3]. Among them, AI technology

B. Brik and S. Nazir (Eds.): BigIoT-EDU 2024, LNICST 660, pp. 136–144, 2026.
https://doi.org/10.1007/978-3-032-18628-7_15

may analyze data such students' learning behaviors, processes, and outcomes to create individualized lesson plans and supplementary resources that pique students' interest in and retention of course content [4].

2. Instantaneous comments

With the use of AI, we can keep tabs on kids in real time and provide them constructive criticism; analyze their data and ideas to help them better their performance; increase their knowledge and abilities in sports; and boost their learning outcomes [5].

3. VR technology

The immersive learning environment that virtual reality technology may give students can greatly enhance their mastery of sports-related information and abilities [6]. Through virtual reality technology, students may experience realistic competition circumstances, study game rules and strategies, and develop practical operation skill and actual battle adaptability [7].

B. *The reform of artificial intelligence to the form of physical education in colleges and universities*

1. Change the established style of teaching

Meeting individuals' unique learning requirements and interests is challenging in the conventional college and university PE model, which relies heavily on instructor instruction and student imitation [8]. Teaching according to aptitude and improving students' learning effect and interest in learning are both made possible with the advent of artificial intelligence technology, which allows for the provision of personalized lesson plans and instructional materials based on students' unique needs and learning circumstances [9].

2. Boost pupils' practical abilities

It is challenging to guarantee that every student gets complete exercise chances with the practical operation that is often used in standard college physical education classes, which mostly include theoretical instruction. With the advent of AI technology, virtual reality may immerse students in a learning environment, give them a greater feel for how sports skills work in practice, and boost their practical operation abilities [11].

3. Pique pupils' curiosity in the subject

It is challenging to pique students' interest in learning when they are taught in a style that is primarily based on instructor instruction and student imitation, as is common in typical college physical education classes [12]. The advent of AI has made it possible to provide students with a fully immersive learning environment via VR, which improves their understanding of competition scenarios and tactics, piques their interest in learning, and increases the learning effect [13].

C. *The future development of artificial intelligence for college physical education*

1. The exchange of pedagogical materials

With the advent of AI, it will be possible to share teaching materials across institutions and regions, which will boost both the quality and efficiency of education. Through the sharing of teaching materials, students may get more diverse and complete teaching resources to support students' learning and growth.

2. Boost student engagement and learning

The use of AI in education has several potential benefits, including the ability to track and respond to students in real time, provide more personalized recommendations and recommendations, boost students' engagement and learning outcomes, and increase their motivation to study.

3. Motivate students to study on their own

Students will be able to enhance their learning efficiency via the realization of autonomous learning with the help of artificial intelligence technology. This will allow students to autonomously choose learning methods and material based on their own learning goals and requirements.

There are fresh perspectives and avenues for investigation into how to improve college physical education that arise from the use of AI technology in this field. Students' learning effects and interests can be enhanced with the help of artificial intelligence technology, which can tailor lesson plans and supplementary materials to each student's unique requirements and learning environment. Higher education Phys Ed will face both new possibilities and new obstacles as a result of the increased and more profound use of AI technology in the future.

The teaching form is one of the key components of physical education in colleges and universities, and it is of considerable relevance for physical education. However, in the process of teaching form, there is an issue of inadequate rationality of the teaching form plan, which introduces certain challenges to the execution of teaching. A number of academics hold the view that college and university physical education classes may benefit from an AI-powered study of their pedagogical scheme and the accompanying reinforcement it offers. Based on this, this research suggests using AI to improve the teaching form scheme and check whether the model is successful.

2 Related Works

A. *Mathematical description of artificial intelligence technology*

In order to optimize the teaching form scheme, locate the unqualified values in college physical education based on the indicators in the teaching form, integrate the teaching form scheme, and finally judgment, artificial intelligence technology is used. The practicality of including PE into higher education. With the use of AI, we can optimize various forms of instruction by combining the best features of computers, applying quantitative methods to college sports education, and more.

First Hypothesis: The Need for a Specific Teaching Form is c_i, the teaching form scheme is set_i, the satisfaction of the teaching form scheme is g, with the evaluation function for the instructional form scheme is $S(c_i \approx 0)$, As illustrated in Eq. (1).

$$S(c_i g) = \begin{pmatrix} 1\,0 \\ 0\,1 \end{pmatrix} \rightarrow \sum_{i=1}^{g} (c_i + S)^2 \cdot \frac{1}{2} \tag{1}$$

B. *Choice of teaching format scheme*

Second Hypothesis: Why College Sports Are Important is $e(c_i)$, together with the weighted average is w_i, Therefore, as shown in Eq. (2), the instructional format necessitates unqualified college physical education.

$$e(c_i) = \frac{e - 2!}{9!(w_i - g)!} \cdot \underset{i \to \infty}{S(c_i)} + \bigcap_{c_i} e \tag{2}$$

C. *Analysis of teaching format schemes*

Before carrying out artificial intelligence technology, it is important to perform multi-dimensional analysis of the teaching form scheme, and map the teaching form requirements to the college physical education teaching library, and remove the unqualified teaching form scheme. To start, we do a thorough analysis of college and university PE classes, and then we establish the teaching form scheme's threshold and index weights to make sure the AI is accurate. There has to be an examination of the college and university physical education program as a whole. The general correctness of college and university physical education curricula might be compromised if their student bodies do not follow a normal distribution. Figure 1 shows the particular program selection that is essential to increase the accuracy of artificial intelligence technology and the level of teaching forms. The choice of teaching form scheme is also important.

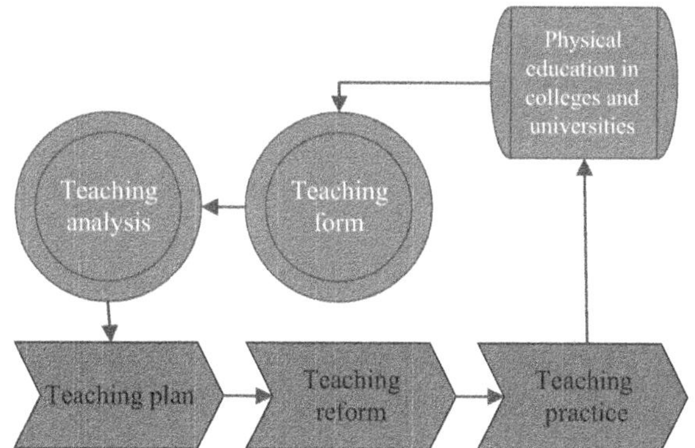

Fig. 1. The results of the selection of the teaching format program

The survey of the teaching form scheme demonstrates that the teaching form scheme displays a multi-dimensional distribution, which is in conformity with the objective facts. The lack of direction in college and university physical education classes suggests a highly randomised instructional form system, making this kind of inquiry very analytical. College PE satisfies standard criteria in large part because computers modify college PE lessons, eliminate unnecessary and redundant plans, and augment the default plan, resulting in a robust dynamic correlation of the whole course outline.

3 Optimization Strategies for Physical Education in Colleges and Universities

By adjusting the characteristics of the instructional form, artificial intelligence technology optimizes the scheme for college physical education by adopting a random optimization method. College and university physical education classes are now organized into tiers according to artificial intelligence criteria, and students are randomly assigned to various classes. In the iterative process, the teaching form schemes of various teaching form levels are optimized and assessed. Once the optimization study is finished, the top college PE programs are determined by comparing their levels of instruction.

4 Results and Discussion

A. *Introduction to the teaching format*

This study uses college physical education teaching in complicated circumstances as its research object; the model includes 12 pathways and a 12-h testing period; and the model is unique to the physical education teaching in higher education. Table 1 displays the scheme.

Table 1. Requirements for the form of teaching in colleges and universities

Scope of application	Grade	Rationality	Teaching format
Freshman	Standard	86.65	85.28
	Higher	88.28	82.67
Sophomore	Standard	87.32	84.20
	Higher	86.08	87.39
Junior	Standard	88.45	86.38
	Higher	84.22	86.30

The teaching format process in Table 1 is shown in Fig. 2.

Artificial intelligence technology's pedagogical framework is more in line with real-world needs than those of conventional approaches. Artificial intelligence technology

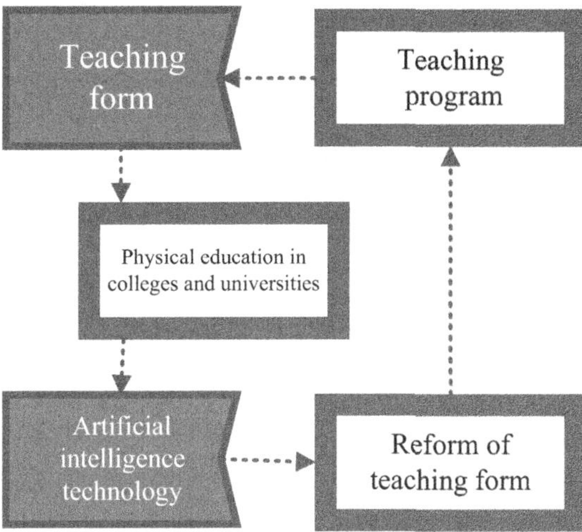

Fig. 2. The analytical process of physical education in colleges and universities

outperforms conventional approaches to college and university physical education in terms of both pedagogical efficacy and logical reasoning. Figure 2 shows that the instructional format scheme has changed, indicating that artificial intelligence technology has a quicker judgment speed. Therefore, the teaching format scheme acceleration, instructing form scheme feasibility, and summation reliability of intelligent innovation are improved.

B. *Physical education in colleges and universities*

College and university physical education curricula make use of three types of information: unstructured, semi-structured, and structural. Preliminary lesson plans for collegiate PE and collegiate PE instruction are generated after the pre-selection of AI technologies. Examination of the practicability of instructional design strategies. Table 2 shows the teaching form method used to choose physical education classes from colleges and universities with varying degrees of formal education in order to more reliably confirm the outcomes of these classes.

Table 2. The overall picture of the teaching format program

Category	Satisfaction	Analysis rate
Freshman	88.62	86.57
Sophomore	89.42	89.86
Junior	89.94	89.38
Mean	88.17	89.55
X^6	89.12	86.56
P = 1.53		

C. *Teaching form and stability of teaching form*

Figure 3 shows the instructional form scheme that was used to compare it with the conventional way in order to validate the correctness of artificial intelligence technology.

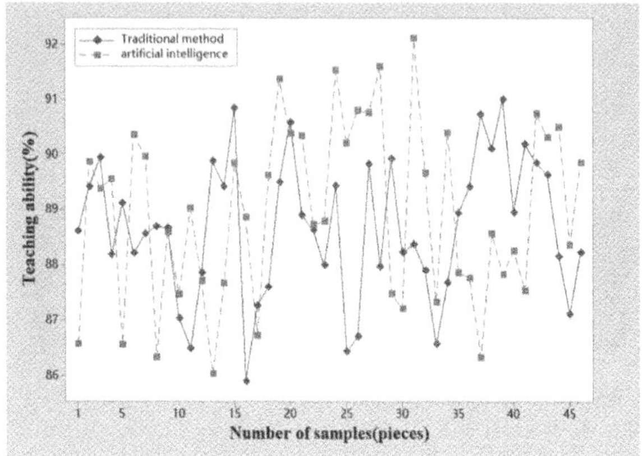

Fig. 3. Teaching forms of different algorithms

Figure 3 shows that the error rate is lower for traditional methods of instruction and has a higher level of stability than AI-based alternatives, suggesting that AI-based methods of instruction are more reliable overall. The methods of instruction vary. The average teaching format plan of the aforementioned three methods is provided in Table 3.

Table 3. Comparison of the accuracy of teaching forms of different methods

Algorithm	Teaching format	Magnitude of change	Error
Artificial intelligence technology	91.88	90.86	90.50
Traditional methods	87.11	88.36	89.60
P	86.02	87.62	88.22

Table 3 shows that the traditional method of teaching college PE has a problem with an unsatisfactory form of instruction, and that college PE instruction has changed a lot and has a high error rate. On the other hand, AI technologies generally teach better than traditional methods, and their teaching forms are over 90% accurate. To further verify AI's superiority and the efficacy of the proposed method, various methods are used to conduct an AI general analysis, as shown in Fig. 4.

Figure 4 shows that compared to the traditional method, the AI teaching form is much better. This is because AI raises the adjustment coefficient for PE classes in universities and sets the thresholds for the form, making it impossible for non-compliant teaching format schemes to be used.

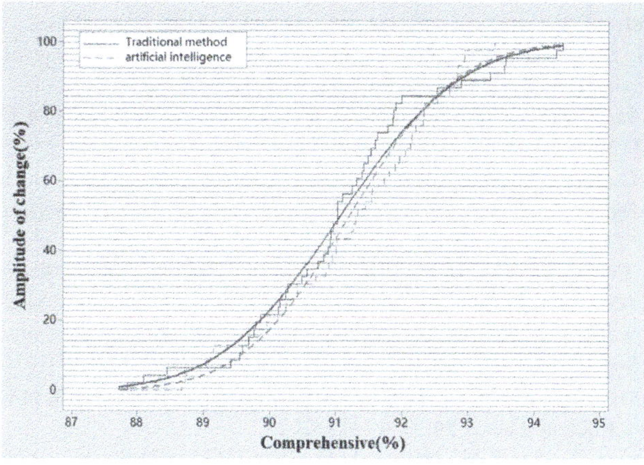

Fig. 4. The teaching form of artificial intelligence technology teaching form

5 Conclusion

This article aims to address the issue of non-ideal college and university physical education programs by suggesting the use of artificial intelligence and computer integration to improve college and university PE programs. Concurrently, a plethora of teaching forms is developed after a thorough analysis of the reform of these forms. It has been shown via research that AI technology has the potential to enhance the effectiveness of college physical education classes and implement generalized teaching methods for these classes. Unfortunately, irrationality in the selection of indicators for teaching forms occurs when artificial intelligence technology focuses too much on analyzing teaching forms.

References

1. Anchia-Umana, I.: Physical Education: the right to a quality education. Mhsalud-Revista En Ciencias Del Movimiento Humano Y La Salud **20**(1) (2023)
2. Banos, R., Espinoza-Gutierrez, R., Calleja-Nunez, J.J., Rodriguez-Cifuentes, G.: Analysis of academic psychological variables, physical education, and physical activity levels of Mexican students. Behav. Sci. **13**(3) (2023)
3. Bartle, G.: An investigation of how physical literacy is enacted in primary physical education. Qual. Res. J. **23**(3), 325–337 (2023)
4. Bernate, J., Fonseca, I.: Digital skills in teachers of physical education degree. Retos-Nuevas Tendencias En Educacion Fisica Deporte Y Recreacion (49), 252–259 (2023)
5. Bezeau, D., Turcotte, S., Desbiens, J.F., Spallanzani, C., Roy, M., Vandercleyen, F., Beaudoin, S.: Physical education teachers' assessment practices in health education. Phys. Educ. Sport Pedag. (2023)
6. Bonilla, D.A., Sanchez-Rojas, I.A., Mendoza-Romero, D., Moreno, Y., Koci, J., Gomez-Miranda, L.M., Rojas-Valverde, D., Petro, J.L., Kreider, R.B.: Profiling physical fitness of physical education majors using unsupervised machine learning. Int. J. Environ. Res. Public Health **20**(1) (2023)

7. Cid, F.M., Ferro, E.F., Mora, J.I., Flores, P.G., Bolados, M.B., Gonzalez, C.C., Munoz, J.M., Ormeno, F.S.: Sexism in physical education students in Chile. Retos-Nuevas Tendencias En Educacion Fisica Deporte Y Recreacion (49), 157–162 (2023)
8. Gonzalez, E.D.: Practice in physical education: case study. Viref-Revista De Educacion Fisica **12**(1), 88–97 (2023)
9. Houser, N., Kriellaars, D.: Where was this when I was in physical education? Physical literacy enriched pedagogy in a quality physical education context. Front. Sports Active Living **5** (2023)
10. Iglesias, D., Fernandez-Rio, J., Rodriguez-Gonzalez, P.: Cooperative learning in physical education: a research overview. Apunts Educacion Fisica Y Deportes (151), 88–93 (2023)
11. Jess, M., Howells, K., McMillan, P.: Becoming physical education: the ontological shift to complexity. Sport Educ. Soc. (2023)
12. Jones, L., Tones, S., Foulkes, G.: Talking the talk: dialogic mentoring in physical education. J. Phys. Educ. Recreat. Dance **94**(5), 40–45 (2023)
13. Liu, C., Dong, C.X., Li, X.H., Huang, H.H., Wang, Q.L.: Analysis of physical education classroom teaching after implementation of the Chinese health physical education curriculum model: a video-based assessment. Behav. Sci. **13**(3) (2023)

Application Analysis of Artificial Intelligence in the Development of Intelligent Teaching System in Colleges and Universities

JunYi Liang(✉)

Beihai Vocational College, Beihai, Guangxi, China
ljynh@163.com

Abstract. Artificial Intelligence (AI) is a branch of computer science that focuses on developing intelligent machines capable of performing tasks that typically require human-like cognition. This includes learning, reasoning, problem-solving, perception, and natural language processing. AI systems can be categorized into three main types: rule-based systems, machine learning, and deep learning. Rule-based systems operate based on pre-defined rules, while machine learning algorithms learn from data to improve performance. Deep learning, a subset of machine learning, uses neural networks to model complex patterns, enabling AI to recognize patterns in images, speech, and text. After comparative analysis, the system established in this paper has high accuracy and fast operation speed of tracking and prediction.

Keywords: Institutions of higher learning · Artificial intelligence · Intelligent teaching · Application

1 Introduction

The integration of AI in education has the potential to revolutionize the way we learn and teach. AI-driven tools can provide personalized learning experiences [1, 2], adapt to individual student needs, and offer real-time feedback. This technology can help bridge the gap in educational resources and accessibility, especially for remote or underprivileged communities [3, 4]. Additionally, AI can automate administrative tasks, such as grading and student assessment, allowing educators to focus on more critical aspects of teaching [5, 6]. Furthermore, AI can facilitate the creation of virtual learning environments, promoting interactive and immersive learning experiences. The process of intelligent knowledge recommendation system in Table 1 is shown in Fig. 1.

Moreover, the rapid pace of technological advancements can lead to obsolescence, requiring continuous updates and maintenance [7, 8]. To overcome these challenges, institutions should consider partnerships with technology providers for cost-effective solutions, explore open-source alternatives, and prioritize investments in scalable and adaptable AI systems that can grow with their needs [9, 10].

B. Brik and S. Nazir (Eds.): BigIoT-EDU 2024, LNICST 660, pp. 145–154, 2026.
https://doi.org/10.1007/978-3-032-18628-7_16

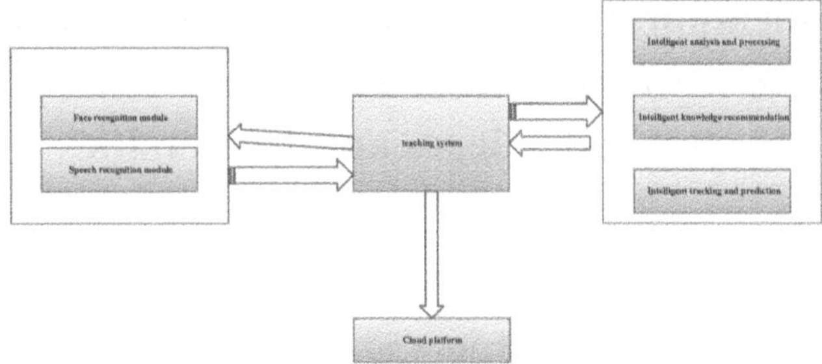

Fig. 1. Construction framework of intelligent teaching system in colleges and universities

2 Related Works

A. *Characteristics and challenges of university teaching systems*

In higher education, AI plays a pivotal role in enhancing the quality and efficiency of learning. It supports the development of adaptive learning platforms that adjust the learning path based on student performance, ensuring that students receive content tailored to their understanding. AI-powered chatbots and virtual assistants can provide instant support to students, answering queries, and guiding them through coursework.

Moreover, AI-driven analytics can help institutions predict student dropout rates, enabling early intervention and support. It can also contribute to research by automating data analysis, identifying patterns, and suggesting new research directions. Additionally, AI-assisted grading systems can save educators time and ensure consistent, objective assessment. Lastly, AI can foster global collaboration by connecting students and professors across borders, promoting cross-cultural understanding and knowledge sharing.

In conclusion, AI's transformative power in higher education lies in its ability to personalize learning, streamline administrative tasks, and foster a more inclusive and data-driven teaching environment. As the technology continues to evolve, it is crucial for educational institutions to embrace AI responsibly, ensuring that it complements rather than replaces human interaction and expertise.

B. *Application of artificial intelligence in university teaching system*

Intelligent Teaching Systems (ITS) are sophisticated software platforms that leverage artificial intelligence (AI) and machine learning technologies to enhance the learning experience in educational institutions. These systems are designed to adapt to individual student needs, provide personalized feedback, and optimize learning resources. By using data analytics, ITS can analyze student performance and suggest tailored learning paths, fostering a more efficient and engaging learning environment. Additionally, they often include interactive elements such as chatbots, virtual tutors, and adaptive quizzes to create a dynamic and responsive educational experience.

The adoption of ITS varies across colleges and universities, influenced by factors such as available resources, institutional priorities, and faculty receptiveness. Some leading institutions have fully embraced ITS, integrating them into their core curricula, while others have piloted programs or adopted them selectively in specific courses. For instance, prestigious universities have implemented AI-powered tutoring systems to support large introductory courses, reducing the workload on instructors and providing personalized feedback to students. Smaller colleges, on the other hand, may opt for cloud-based solutions to leverage the benefits of ITS without significant infrastructure investments.

In the United States, institutions like Carnegie Mellon University and Georgia Institute of Technology have been at the forefront of ITS implementation, while in Europe, universities like the University of Oxford and Technical University of Munich have also incorporated AI-driven tools. In Asia, institutions like Tsinghua University in China and the Indian Institute of Technology have also started exploring the potential of ITS to cater to the diverse needs of their student populations.

C. *The development and application of artificial intelligence in the teaching system of colleges and universities*

Artificial intelligence (AI) has revolutionized the way education is tailored to individual students. By analyzing learning patterns, interests, and performance data, AI-powered systems can create customized lesson plans and learning paths for each student. This personalized approach ensures that the content is tailored to the student's needs, strengths, and weaknesses, allowing for a more effective and efficient learning experience. Moreover, AI-driven adaptive assessments continually evaluate student understanding, providing real-time feedback and adjusting content as needed, ensuring that students remain challenged yet not overwhelmed.

Incorporating AI in intelligent teaching systems streamlines administrative tasks, freeing up educators' time for more impactful activities. Automated grading, for instance, saves teachers hours of manual work, allowing them to focus on providing personalized feedback and guidance. AI can also assist in curriculum planning, suggesting content and resources that align with learning objectives and standards. Furthermore, AI-powered systems can help identify at-risk students early on, enabling timely interventions and support, ultimately reducing dropout rates and improving overall learning outcomes.

AI-driven tools, such as chatbots and virtual assistants, engage students in interactive and immersive learning experiences. These technologies can simulate real-world scenarios, foster collaborative learning, and encourage critical thinking and problem-solving skills. By providing instant feedback and assistance, AI keeps students actively involved and motivated, promoting a deeper understanding of the material. Additionally, AI-powered gamification elements can make learning more enjoyable and memorable, enhancing the overall learning experience.

In the era of remote and blended learning, AI plays a crucial role in maintaining student engagement and connectivity. AI-powered platforms facilitate seamless communication between teachers and students, providing virtual support and resources. These systems can also analyze student participation and engagement, identifying those who may be struggling and requiring additional support. AI-driven content recommendation engines ensure that students have access to relevant and up-to-date materials, regardless of their physical location. Furthermore, AI-powered tutoring systems can offer virtual one-on-one sessions, mimicking the personalized guidance that would typically occur in a physical classroom.

In conclusion, the integration of AI in intelligent teaching systems offers numerous benefits, transforming education into a more personalized, efficient, and engaging experience. By leveraging AI's capabilities, institutions can foster a learning environment that adapts to the unique needs of each student, while empowering educators to focus on their core role of nurturing and guiding learners. As technology continues to evolve, the potential for AI to revolutionize education further is immense, paving the way for a more inclusive and effective educational landscape.

Artificial intelligence has revolutionized the traditional methods of student assessment and feedback. With AI algorithms, intelligent teaching systems can now instantly evaluate student work, providing real-time feedback on performance. These systems can detect patterns, identify common errors, and offer personalized suggestions for improvement. Automated grading not only saves educators time but also ensures objectivity, reducing the potential for bias. Additionally, AI-generated feedback can be more comprehensive and detailed, covering a broader range of learning objectives, which can lead to a more effective learning experience.

3 Optimization Strategy of Intelligent Teaching System in Colleges and Universities

This includes learning how to interpret AI-generated insights, designing personalized learning paths, and addressing the ethical implications of AI use. Providing ongoing professional development programs and fostering a culture of continuous learning is essential to ensure teachers feel comfortable and confident in using AI effectively.Student acceptance plays a crucial role in the success of AI-driven teaching systems. While AI can enhance the learning experience, students may be hesitant to rely on machines for education, fearing the loss of human interaction or potential biases in algorithmic decision-making. To address these concerns, institutions should involve students in the process, explain how AI works, and demonstrate its benefits, such as personalized learning and real-time feedback. Transparency and clear communication about the role of AI can help build trust and foster a positive attitude toward its use.

A. *Mathematical description of artificial intelligence algorithms*

AI-driven content recommendation engines analyze students' learning patterns, interests, and performance data to suggest relevant resources and learning materials. These recommendations can range from specific articles and videos to entire courses, tailored to each student's individual needs.

$$\vec{X}(t+1) = \vec{X}_{best}(t) - \vec{A}\left|\vec{C}\vec{X}_{best}(t) - \vec{X}(t)\right| \tag{1}$$

Among them, the judgment of outliers is shown in Eq. (2).

$$X_i = \left(X_i^1, X_i^2, X_i^3, \ldots X_i^d\right) \tag{2}$$

The system continuously updates its suggestions based on the student's progress, ensuring that they remain engaged and challenged at an appropriate level. By providing personalized content, AI fosters a more efficient and effective learning journey, allowing students to focus on areas where they need the most improvement.

Chat-bots are designed to understand natural language, allowing for seamless communication and a more human-like interaction. They can also adapt their responses over time, learning from student interactions to improve their assistance and provide a more personalized learning experience.

$$\vec{X}(t+1) = \left|\vec{X}_{best} - \vec{X}(t)\right| e^{bl}\cos(2\pi l) + \vec{X}_{best} \tag{3}$$

B. *Selection of intelligent teaching quality programs*

Predictive analytics is a powerful tool in intelligent teaching systems, allowing educators to forecast student performance based on historical data and real-time learning patterns. By analyzing factors such as study habits, engagement, and performance on assessments, AI can identify students at risk of falling behind and provide early intervention.

$$x_j^i = lb_i + (ub_i - lb_i)y_j^i \tag{4}$$

This proactive approach can help prevent academic difficulties, as educators can intervene with targeted support and resources before a student's performance is significantly impacted.

$$\vec{X}(t+1) + x_j^i \leq \max[lb_i + e^{bl}\cos(2\pi l) + \vec{X}_{best}] \tag{5}$$

Additionally, predictive analytics can guide curriculum development and instructional strategies, ensuring that teaching methods align with the needs of the students.

$$\vec{X}(\widetilde{t+1}) + x_j^i \leftrightarrow \max[lb_i + e^{bl}\cos(2\pi l) + \vec{X}_{best}] \tag{6}$$

C. *Intelligent knowledge recommendation system scheme*

The integration of AI with the Internet of Things (IoT) and Big Data has unlocked new possibilities in education. IoT devices, such as smart whiteboards, wearables, and sensors, can collect data on students' learning environments and behaviors. This data, when combined with Big Data analytics, provides a wealth of information on student performance and engagement.

$$y_{j+1}^i = \begin{cases} \mu y_j^i, & y_j^i < 0.5 \\ \mu\left(1 - y_j^i\right), & y_j^i \geq 0.5 \end{cases} \tag{7}$$

Educators can leverage this information to optimize classroom settings, tailor learning materials, and create more effective teaching strategies. Moreover, the synergy between AI, IoT, and Big Data enables real-time monitoring of student progress, enabling educators to make data-driven decisions and improve overall educational outcomes.

$$Td\left(x_j^i\right) = \min\left(\sum \vec{X}(\widetilde{t+1}) + x_j^i\right) \tag{8}$$

The integration of AI in intelligent teaching systems brings with it the need for robust data management practices. Ensuring the privacy and security of sensitive student data is paramount. AI systems often require vast amounts of personal information, including academic performance, learning patterns, and even behavioral data, which can be vulnerable to breaches.

$$ach\left(x_j^i\right) = \frac{\min\left(\sum \vec{X}(\widetilde{t+1}) + x_j^i\right)}{\sum \vec{X}(\widetilde{t+1}) + x_j^i} \times 100\% \tag{9}$$

Institutions must adhere to strict data protection laws, implement encryption and secure storage methods, and educate students and staff about the importance of safeguarding digital identities.

$$ach\left(x_j^i\right) = \frac{\min\left(\sum \vec{X}(\widetilde{t+1}) + x_j^i\right)}{\sum \vec{X}(\widetilde{t+1}) + x_j^i} \times 100\% + tdh\left(x_j^i\right) \tag{10}$$

Adopting AI technology requires a shift in teaching methodology and a deep understanding of the tools. Teachers need to be adequately trained to effectively integrate AI-based systems into their curriculum.

4 Results and Discussion

A. *Introduction to the intelligent knowledge recommendation system*

Implementing AI in teaching systems often involves significant investment in hardware, software, and infrastructure upgrades. Not all institutions have the financial resources to afford cutting-edge AI solutions.

Table 1. Content of intelligent knowledge recommendation system

Basic functionality	Intelligent analytics	Smart recommendations	Image recognition
Face recognition	69.0815	69.7143	71.3739
Speech recognition	67.9340	71.8718	71.7064
Intelligent analytics	65.8253	68.4908	72.0108
Intelligent knowledge recommendation	65.4053	71.3713	72.8525
Intelligently track predictions	69.3629	71.3274	73.5150

B. *Intelligent teaching system in colleges and universities*

Additionally, long-term planning and budgeting for technology upgrades are essential to ensure the sustainability of AI integration in education. Incorporating AI into intelligent teaching systems requires a mindset shift, fostering a culture of innovation that embraces change and continuous improvement. This can be achieved by (Table 2):

Table 2. The overall situation of the intelligent teaching quality program

Teaching content	Functionality	Trace detection
Teaching equipment	75.5692	81.7033
Smart tools	73.4493	81.9742
Teaching modules	76.1717	80.9087
Test the module	77.1044	83.2902
Evaluation module	74.9221	85.1795

C. *Intelligent teaching quality of intelligent knowledge recommendation system*

Promoting experimentation: Encouraging educators to test new AI-driven tools and methods, allowing for iterative development and refining of approaches.

Emphasizing adaptability: Preparing faculty and staff to adapt to new technologies, recognizing that the learning process is ever-evolving.

Celebrating successes and learning from failures: Recognizing and rewarding innovative projects, while also using setbacks as learning opportunities.

Fostering interdisciplinary collaboration: Encouraging collaboration between educators, IT professionals, and AI specialists to create tailored solutions (Fig. 2).

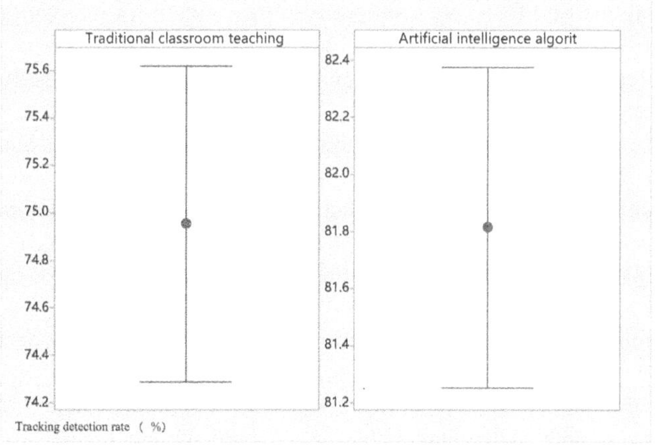

Fig. 2. Intelligent teaching quality of different algorithms

Effective implementation of AI necessitates equipping educators with the skills and knowledge to integrate these tools into their teaching. This involves:

Workshops and seminars: Providing regular training sessions on AI technologies and their pedagogical applications.

Ongoing support: Offering technical assistance and mentorship for teachers during the adoption process.

Continuing education: Encouraging educators to stay up-to-date with AI advancements through conferences, online courses, and professional development programs.

Blended learning: Combining traditional teaching methods with AI-powered tools to enhance teachers' capacity to personalize learning (Table 3).

Table 3. Comparison of the accuracy of intelligent knowledge recommendation systems of different methods

Algorithm	Intelligent teaching quality	Learning efficiency	Security testing
Artificial intelligence algorithms	90.2103	92.5092	91.3201
Traditional classroom teaching mode	82.79	83.08	84.32

Involvement of all stakeholders, including students, parents, and administrative staff, is crucial for successful AI integration. This can be achieved by:

Student engagement: Consulting with students on their learning preferences and using their feedback to refine AI applications.

Parental involvement: Educating parents about the benefits and implications of AI in education, addressing concerns, and seeking their support.

Administrative support: Gaining buy-in from top-level administrators, securing necessary resources, and fostering a supportive environment for innovation.

Collaborative decision-making: Encouraging stakeholders to participate in the selection and implementation of AI tools, ensuring alignment with institutional goals (Fig. 3).

Collaboration with external entities can provide valuable resources and expertise in AI integration. This includes:

Industry partnerships: Working with technology companies to develop AI solutions tailored to educational needs, accessing cutting-edge tools and resources.

Research institutions: Collaborating with universities and research centers to explore the latest AI research and best practices.

Open-source communities: Participating in open-source projects to benefit from collective innovation and cost-effective solutions.

Policy and regulatory engagement: Staying informed about regulatory frameworks and collaborating with policymakers to ensure ethical and responsible AI use in education.

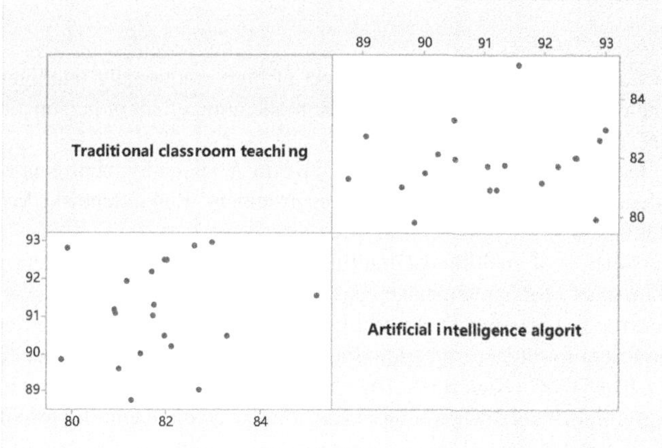

Fig. 3. Intelligent teaching quality of artificial intelligence algorithm intelligent knowledge recommendation system

By focusing on these strategies, institutions can successfully implement AI in intelligent teaching systems, transforming the learning experience and preparing students for a future shaped by technology.

5 Conclusion

As AI algorithms continue to evolve, the potential for refining personalized learning experiences in intelligent teaching systems grows exponentially. These systems can analyze student performance data, learning preferences, and cognitive styles to create tailored learning paths for each individual. Adaptive content delivery, where lessons and assessments adapt to the pace and level of understanding of each student, will become more seamless, reducing the need for one-size-fits-all curricula. Additionally, AI can help identify students who may be struggling early on, allowing for timely interventions and support.

Aiming at the problem that the intelligent teaching quality of intelligent teaching system in colleges and universities is not satisfactory, this paper proposes artificial intelligence algorithms and combines artificial intelligence theory to optimize the intelligent teaching system of colleges and universities. At the same time, the innovation of intelligent knowledge recommendation system and threshold innovation are analyzed in depth to construct a teaching collection. Research shows that artificial intelligence algorithms can improve the accuracy and stability of intelligent teaching systems in colleges and universities, and can be used to intelligently teach systems in colleges and universities Conduct a general intelligent knowledge recommendation system. However, in the process of applying artificial intelligence algorithms, too much attention is paid to the analysis of intelligent knowledge recommendation system, resulting in irrationality in the selection of indicators of intelligent knowledge recommendation system.

References

1. Maamari, B.E.E., Salloum, Y.N.N.: The effect of high emotionally intelligent teachers on their teaching effectiveness at universities: the moderating effect of personality traits. Int. J. Educ. Manag. **37**(3), 575–590 (2023)
2. Masterl, E., Jean, S., Potocnik, J., Burnik, U., Kosir, A.: Socially intelligent communicator: prototype, demo environment and learning environment. Elektrotehniski Vestnik **90**(1–2), 16–22 (2023)
3. Nie, Y.: Application of multimodal multimedia information and big data technology in teaching Chinese as a foreign language course. Int. J. Dig. Multim. Broadcast. (2023)
4. Sajja, R., Sermet, Y., Cwiertny, D., Demir, I.: Platform-independent and curriculum-oriented intelligent assistant for higher education. Int. J. Educ. Technol. Higher Educ. **20**(1) (2023)
5. Shih, S.-C., Chang, C.-C., Kuo, B.-C., Huang, Y.-H.: Mathematics intelligent tutoring system for learning multiplication and division of fractions based on diagnostic teaching. Educ. Inf. Technol. **28**(7), 9189–9210 (2023)
6. Su, B., Peng, J.: Sentiment analysis of comment texts on online courses based on hierarchical attention mechanism. Appl. Sci. Basel **13**(7) (2023)
7. Sun, M.: A Vision sensing-based automatic evaluation method for teaching effect based on deep residual network. Math. Biosci. Eng. **20**(4), 6358–6373 (2023)
8. Tang, J., Zhang, P., Zhang, J.: Design and implementation of intelligent evaluation system based on pattern recognition for microteaching skills training. Int. J. Innov. Comput. Inf. Control **19**(1), 153–162 (2023)
9. Tian, X., Chen, X., Feng, L.: Quality improvement path and countermeasures for future-oriented film and animation teaching: based on fuzzy comprehensive evaluation method. J. Intell. Fuzzy Syst. **44**(2), 2981–2997 (2023)
10. Tuerhong, A., Silamujiang, M., Xianmuxiding, Y., Wu, L., Mojarad, M.: An ensemble classifier method based on teaching-learning-based optimization for breast cancer diagnosis. J. Cancer Res. Clin. Oncol. **149**(11), 9337–9348 (2023)

Intelligent Teaching System Based on Mobile Terminal for Legal Education Scenario Simulation

Xu Jing(✉)

Yantai Vocational College, Yantai, China
tougao667788xj@126.com

Abstract. With the rapid development of science and technology, mobile terminals have penetrated into every corner of daily life, and the field of education is no exception. In legal education, the application of mobile terminals has shown great potential and brought innovation to the traditional teaching mode. The situation simulation intelligent teaching system is a kind of teaching tool that uses the advanced information technology and combines the characteristics of legal education to create the simulated practical situation, so that students can learn and apply the legal knowledge in the simulated environment. Through a highly customized case library, the system provides diverse legal situations, such as court debate, case analysis, contract review, etc., to enable students to improve their legal literacy and professional skills in simulation practice. MED simulation shows that under the condition of certain intelligent teaching standards, mobile terminals have a view to legal education scenarios The accuracy of simulated intelligent teaching and the simulated intelligent teaching time are better than the CSN6.1 education model.

Keyword: Intelligent in education · Mobile terminals · Legal education scenarios

1 Introduction

Mobile terminals provide new possibilities for legal education, promote the combination of theory and practice, and enhance the interest and effectiveness of learning. With the continuous progress of technology, the application potential of mobile terminals in legal education will be further released, bringing infinite imagination to the future of legal education. The simulated intelligent teaching process in Table 1 is shown in Fig. 1.

In addition, the system enhances students' critical thinking and problem solving skills through intelligent q & A, online discussion and moot court exercises. In terms of evaluation, the system adopts a combination of formal and non-formal evaluation, including online testing, mock court performance, case analysis reports, etc., to comprehensively evaluate students' abilities in knowledge mastery, legal application and communication skills. The data analysis module is an important support for the teaching system, which collects and analyzes students' learning data, including learning time, learning content, interaction frequency, speed and quality of task completion, etc.

B. Brik and S. Nazir (Eds.): BigIoT-EDU 2024, LNICST 660, pp. 155–163, 2026.
https://doi.org/10.1007/978-3-032-18628-7_17

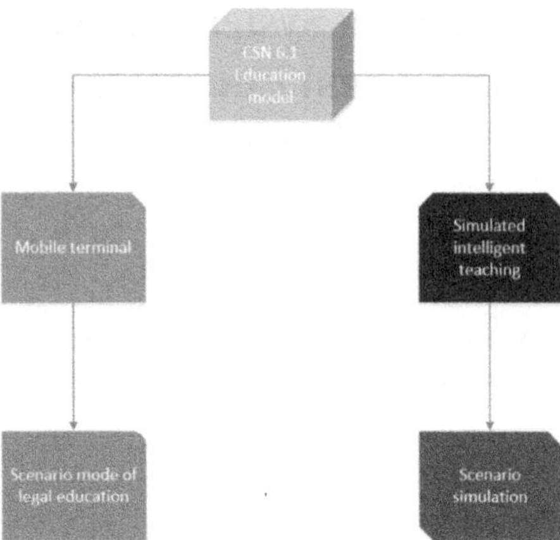

Fig. 1. The analysis process of the scenario model of legal education

2 Related Works

A. *Characteristics of mobile terminals and their impact on the simulation system of rule of law education scenarios*

1. Convenience and Flexibility The portability of mobile terminals makes the law study no longer limited by the time and place. Students can consult laws, cases, participate in discussions, and even conduct moot court exercises anytime and anywhere, which greatly improves the flexibility of learning.
2. Rich multimedia resources Mobile terminals can integrate audio, video, image and other multimedia resources to make legal education more vivid. For example, by watching actual court trial videos, students can intuitively understand the legal process and improve practical perception.
3. Personalized learning experience Using mobile terminals, teachers can customize personalized learning paths and provide customized learning materials and exercises according to each student's learning progress and understanding ability. In addition, the intelligent recommendation system can push relevant courses and information according to students' learning interests and needs.
4. interaction and collaboration Mobile terminals support instant messaging and social media functions. Students can have real-time discussions with their classmates and teachers to form study groups to discuss legal issues together and improve their teamwork ability.
5. Data-driven teaching improvement By collecting students 'learning data on mobile terminals, teachers can understand students' learning habits and difficulties, so as to adjust teaching strategies and realize a student-centered education model.

B. *Methods and strategies for optimizing the simulation system of rule of law education scenarios*

1. Situational generation and Role playing

Scenario generation: automatic generation or different types of legal cases customized by teachers, covering civil, criminal, administrative and other legal fields. Students can play various roles, such as lawyers, judges and prosecutors, to conduct mock court debate and improve their oral expression and logical reasoning ability.

2. Interactive feedback, Resource database and Learning tracking

The system analyzes students' performance in real time, provides feedback and suggestions, and helps students to self-evaluate and improve. Built-in rich legal literature, precedents and regulations for students to consult and learn. Record students' learning progress and performance, and provide teaching data support for teachers.

3. Improve practical ability、Stimulate learning interest and Personalized learning

The system provides students with a safe and convenient platform for practice, so that they can enhance their ability to solve practical problems by simulating real cases while learning theories. The interaction and interest of the simulated situation can stimulate students' interest in learning and improve their participation. According to the performance and needs of each student, the system can provide personalized learning resources and feedback to promote individualized teaching.

4. Teamwork、Evaluation and feedback、Adaptive learning

In the situational simulation, students need to work together, developing their teamwork and communication skills. The data and feedback provided by the system can help teachers to more accurately evaluate students' learning effectiveness and adjust their teaching strategies. The system can adapt to the development of legal education, with the update of laws and regulations, timely update the case database, to ensure that students are exposed to the latest legal knowledge. In general, the situational simulation intelligent teaching system improves the effectiveness of legal education through the innovative teaching mode, and provides strong support for the cultivation of legal talents with practical ability and innovative thinking.

Intelligent recommendation system is the core component of the intelligent teaching system of legal education situation simulation. It uses advanced machine learning algorithms, such as collaborative filtering and content filtering, to provide students with personalized learning resources. The system recommends relevant cases, literature, courses and discussion topics according to students' learning history, interest preferences, learning progress and understanding degree, so as to enhance the pertinence and effectiveness of learning. In addition, the system can also dynamically adjust the learning path, optimize students' learning results according to their learning results, and ensure that they get balanced and in-depth learning in various branches of law.

3 Optimization Strategy of Legal Education Scenario Model

Situational simulation plays a vital role in legal education, transforming abstract legal Works and principles into vivid cases, and allowing students to practice legal application in a simulated environment. When designing the situation simulation module, the first task is to carefully construct the situation to ensure that it is both educational and can arouse students' interest. Case selection should cover all kinds of legal fields, such as criminal law, civil law, administrative law, commercial law, etc., to comprehensively cover all aspects of legal education. The case should be real and representative, reflecting the legal problems in reality, so that students can experience the real legal practice.

A. *Mathematical description of the mobile terminal*

The core of the system design is to realize the efficiency and interactivity of legal education, aiming to provide a convenient and immersive learning environment through mobile terminals. User-friendly: ensure that the system interface is intuitive and easy to use, adapt to the technical level of different users, and convenient for teachers and students to quickly.

$$ned\left(y_i \cdot x_{ij}\right) = z_{ij} \geq maf \sum xi \tag{1}$$

Among them, the judgment of outliers is shown in Eq. (2).

$$maf\left(x_{ij}\right) = \left(xi^2 + \frac{1}{2}\right) \triangleright \min(\sum x_{ij}) \tag{2}$$

Flexibility: The system should be able to meet the needs of different law courses and support multidisciplinary and multi-level teaching content.

Interactivity: use situation simulation to enhance students' sense of participation, improve learning interest and effect.

Intelligence: Using AI technology to provide personalized learning suggestions to assist teaching decisions.

Scalability: The design should take into account the possibility of future function expansion and technology upgrades.

$$Q(y_i) = \sum qi \times \sqrt{yi}.\arcsin\theta \tag{3}$$

B. *Selection of scenario-based schemes.*

Improve learning efficiency: Through situational simulation, students can understand and master legal knowledge in practice. Enhance practical ability: let students develop the ability to analyze and solve problems in simulated legal cases.

$$p(x_i) = \mathrm{x}_i \cdot Q(yi) + ki \tag{4}$$

Promoting teaching innovation: to provide new teaching tools for teachers and promote the diversification of teaching methods. Ensure data security: to ensure the privacy of user data and the stability of the system operation.

$$p(x_i) + Q(y_i) \leq maf\left(x_{ij}\right) \tag{5}$$

Front end: responsive design for a variety of mobile devices, and user interfaces with HTML 5, CSS 3 and JavaScript to ensure consistency across different platforms.

$$p(x_i) + Q(y_i) \leftrightarrow \min(\sum x_{ij}) \tag{6}$$

C. *Analysis of simulated intelligent teaching scheme.*

Integrated virtual reality (VR) or augmented reality (AR) technology to provide a more realistic situational simulation experience. Back-end: Based on the microservice architecture, using technologies such as Node.js or Python, to ensure the scalability and high concurrent processing capability of the system. Back-end services include user management, course content management, situational simulation engine, and intelligent recommendation systems.

$$med(x_i) = \frac{p(x_i) + Q(y_i)}{\min(\sum x_{ij})} \tag{7}$$

Database: use relational database (such as MySQL) to store user information, course content and learning records, and may combine NoSQL database (such as MongoDB) to store unstructured data, such as situational simulation scenario description and user interaction data.

$$Jc(x_i) = \min[\sum p(x_i) + Q(y_i)] \tag{8}$$

Context simulation engine: Using natural language processing (NLP) and machine learning algorithms to analyze and generate complex legal situations to provide dynamic interactive experience. The user makes decisions in the simulation, systematically feedback the corresponding results, and simulate the real legal practice process. Intelligent recommendation system: Based on user learning history and behavioral data, collaborative filtering or deep learning models are adopted to recommend personalized learning resources and paths.

$$abhf(x_i) = \frac{\min[\sum p(x_i) + Q(y_i)]}{\sum p(x_i) + Q(y_i)} \times 100\% \tag{9}$$

Security and privacy protection: the system adopts HTTPS encrypted communication to ensure the security of data transmission; implement user rights management and protect user privacy; meanwhile, regularly conduct security audit and vulnerability repair to ensure the stable operation of the system. Through the above technical framework, the system can realize the intelligent, personalized and situational transformation of legal education, and provide efficient and innovative teaching tools for both sides.

$$abhf(x_i) = \frac{\min[\sum p(x_i) + Q(y_i)]}{\sum p(x_i) + Q(y_i)} \times 100\% + vgxd(x_i) \tag{10}$$

Cooperate with legal experts to create a diverse case bank covering a variety of legal fields to ensure the educational value and authenticity of situational simulation. System integration: the situation simulation module is seamlessly connected with the intelligent teaching function to realize the functions of learning progress tracking, personalized recommendation and data analysis.

4 Results and Discussion

A. *Introduction to simulated intelligent teaching*

The personalized learning tutoring function is designed to provide customized learning support for each student. The system understands students' problems and puzzles in the simulated situation through natural language processing technology, provides real-time answers and guidance, and simulates the real legal consultation process.

Table 1. Analog intelligent teaching requirements

Scope of application	Grade	Innovative effect	Scenario simulation
Sample one	I	33.61	33.51
	II	34.15	34.58
Sample two	I	33.48	34.25
	II	33.49	34.36
Sample three	I	35.51	33.52
	II	33.48	32.45

B. *Situation of legal education scenarios*

Through big data technology and artificial intelligence algorithms, the system can identify learning patterns, find students' learning difficulties, and predict learning results. These insights provide faculty with decision support, helping them adjust teaching strategies, conduct individual coaching, or optimize course content. At the same time, the systematically generated learning report also provides a basis for students to self-monitor and adjust their learning strategies, and promote their independent learning ability. In implementing the intelligent teaching system of legal education situation simulation based on mobile terminals, the primary task is to ensure the close integration of technology and educational objectives (Table 2).

Table 2. The overall picture of the scenario-based scenario

Category	Satisfaction	Analysis rate
Sample one	84.46	73.05
Sample two	83.16	73.48
Sample three	83.62	75.26
Mean	82.26	73.29
X6	34.15	33.91
P = 3. 255		

C. *Scenario simulation and stability of simulated intelligent teaching*

The design of the simulation process should focus on interactivity and operability. Students should be able to play the role of lawyers, judges and prosecutors in the simulated environment, and participate in the investigation, litigation and mediation of the case (Fig. 2).

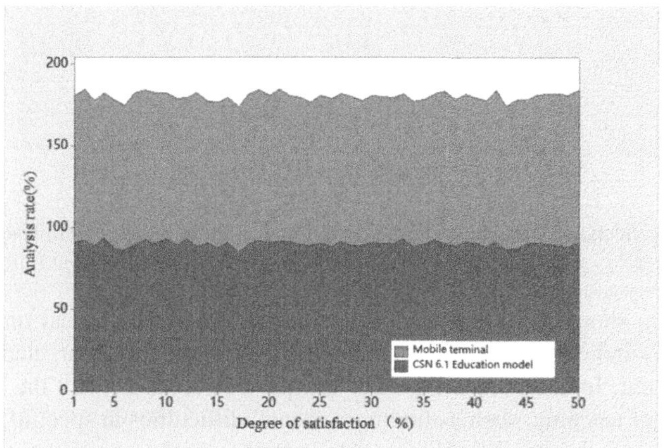

Fig. 2. Scenario simulation of different algorithms

Improve their legal thinking and practical skills through the writing of legal documents, the simulation of court debate, evidence analysis and other tasks. The optimization simulation process requires the system to be able to dynamically adjust the difficulty of the case according to the students' selection and performance, provide real-time feedback, and ensure the gradual and challenging learning (Table 3).

Table 3. Comparison of the accuracy of simulated intelligent teaching of different methods

Algorithm	Scenario simulation	Magnitude of change	Error
Mobile terminals	93.26	93.51	95.25
CSN6.1 education model	82.25	83.26	84.95
P	35.152	33.251	35.853

In addition, the simulation should support multi-person collaboration and cultivate students' teamwork ability. User interaction is a core component of the context simulation module. The system should provide an intuitive user interface for students to interact easily. At the same time, various interactive elements should be set up in the simulation process, such as dialog box, decision tree, prompt information, etc., to guide students to think deeply. The feedback mechanism is an indispensable part of the learning process (Fig. 3).

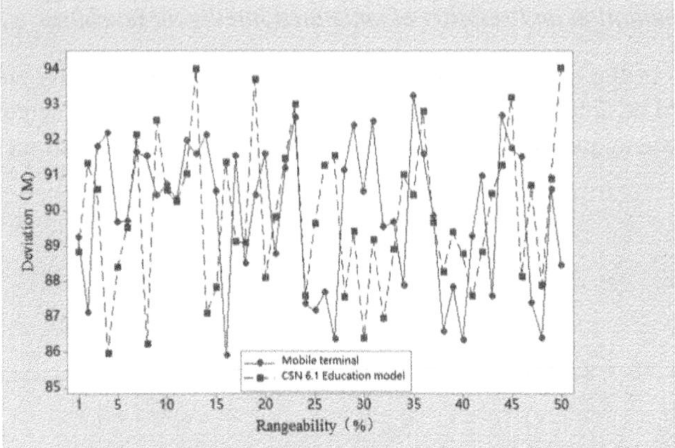

Fig. 3. Scenario simulation of mobile terminal simulation intelligent teaching

The system should be able to evaluate students' decisions in real time, point out the correctness and error of their legal understanding, and provide targeted suggestions for improvement. In addition, the system can provide teachers with the basis for the improvement of teaching, such as finding students' difficulties in specific fields, adjust the teaching content or provide additional learning resources.

5 Conclusion

To fully understand the needs of legal education, including students 'learning habits, teachers' teaching methods, and the specific requirements of the curriculum, to ensure the pertinence of the system design. Optimize the system to accommodate a variety of mobile devices, including iOS and Android systems, ensuring a smooth user experience on different devices. Test and feedback: test in a small range, collect user feedback, adjust and improve the system performance. Training and Support: Provide adequate training and use guidelines for teachers and students to ensure that they can effectively use the system for teaching and learning. Through the above intelligent teaching functions, the intelligent teaching system of legal education situation simulation not only improves the teaching efficiency, but also promotes the students' deep learning and comprehensive development of students in the field of law. Through continuous learning and iteration, the system continuously optimizes its recommendation, tutoring and evaluation mechanisms to meet the change of education and the needs of students.

References

1. Alabdulqader, S., et al.: Emergency physicians' awareness of medico-legal case management: a cross-sectional study from Saudi Arabia. Saudi J. Med. Med. Sci. **11**(1), 60–66 (2023)
2. Allison, N.G.: From semantic weight to legal ontology via classification of Works in legal texts. Law Teacher **57**(2), 201–217 (2023)

3. Anders, S., et al.: Adventure legal medicine: a free online serious game for supplementary use in undergraduate medical education. Int. J. Legal Med. **137**(2), 545–549 (2023)
4. Ballakrishnen, S.S.: Law school as straight space. Fordham Law Rev. **91**(4), 1113–1138 (2023)
5. Benediktsson, A.I.: The place of multicultural education in legal acts concerning teacher education in Norway. Multicul. Educ. Rev. **14**(4), 228–242 (2022)
6. Blackburn, L.: Qualifying work experience: do street law projects provide a "legal service "? Law Teacher **57**(1), 84–88 (2023)
7. Chuikov, O.E., Rozhnov, S.N., Tyurin, I.V., Gordeev, I.A.: Statutory regulation of the operation of female gymnasiums and Progymnasiums in the Russian empire. Europ. J. Contemporary Educ. **12**(1), 279–285 (2023)
8. Diskin, T.: Legal socialisation through literature in Israel's education system. Israel Affairs **29**(4), 758–773 (2023)
9. Ducarre, L.M.: Redefining inclusive education for autistic children in international and European law. Int. J. Childrens Rights **31**(2), 326–351 (2023)
10. Fakih, A., Kassab, S., Lizzaik, Z.: Employability of Syrian refugees in Lebanon: the role of legal residency. Defence and Peace Econ. (2023)
11. Hewitt, A., Henderson, S., Covark, K.: Minimising risks for South Australia's legal interns. Alternat. Law J. **48**(2), 143–147 (2023)
12. Hews, R., Beligatamulla, G., McNamara, J.: Creative confidence and thinking skills for lawyers: making sense of design thinking pedagogy in legal education. Thinking Skills and Creat. **49** (2023)
13. Leheza, Y., Vlasenko, D., Shcherbyna, Y., Moroz, V.: Service legal relations: international legal and administrative-criminal aspect. Dixi **25**(1) (2023)
14. Markova, S.V., Nikitskaya, C.A.: Formation of legal awareness as a component of the professional identity of specialists in the social sphere at the stage of study at the university. Psychol. Law **13**(1), 221–231 (2023)
15. Masbernat, P.: Tax education and development of ethics and tax compliance. Revista De Educacion Y Derecho-Educat. Law Rev. **26** (2023)
16. McKinsey, E., Desmarais, S.L.: Impact of growth mindset-enhanced trauma education on criminal legal professionals' attitudes and perceptions. Crim. Justice Behav. **50**(4), 578–599 (2023)

Optimization of College Physical Education Curriculum Management System and the Construction of Service Functions Based on Artificial Intelligence

Xiaopeng Ji(✉)

Physical Education Research Department, Xinjiang University, Urumqi, Xinjiang, China
Jxp13565834075@126.com

Abstract. Since the dawn of AI, the current system for managing educational administration has been fine-tuned and enhanced on a regular basis. Now that we live in the Internet age, students and the general public may interact via streaming media. In order to create a new system for managing educational administration and its services, the physical education department will draw on the existing teaching service system. This article's goal is to help college and university administrators improve their physical education course management systems by building AI-based service functionalities. Academic staff, instructors, students, and others involved in the day-to-day operations of a university's educational administration management system are the focus of this article's research and analysis, which then proceeds to dissect and integrate the system's many business modules in order to extract its many functional modules. Management of teachers, lesson plans, scheduling, and systems are all part of this. We break down the sub-functions of each functional module and examine their corresponding specific business processes. The survey data analysis shows that students are most concerned about two functions that should be added to the physical education management system: online course selection and query functions (with 263 respondents accounting for 90.69%) and physical education results query functions (with 232 respondents accounting for 80%). Similarly, this is the primary role of the system for managing educational administration in sports.

Keywords: Artificial intelligence · College physical education curriculum · Educational administration management · Service function

1 Introduction

Colleges and universities achieve their missions and educate students via effective educational administration. Organizing, planning, and directing school teaching work revolves around educational work [1, 2]. Physical education management system optimization may help students learn more about sports than they would in a traditional classroom setting, make more comprehensive and reusable teaching materials available to them,

B. Brik and S. Nazir (Eds.): BigIoT-EDU 2024, LNICST 660, pp. 164–172, 2026.
https://doi.org/10.1007/978-3-032-18628-7_18

and better realize the expansion of classroom instruction [3, 4]. Simultaneously, physical education curriculum management system optimization may boost teacher productivity by assisting them with transactional chores that aren't directly related to instruction [5, 6]. The physical education curriculum management system has the potential to enhance the quality of instruction by facilitating more precise transfer of relevant information [7, 8].

Academics from all over the world have delved into the topic of physical education curriculum optimization and educational administration management system study from all sorts of different perspectives. An interactive educational administration system was created by Yang [10]; Santos introduced the data flow processing method to optimize data sharing and transmission, and the system's processing speed was increased [11]; Ryan believes that physical education teachers should be better at using the system and should arrange teaching time more scientifically so that students can get physical exercise without delaying other learning arrangements [12]; and Liu introduced workflow technology to design an educational administration management system based on business processes according to user needs [9].

The goal of this article's study is to optimize and create service functions for college physical education curricula. The first step is to assess and integrate the different business modules of the college education management system after conducting a questionnaire survey to identify the inadequacies of the ordinary system and to designate new roles. After that, it proposes AI-era optimization countermeasures for college PEMSs, optimizes the PEMS based on four modules—teacher management, lesson plan management, timetable management, and system management—and examines the specifics of each functional module. The sub-tasks of every module have been broken down by the business process.

2 Related Works

2.1 Optimization of College Sports Educational Administration Management System

(1) A method for managing PE programs that makes use of AI

College students' interest in and engagement with sports can be fostered through the use of sports information technology in the classroom, which provides students with a range of resources including text, images, and audio to create a more engaging and effective visual and auditory multisensory experience. Modern pedagogy makes use of network technologies. Teachers have a lot of leeway when it comes to using audio and graphics to spark students' imaginations, make the often difficult-to-explain physical education material more vivid, and make class more enjoyable overall, all with the goal of facilitating effective sports learning.

(2) Make use of the ERAMS to establish communication amongst faculty members

Students have access to a wider training field thanks to the school's use of sports apps for physical education, which allows for more room for exercise and training. It may also help pupils exercise regardless of the time or technique they choose to exercise. Also, when the scheduled training is over, students may take advantage of free training to fully use the Internet and artificial intelligence, which is beneficial for everyone involved: schools, students, and instructors.

After APP is integrated into PE administration, teachers can use it to get to know their students better. This improves communication between the two parties, which in turn helps teachers meet their students' specific needs and gain their acceptance. Students may enhance their activity level by gaining a better grasp of professional information via the recommended physical education curriculum. From a school's perspective, the APP data allows them to better manage their resources, provide better service, and raise the quality of instruction their kids get. Schools may also use the app to organize student-centered contests that address the app's stated goals.

Thirdly, a fair course-to-student ratio is encouraged by physical education administration.

Physical education curriculum has, historically speaking, evolved from fully mandatory to a hybrid model that includes both mandatory and optional components. There has been a general downward trend in the ratio of required to optional courses. Course material in physical education reflects the systematic character of the discipline. In particular, it alludes to the interdependent and mutually influential nature of technology, as well as the inescapable link between course material, projects, and technology in general. Secondly, the physical education course schedule is well-aligned with the school's aims, the students' real circumstances, their personal development, the classroom setting, and other factors. This means that the curriculum is structured according to rules and linkages within itself. Planners of PE curricula have ideas for and The physical education classes are structured in a way that is specifically designed for each grade and school.

2.2 Construction of the Service Function of the Educational Administration Management System for College Physical Education Courses

(1) A sub-function of teacher management

College and university faculty members are both the focus of management in educational administration and the backbone of the teaching force on a daily basis. Consequently, it is important to keep track of instructors' fundamental information, information about their jobs in the classroom, information about their performance in both classroom instruction and scientific research, and information about their incentives and penalties. Educational management relies on data like teacher evaluations. Thus, the teacher management sub-function module primarily consists of the following modules: teacher assessment, performance management, reward and punishment management, basic information management, and instructional task management.

(2) A sub-function for managing lesson plans

The systematic execution of day-to-day pedagogical tasks at higher education institutions is impossible without a well-thought-out lesson plan. The teaching plan management sub-function primarily consists of the following modules: professional setting management, curriculum setting management, and teaching plan revision management.

The content of this part of the work includes professional settings, curriculum settings, teaching arrangements, and more. As a result, the primary goal of this sub-function is to provide support for various daily tasks and to realize the teaching plan.

(3) Particular duty of timetable administration

An essential part of educational administration's day-to-day job is course schedule management. It has to do with how the school's overall instructional activities—including those of individual instructors and students—typically progress. No courses may show up without first carefully considering how to distribute and modify many instructional resources, including professors, students, classrooms, etc. The features of teaching should inform a rational and fair approach to scheduling that minimizes conflicts among students, instructors, classrooms, class time, etc. There are a lot of moving parts in manual scheduling, which makes the process laborious and prone to error. The use of an intelligent, computerized lesson scheduling algorithm substantially enhanced the effectiveness of lesson scheduling. The Academic Affairs Office administrative personnel makes any required manual revisions to the automatically scheduled courses. Managing schedule parameters, managing the schedule itself, and managing the schedule itself make up the bulk of the schedule management sub-function module.

Section four: sub-functions of system management.

As a management function module inside the educational management system, system management is primarily responsible for the day-to-day administration and upkeep of the system. To give just a few examples, the system's registration/login management ensures that users can easily register and log in to the interface, the system's backup/restore management allows users to control the backup or restoration of important data, and the system's assistance with managing dynamic help files enhances user convenience and proficiency. System log management records the daily operation information of the system to facilitate system maintenance and management, system code maintenance and management, and other system maintenance tasks; authority/password management can set initial passwords for users or grant them different permissions.

(4) How the sports education administration management system is put into practice by students

More and more schools are letting students choose their own classes, including PE, so they may tailor their college experience to their interests. This is excellent student work that reflects the students' individual interests and gives them the freedom to make decisions that are relevant to their lives. Course selection will significantly boost student engagement, which in turn will aid in the growth and steady advancement of physical education management. Many institutions have embraced this concept, which has gained the respect of many students, and the method for selecting courses for students is maturing nowadays. Hence, this model will be used to manage future physical education activities in order to enhance its internal structure, management efficiency, and teaching quality continually.

2.3 Application of Artificial Intelligence Algorithms in Educational Administration Management System

The gene sequences are substituted with random integers that follow normal distributions for the mean and variance of the associated mutation process when using the Gaussian mutation approach, instead of σ and μ. In the evolution strategy, it mainly includes two elements (X, σ). Where X represents the next visited node and σ represents the variance. Its node descendant generation formula is as follows:

$$\sigma^{\cdot} = \sigma \ell N(0, \nabla\sigma) \quad (1)$$

$$x^{\cdot} = x + N\left(0, \nabla\sigma^{\cdot}\right) \quad (2)$$

The mean of $N(0, \nabla\sigma^{\cdot})$ is 0, the variance is σ, and the two are independent and Gaussian random number vectors.

3 Optimization and Service Functions of College Physical Education Management System Based on Artificial Intelligence

3.1 Research Content

This study communicates with the educational administration departments of various colleges and universities to gather relevant information, analyze the functional design of the PE management system, and incorporate new concepts into undergraduate physical education; it takes as its research object the optimization and service functions of the college PE curriculum management system. Concurrently, the teaching management system enhances the varied system that use management to direct instruction and oversee students' well-being, and it transforms this one-way service into a two-way one.

3.2 Implementation and Testing of the Questionnaire Survey

From 2018 to 2020, students enrolled in 8 different undergraduate institutions in H Province filled out an online survey. There were a total of 300 surveys sent out; 296 were returned, with 290 of them being genuine. The effective rate was 96.67% and the recovery rate was 98.67%, both of which were statistically acceptable.

Assessment of the survey's dependability: The reliability coefficient value is more than 0.80, indicating a high reliability level, and the statistics of the correlation coefficient r = 0.972 indicate that it satisfies the reliability standards of the questionnaire survey.

4 Results and Discussion

4.1 Function Analysis of Sports Educational Administration Management System

Students were asked to tell us "what do you think the physical education management system should have in the summary of the physical education management system" using a survey questionnaire. Table 1 displays the outcomes. Of the total, 54.14% were attributed to fitness-related questions, while 47.33% were attributed to physical fitness classes taken outside of the classroom. A total of 36.9% were fitness counseling bookings. A total of 263 individuals, or 90.69%, feel that features to help choose and search among available online courses should be included. A total of 232 individuals, or 80% of the total, feel that the ability to query PE findings should be included.

Table 1. Functions that the sports educational administration management system should have

Features	Proportion (%)	Number of people
Online course selection and inquiry	90.69%	263
Physical education class results query	80%	232
Body side health test query	71.03%	206
APP and network synchronization	54.83%	159
Answers to fitness questions	54.14%	157
Extracurricular physical fitness course	47.93%	139
Introduction and videos of sports events	41.72%	121
Announcement	38.97%	113
Online fitness coaching appointment	36.90%	107

(This question is multiple choices, so the percentages add up > 100%)

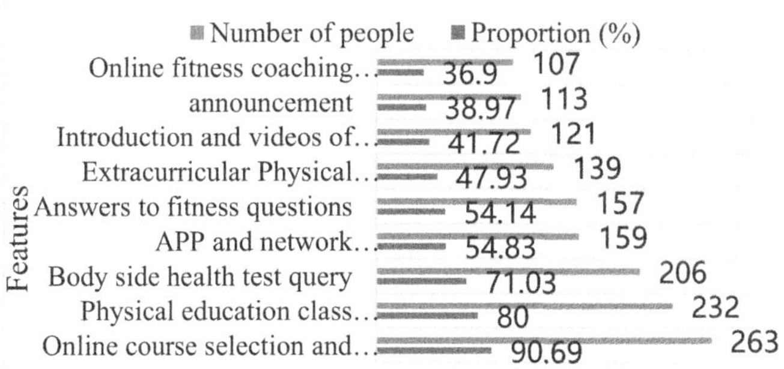

Fig. 1. Functions that the sports educational administration management system should have

The functions that students value and are most concerned about in a sports educational administration management system are online course selection and inquiry, physical education class score inquiry, and sports health test inquiry (as shown in Fig. 1). Also built on this foundation is the system for managing educational administration in sports. Students start to focus on finding solutions to their health concerns and participating in extracurricular physical exercise classes after they finish tasks connected to their essential interests. The students' continued preoccupation with academic material and the lack of integration of physical exercise—particularly extracurricular physical exercise—into their daily lives is evident from the relatively little attention given to the content of extracurricular sports activities compared to the former.

4.2 Analysis of the Communication Form of the Sports Management System

Table 2 shows the results of the poll asking "Which form of communication in the sports management system do you prefer?" Of the total respondents, 45 are agnostic (15.52%), 161 are in favor of the Internet + APP combo (55.52%), and 84 are fans of the sports management system's online version (22.97%).

Table 2. Investigation on the form of communication in the sports management system

	Proportion (%)	Number of people
It doesn't matter	15.52%	45
Network + APP	55.52%	161
Online version	28.97%	84

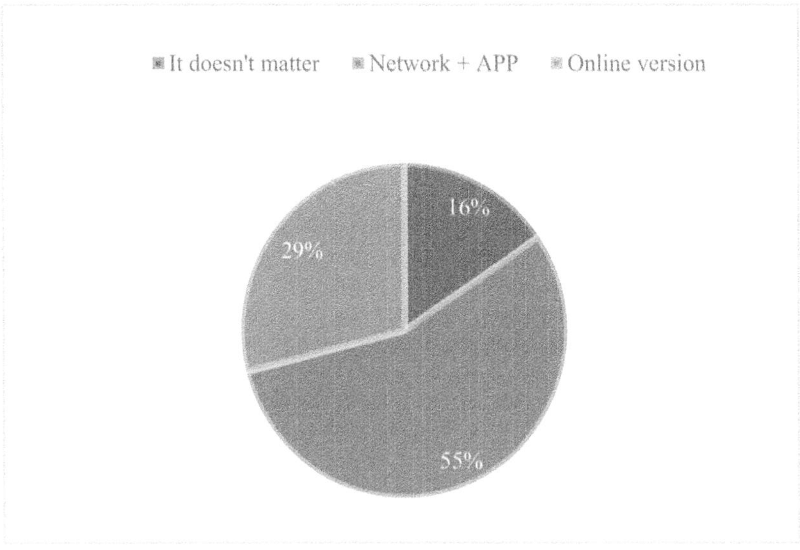

Fig. 2. Investigation on the form of communication in the sports management system

Figure 2 shows that compared to students who say they aren't interested in using the Internet at all, a much larger percentage of students favor communications that combine the two. This is due to the fact that when the APP is integrated into the management of physical education administration, the teacher gets to know their students better through the app. This facilitates communication between the students and the teacher, which in turn helps the teacher understand the students' needs. Finally, the app suggests physical education courses that students are more likely to accept, which in turn helps students exercise more regularly based on a better grasp of professional knowledge.

5 Conclusion

College and university physical education program service function development and educational administration management system optimization are the primary topics of this essay. This article lays forth the groundwork for the system study by analyzing and comprehending the present state of educational administration systems domestically and internationally. College sports educational administration management system functionality should encompass administrator sports educational administration management, teacher sports educational administration management, and student sports educational administration management, as determined by an examination of the system requirements from three distinct users: students, instructors, and educational administration administrators. There will be a significant role for online instruction in PE as well. Incorporating sports applications into the classroom may let students practice autonomously and maximize their workout time by removing constraints related to location, time, and sports approaches.

Acknowledgments. National Social Science Foundation of China (N0:BLA200218).

References

1. Ahmed, M.: Study to develop leadership skills and administrative in colleges of physical education and sports science according to the comprehensive quality system. Int. J. Psychosoc. Rehabilit. **24**(4) (2020)
2. Sun, H.: Study on application of data mining technology in university computer network educational administration management system. J. Intell. Fuzzy Syst. **37**(122), 1–8 (2019)
3. Aria, R., Archer, N.: Using an educational video versus in-person education to measure patient perceptions of an online self-management support system for chronic illness. Comput. Human Behav. **84**, 162–170 (2018)
4. Akkaya, A.: Theories of educational management and leadership: by Tony Bush, California, SAGE Publications, 2020, 208 pp. 89.00. (Hardback), ISBN 978-1526432124; 26.02 (Paperback), ISBN 978-1526432131; Educat. Rev. 2021(3):1–2
5. Hallinger, P., Kovacevic, J.: Mapping the intellectual lineage of educational management, administration and leadership, 1972–2020. Educ. Managem. Adminis. Leadership **1**, 17411432211 10060 (2021)
6. Shaari, I., Hung, D.: Partnership between a central agency and its schools: towards fostering laterality. Educ. Managem. Adminis. Leadership **46**(4), 578–601 (2018)
7. Hughes, B.: Processing of biological growth media based on measured manufacturing characteristics. Rev. Educ. Res. **22**(3), 169–174 (2018)
8. Belousov, Y.V., Timofeeva, O.I.: International experience of community participation in the school education management. Manage. Sci. **10**(3), 48–60 (2020)

9. Liu, G.: Research on the status quo of the curriculum of public physical education in high schools. J. Contemporary Educ. Res. **4**(2), 50–53 (2020)
10. Yang, Y., Liu, W.: The influence of public physical education curriculum on college students' physical health. Revista Brasileira de Medicina do Esporte **27**(spe), 83–86 (2021)
11. Santos, F., Rui, N., Pereira, P., et al.: The physical education curriculum and life skills: processes and intervention strategies. Motricidade **16**(2), 135–143 (2020)
12. Ryan, T.G., Ryan.: The evolving health and physical education curriculum of Ontario. Int. J. Phys. Educ. **59**(1), 1–11 (2020)

Knowledge Graph Construction and Visualization Technology of Online Courses for Intelligent Education

Yibao Huang(✉)

Guangdong Preschool Normal College In Maoming, Maoming, China
selves82@163.com

Abstract. Knowledge graphs of online courses for intelligent education rely heavily on research into knowledge graph generation and visualization technologies; yet, this area has a problem with incorrect performance placement. The problem of incorrect construction and location in the knowledge graph of online courses for intelligent education is too big for the conventional bee colony algorithm to handle, and the output is inadequate. Therefore, this study presents and evaluates research on the building and visualization technologies of online course knowledge graphs for intelligent education, and it uses particle swarm arithmetic to inform its findings. We start by applying swarm intelligence theory to identify the factors that will have an impact, and then we divide the indicators according to the requirements of knowledge graph construction and visualization technology research, with the goal of reducing interference factors in this field. After that, we take a look at the results of our study on knowledge graph creation and visualization technology by applying particle swarm arithmetic to a scheme we made using swarm intelligence theory. While researching knowledge graph construction and visualization technology, the MATLAB simulation results show that Particle swarm arithmetic works better than the typical Bee colony method under specific evaluation circumstances in terms of accuracy and time of influencing factors.

Keywords: swarm intelligence theory · particle swarm arithmetic · Research on knowledge graph construction and visualization technology · Smart education · Online courses

1 Introduction

Knowledge graphs for intelligent online education [1] rely heavily on research into knowledge graph building and visualization technologies, which in turn may speed up the process of precisely controlling aging performance [2] by reducing the prevalence of incorrect design and placement. On the other hand, studies on knowledge graph construction and visualization technology have been conducted, but there is a lack of precision in the research on knowledge graph construction and visualization technology scheme [5]. This has a negative effect on the research on knowledge graph construction

B. Brik and S. Nazir (Eds.): BigIoT-EDU 2024, LNICST 660, pp. 173–184, 2026.
https://doi.org/10.1007/978-3-032-18628-7_19

and visualization technology [6]. Particle swarm arithmetic [8] applied to the study of the aging performance assessment mode may successfully analyze and support research on knowledge graph construction and visualization technology schemes, according to certain researchers [7]. Based on this information, a Particle swarm algorithm is proposed [9] to test the model's effectiveness and optimize research on knowledge graph creation and visualization technology schemes.

2 Related Concepts

2.1 The Particle Swarm Arithmetic is Described Mathematically

Particle swarm analysis will enhance computer-based knowledge graph construction and visualization technology research, as will index parameters in this field, it is y_i. Results from studies examining knowledge graph building and visualization technologies using unqualified value parameters indicate that z_i, and the research on knowledge graph construction and visualization technology scheme is $tol\left(y_i \cdot t_{ij}\right)$. Together with the function to determine, using the computation indicated in Eq. (1), the practicability of research on knowledge graph building and visualization technology.

$$\lim_{x \to \infty} \left(y_i \cdot t_{ij}\right) = \frac{\partial^2 \Omega}{\partial v^2} y_{ij} \geq \max(t_{ij} \div 2) \tag{1}$$

Outliers among them are evaluated using the equation.

$$\max(t_{ij}) = \frac{\partial^2 \Omega}{\partial v^2} \succ \sqrt{2}\left(\sum t_{ij} + 4\right)\mathfrak{M} \tag{2}$$

By integrating computational advantages, particle swarm arithmetic quantifies studies on knowledge graph creation and visualization technologies, which might lead to more precise studies in these areas.

What if I were to Information graph building and visualization technology research needs t_i that the research on knowledge graph construction and visualization technology scheme is set_i, as a means of fulfilling research on knowledge graph building and visualization is y_i. Together with the scheme's evaluative role in knowledge graph building and visualization technologies is $F(t_i \approx 0)$ as shown by Eq. (3).

$$F(d_i) = \frac{\delta y}{\delta x} \sum t_i \cap \xi \cdot \sqrt{2} \to \oint y_i \cdot 7 \tag{3}$$

2.2 Selection of Research on Knowledge Graph Construction and Visualization Technology Scheme

Second Hypothesis Studying the role of knowledge graphs in building and displaying technological information is $g(t_i)$, The weighting factor is w_i. Therefore, as shown in

Equation, study on knowledge graph creation and visualization technologies need the unqualified research on the subject.

$$g(t_i) = \ddot{x} \cdot z_i \prod F(d_i) \frac{dy}{dx} - w_i \Phi \tag{4}$$

Assumptions I and II of the study on knowledge graph creation and visualization technology allow for the entire function of the research to be acquired, and the outcomes are represented in Eq. (5).

$$\lim_{x \to \infty} g(t_i) + F(d_i) \leq \bigcap \max(t_{ij}) \tag{5}$$

Data standardization is essential for conducting effective research on knowledge graph creation and visualization technologies; Eq. (6) presents the findings.

$$g(t_i) + F(d_i) \leftrightarrow \lim_{\delta x \to 0} \left(\sum t_{ij} + 4 \right) \tag{6}$$

2.3 Analysis of Research on Knowledge Graph Construction and Visualization Technology Scheme

Prior to implementing particle swarm math, it is necessary to conduct a thorough analysis of the research on knowledge graph construction and visualization technology scheme. The needs of this research should be compared to the existing library of research on this topic, and any unqualified research should be removed. Equation (7) shows the results of the anomaly assessment system, which is $No(t_i)$, and Eq. (6) shows how to deliver it.

$$No(t_i) = \frac{g(t_i) + F(d_i)}{mean\left(\sum t_{ij} + 4\right)} \lim_{\delta x \to 0} \Phi \tag{7}$$

Among them, it is $\frac{g(t_i)+F(d_i)}{mean(\sum t_{ij}+4)} \leq 1$ specified that the scheme must be $Z(t_i)$ suggested; otherwise, the scheme integration is necessary; the outcome is illustrated in Eq. (8).

$$Zh(t_i) = \lim_{x \to \infty} \left[\sum g(t_i) + F(d_i) \right] \lim_{x \to \infty} \tag{8}$$

The study on knowledge graph construction and visualization technology has been $accur(t_i)$ examined in depth, and in order to guarantee the accuracy of the Particle swarm calculation, its threshold and index weight have been set. Research on knowledge graph creation and visualization technologies is $unno(t_i)$, a well-tested research strategy, and it has to be investigated carefully. According to Eq. (9), the overall accuracy of research on knowledge graph construction and visualization technology will be reduced if the distribution of the research is non-normal. This is because the research on knowledge graph construction and visualization technology scheme is affected.

$$accur(t_i) = \frac{\min\left[\sum g(t_i) + F(d_i)\right]}{\sum g(t_i) + F(d_i)} \Lambda \tag{9}$$

Evidence from studies on knowledge graph building and visualization technologies shows that the scheme follows a multi-dimensional distribution, in line with what is known to be true. Because there is no clear path to the study on knowledge graph construction and visualization technology, it is called high analytical research by $randon(t_i)$. This indicates that the scheme is very unpredictable. One possible representation of the calculation of Eq. (9) is Eq. (10), if the study on knowledge graph construction and visualization technology's stochastic function is.

$$accur(t_i) = \dddot{x}\frac{\min[\sum g(t_i) + F(d_i)]}{\frac{1}{2}\sum g(t_i) + F(d_i)} + randon(t_i) \tag{10}$$

Knowledge graph construction and visualization technology research, for example, satisfies all norms because of computational adjustments that clean up the research, do away with superfluous and redundant schemes, and augment the default scheme, all of which leads to a robust dynamic correlation across the board.

3 Research on Knowledge Graph Construction and Visualization Technology Optimization Approach

The optimization of research on knowledge graph construction and visualization technology is accomplished through the use of particle swarm arithmetic, which modifies the parameters of the Internet and employs a random optimization method. The evolutionary algorithm divided the study of knowledge graph building and visualization technologies into many phases, after which it randomly selected several approaches. During the iterative phase, the study on knowledge graph construction and visualization technology scheme is enhanced and revised based on the different grades. Once the optimization study is finished, the research on knowledge graph construction and visualization technology level of different schemes is put together, and the best of this research is documented.

4 Results and Discussion

4.1 Introduction to the Research on Knowledge Graph Construction and Visualization Technology

Using complex cases as an example, this study employs knowledge graph construction and visualization technology as its research object; the study employs a 12-h testing period and displays the research scheme for knowledge graph construction and visualization technology in Table 1.

The research on knowledge graph construction and visualization technology process in Table 1 is shown in Fig. 1.

Particle swarm mathematics, which incorporates the Bee colony method, is more in line with the actual requirements of research on knowledge graph creation and visualization technology when it comes to its scheme for studying these topics. When it comes to research on knowledge graph creation and visualization technologies, particle swarm

Table 1. Research on knowledge graph construction and visualization technology research on knowledge graph construction and visualization technology requirements.

Scope of application	Grade	Accuracy	Research on knowledge graph construction and visualization technology
Swarm intelligence theory	I	89.23	90.14
	II	90.47	90.11
Intelligent coaching and reasoning	I	91.09	88.43
	II	92.65	86.6
Teaching research and decision support	I	87.82	89.81
	II	86.68	89.71

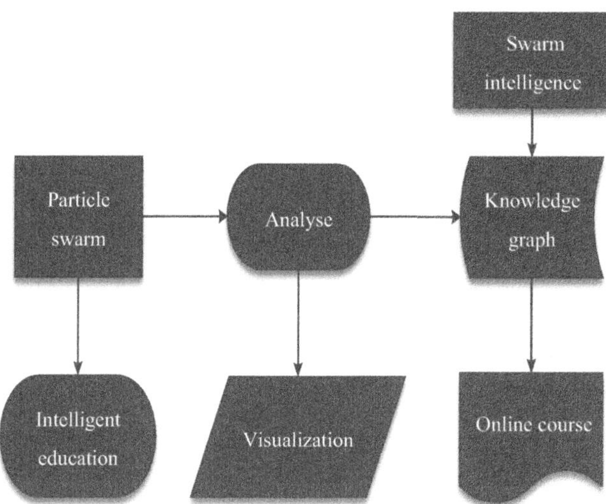

Fig. 1. Analysis process of research on knowledge graph construction and visualization technology

arithmetic is more accurate and logical than the bee colony method. Modifying the study on knowledge graph building and visualization technology method in Fig. 2 improves the precision and reliability of particle swarm arithmetic. Hence, the study on knowledge graph building and visualization technology scheme by the evolutionary algorithm has become more efficient, accurate, and stable in terms of summation.

4.2 Research on Knowledge Graph Construction and Visualization Technology

Research on knowledge graph building and visualization technology demands are more closely fulfilled by the Particle swarm arithmetic scheme, which contains the Bee colony method. In terms of logic and accuracy of research on knowledge graph creation and visualization technologies, particle swarm arithmetic beats the bee colony method. In Fig. 2, we can see how modifying the study on knowledge graph building and visualization technology scheme improves the accuracy and reliability of particle swarm analytics. This led to faster, more accurate, and more stable summation in the evolutionary algorithm's study of knowledge graph building and visualization technology schemes (Table 2).

Table 2. The overall situation of the research on knowledge graph construction and visualization technology scheme

Category	Random data	Reliability	Analysis rate
Swarm intelligence theory	91.69	91.83	88.29
Intelligent coaching and reasoning	88.56	90.06	89.45
Teaching research and decision support	88.59	92.66	85.75
Mean	88.87	87.75	87.1
X6	90.6	83.44	90.68
	P =.249		

4.3 Research on Knowledge Graph Construction and Visualization Technology and Stability

Research on knowledge graph building and visualization technology scheme is presented in Fig. 2. It is consisted of the Bee colony method, which is used to assess the accuracy of particle swarm arithmetic.

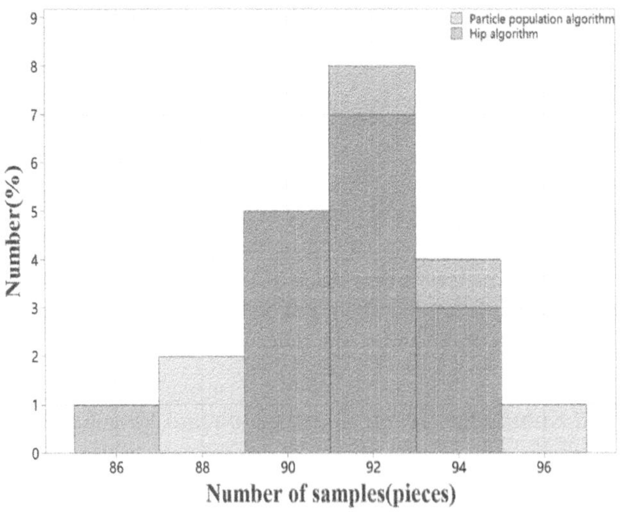

Fig. 2. Inaccurate construction and positioning of aging performance of different algorithms.

Figure 2 shows that compared to the Bee colony algorithm, Particle swarm arithmetic has more research on knowledge graph construction and visualization technology, but with a lower error rate. This suggests that Particle swarm arithmetic's research on these topics is more consistent, in contrast to the inconsistent research on these topics by the Bee colony algorithm. All three of the aforementioned approaches have their average study on knowledge graph construction and visualization technology schemes shown in Table 3.

Table 3. Compares the accuracy of several research on knowledge graph construction and visualization technology.

Algorithm	Survey data	Research on knowledge graph construction and visualization technology	Magnitude of change	Error
Particle swarm arithmetic	85.33	85.15	82.88	84.95
Bee colony algorithm	85.20	83.41	86.01	85.75
P	87.17	87.62	84.48	86.97

Research on knowledge graph creation and visualization technology varies greatly with a huge mistake rate, and the Bee colony technique has shortcomings in terms of accuracy (as shown in Table 3). When compared to the ant colony method, particle swarm analysis yielded superior results in studies concerning knowledge graph building and visualization technologies. Particle swarm analysis has also shown that knowledge graph creation and visualization technologies may achieve an accuracy of over 90% with little to no change in precision. For the purpose of proving that particle swarm arithmetic is superior. Figure 3 shows the results of a comprehensive analysis of the Particle swarm algorithm using a variety of approaches, which further supports the effectiveness of the proposed method.

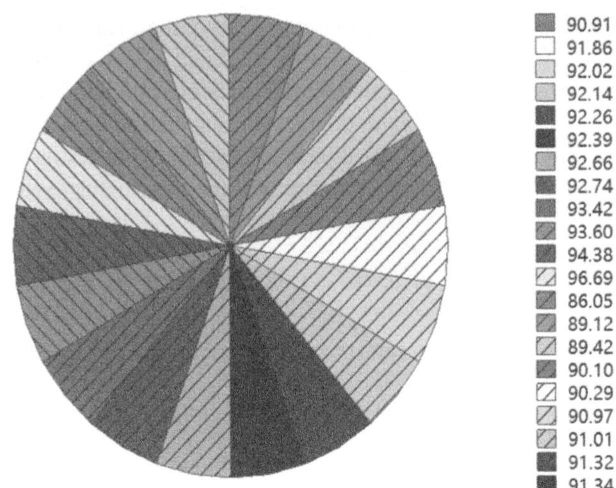

Fig. 3. Research on knowledge graph construction and visualization technology of Particle swarm arithmetic

Figure 3 demonstrates that compared to the Bee colony method, Particle swarm arithmetic's study on knowledge graph creation and visualization technologies is drastically superior. This is due to the fact that Particle swarm arithmetic raises the adjustment coefficient for research on knowledge graph construction and visualization technology and establishes the threshold for Internet information in order to exclude research on knowledge graph construction and visualization technology schemes that falter.

4.4 Rationality of Research on Knowledge Graph Construction and Visualization Technology

To ensure that the Particle swarm arithmetic is proper, the study on knowledge graph construction and visualization technology scheme is linked with the Bee colony algorithm. Figure 4 depicts this research.

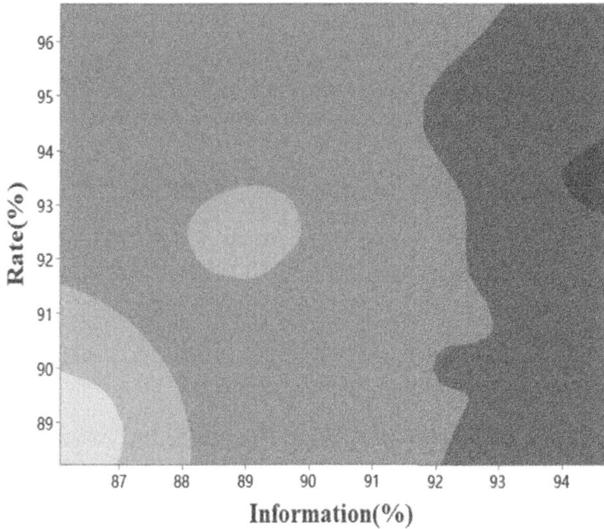

Fig. 4. Inaccurate construction and positioning of aging performance of different algorithms.

Figure 4 demonstrates that compared to the Bee colony algorithm, the research on knowledge graph construction and visualization technology conducted by particle swarm arithmetic is more rational. Furthermore, it is possible to further improve this research by incorporating particle swarm arithmetic into future endeavors. Particle swarm analytics allows for the development of a decentralized data storage and administration platform, which guarantees the secure storage and preservation of discoveries. Particle swarm arithmetic allows for the generation of unique identifiers for each, as well as the storage of suitable data and schemes.

4.5 Validity of Research on Knowledge Graph Construction and Visualization Technology

Figure 5 shows the results of the research on the knowledge graph construction and visualization technology scheme, which includes the Bee colony algorithm, in order to validate the efficacy of the Particle swarm arithmetic.

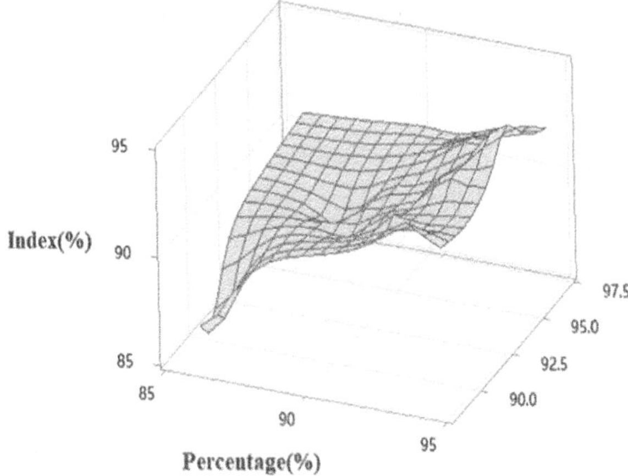

Fig. 5. Research on knowledge graph construction and visualization technology of different algorithms.

Figure 5 demonstrates that compared to the Bee colony algorithm, particle swarm arithmetic has more research on knowledge graph construction and visualization technology, but with a lower error rate. This suggests that particle swarm arithmetic's research on these topics is more consistent, in contrast to the uneven research on these topics by the Bee colony algorithm. All three of the aforementioned approaches have their average study on knowledge graph construction and visualization technology schemes shown in Table 4.

Table 4. Compares the efficacy of several research on knowledge graph construction and visualization technology.

Algorithm	Survey data	Research on knowledge graph construction and visualization technology	Magnitude of change	Error
Particle swarm arithmetic	92.96	92.83	85.01	84.23
Bee colony algorithm	88.53	90.67	89.78	87.71
P	88.14	87.23	91.22	91.56

As can be seen from Table 4, there are some issues with the accuracy of the research on knowledge graph construction and visualization technology when using the Bee colony algorithm. Specifically, there is a high error rate and significant variation in the research. When compared to the ant colony method, particle swarm analysis yielded superior results in studies concerning knowledge graph building and visualization technologies. Particle swarm analysis has also shown that knowledge graph creation and visualization technologies may achieve an accuracy of over 90% with little to no change in precision. For the purpose of proving that particle swarm arithmetic is superior. In order to further evaluate the effectiveness of the presented technique, the Particle swarm algorithm was routinely investigated by many ways, as shown in Fig. 6.

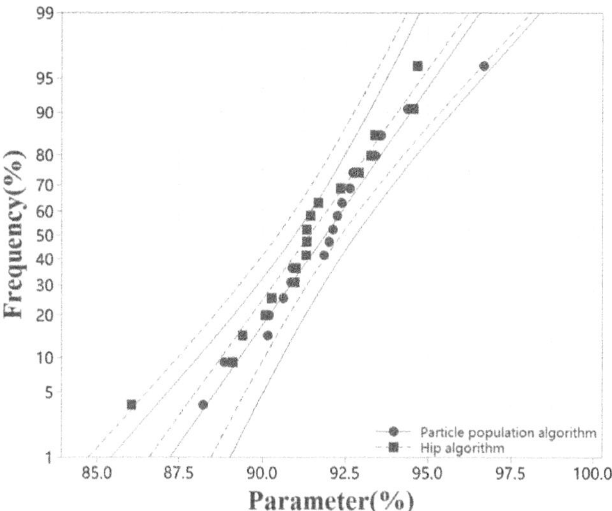

Fig. 6. Particle swarm arithmetic research on knowledge graph construction and visualization technology

Figure 6 demonstrates that compared to the Bee colony method, Particle swarm arithmetic's research on knowledge graph generation and visualization technologies is much superior. This is due to the fact that Particle swarm arithmetic raises the adjustment coefficient for research on knowledge graph construction and visualization technology and establishes the threshold for Internet information in order to exclude research on knowledge graph construction and visualization technology schemes that falter.

5 Conclusion

This study proposes a particle swarm algorithm that utilizes computer technology to improve research on knowledge graph building and visualization technology. It aims to solve the problem of suboptimal research in this area. At the same time that web-based data collection is being developed, the validity and trustworthiness of studies pertaining to knowledge graph building and visualization technologies are being investigated extensively. The results show that using particle swarm arithmetic improves the accuracy of research on knowledge graph construction and visualization technology, and that generic research on the same topic can be applied to this specific area of study. Nevertheless, the Particle swarm algorithmic procedure focuses excessively on studying research on knowledge graph construction and visualization technologies, leading to illogical indicator selection based on this research.

References

1. Li, B., Hongshen, W., Zhongjin, H., Yadong, L.: Research on the construction and visualization of complex surface precision machining knowledge graph for process planning reuse. Modern Manufact. Eng. (000–003) (2022)
2. Guo, Y., Dan, L.: A review of research on artificial intelligence in education in China in the Last decade—based on citespace knowledge graph analysis software guide **21**(1), 6 (2022)
3. Dong, X., Dongdai, Z., Xuejiao, H., Hengnian, G., Zhen, L.: Research on the construction method of knowledge graph model in the education field under the guidance of discipline core literacy development research on audiovisual education **43**(5), 76–83 (2022)
4. Lin, B.: The current situation and frontier evolution of higher education evaluation research in China in the last decade—visual analysis based on citespace knowledge graph. J. Southwest Univer. Nationalities: Humanit. Soc. Sci. Edition **43**(5), 8 (2022)
5. Zhang, Y., Zhongyuan, D., Junfeng, Z., Yasha, W.: A method for constructing and evolving knowledge graph instances based on intelligent mapping recommendation. Comput. Sci. **50**(6), 142–150 (2023)
6. Zhu, J., Rui, C.: Design of course knowledge graph system based on Neo4j computer knowledge and technology: academic edition **19**(8), 40–42 (2023)
7. Han, Z., Jiansheng, Z.: Research on the construction method of fault knowledge graph for multiple unit trains railway rolling stock (2023)
8. Feng, J.: A parallel construction method of knowledge graph for massive structured data CN116383318A (2023)
9. Zhao, X., Yuyu, Z., Shoucai, J., Fei, H., Jianbei, L.: A generalization generation method and system for dangerous lane changing scenarios for autonomous driving testing. J. Autom. (2023)
10. Qi, C.: Creation and application of knowledge graph in the field of modern educational technology curriculum. J. Heilongjiang Teachers' Developm. College **41**(1), 52–54 (2022)
11. Zhou, Z., Junping, Q.: The distribution characteristics and development trends of knowledge graph research in China towards artificial intelligence. Inform. Sci. **40**(1), 9 (2022)
12. Dilinur K í mu.: Research on the importance of constructing a curriculum knowledge graph—taking the course of "Data Structure" as an example electronic components and information technology, **6**(7), 4 (2022)
13. Yu, J., Zhixian, Z.: The current situation and hot spots of intelligent education research in China—A visual analysis based on CNKI literature from 2000 to 2021. J. Jiangxi Radio Television Univer. **24**(2), 17–25 (2022)

The Improvement of English Teaching Content Through the Cross-Cultural Iterative Approach

Hui Yue(✉) and Jin Yue

Air Force Aviation University, Changchun, Jilin, China
{18943983888,18088662870}@189.cn

Abstract. In view of the limitations of the traditional D-P algorithm in English teaching content, an improvement scheme based on cross-cultural iterative method was proposed. Firstly, the influencing factors is accurately located through the theory of cross-cultural communication, and the indicators is reasonably divided to reduce interference, and the cross-cultural iterative method is used to construct an improvement plan for teaching content. Experimental results show that under certain evaluation criteria, the proposed scheme is superior to the traditional D-P algorithm in terms of the improvement accuracy of teaching content and the processing time of influencing factors, and has obvious advantages. The improvement of teaching content plays an extremely important role in English, which can accurately predict and optimize the growth characteristics and product generation of English. However, the traditional D-P algorithm has certain limitations in solving the simulation problem of teaching content improvement, especially when dealing with complex problems. In this regard, this paper proposes an improvement scheme for teaching content based on cross-cultural iteration method to better solve this problem. The scheme accurately locates the influencing factors through the theory of cross-cultural communication, so as to determine the division of indicators, and uses the cross-cultural iterative method to construct the scheme. Experimental results show that under certain evaluation criteria, the accuracy and speed of the scheme is significantly improved for different problems, and it has better performance. Therefore, the simulation scheme based on cross-cultural iterative method can better solve the limitations of traditional D-P algorithms and improve the accuracy and efficiency of simulation by adopting the cross-cultural iterative method in English teaching content.

Keywords: Theory of intercultural communication · Cross-cultural iterative method · English · Improvement of teaching content · Research

1 Introduction

The importance of improving teaching content in English cannot be overstated. Through simulation, various parameters and changes in this process can be predicted and understood, providing guidance and support for actual production. However, the traditional improvement scheme of teaching content has certain deficiencies in accuracy, which

B. Brik and S. Nazir (Eds.): BigIoT-EDU 2024, LNICST 660, pp. 185–196, 2026.
https://doi.org/10.1007/978-3-032-18628-7_20

limits its effect in practical application. In order to solve the problem of accuracy of the improvement of traditional teaching content, researchers have introduced the cross-cultural iterative method into the improvement analysis of teaching content in recent years [1, 2]. The cross-cultural iterative method is a computational method based on group behavior, which simulates the interaction and cooperation between individuals to achieve the goal of global optimization. The algorithm has the characteristics of decentralization, immutability and smart contract, which can effectively solve the accuracy problems existing in traditional schemes [3, 4]. The improvement and optimization model of teaching content based on cross-cultural iteration method further improves the accuracy and reliability of simulation by optimizing the parameters and algorithms in the improvement process of teaching content. The model adjusts and optimizes the various parameters in this process to achieve the best improvement of teaching content [5, 6]. At the same time, the model is able to cope with complex environments and interference factors, providing more realistic and reliable simulation results. The researchers used extensive experiments and data analysis to evaluate the effectiveness of the improved optimization model for teaching content based on the cross-cultural iterative method. The results show that the proposed model has significant advantages in many aspects compared with the traditional teaching content improvement scheme.

2 Related Concepts

2.1 Cross-Cultural Iterative Approach

Cross-cultural iteration is based on the different requirements of each core, thereby improving the computational or real-time performance of the application. The intrinsic relationship between the variables is constructed into a "model for dealing with sharing-creativity-improvement of teaching content" [7, 8]. The cross-cultural iterative method has obvious advantages, which can carry out efficient integration of archives and has the advantage of sustainability. An improved analysis of the teaching content of unstructured data by the cross-cultural iterative approach, but in accordance with the following assumptions [9, 10].

Hypothesis A: Pit is the result of the development of the improvement of the teaching content, the time is at time t, and the set of improvement of the teaching content is constructed set(Det) [11]. Where any data x belongs to Pi, and the performance result for the improvement of teaching content is $P_j(x)$, and the calculated result is shown in Eq. (1).

$$P_j(x) mathbbS \frac{\delta y}{\delta x} = \sum_{i=1}^{n} X_i Y_i \frac{\Delta y}{\Delta x} \sum_{i,t=1}^{n} x_{it}^{j} \tag{1}$$

where, belongs to the mapping result. In order to improve is $k \in (1, \cdots + \infty)$ the accuracy of the calculations is $Re(k)$ of the teaching content, the immunodeficient of x-sum is $C(x, \beta)$ integrated. In Eq. (1), if the calculation accuracy is ζ low, and if it is $x_{it} = \theta(\rho \tan t)$, the calculation is $x_{it} < \sum_{i,j,t=1}^{n} x_{it}^{j}$ accuracy meets the requirements.

2.2 Classification of Improved Teaching Content

Hypothesis B: The results of the analysis of the improvement of the teaching content is $P_n(x)$, the results of the improvement of the mobile technology of the different teaching content is $\varphi(x \cdot k)$, as shown in Eq. (2).

$$P_h(x) = \int_h k \prod \frac{\partial^2 \Omega}{\partial u^2} \underset{<}{\leftrightarrow} \overline{\varepsilon \sum_{j=1}^{h} f(P_j(x))} \sum_{i=1}^{n} X_i^2 \tag{2}$$

Among them, the comprehensive analysis is $f(x)$ function of different dimensions.

Assuming C: The comprehensive classification function is $w(x)$ a function that satisfies the following conditions, and, then the judgment of the results of distributed computing autonomous information is $w(x) < \wp$ technology is $w(x)^{Prime} < \frac{\Delta \wp^2}{2}$ shown in Eq. (3).

$$w(x) = \frac{\int_h kw(x)^{Prime}}{2} \frac{x - \mu}{\sigma} \tag{3}$$

Hypothesis D: The improvement point of any teaching content is on the axis of autonomous information technology development, and the derivative of the improvement point of any teaching content will represent the direction of information technology development, which is y_{it} calculated as shown in Eq. (4).

$$D\left(y, f(y)^{Prime} | p\right) = \bigcup \sum_{i=1}^{n} \left(X_i - \overline{X}\right)^2 \tag{4}$$

Among them, it is α represents the development direction of distributed computing independent information technology.

From the above theorem, it can be seen that the nonlinear relationship between different economic data x can be calculated by using the improvement of teaching content, and the influence of i dimension and t time on the results of economic characteristics can be reduced. Therefore, the improvement processing of teaching content provides a good foundation and reduces the influence of data structure on the improvement results of teaching content [12, 13]. It can be seen from theorem 3 that the multi-dimensional judgment accuracy of independent information technology is $\alpha \cdot lin\left(\frac{1}{x}\right)$ as follows, indicating that the multi-dimensional judgment accuracy meets the requirements, and further reduces the impact of the improvement of teaching content on the results.

2.3 Mining for the Improvement of Teaching Content

In this paper, the cross-cultural iterative method is selected for model construction, which is an improved classification technology for teaching content, which has the advantages of fuzziness and adaptability, and can realize cyclic calculation and continuously revise the classification set. The cross-cultural iterative method can be constrained by the IF pattern to form constraint M, and its classification process is as follows:

$$\text{IF} : x_i < d_{ij}, \text{ and } \; M(x) \Lambda C(x_i, x_{i-1}), \tag{5}$$

$$\text{then } y \wedge \sum_{i=1}^{n} y_i \vee \frac{1}{2} \sum_{i=1}^{n} M(x_i) \frac{\partial^2 \Omega}{\partial u \partial v} \tag{6}$$

Among them, it is $\lambda(x_i)$ the adjustment function of autonomous information technology, the set of adjustment results of distributed computing information technology, the constraints, and the results of distributed computing autonomous information is d_{ij} technology. The cross-cultural iterative method prepossess the distributed computing information technology, and the cross-cultural iterative method is $M(x)$ used in the processing process, and the accurate results is y finally obtained. Therefore, the output results can be deduced using the cross-cultural iterative method and the results of comprehensive teaching content improvement can be obtained.

Hypothesis E: The improvement of any teaching content is x_i to analyze the relationship between the input variables is x_i and the output variables by constraint M, is y_i shown in Eq. (7).

$$\alpha \cdot g_{ij} mathfrakM \prod \notin = \sum_{i,j=1}^{n} x \cdot \left\{ \frac{(x_i \wedge c_{ij})}{b_{ij}} \right\} \lim_{\delta x \to 0} \frac{\partial^2 \Omega}{\partial u \partial v} \frac{\Delta y}{\Delta x} \tag{7}$$

Among them, the transformation is c_{ij} of the results of the improvement is b_{ij} of different teaching contents; is g_{ij} a prepossessing collection for performance.

According to the improvement of the above teaching content, the continuous operator of the improvement of the teaching content is obtained, and the calculation result is shown in Eq. (8).

$$g_{ij} \frac{n!}{r!(n-r)!} = \oint \quad \sum_{i,j,k=1}^{n} g_{ij}{}^{k} \wedge (x^2) \frac{\Delta y}{\Delta x} \tag{8}$$

Among them, the performance coefficient for the improvement of teaching content, k is δ the class. According to the results of the improvement of the teaching content, the output value of the improvement of the teaching content can be obtained, as shown in Eq. (9).

$$y\sqrt{a^2 + b^2} = \sum_{i,j,k=1}^{n} g_{ij}^{k}(x) \Rightarrow f(P_j(x) \tag{9}$$

The cross-cultural iterative approach can shorten the processing time for the improvement of teaching content and increase the amount of pee-processing performance. According to the initial performance volume, the multi-dimensional improvement of teaching content is carried out to form continuous improvement results of teaching content.

3 Judgment of the Model for the Improvement of Teaching Content

3.1 Initialization of the Improvement of the Teaching Content

Data structure optimization time may be reduced and distributed computing's independent information technology capabilities can be enhanced with the better model of instructional material. This is shown in the thorough examination of both the original and multi-dimensional data volumes, and it employs the enhanced alarm settings of the lesson plans to achieve the thorough evaluation of the lesson plans' enhancements and provide the best possible outcomes.

(1) enhancing self-paced, dispersed computing instruction

Data from autonomous information technology systems is both dispersed and lacks a consistent structure. There will be more math involved and less precision in the overall computation if the quantity of performance data does not follow a normal distribution. The precision of data calculations can only be enhanced by increasing both the quantity and diversity of data. Figure 1 shows the outcomes of increasing the quantity of data in the original data set, which improves the variety of data volume in this research.

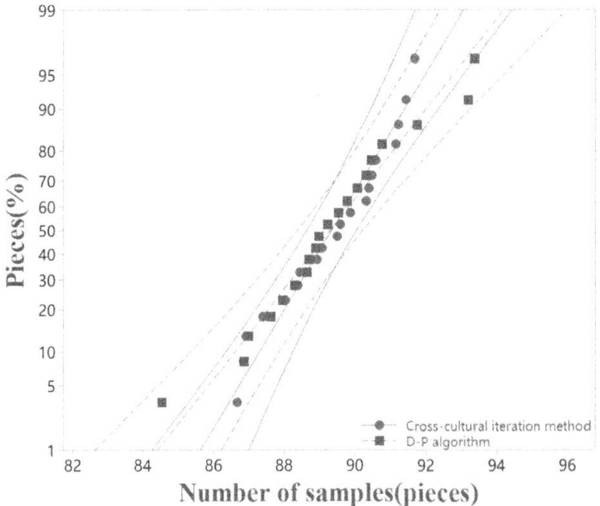

Fig. 1. Results of improved processing of teaching content in different processing aspects

Both the D-P algorithm and the cross-cultural iterative approach were used to handle the original huge data, as shown in Fig. 1. By comparing, we find that the D-P method produces a chaotic and non-directional beginning data set. With the cross-cultural iterative technique, data is processed in a more focused and directed manner. Proofs 1 and 2 of the cross-cultural iterative technique show that the algorithm's output has nothing to do with location, leading to more precise processing and enhancement of course material. When processing the initial data volume, the cross-cultural iterative approach is used since the distribution impact is constant with each data point and the data set is quite stable.

(2) A distributed computing IT comprehensive judgment technique

In order to facilitate the distributed cooperation of multi-dimensional information technology data and to finish the comprehensive judgment process, the algorithm uses a heterogeneous approach for the performance data of various dimensions and changes the relevant parameters. The model's five multi-dimensional breakdown of the huge data allows each dimension to stand in for a subspace of the solution space. The five dimensional instructional materials' improvement data developed simultaneously during the iterative procedure. At the end of the iterative computation, we compare the adaption values of various dimensions, note the improvement information for each multi-dimensional teaching content, and finally, note where the comprehensive teaching content stands in terms of improvement outcomes. The next step is to add up the improvement data from each sub-multi-dimensional teaching component until it reaches the comprehensive teaching content's improvement results. Then, to make the improvement calculation faster and more accurate, find the best place to put the sub-multi-dimensional teaching component's improvement data.

3.2 Improved Judgment Techniques for Teaching Content of Cross-Cultural Iterative Method

The basic idea of the cross-cultural iterative method is to make a comprehensive judgment of the improvement information of multi-time and multi-dimensional teaching content, and adjust and optimize the improvement standard of the initial teaching content of big data and the improvement alarm condition of the teaching content, so as to obtain the optimal solution and reduce the independent information technology rate of distributed computing, as shown in Fig. 2.

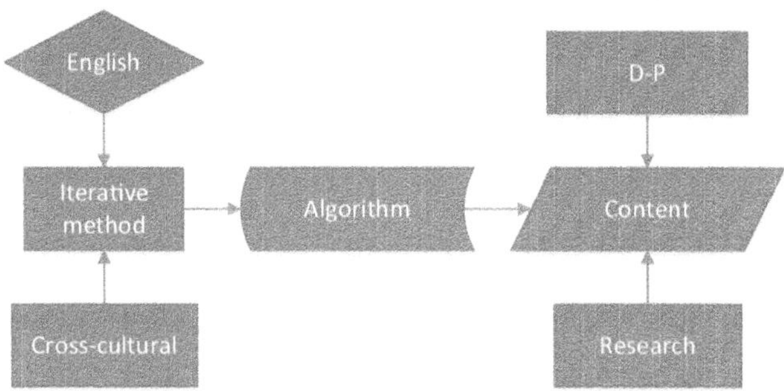

Fig. 2. Computational flow chart of cross-cultural iteration method and big data

The first step is to analyze the data characteristics and problem-solving requirements to find the best way to enhance the data structure of the distributed computing instructional material. Each huge data set represents an opportunity for the improvement alarm condition of the weight and teaching content, and the starting weight of the full data set and the improvement alarm condition of the teaching content are mapped to the big data set as a whole. In this work, we find that the improvement information of the big data teaching material is $D = 433$, based on the real application scenario.

Next, we will initialize the data. Parameters related to unstructured initialization of huge data.

Create a moderation feature as the third step. In order to create the initial data volume for big data and to map it to big data, the idea of cross-cultural iteration approach is used.

Each huge data set's correctness is determined using a modest function that takes the absolute value of its total of squibs.

Fourth, enhance the substance of instruction: The ideal spot for big data and the improvement domain in every subject area for instruction. After splitting the original huge data into five smaller datasets, we can calculate the fitness ratio, find the best overall position, and note the best position for each dataset individually.

Step 5: Refine the ideal location and speed via iteration. The non-structure selects one of the five seed data quantities for evolution, as shown in Eqs. (7) through (9).

The iteration will be terminated and the outcomes of the improvement alert conditions, weights, and optimal locations of the instructional material will be returned in Step 6 unless the number of iterations d is less than the maximum number of iterations D.

4 Practical Case Analysis

4.1 Performance Judgment of the Model

The cross-cultural iterative method was tested with single-index performance, multi-indicator performance, multi-dimensional indicators and other indicators to verify the performance of the model proposed in this paper.

Single-metric performance is the only minimum function of the test model synthesis, and the formula is as follows:

$$A(x) = \sum_{i=1}^{n}\left[x_i^2\right]\frac{-b \pm \sqrt{b^2 - 4ac}}{2a} \tag{10}$$

Multi-index performance is a cosine modulation transfer function that frequently generates a single minimum value to verify the practicability of the model solution, and the formula is as follows:

$$B(x) = \frac{dy}{dx}\lim_{x \to \infty}\sum_{i=1}^{n}\cos\alpha e^{x_i^2} \tag{11}$$

The multi-dimensional indicator is a gradient optimization function of multi-dimensional points, which tests the calculation speed of multi-dimensional data to detect the judgment speed of synthesis, and the formula is as follows:

$$C(x) = \frac{\sqrt{a^2 + b^2}}{2a} - \alpha e^{\sqrt{\frac{1}{n}\sum_{i=1}^{n} x_i^2}} \tag{12}$$

where n is the total number of indicators for which data is calculated, and the number of arbitrary indicators is x_i used.

This paper's instructional material has undergone 1200 modifications, with the most recent iteration being 30 times and the longest duration being 24 months, all for the sake of simplicity in computation. Table 1 shows the precise calculation findings, which

Table 1. Detection results of different test functions

Test metrics	Test the function	Equation parameter	Standard Error	Wald chi-squid	95% Confidence interval
Single-metric performance	Cross-cultural iterative approach	0.3488	2.3331	1.4710	2.6079 ~ 0.1640
	D-P algorithm	1.5890	0.2832	1.9927	
Multi-metric performance	Cross-cultural iterative approach	0.3686	0.1457	3.0717	0.5460 ~ 1.2811
	D-P algorithm	1.4262	2.1513	1.9777	
Multi-dimensional metrics	Cross-cultural iterative approach	1.1866	2.6480	0.9582	3.5760 ~ 0.2947
	D-P algorithm	1.4513	3.7818	0.7362	

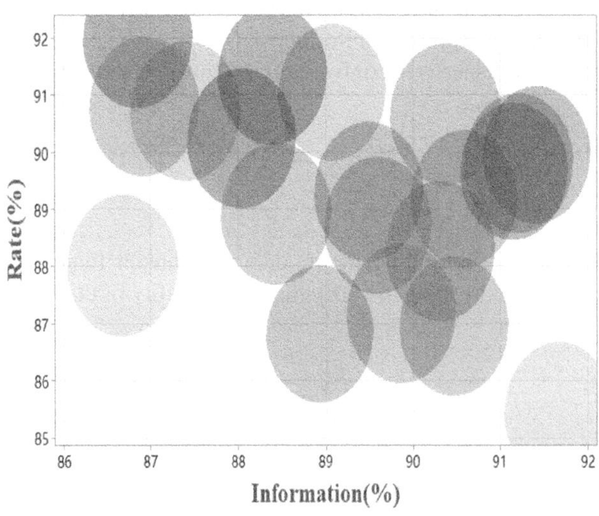

Fig. 3. Comparative study of the research scheme of the algorithm

were averaged across ten times to lessen the impact of non-structural features on the outcomes.

The convergence plots for each data in Table 1 is shown in Fig. 3.

As can be seen from Table 1, compared with the D-P algorithm, the cross-cultural iterative method proposed in this paper is closer to the improvement results of comprehensive teaching content. In terms of standard deviation, mean, and value range, the cross-cultural iterative method is superior to the other two algorithms. From the surface changes in Fig. 4, it can be seen that the cross-cultural iterative method has better stability and faster judgment speed. Therefore, the judgment speed, performance level judgment, and summation stability of the cross-cultural iteration method is better.

4.2 Examples of Improvement of Teaching Content

The judgment data set for the improvement of teaching content includes the improvement of digital teaching content, the improvement of bionic teaching content, the improvement of natural teaching content, the improvement of psychological teaching content, and the improvement of expected teaching content. After the preliminary prepossessing of the data, 43 rows of structured data and 32 rows of semi-structured data were obtained. In order to facilitate information efficiency, data in different fields is selected, namely: financial field, public service field, information security field, and Internet of Things field, and the data processing results is shown in Table 2.

Table 2. Classification and proportion of improvement of teaching content

Different types	Mean	SD
Student	43.60	0.98
Professionals	44.12	0.90
Immigrant	45.34	0.85
Tourist	43.79	1.24
Test items	Test value	p-value
−2Ln LR(L^2)	15.52	0.34
Pearson chi-squid	12.61	0.55
Scaled deviance	15.52	0.34
Degrees of freedom = 14		

4.3 Test Results

In order to verify the cross-cultural iterative method proposed in this paper, the results is compared with the D-P algorithm and big data, and the results is shown in Fig. 4.

Fig. 4. Test results for different algorithms

As can be seen from Fig. 4, the accuracy of the cross-cultural iterative method is higher than that of the D-P algorithm and big data, but the error rate is lower, indicating that the calculation of the cross-cultural iterative method and big data is relatively stable, while the calculation of cross-cultural iterative method and big data is uneven. Table 3 shows the average results of the above two algorithms.

Table 3. Comparison of judgment accuracy at different levels

Algorithm	Size of samples	Mean R	Se	99% Confidence interval	P-value	Accuracy
Cross-cultural iterative approach	673	0.6008	0.7350	0.6722 ~ 0.7294	0.7362	1.4513
D-P algorithm	679	0.7985	3.7818	0.6700 ~ 0.8270	0.1542	4.1704

Table 3 shows that both the cross-cultural iterative approach and the single D-P algorithm suffer from inadequate precision and a wide range of calculation outcomes when it comes to evaluating and improving educational material. This research presents an algorithm that much outperforms the cross-cultural iterative technique in terms of accuracy. While the D-P algorithm has a lower accuracy rate, the suggested approach is competitive with the cross-cultural iterative technique, both of which have accuracy rates over 80%. Figure 7/8 displays the outcomes of a comparison of the optimum fitness values of various algorithms, which further proves the superiority of the cross-cultural iterative technique.

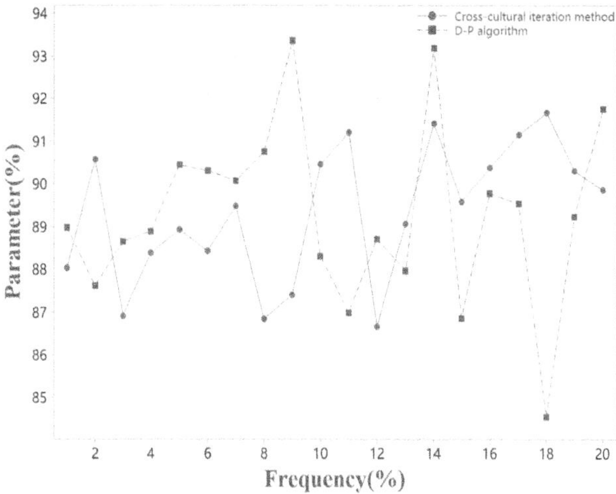

Fig. 5. Performance process of eigenvalues

As can be seen from Fig. 5, the results of the cross-cultural iterative method is significantly better than those of the D-P algorithm, and the reason for this is that the cross-cultural iterative method increases the synergy coefficient, improvement weight, and convergence factor of different dimensions.

5 Conclusion

Aiming at the accuracy problem of improving teaching content, a new comprehensive optimization scheme was proposed, which was based on cross-cultural iteration method and advanced computer technology. Initially, the security of information and the credibility of tampering with it were ensured by applying the decentralized nature of the cross-cultural iterative method and its data consistency guarantee. Then, combined with computer technology, the collected data is deeply analyzed and processed in detail, so as to dig out the intrinsic attributes and potential value of the data. The study also delves into the key performance indicators needed to ensure that the improvement of teaching content is accurate and credible, and constructs a comprehensive web-based information collection platform that plays a crucial role in ensuring the accuracy of the research output. However, it is worth noting that when applying the cross-cultural iterative method, the selection of the evaluation system for the improvement of teaching content must be cautious, so as to effectively explore and make use of the advantages of the cross-cultural iterative method and further improve the accuracy and practical application value of the research results.

References

1. Luhui, F.: Analysis and improvement strategies for scaffolding construction in middle school English writing teaching foreign language teaching in primary and secondary schools. **46**(7), 7 (2023)

2. Zhang, X., Zhang, J.: Exploring the improvement of practical English teaching methods—an evaluation of innovative strategies for college English language practice activities Chinese. J. Educ. (4), 1 (2022)
3. Li, J.: Reflection on strategies for improving high school English reading teaching in and out of the classroom (high school teaching and research). (6), 69–71 (2023)
4. Wu, Y.: Analysis of strategies for improving high school English reading teaching good parents: innovative education. (6) (2022)
5. Zhao, J.: The current situation and improvement strategies of middle school English pronunciation teaching Henan education: teacher education (Part 2). (5), 1 (2022)
6. Zhang, Y., Niu, X.: Exploration and practice of teaching reform for surveying and mapping professional English reading course based on engineering education certification surveying and spatial geographic information **46**(8), 13–15 (2023)
7. Liu, K.: On the teaching methods of middle school English classroom study weekly B edition (12), (2022)
8. Wang, Y.: *The Application of Process Writing Method in High School English Writing Teaching* (Doctoral dissertation) (2022)
9. Hu, L.: Exploring the interactive teaching model for high school English education (2) (2022)
10. Li, Y.: The problems and improvement strategies in the management of college English pronunciation teaching (16) (2022)
11. Shi, X.: A survey on the current situation of the application of thematic teaching mode in middle school English reading teaching. Front. Soc. Sci. **12**(11), 9 (2023)
12. The party will rise forever.: Improvement strategies for overall reading teaching of middle school English story based discourse. Foreign Lang. Teach. Primary Secondary Sch. **45**(1), 6 (2022)
13. Miao, L.: Improvement of English teaching from the perspective of applied linguistics: a new exploration of contemporary English teaching from the perspective of applied linguistics. Chin. J. Educ. (4), 1 (2022)

The Design of the Information Talent Training System of Applied Undergraduate Engineering Management Based on Knowledge Embedding

Xiaowen Hu[1](✉), Feng Yang[2], and Yanfei Ge[3]

[1] Nantong Institute of Technology, Nantong, China
huxiaowen870528@126.com

[2] Nanjing Tianxing Engineering Survey Co., Ltd., Nanjing, China

[3] Nantong Huayuan Surveying and Mapping Co., Ltd., Nantong, China

Abstract. Engineering information talents are the main talents in the existing employment. Group engineering plays an important role in promoting social development and belongs to the development of basic construction. But how to effectively manage talents, make them. Knowledge and ability have been significantly improved, which has become the focus of research. I combine the knowledge embedding analysis method with talents, optimize it, and better tap the development potential of talents. The results show that the knowledge embedding analysis method has a significant impact on the utilization and matching of talents and the evaluation of practical application effects, which can keep it between 70% and 80%. It shows that knowledge embedding can better identify talents, manage them, and provide support for social development, and the matching rate of talents reaches more than 85%. Therefore, the embedded knowledge-based method has a significant measure effect on talent management.

Keywords: Information superposition theory · Knowledge embedding · Applied undergraduate engineering management · Talent training system design · Design studies

1 Introduction

The process of talent training is a complex analysis process, which involves many factors such as knowledge points, abilities, interests and scores [1–3]. How to effectively cultivate talents has become the focus of research. Some scholars believe that dynamic tracking of talents and in-depth analysis combined with their own conditions can more effectively identify the characteristics of talents. Some scholars also believe that systematic knowledge training can meet the needs of knowledge cultivation and provide social practical talents [4, 5]. Some scholars also believe that in the process of talent analysis, it is necessary to integrate the characteristics and characteristics of talents to form a comprehensive analysis. In the process of talent cultivation, it is necessary to analyze talents from multiple angles, including their interests [6–8]. Conditions, their

B. Brik and S. Nazir (Eds.): BigIoT-EDU 2024, LNICST 660, pp. 197–204, 2026.
https://doi.org/10.1007/978-3-032-18628-7_21

own development direction and goals are comprehensively judged to form an effective talent training plan. The talent training plan should be practiced and promoted, and the training indicators and content should be constantly adjusted to improve the comprehensive effect of its training. Some scholars believe that integrating talent training and analysis with intelligent analysis methods can tap the characteristics of talents [9–11]. On the basis of the above analysis, I integrate the knowledge points and contents of talents, aiming at promoting the effective training of talents and building a talent training system [12, 13].

2 Construction of a Theoretical Model for the Design and Research of Information Talent Training System

In the process of talent training, its characteristic points need to be refined, including ability, knowledge points, own knowledge, information and experience., and analyzes is W_i the parameter values is E_i that do not meet the standards, the parameter values is $\hat{e}_i = E_i/|E_i|\hat{e}_i = E_i/|E_i|$, into the design and research can be referred to Eqs. (1) and (2).

$$W_i = \frac{1}{2}E_i \times H_i^* = \frac{|E_i|^2}{2\eta_o}\hat{e}_i \times \hat{h}_i^*, |W_i| = \frac{|E_i|^2}{2\eta_o} \tag{1}$$

$$P = \sigma|W_i| = \frac{\sigma}{2\eta_o}|E_i|^2\overline{XY} \tag{2}$$

Knowledge embedding is to internalize knowledge, integrate it with the actual situation and conditions of students and talents, form a comprehensive analysis, and improve students and talents' own learning ability. Realize the practice of knowledge in various fields and contents. Therefore, talent cultivation is the result of comprehensive analysis of knowledge, and it is also the result of overall judgment of knowledge points. To make a holistic judgment on it, it needs to be combined with the needs of practice. Optimize the original results. Therefore, the knowledge points should be quantified. The search is E_i implemented, and the formula is W_s described as follows:

$$|W_s| = \frac{P}{4\pi R^2} = \frac{\sigma|E_i|^2}{8\pi\eta_o R^2}\sqrt{2}\text{O} \tag{3}$$

Comprehensive analysis of points and holistic dialogue of knowledge content. Pheromone value is E_s set, and the formula is η_o described as follows:

$$|W_s| = \frac{1}{2\eta_o}|E_s|^2 \tag{4}$$

The holistic analysis and judgment of knowledge are consistent with the needs of talents and their practical abilities. Therefore, a comprehensive judgment of talent demand can complete the combination of overall knowledge demand. Embedded knowledge learning can optimize the original knowledge points, and the results is shown in Eq. (5).

$$\sigma = 4\pi R^2\frac{|E_s|^2}{|E_i|^2}\lim_{x\to\infty}\frac{n!}{r!(n-r)!} \tag{5}$$

The reliability of the design and research of the information talent training system, is shown in Eq. (6).

$$\sigma = \sum_{i=1}^{n} X_i^2 4\pi R \frac{E_s \times E_s^*}{E_i \times E_i^*} \tag{6}$$

The comprehensive judgment of knowledge points, the optimization of knowledge content and the holistic analysis of knowledge, the existing analysis contents and conditions are talent embedded research. As a result, it is necessary to make an in-depth judgment on the talent conditions and content, and the results is $No(t_i)$ shown in Eq. (7).

$$No(t_i) = \frac{g(t_i) + F(d_i)}{mean\left(\sum v_{ij} + 4\right)} X_1, \ldots, X_n \tag{7}$$

3 A Practical Case of Research on the Design and Research of Information Talent Training System

3.1 The Relevant Concepts of the Design and Research Model Construction of the Information Talent Training System

The knowledge optimization, it is necessary to carry out knowledge conditions and knowledge integrity results. Practical analysis verifies the rationality results, and at the same time, it is necessary to judge the relevance and content of knowledge. On the whole, the comprehensive analysis and conditional analysis of knowledge points, it is necessary to realize the overall planning and optimization of knowledge, and complete the diversity analysis and demand of knowledge. Therefore, in the process of talent training and talent planning, the knowledge content should conform to the actual situation and optimize the original actual conditions.Simulate the research process of the design of the information talent training system, as shown in Fig. 1.

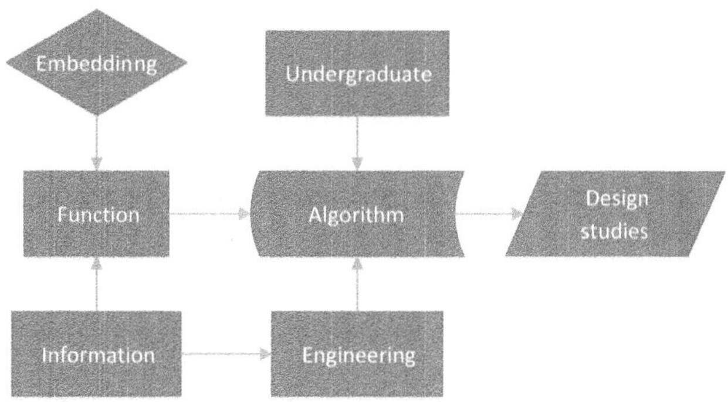

Fig. 1. The analysis process of the design and research of the information talent training system

From the analysis in Fig. 1, it can be seen that in the process of knowledge planning and knowledge content analysis, it is necessary to judge the actual needs of talents, the development direction and potential of talents, and realize the matching between talents and social needs. The optimization and conditions of talents should also meet the actual requirements. Therefore, it is necessary to evaluate the integrity and integrity of talents. Forecast the development potential of talents and form an effective plan. The results, practices and contents of comprehensive talent analysis complete the diverse needs and development of talents. Provide support for later talent training and talent index setting.

3.2 Research on the Design and Research of Information Talent Training System

The embedded analysis of talents is mainly to judge the cultivation of talent ability and the practical application of talents. Therefore, embedded knowledge belongs to a long-term process. I have. Graduate students in colleges and universities make in-depth analysis as the research object, and the condition of analysis is mainly the practical ability of talents. Based on various indicators such as knowledge transformation ability, talent knowledge conditions and talent development potential. Test data. Sourced from actual survey results. There are 120 cases investigated, and invalid cases and valid cases are excluded from the research results. Anomalous cases. The results show that all 120 copies meet the actual requirements, and the specific results are summarized in Table 1.

Table 1. Subject-related parameters of the study

Category	Knowledge competence	Improve one's comprehensive ability	Results of comprehensive talent training	Diversification analysis
Curriculum	88.56	92.49	95.71	88.56
Hands-on teaching	88.92	94.07	90.61	88.92
Talent development program	91.71	92.22	93.08	91.71
Faculty building	92.22	90.13	93.07	92.22

3.3 Research and Stability of the Design and Stability of the Information Talent Training System

The process of talent analysis is a complex process, and it is necessary to dynamically optimize and judge talents. The dynamic judgment process of talents involves the promotion of practical ability, practical knowledge and their own knowledge structure. Therefore, the dynamic judgment process is also a complex condition, which should be optimized and diversified analysis completed. Verify the accuracy of knowledge embedding, the research scheme is compared with the divide and conquer algorithm, and the research scheme of the information talent training system design is shown in Fig. 2.

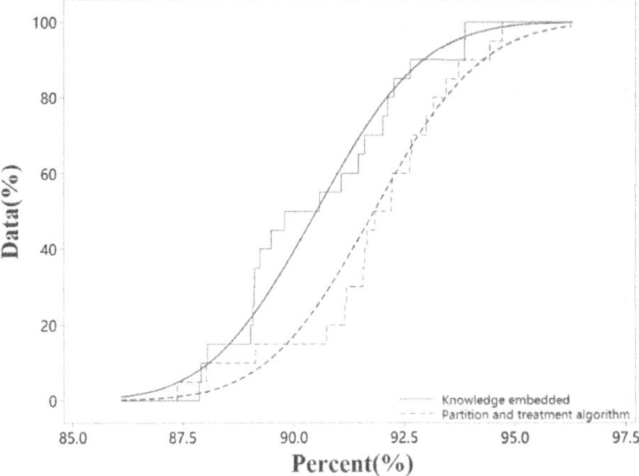

Fig. 2. Research on the design of information talent training system with different algorithms

The data and the chart in Fig. 2, The dynamic change process, as well as the analysis and correlation between indexes and curvature, also present complex problems. In order to make in-depth judgment, it is necessary to verify and identify the effectiveness of the distribution of talents and the weights of talents. Then improve the comprehensive analysis level of talents. Specific analysis results are shown in Fig. 3.

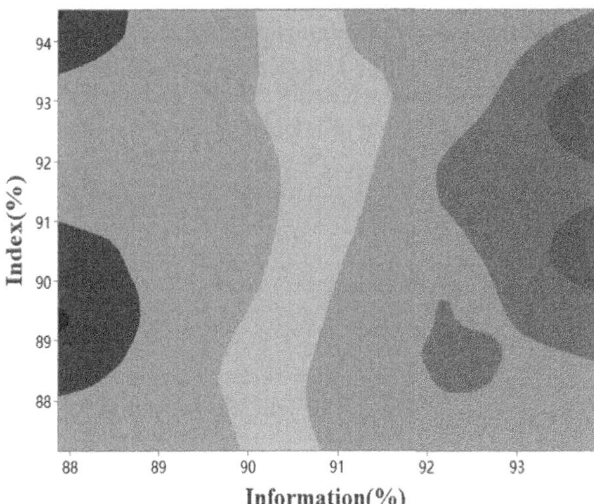

Fig. 3. Research on the design of information-based talent training system embedded in knowledge

Figure 3 shows the distribution of talents is polarized, which shows that in the process of talent cultivation, ineffective talents should be removed. Let effective talent and higher value talent be highlighted. In the overall cultivation process of talents, the phenomenon of talent polarization can eliminate talents, and then provide more talents. Comprehensive results in talent. In the process of elimination, targeted testing of technical knowledge can be carried out to make up for its shortcomings, so as to optimize the integrity of talents. Results. In the case of the differentiation of the two sentences, we can teach students in accordance with their aptitude and cultivate talents from person to person. And realize and improve the training effect of talents.The specific talent training results are shown in Table 2.

Table 2. Rational comparison of different methods of information talent training system design and research

Algorithm	The cultivation of basic knowledge	Cultivation of practical ability	Cultivation of comprehensive effects	Holistic cultivation results
Knowledge embedding	93.87	93.73	90.50	90.50
Divide and conquer algorithm	92.02	91.57	89.92	94.23

The results of the above analysis show that in the process of talent cultivation, all indicators meet the requirements, indicating that in-depth judgment in comprehensive ability, knowledge points and knowledge structure can realize the optimization of talent cultivation, talent structure and optimization, and complete the comprehensive analysis of talents. In order to further find the content of talent training, quantify the overall optimization results and talent training conditions, form a correlation, and complete the comprehensive analysis and judgment of talents. The specific talent training process is shown in Fig. 4.

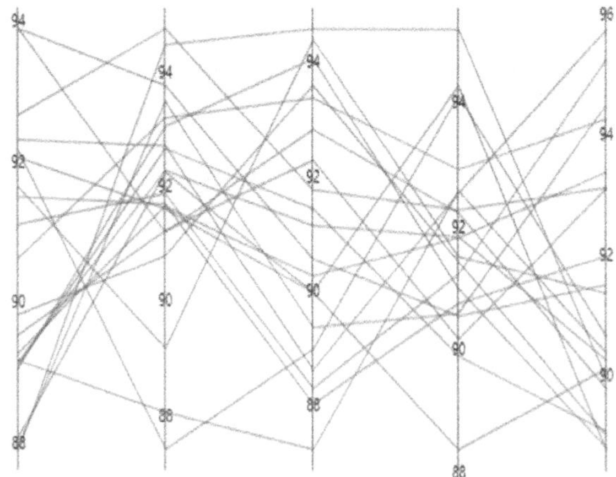

Fig. 4 Comparative study of the research scheme of the algorithm

From Fig. 4, In the process of comprehensive analysis of talents and comprehensive condition judgment, it also belongs to the holistic analysis of talents. In the process of overall judgment and overall optimization of talents, the overall adjustment of related talents and the diversified analysis of talents are also realized, which can complete the diversified result judgment of talents, and realize teaching students in accordance with their aptitude, which varies from person to person and from place to place. In addition, talents are also carried out. Comprehensive judgment and analysis results to realize the mapping of diversified indicators and diversified contents of talents. Lay the technology for talent cultivation, talent association and later application of talents.

4 Conclusion

The process of talent cultivation is a complex process, and talent cultivation is a dynamic process. It is a complex content to analyze and cultivate talents' knowledge points, practical abilities and comprehensive indicators. How to judge effectively, improve the rationality of its analysis results and verify the comprehensiveness of the results has become the focus of current research. Therefore, in the process of talent training, talent planning should be carried out. The promotion of talents, whether talents are effective or not, and the rational use of talents are also the focus of research. The results of this paper show that in the process of embedded knowledge training, talents are polarized, but the compound rate of talent training reaches more than 80%, and the accuracy of talent compound improves by 20%. The promotion rate and promotion effect of talents have been remarkable. Therefore, in the process of multi-index analysis and multi-content judgment of talents, the integrated judgment of talents is realized. However, the research results of this paper also have some shortcomings, mainly because there is some irrationality in the process of talent planning. There are differences between trend analysis and talent case analysis, which will make up for the above analysis deficiencies in the future.

Acknowledgements. Jiangsu University philosophy and social science research project (source), Research on training of applied undergraduate engineering management information talents based on knowledge embedding (name), 2023SJYB1719 (No.).

References

1. Hou, X., Zhou, X., Han, Z., Jiang, Y.: Research on the training model of mechanical and electrical innovation talents based on system thinking equipment manufacturing technology (5), 196–1999 (2022)
2. Sui, S., Zhang, G., Liu, H.: Exploring the blended teaching model of tax law courses based on the goal of cultivating applied talents. China Manage. Inf. **26**(9), 225–229 (2023)
3. Jie, S.: Research on the curriculum reform of management information systems in applied private undergraduate universities computer application abstracts **39**(11), 10–12 (2023)
4. Xu, Y.: Research on talent training mode of traditional culture education in engineering application-oriented undergraduate colleges—based on information technology, from the perspective of internet plus+morality cultivation. Sci. Educ. Guide (5), 3 (2022)

5. Zhu, L.: Exploration of database principle teaching reform under the applied talent training model technology wind (22), 131–133 (2022)
6. Liu, F., Han, Y.: Research on key technologies for network security of railway design enterprise management information system railway computer applications **32**(11), 68–72 (2023)
7. Huang, D., Fan, X.: Exploration of teaching methods for linear algebra based on application examples. Educ. Prog. **13**(11), 6 (2023)
8. Yu, S., Gan, X., Luo, L., Guo, Q., Zheng, Q., Bian, C.: The role of Internet plus+317 care mobile app information platform education in improving the implementation rate of postpartum contraception and reproductive health. Int. J. Nurs. **42**(23), 4301–4303 (2023)
9. Luo, J., Zhang, R., Dong, S., Yang, J., Li, X.: Research on the current situation and construction model of grassland informatization construction in China. J. Grassland **31**(11), 3227–3232 (2023)
10. Lin, J., Zhou, Z., Pan, C.: Strategic thinking on the reform of applied talent training model and curriculum system construction in undergraduate colleges knowledge economy (2022)
11. Chen, L.: Reform of the training mode for financial management talents in universities under the information environment (17), 2 (2022)
12. Wang, W., Huang, S.: Research on the three integration training model for practicing ability of engineering management applied talents under the background of building informatization—based on the practical analysis of Guilin aerospace industry college educational observation **12**(1), 4 (2023)
13. Zhou, X.: A study on the training model of applied undergraduate talents based on the integration of competition and certification courses—taking the engineering management major of S school in Shanghai as an example Jiangsu business theory (9), 119–121 (2022)

Application of Network Platform in Intelligence Education

Design and Implementation of the Network Education Resource Database System in Colleges and Universities

Lulu Wang[1](✉) and Linlin Wu[2]

[1] School of Chinese Classics, Xiamen Institute of Technology, Xiamen, Fujian, China
935748819@qq.com

[2] Research and Discipline Department, Xiamen Institute of Technology, Xiamen, Fujian, China
wulinlin@xit.edu.cn

Abstract. Network education resources are comprehensive contents and resources for systematic and learning. However, the comprehensiveness and application degree of each resource have a significant effect on educational effect. However, there are problems in the current realization and system design of network education resources in colleges and universities, so it is necessary to use intelligent analysis methods to carry out overall planning and promotion. The results show that improving the analysis method through online educational resources and system settings can effectively improve the educational effect, and the improvement range is more than 20%, which can make the satisfaction of the network interest rate reduction effect reach more than 85%. Therefore, through the network education and system setting in colleges and universities, comprehensive analysis can be realized, and the analysis effect and content can be improved.

Keywords: Biological behavior phenomenon · Universities · Education · System design · Generators

1 Introduction

Educational resources, network resources and systematic comprehensive analysis have significant effects on educational level and educational results. However, how to conduct educational analysis and comprehensive analysis? It is necessary to make a comprehensive judgment in combination with the actual needs, and at the same time, it is necessary to make a systematic setting according to the integrity and diversity of education [1, 2]. The information content of the database should be optimized for the overall conditions and structure of the information [3]. At the same time, it is necessary to analyze the overall action and comprehensiveness of education to enhance the effect of educational upgrading [4, 5]. At the same time, we should also improve the comprehensiveness of education, the effect of education, theoretical ability and practical ability [6]. Optimize the diversified analysis and form the overall planning of the education system [7]. In the process of overall judgment and multivariate analysis of the education system, it is

B. Brik and S. Nazir (Eds.): BigIoT-EDU 2024, LNICST 660, pp. 207–216, 2026.
https://doi.org/10.1007/978-3-032-18628-7_22

also necessary to deepen and excavate the diversified contents and levels of education [8], and their related values and characteristics. Therefore, in the process of educational analysis and diversified judgment, it is necessary to integrate the original system with the help of intelligent analysis methods [9, 10].

2 Related Concepts

2.1 The Whale Algorithm is Described Mathematically.

The integrity of educational content is $\mathrm{y_i}$, A pluralistic analysis of education is $\mathrm{z_i}$, and Associated content as well as associated resources is $\mathrm{tol}\left(\mathrm{y_i} \cdot \mathrm{t_{ij}}\right)$ is shown in Eq. (1).

$$\lim_{x\to\infty}\left(y_i \cdot t_{ij}\right) = \frac{-b \pm \sqrt{b^2 - 4ac}}{2a} y_{ij} \geq \max\left(t_{ij} \div 2\right) \tag{1}$$

In the process of educational planning, the characteristics, contents and points of education are excavated for overall optimization, and at the same time, educational resources are deeply excavated and judged (2).

$$\max(t_{ij}) = \partial\left(t_{ij}^2 + z \cdot t_{ij}\right) \succ \sqrt{2}\left(\sum t_{ij} + Jin\right) \tag{2}$$

The relevance content of education, diversity and plurality of content of education, and the mining of educational content are the key points of comprehensive analysis and diversification analysis. However, in the process of comprehensive judgment and diversified analysis of education, it is also necessary to realize the diversified analysis and judgment of educational resources and contents. Specific judgment process is $F(t_i \approx 0)$ as shown by Eq. (3).

$$F(d_i) = \frac{n!}{r!(n-r)!} \sum t_i \cap \xi \cdot \sqrt{2} \to \oint y_i \cdot 7 \tag{3}$$

2.2 Selection of Techniques for Safeguarding and Accessing Resources Scheme

Dig deep into the diversified conditions and integrity of education, and make an in-depth analysis of the content and diversified indicators of education is $g(t_i)$, The overall planning of education, the integration of content and the diversified content of education need to be constructed to construct corresponding data and results. The specific construction process is shown in Formula (4).

$$g(t_i) = \ddot{x} \cdot z_i \prod F(d_i) \frac{dy}{dx} - w_i \Phi \begin{pmatrix} a_{11}\ a_{12}\ a_{13} \\ a_{21}\ a_{22}\ a_{23} \\ a_{31}\ a_{32}\ a_{33} \end{pmatrix} \tag{4}$$

To form comprehensive educational conditions for educational content and educational results, it is also necessary to set the limit of educational content and optimize the overall educational content, systems and educational content optimization results is shown in Eq. (5).

$$\lim_{x \to \infty} g(t_i) + F(d_i) \leq \cap mit \ \max(t_{ij}) \tag{5}$$

Through multi-content, holistic judgment and comprehensive analysis, this paper verifies the comparison and mapping of feature points of educational resources, and constructs the changes of feature points of educational resources in Eq. (6).

$$\int g(t_i) + F(d_i) \leftrightarrow \sqrt{b^2 - hit \cdot ac}\left(\sum t_{ij} + Tir\right) \tag{6}$$

2.3 Analysis of Techniques for Safeguarding and Accessing Resources Scheme

The comprehensive analysis of education and the comparison of educational resources and education need conditional constraints. Generally, in the process of system setup analysis, it is divided into two types: input and output, and input and output need to build a matrix. The specific content in the process of building the matrix is $No(t_i)$ shown in Eq. (7).

$$No(t_i) = \frac{g(t_i) + F(d_i)}{mean\left(\sum t_{ij} + 4\right)} \begin{pmatrix} 1 & 0 \\ 0 & 1 \end{pmatrix} \tag{7}$$

Among them, is $\frac{g(t_i)+F(d_i)}{mean(\sum t_{ij}+4)} \leq 1$ specified that the scheme must be $Zh(t_i)$ suggested; in Eq. (8).

$$Zh(t_i) = \lim_{x \to \infty} \left[\sum g(t_i) + F(d_i)\right] \lim_{x \to \infty} \tag{8}$$

Analyze the accuracy judgment of industrialized education and the comprehensive application strength judgment of education to verify students' academic performance, educational resources, educational conditions and the actual situation of employment permits, and make overall planning. It is also necessary to obtain the minimum value in the planning process, so as to reduce the cost in educational analysis. Data redundancy improves the accuracy of educational analysis, as stated in Eq. (9).

$$Ter(t_i) = \frac{\min[\sum g(t_i) + F(d_i)]}{\sum g(t_i) + F(d_i)} \times 100\% \tag{9}$$

Educational resource analysis and holistic judgment should have certain randomness, random process, and holistic planning and analysis should be carried out. Random content should be based on the objective conditions of educational needs is $randon(t_i)$ as Eq. (10).

$$accur(t_i) = \frac{\min[\sum g(t_i) + F(d_i)]}{Pio \sum g(t_i) + F(d_i)} + \int randon(t_i) \tag{10}$$

3 Techniques for Safeguarding and Accessing Resources Optimization Approach

In the process of comprehensive analysis, holistic planning and diversified judgment of educational content, the content of holistic planning of educational resources and the importance of comprehensive cooperation in education need to be verified. In the process of verification, the data content, resource content and database content are mainly judged, and the related contents are also planned. In the process of planning, analysis and comprehensive judgment, the content conditions, implementation and overall structure also need to be optimized. Therefore, it is necessary to make judgments through actual specific analysis and specific situations. In the process of judgment, it is necessary to plan the content structure of educational resources, the distribution of resources and the satisfaction of resources, and realize the standardized analysis, so as to meet the system's information input and output and comprehensive analysis of information.

4 Practical Examples of Techniques for Safeguarding and Accessing Resources

4.1 Introduction to the Techniques for Safeguarding and Accessing Resources

Students from freshman to sophomore are analyzed as the research object, which mainly makes judgment research based on mathematical achievements and mathematical contents, and the effects include academic achievements, students' theory and ability to apply practice. At the same time, the obtained data should be standardized and analyzed. The results of the standardized analysis are shown in Table 1.

Table 1. Techniques for safeguarding and accessing resources techniques for safeguarding and accessing resources requirements.

Scope of application	Grade	Student's academic performance	The comprehensive effect of students
College teachers and students	I	16.81	39.82
	II	47.79	59.29
Education managers	I	38.05	50.44
	II	56.64	45.13
Educational technicians	I	52.21	37.17
	II	16.81	39.82

Analyze students' learning situation, judge students' academic achievements, actual situation and students' abilities, and draw a correlation diagram between students' academic achievements and abilities is shown in Fig. 1.

The analysis in Table 1 shows that there is a logical relationship among the data in the process of correlation analysis of students' academic achievements. There are also

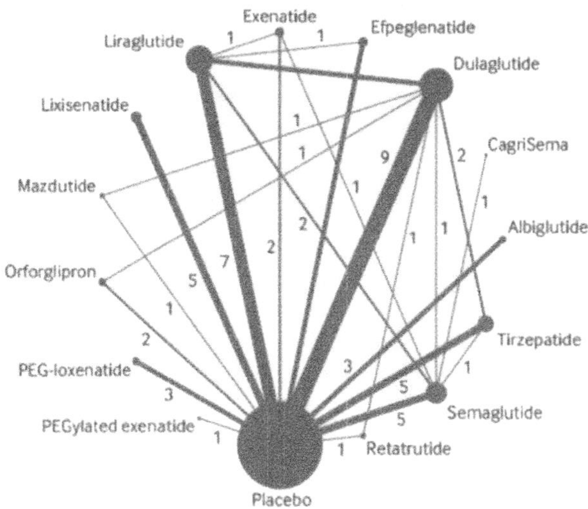

Fig. 1. Analysis process of techniques for safeguarding and accessing resources

specific differences in logical relations and contents. It shows that there are significant differences in the distribution, systematic utilization and comprehensive judgment of academic achievements. Therefore, it is necessary to optimize the specific content to improve students' learning effect.

4.2 Techniques for Safeguarding and Accessing Resources

Students' learning effect is a process of comprehensive analysis, diversified analysis and holistic judgment. However, whether students' learning effect can meet the requirements needs to be summarized as a whole. The holistic analysis process is shown in Table 2.

Table 2. The overall situation of the techniques for safeguarding and accessing resources scheme.

Category	Comprehensive judgment of students' academic performance	The deepening of results	Optimization of learning content
College teachers and students	78.64	81.55	77.67
Education managers	76.70	73.79	79.61
Educational technicians	79.61	78.64	79.61

4.3 Techniques for Safeguarding and Accessing Resources and Stability

In the process of analyzing students' academic achievements, we should also judge students' learning ability and the role of the system. It is mainly reflected in two aspects, the auxiliary role and effect of the system. Students' learning ability, the need for practical knowledge is shown in Fig. 2.

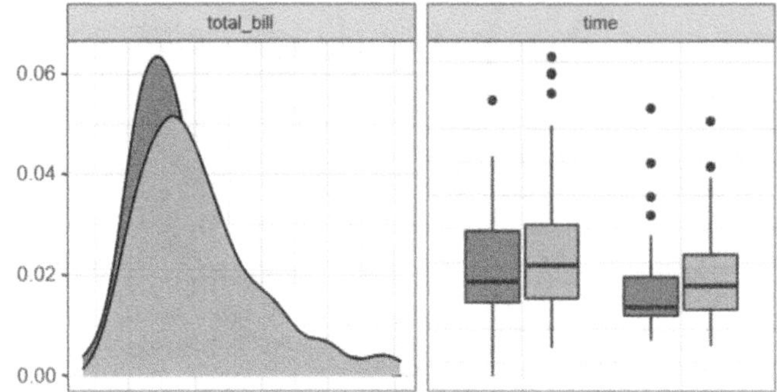

Fig. 2. Evaluation model of aging performance of different algorithms

Figure 2 shows that In the process of analysis, it will be found that students' learning ability and systematic participation show the same changes. Moreover, the change between them is relatively large, and the improvement of students' learning ability is relatively good. On the whole, the improvement degree is greater than 2%, indicating that students' learning ability has been significantly improved in the process of system auxiliary line and optimization, and the analysis results will be summarized. The summary results are shown in Table 3.

Table 3 Compares the accuracy of several techniques for safeguarding and accessing resources.

Algorithm	Students' comprehensive analysis effect	On the ability to transform practice	Comprehensive comparison	Judgment of the overall result
Whale algorithm	59.29	46.90	43.36	80.58
Grey Wolf algorithm	37.17	58.41	44.25	78.64
P	53.10	48.67	37.17	73.79

Table 3 shows that the comprehensive analysis, diversified analysis and authenticity result analysis of life are all greater than 40%, and some analysis contents are relatively good, which shows that in the process of learning analysis and overall planning, the role of students can relatively meet the actual requirements, optimize students' learning and improve their teaching effect, as shown in Fig. 3.

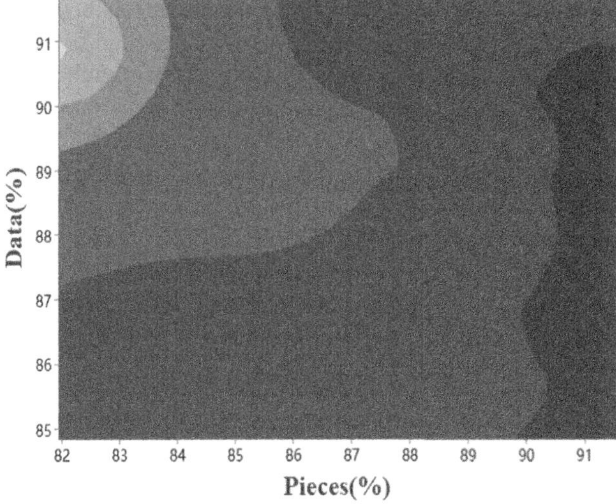

Fig. 3. Techniques for safeguarding and accessing resources of Whale algorithm

Figure 3 shows that Students' learning situation is analyzed distributively, and students' overall analysis effect and analysis situation are studied through judgment. The results show that in the process of comprehensive analysis, the content of students is relatively good and meets the actual requirements. Moreover, students' overall planning and students' overall content also meet the requirements, which shows that in the process of comprehensive judgment and comprehensive content analysis, all indicators are evenly distributed and gradually improved. This shows that under the action of auxiliary system, students' learning effect has been significantly optimized.

4.4 Rationality of Techniques for Safeguarding and Accessing Resources

Investigate and analyze knowledge points, investigate the results between knowledge points, and judge students' learning situation and content through the contents of each chapter, so as to judge the auxiliary nature of the system. The effect of the system action is verified by color contrast in Fig. 4.

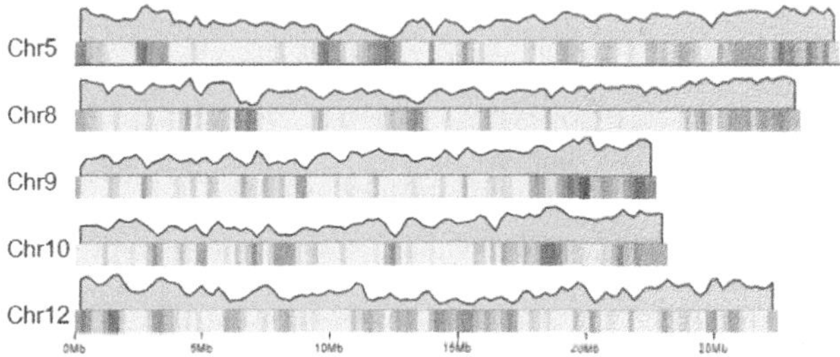

Fig. 4. Distribution pattern evaluation across multiple chromosomes

Figure 4 shows that in the process of systematic analysis, there is a gradual change between red and blue, and students' academic performance changes evenly in chapters. Although there is a trend of up and down distribution, the overall change is relatively stable.

4.5 Validity of Techniques for Safeguarding and Accessing Resources

Academic achievements also need to be judged continuously, and the continuous increase can judge the evaluation results and effects among academic achievements. Through the continuity of academic performance and the overall effect of verification, students' comprehensiveness can be improved. Analyze students' holistic planning and holistic content. Specifically is shown in Fig. 5.

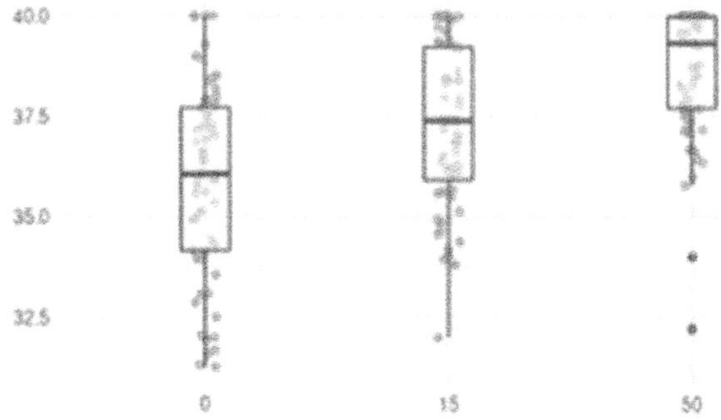

Fig. 5. Techniques for safeguarding and accessing resources of different algorithms

Figure 5 shows that when students analyze at different stages, they will find that their academic performance is on the rise. Moreover, in the process of color contrast, it will be found that the auxiliary role of the system has also played a significant role in improving academic performance. This shows that in the process of comprehensive judgment of students' achievements, the optimization of the system can improve the learning effect, and at the same time, the learning effect should be summarized. The summary process is mainly to analyze whether the continuous analysis results can effectively improve the function, the improvement process and the summary results. As shown in the Table 4.

Table 4. Compares the efficacy of several techniques for safeguarding and accessing resources.

Algorithm	The comprehensive effect of students' academic performance	Improve the holistic content of academic performance	Holistic planning of life	Holistic judgment of students' academic achievement
Whale algorithm	74.76	81.55	76.70	77.67

(continued)

Table 4. (*continued*)

Algorithm	The comprehensive effect of students' academic performance	Improve the holistic content of academic performance	Holistic planning of life	Holistic judgment of students' academic achievement
Grey Wolf algorithm	73.79	81.55	81.55	79.61
P	79.61	75.73	72.82	76.70

Table 4 shows that through comprehensive analysis and the overall judgment of students' academic performance, it is verified whether there is uniformity and logical relationship among the analysis results, and whether the logical relationship can be optimized as a whole. By continuously tracking the teaching content, teaching effect, academic performance and practical ability, and analyzing and judging through the form of points, it will be found that the analysis results show a trend of obvious distribution boundaries, indicating that the results are not correlated, and the results are significantly representative, as illustrated in Fig. 6.

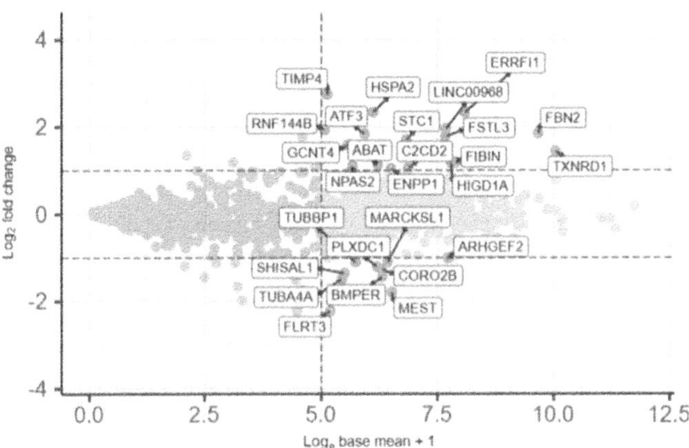

Fig. 6. Whale algorithm techniques for safeguarding and accessing RESOURCES

Figure 6 shows that this academic achievement shows a change from simplicity to complexity, and in the process of complex change, there is a gradual trend in the correlation between data, the degree of change of data and the overall structure of data, but the overall change still exists. The distribution of securities shows that the logic and logical points between each data are also evenly up and down. Therefore, it is proved that educational resources have been effectively utilized in the process of analysis and system optimization.

5 Conclusion

The optimization and judgment of the integrity of educational resources are the main contents in the teaching process. However, how to effectively improve its educational effect, optimize the original educational form and enhance its practical ability has become the focus of research. Therefore, in terms of overall judgment and comprehensive analysis, it is necessary to use intelligent analysis methods for planning. The results of this paper show that through intelligent analysis method, it can have a significant impact on the education system, database and data resources, with an increase of more than 40%, and promote the overall level of education resources, with a travel rate of more than 35%. It shows that intelligent aircraft law plays a major role in the management of educational resources and the overall judgment process. However, there are some shortcomings in my research, mainly due to the deviation between the survey samples and the survey data.

References

1. Zang, X., Wang, Z., Guo, L.: A data-driven modeling based reactive power and voltage optimization control method for wind farms CN202210108334.5 (2022)
2. Bai, W., Liu, Y., Wang, X., Happy, Zhang, S.: A data-driven method for identifying the optimal pitch angle of wind turbines. Electr. Power Sci. Eng. (009), 038 (2022)
3. Lei, D.: Design of speed control system for marine diesel generators ship science and technology (2023)
4. Yue, W., Wang, H., Wu, T., Li, J.: Non-contact shaking pulse generator and method based on programmable nano friction power generation mechanism CN115912982A (2023)
5. Takada, M., Takazawa plows flat.: Engine driven generator CN116263141A (2023)
6. Xie, G., Li, D., Liu, Y., Xu, R., Zhan, H., Xia, H., et al.: An online monitoring method and system for the margin of generator safety phase advance capability CN202010915154.9 (2022)
7. Zhang, C., Zhang, S.: A method for identifying abnormal bearings at the driving end of wind turbine generators based on SCADA temperature data bearing (006), 000 (2022)
8. Wang, H., Sun, W., Zhang, X., He, L.: Research on fault diagnosis method for wind turbine gearbox based on optimized VMD composite multi-scale dispersion entropy and LSTM. J. Solar Energy (004), 043 (2022)
9. Zhu, T., Zhao, S., Cao, Q.: Calculation of generator loss of excitation protection setting based on admittance plane. Electr. Eng. (3), 34–37 (2023)
10. Qiu, J., Yang, D., Cai, G., Wang, L., Duan, F.: A data-driven damping modulation strategy for AC/DC hybrid power systems. J. Power Syst. Autom. **35**(1), 59–67 (2023)

Scientific Research Construction and Management Based on Network Platform

Yang Song(✉)

Jilin Communications Polytechnic, Jilin, China
297145462@qq.com

Abstract. A major issue with the scientific research information management system is the wrong appraisal of results, which has prompted a reform of scientific research management in response to the widespread use of Internet technology. The conventional management mode cannot accomplish the efficient management level in the scientific research information management system, and the assessment is inappropriate. Consequently, this paper suggests an AI-powered network algorithm for assessing and evaluating technological and scientific advancements in management. Firstly, the deep learning theory is utilized to assess scientific researchers, and the indicators are split according to the management evaluation needs to eliminate the interference elements in management evaluation. Following this, a management evaluation scheme is developed and the outcomes of this scheme are thoroughly examined using the principles of deep learning theory, which has been applied to the assessment of services related to technical and scientific innovation. When compared to more conventional management models, MATLAB simulations reveal that intelligent network algorithms outperform them in terms of management evaluation efficiency and accuracy when it comes to services related to technological innovation and scientific research.

Keywords: Scientific research construction · Web platform · Scientific and technological innovation · Management

1 Introduction

Scientific research network platforms are increasingly being built as a result of the fast advancement of information technology. The goal of the research network platform is to create a shared [1], interactive, and readily available system for managing data, information, and knowledge in order to encourage academics from diverse domains to work together and innovate. When it comes to building a platform for scientific research networks, information technology not only offers technical assistance, but also offers limitless optimization opportunities [2]. In this piece, we'll take a look at how IT improves the building blocks of research network platforms, which in turn fosters cooperation and the exchange of information in the scientific community.

A. *Application of information technology in the construction of scientific research network platform*

B. Brik and S. Nazir (Eds.): BigIoT-EDU 2024, LNICST 660, pp. 217–226, 2026.
https://doi.org/10.1007/978-3-032-18628-7_23

1. Online storage and processing

Storage, processing, networking, databases, and other services may be made available via the use of elastic, efficient, and shared computer resources through the use of cloud computing [3]. In the building of the scientific research network platform, cloud computing may offer elastic computing power, enable large-scale data processing and storage, and high concurrent network access, therefore boosting the performance and stability of the scientific research network platform [4].

2. Technologies for big data

The scientific research network platform has amassed a considerable quantity of data, including scientific research publications, experimental data, project information, etc., which are of tremendous relevance for the joint creativity of researchers [5]. With the help of big data technologies, researchers can quickly and easily process and analyze this data, uncover useful insights, and make better decisions.

3. Technology for social networking

By facilitating communication and interaction, social network technology can enhance scientific research network platforms, encouraging researchers to work together and share information. As an example, scientific research teams may benefit from social networking technologies by creating a platform that allows team members to easily communicate and collaborate.

4. Technology based on artificial intelligence

Intelligent services, such intelligent question answering and intelligent suggestion, may be provided by artificial intelligence technology for the scientific research network platform. The use of AI allows for the provision of tailored services, which in turn increases the efficiency of scientific research by facilitating the rapid acquisition of relevant information and knowledge [6].

B. *Optimization of information technology for the construction of scientific research network platform*

1. Make the platform for scientific research network more efficient and stable.

With the use of cloud computing, the scientific research network platform may access storage and computing resources more efficiently, which boosts the platform's speed and reliability. Furthermore, cloud computing's elastic resource scheduling feature may automatically scale up computer resources during times of high scientific research demand [7].

2. Enhance data processing and analysis capabilities

The scientific research network platform can now handle and analyze huge amounts of data effectively with the use of big data technologies, allowing for the extraction of vital information and knowledge. This has the potential to increase the speed and efficiency of scientific research while also helping academics find new research trends and directions more easily [8].

3. Encourage collaboration and information sharing among academics

The research network platform may facilitate interaction and collaboration among researchers by using social networking technologies, which creates an accessible and participatory platform. Because of this, research teams can work together more effectively, which in turn boosts both the quantity and quality of their findings [9].

4. Give wise, individual assistance.

The scientific research network platform can now provide intelligent tailored services, such intelligent question answering and intelligent suggestion, thanks to the integration of AI technology. This may assist researchers have quicker access to the information and expertise they require, boosting the efficiency and quality of their research [10].

C. *The impact of information technology on the optimization of scientific research network platform*

Incorporating IT optimization into the scientific research network platform has several benefits, including a more stable and efficient platform overall, better data processing and analysis capabilities, easier researcher-to-researcher communication and collaboration, and more tailored intelligent service provision. The method and outcomes of scientific research are impacted by these improvements, which also enhance the quality and efficiency of scientific research while promoting collaboration and the sharing of information.

Cloud computing, big data, social networks, and artificial intelligence are some of the topics covered in this article as they pertain to the development of a platform for scientific research networks. All of these tweaks make the scientific research network platform more reliable and fast, better at processing and analyzing data, easier for researchers to talk to each other and work together, and more capable of providing intelligent, tailored services. The process and outcomes of scientific research have been positively affected by these improvements, which have also increased the effectiveness and quality of scientific research while fostering collaboration and the exchange of information.

An integral aspect of the overall scientific research management system, scientific research project management encompasses the primary components of scientific research information release, scientific research project management, and the management of scientific research results, among others. However, in the process of management assessment, there is an issue of low accuracy in the management evaluation program, which has a certain influence on scientific research management. Some researchers claim that the use of intelligent network algorithms to the analysis of scientific research information management system may effectively evaluate management evaluation schemes and give commensurate assistance for management evaluation. On this premise, an intelligent network method is presented to optimize the management evaluation scheme and test the efficacy of the model.

2 Related Works

A. *Mathematical description of intelligent network algorithms*

Based on management evaluation indicators, the intelligent network algorithm optimizes the management evaluation scheme using management theory, find the unqualified values in the scientific research information management system is x_i, and integrate the management evaluation scheme is a, and finally judge the feasibility of the scientific research information management system is p_i, calculated as shown in formula (1).

$$p_i = x_i - ab \tag{1}$$

Equation (2) shows the judgment of outliers among them.

$$x_i - ab = \prod_{i=1}^{n} \theta + u \tag{2}$$

In order to enhance the management assessment of the scientific research information system, the intelligent network algorithm integrates the benefits of management theory with the scientific research information management system for quantification.

Suppose I. The management evaluation requirement is y, that the management evaluation program is W_{ij}^2, the efficiency of the management evaluation program is c_i, and the management evaluation program judgment function is $R(t_i)$, as shown in Eq. (3).

$$R(t_i) = W_{ij}^2 - y + c_i \tag{3}$$

B. *Selection of scientific research information system programs*

Hypothesis II. The function of the scientific research information management system is $Y(v_i)$, the weight coefficient is P_i, Consequently, as shown in Eq. (4), the management assessment calls for an unqualified system for managing scientific research information.

$$Y(v_i) = P_i + y - t \tag{4}$$

Equation (5) shows that a complete function of scientific information can be obtained by combining Hypotheses I and II.

$$R(t_i) + Y(v_i) \leq x_i - ab \tag{5}$$

In order to increase the efficacy of management evaluations, all data has to be normalized and the outcomes are indicated in Eq. (6).

$$R(t_i) + Y(v_i) \leftrightarrow \prod_{i=1}^{n} \theta + u \tag{6}$$

C. *Analysis of management evaluation programmed*
C. *Analysis of management evaluation programmed*

Before carrying out the intelligent network algorithm, it is necessary to conduct a multi-dimensional analysis of the management evaluation scheme and map the management evaluation requirements to the scientific research information management system database and eliminate the unqualified management evaluation scheme is $J(a_i)$. According to Eq. (6), the anomaly evaluation scheme can be proposed, and the results are shown in Eq. (7).

$$J(a_i) = \frac{R(t_i) + Y(v_i)}{\prod_{i=1}^{n} \theta + u} \tag{7}$$

Among them, it is $\frac{R(t_i)+Y(v_i)}{\prod_{i=1}^{n} \theta+u} \leq 1$, stated that the scheme needs to be proposed, otherwise the scheme needs to be integrated into it is $N(x_i)$, and the result is shown in Eq. (8).

$$N(x_i) = \min[\sum R(t_i) + Y(v_i)] \tag{8}$$

After a thorough analysis of the scientific research information management system, the management evaluation scheme's threshold and index weight are set to guarantee the intelligent network algorithm's accuracy. The scientific research information management system is a systematic test management evaluation scheme, which has to be innovatively assessed. When managing data for scientific studies, if the distribution is non-normal, its management evaluation scheme will be affected is $No(y_i)$, reducing the accuracy of the overall management evaluation is $\lim b$, and the calculation result is shown in Eq. (9).

$$\lim b = \frac{\min[\sum R(t_i) + Y(v_i)]}{\sum R(t_i) + Y(v_i)} \times 100\% \tag{9}$$

In accordance with the factual facts, the scientific research information system scheme displays a multi-dimensional distribution, as shown by the survey management evaluation scheme. This kind of study is considered to be very analytical since the scientific research information system is not directed, which suggests that the plan of the system is quite random. If the stochastic function of the research information management system is $arcsec(x_i)$, then the calculation of Eq. (9) can be expressed as formula (10).

$$\lim b = \frac{\min[\sum R(t_i) + Y(v_i)]}{\sum R(t_i) + Y(v_i)} \times 100\% + arcsec(x_i) \tag{10}$$

Of these, the scientific research information management system satisfies typical standards; this is largely attributable to the fact that the management theory modifies the system, gets rid of unnecessary and duplicate schemes, and enhances the default scheme, resulting in a robust dynamic correlation throughout the management evaluation scheme.

3 Optimization Strategy of Scientific Research Information Management System

The intelligent network algorithm adopts the random optimization strategy for the scientific research information management system and adjusts the parameters of scientific researchers to realize the optimization of the scientific research information management system. A number of management evaluation levels are used by the intelligent network algorithm to randomly select different schemes for the scientific research information management system. Management evaluation schemes with varying degrees of evaluation are optimized and studied iteratively. We evaluate the management evaluation levels of several schemes once the optimization analysis is finished, and we record the best scientific research information management system.

4 Results and Discussion

A. *Introduction to management evaluation*

Table 1 shows the management evaluation scheme for the specific scientific research information management system; the paper uses the scientific research information management system in complex situations as its research object; the test lasts 12 h; and there are 12 paths.

Table 1. Scientific research management evaluation requirements

Scope of application	Grade	Scientific	Innovative
Information on scientific research results	I	78.54	38.04
	II	76.85	38.98
Research project information	I	76.11	37.38
	II	76.19	36.95
Share resource information	I	75.65	36.72
	II	80.14	37.75

The management evaluation process in Table 1. is shown in Fig. 1.

By comparing it to the conventional management mode, the intelligent network algorithm's management evaluation scheme is more in line with the actual management evaluation requirements. When it comes to the scientific research information management system's rationality and fluctuation range, the intelligent network algorithm outperforms the conventional mode. Figure 1 shows that the intelligent network algorithm's management evaluation scheme changes lead to better stability and higher management efficiency. Consequently, the intelligent network algorithm's management evaluation scheme, the scientific research information system scheme, the management evaluation scheme, and the summation stability are all superior.

B. *Scientific research information management system*

Information that is neither structural nor semi-structural, as well as information that is structural, make up the management evaluation scheme of an information management system for scientific research. After the pre-selection of intelligent network algorithm,

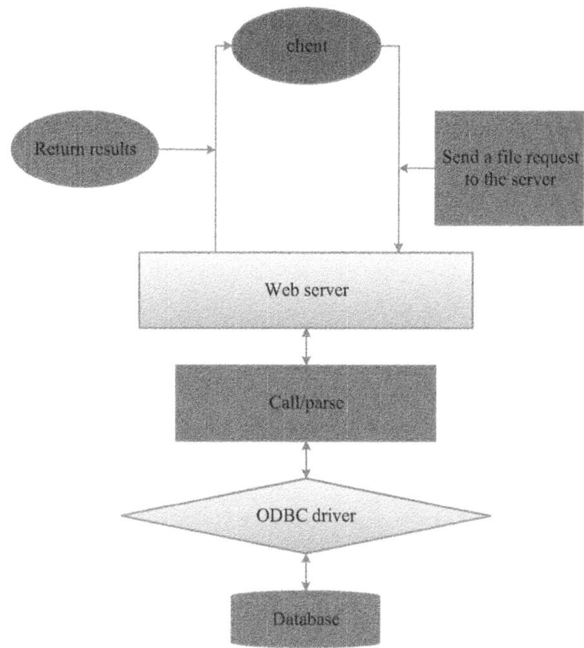

Fig. 1. The analysis process of the research information management system

the preliminary management evaluation scheme of scientific research information management system is generated, and the feasibility of the management evaluation scheme of scientific research information management system is assessed. In order to more correctly verify the innovation impact of scientific research information management system, pick scientific research information management system with various management evaluation levels, and manage the evaluation scheme, as indicated in Table 2.

Table 2. The overall situation of the research information system program

Category	Efficient	Accuracy
Teacher management	80.15	83.07
Student management	78.38	83.64
Scientific instrument management	81.59	81.90
Mean	81.65	81.68
X^6	38.28	39.01
P = 4.57		

C. *Research information system and stability of management evaluation*

By contrasting the management evaluation scheme (shown in Fig. 2) with the conventional management mode, we can confirm that the intelligent network method is accurate.

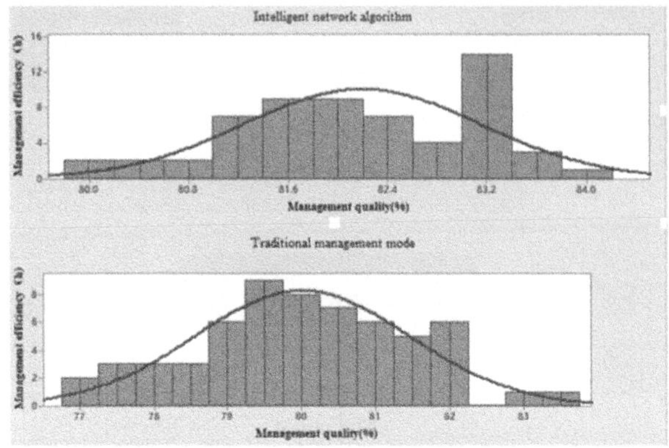

Fig. 2. Research information system with different algorithms

Figure 2 shows that the intelligent network algorithm's scientific research information system is higher than the traditional management mode's, but with a lower error rate. This suggests that the intelligent network algorithm's management evaluation is relatively stable, in contrast to the traditional mode's uneven evaluation. Table 3 displays the average management assessment scheme for the two methods mentioned before.

Table 3. Comparison of management evaluation accuracy of different methods

Algorithm	Research information System	Magnitude of change	Error
Intelligent network algorithms	90.76	91.28	0.52
Traditional management model	84.94	88.97	4.03
P	36.37	38.46	2.09

Table 3 shows that traditional management has poor scientific research information system stability and performance in terms of scientific research information management system. The scientific research information management system has changed a lot and has a high error rate. In comparison, intelligent network algorithms perform better and have higher scientific research information systems. Furthermore, the intelligent network algorithm's scientific research information system has an accuracy level of over 90.76 percent and has not changed much. To confirm its effectiveness and superiority, the intelligent network algorithm's general analysis was conducted.

The intelligent network algorithm improves the scientific research information management system by increasing the adjustment coefficient, setting the threshold for scientific researchers, and eliminating management evaluation schemes that fail to meet

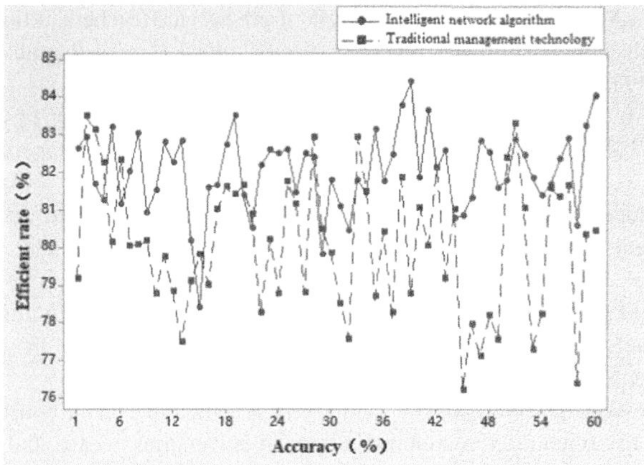

Fig. 3. Scientific research information system for intelligent network algorithm management evaluation

requirements (as seen in Fig. 3), making it far superior to the traditional management mode.

5 Conclusion

This study presents an intelligent network algorithm that integrates management theory in an effort to improve the current scientific research information management system, which is not optimal. Simultaneously, a group of academics is put together by doing extensive study on management assessment innovation and threshold innovation. Based on the findings, the intelligent network algorithm may enhance the reliability and consistency of the system for managing scientific research data, as well as perform an overall assessment of the system's administration. Realizing a more contemporary approach to managing scientific research information, raising the bar for scientific research management, and offering services related to technical and scientific innovation are all critically important.

References

1. Ambriz, G.S., Hernandez, A.Y., Ambriz, M.L.S.: Informational competencies: instrumentation of teaching strategies for their development, graduate students in administration sciences. Revista De Gestao E Secretariado-Gesec **14**(3), 3063–3096 (2023)
2. Araoz, E.G.E., Bautista-Quispe, J.A., Cordova-Rojas, L.M., Reyes, B.V., Chayna, E.T.: Scientific production of the thesis advisors of a public university in the peruvian amazon. Revista Universidad Y Sociedad **15**(3), 453–459 (2023)
3. Arslan, F.: Anxiety and attitudes of midwifery students toward scientific research. J. Balt. Sci. Educ. **22**(3), 381–392 (2023)
4. Boldyrev, V.A., Lisitsa, V.N., Baukin, V.G.: Scientific schools: analysis of data on indexed publications. Sociologia Nauki I Tehnologij-Sociol. Sci. Technol. **14**(1), 166–185 (2023)

5. Bozoglu, G.N., Yavuz, E.: The mediating role of pre-service teachers' attitudes towards scientific research. Pamukkale Universitesi Egitim Fakultesi Dergisi-Pamukkale University J. Educ. (58), 349 (2023)
6. Chen, C., Zhe, C., Zheng, Y. Y., Xiong, X., Xiao, T., Lu, X.F.: Evaluation of scientific research in universities based on the theories for sustainable competitive advantage. Sage Open, **13**(2) (2023)
7. Colen, L., Belderbos, R., Kelchtermans, S., Leten, B.: Many are called, few are chosen: the role of science in drug development decisions. J. Technol. Transf. (2023)
8. Corrales-Reyes, I.E., Villegas-Maestre, J.D., Valdes-Gamboa, L., Garcia-Raga, M., Veliz-Concepcion, O.L., Torres-Fernandez, L.S., Tusell-Hormigo, D., Viton-Castillo, A.A., Torrecilla-Venegas, R., Mejia, C.R.: Factors associated with interest in scientific research in dental students of six Cuban universities. Front. Educ. **8** (2023)
9. Guanglong, Z., Wei, S., Yongzhong, C., Guisheng, Z.: Thoughts on the construction and management of entity scientific research institutions in universities: a case study of international joint laboratory of Yangzhou University[J]. Volkswagen Standardiz. (21), 163–164 2020
10. Yaqing, M.: Useful exploration on the construction and management of scientific research and innovation teams in local universities in the new era——Review of "Construction and Management of Scientific Research and Innovation Teams in New Undergraduate Colleges"[J]. J. Shaanxi Preschool Normal Univ. **36**(08), 133 (2020)
11. Hyun-chul, Y.: Research on the construction and management of scientific research faculty in university research institutes[J]. Agrotechnic. Econ. **07**, 143 (2020)

Research and Implementation of Web-Based Foreign Language Learning System Platform

Sijia Tan(✉)

Shanghai Urban Construction Vocational College, Shanghai, China
sagayoga2023@163.com

Abstract. In the accelerating globalization today, language as a bridge of communication, its importance is self-evident. Foreign language learning is no longer limited to the traditional classroom education, and the networked learning mode is gradually becoming the mainstream. The big data, foreign language learning platform provides a rich and variety of resources and personalized services, enabling learners to learn anytime and anywhere, breaking the limitation of time and space. Networked foreign language learning not only improves the convenience of learning, but also improves the learning efficiency and effect through the functions of interactive communication, real-time feedback and adaptive learning. Moreover, it encourages self-driven and lifelong learning, providing equal learning opportunities for learners of different ages and backgrounds. The research platform can promote the development of foreign languages, integrate corresponding resources, the integration rate reaches 90%, and associate the optimized content to promote the overall change of content, and the correlation degree reaches 15%. Therefore, the research platform can realize the comprehensive analysis of foreign languages and improve the relationship effect.

Keywords: Computer technology · Network algorithms · Foreign language learning · System platform

1 Introduction

With the continuous growth of the online education market, the competition of foreign language learning platforms is becoming increasingly fierce. However, the existing platforms still have deficiencies in personalized teaching, integration of learning resources, user engagement, and learning effect tracking. Therefore, it is particularly necessary to study and develop a networked foreign language learning system with perfect functions and excellent user experience. The system should be able to provide customized learning path according to the abilities and needs of learners, and at the same time, dynamically adjust the learning content and methods through data analysis and intelligent algorithms, so as to improve the pertinence and efficiency of learning. In addition, with the popularization of new technologies such as 5G and artificial intelligence, foreign language learning platforms also need to constantly update their technical means to meet users'

B. Brik and S. Nazir (Eds.): BigIoT-EDU 2024, LNICST 660, pp. 227–236, 2026.
https://doi.org/10.1007/978-3-032-18628-7_24

pursuit of efficient, intelligent and interesting learning experience. Therefore, the study of the networked foreign language learning system is not only an inevitable trend of the development of educational technology, but also an urgent need to improve the quality and penetration rate of foreign language education.

The networked foreign language learning system platform adopts a service-oriented architecture (Service-Oriented Architecture, SOA) to improve the scalability and flexibility of the system. The architecture consists of multiple independent micro-services, each of which is responsible for specific functional modules, such as user management, course content, learning progress tracking, etc. These microservices communicate through the API interface, allowing the system to respond quickly to user needs and data changes. In addition, the platform uses cloud deployment that leverage distributed computing and storage resources to ensure high availability and scalability.

The front-end interface uses a modern Web development technology stack, including front-end frameworks. With HTML 5, CSS 3, and JavaScript, developers build an interactive, rich user interface for dynamic loading, real-time updates, and offline caching. Also, the front end integrates third-party libraries and API, such as Google Fonts for font beautification, Font Awesome for icons, and Axios for processing HTTP requests.

2 Related Works

A. *Comprehensive analysis of learning and resources*

The backend uses Node.js or Java Spring Boot as the main development framework to provide efficient data processing and business logic. RESTful API Design principles are used to build back-end services to ensure seamless connection with the front end. Use Express or Spring MVC as a routing controller to process HTTP requests and return the response. To achieve inter-service communication, message queues (such as RabbitMQ or Kafka) are used for asynchronous processing to improve system performance and maintainability. In addition, the authentication and authorization functions are implemented through JWT (JSON Web Tokens) to ensure the security of user data.

$$tol\frac{n!}{r!(n-r)!}\frac{1}{2}\left(y_i \cdot t_{ij}\right) = \lim_{x\to\infty} y_{ij} \geq \max(t_{ij} \div 2) \tag{1}$$

The correlation effect between comprehensive platform and resources is shown in Eq. (2).

$$\max(t_{ij}) = iintmean\left(\sum t_{ij} + 4\right) \tag{2}$$

The database uses relational database MySQL or non-relational database MongoDB, selected according to the characteristics of the data. For structured data such as user information and course content, it is suitable for using a relational database for storage and query. For unstructured or semi-structured data such as learning history, user behavior and other non-structured data, non-relational databases can provide better flexibility. The database design follows the principle of normalization, reducing redundant data and improving data consistency. At the same time, the index is used to optimize the query performance and adopt the library and table strategy to meet the challenge of large data volume. In addition, caching technologies such as Redis are used to cache the data of high-frequency access to further improve the system response speed.

$$F(d_i) = \frac{-b \pm \sqrt{b^2 - 4ac}}{2a} \cdot \sum t_i \cap \xi \cdot ointy_i \tag{3}$$

B. *Resource call plan and plan*

The user management module is the core component of the system, responsible for user registration, login, permission management and personal information maintenance. Users can register through their email or mobile phone number, and the system ensures the account security by verifying the uniqueness of user input. The login process adopts encrypted transmission to protect the user information security. User information includes name, age, learning goals, etc. This information helps the system to provide personalized learning advice for users. At the same time, the module also includes password retrieval, account activation, authority upgrade (such as upgrading from ordinary user to teacher) and other functions to meet the needs of different user groups.

$$g(t_i) = \ddot{x} \cdot z_i \cdot 7 \cdot \frac{1}{2} \frac{n!}{r!(n-r)!} \tag{4}$$

The course management module provides users with rich learning resources, covering different languages and different levels of courses.

$$iintg(t_i) + F(d_i) \leq \sum \max(t_{ij}) \tag{5}$$

The course is divided into elementary, intermediate and advanced courses, including grammar, vocabulary, listening, speaking, reading and writing. Teachers can upload teaching videos, audio, documents and quizzes, and the system automatically generates learning paths according to the course content.

$$g(t_i) + F(d_i) \leftrightarrow \iiint mean\left(\sum t_{ij} + 4\right) \cdot \cup_{i=1}^{n} t_i \cdot \sqrt{5} \tag{6}$$

C. *Analysis of system platform scheme*

In addition, the course has a fixed schedule and an optional custom learning plan, which users can flexibly adjust to their own time and learning speed.

$$No(t_i) = \frac{g(t_i) + F(d_i)}{\cup_{i=1}^{n} t_i \cdot \sqrt{5}} \tag{7}$$

The interactive learning module encourages communication and cooperation between users, providing features such as discussion areas, real-time chat and group projects. Users can share their learning experiences, answer their questions, and practice their language with others here. In addition, the system provides speech recognition and speech synthesis technology, where users can practice speaking, and the system will provide feedback and scoring. Virtual role-playing and simulated dialogue scenarios to further enhance the practical use of language.

The learning progress and evaluation module tracks the user's learning status in real time, and records the learning time, completed courses, test scores and other data. Users can view their study reports to understand their strengths and weaknesses. The system is based on machine learning algorithm and intelligently recommends appropriate review content and improvement strategy according to the user's learning performance. In addition, regular comprehensive assessments provide users with clear indicators of progress and stimulate the motivation for continuous learning.

$$accur(t_i) = \frac{\min\left[\sum g(t_i) \cdot F(d_i)\right]}{op} + t \tag{8}$$

The data analysis and visualization module collects and analyzes users' learning data, including learning duration, activity, completion rate, etc., to generate intuitive charts. These data can help teachers to understand the students' learning situation and conduct personalized teaching. At the same time, administrators can optimize the course content and system functions through these data to improve user satisfaction. Users can also use these charts to understand their own learning patterns, adjust their learning strategies, and achieve more efficient learning.

$$accur(t_i) = \frac{\min[\sum g(t_i) + F(d_i)]}{\sum g(t_i) + F(d_i)} + \iiint randon(t_i) \tag{9}$$

Personalized learning path recommendation algorithm is the core component of the foreign language learning platform. It generates the most suitable learning path for each user by analyzing their learning history, learning level, learning preferences and available time. The algorithm combines collaborative filtering, content filtering and rule-based methods to consider the user's behavioral data, such as completed courses, accuracy of exercises, learning time, etc. Through machine learning models, such as matrix factorization or deep neural networks, the algorithms are constantly optimized to provide dynamic and updated personalized recommendations to ensure that users improve their foreign language skills in the most efficient path.

3 Optimization Strategies for Foreign Language Learning

The intelligent evaluation mechanism is an integral part of the platform, using automatic scoring systems and natural language processing technology to assess user performance in real time in listening, speaking, reading and processing. The mechanism can not only accurately analyze the user's language output, but also identify and feedback the error types, such as grammar, vocabulary, or pronunciation problems. In addition, it provides immediate feedback to help users understand their strengths and weaknesses.

4 Results and Discussion

A. *System platform introduction*

As the virtual teacher of the platform, the AI teaching assistant uses the natural language understanding and generation technology to conduct real-time dialogue with the users and simulate the real language communication situation. It understands the user's input, provides an appropriate response, and adapts to the user's language level and learning progress.

Table 1. Reign language learning system platform requirements

Scope of application	Platform form	Get data	Get resources
English	I	73.79	72.82
	II	74.76	77.67
French	I	77.67	82.52
	II	74.76	76.70
German	I	75.73	73.79
	II	82.52	76.70

The system platform procedure in Table 1. The premise of the construction of the resource platform is the acquisition, integration, and comprehensive utilization of resources, which is shown in Fig. 1.

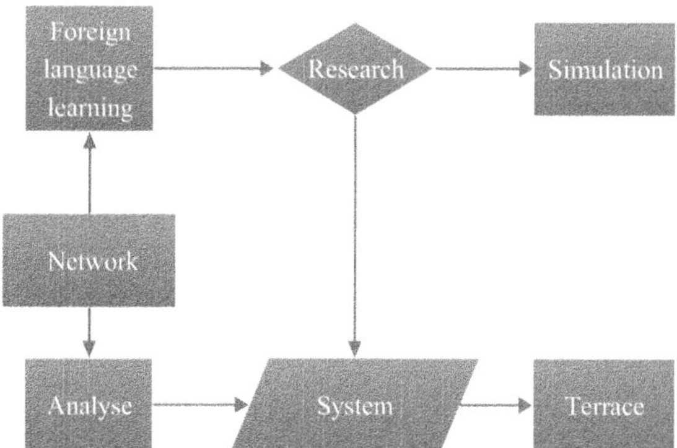

Fig. 1. The analytical process of foreign language learning

AI teaching assistants also have the ability to make teaching plans, and recommend appropriate dialogue exercises, situational simulation or role-playing activities according to users 'needs and progress, so as to improve users' language use ability.

B. *Foreign language learning*

Deep learning models are used to understand and generate natural language to enable an adaptive dialogue system and context-aware question-answering functions on the platform. These models are able to handle complex linguistic structures, understand and generate continuous streams of text, allowing the AI TA to interact more naturally with users. At the same time, deep learning is also applied in speech recognition and speech synthesis to improve the accuracy of speech input, generate smooth speech feedback, and enhance the immersion of learning. Through the integrated application of these intelligent learning algorithms, the system platform can not only provide personalized learning experience, but also create an efficient, dynamic and highly adaptable foreign language learning environment through continuous evaluation and feedback, as well as the interaction of AI teaching assistants (Table 2).

Table 2. The overall picture of the system platform solution

Category	Random data	Reliability	Analysis rate
English	85.32	85.90	83.95
French	86.36	82.51	84.29
German	84.16	84.92	83.68
Man	86.84	84.85	84.40
X^2	83.04	86.03	84.32
	P = .249		

C. *System platform and stability*

The design of the user interface (UI) is a key factor to the success of the system platform, and its goal is to provide an intuitive, easy to use and attractive interactive environment. The design philosophy is user-centered and emphasizing simplicity, consistency, discoverability and accessibility. The interface design follows the following principles: Concicity: The interface should avoid too many complex elements to reduce the cognitive burden and enable users to quickly understand and operate (Fig. 2).

Consistency: The design should maintain consistent interface elements, icons and layout to enhance user learning efficiency and usage habits. Disverability: Key functions should be easy to discover, such as obvious locations, icons or prompts to allow the users to naturally find the required functions, as Table 3.

To accommodate the different devices and screen sizes, the system platform adopts a responsive design. This ensures that the same great experience is achieved on a desktop, tablet, or smartphone. The responsive layout automatically adjusts the way the content is displayed through media queries, streaming grids, and adaptive images. At the same time, the mobile terminal has optimized the touch operation to ensure that the button size is moderate, reasonable spacing, easy for fingertip operation (Fig. 3).

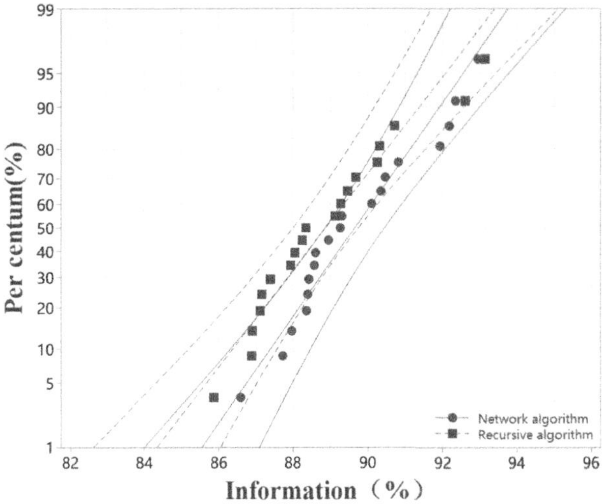

Fig. 2. System platforms for different algorithms

Table 3. Caparison of system platform accuracy of different methods

Algorithm	Resource integration	Resource utilization	Comprehensive analysis	Overall change
Network algorithm	85.33	46.02	43.36	72.82
	85.75	83.44	85.65	84.03
Recursive algorithms	85.20	83.41	86.01	85.75
P	87.17	87.62	84.48	86.97

The user experience is not done all at once, but requires continuous monitoring, evaluation, and improvement. Through the analysis of user behavior data, we can understand the behavior patterns of users on the platform, and find out the pain points and bottlenecks. User feedback systems are also important ways to optimize, encouraging users to share their experiences and suggestions.

D. *Effectiveness of the system platform*

Based on this information, A / B tests are conducted to compare the effects of different design versions, with data-driven decisions, and continuous iterative optimization. At the same time, follow the design principles, regularly update the interface style, to keep the modern and attractive platform.

From Fig. 4, it can be seen that there is an inevitable connection between the teaching platform and the implementation effect, and the distribution of resources is diversified, so

Fig. 3. The system platform of the network algorithm system platform

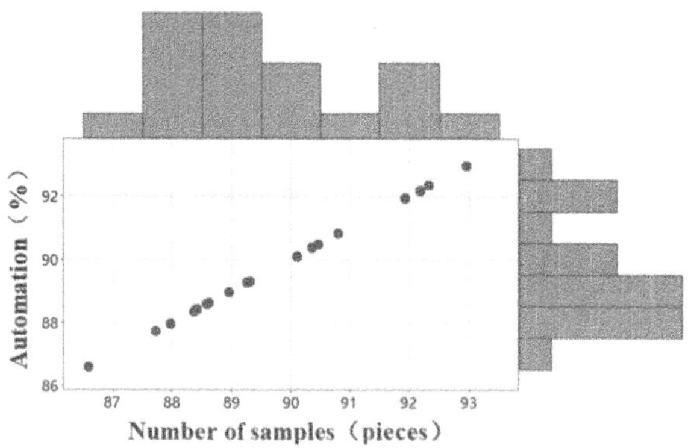

Fig. 4. Distribution of educational resources and language learning effects

the integrity of resources should be judged. At the same time, it is also necessary to constrain the planning, planning content, and multiple conditions of educational resources, and the results are shown in Table 4.

Table 4. Comparison of system platform effectiveness of different methods

Algorithm	Outcome	Resource distribution	Web construction	Language integrity
Network algorithm	80.58	82.52	78.64	74.76
Recursive algorithms	77.67	73.79	81.55	82.52
P	74.76	72.82	78.64	73.79

The networked foreign language learning system platform, it is necessary to build an efficient and safe development and testing environment. This includes setting up development workstations, selecting and configuring suitable development tools such as IDE (Integrated Development environment) and version control systems (e. g. Git), and establishing a Continuous Integration / Continuous Deployment (CI / CD) pipeline (Fig. 5).

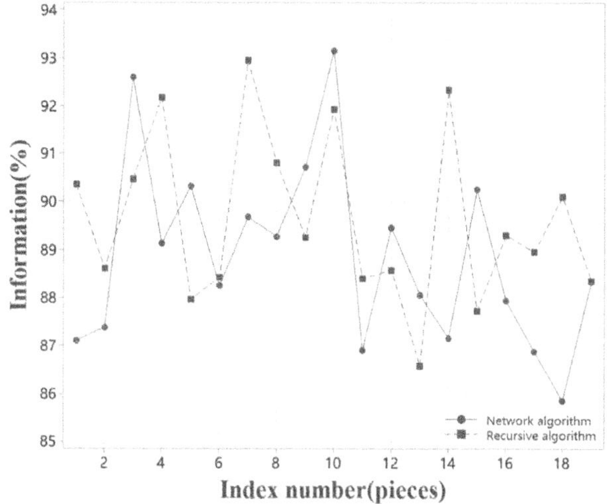

Fig. 5. The system platform of the network algorithm system platform

At the same time, it is necessary to establish an isolated test environment to simulate real user scenarios to test the various functions and performance of the platform. The test environment should be similar.

5 Conclusion

The comprehensive utilization of resources and the distribution of resources with the help of the network can improve the teaching effect. At the same time, the integration of online English resources can improve the planning effect of resources. The results of this paper show that network analysis can promote the rational distribution of resources, complete the overall resource integration, deepen the content and structure of knowledge, and promote the effective application of knowledge, with an improvement rate of 80%. Therefore, optimizing network technology and promoting the overall planning of resources can realize the diversified development of resources. However, there are also certain shortcomings in this study, mainly the research process and research samples.

References

1. Zhiqiang, H.: Research on foreign language learning under computer network algorithm[J]. J. Foreign Lang. Learn. Res. **46**(01), 107–111 (2024)

2. Aowei, W., Yu, W., Jiehui, F., Yongkang, Y., Guohua, Z., Huawei, H.: Intelligent foreign language learning system based on multi-source network algorithm [J]. Wisdom For. Lan. Learn. Guide, **3**(09), 1–4
3. Xiuwu, Y., Pei, Y., Yong, L., Luping, H.: WSN network algorithm based on fireworks optimization[J]. J. Huazhong Univ. Sci. Technol.(Natural Science Edition) **51**(05), 112–118 (2023)
4. Wei, L., Xinghui., X.: Development strategy of foreign language learning informatization in the era of mobile Internet[J]. Rural Sci. Technol. (27), 122–123 (2018)
5. Jianxin, H.E.: Research on urban foreign language learning information service model under the background of "Internet + Foreign Language Learning"[J]. Southern Rural Areas **34**(04), 14–21 (2018)
6. Ban, L.: Analysis of the degree of internet acceptance of foreign language learning information[J]. Hunan Agricult. Mach. **41**(08), 81+96 (2014)
7. Yunping, Z.: The influence of information network dissemination on the production mode of traditional foreign language learning in China[A]. Office of the Rural Work Leading Group of the Shandong Provincial Party Committee, China Rural Professional and Technical Association, Shandong Science and Technology Association, Popular Press Group, Weihai Municipal People's Government, Japan Nongshan Fishing Village Cultural Association.Modern Foreign Language Learning Innovation and Development-Proceedings of the Sino-Japanese Modern Foreign Language Learning Innovation Forum[C].Office of the Rural Work Leading Group of the Shandong Provincial Party Committee, China Rural Professional and Technical Association, Shandong Science and Technology Association, Popular Press Group, Weihai Municipal People's Government, Japan Nongshan Fishing Village Cultural Association: Shandong Association for Science and Technology, 278–282 (2008)
8. Fang, Y.: On the principles and methods of internet foreign language learning information classification[J]. Anhui Foreign Language Learn. Sci. (22), 7000–7001 (2007)
9. Fang, Y., Weizhi., H.: Collection and utilization of internet foreign language learning information resources[J]. Sci. Eng. Stud. High. Educ. (03), 133–134+137 (2006)
10. Qin, Z., Guilian, M.A.: Development and application of foreign language learning information resources on the internet[J]. J. Mod. Inform. (03):140–141+144 (2004)

Research on the Construction of University English Course Service Platform in Network Environment

Feng Hu(✉)

Liaoning Mechatronics College, Dandong, Liaoning, China
xiaoxiao181@163.com

Abstract. The significance of oral and listening English in higher education Despite the critical nature of the English language, many people struggle with basic communicating verbally and aural skills. Conventional pedagogical approaches provide less than satisfactory outcomes when it comes to improving students' hearing and speaking abilities in college-level English. Consequently, this article suggests a platform for English language courses that analyzes communicating verbally and aural. Starting with the design and construction of the platform using the MVC architecture, the indicators are segregated according to the needs of English communicating verbally and aural, with the goal of reducing interference factors in these areas. After that, an MVC architecture creates a platform for the English course service, formulates a plan for the English communicating verbally and aural, and conducts a thorough analysis of the outcomes. Under certain assessment criteria, the MATLAB simulation demonstrates that the English course service platform for colleges and universities achieves particular learning outcomes in terms of both hearing and speaking English. All are superior to traditional teaching courses.

Keywords: MVC architecture · English course service platform · College English · English communicating verbally and aural

1 Introduction

As computing power has increased, the Internet has emerged as a vital medium for individuals to obtain information and learn [1]. In English courses, the online environment not only provides students with broader English learning resources, but also provides teachers with more teaching tools and technical means [2]. However, the network environment can also have an impact on the service level of English courses. This paper will discuss the impact of the network environment on the service level of English courses from the aspects of network environment [3], English teaching objectives, curriculum design and evaluation.

A. *Definition and significance of network environment*

B. Brik and S. Nazir (Eds.): BigIoT-EDU 2024, LNICST 660, pp. 237–246, 2026.
https://doi.org/10.1007/978-3-032-18628-7_25

The network environment refers to the environment in which people communicate and learn on the Internet. It can provide people with various resources and services, such as online courses, online dictionaries, search tools, literature downloads, etc., thus providing more convenient and extensive channels for English learning [4]. At the same time, the network environment can also provide more technical support and teaching methods for English teaching, such as online classrooms, courseware production, etc. [5].

B. *The impact of the network environment on the service level of English courses*

1. The influence of the network environment on the objectives of English teaching

The network environment can provide a wider range of teaching resources and channels for English teaching, so as to achieve more teaching goals [6]. For example, through search tools and online dictionaries, students can access English learning materials and vocabulary information more quickly; Through online classes and courseware production tools, teachers can innovate teaching methods and methods to further improve teaching effectiveness. Therefore, the network environment has a positive impact on the service level of English courses [7].

2. The impact of the network environment on course design

Additional components and opportunities for course creation are introduced by the network environment [8]. For instance, educators may create more engaging and participatory course materials with the use of supplementary tools and resources available online; students can experience a more authentic and relevant learning environment for English via the use of the Internet and multimedia technologies. Consequently, the efficacy and quality of English course design are greatly affected by the online environment [10].

3. The impact of the network environment on course assessment

Course evaluations benefit from the network environment's wealth of data and information. For instance, online communication and Q&A platforms allow students to ask more questions and get prompt responses and assistance; online testing and assessment tools[11] provide instructors with a more complete and accurate view of students' learning outcomes and levels. In order to assess and enhance English language education, the network environment is crucial [12].

C. *Measures to optimize the network environment*

1. Improve network facilities and technical support

The key to optimizing the network environment is to improve network facilities and technical support, especially in some areas and schools [13], the network facilities and technical level is relatively low, which will have a negative impact on English teaching. Therefore, education departments and schools should actively take measures to optimize network facilities and technical support and improve the service level of the network environment [14].

2. Build an online teaching resource library

One key approach to improve the network environment is building an online instructional resource library [15]. The development of an online teaching resource library has several potential benefits, including the enhancement of the quality of English language courses offered, the provision of students and instructors with more varied and thorough materials for learning the language, and the satisfaction of students' varying learning requirements and skill levels [16].

3. Introduce intelligent English learning system

To further enhance the quality of service for English language instruction in a network setting, an intelligent learning system for the language might be implemented. The implementation of an intelligent learning system has the potential to raise the bar for English course service, empower students to become more self-reliant learners, and customize their educational experience.

An essential factor influencing the quality of English language instruction is the network environment. Teachers may improve their teaching techniques and create more efficient and effective learning channels for students in the network environment, while students can access more materials and channels to learn English. Optimization of the network environment may be achieved by the implementation of intelligent learning systems, the improvement of network facilities and technical support, and the construction of an online library of teaching resources. By implementing these changes, we can raise the bar for English course service and push for the field's continued growth and improvement.

There is a tremendous deal of importance in studying college English, and one of the main components is hearing and speaking English. Unfortunately, there is an issue with the English communicating verbally and aural scheme's lack of accuracy that makes learning the language challenging. There are academics who think that by analyzing college and university English using the English course service platform, we can better understand the English communicating verbally and aural scheme and provide appropriate assistance for it. Aiming to optimize the English communicating verbally and aural scheme, this study offers and tests an English course service platform based on this.

2 Related Works

A. *Mathematical description of the English course service platform*

Based on indications in English hearing and speaking, the English course service platform optimizes the communicating verbally and aural program using artificial intelligence is y_i, discovers the absolute principles in university English is z_i, and integrates the English communicating verbally and aural program is $tol(y_i \cdot q_{ij})$, before deciding whether or not the platform for providing college-level English courses is feasible, using the results from formula (1).

$$tol\left(y_i \cdot q_{ij}\right) = y_{ij} \geq \max(q_{ij}) \tag{1}$$

Equation (2) shows the evaluation of outliers among them.

$$\max(q_{ij}) = \left(q_{ij}^2 + 1\right) \succ mean\left(\sum \lim_{q \to \infty} \frac{dy}{dq} q_{ij}\right) \tag{2}$$

If you want to enhance your English hearing and speaking abilities, you should check out the English course service platform. It combines the benefits of artificial intelligence with quantification using collegiate English.

Suppose I. English communicating verbally and aural requirements is q_i, English communicating verbally and aural scheme is set_i, English communicating verbally and aural program satisfaction is y_i, English communicating verbally and aural scheme judgment function is $A(q_i \approx 0)$, as shown in Eq. (3).

$$A(q_i) = \sum q_i \cap \xi \to \oint y_i \lim_{\delta q \to 0} \bigcap_{i=1}^{n} Q_i \frac{1}{2} \arcsin \theta \tag{3}$$

B. *Choice of English communicating verbally and aural program*

The Second Hypothesis: college English function is $s(q_i)$, and the weight coefficient is w_i, then, English communicating verbally and aural requires unqualified college English as shown in Eq. (4).

$$s(q_i) = z_i \cdot \prod A(q_i) - w_i \sum_{i=1}^{n} Q_i Y_i \frac{1}{n} \partial \sqrt{\frac{1}{n}} \tag{4}$$

As shown in Eq. (5), the complete function of college English may be determined in accordance with hypotheses I and II.

$$s(q_i) + A(d_i) \le \max(q_{ij}) \tag{5}$$

The outcomes of standardizing all data may be seen in Eq. (6), which can help increase the efficacy of oral and auditory English communication in higher education.

$$\widetilde{s(q_i) + A}(x_i) \leftrightarrow mean\left(\sum \lim_{q \to \infty} \frac{dy}{dq} q_{ij}\right) \tag{6}$$

C. *Analysis of English communicating verbally and aural programs*

Conducting a multi-dimensional analysis of the English communicating verbally and aural scheme, mapping the requirements to the university English database, and eliminating the unqualified English communicating verbally and aural scheme are all necessary before implementing the English course service platform is $No(q_i)$, Eq. (7) displays the outcomes, while Eq. (6) allows for the proposal of the anomaly assessment method.

$$No(q_i) = \frac{s(q_i) + A(x_i)}{mean\left(\sum \lim_{q \to \infty} \frac{dy}{dq} q_{ij}\right)} \tag{7}$$

Among them, $\frac{s(q_i)+A(x_i)}{mean\left(\sum \lim_{q\to\infty} \frac{dy}{dq} q_{ij}\right)} \leq 1$ it is stated that the scheme needs to be proposed, otherwise the scheme integration required is $Zh(q_i)$, and the result is shown in Eq. (8).

$$Zh(q_i) = \min\left[\sum \frac{1}{n} \lim_{q\to\infty} \frac{1}{2} \frac{\Delta y}{\Delta q} \frac{1}{2} \pi s(q_i) + A(x_i)\right] \tag{8}$$

In order to guarantee the precision of the English course service platform, College English does thorough analyses and establishes the threshold and index weight of English communicating aurally and vocally. College English is an analytically rigorous examination of oral and written communication skills in English. Assuming that academic English follows a nonnormal distribution $unno(q_i)$, The plan for verbal and auditory English communication will be impacted, lower the overall accuracy of verbal and auditory English communication $accur(q_i)$, and the calculation result is shown in Eq. (9).

$$accur(q_i) = \frac{\min\left[\sum \frac{1}{n} \lim_{q\to\infty} \frac{1}{2} \frac{\Delta y}{\Delta q} \frac{1}{2} \pi s(q_i) + A(Q_i)\right]}{\sum \frac{1}{n} \lim_{q\to\infty} \frac{1}{2} \frac{\Delta y}{\Delta q} \frac{1}{2} \pi s(q_i) + A(X_i)} \times 100\% \tag{9}$$

A multidimensional distribution is shown by the survey of English verbal and auditory communication systems, which is consistent with objective facts. As a highly analytical field of study, college English is characterized by a lack of directionality, which suggests that the auditory and verbal English communication scheme is quite random. Assuming that the collegiate English random function is $randon(q_i)$, then formula (10). This is the expression that represents the computation of formula (9).

$$accur(q_i) = \frac{\min\left[\sum \frac{1}{n} \lim_{q\to\infty} \frac{1}{2} \frac{\Delta y}{\Delta q} \frac{1}{2} \pi s(q_i) + A(x_i)\right]}{\sum \frac{1}{n} \lim_{q\to\infty} \frac{1}{2} \frac{\Delta y}{\Delta q} \frac{1}{2} \pi s(q_i) + A(x_i)} \times 100\% + randon(q_i) \tag{10}$$

Of them, college English satisfies typical standards; primarily, AI modifies college English, gets rid of redundant and unneeded schemes, and augments the default scheme, resulting in a robust dynamic connection between the complete English communication scheme and auditory scheme.

3 Optimization Strategies for College English

In order to optimize college English, the English course service platform uses a random optimization technique and tweaks the platform's settings. The online English language learning platform sorts college-level English into several verbal and auditory communication levels and then chooses a solution at random from among them. The iterative approach involves optimizing and analyzing strategies for English verbal and auditory communication at various levels. Once the optimization study is finished, you may choose the finest college English by comparing the verbal and aural levels of various programs.

4 Results and Discussion

A. *Introduction to English communicating verbally and aural*

Table 1 shows the English communicating vocally and aurally scheme of specialized college English; this study uses college English in difficult circumstances as its research target; the exam has 12 pathways and lasts 12 h.

Table 1. College English communicating verbally and aural requirements

Scope of application	Grade	Level of competence	English communicating verbally and aural
Hearing	Normal	85.50	86.17
	Higher	85.90	82.39
Read	Normal	82.91	85.06
	Higher	86.72	85.11
Read and write	Normal	84.42	80.45
	Higher	83.95	82.55

The English communicating verbally and aural process in Table 1 is shown in Fig. 1.

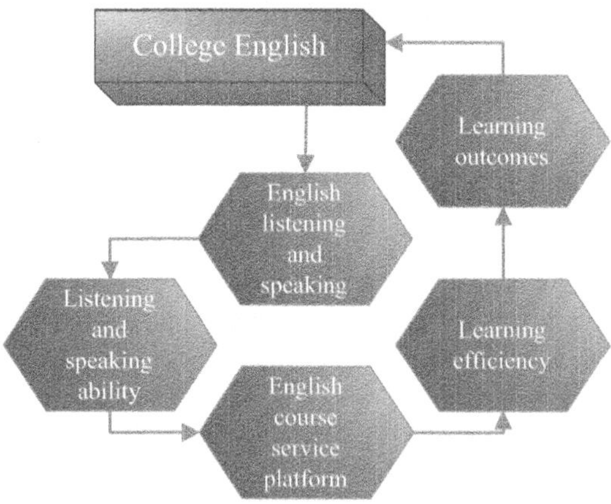

Fig. 1: Analysis process of college English

The program for hearing and speaking English on the English course service platform is more in line with real-world needs than those of conventional classroom instruction. Compared to more conventional methods of instruction, the English course service platform provides a more reasonable and efficient means of studying college-level English. Figure 2 shows the modifications in the English verbal and auditory communication scheme, demonstrating that the English course service platform has a greater learning efficiency. Consequently, the summation stability, quickness, and logic of the English course service platform's verbal and auditory plans are all much improved.

B. *College English*

There is both organized and unstructured data in the College English program's spoken and auditory communication component. Following the pre-selection of the English course service platform, the first plan for college-level verbal and auditory communication was gathered and evaluated for practicability. Using the options in Table 2 to choose college English with varying degrees of verbal and auditory communication skills and strategies for verbal and aural communication will allow for more precise verification of the learning outcomes of college English.

Table 2. The overall situation of the English communicating verbally and aural program

Category	Quality of learning	Analysis rate
Hearing	86.69	88.43
Read	87.67	85.58
Read and write	87.82	88.04
Mean	85.12	87.81
X^6	86.07	87.42
P = 1.767		

C. *English communicating verbally and aural English communicating verbally and aural and stability*

Figure 2 compares the English communicating vocally and aural scheme with the conventional teaching course's scheme in order to test the correctness of the English course service platform.

Based on Fig. 2, it is evident that the English course service platform has higher verbal and aural communication skills than the traditional teaching course. However, the error rate is lower, suggesting that the English course service platform's verbal and aural communication is relatively stable, in contrast to the traditional teaching course's uneven verbal and aural communication. Table 3 displays the average spoken and auditory communication method for the three algorithms mentioned earlier.

Table 3 shows that college-level English has evolved much, and the mistake rate is considerable, and that conventional methods of instruction fall short when it comes to students' ability to communicate orally and aurally in the language. The overall outcomes of the English course service platform outperform those of conventional classroom instruction when it comes to oral and written communication in English. The accuracy rate has been relatively constant at around 92% for the English course service platform's spoken and auditory communication. So that the English course service platform's excellence might be confirmed to us. Figure 3 shows the results of a general study of the English

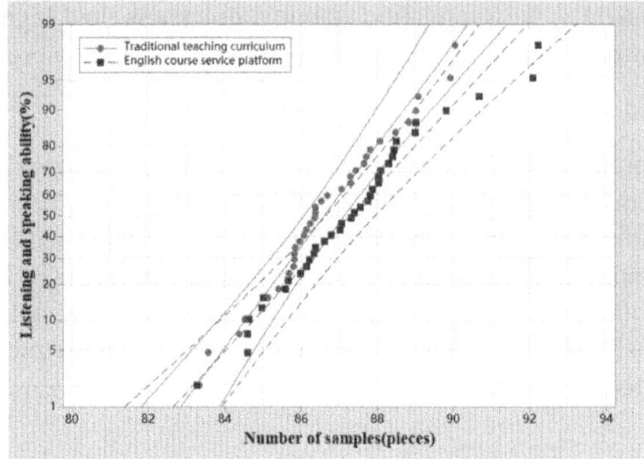

Fig. 2: English communicating verbally and aural with different algorithms

Table 3. Comparison of English communicating verbally and aural accuracy by different methods

Algorithm	English communicating verbally and aural	Magnitude of change	Error
English course service platform	92.38	92.88	93.26
Traditional teaching curriculum	91.91	91.64	92.00
P	88.70	88.17	89.64

course service platform using various methodologies, which was conducted to further confirm the efficacy of the suggested strategy.

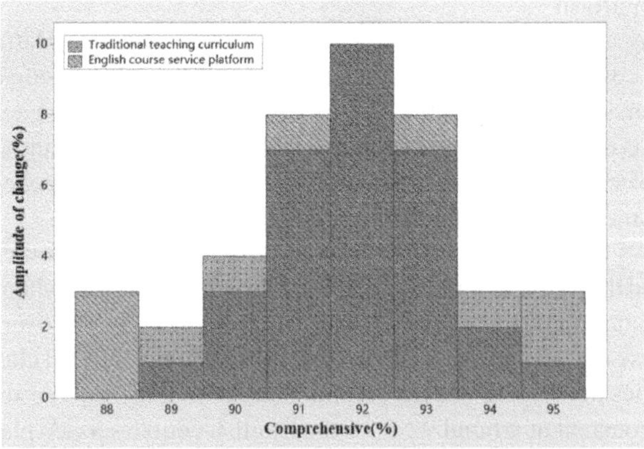

Fig. 3. English course service platform English communicating verbally and aural

Figure 3 shows that compared to traditional classroom instruction, the English course service platform excels in verbal and aural communication. This is because the platform raises the college English adjustment coefficient and filters out subpar schemes to ensure that all students reach their full potential.

5 Conclusion

In response to the widespread dissatisfaction with college students' oral and written English proficiency, this article suggests a platform for English course services that integrates AI in an effort to improve students' academic English. Concurrently, a platform collection is built by in-depth analysis of the English language's verbal and auditory communication levels. The research indicates that the English course service platform may enhance the learning efficiency and quality of college-level English, as well as general English listening and speaking skills. Unfortunately, the English course service platform pays too much emphasis to the analysis of auditory and vocal English communication, leading to illogical indication selection.

Acknowledgements. "College English Curriculum Development and Practice under the Model of Joint Training of Higher Education" (JYLX2022029) 2022 teaching research project of Liaoning Mechatronics College.

Funding. This work was supported by: Research on The Construction of the New-form of Textbook and Online Resources for Professional English under The Background of Integration of Production and Teaching (WYJZW-2024-1007), Special Project on "Three Integration" Foreign Language Teaching Reform, Foreign Language Teaching Advisory Board for Vocational Colleges, Ministry of Education; Research on the Construction and Application of New-form "Golden Textbooks" for Vocational College English with Integrating Curriculum Ideology and Politics (YW2025A35) Special Research Project on Foreign Language Education Reform in Vocational Colleges, Foreign Language Education Committee, Chinese Society of Vocational and Technical Education.

References

1. Ahmad, S., Aoun, N.B., Ali, G., El-Affendi, M.A.A., Anwar, M.S.: Multi-clustered mathematical model for student cognitive skills prediction optimization. IEEE Access **11**, 65371–65381 (2023)
2. Alhmiedat, T., Marei, A. M., Messoudi, W., Albelwi, S., Bushnag, A., Bassfar, Z., Alnajjar, F., Elfaki, A. O.: A SLAM-based localization and navigation system for social robots: the pepper robot case. Machines **11**(2) (2023)
3. Alkadi, R., Shoufan, A.: Unmanned aerial vehicles traffic management solution using crowd-sensing and blockchain. IEEE Trans. Netw. Serv. Manage. **20**(1), 201–215 (2023)
4. Allerton, F., Russell, J.: Antimicrobial stewardship in veterinary medicine: a review of online resources. JAC-Antimicrobial Resistance **5**(3), dlad058-dlad058 (2023)
5. Ambroz, M., Pernaa, J., Haatainen, O., Aksela, M.: Promoting STEM education of future chemistry teachers with an engineering approach involving single-board computers. Appl. Sci.-Basel **13**(5) (2023)

6. Bendezu-Quispe, G., Caira-Chuquineyra, B., Fernandez-Guzman, D., Casanova-Perez, R., Bendezu-Martinez, A.G.: Massive open online courses: learning opportunities about global health for Latin American countries. Biomedica: Revista del Instituto Nacional de Salud **43**(2), 261–269 (2023)
7. Chytas, K., Tsolakidis, A., Triperina, E., Karanikolas, N.N., Skourlas, C.: Academic data derived from a university e-government analytic platform: an educational data mining approach. Data Brief **49**, 109357 (2023)
8. Dinh Ba, P., et al.: Balancing and tracking control of ballbot mobile robots using a novel synchronization controller along with online system identification. IEEE Trans. Industr. Electron. **70**(1), 657–668 (2023)
9. Dong, X., Wang, X., Peng, L., Wang, M., Wang, G.: An efficient task synthesis method based on subspace differential patterns for arrangements of event intervals mining in the avionics cloud system architecture. Aerospace **10**(3) (2023)
10. Esh, N., Michael, S., Paetzholdt, J., Samaras, K.: Bridging public and private health services to best meet the cardiometabolic needs of people with severe mental illness: a retrospective cohort study. Australasian psychiatry: bulletin of Royal Australian and New Zealand College of Psychiatrists: 10398562231190781–10398562231190781 (2023)
11. Fernandes, B., Almeida, V.M.C.D.:Trinks.com—plataforma digital a serviço da beleza. Cadernos EBAPE.BR **21**(1), e2022–0073–0073 (2023)
12. Galehdar, N., Heydari, H.: Exploring caregivers' perceptions of community-based service requirements of patients with spinal cord injury: a qualitative study. Bmc Primary Care **24**(1) (2023)
13. Giuliano, R., Innocenti, E.: Machine learning techniques for non-terrestrial networks. Electronics **12**(3) (2023)
14. Grieco, G., Iacovelli, G., Boccadoro, P., Grieco, L.A.: Internet of drones simulator: design, implementation, and performance evaluation. IEEE Internet Things J. **10**(2), 1476–1498 (2023)
15. Guiney, H., Mahoney, A., Elders, A., David, C., Poulton, R.: Internet-based cognitive behavioural therapy in the real world: naturalistic use and effectiveness of an evidence-based platform in New Zealand. Australian and New Zealand J. Psychiatry (2023)
16. Herren, T., et al.: Development of a pilot introductory advanced cardiovascular resuscitation course for senior medical students in Switzerland: student-driven implementation study. Interact. J. Med. Res. **12**, e46075–e46075 (2023)

Research on the Application of Neural Network in the Analysis of College Students' Mental Health

Wenjun Li[1](✉) and Yuhang Li[2]

[1] Changchun Humanities and Sciences College, Jilin 130117, China
wenjun.1@163.com
[2] Jilin University of the Arts, Jilin 130021, China

Abstract. College students' mental health analysis relies heavily on health analysis applications, yet there is an issue with erroneous result assessment. It was illogical to use questionnaire analysis to determine college students' mental health since it did not address the issue of health analysis application. Thus, in order to analyze the mental health of college students, this research suggests a neural network approach. First, college students' health is assessed using neural network theory; indicators are then split according to the needs of the health analysis application in order to lower their overall number. Distractions in health analytic applications. After that, we take a look at how college students' mental health is examined using neural network theory, develop a plan for applying health analysis, and last, apply the plan and analyze the findings thoroughly. Neural network techniques are useful for college students, according to MATLAB simulations, given certain assessment criteria. When compared to questionnaire analysis, health analysis provided more accurate results and took less time to apply to college students' psychological well-being.

Keywords: Health · Neural network algorithms · College Student Psychology · Analysis

1 Introduction

More and more people are paying attention to how college students are doing mentally in recent years. The area of psychology has made extensive use of neural network technology, a developing AI technology [1]. This article delves into the ways neural network technology has been used and its effects on studies concerning the mental health of college students.

A. *Current situation of college students' mental health*

The prevalence of mental health issues among college students is on the rise right now, thanks to society's relentless progress. On the one hand, college students are under multiple pressures such as academic pressure, life pressure, and employment pressure

B. Brik and S. Nazir (Eds.): BigIoT-EDU 2024, LNICST 660, pp. 247–256, 2026.
https://doi.org/10.1007/978-3-032-18628-7_26

[2], on the other hand, college students' self-awareness, interpersonal communication, emotional management and other abilities are relatively weak, and they are easily troubled by psychological problems. According to statistics, there are obvious psychological problems such as emotional disorders, anxiety disorders, and depression in the group of college students, which have a negative impact on the physical and mental health and academic development of college students, and have also attracted social attention [3].

B. *Fundamentals of neural network technology*

One kind of computer model that attempts to capture human intelligence is the neural network nervous system, consisting of multiple interconnected neurons. Neural networks can learn sample data and independently discover the intrinsic relationship between data [4], so as to achieve better prediction and classification effects. The basic principle is that the input data is processed and transformed through multi-level neuronal connections, and the final output result [5].

C. *Application of neural network technology in the study of mental health of college students*

1. Prediction of psychological problems

Neural network technology can predict the possible issues related to mental health among university students through the analysis of their individual psychological characteristics. For example, by collecting a large number of psychological test data of college students, establishing corresponding neural network models, and optimizing the model through training data, different psychological problems that different college students may have in the future can be predicted. In this way, college students with psychological problems can be detected in time and timely help and intervention can be provided [6].

2. Classification of psychological problems

Neural network technology can classify the issues related to mental health among university students and formulate targeted psychological intervention programs. For example, by training a neural network model, known psychological problems can be classified [7], and then psychological problems with the same category can be identified through the analysis of new data, so that psychological intervention methods can be used in a targeted manner [8].

3. Treatment of psychological problems

Neural network technology can play an important role in psychotherapy. For example, patient confidence and effectiveness in treatment can be increased by simulating human-machine interactions. In addition, neural networks can also be used to formulate more effective treatment plans, such as personalized treatment plans, based on the individual characteristics of patients, to design psychological treatment plans suitable for them [9].

4. Psychological research analysis

Neural network techniques can also be used to conduct large-scale psychological research. For example, the neural network technology can be used to analyze the psychological models of college students of different genders, different disciplinary backgrounds and different cultural backgrounds to find the patterns and characteristics [10].

D. Impact of neural network technology in college students' mental health research

1. Improve forecast accuracy

Neural network techniques can be trained to improve the accuracy and reliability of predictions. Therefore, in the research of college students' mental health, neural network technology can play an important role in better prediction effect, timely detection and intervention of college students' psychological problems, and ensure their physical and mental health [11].

2. Improve the treatment effect

Neural network technology can help formulate personalized treatment plans, accurately intervene in college students' psychological problems, and improve treatment effects. Therefore, the application in psychotherapy is promising.

3. Discover new patterns

Neural network technology can conduct large-scale psychological research and discover its laws and characteristics. This will help to gain an in-depth understanding of the nature and law of college students' mental health problems, and provide a theoretical basis for effective intervention and treatment.

4. Risk and Privacy Issues

There is an immediate need to address data privacy and security concerns associated with the processing of massive amounts of personally identifiable information (PII) generated by neural network applications. Hence, it is important to enhance management and security measures when using neural network technology to study college students' mental health to prevent the exploitation or leakage of personal information.

One problem that requires immediate addressing is the mental health of college students. The study of college students' mental health, along with advancements in prediction accuracy, treatment efficacy, and rule discovery, may all benefit from neural network technology, a relatively new kind of artificial intelligence. However, there are also worries about privacy and potential hazards. Thus, it is critical to think about the issue from every angle to make sure neural network technology is used correctly and effectively in studies on college students' mental health.

The mental health of college students is greatly impacted by health analysis applications, which are a significant part of college students' mental health. Nevertheless, there is an issue with the health analysis application scheme's lack of precision, which has negative effects on college students' emotional and physical well-being. Applying neural network algorithms to college students' mental health assessments, according to some researchers, may help with both the analysis of the application scheme and the provision of supporting evidence. This research uses this information to suggest a neural network approach that may improve the health analysis application scheme and check whether the model is successful.

2 Related Works

A. *MathemSatical description of the neural network algorithm*

Based on the indicators in the health analysis, the neural network algorithm determines the unqualified values in the mental health analysis of college students by optimizing the application scheme using neural network theory application z_i The health analysis application scheme is $tol(y_i \cdot x_{ij})$ integrated, and the computation is shown in Eq. (1), the feasibility of mental health analysis among college students is then evaluated.

$$tol(y_i \cdot x_{ij}) = \frac{1}{2} y_{ij} \geq \max(x_{ij}) \tag{1}$$

Equation (2) shows the evaluation of outliers among them.

$$\max(x_{ij}) = \lim_{x \to \infty} \left(x_{ij}^2 + 2\right) \succ mean\left(\sum x_{ij}\right) \tag{2}$$

With the use of quantitative data from college students' mental health assessments, the neural network algorithm incorporates the best features of neural network theory to enhance the practicality of health analysis.

I. The health analysis application's prerequisites are, and the application's framework is x_i, the satisfaction of the health analysis application scheme is set_i, and the health analysis application is y_i. The scheme judgment function is $F(x_i \approx 0)$ shown in Eq. (3).

$$\lim_{x \to \infty} F(d_i) = \lim_{x \to \infty} \sum x_i \cap \xi \to ointy_i \tag{3}$$

B. *Selection of health analysis application schemes*

Second Hypothesis The purpose of analyzing college students' mental health is $g(x_i)$, the weight coefficient is w_i, then, the health analysis application requires unqualified college student mental health analysis as in the formula (4) shows:

$$\int g(x_i) = z_i \cdot \prod F(d_i) - \lim_{x \to \infty} w_i \tag{4}$$

Equation (5) shows the outcome of obtaining the synthetic function of the neural network from assumptions I and II.

$$\lim_{x \to \infty} g(x_i) + \lim_{x \to \infty} F(d_i) \leq \max(x_{ij}) \tag{5}$$

The consequences of standardizing all data may be seen in Equation (6), which can be used to increase the efficacy of health analytics systems.

$$g(x_i) + F(d_i) \leftrightarrow \frac{1}{2} mean\left(\sum x_{ij}\right) \tag{6}$$

C. *Analysis of health analysis application schemes*

Prior to implementing the neural network algorithm, it is recommended to conduct a multi-dimensional analysis on the health analysis application scheme. Students' mental health analysis libraries should then be used to map the requirements of the health analysis application, allowing for the elimination of unqualified health analytic applications $No(x_i)$. Equation (7) shows the findings, while Eq. (6) allows for the proposal of the anomaly assessment system.

$$No(x_i) = \frac{g(x_i) + F(d_i)}{\frac{1}{2}mean(\sum x_{ij})} \tag{7}$$

Among them, it is $\frac{g(x_i)+F(d_i)}{mean(\sum x_{ij})} \le 1$ stated that the scheme needs to be proposed, otherwise the scheme integration is $Zh(x_i)$ required, and the result is shown in Eq. (8).

$$Zh(x_i) = \min[\sum g(x_i) + F(d_i)] \tag{8}$$

In order to guarantee the correctness of the neural network algorithm, we conduct a thorough study of college students' mental health and determine the thresholds and index weights of the health analysis application scheme. A new kind of analysis is needed to systematically examine health analysis application systems on college students' mental health. If assessments of college students' psychological well-being are $unno(x_i)$ in a manorial distribution, their health analysis application scheme will be affected, reducing the accuracy of the overall health analysis application, the calculation result is $accur(x_i)$ shown in Eq. (9).

$$accur(x_i) = \frac{1}{2}\frac{\min[\sum g(x_i) + F(d_i)]}{\sum g(x_i) + F(d_i)} \times 100\% \tag{9}$$

According to objective facts, the health analysis application scheme exhibits a multi-dimensional distribution, as shown in the survey of the scheme. This research is considered to be very analytical since the results of the college students' mental health analysis do not show any discernible patterns, suggesting that the health analysis application scheme is very stochastic. Assuming that the examination of college students' mental health is $randon(x_i)$, then the calculation of Eq. (9) can be expressed as formula (10).

$$accur(x_i) = \frac{\min[\sum g(x_i) + F(d_i)]}{\sum g(x_i) + F(d_i)} \times 100\% + randon(x_i) \tag{10}$$

College students' mental health assessments are up to par; primarily, the gray theory tweaks these assessments, gets rid of unnecessary and duplicate schemes, and augments the default one, resulting in a robust dynamic correlation across all health analysis application schemes.

3 Optimization Strategies for College Students' Mental Health Analysis

With the help of health parameter adjustments, the neural network algorithm optimizes the scheme for analyzing college students' mental health using a random optimization technique.The neural network algorithm randomly chooses several schemes after dividing the college students' mental health analyses into different degrees of health analysis applications. Various health analysis application levels' solutions are optimized and evaluated in the iterative process. Once the optimization analysis is finished, many programs' health analysis application levels are combined to record the finest mental health analysis for college students.

4 Results and Discussion

A. *Introduction to the application of health analysis*

With a 12-h testing period and twelve pathways, this study aimed to improve health analysis's practical applicability by analyzing college students' mental health in complicated scenarios. In Table 1, we can see the mental health analysis application method for college students.

Table 1. University health analysis application requirements

Scope of application	Grade	Health effects	Health analytics applications
Freshman	I	76.97	75.42
	II	76.89	77.33
Sophomore	I	74.56	75.95
	II	75.48	76.64
Junior	I	74.98	79.22
	II	76.76	74.03

The health analysis application in Table 1 is shown in Figure 1.

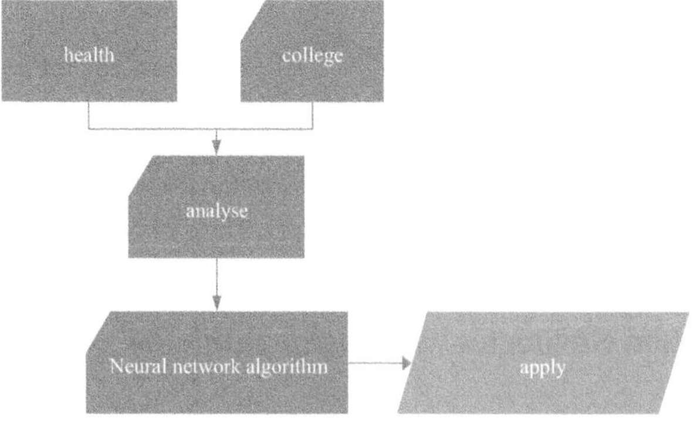

Fig. 1. The analysis process of college students' mental health analysis

The neural network algorithm's health analysis application scheme, which includes questionnaire analysis, is more in line with the needs of real health analysis applications. Compared to questionnaire analysis, neural network algorithm provides a more reasonable and fluctuation-free assessment of college students' mental health. Figure 2 shows the modifications made to the health analysis application scheme, which result in a more stable neural network method and quicker judgment speed. As a result, the neural network algorithm's health analysis application scheme is more stable, accurate, and quick.

B. *Analysis of college students' mental health*

When it comes to college students' mental health, there are three types of data: non-fixed, semi-fixed, and fixed. A prototype health analysis application plan for college students' mental health analysis was developed after the ore-selection of neural network algorithm. The scheme was then evaluated for viability. Using health analysis application methods with varying degrees of rigor may help us better confirm that college students' mental health analyses are having an innovative impact. The results may be shown in Table 2.

Table 2. The overall picture of the health analytics application scenario

Category	Satisfaction	Analysis rate
Freshman	84.36	73.04
Sophomore	83.01	73.54
Junior	83.52	75.27
mean	82.63	73.34
X6	34.25	33.34
P = 3.074		

C. *Health analysis application stability*

Pictured in Figure 2 is the health analysis application scheme, which incorporates questionnaire analysis to validate the neural network method.

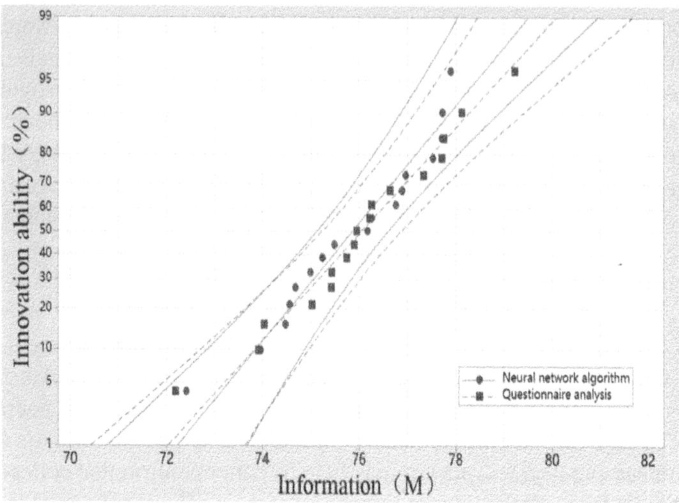

Fig. 2. Health analysis applications with different algorithms

Figure 2 shows that the neural network algorithm's health analysis application is more prevalent than the questionnaire analysis application, with a lower mistake rate. This suggests that the neural network algorithm is more applicable to health analysis. In contrast to the erratic results from health analysis questionnaires, it was quite steady. Presented in Table 3 is the typical methodology for applying the aforementioned three algorithms to health analysis.

Table 3. Comparison of the accuracy of health analysis applications of different methods

Algorithm	Health analytic applications	Magnitude of change	Error
Neural network algorithms	93.67	93.41	95.61
Questionnaire analysis	82.79	83.08	84.32
P	35.012	33.827	35.810

As seen in Table 3 The analysis of college students' mental health has undergone substantial changes, and the mistake rate is considerable. It is evident that questionnaire analysis has limitations in terms of the stability and applicability of health analysis. As a whole, neural network algorithm turns out superior than questionnaire analysis when it comes to health analysis. Additionally, there has been no discernible change in the accuracy of health analysis applications using neural network algorithms, which now reach over 90%. In order to further validate the superiority of the neural network method. Figure 3 shows that several methodologies are often used to examine the neural network algorithm in order to further validate the efficiency of the suggested method.

In light of Figure 3 Because neural network algorithms have raised the number of college students, it is clear that their use in health analysis is much superior than

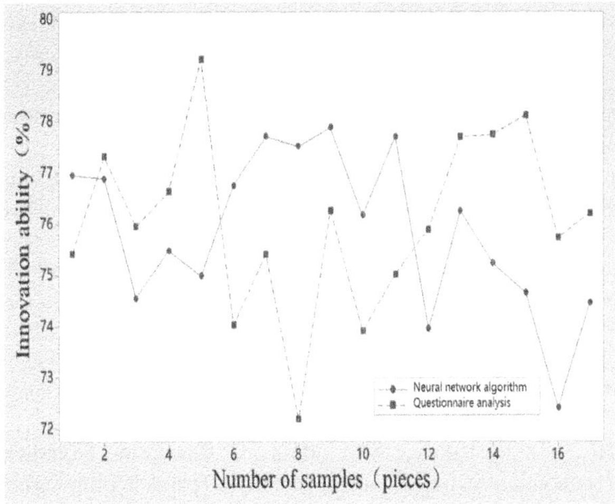

Fig. 3. Health analysis application of neural network algorithm health analysis application

questionnaire analysis. By adjusting the coefficient and establishing a health criterion for college students, mental health analysis may weed out health analysis application schemes that fall short of standards.

5 Conclusion

This study presents a neural network method that integrates neural network theory to maximize college students' mental health diagnosis, aiming to address the issue of less-than-ideal implementation of such an approach. Also, in order to build the college students' health collection, we thoroughly examine the innovations in health analysis applications and threshold innovations. The neural network method has the potential to enhance the reliability and consistency of college students' mental health analyses, as well as their general health analytic applications, according to research. Irrationality in the selection of health analysis application indicators occurs because the neural network algorithm pays too much attention to the examination of health analysis applications.

References

1. Bautista, J., Schueller, S.M.: Understanding the adoption and use of digital mental health apps among college students: secondary analysis of a national survey. JMIR Ment. Health 10 (2023)
2. Beasley, L., Hoffman, S., Houtz, J.: Health literacy and mental well-being among university students in the United States. J. Am. Coll. Health (2023)
3. Bowness, B., Hayes, D., Stepanian, K., Anfossi, A., Taylor, A., Crowther, A., Meddings, S., Osman, Y., Grant, J., Repper, J., Ronaldson, A., Henderson, C., Slade, M.: Who uses recovery colleges? Casemix analysis of sociodemographic and clinical characteristics and representativeness of recovery college students. Psychiatr. Rehabil. J. (2023)

4. Hirshberg, M.J., Colaianne, B., Inkelas, K.K., Oke, G., Van Doren, N., Davidson, R.J., Roeser, R.W.: COVID-19 pandemic effects on college student mental health: A cross-sectional cohort comparison study. J. Am. Coll. Health (2023)
5. Kim, Y., Murphy, J.: Mental health, food insecurity, and economic hardship among college students during the COVID-19 pandemic. Health Soc. Work (2023)
6. Kook, Y., Le, T.P., Robey, N., Raposa, E.B.: Mental health and resource utilization among underrepresented students transitioning to college in the United States. J. Divers. Higher Educ. (2023)
7. Lourie, A., Kennedy, S., Henshaw, E.J., James, D.: College transition Fall 2020 and 2021: understanding the relationship of COVID-19 experiences and psychosocial correlates with anxiety and depression. Plos One **18**(7) (2023)
8. Ma, H., Ren, L., Zong, X.L., Zhang, J., Zhang, Z.J., Jia, L., Chen, Q.L., Niu, S.L.: Death attitudes and Chinese college students' mental health: a latent profile analysis. Death Stud. (2023)
9. Ramirez, A., Rivera, D.B., Valadez, A.M., Mattis, S., Cerezo, A.: Examining mental health, academic, and economic stressors during the COVID-19 pandemic among community college and 4-year university students. Commun. Coll. Rev. (2023)
10. Tambling, R.R., D'Aniello, C.: Mental health literacy and relational health literacy among college students. J. Am. Coll. Health (2023)
11. Zhu, X.L., Wen, Z., Yu, W.B.: Effects of media exposure on PTSD symptoms in college students during the COVID-19 outbreak. Front. Publ. Health **11** (2023)

Research on the Application of ANN Algorithm in the Construction of Intelligent Student Management Assessment Information System

Ran Huzhen(✉)

Railway Technical College, Lanzhou Jiaotong University, Lanzhou 730070, China
gjprhz123@163.com

Abstract. Despite the critical importance of education management assessment in assessing intelligent student management, the issue of erroneous result evaluation persists. Traditional evaluation techniques struggle to match the system's accuracy and efficiency criteria because of the high complexity and massive quantity of data, rendering the assessment unrealistic. So, to assess and analyze education management in a novel way, this research suggests an ANN algorithm. In order to minimize interference elements in education management assessment, the indicators are split according to the needs of the evaluation, and the information system data is managed using database theory. The next step is to use database theory to assess intelligent student management assessment management, create an evaluation scheme for educational management, and then thoroughly examine the evaluation outcomes. When compared to more conventional evaluation methods, MATLAB simulations reveal that ANN algorithms provide superior accuracy, efficacy, and educational management efficiency when building intelligent student management evaluation information systems.

Keywords: Database theory · ANN algorithm · Intelligent · Evaluation of educational management

1 Introduction

Informatization, digitalization, and intelligence have been the steady paths taken by school management with the expansion of IT [1]. Smart student management evaluation information system is an IT-based education management system that gives parents and schools a leg up when it comes to making decisions about students' education by keeping tabs on their attendance, grades, and performance in class, among other things [2]. Accordingly, a number of academics hold the view that intelligent student management assessment analysis using ANN algorithms may give useful insights into the education management evaluation scheme and provide relevant backing for this evaluation [3]. In order to improve the assessment scheme of education management and evaluate the efficacy of the model, this research presents an ANN algorithm [4].

B. Brik and S. Nazir (Eds.): BigIoT-EDU 2024, LNICST 660, pp. 257–268, 2026.
https://doi.org/10.1007/978-3-032-18628-7_27

2 Related Works

A. *Mathematical description of the ANN algorithm*

For learning and cognitive activities, the ANN algorithm can simulate the connections and information transfer between neurons in the human brain [5]. Automatic feature extraction, sample classification, and prediction are all within the ANN algorithm's purview of efficiency and accuracy. The next step is to optimize the educational management assessment scheme using data mining theory. The results show that, based on the evaluation's distinctive characteristic the τ_i characteristic values that do not meet the requirements in the intelligent student management evaluation is D_i, in order to determine if intelligent student management assessment is feasible, the educational management evaluation scheme's integration function is executed is $R\left(d_i \cdot x_{ij}\right)$, which is calculated as shown in Eq. (1).

$$R\left(d_i \cdot x_{ij}\right) = \tau_i + u \tag{1}$$

Among them, Equation displays the evaluation of out-of-the-ordinary feature values (2).

$$\tau_i + u = \sum y_{ij} - D_i \tag{2}$$

Education management assessment and assessment information systems may benefit from the ANN algorithm's usage of intelligent student management evaluation for quantification, which integrates the best of data mining theory.

Assume I. The criteria for evaluating educational administration is v_i, the educational management evaluation scheme is x_{ij}, the practicality of the assessment plan for educational administration is μ, and the prediction function of the educational management evaluation scheme is $Q(z_i)$, as shown in Eq. (3).

$$Q(z_i) = \sum_{i=1}^{t} v_i - x_{ij} \cdot \mu \tag{3}$$

B. *Evaluate the choice of information system options*

Part II: The Intelligent Evaluation Function for Student Management is $H(r_i)$, and the weight coefficient is d_i, then Eq. (4) shows that the unqualified intelligent student management assessment is required for the education management evaluation.

$$H(r_i) = \int d_i \cdot (p - 2) \tag{4}$$

Equation (5) shows that a complete function for assessing information systems may be derived from Hypotheses I and II.

$$Q(z_i) + H(r_i) \leq \tau_i + u \tag{5}$$

Standardizing the categorization and prediction of all data is necessary to enhance the efficacy of education management evaluation, as seen in Eq. (6).

$$Q(z_i) + H(r_i) \leftrightarrow \sum y_{ij} - D_i \tag{6}$$

C. *Analysis of educational management evaluation programmers*

Prior to implementing the ANN algorithm, it is recommended to conduct a thorough analysis of the education management evaluation scheme from multiple angles. Then, in order to eliminate any education management evaluation schemes that do not fulfill the requirements, the needs should be mapped to the intelligent student management evaluation library is IT_i. According to Eq. (6), the anomaly evaluation scheme can be proposed, and the results are shown in Eq. (7).

$$IT_i = \frac{Q(z_i) + H(r_i)}{\sum y_{ij} - D_i} \tag{7}$$

Among them, it is $\frac{Q(z_i)+H(r_i)}{\sum y_{ij}-D_i} \le 1$, stated that the scheme needs to be proposed, otherwise the scheme integration is required is $M(a_i)$, and the result is shown in Eq. (8).

$$M(a_i) = Q(z_i) + H(r_i) \tag{8}$$

In order to guarantee the ANN algorithm's correctness, the education management evaluation scheme's thresholds and index weights are chosen after a thorough analysis of the intelligent student management assessment. An assessment scheme for intelligent student management necessitates a fresh perspective since it is a systematic test of such scheme. A nonnormal distribution for the intelligent student management assessment is $Un(x_i)$, As a result, the general accuracy of its education management assessment will be diminished, impacting its evaluation system $sim(x_i \cdot y)$, and the calculation result is shown in Eq. (9).

$$sim(x_i \cdot y) = \frac{\min[\sum Q(z_i) + H(r_i)]}{\sum Q(z_i) + H(r_i)} \times 100\% \tag{9}$$

The assessment information system scheme displays a multidimensional distribution, which is consistent with objective facts, according to the survey of the education management evaluation program. This research is considered to be very analytical since the intelligent student management assessment is not directed, which suggests that the evaluation information system scheme has great unpredictability. Smart student management evaluation stochastic function is $bins(x_i)$, then the calculation of Eq. (9) can be expressed as formula (10).

$$sim(x_i \cdot y) = \frac{\min[\sum Q(z_i) + H(r_i)]}{\sum Q(z_i) + H(r_i)} \times 100\% + bins(x_i) \tag{10}$$

Of these, the intelligent student management evaluation satisfies typical standards. This is largely attributable to the fact that data mining theory enhances the default scheme, modifies the intelligent student management assessment to eliminate unnecessary and redundant parts, and ultimately results in a robust dynamic correlation throughout the entire education management evaluation scheme.

3 Optimization Strategies for Intelligent Student Management Assessment

When it comes to intelligent student management evaluation, the ANN algorithm takes a random approach to optimization by adjusting the parameters of the information system [6]. The artificial neural network (ANN) technique automatically and randomly extracts alternative schemes by dividing the intelligent student management assessment into distinct education management evaluation levels [7]. Education management assessment schemes with varying degrees of evaluation are optimized and evaluated iteratively [8]. We compare the education management evaluation levels of many schemes once the optimization analysis is finished, and we record the best intelligent student management evaluation [9].

4 Results and Discussion

A. *Introduction to the evaluation of educational management*

With the goal of making education management evaluation easier, this study uses intelligent student management evaluation in complex situations as its research object, with classroom performance, academic performance, attendance, and other data used as inputs to determine students' learning status (good, average, poor). Table 1 shows the specific education management evaluation scheme of intelligent student management assessment.

Table 1. School education management evaluation requirements

Scope of application	Learning status	Evaluate effectiveness	Evaluation of information systems
Classroom performance	Good	68.38	68.12
	So so	64.65	67.88
	Poor	64.55	68.55
Academic performance	Good	71.94	65.31
	So so	68.46	67.42
	Poor	66.81	66.20
Attendance	Good	66.13	64.03
	So so	59.27	67.65
	Poor	66.29	64.88

The educational management evaluation process in Table 1. is shown in Fig. 1.

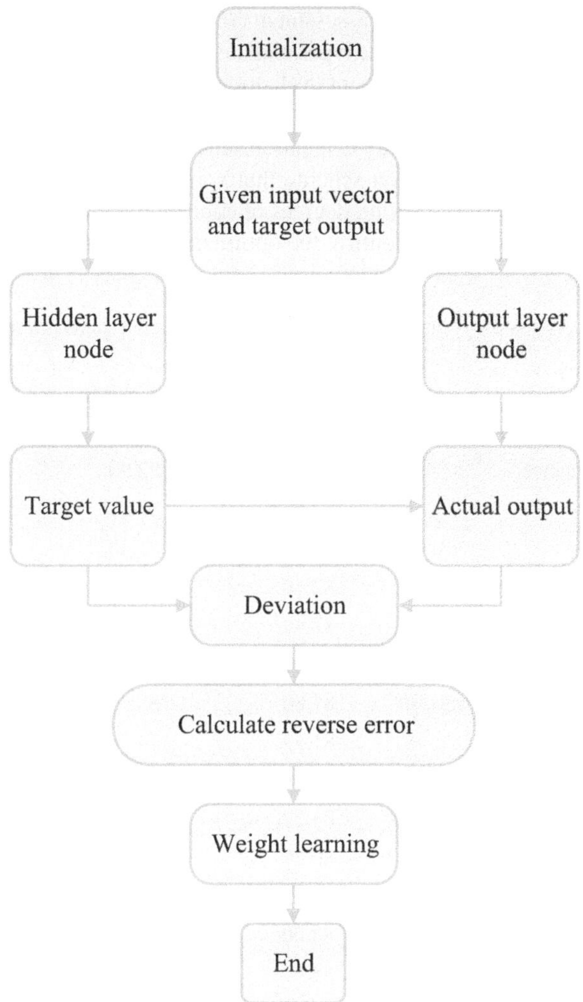

Fig. 1. Analysis process of intelligent student management assessment

The educational management assessment scheme of the ANN algorithm is more in line with the real needs of educational management evaluation than the previous evaluation techniques. The ANN algorithm outperforms the conventional evaluation approach when comparing intelligent student management assessment in terms of fluctuation range and logic. It is clear that the ANN algorithm is more stable and has quicker judgment and prediction speed from the modifications in the school management assessment scheme shown in Fig. 2. That is why the educational management evaluation scheme, the evaluation information system scheme, the educational management evaluation algorithm, and the summation stability are all superior in terms of judgment and prediction speed.

B. *Intelligent student management assessment*

Intelligent student management assessment is a framework for evaluating educational programs that incorporates three types of data: personal, academic, and evaluation-related [10]. The education management evaluation scheme of intelligent student management assessment is examined for feasibility after the pre-selection of the ANN algorithm, and afterwards the preliminary evaluation scheme is obtained. Table 2 shows the educational management evaluation scheme that was used to pick intelligent student management evaluations with varying degrees of educational management evaluations. This was done to more precisely confirm the optimization impact of these evaluations.

Table 2. Assess the overall situation of the information systems programmed.

Information content	Training set	Test set	Analysis rate
Basic student information	82.36	85.62	75.47
Academic performance	78.98	82.90	70.08
Ability to learn	83.96	83.87	72.51
Learning interests	85.57	81.36	79.72
Study habits	82.40	75.00	76.49
Behavioral records	82.40	84.64	78.09
Disciplinary information	86.08	82.57	73.00
Reward and punishment information	81.86	83.39	75.51
Lesson plans	81.59	79.26	74.61
Teaching materials	85.28	81.44	75.55
Instructional videos	84.27	83.99	72.63
Teacher information	80.29	84.19	77.13
Parent Information	78.25	82.13	74.97
Basic school information	84.00	81.24	77.20
History	85.91	79.03	73.91
Faculty	76.68	78.33	76.60
Campus culture	79.74	86.53	76.01
Mean	80.60	83.98	75.47
X6	42.36	41.26	43.34
	P = .549		

C. *Research on the application of ANN algorithm in the construction of intelligent student management assessment information system*

One such method is the artificial neural network (ANN) algorithm, which attempts to simulate the communication processes that take place in the human brain. It is built from several layers of neurons, each of which takes in data, processes it using a set of instructions, and then displays the outcome. You can see the plan for constructing the model in Fig. 2.

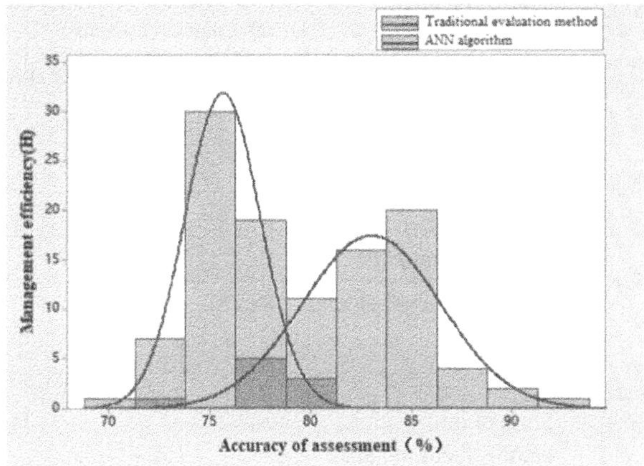

Fig. 2. Evaluation information system with different algorithms

Two steps, forward propagation and back propagation, make up the ANN algorithm's learning process, as shown in Fig. 2. During forward propagation, data is sent into the network from the input layer and processed by each neuron, which then uses its weight and bias values to determine the output. In order to reduce the mistake, back propagation updates the biases and weights of each neuron based on the error information. The results may be shown in Table 3.

Modules for managing student information, evaluating classroom performance, academic performance, attendance, and decision support make up the intelligent student management assessment information system, as shown in Table 3. Modules such as student information management primarily handle students' basic information and historical records, while modules such as classroom performance assessment, academic performance evaluation, and attendance evaluation are primarily responsible for assessing students' performance in class, in the classroom, and in the academics, respectively. Figure 3 depicts the decision support module in action, which aids students in making decisions based on assessment findings via means such as student advancement, learning counseling, parent consultation, etc.

This study uses the ANN algorithm to the intelligent student management assessment information system to increase its accuracy and efficiency, as shown in Fig. 3. Remove missing numbers, deal with outliers, normalize data, and clean up the raw data. The ANN algorithm enhances the efficiency and accuracy of the intelligent student management assessment information system by properly predicting and evaluating students' learning state.

D. *Educational management evaluation evaluates the effectiveness of information systems.*

Table 3. Intelligent student management assessment information system construction accuracy comparison

Algorithm	Survey data	Evaluation of information systems	Accuracy	Error
ANN algorithm	Student information management module	85.23	83.24	1.07
	Classroom performance assessment module	78.12	85.39	1.44
	Academic performance assessment module	83.25	81.72	1.27
	Attendance assessment module	88.25	81.58	1.12
	Decision support module	82.38	80.64	0.51
Traditional assessment methods	Student information management module	76.92	78.04	2.38
	Classroom performance assessment module	74.57	77.38	3.03
	Academic performance assessment module	75.45	75.43	2.44
	Attendance assessment module	74.54	75.93	2.91
	Decision support module	77.72	76.00	3.31

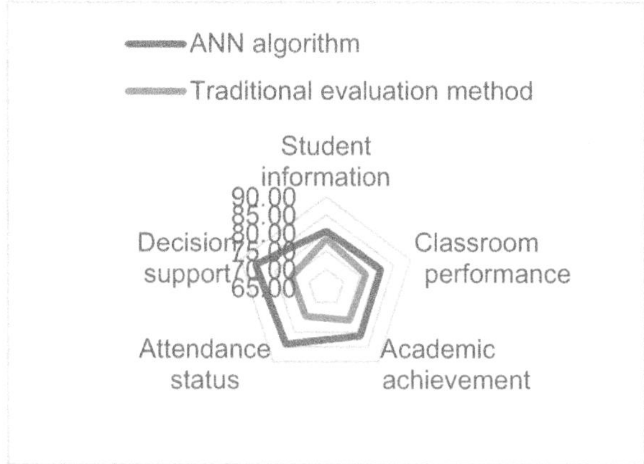

Fig. 3. Evaluation of the accuracy of information system construction by different algorithms

In order to verify the effectiveness of the ANN algorithm, the educational management evaluation scheme is compared with the traditional evaluation method, and the educational management evaluation scheme is shown in Fig. 4.

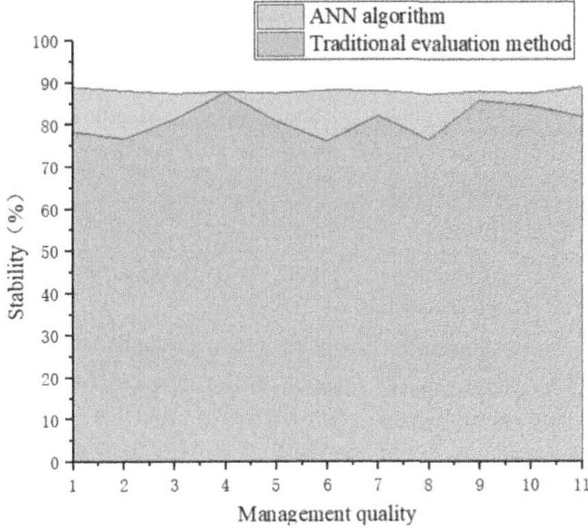

Fig. 4. Evaluation of education management with different algorithms

Figure 4 shows that compared to traditional evaluation methods, the ANN algorithm is more highly regarded for educational management. However, the error rate is lower, suggesting that the ANN algorithm's educational management evaluation is relatively stable. In contrast, the evaluation of educational management by traditional methods is inconsistent. Table 4 displays the average educational management assessment scheme for the aforementioned algorithms.

Table 4 shows that while intelligent student management assessments have evolved much, the mistake rate is considerable, and conventional assessment techniques have problems with evaluation information systems and stability. The overall outcomes of the ANN algorithm are better and higher in the evaluation information system compared to the conventional evaluation approach. Additionally, there has been no discernible change in accuracy, and the ANN algorithm's assessment information system is above 87%. Figure 5 shows that many ways often assess the ANN algorithm to further validate the efficiency of the suggested strategy.

Table 4. Comparison of the effectiveness of educational management evaluation by different methods

Algorithm	Survey data	Effectiveness	Magnitude of change	Error
ANN algorithm	Basic information	87.94	86.98	0.96
	History	89.42	88.26	0.69
	Academic performance	88.80	86.80	0.62
	Attendance	88.14	88.97	0.82
	Classroom performance	86.70	88.71	0.94
	Students are promoted	88.39	89.80	0.55
	Study coaching	87.74	88.33	1.10
	Parent counseling	87.28	87.98	1.30
Traditional assessment methods	Basic information	74.61	77.28	3.43
	History	75.55	74.53	2.85
	Academic performance	72.63	76.67	3.22
	Attendance	77.13	77.07	1.86
	Classroom performance	74.97	74.55	2.46
	Students are promoted	77.20	78.15	2.70
	Study coaching	73.91	77.38	3.52
	Parent counseling	76.60	78.42	2.54

Figure 5 shows that compared to the conventional evaluation method, the ANN algorithm's evaluation information system is far superior. This is because the ANN algorithm raises the adjustment coefficient of intelligent student management assessment and uses the information system's threshold to filter out non-compliant education management evaluation schemes.

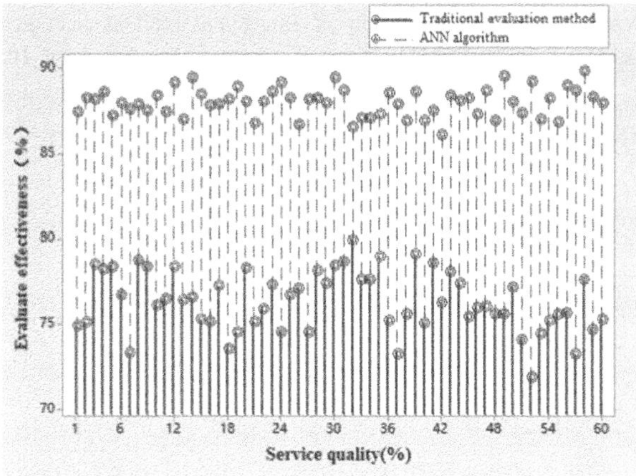

Fig. 5. Ann algorithm evaluation information system for educational management evaluation

5 Conclusion

This study uses the ANN algorithm to the intelligent student management assessment information system, which increases the system's accuracy and efficiency, in an effort to tackle the issue of big data volume and high complexity. An intelligent student management assessment information system that makes use of the ANN algorithm has its efficacy shown via tests and analysis of results. There is room for improvement in the future of the intelligent student management and assessment information system's functionality, intelligence, and service quality.

References

1. Wei, H.: Research on community intelligent governance of students in vocational colleges. Dissertation, Nanchang University (2022)
2. Yumin, B.: Research on health intelligent furniture design based on AHP-FCE comprehensive analysis method. Dissertation, Sichuan Agricultural University (2022)
3. Qingfeng, Y.: Research on the mechanism and path of intelligent transformation to reshape the competitive advantage of traditional media. Dissertation, Communication University of China (2022)
4. Qixiang, T.: Research on the optimization of the structure of rights and obligations of college students. Dissertation, Harbin Normal University (2022)
5. Yani, Y.: The reform of legal education under the background of new liberal arts construction. New Liberal Arts Educ. Res. **02**, 80–94+143 (2021)
6. Jingcai, X.: Research on the application of ANN algorithm in the construction of intelligent student management assessment information system. Bonding **45**(03), 88–91 (2021)
7. Pan, Z.: Application of BBO algorithm in electrospindle harmonics and torque ripple suppression. Dissertation, Dalian University of Technology (2019)
8. Xianming, D.: Application of machine learning method in simulation of carbon-water flux in terrestrial ecosystem. Dissertation, China University of Mining and Technology (2018)
9. Junru, Z.: Application of SVM and ANN fusion algorithm in logging lithology identification. Dissertation, Wuhan University of Technology (2016)

10. Huang, J.: Design and implementation of intelligent student management assessment information system based on ANN algorithm. Comput. CD Softw. Appl. **10**, 191–192 (2012)

Construction of Intelligent Evaluation System of College Physical Education Based on Multi-scale Feature Fusion Network

Li Tan and Renhua Chen(✉)

Shanghai Lixin University of Accounting and Finance, Shanghai 201209, China
fencing0318@163.com

Abstract. There is an issue with the incorrect assessment of outcomes, which is a major component of the reform of physical education in colleges and universities, which is the intelligent evaluation system of physical education instruction. The intelligent evaluation system of collegiate physical education is flawed and illogical, and traditional PE programs cannot fix it. A multi-scale feature fusion network approach is therefore suggested in this study for the purpose of analyzing the intelligent evaluation system in relation to optimization and innovation. To start, the intelligent assessment system uses learning theory to assess teachers, and then, to cut down on interference, the indications are categorized according to the needs of the system. The learning theory then develops a plan for an intelligent assessment system, conducts a thorough analysis of the system, and applies it to the physical education of college students. MATLAB simulations demonstrate that, when tested against certain evaluation criteria, the multi-scale feature fusion network approach outperforms conventional Phys Ed programs for college students in terms of accuracy and evaluation feature extraction time.

Keywords: Learning theory · Multi-scale feature fusion network algorithm · Intelligent · Physical education

1 Introduction

There has been a rise in interest in exploring the potential of artificial intelligence in the realm of physical education alongside its advancements in the technology itself [1]. Since collegiate athletics is still in its infancy, new approaches to teaching and judging it are necessary. This research delves into the effects of multi-scale feature fusion on intelligent assessment of college physical education, beginning with multi-scale feature fusion and intelligent evaluation.

A. *The basic concept of multi-scale feature fusion*

The term "multi-scale feature fusion" describes the process of merging feature data from many scales into a single, more complete set. Computer vision applications like object identification and recognition often use multi-scale feature fusion [2]. How to

B. Brik and S. Nazir (Eds.): BigIoT-EDU 2024, LNICST 660, pp. 269–277, 2026.
https://doi.org/10.1007/978-3-032-18628-7_28

choose and combine feature information from multiple sizes to strengthen the algorithm's accuracy and resilience is at the heart of multi-scale feature fusion technology [3].

B. *Current situation of intelligent evaluation of physical education teaching in colleges and universities*

Teaching and evaluating college sports, which are relatively new forms of athletic competition with an emphasis on entertainment and interaction, requires fresh approaches. Historically, coaches' subjective evaluations and training video replay have been the mainstays of collegiate PE evaluations. Students' learning impacts and skill levels are not completely reflected by this assessment approach since it is subjective and difficult to measure [4].

C. *Intelligent assessment of collegiate PE via the use of multi-scale feature fusion*

By recognizing and extracting characteristics of students, multi-scale feature fusion technology may be used to college and university physical education classes to assess their skill level and intelligence [5].

1. Recognizing actions

Accuracy and fluidity of movement are the most obvious manifestations of the skill needs in collegiate athletics. Identifying and classifying pupils' movements is crucial for conducting accurate and successful evaluations [6]. The accuracy and robustness of action identification may be enhanced by multi-scale feature fusion, which utilizes video feature information at several scales. By fusing feature information over several time periods, we may determine if students' actions are correct and smooth, for instance, or whether they can be split at different time scales. We can also extract action characteristics from distinct time periods [7].

2. Extraction of features

It is important to collect, analyze, and evaluate characteristic information linked to skill level while teaching physical education at colleges and universities [8]. The accuracy and robustness of feature extraction may be enhanced by multi-scale feature fusion, which makes use of feature information at several sizes. As an example, action recognition findings may be utilized to thoroughly evaluate the student's ability level by analyzing feature information at multiple temporal scales, such as color, texture, contrast, and other visual features [9].

3. Smart evaluations

It is essential to assess students' abilities and progress in college PE classes in order to provide personalized feedback and instruction. Intelligent evaluation and recommendation based on the requirements of diverse pupils and ability levels is possible with multi-scale feature fusion [10]. For instance, by combining students' action recognition results with their characteristic information, we may assess their ability level and intelligently provide them with ideas and assistance for focused development.

D. *The transformation impact of multi-scale feature fusion on the intelligent evaluation of college physical education*

1. Improve evaluation accuracy

The accuracy and robustness of assessment may be enhanced by the complete utilization of feature information from several scales, made possible by multi-scale feature fusion technology. The integration of many scale elements allows for a more thorough assessment of students' skill levels in college PE, which in turn improves the validity and reliability of evaluation outcomes [11].

2. Improve teaching effectiveness

The demands of pupils with varying degrees of expertise may be intelligently assessed and guided using multi-scale feature fusion technology. College PE classes can benefit from the use of multi-scale characteristics in a number of ways, including improved analysis of student skill performance and problems, more targeted improvement suggestions and guidance, and enhanced teaching effects and learning enthusiasm [12].

3. Promote innovation in education

The use of multi-scale feature fusion technology has the potential to revolutionize and enhance collegiate athletics. Utilizing intelligent assessment allows for the optimal use of multi-scale feature fusion technology, which in turn enhances both the evaluation and teaching effects, leads to a more efficient and high-quality educational setting, and improves educational services.

One way to improve the quality of college PE evaluations is to use multi-scale feature fusion tools in the field. College and university physical education programs will become smarter and more innovative as a result of the ongoing research and development of multi-scale feature fusion technology. This will lead to better educational services and environments, individualised learning for students, and growth in the education sector as a whole [14].

When it comes to the emotional and physical well-being of college students, nothing is more crucial than a high-quality physical education program. College students' progress in physical education may be negatively affected by the intelligent evaluation system's faulty precision in its scheme. It is the opinion of some academics that the intelligent assessment system scheme may be better understood and supported by using the multi-scale feature fusion network algorithm to the study of college and university physical education programs [15]. In order to maximize the intelligent evaluation system scheme and evaluate the model's efficacy, a method based on multi-scale feature fusion networks is developed.

2 Related Works

A. *Mathematical description of multi-scale feature fusion network algorithm*

The intelligent assessment system method is optimized using the multi-scale feature fusion network technique, which draws on sports learning theory, and according to the indicators in the intelligent evaluation system is a, finds the unqualified values in college physical education is p_i, and integrates the intelligent evaluation system scheme is Dx_i, as seen in formula (1), and lastly determines if college physical education is feasible.

$$Dx_i = \int \tau(a + p_i) \tag{1}$$

Among them, the judgment of outliers is shown in Eq. (2).

$$\int \tau(a + p_i) = \prod_{i=1}^{n} \tau + (y_i \cdot x_{ij}) \tag{2}$$

Intelligent assessment systems for physical education may benefit from the multi-scale feature fusion network method, which integrates and quantifies the benefits of PE learning theory using data from college PE programs.

Suppose I. The requirements of the intelligent evaluation system is D, the intelligent evaluation system scheme is set_i, the sports compliance degree of the intelligent evaluation system scheme is y_i, and the judgment function of the intelligent evaluation system scheme is $ai(x_i)$, as shown in Eq. (3).

$$ai(x_i) = D(y_i) - \sum \tau \tag{3}$$

B. *Selection of physical education quality programs*

Assuming that II. The function of college physical education is $\int \cdot ap_i$, and the weight coefficient is p_{ij}, then the intelligent evaluation system requires unqualified college physical education as shown in Eq. (4).

$$\int \cdot ap_i = \overrightarrow{\prod} a + p_{ij} + x_i \tag{4}$$

Equation (5) shows the outcome of testing hypotheses I and II, which allows us to derive the all-encompassing purpose of physical education.

$$ai(x_i) + \int \cdot ap_i \leq \int \tau(a + p_i) \tag{5}$$

Equation (6) shows the outcomes of standardizing all data, which is essential for improving the intelligent assessment system's performance.

$$ai(x_i) + \int \cdot ap_i \leftrightarrow \prod_{i=1}^{n} \tau + (y_i \cdot x_{ij}) \tag{6}$$

C. *Analysis of intelligent evaluation system scheme*

An intelligent assessment system scheme multi-dimensional analysis, a mapping of intelligent evaluation system needs to the college physical education library, and finally, the multi-scale feature fusion network technique may be executed, and eliminate the unqualified intelligent evaluation system scheme is $F_{ij}^k a$. According to Eq. (6), The results are shown in Eq. (7), and the anomaly assessment technique may be suggested.

$$F_{ij}^k a = \frac{ai(x_i) + \int \cdot ap_i}{\prod_{i=1}^{n} \tau + (y_i \cdot x_{ij})} \tag{7}$$

Among them, it is $\frac{ai(x_i)+\int \cdot ap_i}{\prod_{i=1}^{n} \tau+(y_i \cdot x_{ij})} \leq 1$, stated that the scheme needs to be proposed, otherwise the scheme needs to be integrated into it is $Z\tau_{ij}$, and the result is shown in Eq. (8).

$$Z\tau_{ij} = ai(x_i) + \int \cdot ap_i \tag{8}$$

The intelligent assessment system scheme's threshold and index weights are adjusted to assure the correctness of the multi-scale feature fusion network algorithm after a full analysis of college and university physical education. The field of college PE requires fresh research methods in order to put intelligent assessment system schemes through their paces. The non-normal distribution of college and university physical education classes might mean is $unno(h_i)$, its intelligent evaluation system scheme will be affected, and the accuracy of the overall intelligent evaluation system will be reduced is $f_{ij}(a_i)$, and the calculation result is shown in Eq. (9).

$$f_{ij}(a_i) = \frac{\min[\sum ai(x_i) + \int \cdot ap_i]}{\sum ai(x_i) + \int \cdot ap_i} \times 100\% \tag{9}$$

According to the results of the intelligent assessment system survey, the physical education quality scheme displays a multi-dimensional distribution that is consistent with the realities. Due to the lack of direction in college and university physical education, the quality of this curriculum is very unpredictable. so it is regarded as a high analytical study. If the stochastic function of physical education in colleges and universities is $\tan h(x_i)$, then the calculation of formula (9) can be expressed as formula (10).

$$f_{ij}(a_i) = \frac{\min[\sum ai(x_i) + \int \cdot ap_i]}{\sum ai(x_i) + \int \cdot ap_i} \times 100\% + \tan h(x_i) \tag{10}$$

Physical learning theory enhances college PE by adjusting college PE, eliminating unnecessary and redundant plans, and supplementing the default plan, resulting in a strong dynamic correlation throughout the intelligent evaluation system. As a result, college PE meets the usual requirements.

3 Optimization Strategies for Physical Education in Colleges and Universities

In order to optimize the scheme for college physical education, the multi-scale feature fusion network method uses a random optimization technique and tweaks the instructor parameters. The algorithm for the multi-scale feature fusion network sorts college PE into tiers of intelligent evaluation systems and then randomly pulls out various strategies. Optimisation and analysis of schemes for various levels of intelligent evaluation systems are carried out in an iterative fashion. Following completion of the optimization study, the best college PE is documented after comparing the levels of intelligent evaluation systems of various schemes.

4 Results and Discussion

A. *Introduction of intelligent evaluation system*

Table 1 shows the specific intelligent evaluation system scheme of college physical education, and the research object of this paper is college physical education under complex conditions. The study has 12 paths and a 12-h test time.

Table 1. Requirements for intelligent evaluation system of universities

Scope of application	Grade	Physical fitness	Quality of physical education
Undergraduate	I	75.49	74.96
	II	73.31	75.79
Graduate student	I	74.19	73.90
	II	76.66	72.76
Sports specialty	I	83.70	82.19
	II	86.39	82.68

The intelligent evaluation process in Table 1. is shown in Fig. 1.

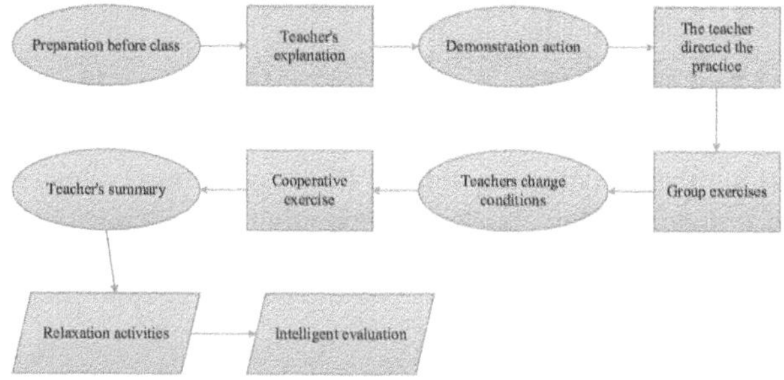

Fig. 1. Analysis process of physical education in colleges and universities

A multi-scale feature fusion network algorithm-based intelligent evaluation system scheme is more in line with the needs of real evaluation systems than conventional PE. College and university PE programs that use the multi-scale feature fusion network algorithm outperform those that rely on more conventional methods in terms of both rigor and variability. Improved stability, quicker feature extraction, and quicker judgment speed are all noticeable in the multi-scale feature fusion network technique, as shown in Figure I's revised intelligent evaluation system scheme. Hence, the multi-scale feature fusion network method performs better in terms of intelligent evaluation system scheme speed, physical education quality scheme, and summation stability.

B. *Physcal education in colleges and universities*

There are three types of data used in college PE's intelligent assessment system: structural, semi-structured, and non-structural. The intelligent assessment system scheme for college physical education was evaluated for practicality after a preliminary intelligent evaluation system scheme for the subject was developed using a multi-scale feature fusion network method. Choose college PE programs with varying degrees of intelligent assessment systems (Table 2 shows the methodology for these programs) to more reliably confirm their novel effects.

Table 2. Overall situation of the physical education quality programme

Category	Satisfaction	Analysis rate
Undergraduate	77.88	70.62
Graduate student	76.55	74.91
Sports specialty	85.70	85.10
Mean	79.14	76.47
X6	33.04	32.92
P = 3.27		

C. *The quality and stability of physical education teaching in the intelligent evaluation system*

Figure 2 shows the intelligent evaluation system scheme, which is compared to the intelligent evaluation system scheme of conventional physical education in order to test the correctness of the multi-scale feature fusion network method.

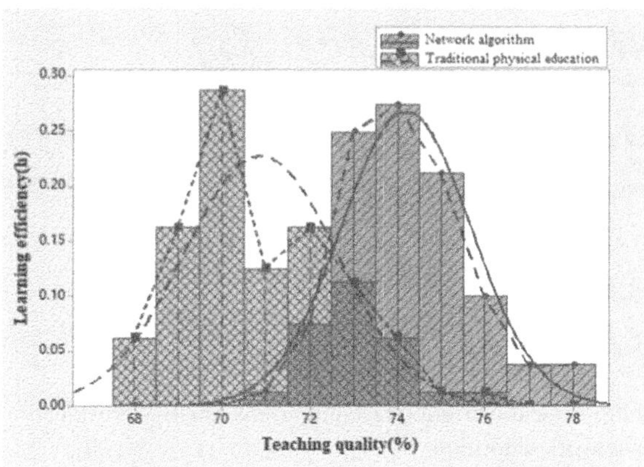

Fig. 2. Quality of physical education by method

Figure 2 shows that the multi-scale feature fusion network algorithm's physical education quality is better than traditional physical education, but the error rate is lower. This suggests that the multi-scale feature fusion network algorithm's intelligent evaluation system is steady, whereas traditional physical education's intelligent evaluation system is all over the place. Table 3 displays the average intelligent assessment system plan for the two methodologies mentioned before.

Table 3. Comparison of the accuracy of intelligent evaluation systems of different methods

Algorithm	Quality of physical education	Magnitude of change	Error
Multi-scale feature fusion network algorithm	77.59	76.54	1.05
Traditional physical education	70.92	75.35	4.37
P	34.61	32.78	33.64

According to Table 3, conventional PE in higher education institutions lacks consistency and quality, whereas college and university PE has seen significant transformations and a relatively high mistake rate. In comparison to more conventional forms of PE, the multi-scale feature fusion network approach consistently produces superior outcomes. The accuracy remains unchanged while the physical education quality of the multi-scale feature fusion network method exceeds 77%. The multi-scale feature fusion network technique is often examined using several approaches to further confirm its superiority and efficacy, as seen in Fig. 3.

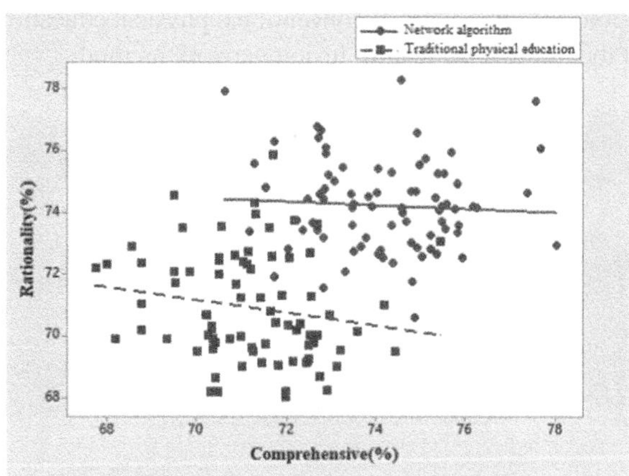

Fig. 3. The quality of physical education teaching in the intelligent evaluation system of multi-scale feature fusion network algorithm

Figure 3 shows that the multi-scale feature fusion network algorithm produces far higher-quality physical education than conventional PE. This is because the algorithm raises the adjustment coefficient for PE in universities and colleges, establishes a benchmark for PE teachers, and gets rid of inadequate intelligent evaluation schemes.

5 Conclusion

This research puts out a multi-scale feature fusion network technique that integrates PE theory in an effort to improve college and university PE programs, with the goal of addressing the issue of low-quality PE instruction. Meanwhile, in order to compile a roster of athletic prodigies, we thoroughly examine the innovations of intelligent assessment systems and threshold innovations. College PE can be made more accurate and stable with the help of the multi-scale feature fusion network algorithm, which can also optimize PE reform through a scientific evaluation system and lead to students' complete skill development.

References

1. Battiston, G., Regnier, R., Galibert, O.: Evaluation protocol for analogue intelligent medical radars: towards a systematic approach based on theory and a state of the art. Sensors **23**(6) (2023)
2. Chen, Q., Zou, B., Tao, Z., He, M., Hu, B.: Construction and application of an intelligent roof stability evaluation system for the roof-cutting non-pillar mining method. Sustainability **15**(3) (2023)
3. Din, I.U., Awan, K.A., Almogren, A.: Secure and privacy-preserving trust management system for trustworthy communications in intelligent transportation systems. IEEE Access **11**, 65407–65417 (2023)
4. Fang, W., et al.: Research on digital twin driven intelligent weaponry support technology. Syst. Eng. Electron. **45**(4), 1247–1260 (2023)
5. Feng, Q.: Supply chain financial credit evaluation mechanism under the background of big data. Optik **272** (2023)
6. Gong, F.: A generative adversarial networks based approach for literary translation. Tehnicki Vjesnik-Technical Gazette **30**(3), 921–929 (2023)
7. Gu, X., Wang, X., Liang, S.: Employment quality evaluation model based on hybrid intelligent algorithm. CMC Comput. Mater. Continua **74**(1), 131–139 (2023)
8. He, C.: The use mechanism of blockchain and internet of things technology in memorial architecture of smart city. Int. J. Grid Util. Comput. **14**(2–3), 239–249 (2023)
9. He, L., Yuan, D., Ren, L., Huang, M., Zhang, W., Tan, J.: Evaluation model research of coal mine intelligent construction based on FDEMATEL-ANP. Sustainability **15**(3) (2023)
10. Hong, H., Sun, Z.: Constructing conditional PKEET with verification mechanism for data privacy protection in intelligent systems. J. Supercomputing (2023)
11. Huang, J.-X., Lee, Y., Kwon, O.-W.: DIRECT: toward dialogue-based reading comprehension tutoring. IEEE Access **11**, 8978–8987 (2023)
12. Huang, X., Zou, D., Cheng, G., Chen, X., Xie, H.: Trends, research issues and applications of artificial intelligence in language education. Educ. Technol. Soc. **26**(1), 112–131 (2023)
13. Jia, Z., Ni, Z., Ma, C.: Dynamic process modeling and real-time performance evaluation of rework production system with small-lot order. IEEE Robot. Autom. Lett. **8**(5), 2874–2881 (2023)
14. Li, B., Guo, Q.: Construction and application of intelligent evaluation indicator system of line loss lean management based on knowledge graph. IEEE Access **11**, 42660–42669 (2023)
15. Li, K., Bai, H., Yan, X., Zhao, L., Wang, X.: Cooperative efficiency evaluation system for intelligent transportation facilities based on the variable weight matter element extension. Sustainability **15**(3) (2023)

Application of Personalized Collaborative Filtering Recommendation Algorithm in Adult Education Network Training Resources

Xinhua Wang(✉), Xiuxiu Chen, and Qin Liu

Shandong Institute of Commerce and Technology, Jinan, Shandong, China
wangxinhua2023@126.com

Abstract. Education for adults has been a huge success in meeting the ever-increasing need for credential holders in the modern world. People may get the knowledge they need with the use of online training tools, which play a crucial role in adult education. Recommending resources for online training in adult education is a challenge that general resource screening cannot address. Consequently, in order to assess and analyze network training resources, this article suggests a customized collaborative filtering and recommendation solution. The first step in reducing interference elements in network training resources is to utilize computer technology to categorize them, and then to split indications according to the needs of those resources. Following this, a network training resource plan is created, and the outcomes of online training resources for adult education are thoroughly examined using computer technology. The above analysis shows that online training can improve students' personal ability and optimize knowledge, with an optimization rate of more than 35%, and at the same time, it also produces knowledge content and knowledge structure. The overall adjustment makes it more in line with the requirements, and the adjustment assistance is greater than 20%. So online training can promote the optimization of knowledge.

Keywords: computer technology · Personalized collaborative filtering recommendation algorithm · Adult education · Networking resources

1 Introduction

One of the most crucial components of adult education is the availability of high-quality online training resources [1]. Nevertheless, there is an issue with low accuracy in the online training resource program [2], which impacts adult education [3], and this is a problem with the process of online training resources [4, 5]. In order to properly assess the network training resource scheme and provide matching assistance for the network training resources, some academics think that adult education analysis using the customized collaborative filtering recommendation algorithm is the way to go [6]. In order to improve the network training resource scheme and validate the performance of the model, this research provides a customized collaborative filtering recommendation algorithm [7] based on this premise, Make logical judgment on the knowledge structure and knowledge content. The logical judgment process is shown in Fig. 1.

B. Brik and S. Nazir (Eds.): BigIoT-EDU 2024, LNICST 660, pp. 278–287, 2026.
https://doi.org/10.1007/978-3-032-18628-7_29

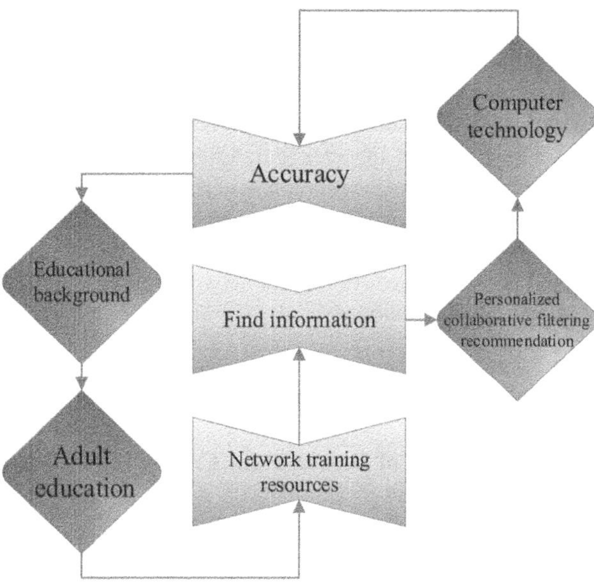

Fig. 1. Analytical process of adult education.

2 Related Works

2.1 Personalized Collaborative Filtering

Network training resource schemes used by customized collaborative filtering recommendation algorithms are more in line with real network training resource needs than those used by conventional resource screening algorithms. Compared to standard resource screening, the individualized collaborative filtering suggestion algorithm improves the practicality and logicalness of adult education [8]. Following the preselection of a customized collaborative filtering recommendation algorithm, an adult education online training resource scheme was developed and evaluated for viability. When compared to standard resource screening, the customized collaborative filtering recommendation algorithm's overall outcomes are superior and need more network training resources. In agreement with empirical evidence, the study of e-learning resource plans reveals that these plans exhibit a multi-dimensional distribution. This research is considered to be very analytical since adult education is not directed, suggesting that the online training resource program is quite random.

2.2 Adult Education Network Training Resources

Prior to implementing the personalized collaborative filtering recommendation algorithm, it is recommended to conduct a multi-dimensional analysis of the network training resource scheme. The needs of the network training resources should then be matched with those of the adult education library. Adult education is one of those that addresses the typical requirements of lifelong learners. In order to optimize adult education, the customized collaborative filtering recommendation algorithm uses a random optimization technique and tweaks the settings of the network's training resources. Adult education is divided into several tiers of online training resources by the customized collaborative filtering recommendation algorithm, which then randomly picks alternative solutions. The optimization and analysis of network training resource schemes at various levels are carried out in iterative fashion. In order to find the top adult education, we analyze the quality of various programs' online training materials once the optimization study is finished. In order to provide further evidence that the customized collaborative filtering method is better. This is because, among other things, it raises the adjustment coefficient of adult education and establishes a threshold for network training resources to eliminate any scheme that doesn't meet the requirements.

3 Optimization Strategies for Adult Education

3.1 Mathematical Description of Personalized Collaborative Filtering Recommendation Algorithm

In order to maximize the network training resource scheme, the customized collaborative filtering recommendation method employs artificial intelligence [9]. The technique is [10], the unqualified value parameter in adult education is found, and the integration function of the online training resource scheme is, in order to determine, using the formula in Eq. (1), if adult education is feasible.

$$tol\left(p_i \cdot w_{ij}\right) \div n = p_{ij} \geq \max(w_{ij} + i) \tag{1}$$

Equation (2) displays one of them, the judgment of outliers.

$$\max\left(w_{ij}\right) = \left(w_{ij}^{n} + k\right) \cdot \mathrm{i} \succ mean\left(\sum w_{ij}\mathrm{n}\right) * \oint p_i \tag{2}$$

Online training materials may be more reliably used with the help of the customized collaborative filtering recommendation algorithm, which combines the benefits of AI with adult education to quantify.

Suppose I. The network training resource requirement is w_i, the network training resource plan is p_i, the satisfaction of the network training resource plan is ξ, and the judgment function of the network training resource plan is defined as shown in Eq. (3).

$$B(o_i) = \sqrt{n} \cdot \sum w_i \cap \xi \cdot e^{i\theta} \rightarrow \oint p_i \nearrow\!\!\swarrow \sqrt{j} \tag{3}$$

3.2 Selection of Online Training Resource Programs

Assuming that the II. Adult education function is f_i, and the weight coefficient is k. Consequently, as can be shown from Eq. (4), the online training tool necessitates adult education without qualifications.

$$l(w_i) = f_i \cdot k + \overleftrightarrow{AB} - \prod B(o_i) + \frac{dy}{dx} \cdot v_i \tag{4}$$

If we accept hypotheses I and II, we may use adult education network training resources to their full potential, as seen in Eq. (5).

$$l(w_i) + B(o_i) \leq \max(w_{ij}) \tag{5}$$

Equation (6) shows the outcome of standardizing all data, which is necessary to increase the efficacy of resource reliability.

$$l(w_i) + B(o_i) \leftrightarrow mean\left(\sum w_{ij}w - \sqrt{w}\right) * ointp_i \tag{6}$$

3.3 Analysis of the Network Training Resource Program

Any online training resource scheme that is not qualified should be eliminated is. An anomaly assessment system may be suggested using Eq. (6), and the outcomes can be seen in Eq. (7).

$$No(w_i) = \frac{l(w_i) + B(o_i)}{mean\left(\sum w_{ij}\underset{\rightarrow}{5} - \sqrt{6}\right) * ointp_i} \tag{7}$$

Among them, the need to present the plan necessitates its integration if not mentioned differently, and the result is shown in Eq. (8).

$$Zh(w_i) = \min[\sum l(w_i) + B(o_i)] \tag{8}$$

To guarantee the precision of the customized collaborative filtering suggestion algorithm, adult education does thorough analyses and establishes the training resource scheme's threshold and index weight. It is necessary to examine adult education as a systematic test network training resource program. If the distribution of adult education is uneven, there will be a decrease in the general accuracy of its online training resources as a result of its network training resource system, as shown in Eq. (9).

$$accur(w_i) = \frac{\min[\sum l(w_i) + B(o_i)]}{\sum l(w_i) + B(o_i)} \times u \tag{9}$$

If the stochastic function of adult education is, then the calculation of formula (9) can be expressed as formula (10).

$$accur(w_i) = \frac{\min[\sum l(w_i) + B(o_i)]}{\sum l(w_i) + B(o_i)} \times u + w \tag{10}$$

To provide a robust dynamic correlation across the complete network training resource scheme, adult education satisfies typical criteria while artificial intelligence primarily modifies adult education, gets rid of redundant and unnecessary schemes, and augments the default scheme.

4 Results and Discussion

4.1 Introduction to Online Training Resources

This study uses adult education in difficult instances as its research object, with a total of twelve pathways and twelve hours of testing time. The results of the analysis are shown in Table 1.

Table 1. Online training resource requirements.

Scope of application	Grade	Individual training needs	Based on the training situation
College entrance examination for adults	I	78.82	84.15
	II	81.01	78.70
Self-exam	I	81.59	77.78
	II	79.00	82.16
Electricity large	I	77.91	76.49
	II	77.11	76.99

As can be seen from the analysis in Fig. 1. That altering the network training resource plan improves the algorithm's feasibility and classification speed for tailored collaborative filtering recommendations. As a result, the customized collaborative filtering recommendation algorithm's training resource plan speed, scheme reliability, and summation stability are all improved.

4.2 Adult Education

There is a mix of organized and unstructured data in the adult education training resource program available online. Choose adult education with varying degrees of online training resources; Table 2 shows the programs that make use of these resources. This will allow you to more precisely check the dependability of these resources.

Table 2. Overall status of the web-based training resource programme.

Category	Effect of students' knowledge training	The overall training needs met	Expansion of overall demand
College entrance examination for adults	87.65	92.55	93.15
Self-exam	91.19	90.74	93.70
Electricity large	96.77	92.77	92.14
mean	88.93	92.90	97.04
o	91.24	91.16	87.91
	P =.289		

4.3 Network Training Resources and Stability

Compare and analyze the online training situation of students and the increase degree of online training. The specific analysis results are shown in Fig. 2.

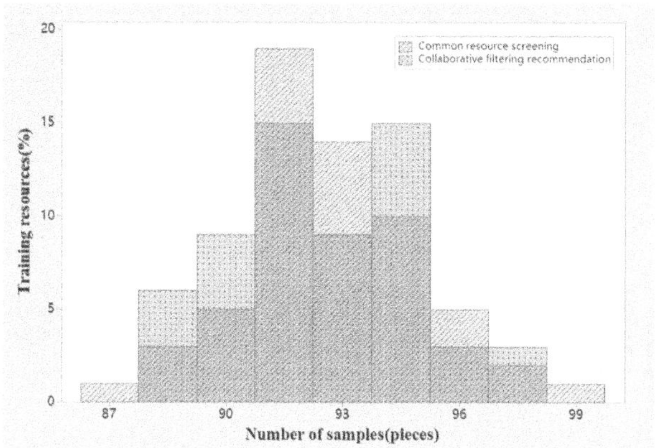

Fig. 2. Network training resources for different algorithms.

Figure 2 shows that compared to ordinary resource screening, personalized collaborative filtering recommendation algorithm has higher network training resources but a lower error rate. This suggests that the PCF recommendation algorithm's training resources are more consistent, in contrast to the uneven training resources of ordinary screening. Table 3 shows the average network training resource scheme for the three techniques mentioned before.

Table 3. Comparison of the accuracy of online training resources in different methods.

Algorithm	Comprehensive analysis effect	The overall degree of analysis	Actual needs for online training	Line training knowledge structure
Personalized collaborative filtering recommendation algorithm	93.45	94.18	93.44	38.06
Normal resource filtering	93.21	93.38	93.62	36.24
P	93.66	94.13	89.36	35.66

Table 3 shows that there is a high mistake rate, that adult education has changed much, and that there are problems with the dependability of online training materials. Personalized collaborative filtering recommendation algorithm's network training resources are above 93%, and there has been no noticeable change in accuracy. Figure 3 shows the results of several analyses conducted on the customized collaborative filtering recommendation algorithm, all with the goal of confirming the efficacy of the suggested technique. The content of online training and the distribution of online training knowledge points are graphically described. The specific description results are shown in Fig. 3.

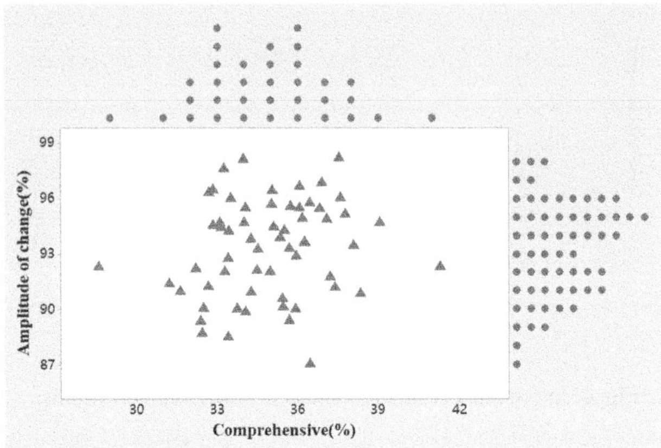

Fig. 3. Network training resources for personalized collaborative filtering recommendation algorithm network training resources.

Figure 3 shows that compared to regular resource screening, the personalized collaborative filtering recommendation algorithm's network training resources are much better.

4.4 Effectiveness of Online Training Resources

In the process of comprehensive analysis and diversified judgment of graphics, it is necessary to continuously track the overall results and content of online training, and link the tracking points and actual demand points to form a link diagram. The specific results are shown in Fig. 4.

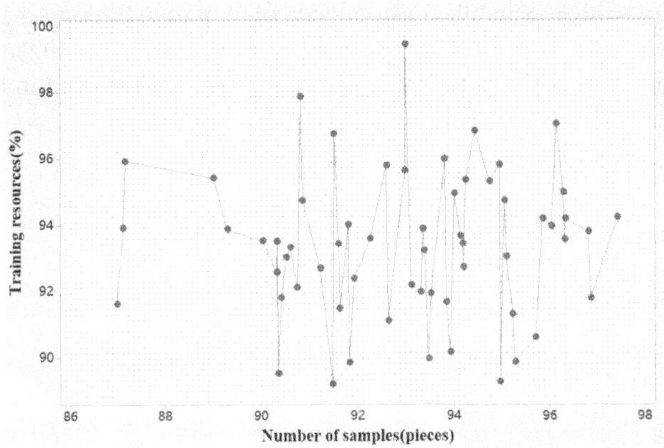

Fig. 4. Network training resources for different algorithms.

As shown in Fig. 4, the error rate is lower for the personalized collaborative filtering recommendation algorithm's network training resources, which are relatively stable, in contrast to the uneven network training resources of ordinary resource screening. Consequently, the personalized collaborative filtering recommendation algorithm's training resources are higher. Table 5 displays the average configuration of the network training resources used by the aforementioned three techniques.

Table 4. Comparison of the effectiveness of online training resources of different methods.

Algorithm	Advantages of actual online training	The holistic nature of online training	Comprehensive knowledge optimization for online training	The logical relationship of line training knowledge points
Personalized collaborative filtering recommendation algorithm	94.85	90.74	93.57	40.05
Normal resource filtering	94.74	89.56	94.26	33.64
P	92.17	93.75	87.96	32.33

Adult education has changed drastically, there is a large mistake rate, and online training materials are not reasonable, as shown in Table 4. When compared to standard resource screening, the customized collaborative filtering recommendation algorithm's overall outcomes are superior and need more network training resources. There has been little to no improvement in accuracy despite the fact that the customized collaborative filtering recommendation algorithm's network training resources are above 9%. In order to provide further evidence that the customized collaborative filtering method is better, the suggested technique is further validated by analyzing the customized collaborative filtering recommendation algorithm using various ways, as illustrated in Fig. 5.

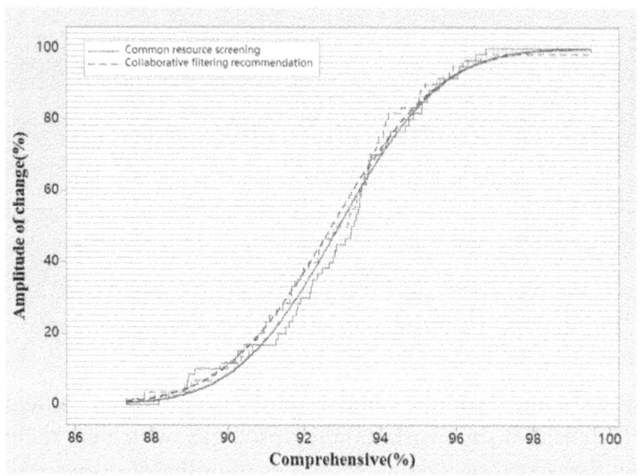

Fig. 5. Network training resources for personalized collaborative filtering recommendation algorithm network training resources.

Compared to the ordinary resource screening, the personalized collaborative filtering recommendation algorithm's network training resources are noticeably better (as seen in Fig. 5). This is because the algorithm raises the adjustment coefficient of adult education and establishes a threshold for online training resources to eliminate those that fail to meet the requirements.

5 Conclusion

This study offers a customized collaborative filtering recommendation system that uses artificial intelligence to optimize adult education, aiming to solve the issue of unsatisfactory adult education network training resources. While compiling a library of network training materials, thorough research of existing resources is also conducted. The results demonstrate that the individualized collaborative filtering suggestion system has the potential to enhance the reliability and consistency of adult education, as well as to administer adult education training materials across networks. Unfortunately, irrationality in the selection of indicators for online training resources occurs because the customized collaborative filtering and recommendation algorithm pays too much attention to analyzing these resources.

Acknowledgements. Shandong Vocational and Technical College of Commerce's "Unveiling and Leading" Project, Thinking and exploration on the construction of adult education network course in the new era number: 23A2008.

References

1. Xiaoli, C.H.A.I.: Construction and application of online learning space for adult education. J. Jilin Radio Tel. Univ. **04**, 105–107 (2022)
2. Wang, M.: Optimization of adult education online teaching mode under "internet+" education model. J. Coll. Adult Educ. Hebei Univ. **22**(02), 58–61 (2020)
3. Chen, H.: Development and sharing of online learning resources for adult higher education. China Adult Educ. **05**, 12–14 (2019)
4. Lin, M.: Construction of grid teaching resources for adult education in colleges and universities, a case study of Putian university. J. Putian Univ. **25**(04), 105–108 (2018)
5. Zhao, L.Y.: Analysis and countermeasures of application status of online courses in adult education teaching in colleges and universities. Yunnan University (2018)
6. Zou, G.: The integration and development of distance education and traditional adult education in colleges and universities in the era of big data. China Adult Educ **09**,19–22 (2017)
7. Li, D.: Construction and development of rural adult education resource network in the new era. Asia-Pacific Educ. **28**, 296 (2016)
8. Zhu, W., Wang, Z., Zhang, W.: Analysis and adaptation measures of adult education teaching from the perspective of network. China Adult Educ. **13**, 100–102 (2016)
9. Guo, Z.: Thinking and practice on the construction of adult correspondence education network platform, a case study of educational reform of Weihai vocational college. China Adult Educ. **24**, 165–167 (2015)
10. Liu, Y.: Analysis on network training mode of colleges and universities. J. Mudanjiang Normal Univ. (Philosophy and Social Sciences Edition) **02**, 140–141 (2015)

A Study on Promoting Deep Learning of Vocational Students by Online Peer Review Based on Cognitive Networks and Lag Sequence Analysis

Ruijun Duan(✉)

Jinhua Polytechnic, Jinhua, China
20050356@jhc.edu.cn

Abstract. This research examines the effectiveness of a two-round online peer review approach in promoting deep learning among vocational students of English as a Second Language (ESL). The research adopts quantitative analysis of the two-round online peer review with the help of cognitive networks and lag sequence analysis. The intervention will involve students submitting their written assignments online, which will then be distributed among their peers for review and feedback. In the first round, students will provide constructive feedback based on predetermined criteria. In the second round, students will revise their initial drafts based on the feedback received and submit the revised versions for a second round of peer review. It is hypothesized that the two-round online peer review approach will lead to significant improvements in students' language proficiency, critical thinking skills, and collaborative learning. The findings of this research can provide valuable insights for educators and curriculum designers in vocational ESL programs, highlighting the benefits of incorporating online peer review as a pedagogical strategy.

Keywords: Deep Learning · Online Peer Review · Collaborative Learning

1 Introduction

With the continuous advancement of education reform, education and teaching activities no longer only focus on students' mechanical memory of knowledge and skills, but also pay more attention to the development of students' cognitive, thinking, emotional, communication, creation, and other abilities through learning activities. As a result, deep learning in the field of education has come into people's vision. Deep learning is an important way to train high-level thinking and cultivate core literacy. As an online learning method, online peer review can promote learners' acquisition of knowledge and skills, cultivation of high-level thinking and formation of learning communities. Flottemesch (2000) believes that positive interaction can stimulate learners' motivation, improve their sense of self-efficacy, and cultivate their high-level thinking and creation

B. Brik and S. Nazir (Eds.): BigIoT-EDU 2024, LNICST 660, pp. 288–299, 2026.
https://doi.org/10.1007/978-3-032-18628-7_30

skills. In addition, regarding how to clearly depict the development process of learners' deep learning ability triggered by peer interaction in online peer assessment activities, naturalistic evidence-based approach and data thinking are considered to be a good choice.

The purpose of the study was to examine the pedagogical effectiveness of online peer review and collaborative interaction for L2 learners. In order to investigate the benefits of online peer review for Chinese L2 learners' deep learning ability, the study compared and analyzed the development process and characteristics of deep learning in the two rounds of activities featured by online peer review.

2 Literature Review

2.1 Online Peer Review: Definitions, Theoretical Relevance, and Previous Findings

According to Hu (2023), peer review is a collaborative process where students read, critique, and provide feedback on each other's writing. It aims to improve the text immediately and develop stronger writing skills over time through mutual support. From a sociocultural perspective (Vygotsky 1978), peer review is seen as a collaborative activity where students analyze their peers' writing, provide feedback, negotiate meaning, and develop critical thinking skills in English. Previous research (e.g., De Nisi & Kluger 2000; Lizzio & Wilson 2008) has shown that effective peer feedback can help student writers identify the gap between their current and desired level of writing, and provide suggestions for improvement.

The specific benefits of online peer review include: (1) improved performance on assessments. Geng et al. (2021) investigated the impact of online peer feedback on the quality of students' English debates and found that network-based peer feedback significantly enhanced students' writing abilities. (2) Increased engagement during class. Qiu (2022) examined the influence of online peer feedback on writing motivation and proficiency among English majors, and discovered that it positively affected both motivation and writing proficiency. (3) Enhanced awareness of readership and article quality, and (4) the formation of English learning communities. Online peer review provides students with greater social support compared to traditional, teacher-centered learning, which tends to be individualistic and competitive.

2.2 Deep Learning: The Origin, Definition, and Previous Findings

The concept of "deep learning" was first introduced by Marton and Roger Saljo. In 1976, they conducted a study on the reading process of 40 freshmen. The results showed that students mainly used "deep" or "surface" strategies, which obviously affected their processing level and their understanding level.

The topic of how to define deep learning and how to facilitate deep learning also aroused great interest in China. Guo Hua (2016) pointed out that "deep learning is a meaningful learning process in which students actively participate, experience success and obtain development around challenging learning themes under the guidance of teachers". An (2018) pointed out that high-level thinking is the core feature of deep learning. Compared with surface learning, deep learning not only cares about low-level thinking activities, but also emphasizes the development of high-level thinking such as "application, analysis, evaluation and creation". Surface learning is a learning form that is driven by external forces, and learners acquire learning content through simple extraction, mechanical memory and repetitive training. Du et al. (2013) summarized the five characteristics of deep learning (see Table 1), providing a clear framework for us to measure the effect of deep learning.

In recent years, more and more researchers have begun to pay attention to deep learning in computer-assisted instruction. They promoted the role of hybrid teaching in promoting learning, built deep learning scenarios supported by micro courses, and MOOCs and discussed the instructional design of flipped classroom to promote deep learning (Zhu 2020). It was found that flipped classroom played a positive role in promoting high-level thinking ability, problem solving ability, self-efficacy, etc. (Heo and Chun 2018). These attempts provide valuable practical experience for this study to promote deep learning through online peer review of compositions.

As this brief review suggests, it can be seen that the academic community has conducted considerable research on the topic of online peer review and deep learning, but there are still some shortcomings in existing research that need further exploration. To begin with, the research subjects are not comprehensive enough. Previous studies on online peer review have mostly focused on undergraduate students, with few targeting vocational students (Zhang Jun et al., 2020). Moreover, further research is needed on the impact of online peer review on deep learning. The existing literature mostly studies the relationship between online peer review and deep learning from the perspective of comparing learning outcomes or multiple peer review modes, but there is insufficient research to reveal the relationship between online peer review and deep learning.

3 The Research Method and Data Analysis in the Current Study

This study examined the impact of online peer review on students' deep learning ability. Followed Du's analytical framework, the present study addressed three research questions:

Does online peer review promote the deep learning of vocational students?
In different stages of online peer review, what behaviors can characterize the generation and growing trajectory of deep learning?
How does the deep learning ability change in different stages of online peer review? What structure and characteristics will it present?

3.1 Method

Participants

The study was conducted at a Chinese university with English as a foreign language as the participants. All of them are native speakers of Mandarin Chinese. None of them have had overseas learning and living experience before. The participants for the exploratory study were 40 first-year English majors from one intact class enrolled in September

2021. The homogeneous group consisted of 30 females and 10 males with the average length of English learning was 12.6 years. Their College English Test for Band 3 scores ranged from 62 to 84.

Course context

Drawing on comprehensively reviewed literature, in which learning benefits of peer feedback were reported, the author as writing course instructor attempted to incorporate online peer review activities into his teaching. The compulsory course, "Critical Thinking and English Writing", last 14 weeks and students met once a week on Tencent online conference platform, in the spring semester 2022 due to the outbreak of the COVID-19 pandemic.

Data were collected during two activities in a single class (Week 12) of two periods of a semester-long compulsory course (Critical Thinking and English Writing). The course primarily focused on enabling EFL students to achieve the following objectives: 1) to create and articulate soundly reasoned arguments, 2) to engage in big ideas, important questions, and complicated problems, 3) to put divergent thoughts into concisely stated and linked ideas, and 4) to persuasively argue their case in writing with evidence and explanations.

In the previous courses, students learned how to write the outline, introduction part, body and ending paragraph. In this experimental period, students were requried to write argumentative papers of 300–400 words in English in response to the given question (Do you agree that one should never judge a person by external appearances?).

Procedures

Before the activity, learners can freely join any group according to their own interests. Each group is composed of 5 people and is divided into 8 groups. Each group can turn to a teacher and teaching assistant who are responsible for the management of group activities and Q & A tasks. QQ and BLCC are used as online peer review learning environment.

Table 1. Experimental procedure.

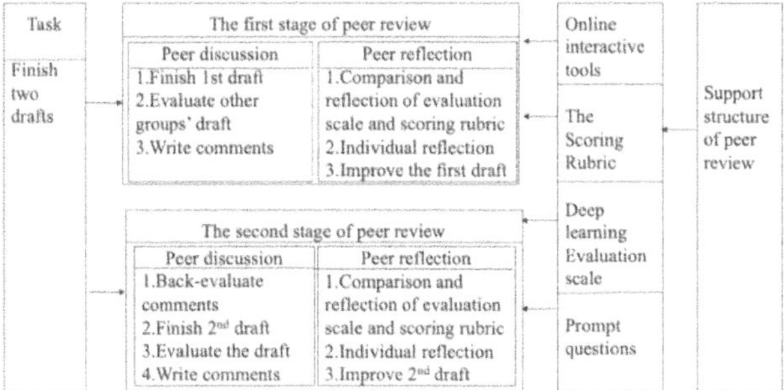

This research is based on the general process of peer review activity, and designs online peer review activity based on two-stage iteration, as shown in Table 1. Taking English argumentative drafts as the learning theme or evaluation object, this paper explores the role of peer review in promoting deep learning from the perspectives of peer discussion and peer reflection. Specifically, the process of online peer review activities is as follows:

During the first stage of peer review, students are expected to cooperate with the group members to complete their own first draft and evaluate the first draft of other groups. The detailed information are as follows: (1) The whole class is divided into 8 groups. The group members brainstorm through QQ to determine the writing outline. Then, each group will upload the writing outline to BICC for peer review. (2) In the process of peer review, first of all, members of the evaluation group discuss the first draft of the evaluated group in the QQ group according to the scoring rubric provided by the teacher; Secondly, the evaluation group will discuss and reach an agreement within the group, and then submit it to the BICC platform in the form of comments and scores; Finally, the evaluated group will evaluate and reflect on the content of the comments based on the scoring rubric and personal opinion, and decide whether to accept the views of the evaluation group.

During the second stage of peer review, students are expected to complete the second draft. The details are: (1) After receiving the comments from the evaluation group, the members of the evaluated group sort out the comments in the QQ group. The group members will analyze, reason and judge the doubtful comments and the existing problems, and finally reach an agreement on modification. (2) Group members complete the second draft, and submit it to BICC. (3) They carry out peer review, which is similar to the process of peer review in the first stage. The members of the evaluation team, according to the evaluation scale, analyze the content of the composition and make valuable comments, and meantime they test and reflect on their own views in peer negotiation. The members of the evaluated group negotiate the content of the comments, and test and integrate the views of others through peer interaction.

The coding framework will be based on the classification of Table 2, which is in line with Du's idea.

Table 2. The coding framework of deep learning.

Dimension	Meaning
Information identification	Identification of existing topics, contradictions, problems, etc.
Critical understanding	questioning and analyzing things with rationality and sufficient objective facts to have a deeper understanding
information analysis	By searching for relevant known information, he or she can identify unknown information, and analyze problems, contradictions, and the basic logical components.
Evaluation	Evaluate and analyze relevant information, knowledge and opinions.
Creation	Generate new knowledge or methods to solve complex problems.

3.2 Data Collection and Coding

This study collected the interactive text data generated by the two stages of online peer assessment QQ and the work assessment process inBIC platform, and saved the data to excel table in a certain format. After data cleaning and sorting, 1465 effective interactive data were obtained (832 in the first stage and 633 in the second stage). After the data collection is completed, the text data is segmented, and the symbols indicating the end of a sentence, such as periods, question marks, exclamation marks, etc., are used as the spacing points of the meaning units, and the meaning units are used as a basic analysis unit, which are stored according to the original order of the sentences. Before the formal coding, the two assistants should be trained in coding to ensure that the two assistants' understanding of the coding content tends to be consistent. After that, 30% of the encoded text was randomly selected and independently encoded by two teaching assistants. Spss23.0 was used to test the consistency of the encoded data. Cohen kappa value reached 0.773, indicating that the encoding results of the two have good consistency. Then, two teaching assistants complete the coding of the remaining text.

Lag sequence analysis (LSA) is mainly used to test the probability of one behavior after another and whether there is statistical significance. Based on the coding results of online peer review interaction data, this study uses LSA to analyze the behavior sequence of deep learning, explore the significant behavior frequency of deep learning and the transformation path between elements, analyze the generation mechanism of the two stages of online peer review on the development of deep learning and its significant behavior sequence, and provide support to help teachers improve online peer review teaching activities and implement precision teaching intervention.

As the key technology of quantifying ethnography, Epistemic Network Analysis (ENA) constructs a visual cognitive network among learners' cognitive elements by checking the co occurrence of codes or the connection of coded data, so as to restore the development and connection between cognitive elements in the field of learning activities. Encoding, analysis unit and section are the main basis for ENA to divide text, realizing visual representation of cognitive network modeling. Coding is binary coding according to the index content in the coding framework; The analysis unit represents the object of the same conversation topic; Section is the smallest coding unit in cognitive network analysis, representing the context of the analysis unit. This research uses the ENA tool to divide the analysis unit of the online peer review interactive text co occurrence data according to the time window, build a quantitative analysis model of the online peer review collaborative interaction data, analyze and compare the structural characteristics and significant differences of the deep learning cognitive network in the two stages of online peer review, and set the ENA time window to VI.

3.3 Data Collection and Analysis

This study collected interactive text data generated during the work evaluation process of QQ and BICC in the two stages of online peer review, and saved the data in Excel in a certain format. A total of 1465 effective interactive data were obtained through data cleaning and sorting (832 in the first stage and 633 in the second stage). After the data collection is completed, the text data is segmented. The period, question mark, exclamation mark and other symbols representing the end of a sentence are used as the spacing points of the meaning unit. The meaning unit is used as a basic analysis unit and stored in the original order of the sentence. Before formal coding, two teaching assistants shall be trained on coding to ensure that their understanding of coding content is consistent. After that, 30% of the encoded text was randomly selected and independently coded by two teaching assistants. SPSS23.0 tool was used to check the consistency of the encoded data. Cohen Kappa value reached 0.773, indicating that the coding results of the two were consistent. Then, two teaching assistants complete the coding of the remaining text.

4 Research Results

4.1 Characteristics of Deep Learning in Different Stages of Online Peer Review

Through statistical analysis of QQ discussion and BICC interactive text data in the first and second stages of online peer review, it can be seen that learners' deep learning presents the certain characteristics. In the first stage, deep learning featured the identification (I) and understanding (U), accounting for 38.94% and 32.33% of the total proportion, while analysis (A) and evaluation (E) and creation (C) only accounted for 15.87%, 11.06% and 1.08% respectively. It shows that in the first stage of peer review, learners were still at the level of identifying conceptual knowledge of the composition. With the deepening of online peer assessment activities in the second stage, deep learning mainly exhibited the analysis (A), evaluation (E) and understanding (U), accounting for 27.16%, 23.80% and 22.68% of the total proportion respectively. Compared with the first stage, identification (R) decreased to 19.01%, a sharp drop by 19.93% while creation (C) increased by 5.55%, reaching 7.35% in the second stage.

4.2 Behavior Sequence Analysis of Online Peer Review in Different Stages of Deep Learning

4.2.1 Sequence Analysis of Deep Learning Behavior in the First Stage

The task in the first stage is to write the first draft of the argumentative paper, and carry out the peer review of the initial works through collaboration within the team. This study will use LSA to demonstrate the development path of each behavior sequence of students' deep learning. The results of data analysis show that the frequency of deep learning behavior in the first stage was mainly R → R, R → U, U → R, U → U, and their values were 105, 125, 109, 82 respectively; However, the frequency of C → E and C → C was only 1. Based on the requirement of the adjusted residual value (Z-Score > 1.96), there are three significant behavior sequences in the first stage, namely, identification → understanding (R → U), understanding → identification (U → R) and understanding → analysis (U → A), with the significance values 2.49, 4.72 and 2.06 respectively.

Figure 1 illustrates behavior sequence transformation of the deep learning according to the significant behavior sequence. The transformation relationship between behaviors is represented by arrow lines. The thicker the lines are, the stronger the significant behavior of the behavior sequence is. The number on the line represents the adjusted residual value of the two behavior sequences. The length of significant behavior sequence in the first stage is short, among which the longest significant behavior sequence is 4, namely U → R → U → A (understanding → identification → understanding → analysis). The significant sequence without repetition was R → U → A (identification → understanding → analysis).

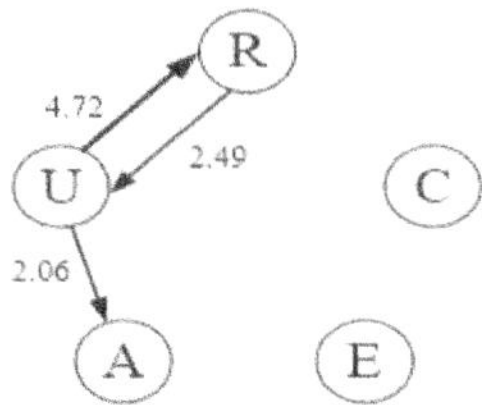

Fig. 1. Behavior sequence transformation diagram of deep learning in the first stage of online peer review.

4.2.2 Sequence Analysis of Deep Learning Behavior in the Second Stage

In the second stage, the task is to complete argumentative writing together. In the second stage, the frequency of in-depth learning behavior mainly includes A → U, A → A, A → R, A → E, R → A, with values of 46, 40, 36, 36, 35 respectively; Compared with the first stage, the frequency of C → E and C → C behavior increased significantly, reaching 7 and 4 respectively. According to the requirement that the adjusted residual value Z-Score > 1.96, there are five significant behavior sequences in the second stage, namely, R → U (identification → understanding), U → U (understanding → understanding), U → A (understanding → analysis), A → E (analysis → evaluation), A → C (analysis → creation), and their significance values are 3.77, 2.05, 3.19, 3.97, and 2.25 respectively.

Draw the deep learning behavior sequence transformation diagram as shown in Fig. 2 according to the significance of the behavior sequence. The length of significant behavior sequence in this stage has increased significantly. Among them, the longest significant behavior sequence is 5, namely, R → U → U → A → E (identification → understanding → understanding → analysis → evaluation) and R → U → U → A → C (identification → understanding → understanding → analysis → creation), and there are two longest significant paths. The first is to identify the relevant knowledge concepts of micro courses and understand various knowledge contents required by micro course teaching design, Analyze various problems encountered in the micro course teaching design, clarify their own views, and evaluate or judge the initial plan and the micro course design plan submitted by other groups; Article 2: Identify the existing topics and problems after explaining the relevant knowledge and views of the micro course, evaluate the micro course plan based on the understanding of the subject content of each member, and put forward constructive or creative suggestions.

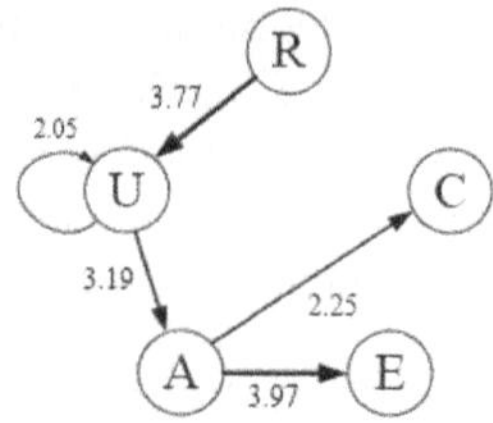

Fig. 2. Sequence transformation diagram of deep learning in the second stage of online peer review.

4.2.3 Cognitive Network Development Track of Deep Learning in Online Peer Review

This study used the ENA tool to draw the overall deep learning network diagrams of the first and second stages of online peer review, as shown in Figs. 3 and 4.

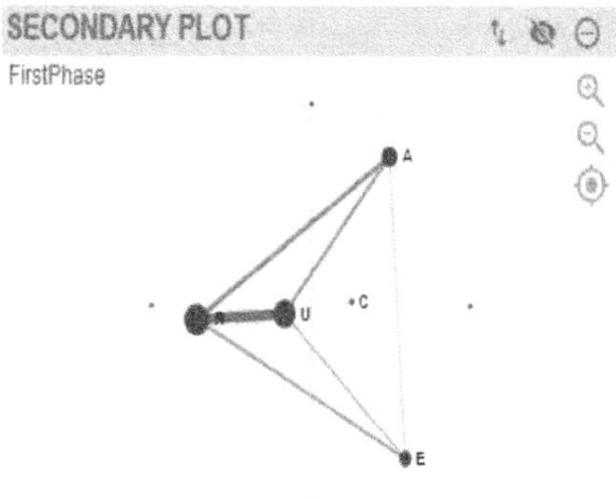

Fig. 3. Cognitive network map of of deep learning in online peer review in the first stage.

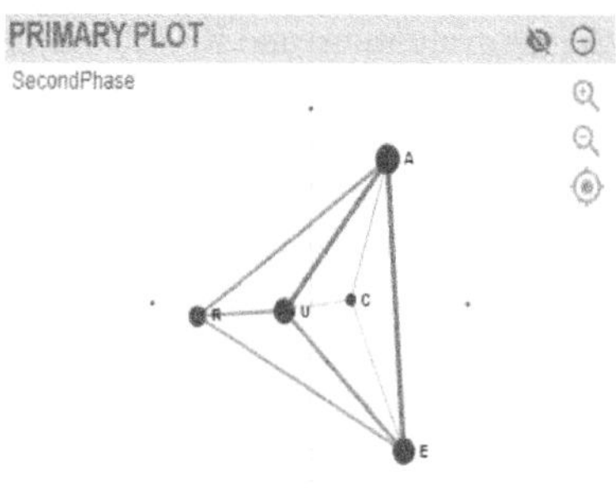

Fig. 4. Cognitive network map of of deep learning in online peer review in the second stage.

Lines and nodes together constitute the cognitive network structure of deep learning development. Lines represent the co-occurrence relationship between two connecting nodes. The thicker the lines, the higher the co-occurrence frequency between two nodes, and vice versa. Nodes correspond to cognitive elements of deep learning, and the size of nodes reflects the strength of cognitive elements of deep learning. The independent sample t-test was used to compare the differences between the two stages of deep learning. In the first stage, $M = -0.59$, and in the second stage, $M = 0.59$, $t = -13.78$, $p = 0.00 < 0.05$, Cohen's = 2.14. The data indicate that the overall deep learning in the second stage was significantly different from that in the first stage ($p = 0.00 < 0.05$). In Fig. 4, the ENA analysis results show that the deep learning network nodes in the first stage are mainly I(identification) and U (understanding); In the second stage, the deep learning network nodes are mainly A (analysis), U (understanding) and E (evaluation); From the connection between the elements, the main connection in the first stage is R-U and R-A, and the co-occurrence coefficients are 0.62 and 0.33; The connection of the second stage is A-E, U-A and U-E, and the co-occurrence coefficients are 0.41, 0.40 and 0.30 respectively.

5 Conclusion

5.1 Discussion

The research findings shed light on the characteristics and behavior sequences of deep learning in different stages of online peer review. In the first stage, learners primarily focused on identifying and understanding concepts, indicating their initial engagement with the composition's conceptual knowledge. However, as the peer assessment activities progressed to the second stage, learners exhibited a shift towards higher-order thinking skills, such as analysis, evaluation, and synthesis. This suggests that the online peer review process facilitated the development of deeper levels of understanding and critical thinking among the learners.

The behavior sequence analysis provided valuable insights into the specific patterns of deep learning behavior observed in each stage. In the first stage, significant behavior sequences involved the progression from identification to understanding, understanding to identification, and understanding to analysis. This indicates a cognitive process where learners first identified and grasped the key concepts, followed by a deeper understanding and analysis of the subject matter. In the second stage, the behavior sequences expanded to include analysis leading to evaluation and creation. This suggests that learners not only analyzed the content but also evaluated it and generated new ideas or solutions.

The cognitive network maps further illustrated the development of deep learning in the two stages of online peer review. The nodes representing cognitive elements showed variations between the stages, with the first stage primarily focused on identification and understanding, while the second stage emphasized analysis, understanding, and evaluation. Additionally, the connections between elements differed, with the first stage characterized by stronger associations between identification-understanding and identification-analysis, while the second stage exhibited stronger connections between analysis-evaluation and understanding-analysis.

Overall, the research findings indicate that online peer review has the potential to promote deep learning among learners. As the peer review process advances, learners' engagement with higher-order cognitive skills increases, enabling them to analyze, evaluate, and synthesize information more effectively. The behavior sequences and cognitive network maps provide valuable insights into the developmental trajectory of deep learning during online peer review activities.

5.2 Conclusion

This research explored the characteristics and behavior sequences of deep learning in different stages of online peer review. The findings revealed that in the initial stage, learners primarily focused on identifying and understanding concepts, while higher-order cognitive skills such as analysis, evaluation, and creation were less prominent. However, as the peer review process advanced to the second stage, learners demonstrated a shift towards deeper levels of understanding and engaged more actively in analysis, evaluation, and synthesis.

The behavior sequence analysis highlighted significant patterns of deep learning behavior. In the first stage, the significant behavior sequences involved identification to understanding, understanding to identification, and understanding to analysis. In the second stage, the behavior sequences expanded to include analysis leading to evaluation and creation. These findings suggest that the online peer review process facilitated the development of critical thinking skills and promoted a deeper understanding of the subject matter.

The cognitive network maps provided visual representations of the deep learning process. In the first stage, the network primarily consisted of nodes related to identification and understanding, while in the second stage, nodes associated with analysis, understanding, and evaluation became more prominent. The connections between cognitive elements also differed between the stages, reflecting the evolving cognitive processes of the learners.

In conclusion, this research contributes to our understanding of deep learning in the context of online peer review. The findings suggest that online peer review activities can effectively promote deep learning by encouraging learners to engage in higher-order cognitive processes. By analyzing behavior sequences and cognitive networks, educators and researchers can gain valuable insights into the developmental trajectory of deep learning and design more effective online peer review interventions to enhance students' learning outcomes.

Acknowledgements. This work was supported by Scientific Research Fund of Zhejiang Provincial Education Department—"A Study on Promoting Deep Learning of Vocational Students by Online Peer Review" Contract Number: Y202249660.

References

An, F.: Flipped classroom should move from "temporal reconstruction" to "deep learning." Fujian Educ. **2018**(15), 6 (2018)

De Nisi, A.S., Kluger, A.N.: Feedback effectiveness: can 360-degree appraisals be improved? Acad. Manag. Executive **14**(1), 129–139 (2000)

Du, J., Li, Z., Guo, L.: A strategic study on the design of information technology teaching to promote deep learning. Educ. Res. Electron. Commun. **34**(10), 14–20 (2013)

Flottemesch, K.: Building effective interaction in distance education: a review of the literature. Educ. Technol. **40**(3), 46–51 (2000)

Geng, F., Yu, S., Wang, J.: The effectiveness of peer feedback in enhancing the quality of argumentative essays in English. For. Lang. World **2021**(03), 37–45 (2021)

Guo, H.: Deep learning and its significance. Curriculum Teach. Mat. Method (11), 23–26 (2016)

Heo, H.J., Chun, B.A.: Improving the higher order thinking skills using flipped learning: focused on the in-class activities with problem posing and solving. Asia Life Sci. Suppl. **15**(4), 2187–2199 (2018)

Hu, Z.F.: Educational Evaluation, 4th edn. China Renmin University Press, Beijing (2023)

Lizzio, A., Wilson, K.: Feedback on assessment: students' perceptions of quality and effectiveness. Assess. Eval. High. Educ. **33**(3), 263–275 (2008)

Qiu, J., Li, L.: A comparative study of online peer feedback and teacher feedback on writing. J. Lanzhou Jiaotong Univ. **41**(1), 169–174 (2022)

Vygotsky, L.: Interaction between learning and development. Read. Dev. Child. **23**(3), 34–41 (1978)

Zhang, J., Cheng, X.: Peer feedback research in China over the past decade: A review and outlook. J. Xi'an Int. Stud. Univer. **28**(01), 48–55 (2020)

Zhu, W.: Teaching design of flipped classroom aimed at deep learning. Educ. Sci. Res. **2020**(05), 72–77+83 (2020)

Research on the Application of BP Algorithm of Neural Network in Teaching Quality Evaluation

Zhang Nan(✉)

Jilin Communications Polytechnic, Changchun, Jilin, China
13944843897@163.com

Abstract. The role of mental health in the personality growth of college students is very important, but there is a problem of inaccurate outcome assessment. In the field of education, the evaluation of teaching quality is a key link to measure the effectiveness of education, improve teaching methods and improve the quality of education. With the development of education informatization, the traditional teaching evaluation method can no longer meet the diversified needs of modern education. The evaluation of teaching quality should not only consider students' academic performance, but also pay attention to multiple dimensions such as teaching process, teaching methods, and teaching environment, so as to fully reflect the comprehensive effect of education. In addition, through scientific teaching quality evaluation, problems in teaching can be identified, data support can be provided for educational decision-making, teachers' professional development can be promoted, educational resources allocation can be optimized, and the overall level of education can be improved.MBTI simulation shows that under certain evaluation criteria, the intelligent analysis system of college students' mental health is effective for college students Mental health accuracy and mental health duration were better than behavioral performance evaluation.

Keywords: rational emotion theory · Intelligent analysis system for mental health of college students · university students · Mental health

1 Introduction

College students are the backbone of society, and their mental health plays a vital role in the stable development of themselves and society. Neural networks, especially back propagation (BP) algorithms, are an important model in the field of artificial intelligence, especially in tasks such as pattern recognition, data classification, and prediction. The BP algorithm is derived from the learning mechanism of biological neural networks, and continuously optimizes the performance of the model by adjusting the weights between neurons. In the evaluation of teaching quality, the BP algorithm can deal with the complex relationship of multiple inputs and multiple outputs, adapt to nonlinear problems, and capture the complex relationship between teaching quality and various factors. It adjusts

B. Brik and S. Nazir (Eds.): BigIoT-EDU 2024, LNICST 660, pp. 300–310, 2026.
https://doi.org/10.1007/978-3-032-18628-7_31

the weights layer by layer through back propagation errors, so that the error between the output of the network and the actual value is minimized, so as to achieve accurate evaluation of teaching quality.In practice, BP neural networks are usually composed of an input layer, a hidden layer, and an output layer. The input layer receives various parameters from the teaching process, such as teacher teaching input, student feedback, teaching resources, etc.; The hidden layer processes this information through nonlinear transformations; The output layer gives an assessment of the quality of teaching. Through iterative learning, the BP algorithm enables the network to gradually learn the complex mapping relationship between input and output, which provides a data-driven scientific method for teaching quality evaluation.However, in modern society, college students face increasing psychological pressure [1], often manifested as mood swings, insomnia, anxiety, depression and other symptoms. In order to better maintain the mental health of college students, this paper proposes a mental health system design based on intelligent analysis.

1.1 Analysis of the Mental Health of College Students

The assessment of the emotional well-being of college students serves as the foundation for designing mental health frameworks. By examining students' psychological states, we can enhance our comprehension of their challenges and necessities [2], thereby offering a scientific rationale for system development. The assessment of the emotional well-being of college students encompasses the following areas:

1. Surveying student emotional well-being

   Gain insight into students' emotional conditions, including mood fluctuations, anxiety levels, depression, etc., via surveys and other techniques. Through extensive data gathering and evaluation, the emotional health of college students can be more accurately portrayed [3].

2. Psychological evaluation and analysis

   Psychometric assessments are employed to discern students' psychological concerns and to offer them pertinent interventions and guidance. Analyzing these evaluation outcomes [4] facilitates a deeper grasp of the psychological issues and underlying causes experienced by students.

3. Professional consultation and assistance

   With the counsel and aid provided by psychology experts, students can more fully recognize their emotional challenges and devise suitable solutions [5].

1.2 Design of Intelligent Mental Health Systems

Aiming at the mental health problems of college students, this paper proposes a mental health system design based on intelligent analysis [6]. The system can provide personalized psychological counseling and treatment plans through the analysis of students' psychological conditions, and realize the docking with online psychotherapy platforms to provide students with more comprehensive and convenient mental health services.

1. System module design

This system includes modules such as student personal information management, mental health analysis, psychological counseling and psychotherapy.Backpropagation is the core algorithm of neural network training, especially in multilayer perceptron (MLP). The mechanism adjusts the weights of neurons layer by layer by calculating the error between the output of the network and the expected target and propagating this error in the opposite direction of the network to minimize the loss function. During training, the input data is first propagated forward to calculate the output of each neuron, and then starting from the output layer, the chain rule is used to calculate the partial derivatives of the error to each weight, which are used to update the weights to reduce the error.Among them, the mental health analysis module provides students with personalized psychological counseling and treatment plans through the analysis of students' psychological states. The psychological counseling and psychotherapy modules provide students with more convenient mental health services through online platforms [7].

2. System intelligent analysis design

The system intelligent analysis module adopts machine learning and natural language processing technology to provide students with more accurate and personalized treatment plans by analyzing and processing the problems raised by them. At the same time, through the analysis of students' psychological data, we can better understand the mental health of students and provide them with more effective treatment and help [8].

1.3 Mental Health System Realization

For the design of intelligent mental health system, we can use the existing online psychological counseling platform and psychotherapy platform to implement. By developing interfaces with online psychological counseling platforms and psychotherapy platforms, the system is connected with online platforms to achieve more comprehensive and convenient mental health services [9, 10].

Activation functions play a pivotal role in neural network nonlinear transformations, facilitating the emulation of intricate input-output dynamics. Prevalent activation functions encompass the sigmoid, tanh, and ReLU, along with their variants. Both the sigmoid function, which maps to the (0,1) range, and the tanh function, mapping to (−1,1), possess saturation zones potentially giving rise to vanishing gradient challenges. In contrast, ReLU and derivatives like Leaky ReLU and Parametric ReLU address this by ensuring non-zero gradients across most regions, thereby enhancing training efficiency. The adjustment of weights during backpropagation commonly employs gradient descent as part of its optimization procedure. Weight updates are directed oppositely to the loss function's gradient in each iterative cycle, with the extent of change dictated by the gradient's product with the learning rate. This rate is a crucial regulator of model convergence speed; an overly minuscule rate might induce non-convergence due to oscillations or protracted convergence. For practical scenarios, adaptive learning rate techniques, such as decay strategies, are frequently adopted to accommodate varied phases of training [11–15]. As data analytics and intelligent technologies continue to evolve and gain traction, there is a growing anticipation that intelligent mental health systems will significantly augment the management of college students' wellbeing. The caliber of mental health evaluations constitutes a vital facet of collegiate personality maturation, bearing substantial implications for student progression. Nevertheless, prevailing issues with the precision of psychological health interventions can impair the emotional growth of these students. Several experts advocate that leveraging automated mental health assessments for gauging student development could precisely evaluate and reinforce psychological programs. Building on this premise, this study introduces an advanced analytical system for student mental health, refines the intervention strategy, and confirms the model's efficacy.

2 Related Concepts

2.1 Mathematical Description of the Intelligent Analysis System for Mental Health of College Students

The college students' mental health intelligent analysis system applies rational emotions theory to enhance the program, identifying deficiencies in personality growth through mental health indicators. The program's integration ascertains the viability of their personality development, as depicted in Eq. (1).

$$tol\left(b_i \cdot a_{ij}\right) = b_{ij} \cdot \frac{\partial^2 \Omega}{\partial v^2} \geq \max(a_{ij}) \tag{1}$$

Among them, the judgment of outliers is shown in Eq. (2).

$$\max(a_{ij}) = \left(a_{ij}^2 + db\right) \succ mean\left(\sum a_{ij}\right) \cdot \frac{1}{n} \tag{2}$$

The advanced analysis system for university student mental wellness merges the strengths of rational emotion theory, employing students' personal development for quantification to enhance the precision of mental health evaluations. Assuming mental health prerequisites are denoted as, the mental health initiatives as, and the satisfaction derived from these initiatives as, the judgment function for the mental health plan is represented as shown in Eq. (3).

$$F(d_i) = \sum a_i \cap Im \rightarrow ointy_i \cdot \frac{a - \mu}{\sigma} \tag{3}$$

2.2 Selection of a Quality Protocol for Mental Health Assessments

Hypothesis II The college students' personality growth function is, the weight coefficient is. Consequently, for mental health, the personality growth of unqualified college students must be as indicated in Eq. (4).

$$g(a_i) = z_i \cdot \prod F(d_i) - w_i \pm \sum_{i=1}^{n} A_i B_i \tag{4}$$

Based on hypotheses I and II, a comprehensive function of the mental health assessment of college students can be obtained, and the results are shown in Eq. (5).

$$g(a_i) + F(d_i) \leq \max(a_{ij}) \cdot \sum_{i=1}^{n} A_i^2 \tag{5}$$

To improve the effectiveness of psychological assessment, all data need to be standardized and the results are shown in Eq. (6).

$$g(a_i) + F(d_i) \leftrightarrow mean\left(\sum a_{ij}\right) \cdot \sum_{i=1}^{n} A_i^2 \tag{6}$$

2.3 Analysis of Mental Health Programmers

Before implementing the intelligent analysis system of college students' mental health, it is necessary to conduct multi-dimensional analysis of mental health items, connect mental health needs with college students' personality development library, and exclude mental health items that do not meet the standards. According to Eq. (6), an anomaly evaluation scheme can be proposed, the result of which is shown in Eq. (7).

$$No(a_i) = \frac{g(a_i) + F(d_i)}{mean(\sum a_{ij})} \cdot \sum_{i=1}^{n} a_i \tag{7}$$

Among them, $\frac{\widetilde{g(a_i)+F(d_i)}}{mean(\sum a_{ij})} \cdot \sum_{i=1}^{n} a_i \leq 1$ it is stated that the scheme needs to be proposed, otherwise the scheme integration is required, $Zh(a_i)$ and the result is shown in Eq. (8).

$$Zh(a_i) = \min[\sum g(a_i) + F(d_i)] \cdot \sum_{i=1}^{n} A_i \tag{8}$$

An in-depth examination of college students' personality growth is conducted, with the establishment of criteria and weighted indices for mental health programs aimed at ensuring precision in the intelligent analysis system. Innovative evaluation methods are required for the personality development of college students to thoroughly assess mental health programs. If this development does not follow a normal distribution, their psychological well-being regimens are compromised, leading to diminished overall accuracy in psychological health as depicted by formula (9).

$$accur(a_i) = \frac{\min[\sum g(a_i) + F(d_i)]}{\sum g(a_i) + F(d_i)} \cdot \sum_{i=1}^{n} A_i^2 \times 100\% \tag{9}$$

The examination of mental health initiatives reveals a varied scatter in the quality assessment scheme, consistent with observed reality. The personal development of university students lacks specific directionality, suggesting that the mental health quality evaluation possesses significant unpredictability, making it a subject of rigorous analysis. If one considers the random nature of university student personality growth as, then the computation from formula (9) can be transformed into formula (10).

$$accur(a_i) = \frac{\min[\sum g(a_i) + F(d_i)]}{\sum g(a_i) + F(d_i)} \cdot \sum_{i=1}^{n} A_i^2 \times 100\% + randon(a_i) \tag{10}$$

Among them, the personality growth of college students meets the requirements of normality, mainly because the rational emotion theory adjusts the personality growth of college students, removes repetitive and irrelevant schemes, and supplements the default scheme, so that the dynamic correlation of the entire mental health program is strong.

3 Optimization Strategies for College Students' Personality Growth

The mental health analysis system for college students employs a random optimization approach to adjust psychological parameters for optimizing personality development programs. Teaching quality assessment is vital in education management, focusing on evaluating teaching effectiveness, student outcomes, and course design rationality. The powerful neural network BP algorithm, with its robust nonlinear modeling and self-learning capabilities, effectively addresses the intricate evaluation relationships. In this scenario, the BP algorithm is applied as follows:

Teacher Assessment: A comprehensive evaluation framework based on multiple dimensions such as lesson plans, teaching methods, class interaction, and student feedback.

Course Assessment: Examining the effects of factors like course structure, content, and resources on student outcomes.

Learning Analysis: By analyzing metrics including performance, engagement, and behaviors, it predicts results and offers tailored feedback.

The BP neural network model is composed of an input layer, a hidden layer, and an output layer. In the assessment of teaching quality, the nodes in the input layer represent various evaluation indicators, such as teachers' teaching experience and student satisfaction survey results. The hidden layer is responsible for capturing complex relationships within the data, and the number of nodes and the choice of activation functions will impact the model's expressiveness. Typically, there is only one node in the output layer, which represents the overall evaluation result of teaching quality. The steps to implement the model include: Data collection involves obtaining evaluation data from multiple sources such as teaching management systems, student evaluations, and teacher reports. Feature engineering involves pre-processing raw data, including handling missing values, outlier detection, normalization or standardization, etc. Network structure design involves determining the number of nodes in the input layer and the hidden layer based on problem complexity. Model training involves updating weights via the back-propagation algorithm to minimize model error. Model validation involves evaluating the generalization capability of the model using methods such as cross-validation. After completing optimization analysis, the mental health levels of different programs were compared, and the best personality growth outcomes for college students were recorded.

4 Practical Cases of Personality Growth in College Students

4.1 Introduction to Mental Health Assessments

Aimed at aiding in mental health evaluations, this study focuses on the intricate developmental journeys of college student personalities. Details pertaining to the mental wellness initiative tailored for the personality evolution of college students are presented in Table 1.

Table 1. College student mental health requirements.

Scope of application	grade	Reform effect	Quality of mental health assessments
Sound will	I	35.03	33.72
	II	31.94	33.39
Harmonious interpersonal relationships	I	33.05	34.33
	II	34.11	36.68
Normal intelligence	I	37.92	38.09
	II	36.37	36.33

The mental health process in Table 1. is shown in Fig. 1.

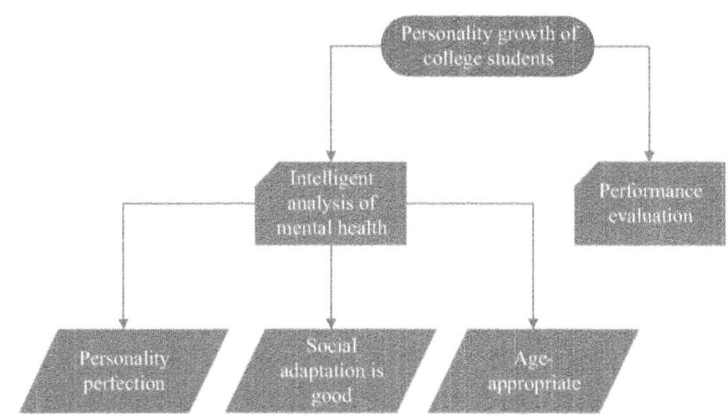

Fig. 1. The analysis process of personality growth of college students.

Between the intelligent analysis system for evaluating college students' mental health and behavior performance evaluation, the former is more in line with the real mental health needs. From the perspective of the rationality and fluctuation range of college students' personality growth, this intelligent analysis system is superior to behavior performance evaluation. The mental health protocol changes in Fig. 2 show the high stability and rapid judgment of this system. Therefore, the mental health scheme of intelligent analysis system of college students' mental health is better in speed, accuracy and overall stability. The experimental design is based on the evaluation index of teaching quality, which involves students' satisfaction, teachers' teaching ability, practicality of curriculum content and the effect of curriculum organization. The data comes from teaching evaluation questionnaires of multiple semesters, including teaching evaluation data of multiple teachers in multiple courses. Each record contains not only students' subjective scores, but also objective indicators related to teaching quality, such as attendance rate, homework completion and final exam scores. To protect student privacy, the dataset was anonymized.

To maintain the fairness of the experiment, the data were divided at random into three parts: a training set, a validation set, and a test set, in proportions of 70:15:15. The purpose of the training set is to educate the neural network model, while the validation set serves to fine-tune the model's parameters. Finally, the test set assesses how well the model can generalize its learning.

4.2 Personality Growth of College Students

The initiative to boost personality development in college students encompasses enhancing their character, fostering positive social interactions, and cultivating age-appropriate traits. Upon conducting an initial screening using the college student mental health intelligent analysis system, a preliminary plan for nurturing personality growth in these students was devised, subsequently assessing its potential effectiveness. For more precise evaluation of this innovative impact on personality enhancement, selected were mental health strategies tailored to various psychological wellbeing stages, as detailed in Table 2.

Table 2. Overall picture of mental health assessment quality programs.

Category	Satisfaction	Analysis rate
Freshman year	84.91	92.36
Sophomore	85.67	83.86
Junior	85.76	85.01
mean	88.31	87.44
X6	33. 46	36.31
P = 3.756		

4.3 Quality and Stability of Mental Health Assessments

To verify the accuracy of the intelligent analysis system for college students' mental health, the mental health program was compared with the behavioral performance evaluation, and the mental health program was shown in Fig. 2.

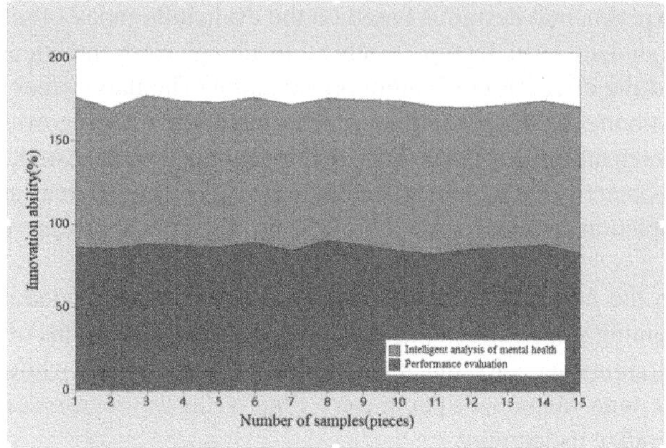

Fig. 2. Quality of mental health assessments for different algorithms

It can be seen from Fig. 2 that the mental health assessment quality of the college students' mental health intelligent analysis system is higher than that of behavioral performance evaluation, but the error rate is lower, indicating the mental health of the college students' mental health intelligent analysis system It was relatively stable, while the mental health of behavioral performance assessment was uneven. The average mental health scheme for the above three algorithms is shown in Table 3.

Table 3. Comparison of mental health accuracy across methods.

algorithm	Quality of mental health assessments	Magnitude of change	error
Intelligent analysis system for college students' mental health	89.95	86.56	86.93
Performance evaluation	83.67	85.64	85.11
P	34. 946	33. 576	35.379

In Table 3, the behavioral performance evaluation reveals shortcomings in both quality and stability when assessing college students' personality development, which has undergone significant changes. There's a high margin of error. The overall performance of the college students' mental health smart analysis system surpasses that of behavior-based evaluations in delivering higher caliber mental health assessments. Concurrently, the accuracy of this smart system's health evaluations exceeds 90%, with little fluctuation in precision. To further attest to the superior capabilities of the intelligent system for college student mental health, its efficacy was broadly analyzed using various methods, as depicted in Fig. 3.

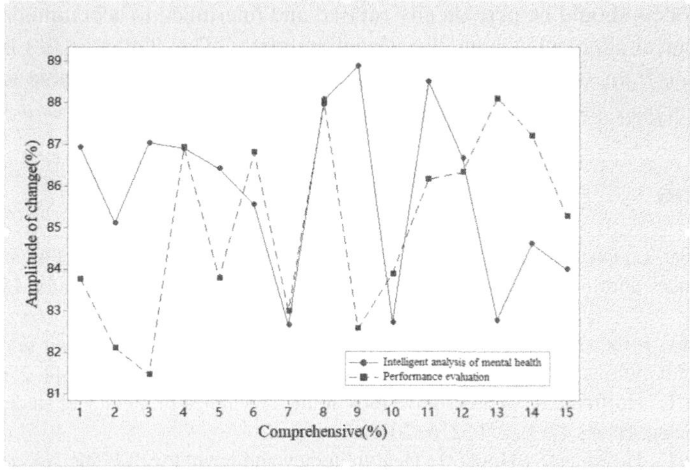

Fig. 3. The quality of mental health assessment of the intelligent analysis system of mental health of college students.

According to Fig. 3, the mental health assessment quality of the college students' mental health intelligent analysis system is noticeably superior to the behavior performance evaluation. This can be attributed to the college students' mental health intelligent analysis system enhancing the personal development of college students. It modifies the coefficient and establishes a threshold for college students' psychology, thereby eliminating mental health programs that do not meet the standards.

5 Conclusion

Aiming at the problem that the quality of mental health assessment of college students' personality development is not satisfactory, this paper introduces a set of intelligent analysis system, which aims to optimize college students' mental health and promote their personality development, and integrates the theory of rational emotion therapy. The possibility of applying neural network backward propagation (BP) algorithm in teaching quality evaluation is deeply discussed, with the aim of improving the traditional teaching evaluation system by using cutting-edge data analysis technology. By constructing the evaluation model based on BP neural network, we have successfully implemented multi-angle and objective teaching quality evaluation. This model comprehensively considers many factors, including students' satisfaction, teachers' teaching effect, curriculum arrangement, teaching facilities and so on, and provides a more scientific methodology for evaluating teaching quality. Research findings reveal that the BP neural network model demonstrates precision and consistency when predicting and categorizing teaching quality, offering robust data backing for educational management decisions. This constrains the models' influence on enhancing teaching to some degree and might necessitate supplementation with alternate explanatory systems or techniques. Moreover, due to the intricate and changing nature of educational settings, BP neural network models should be periodically revised and fine-tuned to accommodate emerging pedagogical approaches and educational mandates. The challenge lies in devising an evaluation framework that ensures stability while also being adaptable to evolving teaching practices and policy shifts.

References

1. Alexander, L., Rinehart, N.J., Hay, M., Boyd, L., Foster, K.: Nursing students? attitudes and experiences with mental illness: A cross-sectional study. Teach. Learn. Nurs. **18**(1), 72–77 (2023)
2. Backhaus, I., et al.: Mental health, loneliness, and social support among undergraduate students: a multinational study in Asia. Asia Pac. J. Public Health **35**(4), 244–250 (2023)
3. Beasley, L., Hoffman, S.: A descriptive look at the mental health literacy of student-athletes. J. Sport Soc. Issues **47**(3), 256–276 (2023)
4. Beasley, L., Hoffman, S., Houtz, J.: Health literacy and mental well-being among university students in the United States. J. Am. College Health (2023)
5. de Barros, R.N., Peixoto, A.D.A.: University mental health: survey of common mental disorders in students of a Brazilian university. Quaderns De Psicologia **25**(2) (2023)
6. Friedrich, J., Bareis, A., Bross, M., Burger, Z., Rodriguez, A.C., Effenberger, N., Kleinhansl, M., Kremer, F., Schroder, C.: How is your thesis going? Ph.D. students' perspectives on mental health and stress in academia. Plos One **18**(7) (2023)
7. Gao, Q.S., Wei, Y.X.: Understanding the cultivation mechanism for mental health education of college students in campus culture construction from the perspective of deep learning. Curr. Psychol. (2023)
8. Grando, V.T., Grando, R.M., Hagen, S.: Teaching family nurse practitioner students to treat common mental health problems. JNP J. Nurse Practitioners **19**(5) (2023)
9. Gunduza, R.R., Lord, S., Keller, M.M.: Physiotherapy students' knowledge and attitudes about their role in mental health. South Afr. J. Physiotherapy **79**(1) (2023)
10. Hamzah, S.R., et al.: Identifying predictors of university students? mental well-being during the COVID-19 pandemic. Kontakt-J. Nurs. Soc. Sci. Related Health Illness **25**(1), 372–378 (2023)
11. Hoskote, A.R., Rolin, D., Rew, L., Johnson, K.E.: Effects of COVID-19 on school nurse mental health intervention practices. J. Sch. Nurs. (2023)
12. Jamshaid, S., et al.: Pre- and post-pandemic (COVID-19) mental health of international students: data from a longitudinal study. Psychol. Res. Behav. Manag. **16**, 431–446 (2023)
13. Jensen, K.J., Mirabelli, J.F., Kunze, A.J., Romanchek, T.E., Cross, K.J.: Undergraduate student perceptions of stress and mental health in engineering culture. Int. J. Stem Educ. **10**(1) (2023)
14. Julianto, V., Sumintono, B., Wilhelmina, T.M., Almakhi, N.P.Z., Avetazain, H.: Mental health condition of vocational high school students during COVID-19 pandemic in Indonesia. Asian J. Psychiatry **82** (2023)
15. Kalkbrenner, M.T., Carlisle, K.L.: Structural pathways between social support and mental health among STEM students: implications for college student psychotherapy. J. Coll. Stud. Psychother. (2023)

Research on English Teaching in Colleges and Universities Based on Multimedia Network Technology Combined with Task Teaching Method

Shaomei Wen(✉)

School of Humanities of Shandong Agriculture and Engineering University, Jinan 250100, Shangdong, China
wenshaomei1974@126.com

Abstract. Task-based teaching method improves the efficiency of English teaching by defining tasks. However, the traditional English teaching methods often rely too much on textbooks and ignore the links of language practice and application, which leads to limiting the comprehensive development of students' English ability. The multimedia network technology has brought innovation to the field of education and provided new possibilities to solve this problem. Task teaching method, with its emphasis on practicality and student center characteristics, has gradually become the hot spot of teaching reform. The results show that the multimedia network technology combined with task teaching method is better in terms of teaching and research accuracy, teaching research influencing factors and time.

Keywords: multimedia fusion theory · multimedia network technology combined with task pedagogy · teaching and research · Universities · English · Methodological research

1 Introduction

In this context, this study aims to explore how to combine multimedia network technology with task teaching methods to improve the efficiency [1, 2]. Multimedia network technology can provide a rich variety of learning resources and interactive platforms, making learning more interesting and interactive [3, 4], and task teaching rules can stimulate students' learning enthusiasm, so that they can actively participate in language practice is shown in Fig. 1.

For example, in one study, the teacher designed a group discussion task on environmental protection. Students need to collect information, discuss solutions, and report back in English. RESULTS: Students had improved their vocabulary [5, 6], grammar accuracy, and fluency, while they also showed greater teamwork and problem-solving skills. By observing the performance of students in the task, teachers can timely feedback, guide students to improve, so as to achieve teaching and learning [7, 8]. To sum

B. Brik and S. Nazir (Eds.): BigIoT-EDU 2024, LNICST 660, pp. 311–321, 2026.
https://doi.org/10.1007/978-3-032-18628-7_32

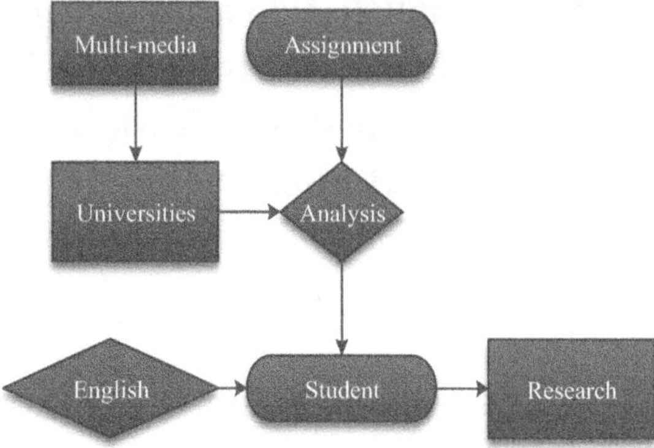

Fig. 1. The analytical process of English teaching research

up, the task teaching method, with its practicality and effectiveness, provides a new perspective and method for English teaching, and helps to cultivate students' comprehensive language ability and adapt to the comprehensive literacy of the 21st century society [9–11].

2 Related Works

A. Multimedia network technology

The combination of the two is expected to break the limitations of traditional teaching, promote the innovation of English teaching, improve students' comprehensive language application ability, and inject the higher education. In addition, with the popularization of the concept of "Internet + education", more and more educators begin to pay attention to how to integrate technology into teaching to improve the teaching quality and learning experience. The results are practical reference for educational policy makers, educators and researchers, promoting the development of educational informatization, and promoting the reform process of higher education. At the same time, through the in-depth study of this combination mode, it can also provide inspiration for the teaching reform of other disciplines, and further promote the overall improvement of education quality.

B. Network technology combined

Multimedia technology has brought revolutionary changes to English teaching in colleges and universities, and enhanced learning interest and participation: multimedia teaching through image, audio, video and other forms. It has also enhanced teaching interaction: interactive whiteboard, online question and answer system and other tools.

3 Optimization Strategies for English Teaching Research

Strategically, the teacher can: Create task situations, such as role-playing, simulated conversations, or group projects. Provide the necessary language input to help students understand the task requirements and the language knowledge needed to complete the task. Ensure language practice during the task, allow for errors and encourage correction. Encourage reflection and evaluation and let students discuss and evaluate their performance after completing the task.

A. Mathematical description of multimedia network technology combined with task pedagogy

Personalized learning: Multimedia resources can provide customized learning paths according to different students' learning needs and progress to meet their personalized learning needs.

$$\lim_{x \to \infty} \left(y_i \cdot t_{ij}\right) = y_{ij} \geq \max(t_{ij} \div 2) \tag{1}$$

Expand learning time and space: Network teaching is not limited by time and place, and students can study independently anytime and anywhere to deepen their understanding of knowledge points.

$$\max(t_{ij}) = \partial\left(t_{ij}^2 + k \cdot t_{ij}\right) \succ mean\left(\sum t_{ij} + n\right) \tag{2}$$

Enrich teaching methods: Multimedia technology enables teachers to use various forms of teaching methods, such as simulated dialogue, role playing, etc., to improve students' language practice ability.

With the development of Internet technology, the rich teaching resources on the Internet provide a broad platform. Online course platform: such as Coursera, EdX and other provide high-quality English courses, students can choose their own learning content and communicate with students around the world. Digital library and academic resources: such as JSTOR, PubMed and others provide massive academic literature to support students' deep learning and research.

$$F(d_i) = R \prod u \cdot \sum t_i \cdot ointy_i \cdot n \tag{3}$$

B. Selection of teaching and research programs

Language learning applications: such as Duolingo, Rosetta Stone, etc., to help students improve their language skills through gamification. Social media and forums: Facebook, LinkedIn and other social platforms provide students with a real language environment and exercise their practical communication skills. Online collaboration tools: such as Google Classroom, Microsoft Teams, etc. to promote collaboration and interaction between teachers and students.

$$g(t_i) = \frac{\ddot{x} \cdot z_i}{w_i} \tag{4}$$

The English teaching research can be shown in Eq. (5).

$$\frac{\lim_{x \to \infty} g(t_i)}{F(d_i)} \cdot \max(t_{ij}) < 0 \tag{5}$$

A university uses mixed teaching in English classes, combining online and offline resources. Students preview through the online platform before class and discuss and practice in class.

$$\sqrt{g(t_i) + F(d_i)} / mean\left(\sum t_{ij} + n\right) \tag{6}$$

C. Analysis of teaching and research programs

According to the students' online learning data, teachers will give targeted explanations and guidance to improve the pertinence of teaching.

$$No(t_i) = \frac{g(t_i) + F(d_i)}{mean\left(\sum t_{ij} + k\right)}^{n} \tag{7}$$

Through VR technology, students can be placed in a simulated English environment, such as virtual travel, business meetings, etc., to improve their situational communication skills. This immersive learning enhances memory and understanding.

$$Zh(t_i) = \sqrt{2}\left[\sum g(t_i) + F(d_i)\right] \tag{8}$$

Faculty design cross-cultural research projects and students work together through online collaboration such as online document sharing and discussion tools. This not only exercises the students' English ability but also cultivates their teamwork and information retrieval skills. Through the above practice, multimedia network technology has played an important role in English teaching in colleges and universities, enriched the teaching means, improved the teaching effect, and provided students with more diversified and efficient learning experience.

$$acc(t_i) = \sqrt{\frac{\min\left[\sum g(t_i) + F(d_i)\right]}{\lim_{x \to \infty} \sum g(t_i) + F(d_i)}} \times n \cdot k \tag{9}$$

The task teaching method, derived from the theory of communicative language teaching, emphasizes the learning and use of language by completing specific tasks, rather than simply learning language structure or vocabulary. This approach regards language as a communication tool rather than an isolated knowledge. Since the 1980s, the task teaching method has been developing and gradually valued by the global education community. The core idea is to allow students to learn and use English by solving problems, expressing opinions and sharing information in a real context, so as to improve the practical application ability of the language.

$$au(t_i) = \frac{\min\left[\sum g(t_i) + F(d_i)\right]}{\sum g(t_i) + F(d_i)} + \Delta t_i \tag{10}$$

Task design is the key link of task teaching method. The following principles will ensure the effectiveness of the task: Authenticity: the task should simulate the situation in real life, so that students can apply what they have learned to practice. Completion: The task should be moderate to ensure that students can complete it in a limited time and avoid frustration. Communicality: tasks should encourage the interaction between students and promote the communication and use of language. Openness: Task results should be diverse, encouraging students to express their personal opinions, rather than just one correct answer. Context related: the task should be related to students' life, interests and learning objectives to enhance their learning motivation.

4 Results and Discussion

A. Introduction to teaching and research

Practice has proved that the task teaching method has a remarkable effect in improving students' comprehensive language ability and problem-solving skills. Students actively participate in the process of the task, active learning, enhance the awareness of language use as shown in Table 1.

Table 1. English teaching research requirements

Scope of application	The mission completion level	Accuracy	Teaching and research
College	I	85.00	78.86
	II	81.97	78.45
University	I	83.81	81.31
	II	83.34	78.19
Research institute	I	79.56	81.99
	II	79.10	80.11

B. Research on English teaching

In the combination mode of multimedia network technology and task teaching method, the design stage first emphasizes the goal setting. According to the curriculum standards and students' needs, teachers set tasks with clear learning objectives, which not only cover the training of language skills, but also cover the cultivation of cultural understanding, critical thinking and teamwork. During the implementation stage, teachers use multimedia resources such as online video, audio, interactive software and virtual learning environment to provide students with rich learning materials and situations. In the process of completing the task, students can cooperate and discuss through the network platform to realize the integration of independent learning and peer learning (Table 2).

C. Comparison of understanding and comprehensiveness of knowledge points

Table 2. The overall picture of the teaching and research programme

Category	Task completion rate	Comprehensive comparison of business	Holistic planning of tasks
College	75.73	72.82	78.64
University	79.61	80.58	80.58
Research institute	80.58	73.79	82.52

Improve the content of knowledge, master the key points of reading, and the relevance of knowledge, and conduct content integration analysis. At the same time, it is necessary to make a comprehensive judgment on the structure of knowledge and personal understanding, complete the sublimation, internalization, and effective expansion of knowledge, and the learning process of knowledge is shown in Fig. 2

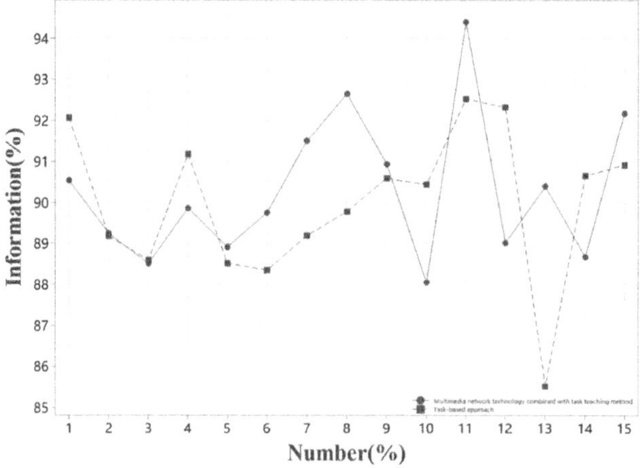

Fig. 2. Teaching and research of different algorithms

The innovation point of this combination mode is that it breaks the traditional teacher-centered mode and puts students in the main position of learning. Multimedia technology provides the interactivity and interest, makes the learning content more vivid, and stimulates the students' interest in learning. At the same time, the task teaching method emphasizes the process of task completion and practice and application, so that language learning is no longer limited to book knowledge. In addition, the use of the network platform enables the teaching process to span the limitations of time and space, so that students can learn anytime and anywhere, and teachers can also track students' learning progress and performance in real time, and provide personalized guidance (Table 3).

In practical teaching, this model shows extremely high applicability. For language learning, it can simulate the real language environment, and by completing tasks, students can improve their language use ability in practice. For example, students can enhance their practical language skills by using online video production projects, practicing

Table 3. Form an effective task volume.

Algorithm	English expression	Word use	Hearing enhancement	Comprehensive expression
Multimedia network technology Combined with task pedagogy	85.33	85.15	82.88	84.95
Task pedagogy	85.20	83.41	86.01	85.75

English presentations and reports, or conducting cross-cultural communication through social media platforms. For other disciplines, such as science and history, multimedia resources can help students understand abstract concepts more intuitively, and tasks can guide them to conduct exploratory learning and improve their problem-solving ability. Furthermore, this model is applicable to students of different levels and backgrounds because it encourages self-directed learning that students can learn at their own pace and interests.

Fig. 3. The distribution of English knowledge points and the ratio of words

As is known from the data analysis in Fig. 3, English Teaching Methods and Task-Based Learning can meet the learning needs of different students by adjusting the task difficulty and multimedia resources. When evaluating students ' learning effect, in addition to the traditional exam, students' learning achievements can also be comprehensively evaluated through diversified evaluation methods such as task completion, activity of discussion, and online learning behavior. In short, the combination of multimedia network technology and task teaching method not only improves the efficiency and effect of teaching, but also provides students with more rich and personalized learning experience, which is a major breakthrough in the application of modern educational technology in teaching.

D. The results of English learning and the stability of knowledge comprehension

The comprehensive application effect of English and the accomplishment of English teaching objectives is shown in Fig. 4.

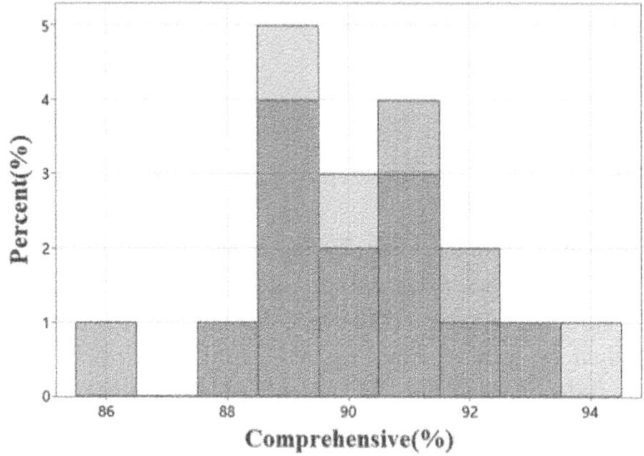

Fig. 4. The proportion of English knowledge points increased

From the analysis in Fig. 4, it can be seen that English knowledge points have increased significantly in terms of analysis and logic improvement, and the increase ratio presents a dual distribution of horizontal and vertical: a horizontal increase of twenty percent, ten percent longitudinal increase. The combination of multimedia network technology and task teaching method has played a significant role in improving students' English listening, speaking, reading and writing ability. By using the online platform, students can have access to a rich variety of audio and video resources, such as English acoustic movies, news reports, academic lectures, etc., which can help them to improve their listening comprehension ability.

E. Effectiveness of teaching and research

At the same time, the interactive speech recognition software and the online oral English practice module enable students to conduct oral English training in a simulated real context, and enhance their expression and communication skills. In terms of reading and writing, the network resource library provides a large number of English articles, books and papers, and students can choose what they are interested in for in-depth reading to improve their reading speed and comprehension. The distribution of knowledge points and the fusion of knowledge logical relationships are displayed. The results shown are shown in Fig. 5.

From the analysis content in Fig. 5, it can be seen that in terms of the distribution of knowledge points and the comparison of core relationships, it will be found that English learning is gradually scattered with tasks as the center, which expands the application scope of words and knowledge points. The real-time feedback and correction functions

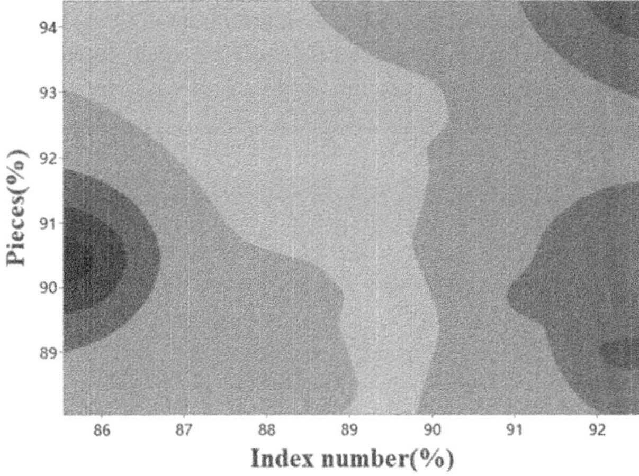

Fig. 5. Teaching research of different algorithms

of online writing tools help students correct grammar mistakes and improve the standardization of writing. By completing the writing tasks in the task pedagogy, such as writing reports, papers or conducting project cooperation, students' organization and expression skills are exercised (Table 4).

Table 4. Judge the relevance of the ratio of English knowledge and the logical distribution of knowledge

Algorithm	Convergence of knowledge	Logical relationships between knowledge	Knowledge Core	Comprehensive distribution of knowledge
Multimedia network technology combined with task pedagogy	82.21	85.92	84.59	82.85
Task pedagogy	83.73	84.23	84.41	83.55
The overall change of knowledge	84.20	87.39	84.76	83.90

The task teaching method combined with multimedia network technology encourages students to participate actively and self-drive. When completing tasks, students need to search and screen information independently, which exercises their ability of information retrieval and critical thinking. The online learning platform provides a personalized learning path, where students can choose the learning content according to their own progress and interests, and cultivate the habit of self-management and self-learning.

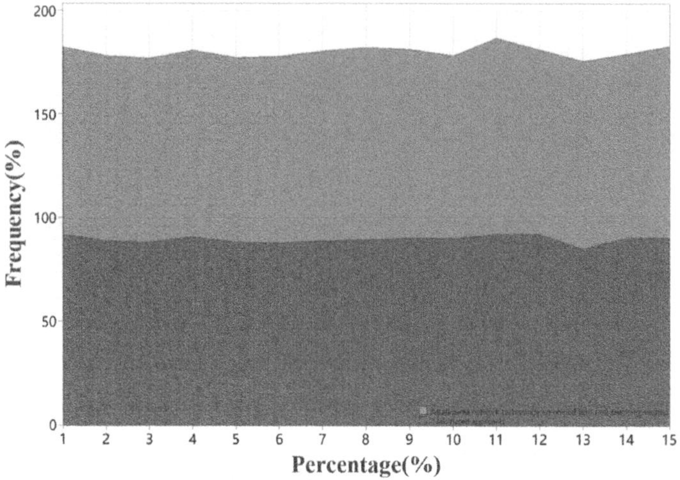

Fig. 6. The growth of knowledge compared with the amount of calculation

From the analysis in Fig. 6, it can be seen that when the amount of tasks increases, the degree of knowledge mastery also improves significantly, and there is a positive distribution between the two. In addition, the group cooperation projects in this teaching model also encourage students to learn to plan themselves, arrange their time properly, and work together with others to solve problems. Through discussion and communication, they can not only improve their English skills, but also develop teamwork and leadership.

5 Conclusion

Multimedia network technology provides a platform for students to have contact with different cultural backgrounds. They can communicate with users from around the world through online forums, social media and international learning communities to learn about the customs, ways of thinking and values of different countries. The cultural contrast research projects that may be involved in the task teaching method enable students to deepen their understanding and respect for the multiple cultures in the process of completing the task. At the same time, viewing and analyzing media content in English-speaking countries, such as movies, music and news, can help students understand the cultural meaning behind the language and improve the sensitivity and adaptability of cross-cultural communication. This ability is particularly important in today's globalization and lays a solid foundation for students' future study and career.

References

1. Peng, F.: Application Research of Multimedia Technology in University English Teaching, vol. 22 (2022)
2. Hou, J.: Integration and application of multimedia WeChat official account in English literature class—review of "Research on the teaching mode of university English based on network multimedia." Sci. Technol. Manage. Res. **42**(5), I0007 (2022)
3. Sun, Y.: Exploration of teaching mode for preschool English teaching method in multimedia network environment. China New Commun. **24**(10), 3 (2022)
4. Ding, G.: Application research of task-based teaching method in college English teaching. Sci. Educ. Guide **4**, 47–49 (2023)
5. Yang, L., Yun, L.: Construction of teaching mode combining multimedia technology and college vocal music teaching—Review of "Research on theory and practice of college vocal music teaching." Science and Technology Management Research **42**(14), I0009–I0009 (2022)
6. Zhu, X.: Research on Online Teaching and Student Autonomous Learning Mode in University English Major, vol. 6 (2022)
7. Zhenglong, B., Guomao, L.: Research on teaching mode combining task-driven teaching method and flipped classroom—taking "Marine Electrical Equipment and Systems" course as an example. J. Wuhan Shipborne Occup. Tech. College **21**(1), 108–111 (2022)
8. Du, J.: Analysis of the advantages and disadvantages of multimedia technology in college English teaching. China Sci. Technol. Period. Database Sci. Res. **12**, 4 (2022)
9. Xu, X.: Exploring the application of task-based teaching method in college English oral teaching. New Curric. Res. **33**, 56–58 (2022)
10. Wei, Z.: Discussion on the ecological characteristics and teaching mode of college English teaching in a multimedia environment. Environ. Eng. **40**(10), 1 (2022)
11. Liu, T.: Reflection on the reform of college English teaching in the multimedia network environment. Growth **8**, 136–138 (2022)

Design of Teaching System of College General Writing Course Based on Network Information Technology

Jinni Xiang(✉)

Department of Basic Courses, Xi'an Eurasia Vocational University, Xi'an 710065, Shanxi, China
xiangjinni@eurasia.edu

Abstract. With the rapid development of information technology, the general writing course of high schools can optimize the teaching system with the help of information technology to achieve the desired teaching effect, and the traditional teaching system can no longer meet the current teaching content. Therefore, this paper proposes a teaching system based on the analysis of teaching system of network information technology. Firstly, based on the effective use of artificial intelligence technology, the content of college writing courses is collected and analyzed in detail, and the indicators are divided according to the requirements of the teaching system to reduce the possible interference factors in the teaching system. Then, artificial intelligence is used to analyze the teaching system of general writing courses in colleges and universities, and then a comprehensive teaching system plan is formed, and the results of the teaching system are comprehensively analyzed. The MATLAB simulation results finally show that under certain evaluation criteria, the rationality of the teaching effect of the university general writing course teaching system based on network information technology is much higher than that of the traditional teaching system.

Keywords: artificial intelligence · Based on network information technology teaching system · College General Writing Course · Teaching system

1 Introduction

General Writing courses are an integral part of the higher education system and are designed to improve students' written communication skills, develop clear thinking logic, and develop critical thinking and innovation. In the era of information explosion, good writing skills not only help students effectively convey ideas in academic research, but also are essential for their communication skills in the workplace and social interactions. Through the General Writing course, students can learn how to organize and express complex ideas, form persuasive arguments, and exercise their reading comprehension and information processing skills. The teaching system process in Table 1 is shown in Fig. 1.

B. Brik and S. Nazir (Eds.): BigIoT-EDU 2024, LNICST 660, pp. 322–332, 2026.
https://doi.org/10.1007/978-3-032-18628-7_33

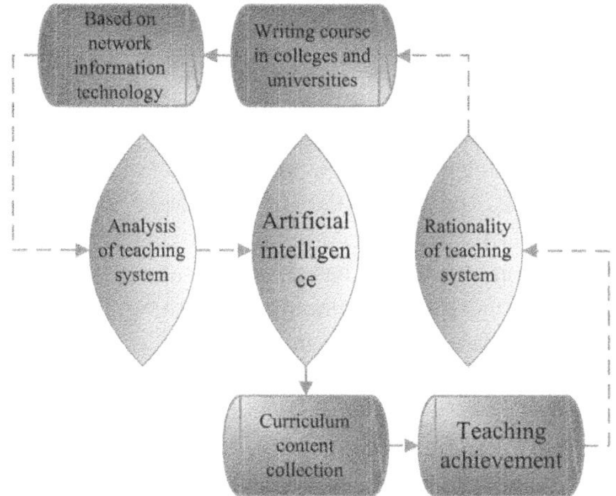

Fig. 1. The analytical process of college general writing courses

Second, using cloud collaboration tools, such as Google Docs or Tencent Docs, enables real-time sharing and collaboration, allowing students to learn from each other and improve their writing skills in the process of co-editing. In addition, utilizing AI writing assistants, such as Grammarly, can provide grammar and spelling checks on the fly, helping students improve the accuracy and standardization of their writing.

2 Related Works

A. *The importance*

With the popularization of the Internet and the progress of science and technology, the application of network information technology in teaching is becoming more and more extensive. Online education platforms, digital teaching materials, and interactive learning tools have become the new normal of teaching. These technologies enable teaching and learning resources to be shared globally, to make learning more flexible, and to provide teachers with new teaching strategies and assessment tools. The application of network information technology can not only enhance the interest and interaction of teaching, but also realize personalized teaching to meet the learning needs of different students.

The purpose of this paper is to explore how network information technology can be deeply integrated with general education writing courses to optimize the teaching effect. Through the analysis of the existing network information technology, we will propose a set of innovative teaching system design to improve students' learning efficiency and enhance the cultivation of writing skills. In addition, this paper will demonstrate the application of information technology in practical teaching through case studies, provide educators with theoretical and practical references, and promote the modernization and reform of general education courses to meet the new needs of education in the information age. This research has important theoretical and practical value for improving the quality of higher education, especially the modernization process of writing education.

B. *The Integration of Network Information Technology and General Writing Courses*

With the rapid development of the information age, network information technology has penetrated into all corners of society, and the field of education is no exception. In the General Education Writing course, this integration is not only reflected in the innovation of teaching methods, but also in the transformation of teaching concepts. The traditional teaching model of writing was often teacher-centered, but now, the introduction of network information technology has enabled students to become the main body of learning, realizing personalized and autonomous learning. Online writing platforms, digital textbooks, and abundant online resources provide students with a rich learning environment, but also put forward new requirements for the role of teachers, who have changed from imparting knowledge to guiding and mentoring learning.

The theoretical basis of the integration of network information technology and general education writing courses is mainly based on the following aspects: First, constructivist theory. It is believed that learning is the process of learners actively constructing knowledge, and the network environment provides rich information resources, which is convenient for students to explore and construct knowledge on their own. Second, multimedia learning theory. The combination of multimedia elements such as images, audio, and video can enhance students' interest in learning and comprehension, and has a significant effect on creative stimulation and situational understanding in writing. Third, social cognitive theory. The online environment fosters interaction and collaboration among learners, and through forums, blogs, social media, and other platforms, students can discuss, share, and give feedback to improve their writing skills. Fourth, adaptive learning theory. Through intelligent algorithms, the network system can provide personalized recommendations based on students' learning situation to help students improve their writing skills in a targeted manner.

In practice, network information technology has penetrated into all aspects of the general education writing course: first, the online teaching platform. Online education platforms such as Coursera, edX, etc., provide a wealth of writing courses that students can learn anytime, anywhere, without time and space limitations. Second, smart writing tools. Tools such as Grammarly, Hemingway, etc., can provide instant feedback on students' writing mistakes, provide suggestions for revision, and improve the quality of writing. Third, a collaborative writing system. Tools such as Google Docs support multi-person collaboration, where students can co-edit and comment to enhance teamwork and critical thinking skills. Fourth, virtual writing workshops. Through video conferencing tools, teachers can organize online workshops for real-time writing instruction and discussions, enhancing teacher-student communication. Fifth, big data analysis. Through the collection and analysis of student writing data, teachers can understand students' learning patterns and optimize teaching strategies.

The integration of network information technology has not only changed the teaching method of general writing courses, but also promoted the all-round development of students' writing ability, opening up new possibilities for the future of education.

(1) Student-centered design principles. In the design of the teaching system of general writing courses in colleges and universities, the concept of student-centered is very

important. This means that teaching and learning activities should take into account students' interests, needs and abilities, and aim to stimulate their initiative and innovation. The role of the teacher has shifted from that of a traditional knowledge transmitter to a facilitator of learning and a mentor. Course content should be flexible, allowing students to choose and adjust according to their own learning style and pace. In addition, teaching methods should emphasize interaction and participation, encouraging students to improve their writing skills through discussion, collaboration, and self-reflection (2). The principle of combining theory and practice. The combination of theory and practice is another important principle in the design of the General Writing course. The theory section aims to provide the basic knowledge of writing, such as linguistic theory, rhetoric, stylistics, etc., to help students understand the essence and skills of writing. The practical part emphasizes the application of these theories through practical writing tasks, such as writing essays, reports, stories, etc., so that students can hone and improve in practice. Teachers can set up a variety of writing projects, such as writing tasks that simulate real-life situations, to guide students to transform theoretical knowledge into practical ability, while providing timely feedback and guidance to promote the continuous development of students' writing skills (3). The principle of interdisciplinary integration. In the information age, writing is no longer confined to a single subject area, but spans multiple disciplines, requiring students to have comprehensive knowledge and interdisciplinary perspectives. Therefore, the design of the teaching system should encourage the integration of interdisciplinarity, combining writing skills with knowledge from various disciplines. For example, the writing of scientific papers can be combined with scientific research methodology, and literary creation can be integrated into the context of literary theory and history. In this way, students can not only improve their writing skills, but also enhance their critical thinking, learn to analyze problems from different perspectives, express their opinions, and thus cultivate a comprehensive quality that can adapt to complex social environments. In implementing these principles, teachers need to use online information technology to provide personalized learning resources, such as online writing platforms, interactive forums and multimedia materials, to support students' self-directed learning. At the same time, online collaboration tools, such as Google Docs or Trello, promote collaboration among students and develop their teamwork skills. This teaching system is designed to create a dynamic, open, and innovative learning environment that fosters the well-rounded writing literacy required in the 21st century.

3 Methods

A. Curriculum System Design

The design of the curriculum system is the basis for constructing the teaching system of general education writing course based on network information technology. In this process, attention should be paid to the systematization and coherence of the course, and ensure that the content covers the basic elements of writing, such as style, structure, language rhetoric, argumentation methods, etc. The curriculum should be divided into basic, advanced and practical modules to suit the needs of students at different levels.

$$tol\left(b_i \cdot s_{ij} \cdot 3\right) = b_{ij} \geq \max\left(s_{ij} \div \frac{1}{6}\right) \tag{1}$$

First, the basic module. It covers the basics of writing, such as grammar, punctuation, paragraph construction, etc., and aims to develop students' basic writing skills. Second, advanced modules. In-depth exploration of writing skills in various genres, such as argumentative essays, reports, storytelling, etc., to improve students' writing skills.

$$\max\left(s_{ij}\right) = \left(s_{ij}{}^2 + 8\right) \succ mean\left(\frac{1}{2} \cdot \sqrt{3} + \sum s_{ij}\right) \tag{2}$$

Third, the practical module. Through real-life writing tasks, students apply theoretical knowledge to practice, including essay writing, news reporting, creative writing, and more.

The application of network information technology provides infinite possibilities for the innovation of teaching methods. The combination of online platforms and multimedia resources can achieve the following teaching strategies: First, interactive teaching. Use online discussion boards and live chat tools to encourage students to discuss inside and outside the classroom to promote deep learning. Second, personalized learning. Personalized learning resources are recommended through intelligent algorithms to adapt to each student's learning pace and interests. Third, multimedia assistance. Use video tutorials, audio tutorials, interactive charts, and more to make abstract concepts more intuitive and easy to understand. Fourth, remote collaboration. Use cloud documents and online collaboration tools to allow students to write in remote teams and develop collaboration skills. Fifth, feedback and correction: With the help of AI automatic grading tools, feedback can be provided quickly to help students correct mistakes in a timely manner.

$$O(q_i) = \sum s_i \cdot \frac{s_i!}{O!(s_i - 1)!} \cdot 3 + \lim_{x \to \infty} \cap \xi \to \frac{1}{2} \cdot \oint b_i \tag{3}$$

B. teaching evaluation system

An effective assessment system should fully reflect students' learning outcomes and progress. With the support of network information technology, teaching evaluation can be realized: first, diversified evaluation. Combined with self-evaluation, peer evaluation, teacher evaluation, and data analysis on online platforms, a comprehensive evaluation perspective is formed.

$$j(s_i) = \mathrm{w}_i v_i \cdot \prod - \iint j \cdot O(q_i) \cdot \frac{j - w_i}{3} \cdot 2 - w_i \tag{4}$$

Second, process evaluation. Pay attention to the learning process of students, such as the activity of participating in discussions, the timeliness of assignment submission, etc.

$$j(s_i) + O(q_i) \leq \max\left(s_{ij}\right) \tag{5}$$

Third, competency-oriented evaluation. Emphasis is placed on assessing students' core competencies such as innovative thinking, critical thinking, and information literacy.

$$j(s_i) + O(q_i) \leftrightarrow mean\left(\frac{1}{2} \cdot \sqrt{3} + \sum s_{ij}\right) \tag{6}$$

Fourth, pay equal attention to form and content. Evaluate the form (e.g., structure, language) and content (e.g., opinions, arguments) of students' writing. Fifth, instant feedback. Through the online platform, students are provided with timely learning feedback so that they can self-adjust and improve.

C. Modular design of courses

The modular design helps students to break down and understand complex knowledge systems. The course can be divided into a basic writing module, a technical application module and a professional application module. Foundation modules teach basic writing theories and skills; The technical application module covers the application of network information technology in writing, such as search engine optimization, HTML and CSS basics, etc.; The professional application module combines various subject areas to allow students to apply what they have learned in practice, such as research report writing, press release writing, etc. Each module should contain theoretical explanations, practical exercises and feedback assessments to ensure that students are able to translate theoretical knowledge into practical skills.

$$No(s_i) = \frac{j(s_i) + O(q_i)}{mean\left(\frac{1}{2} \cdot \sqrt{3} + \sum s_{ij}\right)} \tag{7}$$

In addition, there should be some flexibility between course modules, allowing students to choose different combinations of modules based on their interests and needs for personalized learning. The module design should also take into account the progressiveness of the course to ensure that students can gradually challenge the higher-level content after completing the basic modules, so as to achieve a spiral improvement of ability.

$$Zh(s_i) = \min\left[\sum j(s_i) + O(q_i)\right] \tag{8}$$

Through the selection and arrangement of the above course content, the integration of teaching materials and resources, and the modular design, a general writing curriculum system covering both traditional writing skills and network information technology can be constructed.

$$accur(s_i) = \frac{\min\left[\sum j(s_i) + O(q_i)\right]}{\sum j(s_i) + O(q_i)} \times 100\% \tag{9}$$

so as to meet the educational needs of the 21st century and cultivate students' innovative thinking and practical ability.

$$accur(s_i) = \frac{\min\left[\sum j(s_i) + O(q_i)\right]}{\sum j(s_i) + O(q_i)} \times 100\% + randon(s_i) \tag{10}$$

4 Results and Discussion

A. Application strategy of network information technology

The application of network information technology in general writing courses has greatly broadened the boundaries of teaching and provided infinite possibilities for the innovation of teaching methods. First, with the online learning platform, teachers can create a dynamic library of teaching resources, including various writing examples, writing skills videos, interactive exercises, etc., so that students can study and review on their own anytime, anywhere.

Table 1. Teaching system requirements

Scope of application	Grade	Viability	Teaching system
Transactional style	Standard	91.12	84.69
	Higher	83.62	85.71
Information style	Standard	84.15	81.26
	Higher	87.37	83.38
Litigation style	Standard	84.68	81.58
	Higher	89.09	83.35

B. Methods for the implementation of interactive teaching

Interactive teaching emphasizes the subjective position of students in the learning process, and network information technology provides an effective tool for this. Teachers can design online discussion boards to encourage students to engage in in-depth discussions on specific topics, share ideas, and improve critical thinking. Using online polls or survey tools such as SurveyMonkey, you can gather feedback from students and adjust your teaching strategies. In addition, through online simulated writing tasks, such as using virtual writing workshops, students can experiment with different writing styles and structures in a safe environment, and teachers can provide guidance and feedback on the fly. In this study, we select college general writing courses with different teaching system levels, and the teaching system scheme is shown in Table 2.

C. The teaching system and stability of the teaching system

Self-directed learning is an important goal of the General Writing course, and network information technology supports this goal. Teachers can set personalized learning paths, use learning management systems (LMS) such as Moodle, track students' learning progress, and provide personalized learning resource recommendations. At the same time, through online group projects, students can work together on a writing topic, divide

Table 2. The overall situation of the pedagogical system program

Category	Viability	Analysis rate
Transactional style	90.01	88.14
Information style	85.92	87.75
Litigation style	89.01	87.95
mean	84.74	87.62
X^6	85.18	88.13
P = 2.374		

labor and work together, and improve teamwork skills. Online forums and video conferencing tools, such as Zoom, can facilitate remote collaboration, allowing students to discuss and co-create together, even in different locations (Fig. 2).

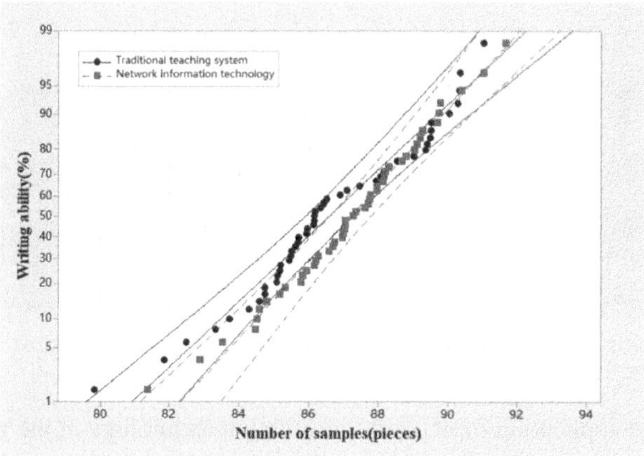

Fig. 2. Teaching system of different algorithms

Through the application of the above-mentioned network information technology, the innovation of teaching methods and means not only improves the learning experience of students, but also improves the efficiency and quality of teaching, and injects new vitality into the general education writing course. The average teaching system scheme of the above three algorithms is shown in Table 3.

In the general writing course of a well-known university, the teacher made full use of network information technology to successfully improve the teaching effect of the course. The course combines an online writing platform with traditional classroom instruction to create a blended teaching model. On the online platform, students can submit assignments in real-time and teachers can provide immediate feedback, facilitating rapid improvement in students' writing skills. In addition, teachers use big data analysis tools to track students' writing habits and progress, providing a basis for personalized

Table 3. Comparison of the accuracy of teaching systems of different methods

Algorithm	Teaching system	Magnitude of change	error
Based on network information technology teaching system	91.54	92.42	90.08
Traditional teaching system	86.51	87.28	89.29
P	88.60	85.72	85.60

instruction. Through online discussion forums, students are able to communicate with each other across time and space, share ideas, and improve critical thinking skills (Fig. 3).

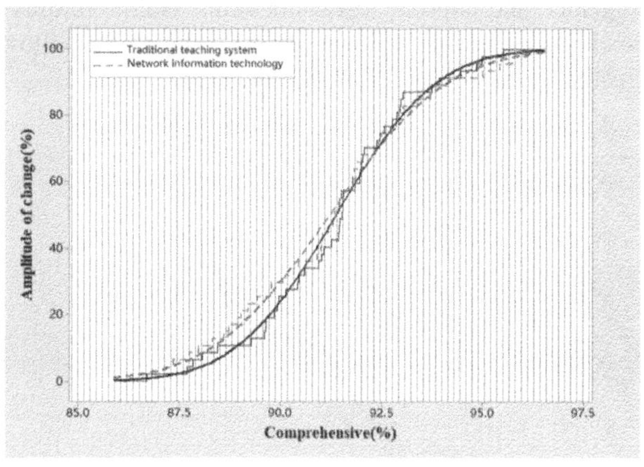

Fig. 3. A teaching system based on the teaching system of network information technology

Although the application of network information technology in the general writing course has achieved remarkable results, it also faces some challenges. First of all, the instability of the network environment may affect the teaching process, such as network latency, server failure, etc., which may interrupt the teaching process and affect the effective communication between teachers and students. Secondly, some students may become dependent on online learning and lack face-to-face communication, which affects the cultivation of teamwork and interpersonal skills. In addition, cyber security issues cannot be ignored, and the supervision of personal information protection and academic integrity has become more difficult. Finally, teachers need to devote more energy to technology learning and maintenance, which can distract them from what to teach and how to teach.

To address these challenges, there are several improvements worth considering. First of all, establish a stable online teaching environment and optimize the online platform to ensure that it can run smoothly during peak hours. Secondly, offline seminars and group activities are regularly organized to make up for the lack of online communication and promote face-to-face communication and teamwork among students. In addition, strengthen cyber security education, raise students' awareness of personal information protection, and strengthen the monitoring of academic integrity through technical means. For teachers, we provide specialized technical training and support to reduce their burden on technology maintenance, so that they can focus more on innovating teaching content and improving teaching quality. At the same time, more intelligent teaching tools can be explored, such as AI-assisted writing guidance, which can automatically identify students' writing mistakes and provide personalized suggestions to further improve teaching efficiency. Finally, regularly evaluate and adjust teaching strategies to adapt to the changing network environment and student needs, and maintain the vitality and adaptability of the teaching model.

5 Conclusion

Through an in-depth study of the integration of network information technology and general writing courses in colleges and universities, this study reveals how information technology can reshape the teaching environment and improve students' learning experience and writing ability. We found that the design of teaching systems combined with network information technology can achieve personalized learning, enhance student engagement, and cultivate their information literacy and critical thinking. The modular design of the course content, combined with the interactive functions of the online platform, makes the teaching more flexible and adapts to the learning needs of different students.

Acknowledgements. The authors acknowledge the The general project of 2021 in the "Fourteenth Five-Year Plan" of:Shaanxi Provincial Education and Science "Innovation and Practice Research on the Teaching Mode of General Writing Course in Shaanxi Universities in the New Era" (SGH21Y0393).

References

1. Al Harrasi, K.T.S.: Reexamining feedback in the context of different rhetorical patterns of writing. Lang. Test. Asia. **13**(1) (2023)
2. Alexander, P.A., Fusenig, J., Schoute, E.C., Singh, A., Sun, Y.T., van Meerten, J.E.: Confronting the challenges of undergraduates' argumentation writing in a "Learning How to Learn" course. Writ. Commun. **40**(2), 482–517 (2023)
3. Aluri, J. et al.: The role of arts-based curricula in professional identity formation: results of a qualitative analysis of learner's written reflections. Med. Educ. Online. **28**(1) (2023)
4. Baker, J., Evans-Tokaryk, T.: Assessing the value of integrating writing and writing instruction into a research methods course. Can. J. Sch. Teach. Learn. **14**(1) (2023)
5. Bernat, F.P., Kraft-Duley, A., Dollar, C., Makin, D.A.: Instruction modality and writing intensive undergraduate research success: a case study. J. Crim. Justice Educ. **35**, 449–469 (2023)
6. Campbell, T.G., Hodges, T., Yeo, S., Rich, E., Pate, K.: Exploring how writing-to-learn in a mathematics methods course influences preservice teachers' beliefs. Int. J. Math. Educ. Sci. Technol. **56**, 231–257 (2023)
7. Christensen, J., Warnsby, A.: Reflective writing in course design for active learning in social work education. J. Soc. Work. Educ. **59**, 756–771 (2023)

8. di Gennaro, K., Choong, K.W.P., Brewer, M.: Uniting CLA with WAW via SLA: learning about written language as a model for college writing courses. J. Second. Lang. Writ. **60**, 100967 (2023)
9. Ezezika, O., Johnston, N.: Development and implementation of a reflective writing assignment for undergraduate students in a large public health biology course. Pedagog. Health Promot. **9**(2), 101–115 (2023)
10. Fitzpatrick, K., Barker, M.K.: Better writing, brick by brick: a student-centered writing exercise using LEGO. J. Microbiol. Biol. Educ. **24** (2023)
11. Goodwin, R., Kirkpatrick, R.: Using rubrics to improve writing skills: a study in Kuwait. Lang. Test. Asia. **13**(1) (2023)
12. Hsiao, J.C., Chang, J.S.: Enhancing EFL reading and writing through AI-powered tools: design, implementation, and evaluation of an online course. Interact. Learn. Environ. **32**, 4934–4949 (2023)
13. Lavoie, E., Cavanagh, M.: Writing instruction for social justice: an investigation into the components of a teacher preparation course. Literacy. **57**(2), 132–148 (2023)
14. Liu, Y., Xiong, W., Xiong, Y., Wu, Y.F.B.: Generating timely individualized feedback to support student learning of conceptual knowledge in writing-to-learn activities. J. Comput. Educ. **11**, 367–399 (2023)
15. Martinez, A.C.L.: Analysis of changes in L2 writing over the time of a short-term academic English programme. Porta Linguarum. **39**, 111–127 (2023)
16. Ozdemir, O.: Using a genre-based writing method in the distance education classroom. Turk. J. Educ. **12**(2), 72–93 (2023)
17. Shooshtari, Z.G., Jalilifar, A., Goudarzi, E.: Teaching for transfer in ESAP writing through collaborative syllabus and multimodal input: the case of Iranian engineering graduates. ESP Today-J. Engl. Specif. Purp. Tert. Lev. **11**(1), 31–52 (2023)
18. Tejero, I.G.G.: Teacher's meanings about academic writing in a distance in-service teacher education course. CPU-E Revista De Investigacion Educativa. **36**, 85–112 (2023)

Research on the Design of Management Platform of Training Room of Higher Vocational Colleges Based on BP Neural Network

Weizeng Huang(✉)

School of Finance and Economics, Guangzhou Vocational College of Technology & Business, Guangzhou, Guangdong Province 511442, China
gzkmuei2023@126.com

Abstract. In today's information society, the management of training rooms in vocational colleges faces many challenges. As an important place to cultivate students' practical skills, the efficient and safe management of the training room is the key to improving the quality of teaching. The traditional management mode of training rooms often relies on manual labor, which not only consumes a lot of manpower, but also easily leads to management loopholes, such as equipment damage, resource waste, security risks, and other issues. The results were comprehensively analyzed. Parallel Distributed Processing simulations show that BP neural network pairs are managed with certain criteria the management accuracy of the training room and the management time of the training room of higher vocational colleges are better than the traditional management mode.

Keywords: management theory · BP neural networks · higher vocational colleges · Management

1 Introduction

With the deepening of education informatization and intelligence, the practical training management platform of vocational colleges and universities has become an indispensable education management tool. The practical training management platform involves a wide range of functions [1], such as practical training resource management, practical training plan management, practical training textbook management, and practical training performance management. How to optimize the efficiency and accuracy of the practical training management platform, improve its management level and user experience has become an important research topic. This paper will discuss the application of BP neural network in the training management platform of vocational colleges, and discuss how to use BP neural network to optimize the management efficiency and accuracy of the training management platform, and improve its management level and user experience [2]. The management process of the training room in Table 1 is shown in Fig. 1.

B. Brik and S. Nazir (Eds.): BigIoT-EDU 2024, LNICST 660, pp. 333–342, 2026.
https://doi.org/10.1007/978-3-032-18628-7_34

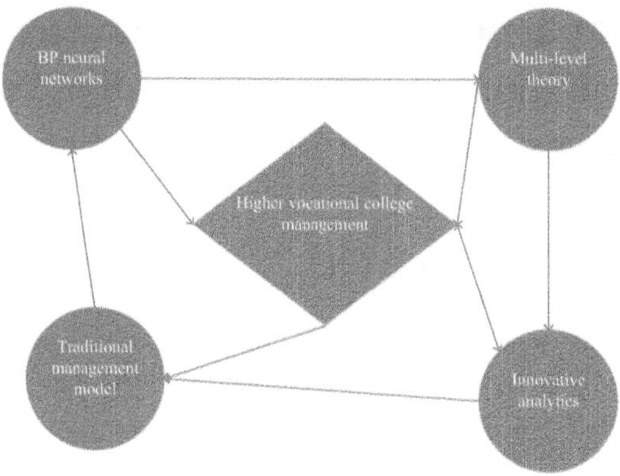

Fig. 1 The analysis process of management of higher vocational colleges

1. Resource prediction and scheduling: The usage demand of training rooms is usually influenced by factors such as course arrangement, number of students, and training projects. BP neural network can learn historical usage patterns, predict future training room needs, and help managers optimize the opening time, allocation, and scheduling of resources in the training room.

2 Related Works

2.1 Overview of the Practical Training Management Platform of Higher Vocational Colleges

The practical training management platform of vocational colleges and universities is a comprehensive education management platform, which is mainly used for the formulation of practical training plans, the management of practical training resources, the management of practical training teaching materials, the management of practical training achievements and other aspects [3]. It is an education management tool that integrates information, intelligence and online. In the training management platform, students can view the training plan, select courses, participate in training, submit training homework, view training results, etc. [4]; Teachers can carry out practical training course management, practical training resource management, practical training performance management, online teaching and other operations; The training administrator can perform operations such as training plan management and training resource management; System administrators can perform operations such as system maintenance and management [5].

The main functions of the training management platform of vocational colleges are as follows:

Practical training plan management: including plan formulation, plan review and other operations [6].

Practical resource management: including resource addition, resource modification, resource deletion and other operations [7].

Practical training performance management: including grade entry, performance review and other operations.

Practical training textbook management: including textbook addition, textbook modification, textbook deletion and other operations [8].

Online teaching: including online courses, online tests, etc. [9].

2.2 Overview of BP Neural Networks

BP neural network is a classical neural network model, which adjusts the weights of neurons through a backpropagation algorithm [10] to achieve fitting and prediction of data. BP neural networks can be used for data analysis and prediction in various fields, such as stock forecasting, price forecasting, etc. [11]. The main feature of BP neural networks is that they can adaptively adjust the network weights, thereby improving the fitting accuracy and prediction accuracy of the network [12].

The application process of BP neural network is as follows:

Design the structure of a neural network.

Initialize the weights of the neural network.

Enter training samples and perform forward and back propagation.

The weights are adjusted according to the error function to maximize the network fitting accuracy and prediction accuracy [13–15].

Repeat steps 3–4 until the stop condition is reached.

2.3 Optimization of BP Neural Network in Practical Training Management Platform

In order to further optimize the efficiency and accuracy of the training management platform, the optimization using BP neural network can start from the following aspects:

1. Data preprocessing

When using BP neural networks for the optimization of the training management platform, it is necessary to preprocess the raw data. The data can be processed by standardization, normalization and other methods, so as to improve the fitting accuracy and prediction accuracy of BP neural network.

2. Parameter tuning

When using BP neural networks for the optimization of the training management platform, parameter tuning is required. The optimal learning rate, impulse and other parameters can be determined through multiple experiments, so as to improve the performance and efficiency of the neural network.

3 Optimization Strategy for the Management of Vocational Colleges

3.1 Mathematical Description of BP Neural Networks

The widespread application of BP neural networks, new solutions have been provided for the management of training rooms in Eq. (1).

$$tol(y_i \cdot x_{ij}) = y_{ij} \oplus \max(x_{ij}) \tag{1}$$

BP neural network is a multi-layer feedforward neural network with backpropagation mechanism, which can model and predict complex nonlinear problems by learning and adjusting weights. In the management of training rooms in vocational colleges, BP neural networks can be used to predict equipment failures, optimize resource allocation, and improve safety management, thereby achieving intelligent management of training rooms is shown in Eq. (2).

$$\max(x_{ij}) = \left({x_{ij}}^2 + 9\right) \succ mean\theta\left(\sum x_{ij}\right) \tag{2}$$

Research Purpose and Problem Definition This study aims to design and implement a training room management platform for vocational colleges based on BP neural network, aiming to solve the following problems: as shown in Eq. (3).

$$G(d_i) = \sum x_i \cap \mathfrak{M} \to \oint y_i \tag{3}$$

3.2 Selection of Management Quality Program for the Training Room

1 Improve management efficiency: Through automated and intelligent management processes, reduce manual intervention and improve the daily operational efficiency of the training room as the Formula (4) shows:

$$g(x_i) = z_i \cdot \prod G(d_i) - \mathfrak{A}_i \tag{4}$$

Preventive maintenance: Use BP neural network to predict equipment failures, perform maintenance in advance, and reduce equipment downtime and maintenance costs is shown in Eq. (5).

$$g(x_i) + G(d_i) \le \max(x_{ij}) \tag{5}$$

Decision support: Provide data-driven decision support for managers, optimize training room planning and management strategies are shown in Eq. (6).

$$g(x_i) + G(d_i) \leftrightarrow mean\left(\sum x_{ij}\right) \tag{6}$$

3.3 Analysis of the Management Plan of the Training Room

Resource optimization: Analyze the usage of the training room, intelligently schedule resources, and avoid resource waste and overuse. Security improvement: Through data analysis, identify security risks, provide timely security warnings and countermeasures are shown in Eq. (7).

$$No(x_i) = \frac{g(x_i) + G(d_i)}{mean\left(\sum x_{ij}\right)} \tag{7}$$

BP, Backpropagation, also known as Backpropagation, is a gradient descent based backpropagation algorithm used to train multi-layer feedforward neural networks. The BP neural network consists of input layer, hidden layer, and output layer, where the hidden layer can be multiple layers. Each neuron has an activation function, such as sigmoid or ReLU, used for nonlinear transformation of input signals is shown in Eq. (8).

$$Zh(x_i) = \min\left[\sum g(x_i) + G(d_i)\right] \tag{8}$$

The calculating the output of each neuron as shown in the Formula (9).

$$accur(x_i) = \frac{\min\left[\sum g(x_i) + G(d_i)\right]}{\sum g(x_i) \oplus G(d_i)} \times 100\% \tag{9}$$

In backpropagation, the network calculates the gradient of prediction error and updates weights along the reverse path. This process is iterated until the error of the network reaches the preset convergence standard. The key to BP neural network lies in its error backpropagation mechanism, which can handle nonlinear problems and adapt to various complex data patterns, making it widely used in many fields is, then the calculation of Formula (9) can be expressed as Formula (10).

$$accur(x_i) = \frac{\min\left[\sum g(x_i) + G(d_i)\right]}{\sum g(x_i) \oplus G(d_i)} \times 100\% + randon(x_i) \tag{10}$$

4 Results and Discussion

4.1 Introduction to the Management of the Training Room

In the management of practical training rooms in vocational colleges, BP neural networks can play multiple roles to improve management efficiency and resource utilization is shown in Table 1.

Table 1 Management requirements for training rooms in vocational colleges

Scope of application	Grade	Manage effects	The quality of management in the training room
Academic building A	I	34.65	33.57
	II	36.28	34.55
Academic building B	I	32.23	34.60
	II	33.77	35.20
Academic building C	I	35.70	33.37
	II	33.72	32.99

4.2 Management of Higher Vocational Colleges

2. Equipment Fault Prediction and Maintenance: By monitoring the working status and maintenance records of the training equipment, the BP neural network can learn the fault mode of the equipment, predict possible faults in advance, and achieve preventive maintenance, reducing equipment downtime and maintenance costs is shown in Table 2.

Table 2 The overall situation of the management quality program of the training room

Category	Satisfaction	Analysis rate
Academic building A	85.36	74.04
Academic building B	84.01	75.54
Academic building C	84.52	74.27
mean	83.63	74.34
X6	34.45	33.24
P = 3.184		

4.3 Management of the Training Room: the Management Quality and Stability of the Training Room

3. Training effectiveness evaluation: Based on student training data, BP neural network can evaluate the training effectiveness and provide a basis for teaching improvement. For example, by analyzing the operational data of students during the practical training process, weak links in teaching can be identified and teaching strategies can be adjusted accordingly is shown in Fig. 2 shown.

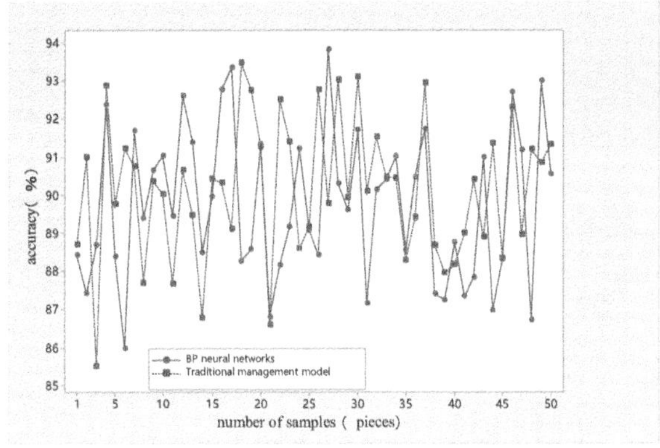

Fig. 2. The quality of management of training rooms with different management models

4. Safety management: The safety of the training room is an important consideration. The BP neural network can analyze the security event records in the training room, identify potential security risks, provide warning mechanisms, and ensure the safety of the training environment is shown in Table 3.

Table 3 Comparison of management accuracy of training rooms with different methods

Management mode	The quality of management in the training room	Magnitude of change	Error
BP neural networks	93.57	93.31	95.41
Traditional management model	82.69	83.28	84.22
P	35.122	33.727	35.920

5. Energy management: The energy consumption of the training room is a part of the operating costs of vocational colleges. BP neural network can predict and optimize the energy use of training rooms, such as achieving energy conservation and emission reduction through intelligent control of air conditioning, lighting and other equipment.
6. Resource allocation optimization: Fig. 3 shown.

Fig. 3. BP neural network training room management the quality of management of the training room

By learning the data used in the training room, the BP neural network can recommend the best resource allocation plan for different courses and training projects, improving the efficiency of the training room's use. In summary, the application of BP neural network can not only improve the automation level of training room management, but also enhance the quality of management through data-driven methods, providing more scientific and efficient support for vocational training education.

5 Conclusion

This article studies the design of a training room management platform for vocational colleges based on BP neural network. By deeply exploring the theoretical basis of neural networks and combining with the characteristics of vocational education, an effective training room management model is constructed. This model can intelligently schedule training room resources, predict training needs, optimize the efficiency of training room utilization, reduce management costs, and improve teaching quality. In the algorithm design phase, we constructed a multi-level BP neural network, including input layer, hidden layer, and output layer. The input layer receives the usage data of the training room, such as the arrangement of training courses, the number of students, the status of training equipment, etc.; The hidden layer is trained with a large amount of data to learn and establish the internal relationship of training room management; The output layer provides management decisions for the training room, such as equipment allocation and appointment management. We used backpropagation algorithm for training, continuously adjusting weights and thresholds to enable the network to more accurately simulate the complex logic of training room management. In practical applications, this platform not only achieves dynamic allocation of training room resources, but also provides fault prediction and preventive maintenance functions, effectively reducing unplanned downtime of training equipment. Meanwhile, through a user-friendly interface and real-time feedback mechanism, the satisfaction of teachers and students with the management of the training room has been improved.

Acknowledgements. In 2021, China University Industry, University and Research Innovation Fund - New Generation Information Technology Innovation Project "Research on the Construction of Training Room Management Mode in Higher Vocational Colleges from the Perspective of Big Data", Project No.: 2021ITA06011; The 2022 Guangzhou Higher Education Teaching Quality and Reform Project - General Project for Higher Education Teaching Reform - "Research on the Construction and Application of a Business Data Analysis Technology Platform for Training New Retail Talents in the Context of Building a High Level Professional Group in Marketing", Project No.: 2022JXGG174; "Research on the Digitalization Strategy of Guangdong Agricultural Product Brands in the Context of Rural Revitalization Strategy", the 2020 Young Innovative Talents Project of General Colleges and Universities in Guangdong Province, Project No.: 2020WQNCX181.

References

1. AlAmer, N.A.: Decision-making styles and managerial creativity of nursing managers in Saudi Arabia: a multi-center cross-sectional study. Healthcare. **11**(12) (2023)
2. Barba-Aragon, M.I., Jimenez-Jimenez, D.: Is training a green innovation driver? The mediating role of knowledge acquisition. J. Knowl. Manage. **28**, 463–483 (2023)
3. Bharadwaj, A.: A 20-20 culture communication template tool for multinational management. Bus. Prof. Commun. Q. **88**, 512–527 (2023)
4. Dalgaard, V.L. et al.: A study protocol outlining the development and evaluation of a training program for frontline managers on leading Well-being and the psychosocial work environment in Danish hospital settings—a cluster randomized waitlist controlled trial. BMC Public Health. **23**(1), 848 (2023)
5. Dankers-de Mari, E. et al.: How does government policy influence the employment and training of nurse practitioners and physician assistants? A realist analysis using qualitative interviews. J. Adv. Nurs. **79**(7), 2553–2567 (2023)
6. Enstroem, R., Schmaltz, R.: A juggler's manifesto: elevating creativity to stay productive amid uncertainty. J. Manage. Dev. **42**(5), 340–351 (2023)
7. Gil, A.J., Rodriguez-Cavides, L., Romero-Daza, D.: Analysis of training effectiveness from the perspective of managers and employees in the Colombian hospitality industry. Ind. Commer. Train. **55**(3), 346–354 (2023)
8. Guidotti, F., Demarie, S., Ciaccioni, S., Capranica, L.: Sports management knowledge, competencies, and skills: focus groups and women sports managers' perceptions. Sustainability. **15**(13) (2023)
9. Jalghef, M.A., Eshah, N., Al-Oweidat, I., Nashwan, A.J.: Self-perceived performance-based training needs among middle-level nursing managers in Jordan. Int. J. Healthc. Manage. **17**, 702–714 (2023)
10. Jiyenze, M.K. et al.: Strengthening health management, leadership, and governance capacities: what are the actual training needs in Tanzania? Health Sci. Rep. **6**(3), e1158 (2023)
11. Jubinville, M., Longpre, C., Nguemeleu, E.T.: Standardized and validated training to support the charge nurse: research protocol. Nurs. Open. **10**(7), 4756–4765 (2023)
12. Kaur, P., Prashar, A., Bhatnagar, J.: Creating resource passageways in cross-cultural virtual work teams: a longitudinal field study. Pers. Rev. **53**, 336–352 (2023)
13. Kebede, A.G., Fikire, A.H.: Exploring factors affecting product innovation practice among micro and small scale enterprises: the case study of Debre Berhan town, Ethiopia. Cogent Bus. Manage. **10**(2) (2023)

14. Liao, L.L., Feng, H., Jiao, J.J., Zhao, Y.A., Ning, H.T.: Nursing assistants' knowledge, attitudes and training needs regarding urinary incontinence in nursing homes: a mixed-methods study. BMC Geriatr. **23**(1) (2023)
15. Manjon, J., Domingo-Ferrer, J., Sanchez, D., Blanco-Justicia, A.: Secure, accurate and privacy-aware fully decentralized learning via co-utility. Comput. Commun. **207**, 1–18 (2023)

Design and Implementation of a Web-Based Quality Evaluation System for the Cultivation of Diversified Grassroots Talents

Jieting Nie(✉)

Yunnan Open University, Kunming, Yunnan, China
Niejieting913@126.com

Abstract. Web Design plays an important role in talent cultivation, but in the process of comprehensive talent cultivation, it is also necessary to integrate many factors and optimize talent cultivation with the help of intelligent analysis methods. The results show that the appearance analysis method can improve the quality of personnel by more than 80%, and it can realize the integration of knowledge and promote the comprehensive development of talents. The attention rate is greater than ten percent. Therefore, the web analysis method can realize the comprehensive promotion of talents and make them develop more stably.

Keywords: Gradient descent theory · Web · Diversified grassroots talent team · Evaluation system · Implementation

1 Introduction

In the process of talent analysis, the diversification of talents and the integration of applications play an important role in social development [1, 2]. The main aspects of education in colleges and universities, how to effectively improve analytical methods and synthesize various knowledge has become the focus of current research. External analysis methods can analyze the research process [3, 4]. Knowledge is integrated, the image is damaged, the direction development is deepened, and the development process of comprehensive performance is formed. But we also form an effective integration of knowledge and key points [5, 6]. However, in the process of analysis, the integration of time nodes and knowledge content is also insufficient. This paper believes that many aspects in the process of talent training can realize the integration of data [7, 8]. Some scholars also believe that the integration of intelligent analysis methods and talent training can improve the comprehensiveness of talents and realize overall planning. Therefore, intelligent analysis methods should be effectively linked with talent training. It can deepen the structure of talents and play a significant role in promoting knowledge content and knowledge change [9, 10].

B. Brik and S. Nazir (Eds.): BigIoT-EDU 2024, LNICST 660, pp. 343–349, 2026.
https://doi.org/10.1007/978-3-032-18628-7_35

2 Theoretical Model Construction for the Design and Implementation of the Training Quality Evaluation System

The system analyzed is W_i, the standards is E_i, In its own knowledge structure. Integrated development of military affairs is $\hat{e}_i = E_i/|E_i|, \hat{h}_i = H_i/|H_i|$, A comprehensive analysis of metaization.the analysis process is shown in formula 1.

$$W_i = \sqrt{\lim_{x \to \infty} \Gamma \times H_i^* |W_i| = \frac{|E_i|^2}{2\eta_o}} \tag{1}$$

The internalization of knowledge and the hierarchical analysis of knowledge integrity also optimize the structure of knowledge and promote the integration of knowledge and demand. The details are shown in Formula 2.

$$P = \sigma |W_i| = \frac{\sigma}{2\eta_o} |E_i|^2 \sum_{i=1}^{n} X_i \tag{2}$$

Knowledge structure and knowledge internalization is E_i. Students' demand for knowledge and the learning effect of knowledge is W_s. The overall change is shown in Eq. 3.

$$|W_s| = \lim_{x \to \infty} \frac{n!}{r!(n-r)!} = \sum_{i=1}^{n} (X_i - \overline{X})^2 \tag{3}$$

Military integrity and educational needs is E_s, diversified development conditions is η_o. The specific results are shown in Formula 4.

$$|W_s| = \frac{1}{2\eta_o} |E_s|^2 \tag{4}$$

Multi-dimensional analysis is needed is shown in Eq. (5).

$$\sigma = 4\pi R^2 \frac{|E_s|^2}{|E_i|^2} \frac{n!}{r!(n-r)!} \frac{-b \pm \sqrt{b^2 - 4ac}}{2a} \tag{5}$$

Continued continuous analysis and overall changes is shown in Eq. (6).

$$\sigma = \lim_{R \to \infty} oR \frac{E_s \times E_s^*}{E_i \times E_i^*} X_1, \ldots, X_n \tag{6}$$

The comprehensive talent training effect can be incorporated into. In the echo function is $No(t_i)$ shown in Eq. (7).

$$No(t_i) = \frac{g(t_i) + F(d_i)}{mean\left(\sum v_{ij} + 4\right)} + \frac{1}{n} \sum_{i=1}^{n} X_i Y_i \tag{7}$$

3 Practical Cases of the Design and Implementation of Quality Evaluation Systems is Cultivated

3.1 Cultivate the Concept of Design and Implementation Model Construction of Quality Evaluation System

Talent cultivation belongs to a gradual process. During the identification process, a direct rest is needed. External databases can be used. Students' learning interests and comprehensive needs are judged. Corresponding knowledge and data according to students' personalized development need to be provided. In the process of knowledge analysis, it is also necessary to transform theory into practice. Effectively blend the two. It can comprehensively improve its analysis effect and content. Therefore, in the process of holistic judgment and comprehensive analysis. Students should conduct comprehensive learning through web technology. The design and implementation process of the culture quality evaluation system was simulated, as shown in Figure 1.

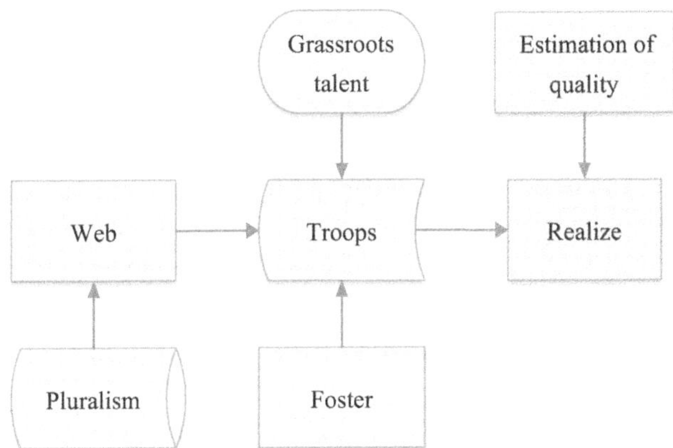

Fig. 1. Cultivating the analysis process of the design and implementation of a quality evaluation system

As can be seen from the analysis in Fig. 1, in the process of knowledge learning and knowledge matching. It is necessary to quantify students' situation and knowledge. Combine the two organically to form a comprehensive contrast. From a three-dimensional teaching and learning direction. At the same time, it is necessary to build a necessary learning system. Through external learning and overall analysis. The process of learning, it is necessary to realize the quantification of knowledge.

3.2 Design and Implementation of the Culture Quality Evaluation System

Taking time as an example, the external learning analysis and external analysis data matching are carried out on freshman to junior students. The survey lasts for six months, and the survey objects are mainly students' learning knowledge, academic achievements and learning contents, and quantify the knowledge and contents. Complete comprehensive judgment. At the same time, it is also necessary to improve students' actual data, data survey and data result analysis, mainly to investigate cases and students' academic performance. The specific learning process is shown in Table I.

Table 1. Subject-related parameters of the study

Category	Acquisition of academic achievement	Understanding of knowledge points	Integrity of diversified data	Results of comprehensive data analysis
Government departments	78.64	75.73	75.73	79.61
Non-profit organizations	79.61	75.73	74.76	82.52
Educational institutions	72.82	75.73	73.79	72.82
Enterprise	77.67	82.52	78.64	81.55

From the analysis results in Table 1, it can be seen that diversification analysis is being performed. And in the process of data judgment and multi-index judgment, it is necessary to realize comprehensive comparison of data. At the same time, it is necessary to integrate the integrity of the data to realize the overall planning of the data.

4 Design, Implementation and Stability of the Culture Quality Evaluation System

The improvement of students' academic performance and comprehensive ability is a gradual process. Therefore, it is necessary to make a continuous judgment on its establishment process. The judgment content is shown in Fig. 2.

The analysis in Figure 2 shows that there are volatile changes in the process of students' learning and ability advancement. The process of advancement and the overall change, out of stability, show that in the process of external information, students constantly manage knowledge absorption and internalization, forming an effective knowledge structure, which can meet their study and work needs. However, whether its knowledge points are integrated or not, and whether the learning knowledge is satisfied, needs further deepening and concrete deepening research. As shown in Figure 3.

Figure 3 shows students' knowledge needs are closely related to the actual external, knowledge points and knowledge structure. Students' actual needs are gradually declining, which shows that they are significantly satisfied. However, the continuous increase of knowledge points provided by the outside shows that the two can achieve effective matching and complete diversified integration. Specific summary results and overall judgment are shown in Table 2.

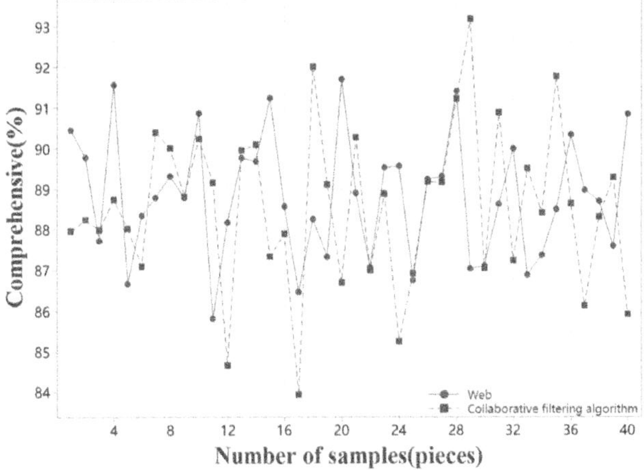

Fig. 2. Design and implementation of a culture quality evaluation system for different algorithms

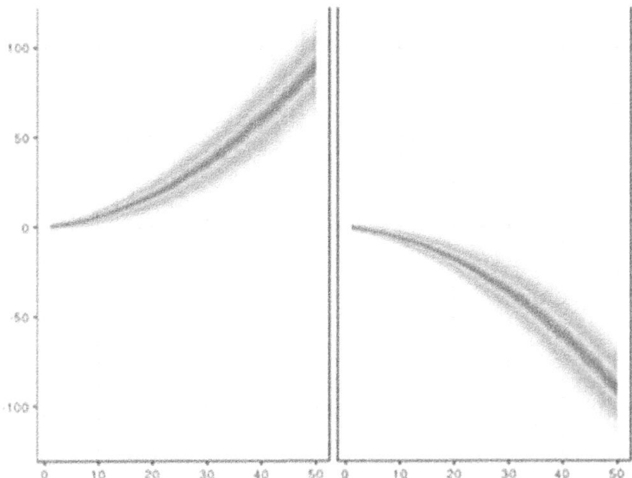

Fig. 3. Design and implementation of a web-based cultivation quality evaluation system

According to the analysis results in Table 2, the overall judgment is made. As well as comprehensive analysis. The integration process and integration rate of students' knowledge and knowledge points are greater than 80%. Therefore, it is necessary to analyze whether students' transformation process is extreme in the process of knowledge internalization, and analyze the causes of extreme problems to find out the causes in the transformation process. Therefore, it is necessary to make a continuous and diversified judgment on it. And show the specific results in the form of three-dimensional diagrams as shown in Fig. 4.

As can be clearly seen from Fig. 4, students do not appear in the process of continuous learning and comprehensive analysis. Extreme points show that in the process of analysis

Table 2. Comparison of the design and implementation of the culture quality evaluation system of different methods

Algorithm	Internalization of student Knowledge	The fusion of knowledge and theory	Enhancement of comprehensive results	Judgment of holistic structure
Web	52.21	38.94	76.70	74.76
Collaborative filtering algorithms	34.51	47.79	82.52	73.79

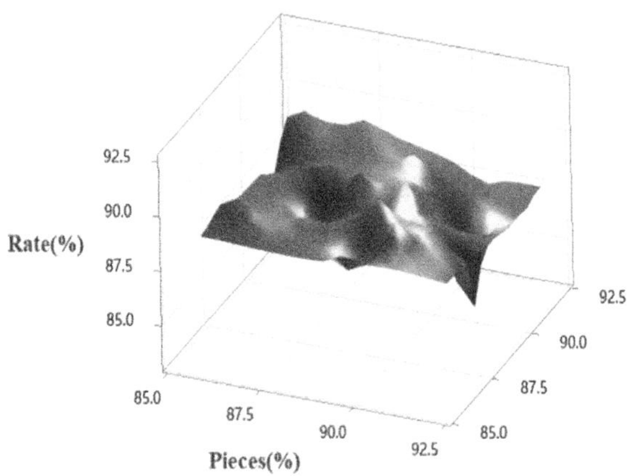

Fig. 4. Comparative study of the research scheme of the algorithm

and diversified judgment, students' knowledge structure is similar to knowledge, content and externally provided knowledge structure, and they are effectively integrated, and there is no difference. The reason of violation, but the appearance part. The deviation is high, mainly because students' individualized differences are obvious. The process of students' comprehensive improvement is complicated. Simple knowledge output can't meet the time needed to improve students' knowledge internalization.

5 Conclusion

The development and comprehensive output of the society require students to have continuous ideas and abilities. How to effectively improve students' comprehensive ability, we need to improve their knowledge and increase their knowledge level, so as to meet the corresponding needs. However, in the process of analysis, whether students can get effective output and improve their comprehensive effect has become a current research problem. Therefore, it is necessary to continuously output students. Instinct to obtain the comprehensive points of students through external forms. Form diversified data content. To meet the actual needs of students, the satisfaction rate is greater than

80%, and it can improve their satisfaction deviation. Therefore, increasing students' learning effect and ability and realizing students' diversified development have become the focus of research.

References

1. Yumei, F., Liang, L., Xiaolong, Y., Xiaohong, Z., Zhijun, Y., Yan L.: Research on the quality evaluation and guarantee system of teacher training talents based on OBE concept. J. Higher Educ. **9**(23), 171–175 (2023)
2. Wei, L., Liang J.: Design of a web online examination system based on wamp architecture automation Technol. Appl. **42**(5), 162–165 (2023)
3. Zhanyong, Q., Xiaoran F.: Construction of a high-quality skilled talent training system based on total quality management modern education management (7), 107–117 (2023)
4. Liqiang, W., Hongyuan, Y., Na, Z., Manhong, L.: Develop a talent training program for art and design majors based on teaching quality monitoring and evaluation. Univ. Educ. (13), 107–111 (2023)
5. Han, Z., Yang, H., Yunlong, Z., Ang, L., Chengxin, G., Tingting, X.: Research on the cultivation path of applied talents in local universities under the background of popularization of higher education—Based on the perspective of constructing a teaching quality evaluation system research and practice of innovation and entrepreneurship theory (17), 131–133 (2023)
6. Lei, W., Lei, Z., Yinqi, M.: The realistic dimension and action path of high quality vocational undergraduate talent training model—Based on text analysis of education quality reports from 21 vocational and technical universities research on chinese higher education (5), 101–108 (2023)
7. Changwu, L.: Design and implementation of a web-based university score management system. Technol. Wind (27), 4–6 (2023)
8. Ziyi, Z., Xiaolan, L., Yuting, L.: Design and implementation of a web-based electronic invoice management system computer knowledge and technology. Acad. Edn. **19**(2), 39–41 (2023)
9. Xinsi, M., Minghe, Y., Hong, W., Tiancheng, Z.: Design and implementation of a student evaluation system based on student portraits software guide, **22**(1), 20–28 (2023)
10. Efendi, F., Tonapa, S.I., Mishbahatal E., Hass, M., Hok Man Ho K. (2023) The impact of seat assisted resistance band exercise on physical function, sleep quality, and depression in elderly individuals: a systematic review. Int. Nurs. Sci. (English), **10**(1), 72–81
11. Yingyue, R., Yinghui, J., Yinglan, X., Hongcai, S., Zhongyu, Z.: Has Chinese and Western medicine truly integrated—a systematic evaluation based on the clinical practice guidelines of integrated traditional Chinese and Western medicine Chinese. J. Evid. Based Med. **23**(10), 1156–1164 (2023)
12. Tong, S., Shiping, H., Xin, W., Feng, L., Yun, R.: A systematic review and re evaluation of radiofrequency ablation combined with transcatheter arterial chemoembolization for the treatment of primary liver cancer. West China Med. **38**(8), 1211–1218 (2023)
13. Bingxing, L. Ying, T., Junling, W., Dai, L., Juntao, Y., Fuming, L., etc.: Systematic evaluation of pharmacoeconomic evaluation of anti novel coronavirus infection Chinese. J. Evid. Based Med. **23**(5), 549–554 (2023)

Design of Athletes' Sports State Monitoring System Based on Artificial Neural Network Algorithm

Lin Zhong(✉)

Jiangxi Vocational Technical College of Industry and Trade, Nanchang, Jiangxi, China
guolao8709052527@126.com

Abstract. Sports training is an important part of competitive sports activities. Its direct purpose is to improve the competitive ability of athletes, and then through participating in sports competitions, the competitive ability that has been obtained will be transformed into sports results. In the current sports training function monitoring, most of them rely on traditional experience and models, lacking scientific evaluation and diagnostic methods and standards. With the rapid development of modern science and technology, this paper analyzes the athletes' sports state based on the ANN (artificial neural network) algorithm. The experimental data shows that the sports state monitoring system established in this paper tests the sports ability by adjusting the sports load before the competition. It is found that the load of runners and swimmers fluctuates greatly before the competition, and the load of bicycles fluctuates relatively smoothly, With the increase of the number of athletes in the test, the proportion of the three types of athletes completing the same intensity load, and the level of blood lactic acid has been improved, indicating that the aerobic metabolism ability is improved. The system designed in this paper increases the speed, breadth and depth of sports training data and information collection, and makes timely feedback through comprehensive and systematic analysis of data and information, thus playing an important role in guiding coaches' scientific decision-making in sports training.

Keywords: Artificial neural network algorithm · Athletes · Motion state · Monitoring system

1 Introduction

In modern competitive sports, the faster, higher and stronger Olympic spirit makes the level of competitive sports continuously improve, and one world record has been refreshed. Sports training can change, consolidate and improve the competitive ability of athletes, and transform it into sports results to the greatest extent through competition. The training process of changing, consolidating and improving athletes' competitive ability is actually a process of scientifically realizing the transfer from the current state of athletes' competitive ability to the specific target state [1]. The intensity and amount

B. Brik and S. Nazir (Eds.): BigIoT-EDU 2024, LNICST 660, pp. 350–358, 2026.
https://doi.org/10.1007/978-3-032-18628-7_36

of training that elite athletes are enduring are increasing. Sports training puts forward higher requirements for sports science and technology. The long-term and systematic scientific monitoring of elite athletes' training process is carried out in order to scientifically diagnose their physical functions, technical characteristics and psychological state. Sports training is an important part of competitive sports activities. Its direct purpose is to improve the competitive ability of athletes, and then to transform the competitive ability obtained into sports results by participating in sports competitions [2]. In the current sports training function monitoring, most of them rely on traditional experience and models, lacking scientific evaluation and diagnostic methods and standards. At the same time, the data processing efficiency of sports training is low, the analysis is not systematic, and the information feedback is slow, which limits the accurate diagnosis and evaluation of training effect and athletes' functional state, and ultimately affects the improvement of athletes' performance. However, whether the athletes' sports state and sports ability can be changed, consolidated and improved according to the training objectives depends to a large extent on the state of the athletes' body bearing the training load, and the state of the athletes' bearing the training load is directly reflected in a series of changes in the body function [3, 4].

It is of great theoretical and practical significance to systematically diagnose and monitor the actual state of athletes' competitive ability in the process of sports training. At the same time, with the rapid development of modern science and technology, we should strengthen the research and application of computer, database, data mining and other technologies in sports training. Based on the ANN algorithm, this paper analyzes the sports state of athletes, and designs a monitoring system for sports state during sports training, which can increase the speed, breadth and depth of sports training data and information collection, and make timely feedback through comprehensive and systematic analysis of data and information, thus playing an important role in guiding coaches' scientific decision-making in sports training [5]. After the training of the ANN algorithm, it is necessary to accelerate the recovery of physical functions by scientific means, effectively improve the training ability of athletes, so as to prevent athletes from overtraining or overtraining. At the same time, it is a problem that needs to be solved in the field of sports science to scientifically regulate the sports state of athletes before major competitions, so as to create the best sports performance in competitions [6].

2 Sports State Monitoring of Athletes

2.1 Evaluation of Athletes' Physical Function

Research and application status of physiological and biochemical detection and evaluation of athletes' physical function, diagnosis system of elite athletes' training load state, screening and application of physiological and biochemical detection and evaluation indexes of elite athletes' training load state, comprehensive evaluation and application of common physiological and biochemical indexes of elite athletes' training load state diagnosis [7]. In sports training, the theory of sports physiology, experimental techniques and methods are used to evaluate the effect of excellent athletes in sports training, and to monitor the ability and functional state of excellent athletes to bear the training load. See Fig. 1 for the main methods of scientific monitoring of athletes' sports training.

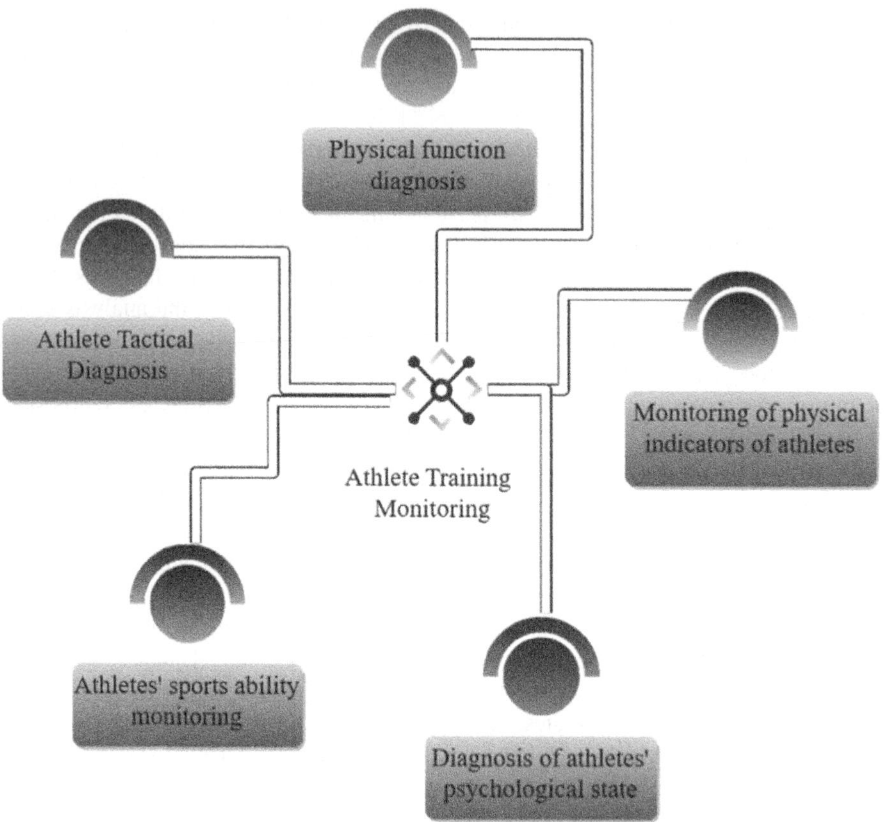

Fig. 1. Main methods of monitoring athletes' sports state

Diagnosing athletes' physical functions can help coaches understand the training effect of exercise load and the state of athletes' physical skills, and accurately evaluate the scientificity and effectiveness of exercise load and training methods. Athletes' function evaluation has become an important content and indispensable link of scientific training [8]. The physical function evaluation of elite athletes involves the neuromuscular system, cardiovascular system, respiratory system, immune system, endocrine system, etc. Through the measurement and comprehensive analysis of many physiological indexes, the degree of diagnosis of exercise fatigue and the recovery of the body are shown in Table 1.

The content and method of body measurement of excellent athletes' health examination, the method and evaluation of medical supervision and inspection of China's excellent athletes' health level, and the method and evaluation of sports trauma of China's excellent athletes' health level examination. Then, it discusses and defines the four basic abilities that constitute the competitive ability, namely physical ability, skill, tactical ability and psychological ability, as well as the level of physical health that has an important impact on the competitive ability, and the state of the body bearing the training load. The physical function of athletes assesses the load intensity and load capacity of athletes

Table 1. Functions of commonly used indicators for physical function evaluation of athletes

Organizational system	Index	Effect
Cardiopulmonary system	Maximum oxygen uptake, anaerobic threshold	Long term training effect
Endocrine system	Testosterone, cortisol	Evaluate training load and functional state
Coach observation system	Athlete plan completion quality	Comprehensive evaluation of athletes

during training, the adaptation of the body to the exercise intensity and volume, and the rationality and effectiveness of training methods and means through the changes of physiological and biochemical indicators of athletes during sports training, so as to help coaches understand the training effect, correctly evaluate and adjust the training program [9].

2.2 Diagnosis and Monitoring of Athletes' Sports Skills

Diagnosis and monitoring is a problem that elite athletes need to solve in training and monitoring in preparation for the Olympic Games and major international competitions. It is mainly aimed at the technical training problems to carry out corresponding applied research and technical services, and is welcomed and approved by coaches. Sports training is a complex, dynamic, individualized and multi-factor influenced process. The technical diagnosis problems put forward by coaches to be solved are different, with distinct special characteristics and individual needs. The lateral measurement methods of aerobic and anaerobic endurance, the measurement methods of endurance, the establishment of the measurement system of endurance training level, the main measurement methods of aerobic and anaerobic endurance, and several basic problems that should be paid attention to in the diagnosis of endurance training level, etc. [10]. Using physiological and biochemical tests to monitor and analyze sports training data, the most commonly used reference evaluation standard is the clinical normal value of each test index. This reference evaluation standard is too wide to effectively and accurately monitor athletes' sports training.

The second, third and fourth working links and functional support of technical training level diagnosis system, on this basis, the diagnosis of elite athletes' bearing sports training load is established. When the exercise value is greater than the rising critical value and the recovery value is less than the recovery critical value, the exercise load is reasonable; when the exercise value is less than the rising critical value and the recovery value is less than the recovery critical value, the exercise load is insufficient; when the exercise value is greater than the rising critical value and the recovery value is greater than the recovery critical value, the exercise load is excessive. Therefore, there are differences in the specific methods and technical details of the technical diagnosis and monitoring conducted by sports researchers for elite athletes preparing for the Olympic Games and major international competitions. Through these methods, the athletes' special sports techniques can be diagnosed qualitatively and quantitatively. On this basis, individual technical optimization is carried out, so as to solve the technical training problems of athletes and continuously improve the scientific level of athletes' sports training.

3 Design of Athlete's Sports Condition Monitoring System Based on Artificial Neural Network Algorithm

3.1 Motion State Monitoring System

Athletes' sports state mainly refers to the relatively highest and relatively stable state of their sports ability during the competition after scientific and systematic training according to training objectives and corresponding training plans. In other words, the best state of its sports ability appears on the scheduled date of the competition. Whether athletes can adapt to the sports load they bear is the key to scientific training. An important content of athletes' physical function evaluation is to scientifically evaluate the athletes' adaptation to the load. If the training load is too small and the body can not get enough stimulation, it will not be able to effectively improve the sports ability; If the exercise load is too large, exceeding the endurance and adaptation threshold of the body, it will cause overtraining, excessive fatigue or sports injury.

Therefore, this paper proposes an ANN algorithm to monitor the athletes' sports state, and its training speed and promotion ability have been greatly improved. The basic idea of the design of the adverse information filtering decision module based on ANN is to first express the text to be monitored as a text vector according to the keywords, take it as the input of ANN, and then make the corresponding decisions according to the calculation results after the neural network calculation. Then, according to the results of long-term training monitoring of excellent athletes, we should study and summarize the indicators of various physiological, biochemical, sports technology and psychological states of excellent athletes when they create the best sports results. Under the ANN algorithm, according to the training experience and observation of coaches, and the athletes' self feelings, we can more accurately establish the best sports state of excellent athletes. In this paper, based on the ANN algorithm, the athletes' sports state monitoring system is designed, as shown in Fig. 2.

The sports condition monitoring system not only involves the diagnosis and monitoring of athletes' competitive ability, that is, physical ability, skills, tactical ability and psychological ability. But also relates to the diagnosis and monitoring of athletes' health level and the state of bearing sports training load; At the same time, it also involves the information storage, information management and information utilization of the above elements. Through the movement state monitoring system of ANN algorithm, coaches and researchers can monitor athletes' achievements in major competitions and training practices, as well as their self-feelings. Assuming that the coordinate position of the athlete's head center is at pixel x_i, then the crowd with N pedestrian head centers is represented as:

$$H(x) = \sum_{i=1}^{N} \delta \tag{1}$$

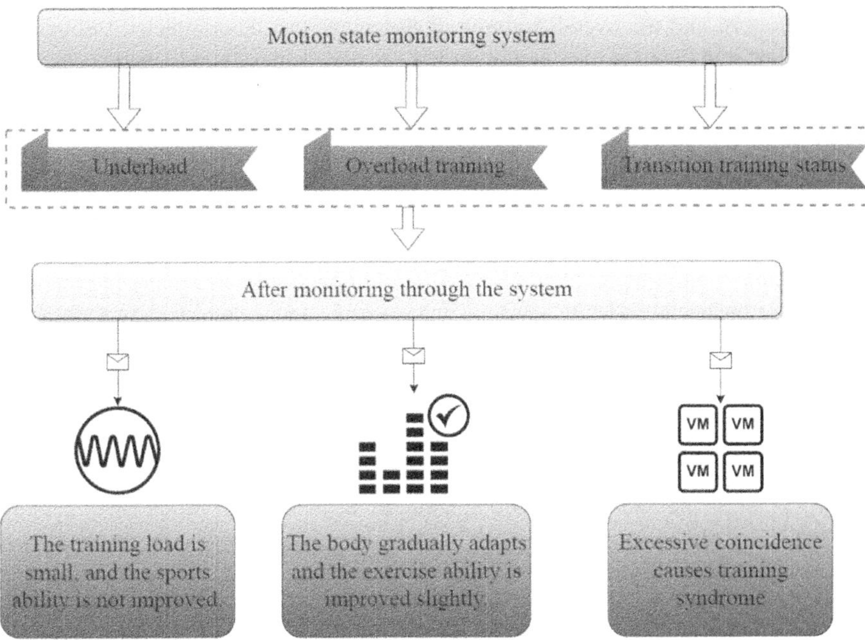

Fig. 2. Motion state monitoring system

The geometric adaptive Gaussian kernel function used in calculation is:

$$F(x) = \sum_{i=1}^{N} \delta(x - x_i) \tag{2}$$

The loss function adopted by the network is:

$$L(\Phi) = \frac{1}{2N} F(X\Phi) \tag{3}$$

Φ is the parameter of continuous training and learning, N is the total number of training images, X is the i image, F is the true density map of i image, $F(X\Phi)$ is the corresponding estimated density map, and L is the loss between the estimated density map and the true density map.

The following general evaluation values are selected for the degree of network pros and cons and the criteria for selecting training models: average absolute error, and the calculation formula of evaluation values is as follows:

$$MAE = \frac{1}{N} \sum_{i=1}^{N} \tag{4}$$

Through the above formula analysis, the speed of ANN training can be accelerated, in addition, the local features of the motion state monitoring image can be extracted more accurately, and the overall training of the image can be completed through the local training, and the final overall monitoring can also achieve good results.

Monitoring the physical function of elite athletes through ANN algorithm is closely related to the exercise load imposed by coaches and the ability of athletes to bear the exercise load. Therefore, the evaluation of excellent athletes' physical functions must be combined with the coaches' training plans and the athletes' training status. It is not possible to simply evaluate whether the athletes are adaptive or overtraining according to the one-time changes of a certain index. The system has become a work and technical platform for China's elite athletes to prepare for the Olympic Games and major international competitions in special scientific research and scientific and technological services, and has provided a testing and experimental technology platform for related basic research and application research, promoting the progress of related research technology.

3.2 Application of the System

In sports practice, the indexes of muscle strength, heart rate and blood lactic acid are often used to evaluate sports effects. In modern competitive sports, the evaluation of athletes' physical functions is characterized by rapidity/accuracy, that is, to accurately capture the instantaneous changes of athletes' relevant indicators on the sports training scene, and quickly evaluate whether the training process of athletes achieves the training effect expected by coaches. Pre competition exercise load adjustment refers to the gradual reduction of pre competition training load to help athletes recover physically and psychologically from high-intensity training, the research method of speed training level diagnosis, the diagnosis method and effective indicators of local action speed and overall action speed, the establishment of speed training level diagnosis system, and the application of speed training level diagnosis of athletes in some sports events. In order to maximize the level of competition. Coaches and sports researchers have realized that reasonable adjustment of sports load can significantly improve the potential of athletes' competitive level. This paper will test the influence of pre match adjustment of sports load on sports ability through the sports state monitoring system, and the experimental results are shown in Fig. 3.

From Fig. 3, it can be found that the load of runners and swimmers fluctuates greatly before the competition, and the load of bicycles fluctuates relatively smoothly. With the increase of the number of test people, the three types of athletes have completed the same intensity of load proportion, and the blood lactic acid level has increased, indicating that the aerobic metabolic capacity has improved. Elite athletes should pay attention to keeping a scientific and reasonable intake ratio of nutrients before competition, as shown in Fig. 4.

It can be clearly seen from Fig. 4 that sugar accounts for the most, reaching 58%, followed by fat, accounting for 26%, and finally protein, accounting for 16%. However, it can be seen that there is no perfect exercise recipe for different athletes in various events or the same event at present. According to the characteristics of long-term scientific monitoring of athletes, dietary and nutritional supplement schemes suitable for different athletes' personality characteristics should be formulated to adjust the best competitive state of athletes.

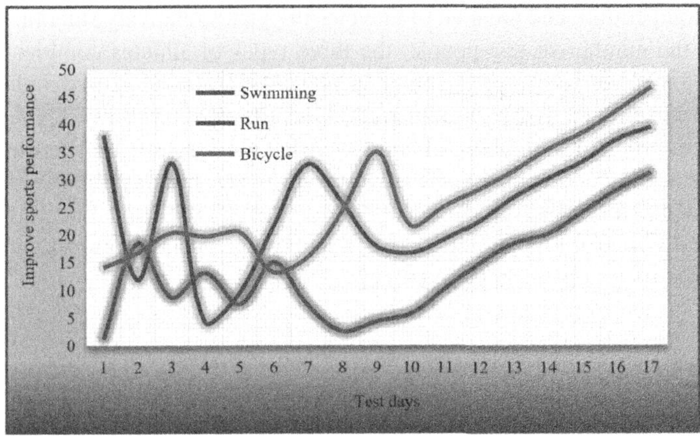

Fig. 3. Effect of adjusting exercise load before competition on exercise ability.

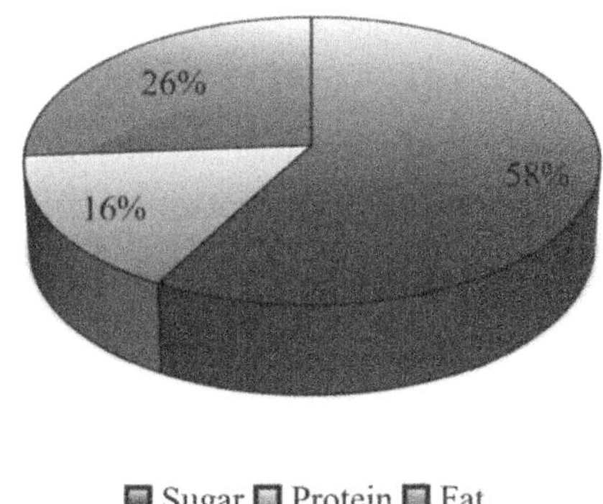

Fig. 4. Scientific and reasonable nutrient intake ratio of athletes before competition

4 Conclusions

Chinese sports science and technology personnel attach great importance to the close combination of scientific research and sports practice. Specifically, in terms of the establishment of research projects, the implementation of research projects, and the application of research results, this paper analyzes the athletes' sports state monitoring based on ANN algorithm, and designs a systematic sports state monitoring system in this paper. The sports state monitoring system not only involves the diagnosis and monitoring of athletes' competitive ability, that is, physical ability, skills, tactical ability, and psychological ability; It also involves the diagnosis and monitoring of athletes' health level and the state of bearing sports training load; At the same time, it also involves the information storage, information management and information utilization of the above elements. Finally, the experimental data shows that the sports state monitoring system established in this paper tests the exercise capacity by adjusting the exercise load before the competition. It is found that the load of runners and swimmers fluctuates greatly before the competition, and the load of bicycles fluctuates relatively smoothly. With the increase of the number of test people, the three types of athletes complete the same intensity of load proportion, and the blood lactic acid level has increased, indicating that the aerobic metabolism ability is improved. After the training of the ANN algorithm, it is an urgent problem in the field of sports science to accelerate the recovery of body functions through scientific means, effectively improve the training ability of athletes, so as to prevent athletes from overtraining or overtraining. At the same time, it is necessary to scientifically regulate the athletes' sports state before major competitions, so as to create the best sports results in competitions.

References

1. Chen, B.H., Huang, S.C., Yen, J.Y.: Counter-propagation artificial neural network-based motion detection algorithm for static-camera surveillance scenarios. Neurocomputing **273**(17), 481–493 (2017)
2. Wang, Z., Jia, S., Xiu, J., et al.: Multi-model target tracking algorithm based on artificial neural network. J. Naval Aeronautical and Astronautical Univ. **58**(20), 36–47 (2019)
3. Sun, X., Huang, M., Liu, Y., et al.: Investigation of artificial neural network algorithm based IGBT online condition monitoring. Microelectron. Reliab. **66**(22), 39–54 (2018)
4. Zhang, G.: Research on safety simulation model and algorithm of dynamic system based on artificial neural network. Soft Comput.: A Fus. Foundat. Methodol. Appl. **38**(15), 26–39 (2022)
5. Zhou, X.: Wearable health monitoring system based on human motion state recognition. Comput. Commun. **150**(10), 62–71 (2020)
6. Fan, J., Guo, X., Wang, C., et al.: The state of motion stereo about plant leaves monitoring system design and simulation. Int. Conf. Comput. Comput. Technol. Agricul. **20**(11), 17–26 (2019)
7. Kim, B.J., Cheon, S.P., Kang, S.J.: Motion estimation and machine learning-based wind turbine monitoring system. Trans. Korean Inst. Electr. Eng. **66**(10), 1516–1522 (2017)
8. Korsakas, S., Vainoras, A., Gargasas, L., et al.: On-line and off-line ECG and motion activity monitoring system for Athletes. Baltic J. Sport Health Sci. **3**(66), 45–63 (2018)
9. Lin, Y.C., Nai-Kuan, C., Lin, G.Y., et al.: A real-time contactless pulse rate and motion status monitoring system based on complexion tracking. Sensors **17**(7), 1490–1499 (2017)
10. Susilawati, S., Sembiring, Z., Muhathir, M.: Motion monitoring system based on IoT. **19**(2), 26–45 (2020)

Research and Application of Higher Education Quality Assessment Algorithm by the Neural-Like Network Architecture

Beibei Wang(✉)

School of Marxism, Lanzhou Institute of Technology, Gansu, Lanzhou, China
13619326766@163.com

Abstract. The quality of education is the goal of higher education, and it is also the external response of various measures of higher education. Neural network can classify and divide similar problems in higher education, improve the quality of education and save this resource. In the process of higher education analysis, the complexity is relatively high and the content involves many points, so it is necessary to optimize it and simplify the analysis content and conditions. The results show that neural network can promote the evaluation of educational quality by more than 20%, make the educational satisfaction rate reach 85%, and promote the optimization of education and the upgrading of content. Therefore, endogenous network can provide corresponding support for the development of higher education.

Keywords: Constitutional network dispensing theory · Neural-like network architecture · Higher education · Resource Query · Systems research

1 Introduction

In the process of educational quality evaluation, it is necessary to make a comprehensive judgment and analysis on teachers' strength, teachers' content, implementation conditions and educational types [1, 2]. However, in the process of testing and analysis, there are differences between indicators and contents, and the evaluation process involves teachers, students and educational contents, and the data among different dimensions are complicated. Therefore, it is necessary to use intelligent analysis methods for analysis. Researchers believe that neural-like networks can comprehensive analysis of similar educational resources and educational contents can improve the effect of analysis [3, 4]. It can also integrate the overall resources and optimize the content structure [5, 6]. At the same time, with the corresponding reasonable educational plan, education can formally carry out education to improve the actual level and actual content of teaching [7–9]. Therefore, intelligent analysis method is combined with intelligent. The integration of data and schemes can improve the overall effect of education. However, in the process of educational analysis, there are also differences in indicators and contents. In order to

B. Brik and S. Nazir (Eds.): BigIoT-EDU 2024, LNICST 660, pp. 359–369, 2026.
https://doi.org/10.1007/978-3-032-18628-7_37

make a better judgment, intelligent analysis methods should integrate similar indicators and data, integrate the original database, realize multi-dimensional analysis of data, and provide support for the improvement of educational structure [10–13]. On the whole, neural networks can promote the development of education and optimize the original ones in the process of judgment in many aspects such as education, cultural education analysis and so on, but there are still some differences. Therefore, optimization analysis should be carried out, and judgment should be made with the support of actual cases.

2 The Concept of Research and Application of the Quality Assessment Algorithm Research Model Construction

In the process of quality evaluation, related concepts such as quality evaluation and neural network should be expounded. Quality evaluation is the evaluation of higher education content and higher education work in the teaching process. An important content is mainly to conduct in-depth analysis of the difficult problems and characteristic points of the teaching center, and integrate various factors to improve the reduction effect. The process of quality evaluation is complex and a continuous process, so in the process of analysis and research of quality evaluation, it is necessary to expand the research scope as much as possible and clarify the corresponding indicators. Neural-like network is an algorithm similar to neural network, which is characterized by fusing the uniqueness of neural network with neural-like network, and obtaining corresponding neurons for data analysis through fuzzy analysis. Therefore, similar to the network is more effective in this range and content, and the results are qualitatively analyzed. Therefore, the intelligent analysis method is fused with neural network and neural network, which have the same attributes, and the test target and test scope do not conflict. Therefore, water-like networks and educational quality assessment. It carries a large connection, but the application process similar to the network requires massive data processing, and its processing process is also very cumbersome. Therefore, the content of intelligent analysis and the scope of teaching effect should be simplified, the indicators should be defined, and characteristic analysis should be carried out. This is the focus and content of this paper.

3 Optimization Strategies for Research and Application of the Quality Assessment Algorithm Research

In the process of analyzing the internal sound network and progressiveness, it is necessary to analyze each link and content. For this judgment, the specific judgment process and research direction is to carry out the main branch points similar to the network. The analysis process is as follows, specifically as follows.

1. The content and indicators to be evaluated are analyzed by analogy.
2. One category of data is integrated and evaluated.
3. The correlation between all kinds of data.
4. First, the correlation points between data.
5. By the overall content of the data.
6. The final evaluation results.

It can be judged that in the process of analysis, each indicator and content is a complicated process. However, the main direction is to expand the data as much as possible, with multiple indicators and multiple contents, and then analyze the feature points and eigenvalues of the data. When the abnormalities are calculated, a preliminary set of outliers is formed, and then output them, and finally output the corresponding quality evaluation scheme. On the whole, in the process of evaluation, the processing of each index, the selection of index and the deletion of index data are the research focus, and they are also a key to ensure the evaluation quality. In the process of quality evaluation and multiple analyses, there are also differences in quality and results, which should be effectively integrated.

4 A Practical Case Study of a Research and Application of the Quality Assessment Algorithm

4.1 Introduction to the Research of Research and Application of the Quality Assessment Algorithm

Conduct an overall analysis of the quality and steps in the process of teaching evaluation, and show the specific process in the form of graphics, as shown in Fig. 1.

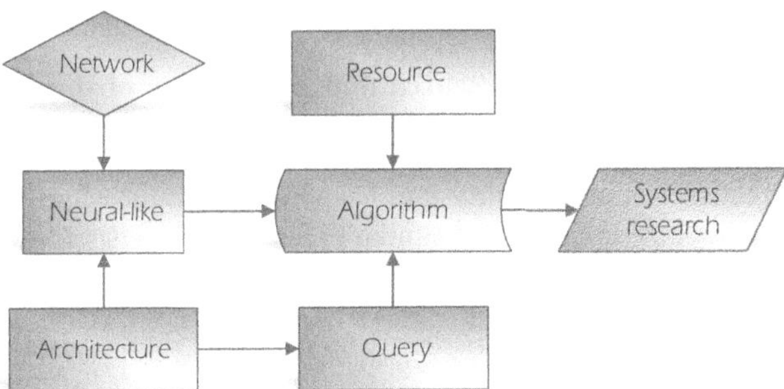

Fig. 1. The analytical process of a research and application of the quality assessment algorithm study

Compare the graphic analysis, graphic data and many aspects of graphic contents, and integrate the data in the graphic to form an effective data content for mapping. In the process of logic analysis of viewpoints, judgments are made on the key points and aspects of the graphics. Therefore, comprehensive analysis and holistic planning are the focus and hot spot of the research, and finally output the corresponding graphic content.

4.2 Research on Research and Application of the Quality Assessment Algorithm

The quality and quality in teaching are analyzed for the research object, the investigation object is 32 cases, the research course is four items, the investigation time is six months, and the characteristic points, contents and multi-index are judged to form an effective data collection. At the same time, the content of the data and the overall results of the data should also be described. The specific description is shown in Table 1.

Table 1. Holistic data description of quality assessment.

Category	General quality analysis	Make indicator judgment of the course	indicator planning	Comprehensive analysis of indicators
Student Reviews:	92.32	88.29	88.76	84.99
Subject, professional assessment	89.58	90.22	89.05	90.51
Assessment of teaching quality	89.37	86.28	89.79	88.88
Student assessment and feedback	90.05	89.51	91.44	91.77
Level of scientific research	86.12	89.90	89.18	87.48

4.3 Research and Stability of Research and Application of the Quality Assessment Algorithm

Check the content of teaching quality and teaching evaluation, and obtain the corresponding data through centralized and similar eigenvalue analysis forms. And the data results. is shown in Fig. 2.

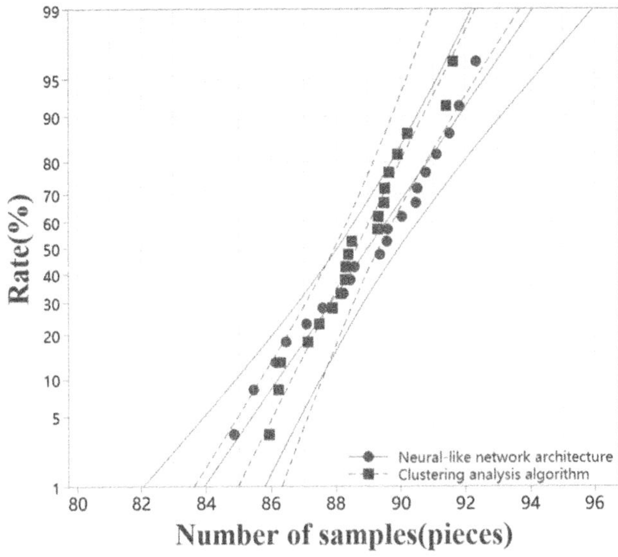

Fig. 2. Research on research and application of the quality assessment algorithm with different algorithms

As can be seen from Fig. 2, In the process of data clustering, data synthesis and data holistic planning, it is necessary to realize digital holistic planning. It will be found that in the process of evaluation, the indicators show a concentrated trend, indicating that in the process of analysis, the content, results and conditions of indicators are gradually simplified, and the forms and types of indicators are relatively concentrated. Therefore, in the overall evaluation process, the evaluation process is more concise. The above results are described and summarized for clarity of presentation. The summary results are shown in Table 2.

Table 2. The process and content of teaching quality evaluation.

Algorithm	Comprehensive evaluation effect	Consistency of human judgment	Comprehensive analysis of	Multiple integrations are required
Neural-like network architecture	91.11	88.14	88.84	92.22
Clustering analysis algorithm	86.47	91.40	87.30	89.88
P	91.52	87.13	88.02	88.11

According to the data analysis in Table 2, Comprehensive analysis and comparison of the contents to form an effective data set, and line judgment of the data results will show that the feature points and fusion points of the data are greater than 80%. Moreover, the correlation between data is relatively good, which shows that there is a strong correlation among multiple indicators in the process of holistic judgment and analysis, which can achieve effective accumulation and provide support for evaluation and evaluation methods. However, whether there are differences between the evaluation methods and whether the evaluation indexes are effective requires linear analysis to show the results in the form of graphs. The specific results are shown in Figure III.

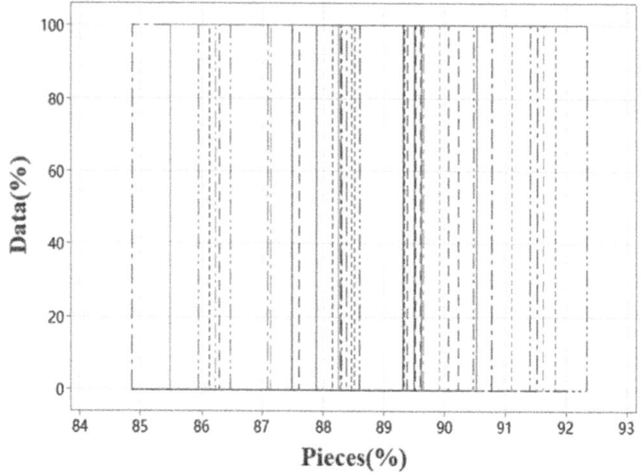

Fig. 3. Research on research and application of the quality assessment algorithm of Neural-like network architecture

Figure 3 shows in the process of comprehensive analysis and overall comparison of graphics, it will be found that the graphics are presented between them. The staggered form of concentration and distribution shows that in the process of class analysis, all kinds of data are aggregated, and the independence of evaluation results is maintained. In the process of analysis and judgment of achievements and related content, it will also be found that the overall structure has a strong correlation. The above analysis proves that in the process of quality evaluation, it is necessary to judge not only the characteristic indexes of quality, but also the relevance, segmentation and comprehensiveness of quality. Therefore, in the process of overall judgment and analysis, there is a strong correlation and logic among various indicators, which can provide support for comprehensive analysis and overall analysis, and summarize the corresponding data, as shown in Table 3.

Table 3. Rationalization and comparison of research and application of the quality assessment algorithm research with different methods

Algorithm	Effect of quality evaluation	Quality assessment satisfaction	Feasibility analysis	Holistic planning	The content of the assessment
Neural-like network architecture	88.59	86.21	89.98	87.18	89.39
Clustering analysis algorithm	90.77	89.64	89.86	88.41	86.90

Table 4. Comparison of the effectiveness of different methods of research and application of the quality assessment algorithm research

Algorithm	The conformity rate of teaching content	The coincidence rate of this effect	This comprehensive compliance rate	Improvement of rational teaching effect
Neural-like network architecture	88.96	93.05	90.21	90.98
Clustering analysis algorithm	90.40	87.62	91.12	91.61
P	90.41	89.66	85.92	92.17

4.4 Comparison of the Effectiveness of the Research on Research and Application of the Quality Assessment Algorithms

In the process, you need to conduct data analysis on the indicators. Among them, teaching content is zk, quality assessment criteria is z_i as, and comprehensive functions for quality assessment is $tol(z_i \cdot v_{ij})$ shown in Eq. (1).

$$\frac{n!}{r!(n-r)!}(z_i \cdot v_{ij}) = \coprod v_{ij} \geq \max(v_{ij} \div 2)\frac{\delta y}{\delta x} \tag{1}$$

When the logical relationship between the contents in the evaluation process meets the conditions. is shown in Eq. (2).

$$max(v_{ij}) = \partial({v_{ij}}^2 + 2 \cdot v_{ij}) \succ \frac{1}{2}(\sum v_{ij} + 4)\mathfrak{M}\frac{\partial^2 \Omega}{\partial u \partial v} \tag{2}$$

The process and time of quantitative evaluation is t_i By using the process and method of judgment is set_i Effect and quality evaluation results of the overall planning is y_i Function of quality evaluation is $F(t_i \approx 0)$ as shown in Eq. (3).

$$F(d_i) = \frac{\Delta y}{\Delta x} \sum t_i \bigcap \xi \cdot \sqrt{2} \rightarrow \oint z_i \cdot 7 \tag{3}$$

Comprehensive evaluation of quality is $g(t_i)$, and Effect judgment of construction site evaluation is w_i, Description of the function to evaluate the effect. as shown in Eq. (4).

$$g(t_i) = z_i \prod F(d_i) \frac{dy}{dx} - \int w_i \frac{n!}{r!(n-r)!} \tag{4}$$

The process of function description is complicated, and there are differences between data, so it is necessary to analyze the difference of functions. is shown in Eq. (5).

$$\lim_{x \to \infty} g(f_i) + \Delta F(x_i) \leq \bigcap \Delta max(v_{ij}) \Delta \sqrt{a^2 + b^2} \tag{5}$$

The overall planning of parameters and the analysis process of quality evaluation, and the results is shown in Eq. (6).

$$g(t_i) + F(d_i) \leftrightarrow \frac{-b \pm \sqrt{b^2 - 4ac}}{2a} (\sum t_{ij} + 4) \tag{6}$$

Summary of analysis results and diversified analysis of analysis content, compare multi-dimensional, multi-content and multi-cluster analysis results to form a final comparison case, and then enter it into the function $No(t_i)$ given in Eq. (7).

$$No(t_i) = \frac{g(t_i) + F(d_i)}{mean(\sum v_{ij} + 4)} \sqrt{b^2 - 4ac} \tag{7}$$

Because the quality evaluation process is not a separate problem, it should be quantitatively analyzed. Quantification is generally divided by dichotomy method, and the analysis results are divided into two parts, so as to reduce the differences between different function results. Provide support for the definition of evaluation indicators and the selection of final results is $unno\sqrt{2}(t_i)$, accuracy of holistic evaluation results is $accur(t_i)$. The quality evaluation results should also be elaborated in the form of percentages, so as to improve the corresponding results. The specific results are shown in Eq. 8.

$$accur(t_i) = \frac{min[\sum g(t_i) + F(d_i)]}{\sqrt{2} \sum g(t_i) + F(d_i)} \times 100\% \tag{8}$$

In the process of quality evaluation, it is necessary to screen it by adding random questions. Judge its rationality and avoid the problem of its blocking. While the setting of random parameters is $randon(t_i)$ The parameters are constrained and analyzed, and the results are described to obtain the limit values. The specific results are shown in Eq. 9.

$$accur(t_i) = \frac{min[\sum g(t_i) + F(d_i)]}{\sum g(t_i) + F(d_i)} \lim_{\delta x \to 0} O \tag{9}$$

Through the above analysis, it will be found that. Mathematical description vs. The integration of quality analysis and teaching content can improve its overall visibility, while the credibility should be displayed by visual results, so as to judge whether the analysis results are reasonable and constraints. Therefore, you must show it in the form of a graph as shown in Fig. 4.

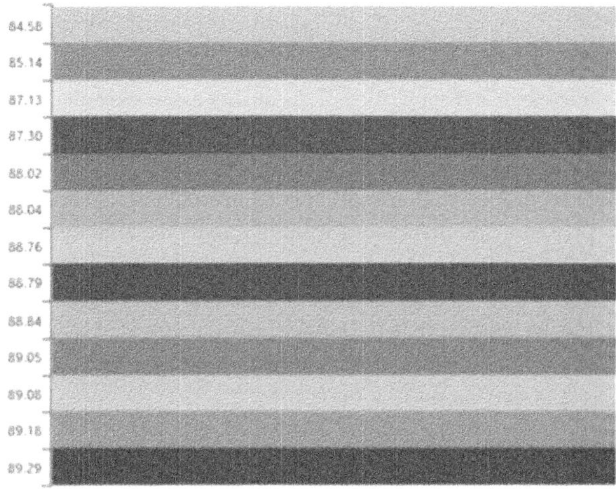

Fig. 4. Research on research and application of the quality assessment algorithm with different algorithms

Figure IV shows that conduct comprehensive analysis and graphic illustration. In the process of analysis, we will find that in terms of quality evaluation and teaching content analysis, we can use similar methods. The form of neural network is used to judge, improve the analysis effect of neural network, and output relatively clear content, and the output conditions are relatively reasonable. The specific results are shown in Table 4.

According to the data in Table 4, through a number of content analysis and overall indicators, the planning will find that in the process of comprehensive judgment and index analysis, there is a strong correlation between the values, and the values meet the actual requirements, and the accuracy and satisfaction of the values are relatively good. It can provide knowledge for quality assessment, but the process of quality assessment is a complex and periodic process. Whether each process is harmonious, as well as the periodic transformation and the deepening of conditional content are also the focus of research. Therefore, it should be continuously analyzed. The persistence analysis process is shown in Fig. 6.

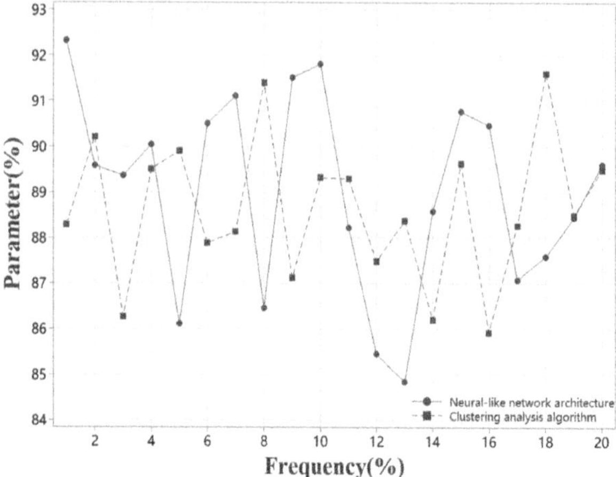

Fig. 6. Research on research and application of the quality assessment algorithm of Neural-like network architecture

As can be seen from Fig. 6, In the process of investment, analysis, comprehensive analysis, holistic planning and diversified volatility analysis, although there are changes among the values, the range of value changes is relatively small, ranging from 84% to 100%. Between 93%. It shows that although the process of data analysis is a complex iterative process, the data structure is reasonable, the data process is relatively good, and the satisfaction rate and conformity of the data are relatively high.

5 Conclusion

Quality evaluation is a multi-content and analysis form of various contents and indicators in the educational process, and it is an objective teaching performance. However, the process of quality evaluation is complicated, and there are great differences between the contents and data. Therefore, neural network-like analysis should be carried out, the feature points should be clarified, the data complexity should be reduced, the original form should be optimized, and the in-depth analysis should be carried out. The results show that neural network can improve the effect of teaching analysis, with an improvement rate of more than 20%, and make the educational effect match the actual demand, with a matching degree of more than 90%. Therefore, in the process of comprehensive analysis, all indicators and values meet the actual requirements. But there are also differences in the results, mainly the differences in data values. In the future, the amount of data samples will be increased to meet the corresponding analysis and improve the analysis effect.

References

1. Hengyang, H.: Application analysis of artificial neural network algorithms in geotechnical engineering. Eng. Technol. Res. **8** (11), 7–9 (2023)

2. Haijun, Z., Jinxiang, W., Zhenhua, Y., Jie, D., Zhenhua L.: A convolutional neural network. Comput. Struct. Appl. Method CN116050490A (2023)
3. Yongjun, Q., Hailin, T., Minhuan, Z.: Research on the algorithm of teaching comprehensive ability evaluation system based on BP neural network Chinese science and technology. J. Database (Full Text Edition) Educ. Sci. (9), 5 (2022)
4. Fengbin, T.: Research on Computing Architecture and Storage Optimization Technology of Neural Network Accelerator. Tsinghua University Press (2022)
5. Shancai, G., Jian, Z., Jianyuan, L.: Optimization of the extraction process and application of total flavonoids from celery leaves based on BP neural network combined with response surface methodology. Chinese J. Food Sci. **23**(8), 263–273 (2023)
6. Yanhan, Z., Yinxin, Z., Zhanhua, H., Kangnian, W.: A dense feature matching algorithm based on improved DFM. Progress in Laser and Optoelectronics, **61**(08) (2024)
7. Peng, G., Wenjian, W., Kequn, Z., Xin, L., Wenjing, F., Ying, M. etc.: Quantitative phase contrast microscopy technology based on convolutional neural networks. Progress in Laser and Optoelectron. **61** (02) (2024)
8. Zerui, W., Shi, C.: A quality aware rotating ship template matching algorithm based on deep features. Comput. Eng. **49** (12), 161–168 (2023)
9. Haifei, Z., Junna, C., Jinding, G.: Research on the application of collaborative filtering algorithm based on convolutional neural network in film recommendation computer knowledge and technology (018–017) (2022)
10. Dongxu, Z., Yonghua, L., Xiaoning, B., Yufeng, W.: Multi objective optimization of steering frame based on rbf clnsga ii algorithm. J. Railway Sci. Eng. **20** (11) (2023)
11. Caoyang, C., Ling, J.: Research and application of neural networks in civil engineering. Shanxi Architecture, **48** (6), 5 (2022)
12. White ice: Research on the application of gabp neural network algorithm model in computer network security. Assessment Automation Technol. Appl. **41** (1), 4 (2022)
13. Xiao, Y.: Research and application of air quality numerical prediction correction method based on multi machine learning algorithm coupling. Environ. Sci. Res. **35**(12), 9 (2022)

The Evaluation Algorithm of Higher Vocational Industry-Education Integration Based on Convolution Neural Network

Pei Liu(✉)

Shandong Institute of Commerce and Technology, Jinan, Shandong, China
liupei1980@163.com

Abstract. The integration of intelligent higher vocational industry and education is greatly aided by research on fusion assessment algorithms; yet, the issue of incorrect evaluation placement remains. In the assessment challenge of intelligent higher vocational industry and education integration, the standard ant colony algorithm fails miserably. As a result, this study reviews previous work on the topic and suggests future research on an assessment method. In order to minimize interference with the fusion evaluation algorithm study, the indicators are first classified according to the needs of the algorithm and then located using gradient descent theory. The next step is to develop a research strategy for a convolution neural network fusion assessment algorithm using gradient descent theory. After that, the research outcomes of this algorithm will be thoroughly examined. According to the findings of the MATLAB simulations, the convolution neural network outperforms the conventional ant colony method in certain evaluation metrics, such as research influencing factor time and research correctness of the fusion evaluation algorithm.

Keywords: Gradient descent theory · Convolution neural networks · Fusion evaluation · Algorithm research · Higher vocational education

1 Introduction

The integration of intelligent [1] higher vocational industry and education[2] relies heavily on fusion evaluation algorithm research, which in turn may expedite the development of more accurate methods for controlling fusion evaluation algorithms [3, 4]. The research scheme of the fusion evaluation algorithm has an issue with low accuracy [5], which has certain negative consequences on the research of the algorithm. This problem has been identified in the course of fusion evaluation algorithm research [6]. When it comes to researching and analyzing fusion evaluation [9] algorithms, some academics think that convolutional neural networks can do a good job of analyzing the research [7] scheme and providing assistance for fusion evaluation algorithm research. This study uses this information to suggest a convolutional neural network, improve the research scheme for the fusion evaluation method, and check that the model is successful [8, 9].

B. Brik and S. Nazir (Eds.): BigIoT-EDU 2024, LNICST 660, pp. 370–380, 2026.
https://doi.org/10.1007/978-3-032-18628-7_38

2 Related Works

2.1 Mathematical Description of Convolution Neural Networks

Using computer technology, a convolutional neural network optimizes the fusion evaluation algorithm's research scheme according to the index parameters, it is y_i. It was discovered that the fusion evaluation algorithm's unqualified value parameters are, and that the integration function of the algorithm's research scheme is z_i conducted, and lastly, the research feasibility of the fusion evaluation algorithm is $tol(y_i \cdot t_{ij})$ judged, calculated as Formula (1).shown.

$$\lim_{x \to \infty} (y_i \cdot t_{ij}) = \lim_{x \to \infty} y_{ij} \geq \max(t_{ij} \div 2) \tag{1}$$

Outlier evaluation is one of them, as illustrated in Eq. (2).

$$\max(t_{ij}) = \partial\left(t_{ij}^2 + k \cdot t_{ij}\right) \succ \sqrt{2}\left(\sum t_{ij} + n\right) \tag{2}$$

The research accuracy of the fusion evaluation method may be enhanced by combining the benefits of computer technology with convolutional neural networks, which quantify utilizing fusion evaluation algorithms.

So what if I The fusion assessment algorithm's research needs is t_i, the research strategy of the fusion evaluation algorithm is set_i, fulfilling the research plan for the fusion evaluation algorithm is y_i, the fusion evaluation algorithm research scheme is $F(t_i \approx 0)$ Industry and teaching process, as shown in Formula (3).

$$F(d_i) = mathbbR \prod \sum t_i \cap \xi \cdot \sqrt{k} \to ointy_i \cdot n \tag{3}$$

2.2 The Integration Content of Industry and Teaching

Test #2 A fusion evaluation algorithm's research purpose is $g(t_i)$ and the weight coefficient is w_i. Therefore, as shown in Eq. (4), studying the qualified fusion evaluation algorithm is necessary for studying the fusion evaluation algorithm research.

$$g(t_i) = x\ddot{\sqrt[n]{k}} \cdot z_i \int F(d_i)\frac{dy}{dx} - \sum n \tag{4}$$

If we accept the first two hypotheses, we can use the ensemble evaluation procedure to find the industrial teaching conditions are as announced, but nothing is shown.

$$\lim_{x \to \infty} g(t_i) + \Delta k \leq \cap \int \max(t_{ij}) \tag{5}$$

Data standardization is essential for improving the research reliability of the fusion assessment method; Eq. (6) shows the outcomes.

$$\lim_{x \to \infty} g(t_i) + F(d_i) \leftrightarrow mean\left(\sum t_{ij} + 4\right) \tag{6}$$

2.3 Analysis of Research Scheme of Fusion Evaluation Algorithm

To ensure the convolution neural network is ready to go, it's important to first conduct a thorough analysis of the fusion evaluation algorithm's research plan, then match the algorithm's research needs to the library of previous studies, and finally, remove any unsuitable studies. Equation (6) allows us to suggest an anomaly assessment system, and the outcomes is $No(t_i)$ shown in Eq. (7).

$$No(t_i) = \frac{g(t_i) + F(d_i)}{mean\left(\sum t_{ij} + 4\right)} \sqrt{b^2 - 4ac} \tag{7}$$

Among them, it is $\frac{g(t_i)+F(d_i)}{mean(\sum t_{ij}+4)} \leq 1$ said that the plan must be put forth in order to avoid the need of integrating the plan, and the outcome is $Zh(t_i)$ shown in Eq. (8).

$$Zh(t_i) = \cap\left[\sum g(t_i) + F(d_i)\right] \tag{8}$$

We established the threshold and index weight of the fusion evaluation algorithm research scheme to assure the correctness of the convolution neural network after completely analyzing the research of fusion evaluation algorithms. A thorough analysis is required of the fusion evaluation algorithm research as it is a systematic test of the fusion evaluation algorithm research plan. Assuming that fusion evaluation algorithm research is $unno(t_i)$ When the data does not follow a normal distribution, it will impact the fusion assessment algorithm's research scheme, leading to less accurate research and calculating results is $accur(t_i)$ shown in Eq. (9).

$$accur(t_i) = \frac{\min\left[\sum g(t_i) + F(d_i)\right]}{\sum g(t_i) + F(d_i)} \times 100\% \tag{9}$$

The fusion assessment algorithm's study plan reveals that it conforms to objective facts by presenting a multi-dimensional distribution. It is considered a very analytical study as the research on the fusion evaluation algorithm is not biased, which suggests that the research plan for the algorithm is quite random. If the ensemble evaluation method examines a random function is $randon(t_i)$, we can rewrite the result of Eq. (9) as Eq. (10).

$$accur(t_i) = \frac{\min\left[\sum g(t_i) + F(d_i)\right]}{\sum g(t_i) + F(d_i)} + randon(t_i) \tag{10}$$

Relatively speaking, in the process of industrial teaching and integration, it is necessary to make a holistic judgment and analysis of multiple contents. This paper studies the integration conditions and supporting points of industries, and makes an in-depth judgment on their contents and characteristic points, finds out the differences between them, and makes effective analysis and deepening. The specific process should be discussed in combination with the actual situation.

3 Optimization Strategy Based on Fusion Evaluation Algorithm

In order to optimize the scheme for the fusion evaluation procedure, the convolutional neural network uses a stochastic optimization technique and tweaks the parameters pertaining to the internet. There are several degrees of fusion evaluation algorithm research [10], and different schemes are chosen at random, in the study of convolutional neural network fusion evaluation algorithms. An iterative technique is used to optimize and examine the research scheme of a fusion evaluation algorithm with various research levels. Following the completion of the optimization study, the research level of various fusion evaluation algorithms is compiled, and the research on the optimal algorithm is documented [11–13].

4 Results and Discussion

4.1 Introduction to the Research of Fusion Evaluation Algorithm

Make in-depth judgment based on the teaching content and conditions of the industry, and make in-depth judgment based on the learning content and practice of freshman, sophomore and third year. Focus on theoretical academic achievements and practical procedures to compare and verify the effectiveness between them, so as to judge the process of industrial integration. The specific test conditions and data are as shown on the Fig. 1.

Table 1. Research requirements for fusion evaluation algorithms

Scope of application	Grade	Three-leaf softening effect	Industrial analysis conditions
Higher vocational colleges	I	57.52	43.36
	II	48.67	47.79
Enterprise	I	51.33	52.21
	II	49.56	48.67
Student	I	50.44	47.79
	II	56.64	44.25

Through the analysis of the data in Table 1, we can know that there are significant differences among the data in the process of industrial upgrading and content analysis. It can be used as the object and content of later analysis, so it is necessary to make an overall judgment on it, and at the same time, it is necessary to make an overall judgment on the industry. Analyze the process to make judgments. The results of Fig. 1 are obtained.

The convolutional neural network fusion evaluation algorithm research plan, which uses the ant colony method, is more in line with the real fusion evaluation algorithm's research needs. The convolution neural network outperforms the ant colony algorithm when it comes to the fusion evaluation method's rationale and accuracy. The improved

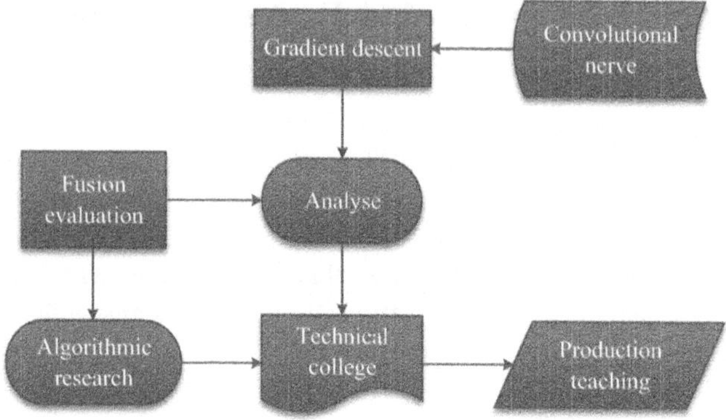

Fig. 1. Industrial integration process and data collection

convolution neural network's correctness and dependability are shown by the revised fusion assessment technique in Fig. 2. As a result, the convolution neural network fusion evaluation algorithm's study scheme is faster, more accurate, and more stable in terms of combination.

4.2 Research on Fusion Evaluation Algorithm

Data that is unstructured, semi-structured, or structural is all part of the study plan for fusion assessment algorithms. The feasibility of the fusion evaluation algorithm research scheme is examined after the election of the convolution neural network. The research scheme is obtained for the research of the preliminary fusion evaluation algorithm. The fusion evaluation algorithm research with various levels and the fusion evaluation algorithm research method are chosen as stated in Table 2 to more properly verify the research impact of the algorithm.

Table 2. Comprehensive analysis conditions of the industry

Category	Practice scores	Improvement of comprehensive capabilities	Holistic judgment
Higher vocational colleges	37.17	61.06	46.02
Enterprise	46.90	56.64	49.56
Student	38.94	59.29	53.98

4.3 Research and Stability of Fusion Evaluation Algorithm

The convolution neural network's correctness is checked by combining the ant colony method with the fusion evaluation algorithm's research plan, which is shown in Fig. 2.

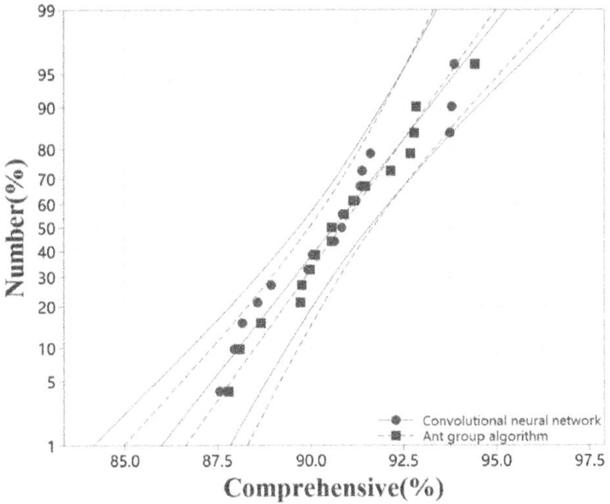

Fig. 2. Research on fusion evaluation algorithm of different algorithms

Figure 2 shows that compared to the ant colony algorithm, the research of the convolution neural network's fusion evaluation algorithm is more consistent and stable, with a lower error rate. In contrast, the research of the ant colony algorithm is more variable and unpredictable. In Table 3, you can see the research plan for the average fusion assessment algorithm of the three methods mentioned before.

Table 3. Comparison of research accuracy of fusion evaluation algorithms of different methods

Algorithm	Fusion analysis	Holistic analysis	Quantitative analysis	Diversification analysis
Convolution neural networks	55.75	44.25	51.33	55.75
Ant colony algorithm	38.94	42.48	40.71	38.94
The overall structure of the analysis	57.52	56.64	45.13	57.52

The research accuracy of the fusion evaluation algorithm has been compromised by the ant colony method, as shown in Table 3. Additionally, the research of the fusion evaluation algorithm has undergone significant changes, and the error rate is rather high. In comparison to the ant colony technique, the fusion assessment algorithm for generic convolution neural network outcomes has been extensively explored and is superior. Research on the convolution neural network fusion assessment technique has also shown an accuracy of over 90% with little to no change over the years. In order to provide further evidence that convolution neural networks are better. Various approaches are used to conduct the general analysis of convolution neural networks, as illustrated in Fig. 3, in order to further validate the efficiency of the suggested method.

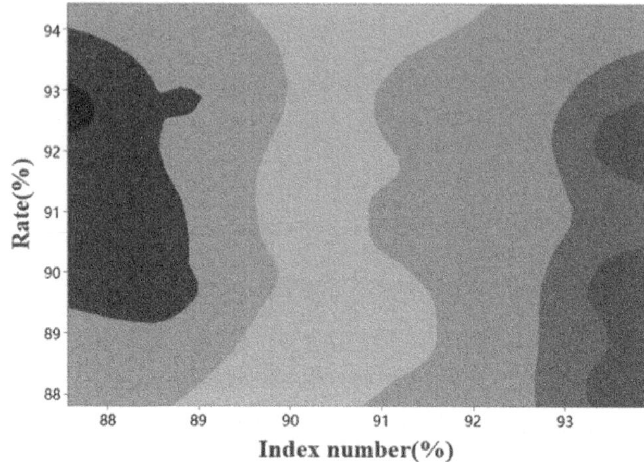

Fig. 3. Research on fusion evaluation algorithm of convolution neural network

Figure 3 clearly shows that the convolution neural network's fusion evaluation algorithm outperforms the ant colony algorithm's. This is because the convolution neural network raises the fusion evaluation algorithm's research adjustment coefficient, establishes the threshold for Internet information, and gets rid of the algorithm's research scheme that doesn't measure up.

4.4 Rationality of Fusion Evaluation Algorithm Research

Incorporating the ant colony algorithm into the fusion evaluation algorithm's research scheme allowed us to confirm the convolution neural network's correctness, as shown in.

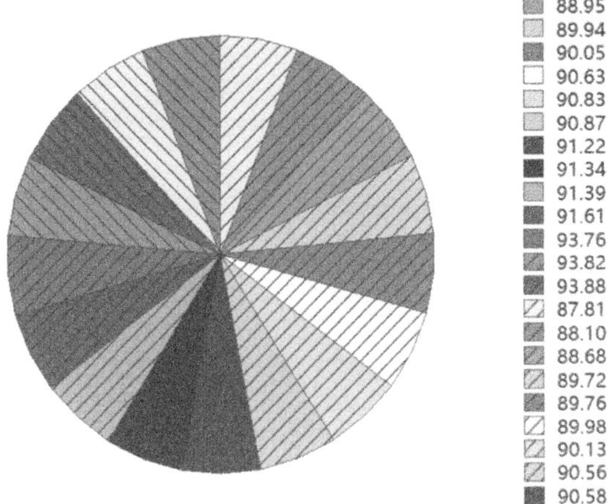

Fig. 4. Research on fusion evaluation algorithm of different algorithms

Figure 4 demonstrates that the convolution neural network fusion evaluation algorithm outperforms the ant colony algorithm in terms of research rationality, and that further improvements to the convolution neural network fusion evaluation algorithm can further increase the research rationality of the algorithm. A distributed infrastructure for data storage and administration, made possible by convolution neural networks, can guarantee the safe recording and storage of findings. Convolutional neural networks allow for the creation of unique identifiers for each and the recording of important data and schemes.

4.5 Fusion Evaluation Algorithm Research Effectiveness

The ant colony algorithm was integrated into the research scheme of the fusion evaluation algorithm to confirm the efficacy of the convolution neural network; Fig. 5 shows the research strategy of the algorithm.

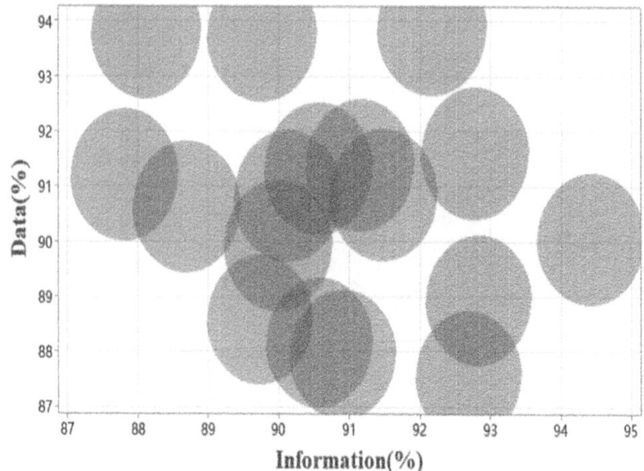

Fig. 5. Research on fusion evaluation algorithm of different algorithms

Figure 5 shows that constitutional neural network fusion evaluation algorithm research is higher than ant colony algorithm research, but with a lower error rate. This suggests that constitutional neural network fusion evaluation algorithm research is relatively stable, in contrast to the uneven research of ant colony algorithm. Table 4 displays the research strategy for the average fusion evaluation algorithm of the three techniques mentioned before.

Table 4. Comparison of the effectiveness of fusion evaluation algorithms of different methods

Algorithm	Comprehensive aircraft conditions	Analyze the effect rationally	Diversified analysis content	Diversified analysis types
Convolution neural networks	51.33	33.63	56.64	51.33
Ant colony algorithm	51.33	44.25	59.29	51.33
Comprehensive analysis effect	41.59	52.21	60.18	41.59

According to Table 4, there are some issues with the ant colony algorithm's research accuracy when it comes to fusion evaluation algorithms. Additionally, there have been significant changes in fusion evaluation algorithms, and the error rate is rather high. In comparison to the ant colony technique, the fusion assessment algorithm for generic convolution neural network outcomes has been extensively explored and is superior. Research on the convolution neural network fusion assessment technique has also shown an accuracy of over 90% with little to no change over the years. In order to provide further evidence that convolution neural networks are better. Various approaches are used to conduct the general analysis of convolution neural networks, as illustrated in Fig. 6, in order to further validate the efficiency of the suggested method.

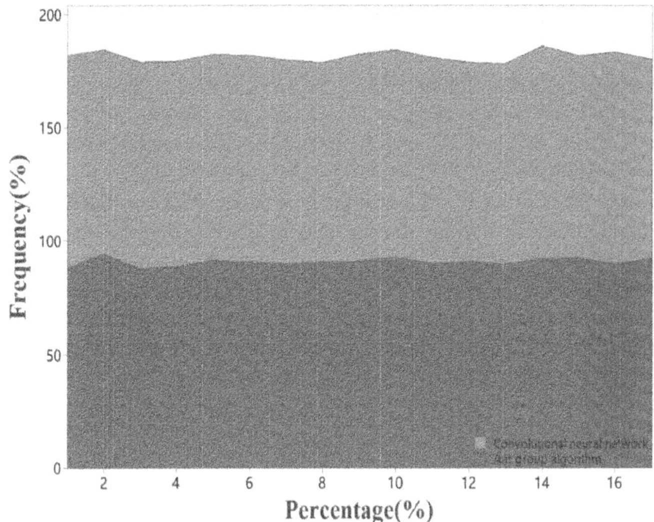

Fig. 6. Research on convolution neural network fusion evaluation algorithm

Figure 6 shows that the convolution neural network's research fusion evaluation algorithm outperforms the ant colony algorithm. This is because the convolution neural network raises the fusion evaluation algorithm's research adjustment coefficient, establishes the threshold for Internet information, and gets rid of the algorithm's research scheme that doesn't work.

5 Conclusion

In response to the fact that current fusion evaluation algorithm research is far from perfect, this study suggests a convolution neural network and uses a combination of computer technologies to enhance fusion evaluation algorithm research. In the meantime, we build the Internet information collecting while we thoroughly examine the research correctness and reliability of the fusion assessment method. Based on the findings, fusion evaluation algorithm research may benefit from using convolutional neural networks to increase accuracy, and more generally, fusion evaluation algorithm research can be conducted. Nevertheless, a fusion evaluation algorithm research indication selection approach that is too focused on in convolution neural network development leads to illogical results.

References

1. Wang, C.: Research on the Application of Fuzzy Mathematics Algorithm in the Evaluation of Industry Education Integration in Vocational Colleges Computer Knowledge and Technology (024), 018 (2022)

2. Wei, D., Liu, D., Rong, G.: Research on recommendation algorithms based on improved convolutional neural networks. Comput. Paradise (1), 0118–0120 (2022)
3. Zhang, H., Cui, J., Ge, J.: Research on the Application of Collaborative Filtering Algorithm Based on Convolutional Neural Network in Film Recommendation Computer Knowledge and Technology (018–017) (2022)
4. Liu, C., Wu, Y., Guo, F., Luo, X., Lu, T.: Research on the Application of Text Box Recognition Algorithm Based on Convolutional Neural Network in Power Business Systems Artificial Intelligence and Robotics Research, vol. 12, issue 3, p. 9 (2023)
5. Liang, K., Zhao, H., Song, W.: Research on the Evaluation Method of Internal Combustion Engine Sound Quality Based on Convolutional Neural Network (2) (2022)
6. Zhang, F., Shi, R., Li, Y., Li, W., Wang, Q., Lu, Z., et al.: A Rolling Sound Classification Method Based on Feature Fusion and Improved Convolutional Neural Network, CN116486834A (2023)
7. Guo, J., Wang, Q., Li, Z., Wu, M., Zhang, H.: A blockchain smart contract classification method based on dual layer twin neural networks. J. Electronics Inf. Technol. **44**, 1–9 (2023)
8. Zou, B., Fang, W., Wang, D.: A Deep Convolutional Neural Network Based Common X-ray Film Detection Algorithm for Circumferential Welds—Review of "Research on Defect Detection Algorithms for Submerged Arc Welding X-ray Welds" Chinese oil, vol. 48, issue 3, p. I0039 (2023)
9. Cao, Z.: Research on power inspection system based on convolutional neural network image fusion algorithm. J. Anyang Normal Univ. (5), 29–32 (2022)
10. Ma, H., Chen, J.: Research on human eye state and blink recognition algorithms based on dual convolutional neural networks. J. China Acad. Electronic Sci. (005), 017 (2022)
11. Wang, C., Zou, H.: Research on diversity recommendation algorithms based on convolutional neural networks. Inf. Technol. **46**(11), 82–89 (2022)
12. Zhang, S.: Research on Course Recommendation Algorithm Based on Graph Convolutional Neural Network Information Systems Engineering, issue 1, pp. 158–160 (2023)
13. Zhao, Z., Gao, T., Wang, H.: A multimodal feature distillation emotion recognition method based on global convolution and affinity fusion. Signal Process. **39**(4), 667–677 (2023)

Higher Vocational Preschool Education Teaching Evaluation System Based on BP Neural Network

Nan Shan(✉) and Yuting Sun

Weifang Engineering Vocational College, Weifang 262500, China
shannan9104@163.com

Abstract. There is an issue with inappropriate assessment, despite the fact that teaching quality evaluation is very crucial in higher vocational preschool education. It is challenging to evaluate students' learning thoroughly and properly using traditional assessment approaches since they often depend on subjective judgment and single indications. In order to enhance the quality of instruction and the overall development of students, this paper suggests a BP neural network algorithm. The algorithm makes use of its robust data analysis and pattern recognition capabilities to create an evaluation system for higher vocational preschool programs. The significance of higher vocational preschool education is firstly examined using the theory of educational data analysis. In order to eliminate interference factors in evaluating teaching quality, the indicators are classified according to the needs of preschool education. The theory of educational data analysis then proceeds to assess the requirements of the system for evaluating teaching, develop the architecture of the system, create the curriculum for preschool, and conduct a thorough analysis of the findings of the assessment of teaching quality. Findings demonstrate that BP neural network-based assessment system for higher vocational preschool education teaching can reliably assess students' progress and provide useful guidance to educators in making informed decisions about their students' education. The goal of using this method is to make higher vocational preschool instruction more effective and efficient.

Keywords: Educational data analysis theory · BP neural network algorithm · Higher vocational pre-school education · Teaching quality evaluation

1 Introduction

Higher vocational preschool education is crucial in today's fast-paced world because it helps to create high-quality talent with an entrepreneurial mindset and strong practical skills [1]. Nevertheless, the education industry has long been preoccupied with, and challenged by, the task of evaluating preschool instruction [2]. When it comes to reflecting students' learning status and the quality of instruction, traditional assessment systems have certain limitations, such as subjective judgment and reliance on a single indicator [3]. Consequently, one of the major concerns in contemporary higher vocational preschool education is the optimization of assessment procedures via the application of

B. Brik and S. Nazir (Eds.): BigIoT-EDU 2024, LNICST 660, pp. 381–390, 2026.
https://doi.org/10.1007/978-3-032-18628-7_39

cutting-edge technology [4]. According to some experts, the preschool education program may be better analyzed and supported by using the BP neural network algorithm to data from higher vocational preschools [5]. Based on this, this research suggests a method using BP neural networks to optimize the preschool teaching scheme and check whether the model is successful [6].

2 Related Concepts

2.1 Mathematical Description of the BP Neural Network Algorithm

BP neural network method optimizes the teaching quality assessment scheme according to the index parameters in preschool education, using the theory of educational data analysis is x_i, it is found that the unqualified value parameters in higher vocational preschool education is D, and the system for assessing the quality of instruction is interwoven with the purpose of determining, in the end, whether or not preschool programs that focus on higher vocational skills are feasible $sum(x_i \cdot y_i)$, which is calculated as shown in Eq. (1).

$$sum(x_i \cdot y_i) \leq tol\left(x_{ij}\tau_i - D\right) \tag{1}$$

Outlier evaluation is one of them, as indicated in Eq. (2).

$$x_{ij}\tau_i - D = \sqrt{a^2 + b^2} \succ soml\left(\sum x_{ij}\right) \tag{2}$$

To enhance the quality of evaluating instruction, the BP neural network method integrates the benefits of educational data analysis theory with higher vocational preschool education for quantification.

Suppose I. The teaching quality evaluation requirements is x_i, the teaching quality evaluation scheme is t, the satisfaction of the teaching quality evaluation program is $x_{ij}\mu$, and the teaching quality evaluation program judgment function is $S(z_i)$, as shown in Eq. (3).

$$S(z_i) = \sum \cdot x_i \cdot \cap \Rightarrow \sum_{i=1}^{t} t + x_{ij}\mu \tag{3}$$

2.2 Selection of Pre-School Education Programmed

Assuming that II. The function of higher vocational preschool education is $sum(D_i)$, and the weight coefficient is G_i, then the teaching quality evaluation requires unqualified higher vocational preschool education as shown in Eq. (4).

$$sum(D_i) = z_i \cdot \prod F(c_i) - G_i \tag{4}$$

Equation (5) shows the outcome of deriving the comprehensive function of preschool education from assumptions I and II.

$$sum(D_i) + S(z_i) \leq tol\left(x_{ij}\tau_i - D\right) \tag{5}$$

Equation (6) shows the outcome of standardizing all data, which is necessary to enhance the efficacy of preschool instruction.

$$sum(D_i) + S(z_i) \leftrightarrow soml\left(\sum x_{ij}\right) \tag{6}$$

2.3 Analysis of Teaching Quality Evaluation Programs

A multi-dimensional study of the teaching quality assessment scheme and mapping of the teaching quality evaluation needs to the higher vocational preschool education library should be carried out before the BP neural network method is executed., and the unqualified teaching quality evaluation scheme should be eliminated is $mit(x_i)$. Equation (7) displays the outcomes, while Eq. (6) allows for the proposal of the anomaly assessment method.

$$mit(x_i) = \frac{sum(D_i) + S(z_i)}{soml(\sum x_{ij})} \tag{7}$$

Among them, it is $\frac{sum(D_i)+S(z_i)}{soml(\sum x_{ij})} \leq 1$, was said that in order for the plan to be implemented, it must first be presented. $Th(x_i)$, and the result is shown in Eq. (8).

$$Th(x_i) = \min[\sum sum(D_i) + S(z_i)] \tag{8}$$

We selected the index weights and threshold of the teaching quality assessment scheme to guarantee that the BP neural network method is accurate after conducting a thorough analysis of higher vocational preschool education. Combining BP neural networks with teaching evaluations of higher vocational preschool education may significantly enhance the impartiality and accuracy of assessment, making it a more effective systematic test teaching quality evaluation scheme. If higher vocational preschool education is in a non-normal distribution is $lem(z_i)$, The overall accuracy of its teaching quality assessment will be reduced as a result of this impact on its teaching quality evaluation methodology. $him(x_i)$, and the calculation result is shown in Eq. (9).

$$him(x_i) = \frac{\min[\sum sum(D_i) + S(z_i)]}{\sum sum(D_i) + S(z_i)} \times 100\% \tag{9}$$

The preschool education program displays a multidimensional distribution, in agreement with objective facts, according to the survey of teaching quality assessment programs. As a result of its lack of directionality, higher vocational preschool education is considered a highly analytical research since it shows that preschool education programs are quite random. If the stochastic function of higher vocational preschool education is $\min(x_i)$, then the calculation of formula (9) can be expressed as formula (10).

$$him(x_i) = \frac{\min[\sum sum(D_i) + S(z_i)]}{\sum sum(D_i) + S(z_i)} \times 100\% + \min(x_i) \tag{10}$$

Among these, higher vocational preschool education satisfies typical standards. This is largely attributable to the fact that educational data analysis theory fine-tunes this type of preschool, does away with unnecessary and redundant programs, and enhances the default program, resulting in a robust dynamic correlation across all programs used to evaluate teaching quality.

3 Optimization Strategies for Higher Vocational Preschool Education

By adjusting parameters and implementing an optimization method for information combinations, the BP neural network algorithm optimizes a preschool vocational education program at the higher level [7]. The program generates several assessment systems at random and splits upper vocational preschool education into degrees of information integration [8]. Iterative analysis and optimization of the teaching quality assessment scheme with varying degrees of information integration is carried out in the process [9]. The optimum higher vocational pre-school education program may be documented after the combinatorial optimization analysis compares the levels of teaching quality assessment of several programs [10].

4 Results and Discussion

4.1 Introduction to the Evaluation of Teaching Quality

This study uses high-complexity pre-vocational learning education as its research target, develops seven testing pathways, and allots twelve hours for testing in order to make it easier to evaluate teaching quality. Table 1 displays the unique assessment system for teaching quality in higher vocational pre-school programs.

Table 1. Teaching evaluation indicators

Level 1 indicators	Secondary indicators	Innovative effect	Teaching effectiveness
Professional quality	Academic Degree	90.28	91.10
	Professional and technical titles	88.24	93.89
Scientific research achievements	Topics and projects	91.22	90.55
	Publication of papers	90.11	88.34
	Teaching, research and reform	89.37	88.85
Teaching attitude	Motivation to teach	93.54	89.93
	Lesson preparation	85.32	92.09

The teaching quality evaluation process in Table 1. is shown in Fig. 1.

The BP neural network algorithm's teaching quality assessment scheme is better in tune with the real demands of preschool education than the standard teaching evaluation technique. Compared to more conventional forms of assessment, the BP neural network algorithm better takes into account variables like the predictability and variability of

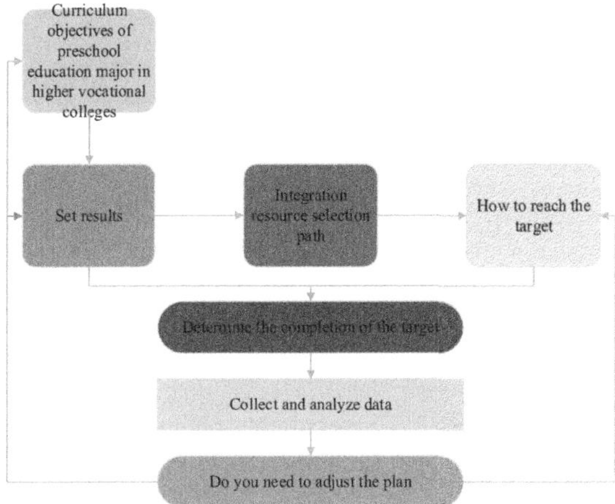

Fig. 1. The analysis process of higher vocational preschool education

preschool vocational programs. We can see that the BP neural network method is more stable and has faster judgment speed with the alteration of the teaching quality assessment scheme in Fig. 2. Consequently, the BP neural network algorithm's teaching quality assessment scheme improves the processing speed, summation stability, and information combination optimization in preschool education programs.

4.2 Higher Vocational Pre-School Education

Evaluations of instructional processes, instructional resources, instructional management, student academic achievement, and so on are all fundamental components of the program for assessing the quality of instruction in higher vocational preschools. After the BP neural network method is pre-selected, we acquire the higher vocational preschool education preliminary assessment combination optimization scheme and examine the feasibility of the teaching quality evaluation scheme. Table 2 shows the evaluation combination optimization processing method that was used to validate the innovative impact of higher vocational preschool education. The higher vocational preschool education was chosen with various teaching quality assessment levels.

Table 2. Overall situation of pre-school education programmed

Category	Degree of demand	Satisfaction	Analysis rate
Teaching objectives	87.10	92.38	89.18
Course content	90.54	92.29	87.84
Teaching methods	89.17	89.77	86.68
Teaching resources	87.50	90.52	91.44
Evaluation and feedback	86.69	92.04	90.13

(*continued*)

Table 2. (*continued*)

Category	Degree of demand	Satisfaction	Analysis rate
Mean	89.89	87.16	90.13
X6	89.39	92.53	92.56
	P = .28		

4.3 Accuracy and Stability of Preschool Education

Figure 2 shows the teaching quality assessment scheme, which was compared with the standard teaching evaluation approach to confirm the correctness of the BP neural network algorithm.

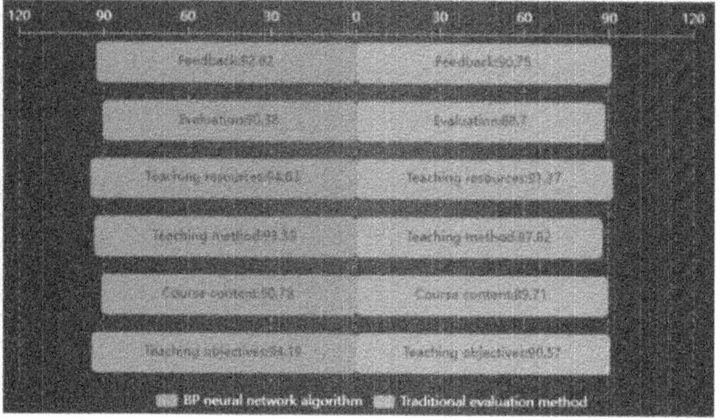

Fig. 2. Teaching quality of preschool education with different algorithms

Figure 2 shows that while evaluating preschool programs, the BP neural network approach performs quite well. The technology is able to automatically evaluate students' learning abilities and any issues by applying BP neural networks to their performance and learning data. The system is able to make more accurate predictions about students' learning outcomes and provide tailored learning recommendations thanks to a mountain of training data and algorithm models. In order to better understand their kids' learning and create effective lesson plans and tutoring strategies, instructors and parents rely on reliable assessment data. Table 3 shows the average criteria for evaluating the quality of instruction for the three methods mentioned earlier.

Table 3. Comparison of teaching quality evaluation accuracy of different methods

Algorithm	System data	Data integrity	Magnitude of change	Outliers
BP neural network algorithm	93.93	94.34	93.75	0.93

(*continued*)

Table 3. (*continued*)

Algorithm	System data	Data integrity	Magnitude of change	Outliers
Traditional methods of teaching assessment	86.81	85.34	90.39	4.53
P	91.15	93.53	93.00	1.62

Table 3 clearly shows that the system is quite stable. We think about data stability and dependability when we build the system. To guarantee the quality and integrity of the data, the system effectively cleans and processes the student data that is input. The system also makes use of the BP neural network method, which is quite stable and resilient; it can continue to function well even when presented with unusual or noisy input. As illustrated in Fig. 3, the assessment system is often subjected to several ways of analysis in order to further confirm the superiority of the BP neural network algorithm.

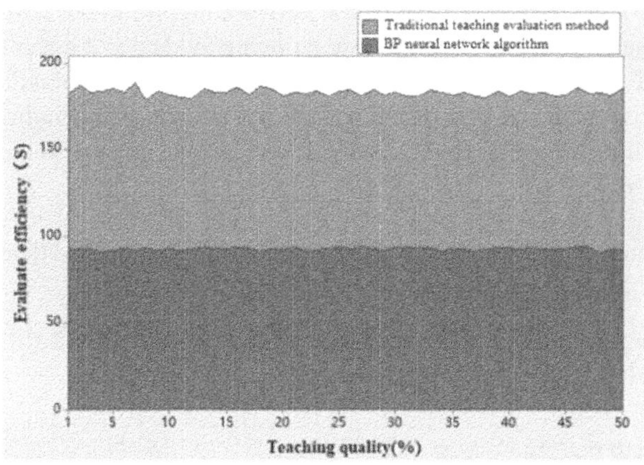

Fig. 3. Teaching evaluation system of BP neural network algorithm

Figure 3 shows that the higher vocational preschool education teaching assessment system using BP neural network technology is very stable and accurate. The system's ability to effectively evaluate students' learning state and provide individualized learning suggestions contributes to the improvement of both students' and teachers' learning and teaching quality. When put into action, the system can consistently assess student and instructor performance and provide dependable instructional assistance.

4.4 Effectiveness of Pre-school Education

Figure 4 shows the teaching quality assessment scheme compared to the conventional teaching evaluation method's teaching quality evaluation scheme in order to test the efficacy of the BP neural network algorithm.

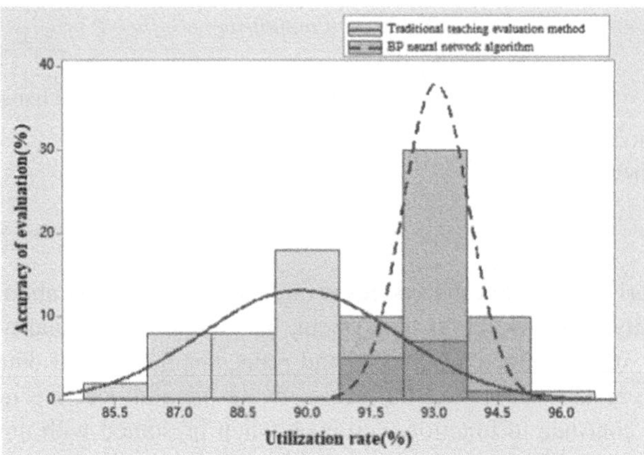

Fig. 4. Preschool education with different algorithms

In Fig. 4, we can observe that BP neural network algorithm has a higher preschool education rate than traditional teaching evaluation methods, but a lower error rate. This suggests that BP neural network algorithm's teaching quality evaluation is relatively stable, in contrast to the uneven teaching quality evaluation of traditional methods. Table 4 displays the average assessment scheme for teaching quality for the three methods mentioned earlier.

Table 4. Comparison of teaching quality evaluation effectiveness of different methods

Algorithm	Survey data	Preschool education	Magnitude of change	Error
BP neural network algorithm	93.09	92.60	92.79	0.97
Traditional methods of teaching assessment	85.81	89.27	87.26	4.38
P	95.47	91.18	93.76	3.61

There have been significant changes in higher vocational preschool education, and the error rate is rather large, as can be shown from Table 4, which shows that conventional teaching assessment techniques have shortcomings in preschool education and stability in higher vocational preschool education. Overall, BP's neural network approach outperforms more conventional forms of evaluating classroom instruction when it comes to preschoolers. Although there has been no gain in accuracy, the BP neural network algorithm's preschool education is above 90%. Various approaches are often used to examine the BP neural network algorithm, as illustrated in Fig. 5, in order to further test the usefulness of the suggested method.

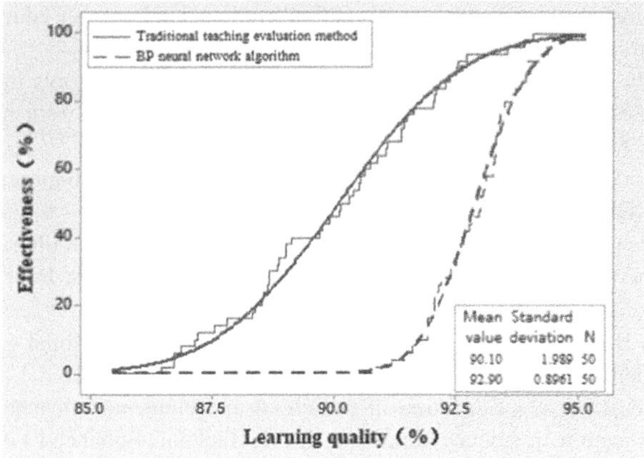

Fig. 5. Preschool education with BP neural network algorithm

Compared to the conventional method of evaluating preschool teachers, the BP neural network algorithm performs much better (as seen in Fig. 5). This is because the algorithm raises the adjustment coefficient for higher vocational preschool programs and establishes a talent threshold to weed out underperforming evaluation schemes.

5 Conclusion

To address the issue of unsatisfactory teaching quality assessment in higher vocational preschool programs, this research presents a BP neural network method that integrates educational data analysis theory to maximize the program's integration. While doing so, a comprehensive analysis is conducted on the innovations of threshold innovation and teaching quality assessment, and a system collection is built. The findings highlight the significance of the BP neural network-based teaching assessment system in enhancing the quality and impact of preschool education in higher vocational settings. A smart evolution of the education sector is possible thanks to the system's design and implementation, which provide valuable reference and investigation. Data security and system scalability are two areas that might need some work and that require more study and development.

References

1. Fridberg, M., et al.: Spanish and Swedish teachers' perspective of teaching STEM and robotics in preschool - results from the botSTEM project. Int. J. Technol. Des. Educ. **33**(1), 1–21 (2023)
2. Habayib, H., Cinamon, R.G.: Preschool teachers' attitudes toward career education: the role of cultural context and teaching self-efficacy. Int. J. Educ. Vocat. Guidance **23**(2), 399–419 (2023)
3. Hayashi, A.: Teaching expertise in three countries: findings and policy implications from an international comparative study in early childhood education. Comp. Educ. **58**(3), 315–327 (2022)
4. Mavric, M., Fetic, M.: Preschool education in Europe. Int. J. Early Childhood Special Educ. **14**(3), 1307–1315 (2022)

5. Mork, S.B.: University-preschool collaboration in pre-school teacher education in Iceland. Learning Environ. Res. **25**(1), 1–16 (2022)
6. Palla, L., Roth, A.-C.V.: Inclusive ideals and special educational tools in and out of tact: didactical voices on teaching in language and communication in Swedish early childhood education. Int. J. Early Years Educ. **30**(2), 387–402 (2022)
7. Palmer, H., Bjorklund, C.: The teaching of numbers in common preschool activities: a delicate balancing act. Early Childhood Educ. J. **51**(5), 971–980 (2023)
8. Timostsuk, I., et al.: Estonian preschool and primary teachers' intercultural competence as shaped by experiences with newly arrived migrant students. Intercult. Educ. **33**(5), 540–557 (2022)
9. Yang, L., Ali, B.: Mathematical statistics technology in the educational grading system of preschool students. Appl. Math. Nonlinear Sci. **8**(1), 593–602 (2023)
10. Zourmpakis, A.-I., et al.: Education of preschool and elementary teachers on the use of adaptive gamification in science education. Int. J. Technol. Enhanced Learn. **14**(1), 1–16 (2022)

Evaluation of Physical Education Level in Higher Education Based on PCA-AHP-GABP Algorithm

Lei Wu(✉) and Wenying He

Wuhan College of Arts & Sciences, Wuhan, Hubei, China
wulei1896@163.com

Abstract. Participation in physical education programs helps kids maintain a healthy lifestyle and become physically capable individuals. Because it may aid in physical and mental development, it is crucial for all students. Sports and their evaluation using the Pca-haph-gabp algorithm are the topics of this essay. To promote the entire growth of society and economy via cultural knowledge, it is necessary to accurately assess its own objective development state and to make rational and scientific judgments on reform and progress.

Keywords: Evaluation of physical education teaching level · PCA-AHP-GABP · Higher Education · Countermeasures and suggestions

1 Introduction

In order to modernize a country, foster scientific and technical innovation, and cultivate top-tier talent, higher education—which is defined as professional education built on general education—is crucial. The fast expansion of higher education in many developed capitalist countries in Europe has been accompanied by an imbalance in regional development, which has gradually caught the attention of many scholars [1]. This is because industrialization has accelerated and the demand for high-quality labor has increased. The reality and development features of higher education may be better understood by assessment and analysis of the level of higher education. This will offer the essential reference for selecting the growth direction and channel of higher education. Higher education has gone from being seen as an ancillary development to the major development in modern society, thanks to the fast growth of the information economy. It has captured the attention of all sections of society. Meanwhile, all parts of society are starting to pay attention to how we can assess the quality of higher education in a way that boosts its quick growth, as well as how we can enhance physical education both in quantity and quality, and how well we manage our institutions. A nation's or region's productivity and the quality of its output are both affected by its citizens' degree of education. Consequently, regional and national rivalry are determined by the degree of higher education. Higher education, and the acquisition of relevant knowledge and skills, are cornerstones

B. Brik and S. Nazir (Eds.): BigIoT-EDU 2024, LNICST 660, pp. 391–401, 2026.
https://doi.org/10.1007/978-3-032-18628-7_40

of both individual and societal advancement. Boosting the region's and country's overall competitiveness requires, among other things, an increase in the quality of higher education available to the public. The only way to reach our end goal of supporting cultural knowledge-based economic and social development is to have a firm grasp of its current objective development status and to make rational, evidence-based reform and development choices.

Numerous physical education instructors have mastered the art of class evaluation over the years. It is possible to make it very obvious even what aspects of a physical education connection are excellent, what aspects are bad, and how to fix the flaws. Gaining experience might be beneficial at times. On the other hand, our assessment of PE classes will be impacted by our lack of knowledge or a variance in our subjective awareness. So, let's dive into the assessment of physical education classes today and find out what it takes. Evaluation purpose, content, topic, methodology, and instrument are the five primary components of our physical education teacher evaluation design. Our next step will be to dissect the question-and-answer format for individual comments.

In order to assess and appraise the current challenges and weaknesses, the assessment aims to answer the question "why?" by understanding how students' sports cognition, skills, physical ability, and emotions are formed during and after learning activities. The primary goal in answering the question "what to evaluate" is to base the substance of the evaluation on the goals of physical education instruction. For instance, knowing that health cognition is a part of sports cognition is essential for evaluating students' sports cognitive objectives [2]. Judgment, rules of events knowledge, and scientific comprehension of sports procedures, strategies, and approaches make up the three pillars upon which sports cognition is tested. Acknowledging the health benefits of physical activity, engaging in sports learning, and participating in extracurricular sports are all ways to measure health cognition. This manner, the assessment of students' sports cognition may be focused, precise, and accurate.

Naturally, we would want to get more experience from other people's lessons in order to progress more rapidly. Still, more theoretical understanding is required in cases when our intellect is inadequate. Analyzing particular incidents in a legalistic manner yields the same outcome as evaluating physical education in the classroom. Beginning with the five components of assessment, identify the process for evaluating physical education instruction in the classroom, examine the blueprint for evaluating instruction in individual units, and finally, evaluate instruction in physical education as a whole. Give you the chops on how to glean the meat from other people's stories.

The purpose of this research is to examine the use of the PCA-AHP-GABP algorithm for the purpose of evaluating the quality of physical education programs offered to college students. Increasing the quality of physical education on college campuses has become more difficult as a result of the program's recent nationwide expansion, and this trend makes it all the more difficult to raise the bar for physical education on college campuses [3]. The first step in finding a solution to this issue is to assess the current state of PE instruction at universities. In order to reform and grow colleges and universities and to increase the quality of physical education instruction in higher education, evaluation is important. The educational level of colleges and universities can be continuously improved, along with economic and cultural development, by speeding up their development process, establishing a reasonable position in society, and assisting decision-makers in improving the operation mode of relevant work. This will help to eliminate disadvantages while retaining advantages.

2 Related Works

2.1 PCA-AHP-GABP Level Evaluation Algorithm

Learning is sluggish, threshold and starting weight rely heavily, and local optimization is simple to achieve since BP neural network uses the gradient descent technique. Nonetheless, genetic algorithms are well-suited to parallel computing, have resilience, are simple and universal, and have good global search abilities. Researchers in the field of water, soil, and air quality monitoring have attempted to enhance neural networks using genetic algorithms. Despite the availability of appropriate and scientific evaluation findings, their application to the assessment of instructional quality is limited. Evaluations of water, soil, air, and educational quality are all part of the broader realm of quality assessment. When it comes to assessing the quality of instruction and classroom instruction, the first three assessment strategies are workable and relevant. The quality of instruction and classroom instruction may be assessed using the same assessment tools as the preceding three. The assessment criteria and indicator items are distinct from one another. The assessment method is more complicated, there are more subjective aspects, and more dimensions are needed to account when evaluating teaching quality compared to the previous three. Using prior research as a foundation, this article presents an efficient technique for evaluating the quality of university instruction by enhancing the institution's model for doing so via the integration of genetic algorithms with BP neural networks.

dimensionality reduction using principal component analysis (PCA) methods for data. Compressing data while accumulating as little information as possible is the goal of principal component analysis, or PCA. It is capable of merging several interconnected signs into a handful of brand-new, completely unconnected metrics. Dimensionity reduction using principal component analysis (PCA) is an evidence-based approach.

The following are the exact procedures:

Standardize the initial data indications and eliminate the impact of magnitude and dimension; Information entropy may be expressed mathematically as (1).

.

$$H_S(p_1, \cdots, p_N) = -K \sum_{i=1}^{N} p_i \log p_i \tag{1}$$

where K is the normal number, p_ I is the probability of the event, H_ S (p_1,.. "", p_N)represents the event's unpredictability.

A lesser information entropy indicates a larger difference between indications, more information means a larger part and weight in the overall judgment, and so on.

In comparison to the subjective weighing approach, the objective entropy method is more accurate and credible, and it also has a theoretical foundation. Furthermore, practical computation is more convenient, and the method is quite straightforward. When determining the index weight from data, the entropy approach may be used to circumvent the inherent subjectivity and unpredictability of the subjective weighting method.

Using the standardised data, determine the correlation coefficient matrix:

$$P_y = \frac{X_y'}{\sum_{i=1}^{n} X_y'} \tag{2}$$

Determine the weight of the jth index:

$$D_j = \frac{\left(1 - e_j\right)}{\sum_{j=1}^{m} \left(1 - e_j\right)} \tag{3}$$

Determine the individual primary components' contribution rates as well as their cumulative contribution rates.

The indicator weight is acquired by AHP. The hierarchical and improved index system of the degree of physical education instruction in higher education is eventually achieved by data dimensionality reduction. The processed index value is forced to fall inside the range [0,1] by pretreating the original index using the extreme value approach, which removes the impact of various dimensions. Furthermore, it is essential to move all the dimensionless data to the right by at least 0.0001 when certain indicators are 0 after processing. Only then will the following computation make sense.

network of GABP neurons. The BP neural network model is one of the most popular feedforward neural network types currently in use. In contrast to the error's reverse propagation, its signal always travels forward. In order to reduce the error and find the ideal weight for the model, the steepest descent approach is used. The input, hidden, and output layers make up a BP neural network. From the input layer to the hidden layer, the Sigaoidl function is used for activation, and from the hidden layer to the output layer, the Purelin function is used. Many parameters must be fine-tuned before a BP neural network can be used to real-world situations; these factors could have an impact on the accuracy of predictions, the rate of convergence, the amount of time needed to train the network, and other issues [5]. Hence, to increase its efficacy, the BP neural network model must be enhanced. Now let's use the network in Fig. 1 to explain how the BP algorithm calculates.

The calculation steps of BP algorithm are as follows:

Forward transmission of information

1) The output of the ith neuron in the hidden layer is shown in formula (4):

$$a1_i = f1\left(w1_j p_j + b1_i\right), (i = 1, 2, \cdots, r) \tag{4}$$

2) The output of the k-th neuron in the output layer is shown in formula (5):

$$a2_k = f2\left(\sum_{i=1}^{s1} w2_k a1_i + b2_k\right), (k = 1, 2, \cdots, s1) \tag{5}$$

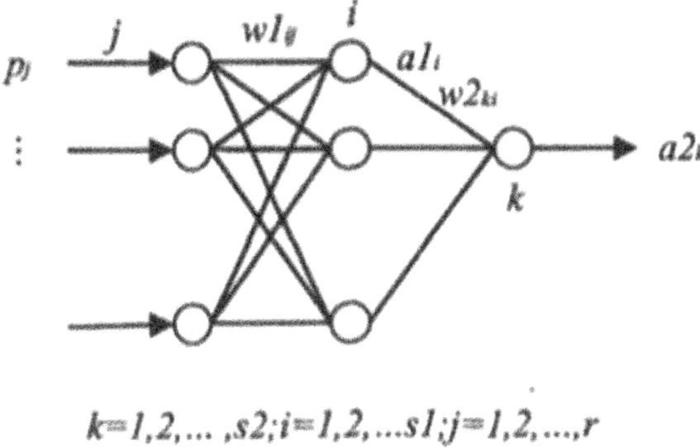

Fig. 1. Simplified network node of hidden layer

3) Define the error function, as shown in Formula (6):

$$E(W, B) = \frac{1}{2}\sum_{k=1}^{s2}(t_k - a2_k)^2 \tag{6}$$

Learn all the samples in the training set by modifying the weights and thresholds of each network layer, picking the next sample in turn, and feeding the eigenvector of one training sample into the input layer. A continuous training number greater than the pre-defined allows you to learn iteratively till the result's error range is inside the given range. Put an end to training and save the neural network for later use.

2.2 PE Teaching Quality Evaluation System

In order to facilitate prompt and effective evaluation of PE teaching quality, increase instructors' excitement, raise the level of PE teaching, and lessen students' burden, a rating system for PE teaching quality was established. Establishing and using the PE teaching quality assessment system is not without its challenges. These include issues with deciding on evaluation indicators, choosing evaluation topics, implementing evaluation methodologies, and collecting evaluation data. The ability to conduct a reasonable and scientific assessment of the quality of physical education instruction is severely compromised by these issues.

The following are some of the issues we identified with the current process of evaluating the quality of physical education instruction at universities based on our interviews with department heads and classroom instructors, conversations with undergraduate student representatives, and research into the issues plaguing university physical education programs:

(1) All of the assessment criteria are lacking

First and foremost, the assessment method for physical education teaching quality looks at instructors' attitudes towards PE, how well they know the PE material, and how well they know the basics of PE. In many cases, specialists' opinions are sought for when deciding what should be included in the many indicators used to assess the quality of physical education classes. Due to the high degree of subjectivity and the impossibility of using it to evaluate the indicator system's contents, the assessment findings are only useful as a point of reference and not as binding authority [6].

The evaluation index system of physical education teaching quality should take into account a wide range of factors when deciding how to rank instructors' performance in the classroom. These factors include, but are not limited to, instructors' levels of expertise, their capacity for scientific research and innovation, the impact of physical education on students' problem-solving skills, and their capacity for innovative practice.

The second point is that there is only one way to measure the quality of physical education instructors' classes; all classes, whether they cover fundamentals, practical applications, or extensive topics, utilize the same assessment index or weight.

(2) The ratio of assessment metrics need some work to make it more reasonable.

It is important to provide varying amounts of weight to the various assessment indications since they all contribute in their own unique ways to the final score. In their rush to get things done, many schools have started giving the same weight to all of the physical education teaching quality assessment indices, but nobody has come up with a consistent way to tell whether this is fair and objective. We can't get an objective and trustworthy assessment of PE quality when we use an irrational percentage of the evaluation index, which leads to a lack of reasonable focus and, as a result, lowers the effectiveness and scientific validity of the results.

Strong subjective considerations are a part of the appraisal technique.

Due to its inadequacy in handling complicated and non-linear practical situations, the conventional approach to evaluating the quality of physical education instruction yields insufficiently compelling assessment results. The physical education teaching quality assessment database has a wealth of information, yet conventional data analysis methods can only scrape the surface.

If we want to know how well college and university PE programs are doing, we need to look at how well they align with school goals while also taking into account the specifics of each PE teacher's approach. Standardizing and guiding instructors' conduct in physical education may be achieved by a reasonable and scientific assessment of teaching quality [7]. Consequently, enhancing the management level of physical education is an immediate necessity, and developing and refining an evaluation model of the quality of physical education instruction in higher education institutions is an effective means of doing so.

3 Evaluation of Physical Education Level in Physical Education Teaching of Higher Education Based on PCA-AHP-GABP Algorithm

It will be challenging for assessment findings to accurately represent the fundamental level of teaching quality if the methods of evaluating teaching quality converge. Colleges and universities of all stripes should, taking into account both the national education policy's talent training standards and requirements and their own unique situations, outline the pros and cons of school administration, and propose fair and reasonable scientific goals and criteria for school management. Colleges and universities should revise their own pedagogical models and approaches in response to societal demands, shifting their focus from the uniformity and similarity of higher education to its unique qualities and distinctions.

In order to reflect the common law of teaching and the characteristics of different types and levels of college instructors' teaching, as well as to promote individual development, respect commonality, pay attention to individuality, and establish a teaching quality evaluation system, one should look at models and methods that do just that [8]. The timely elimination of idle and wasted educational resources and the realization of optimal resource allocation may be achieved via the construction of a diverse, reasonable, and unique method for evaluating teaching quality.

Courses are categorized according to the school's unified standards and based on course characteristics, disciplines, grades, etc., in accordance with the principles of comprehensiveness, directionality, motivation and improvement, objectivity, and subjectivity. This system is based on a summary of the problems with the current teaching quality evaluation system that is based on survey results. To address issues with a single evaluation type of teacher teaching quality, an excessive proportion of evaluation indicators, and strong subjective factors in evaluation methods, it is recommended to use alternative evaluation indicators or weights. Artificial intelligence and other objective evaluation methods are capable of handling nonlinear problems.

This approach is based on the PCA-AHP-GABP neural network. As a research object, consider the level of physical education instruction at the university level. We thoroughly examine ten factors that impact the total score. Given the intercorrelation of the indicators, we have employed principal component analysis (PCA) to lower their dimensionality. This will allow the indicator variables to keep items, do away with the intercorrelation, decrease the input layer variables, and boost the model's overall efficiency.

$$P = (P_1 + P_2)/2 = (P_0 - \left(P_0 - P_{\min})^* m/M + P_0^* \max_{X_k=\Omega} F(X_K)/ \dot{F}\right)/2 \quad (7)$$

The variables M, m, R, P, 0 (assumed initial variation probability), P_ Min (minimum value of the range of variation probabilities), and P_ inversely proportional to the average fitness value are all used in this context. In Fig. 2, you can see the neural network evaluation vector model.

P is the input vector of the neural network, with the size of Rx1, as shown in formula (8).

$$p = \left[p_1, p_2, \cdots, p_R\right] \quad (8)$$

B is the threshold vector of neurons in the input layer, with the size of Sx1, as shown in formula (9).

$$b_1 = \left[b_{1,1}, b_{2,1}, \cdots, b_{s_{1,1}}\right] \quad (9)$$

IW is the connection weight vector between the input layer neuron and the input vector, with the size of S.xR, as shown in formula (10).

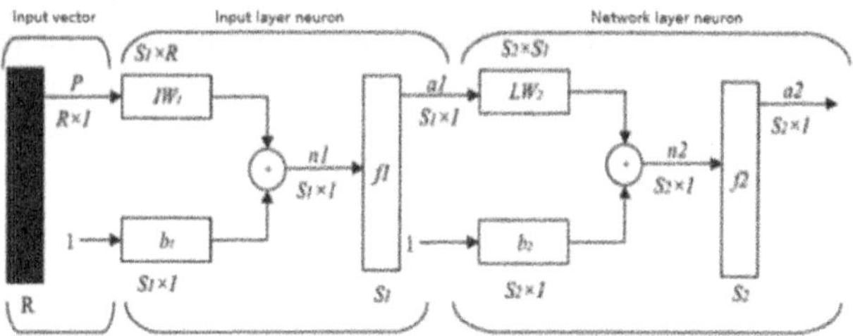

Fig. 2. Neural network evaluation vector model

Shows.

$$IW_1 = \begin{bmatrix} iw_{1,1}^{11} & iw_{1,2}^{11} & \cdots & iw_{1,k}^{11} \\ iw_{2,1}^{11} & iw_{2,2}^{11} & \cdots & iw_{2,k}^{1,1} \\ \cdots & \cdots & \cdots & \cdots \\ iw_{5,1}^{1,1} & iw_{5,2}^{1,1} & \cdots & iw_{5,k}^{1,1} \end{bmatrix} \tag{10}$$

The dimensionality of the goal variable in the real issue determines the output layer's number of nodes. One such tool is the nonlinear transfer function. The hyperbolic function formula (11) is the nonlinear transfer function that is most often utilized.

$$f(x) = \frac{1}{1 + e^x} \tag{11}$$

3.1 Experimental Analysis

This research investigates the use of the PCA-AHP-GABP method for evaluating the quality of physical education courses offered at the university level. This genetic operation makes use of adaptive mutation probability, which streamlines training while simultaneously increasing neural network convergence speed. This approach utilizes BP neural networks in nonlinear mapping and better evolutionary algorithms for global search, and it also minimizes the impact of non-objective elements.

The physical education (PE) teaching quality assessment methodology primarily consists of the following steps:

(1) Identifying and fixing current issues with PE teaching quality evaluation allows us to create a better and more accurate index system.
(2) Separate the data acquired from the quality assessment of physical education (PE) instruction into training and test samples; then, choose evaluation indicators based on the features of PE instruction provided by instructors.
(3) Thirdly, make a note of all the BP neural network algorithm's settings, such as the learning rate, hidden layer neuron count, maximum iterations, minimal error accuracy, transfer function, training frequency, etc.
(4) The evaluation model is fed data, and recurrent training continues until the trigger algorithm stops.

(5) To determine whether the BP neural network model's training impact is satisfactory, input the test sample from the physical education teaching quality assessment. The model was optimized using an upgraded genetic algorithm. Proceed to the next phase if the prediction passes the stop criteria; otherwise, go back one step and train the network once again, that is, go back to step (3).
(6) Enter the sample into the physical education teaching quality assessment model to get the evaluation result.

One frequent method of gathering information is via the use of questionnaires. Using a combination of existing theories and methods, this research compiles a list of elements that affect assessment outcomes, creates an indicator system, designs and issues a questionnaire, and last, issues a recovery questionnaire. Conducting a reliability test entails analyzing the questionnaire's dependability, which is known as reliability analysis [9]. In order to ensure that the findings of the questionnaire are consistent and accurately represent the dependability of the measured indicators, data analysis and testing methods are used to determine reliability. Simply said, the error will be less, the reliability will be better, and fewer difficulties will occur when the questionnaire is circulated if the two indications are reliable and consistent. For the criteria for classifying dependability coefficients, see Table 1.

Table 1. Reliability coefficient

Reliability coefficient	Meaning
0.60–0.65	Better not
0.65–0.70	Minimum acceptable value
0.70–0.80	Pretty good
0.80–0.90	very nice

The effectiveness of the teaching quality assessment model is dependent on the structure and parameters of the adaptive evolutionary algorithm and BP neural network that are involved in the model, which are detailed in this study. Analyzed and compared to other methods, the AHP-GABP model outperforms them in terms of evaluation performance, reduction of subjective factors, shorter evaluation periods, more reasonable factors to consider, and smaller errors [10]. This is due to its use of the principal component analysis method to reduce the dimensionality of index data. The findings of the neural network assessment simulation, as illustrated in Fig. 3, are shown below.

Improving the model's performance and lowering the inaccuracy of the final assessment result are both achieved by neural network optimization using a genetic algorithm. The model suggested in this research has room for improvement with the addition of data indicators and ongoing training of neural networks with larger training sets. It may prove to be more practical throughout the application procedure in the future. Obtaining the equivalent score for higher education level is as simple as entering the indicator data of various nations.

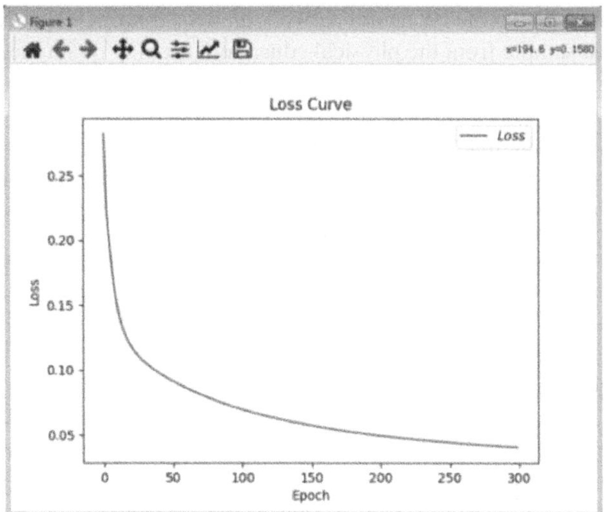

Fig. 3. Neural network evaluation of mean square error simulation results

4 Conclusion

The faster a region's economy can grow, the more clearly defined its advantages in the higher education market are, and the more effectively those resources are distributed. Each region's higher education growth is constrained by its own unique set of objective social circumstances, technical policies, and economic policies; they represent the present state of affairs and the challenges associated with developing and making use of higher education resources. The process of evaluating the quality of instruction is intricate, nonlinear, and fraught with uncertainty. Mathematical model building becomes increasingly complicated due to the large number of components and variables involved in this process. There is room for improvement in the conventional wisdom on the assessment of educational excellence. A credible and scientific model for evaluating teaching quality can only be achieved by combining a plausible system with the appropriate intelligent optimization algorithm.

Acknowledgements. Title: The Relationship between Burnout and Mental Health of Young Teachers in Higher Education: The Moderating Role of Psychological Capital.

Project Source: Jilin Association for Higher Education.

Project Number: JGJXZ2019D54.

References

1. Hu, C.: Application of E-learning assessment based on AHP-BP algorithm in the cloud computing teaching platform. Int. J. Emerg. Technol. Learn. **11**(8), 27 (2016)
2. Zhang, N.: Construction cost optimization system based on AHP-BP neural network algorithm. In: International Conference on Machine Learning and Big Data Analytics for IoT Security and Privacy. Springer, Cham (2022)

3. Cui, Z.W., Shen, Z.Z., Xu, L.-Q., et al.: Back analysis method of seepage coefficient for concrete faced rockfill dam based on AHP-GA. In: Water Resources and Power (2016)
4. Jing, Y., Cheng, W., Gan, C., et al.: Discrimination of liver cancer in cellular level based on backscatter micro-spectrum with PCA algorithm and BP neural network. In: Optics in Health Care & Biomedical Optics VII. International Society for Optics and Photonics (2016)
5. Qingju, T., Jingmin, D., Junyan, L., et al.: Quantitative detection of defects based on Markov-PCA-BP algorithm using pulsed infrared thermography technology. Infrared Phys. Technol. **77**, 144–148 (2016)
6. Li, T., Sun, J., Zhang, X., et al.: Competition prediction and fitness behavior based on GA-SVM algorithm and PCA model. J. Intell. Fuzzy Syst. Appl. Eng. Technol. (5 Pt.1), 37 (2019)
7. Hu, C.: Paper Application of e-learning Assessment Based on AHP-BP Algorithm in the Cloud Computing Teaching Platform (2018)
8. Carbinatto, M.V., Nunomura, M.: Gymnastics in higher education: reflections on assessment. Revista Brasileira De Educação Fisica E Esporte **30**(1), 171–181 (2016)
9. Liu, X., Liao, L.: Research and implementation of performance evaluation system for physical education teachers based on load weight algorithm. In: CIPAE 2020: 2020 International Conference on Computers, Information Processing and Advanced Education (2020)
10. Sun, Y., Shan, H., Zhang, W., et al.: Reliability prediction of distribution network based on PCA-GA-BP neural network. In: Materials Science, Energy Technology and Power Engineering III (MEP 2019), 2154 (2019)

Evaluation and Improvement of Human Resources Training Effect Based on Basic Network Technology

Yang Liu[1(✉)], Xiaolian Chen[2], Hongming Wang[2], and Jun Ni[2]

[1] JiangSu Electric Power Company, Nanjing 210000, Jiangsu, China
lvbaoshi@163.com

[2] State Grid Wuxi power supply company, Wuxi 214000, Jiangsu, China

Abstract. Human resources, as the most precious resource of society, are an indispensable and important factor in promoting economic development and realizing the improvement of people's living standards. However, there are many problems in human resource management in our country. Therefore, studying the evaluation and improvement of the effect of human resource training is a way to make enterprise human resource management easier. Based on basic network technology, this paper conducts research on the evaluation and improvement model of human resource training through experimental design and questionnaire survey. The results of the questionnaire show that 68.7% of people want to conduct training effect evaluation and improved model design. Therefore, the research topic of this article is of practical significance.

Keywords: Basic Network Technology · Human Resources · Training Effect · Evaluation and Improvement

1 Introduction

With the continuous development of human resource management, training has also become an important part of the enterprise. However, due to the misunderstanding of the employee induction training in our country, the disconnection in the actual operation process, and the inadequate learning of new knowledge, the serious problems of manpower waste and brain drain have always plagued managers. The basic network technology of human resources can collect and process data information through computer, Internet and other means, and analyze the obtained data, and then provide it to business managers after drawing conclusions. Therefore, this article also studies the human resource evaluation model from the perspective of basic network technology.

There are many research results for the evaluation and improvement of human resource training effects. For example, Cao Qingwen said that human resource training evaluation has a certain role in the introduction of talents [1]. Yu Yanyan said that personnel training and development, as a vital part of human resource management, play an irreplaceable role in the development of an enterprise [2]. Chen Xuanfang believes that

B. Brik and S. Nazir (Eds.): BigIoT-EDU 2024, LNICST 660, pp. 402–410, 2026.
https://doi.org/10.1007/978-3-032-18628-7_41

under the current social environment, strengthening the effect of human resource training is an issue that every manager should pay attention to [3]. Therefore, this article focuses on the model design of human resource training effect evaluation and improvement and the current situation of human resource training.

This article first studies the relevant theoretical knowledge of training, and makes a preliminary exploration of the model of human resource training. The second thing to study is the key to basic network technology, that is, data processing. Subsequent research is the principle and direction of effect evaluation and improvement model. Finally, a questionnaire survey was conducted, and data support was provided based on the results of the questionnaire.

2 Human Resource Training Effect Evaluation and Improvement Methods Based on Basic Network Technology

2.1 The Basic Theory of Human Resource Training

(1) Training

In a broad sense, training is a way to create intellectual capital. In a narrow sense, it is an organized and implemented planned intervention to improve people's practical work ability. The company plans and organizes training courses that help improve employees' work and study skills. The purpose is to improve the knowledge, skills, attitudes and behaviors of the trainees in a targeted manner to ensure that the trainees can perform the corresponding work tasks in accordance with the prescribed level or standards [4, 5].

(2) Training can be divided into multiple types

Classified by content, it can be divided into skills training, performance training and development training. According to the relationship between the trainees and the workplace during the training period, it can be divided into new employee induction training, workplace employee training and employee training outside the workplace.

(3) Current status of human resource training

From the perspective of the entry period, the company pays more attention to the entry of new employees and management personnel. In general, the company provides more onboarding time for new employees or front-line employees. The main motivation of enterprise groups for employee training is to improve their skills. Training mainly stays at the company level and has not yet reached the strategic level. In addition, the needs analysis of employee training is not considered, the training expenditure is low, and the evaluation of training effects is not emphasized [6, 7].

(4) Training system model

Human resources are an important foundation for an enterprise to survive and develop in the fierce market competition. Staff training is the support for an enterprise to implement strategic development and improve market competitiveness. To do a good job in staff training, it must be regarded as a system engineering [8, 9]. The talent training model is shown in Fig. 1:

In order to meet the actual needs of enterprise competition and development, human resources training must first find out the exact needs of the enterprise in terms of human resources, and implement corresponding training according to the actual situation. The first is organizational analysis, the second is employment analysis, and the third is personal analysis. The implementation of training measures is often affected by the size and structure of the company. After completing a specific project or course, a summative evaluation of the project is usually required [10, 11].

(5) Systematic training mode

The global application of the system training model is of great significance to the development of talent training theory, provides a tool for the establishment of a scientific and standardized training operation system within the organization, and effectively promotes the development of organizational training culture [12].

1) Consultant training model

The advisory model provides training managers with the possibility to perform training support functions when acting as an intermediary for the organization. The model focuses on the training delivery process and training effects.

2) Self-development model

The self-development model is a model closely related to "autonomous learning". The main value of this model lies in the potential opportunities.

3) Transitional training model

The transitional training model is a double cycle of organizational strategy and learning.

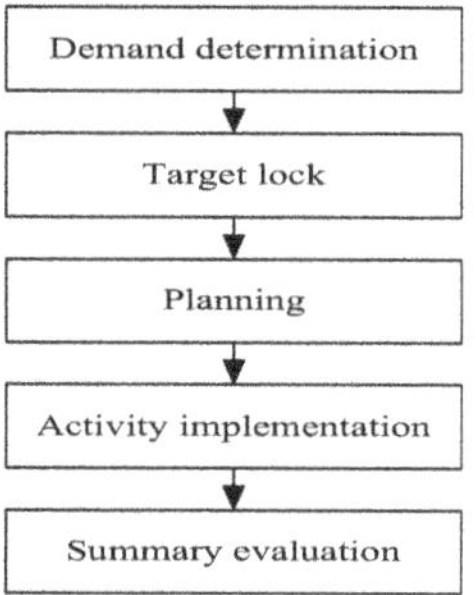

Fig. 1. Human resource training system model

2.2 Application of Basic Network Technology in Effect Evaluation

Among basic network technologies, the most basic and key technology lies in data processing. This paper studies the integrated processing of multi-source heterogeneous data. The purpose is to realize the evaluation and improvement of human resources training through data processing.

Data integration processing jobs can complete the following tasks: correct wrong data and delete redundant data. Convert the wrong data format to the required format and eliminate redundant data attributes. Select the required data and merge the data.

The principle of data cleaning is to use existing technical means and methods to clean up "dirty data". Another important content of data cleaning is the conversion of data types.

Data conversion converts data into a form that meets the requirements of the data format. The main task of data transformation is to find the characteristic representation of the data, reduce the number of valid variables, or use XML transformation to find the invariants of the data, including operations such as normalization, induction, switching, rotation, and projection. Smoothing is the process of removing noise from data. Aggregation is the synthesis and aggregation of data. Normalization refers to the combination of tuple sets under normalization conditions, and generalization refers to the semantic IS-A relationship between the attribute values of tuples.

Data merging removes the attributes that cannot be described by the key features of the system, and merges the same type of key data, so that a set of concise attributes can completely describe the object.

2.3 Model Construction for Effect Evaluation

(1) Principles of model construction

The human resource scorecard's evaluation of the implementation effect of strategic human resource management determines the status of human resource management in the enterprise and plays a key role in establishing the credibility of human resource management. At the same time, it also affects the organization's ability to use human resource management as a strategic asset.

1) The principle of strategic orientation

The human resource scorecard is used in strategic human resource management based on the corporate development strategy, guided by the strategic goal, and decomposes the goals hierarchically, combined with the requirements of the employees to complete the strategic goals to determine the competence and behavior of each employee, thereby ensuring the effective combination of company strategy and specific human resource management activities.

2) Principle of easy operation and execution

The effect evaluation model developed is to be implemented in actual application, and specific indicators need to be used to ensure the accuracy and efficiency of the operation. Therefore, the indicators required to be measured must be easy for all employees to understand and master.

3) The principle of full participation

Applying the human resource scorecard to strategic human resource management is a top-down operation process. It not only clarifies the tasks of human resource management professionals and line managers, but also enables managers and employees outside the human resource management department to participate in the completion of strategic goals.

4) Consistency principle

The consistency of application reflects two aspects. On the one hand, it is necessary to grasp the gap between the status quo of the enterprise and its strategic goals as a whole, consider the enterprise structure horizontally and vertically, and combine the enterprise culture to construct the idea of application.

5) Principle of flexibility

In the process of application, it is required to pay attention to the implementation of corporate strategy, and the implementation of corporate strategy requires continuous change. Therefore, applying the human resource scorecard to strategic human resource management requires flexibility to adapt to the needs of change.

(2) The content of the effect evaluation model

1) Strategic choice
   Comprehensively considering the external environment and internal strengths and weaknesses of the enterprise, the analysis of the internal and external environment of the enterprise can maximize its strengths and avoid weaknesses, realize its strategic nature of success in competition, and thus have a stronger adaptability to changes in the environment.
2) Strategic human resource management
   Strategic human resource management starts from the strategic goals of the enterprise, analyzes and evaluates the characteristics of the individual, organization, and work of the enterprise, formulates specific activities of enterprise human resource management, and develops the capabilities and behaviors of employees that can achieve the strategic goals of the enterprise. Output the corresponding strategic results to improve the performance of the organization.
3) Measurement index system
   In terms of effect evaluation, it uses the four dimensions of the human resource scorecard to evaluate the entire process of strategic human resource management activities. The human resource plan regards management activities, employee capabilities and behaviors, strategy-related output, organizational performance, and corporate strategic goals as a progressive causal relationship, and measures the effects of human resource training from strategy, finance, customers, and operating processes.

(3) Related algorithms for human resource training effect detection
   For several dimensions of human resource training, the reaction test and standard deviation can be used to calculate the degree of ability training.

Assuming that the response to a certain task G is expressed as x, the total response and average range R or standard deviation of each training item can be calculated on this basis. The calculation formula is:

Total response:

$$S = \sum (s \times g) / \sum g \tag{1}$$

Average range:

$$P = \sum (p \times g) / \sum g \tag{2}$$

Standard deviation:

$$\delta = \sqrt{\sum (s - S)^2 g / \sum g} \quad (3)$$

3 Investigation on the Effect of Human Resource Training Based on Basic Network Technology

3.1 Investigation Background

With the adjustment of the country's human resources policy, my country's economic development has entered a new normal stage. In this case, how to improve the competitiveness of enterprises and promote sustainable development is an urgent problem to be solved. How to improve one's own quality and comprehensive ability has become the company's human resource training that faces huge challenges and opportunities. It is urgent to solve the problems, and these problems are inseparable from the establishment of a sound scientific and effective evaluation system.

3.2 Questionnaire Design

The content of the questionnaire designed in this paper is mainly to explore related issues around the effect model of human resource training. The content of the questionnaire has the following aspects:

(1) Fill in the relevant information of the person in the questionnaire, such as gender, occupation, length of service, etc.;
(2) What aspects of training should be included in human resource training;
(3) What aspects of human resource training should be paid attention to in the eyes of the questionnaire;
(4) Available methods for human resource training;
(5) The importance of effect testing and improvement models in the training process;

3.3 Questionnaire Process

This questionnaire is mainly for the company's employees. The survey subjects are mainly employees, plus some supervisors and CEOs. A total of 10 main questions were designed, 150 copies were copied, and 150 people were invited to fill in the online and offline questionnaires. A total of 140 questionnaires were collected, of which 131 were valid, and the effective response rate reached 87.3%. The questionnaire lasted 1 week. Finally, organize the data.

4 Result Analysis

4.1 Survey on the Status Quo of Enterprise Human Resource Training

According to the results of the questionnaire survey, the training of human resources is mainly from the training of new employee manual, business ability, comprehensive ability and management. The company's employees' specific views on the training content are shown in Table 1:

Table 1. Employees' attitudes towards the effects of human resource training

	New employee orientation	Business skills training	Comprehensive quality training	Operation management training
Not satisfied at all	3	5	6	9
Not very satisfied	6	7	8	16
Quite satisfied	5	10	10	10
Very satisfied	6	7	12	11

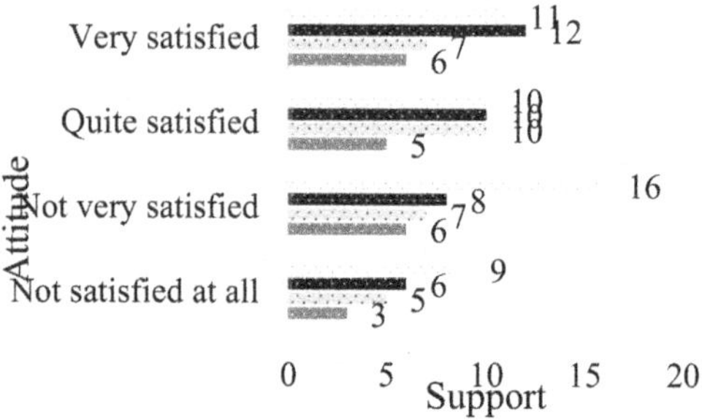

Fig. 2. Employees' attitudes towards the effects of human resource training

As shown in Fig. 2, we can see that many people are most dissatisfied with the training on operation management. The second is dissatisfaction with the training of comprehensive ability. However, the most satisfactory is the cultivation of comprehensive ability. This shows that attention has been paid to comprehensive capabilities, but there are some problems.

4.2 The Importance of Effect Testing and Improvement Models in the Training Process

According to the survey results, we concluded that the design of the model is of different importance in the eyes of people in different positions. But the overall trend is consistent. The specific situation is shown in Table 2:

Table 2. The importance of effect testing and improvement models in the training process

	Staff	Principal	CEO
Not important at all	13	2	0

(continued)

Table 2. *(continued)*

	Staff	Principal	CEO
Not very important	17	8	1
Quite important	24	11	4
Very important	27	19	5

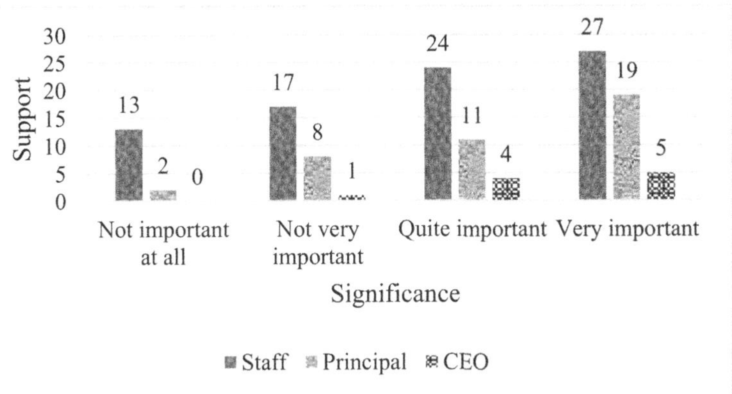

Fig. 3. The importance of effect testing and improvement models in the training process

As shown in Fig. 3, based on this figure, we can find that the number of people who think training effect testing and improved model design are very important is in the first place. Most people think this idea is worth trying. Only a small part of the research on the model considers it unimportant. Among them, the CEO fully supports the design of the model, and 75% of the principals also approve of this design.

5 Conclusion

As the core competitiveness of enterprises, human resources are particularly important in this era. With the rapid development of social economy, market competition has become increasingly fierce. Talent is one of the most valuable resources of a company. In this case, how to improve the competitiveness of enterprises and promote sustainable development is an urgent problem to be solved. And training plays a vital role in improving the overall quality of employees, enhancing the attractiveness of talents, and increasing their internal competitive advantages. This article uses special technology to collect basic information data collection system and human resources department personnel performance management system to analyze and put forward relevant suggestions, and provide certain help and reference value for the company's human resources department to better carry out training work in the future. The survey result data in this article is a big motivation to support the research and improvement of the model.

References

1. Cao, Q., Cheng, X.: Problems and research in the effect evaluation of human resources training. Hum. Resour. Manag. (11), 186–187 (2017)
2. Yu, Y.: Research on the application of offset model in the evaluation of human resources training effects in tourism enterprises. Mark. Mod. (004), 107–108 (2018)
3. Chen, X.: Evaluation of the effectiveness of human resource training in power companies. Manag. Sci. (009), 94–95 (2018)
4. Liu, H.: Problems and countermeasures in the evaluation of corporate human resource training effects. Mark. Mod. **11**(463), 109–110 (2017)
5. Chen, N.: Problems and analysis in the effect evaluation of human resources training. China Civil Bus. **64**(04), 282–282 (2018)
6. Dong, L.: Problems and countermeasures in the effect evaluation of human resource management training. Invest. Entrep. (008), 183–184 (2019)
7. Zhang, R.: Problems and case analysis in the evaluation of human resources training effects. Enterp. Reform Manag. (11), 80–80 (2017)
8. Zuo, X.: Problems and countermeasures in the effect evaluation of human resources training. Chin. Foreign Entrep. (023):149–150 (2017)
9. Zhao, X., Xu, L.: The method innovation and application of the evaluation of skills training effect. China Train. **329**(08), 18–18 (2017)
10. Qiu, X.: Evaluation of enterprise employee training effects and analysis of influencing factors. Zhifu Times. (03X), 70–70 (2018)
11. Zhou, Z.: Thoughts on optimizing the effect of enterprise human resource training. Bus. Stories. **10**, 125–125 (2018)
12. Du, F.: Analysis on the influencing factors of enterprise human resource management training effect. Hum. Resour. Dev. (016), 187–188 (2017)

English Pronunciation Error Detection and Correction System Based on Artificial Neural Network

Yang Yang(✉)

Wuhan Donghu University, Wuhan 430000, Hubei, China
76949549@qq.com

Abstract. The mistake detection and correction system is crucial in the pronunciation of spoken English, yet it has a problem with erroneous performance placement. The usual genetic algorithm fails miserably when it comes to correcting the positioning of incorrect corrections in spoken English pronunciation. This study concludes with the provision of an assessment of the research on an English speech mistake detection and correction system based on artificial neural networks. First, in order to reduce interference factors in the error detection and correction system, the indicators are separated according to the demands of the system, and the influencing components are discovered using gradient descent theory. We then use gradient descent theory to the design of an artificial neural network (ANN) error detection and correction system, and we analyze the results in detail. In terms of accuracy of error detection and correction systems and time of influencing variables, the MATLAB simulation results show that artificial neural networks beat the standard genetic algorithm under specific evaluation conditions.

Keywords: gradient descent theory · Artificial neural networks · artificial neural networks · Error detection · Correction system · Spoken English · Pronunciation

1 Introduction

The mistake detection and correction system is a key aspect of spoken English pronunciation [1], allowing for more rapid and accurate management of the aging performance assessment model [2]. Nevertheless, the error detection and correction system is negatively affected [6] by the lack of precision in the error detection and correction system scheme [5], which occurs during the process [3] of the error detection and correction system [4]. Researchers have shown that employing artificial neural networks [8] to explore the aging performance evaluation mode [9] and effectively analyzing the error detection and correction system scheme are both possible. Using this data, we propose an artificial neural network (ANN) to verify the model's efficacy [10] and optimize the error detection and repair system method. The error detection and correction system process in Table 1 is shown in Fig. 1.

B. Brik and S. Nazir (Eds.): BigIoT-EDU 2024, LNICST 660, pp. 411–420, 2026.
https://doi.org/10.1007/978-3-032-18628-7_42

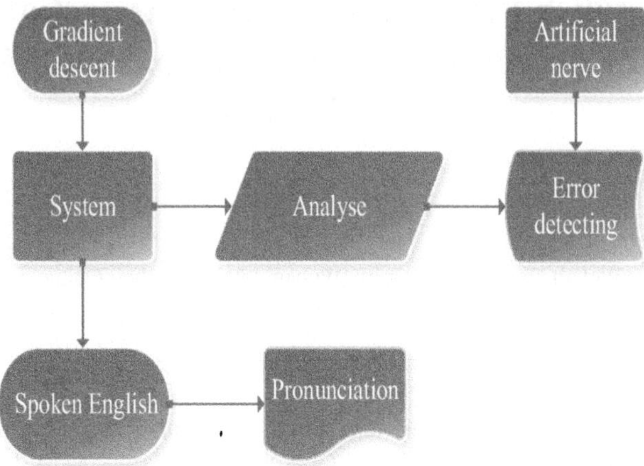

Fig. 1. Analysis process of error detection and correction system

2 Related Works

A. **Artificial Neural Network**

To accomplish the scheme optimization of the error detection and correction system, the Artificial neural networks employs a random optimization approach for the error detection and correction system and updates the Internet information parameters. The evolutionary algorithm split the mistake detection and correction system into numerous phases and then randomly chose alternate techniques. During the iterative process, the error detection and correction system scheme is improved and examined for different grades. After the optimization research is finished, we compile the error detection and correction system levels of several schemes and record the best one.

B. **English Pronunciation Error Detection and Correction System**

Using a genetic algorithm and other artificial neural network features, the mistake detection and repair system is more in line with what is really required. When it comes to logic and the precision of the mistake detection and repair system, artificial neural networks perform better than genetic algorithms. The error detection and correction system scheme of the evolutionary algorithm has improved in terms of speed, accuracy, and summation stability, while the error detection and correction system scheme of the artificial neural networks—which includes the genetic algorithm—is closer to the real needs of the error detection and correction system. The artificial neural networks also outperform the genetic algorithm in terms of the error detection and correction system's logic and accuracy.

3 Error Detection and Correction System Optimization Approach

3.1 The Artificial Neural Networks Is Described Mathematically

The Artificial neural networks will enhance the error detection and correction system scheme utilizing computer technology and the index parameters in the error detection and repair system, it is discovered that the mechanism for detecting and correcting errors uses unqualified value parameters as, and the error detection and correction system scheme is Eq. (1) shows the calculation that is integrated with the function to determine the feasibility of the error detection and correction system.

$$\lim_{x \to \infty} \left(y_i \cdot t_{ij} \right) = y_{ij} \geq \max\left(t_{ij} \div 2 \right) \tag{1}$$

Equation depicts the examination of outliers among them.

$$\max\left(t_{ij} \right) = \partial \left({t_{ij}}^2 + 2 \cdot t_{ij} \right) \succ \lim_{x \to \infty} \frac{-b \pm \sqrt{b^2 - 4ac}}{2a} \tag{2}$$

In order to quantify the error detection and correction system, artificial neural networks integrate the advantages of computer technology; this might lead to an improvement in the accuracy of the system.

So what if I The system for detecting and correcting errors must meet the following requirements is that the error detection and correction system scheme is, the method for meeting the requirements of the system for detecting and correcting errors is, and the judgment function of the error detection and correction system the scheme is as shown by Eq. (3).

$$F(d_i) = \mathfrak{M} \sum t_i \cap \xi \cdot \sqrt{2} \to \oint y_i \cdot 7 \tag{3}$$

3.2 Selection of Error Detection and Correction System Scheme

Second Hypothesis One of the functions of the error detection and correction system is, The weighting factor is, As shown in Equation, the error detection and correction system (4) requires the unqualified error detection and correction system.

$$g(t_i) = \ddot{x} \cdot z_i \prod F(d_i) \frac{dy}{dx} - w_i \Phi \boxed{\Gamma} \tag{4}$$

Based on the assumptions I and II of the error detection and correction system, the entire functionality of the system may be achieved, as indicated in Eq. (5).

$$\lim_{x \to \infty} g(t_i) + F(d_i) \leq \cap \max\left(t_{ij} \right) \tag{5}$$

Eq. (6) shows the outcomes of standardizing all data, which improves the mistake detection and repair system's effectiveness.

$$g(t_i) + F(d_i) \leftrightarrow \frac{n!}{r!(n-r)!} \left(\sum t_{ij} + 4 \right) \tag{6}$$

3.3 Analysis of Error Detection and Correction System Scheme

It is important to conduct a thorough analysis of the error detection and correction system scheme before implementing artificial neural networks. The requirements of the system should be mapped to the error detection and correction system library, and any unqualified schemes should be removed. The anomaly assessment system may be provided using Eq. (6), and the outcomes is shown in Eq. (7).

$$No(t_i) = \frac{g(t_i) + F(d_i)}{mean\left(\sum t_{ij} + 4\right)} \sqrt{b^2 - 4ac} \tag{7}$$

Among them, it is specified that the scheme must be suggested; otherwise, the scheme integration is necessary; the outcome is illustrated in Eq. (8).

$$Zh(t_i) = \lim_{x \to \infty} \left[\sum g(t_i) + F(d_i) \right] \lim_{x \to \infty} \tag{8}$$

The ASD error detection and correction system has been tested extensively, and its threshold and index weight have been set to ensure the correctness of the Artificial neural networks. The ZXC error detection and correction system is a systematic test that must be tested extensively; if the error detection and correction system does not follow a normal distribution, its scheme will be affected, and the overall accuracy of the system will be reduced, as stated in Eq. (9).

$$accur(t_i) = \frac{\min\left[\sum g(t_i) + F(d_i)\right]}{\sum g(t_i) + F(d_i)} \times 100\% \tag{9}$$

In line with empirical evidence, the error detection and correction system scheme exhibits a multi-dimensional distribution, as revealed by the analysis. The error detection and repair method has no directional, implying that the scheme has large unpredictability, and so it is recognized as a high analytical research. You may rewrite the calculation of Eq. (9) as Eq. (10), assuming that is the stochastic function of the error detection and correction system.

$$accur(t_i) = \frac{\min\left[\sum g(t_i) + F(d_i)\right]}{\frac{1}{2} \sum g(t_i) + F(d_i)} + randon(t_i) \tag{10}$$

Computer technology enhances the error detection and correction system, eliminates unnecessary and duplicate schemes, and augments the default scheme, leading to a robust dynamic correlation of the entire system. As a result, the error detection and correction system satisfies standard requirements.

4 Results and Discussion

4.1 Introduction to the Error Detection and Correction System

With 12 pathways and a 12-h test duration, the error detection and correction system in complicated circumstances is used as the research goal. Table 1 shows the scheme of the particular error detection and correction system.

Table 1. Error detection and correction system error detection and correction system requirements

Scope of application	Grade	Accuracy	Error detection and correction system
English learners	I	87.68	86.17
	II	89.99	87.09
Online English learning platform	I	90.89	86.64
	II	88.35	83.82
Training institutions	I	84.87	86.84
	II	85.96	88.91

By modifying the design of the error detection and repair system shown in Fig. 2, the accuracy and reliability of the artificial neural networks are enhanced. As a consequence, the evolutionary algorithm's error detection and repair system scheme has improved in terms of speed, accuracy, and summation stability.

4.2 Error Detection and Correction System

By changing the error detection and correction scheme in Fig. 2, the accuracy and reliability of the artificial neural networks are enhanced (Table 2).

Table 2. The overall situation of the error detection and correction system scheme

Category	Random data	Analysis rate
English learners	88.22	87.39
Online English learning platform	91.87	85.82
Training institutions	91.19	85.82
Mean	86.06	85.95

4.3 Error Detection and Correction System and Stability

In Fig. 2, we can see the error detection and repair system scheme that incorporates the genetic algorithm. This allows us to evaluate the accuracy of the artificial neural networks.

Fig. 2. Evaluation model of aging performance of different algorithms

Figure 2 demonstrates that the Artificial Neural Networks have a more robust error detection and correction system than the Genetic algorithm, with a lower error rate. This suggests that the Artificial Neural Networks system is more stable, in contrast to the Genetic algorithm system, which is more prone to errors. For each of the three approaches we've just covered, Table 3 shows the typical layout of the error detection and repair system.

Table 3. Compares the accuracy of several error detection and correction system.

Algorithm	Survey data	Error detection and correction system	Magnitude of change	Error
Artificial neural networks	89.36	88.60	86.75	90.59
Genetic algorithm	88.82	88.17	91.41	90.34
P	89.20	87.89	89.20	89.77

Figure 3 shows that the Artificial Neural Networks were generally examined using various methodologies to validate the efficiency of the suggested technique and confirm that the Genetic algorithm has flaws in its error detection and correction system. Table 3 shows that the Genetic algorithm's error detection and correction system varies dramatically with large error rates, and that Artificial Neural Networks outperformed the Ant Colony approach in this regard. Additionally, the Artificial Neural Networks' error detection and correction system is higher than 90%, and the accuracy has not changed much.

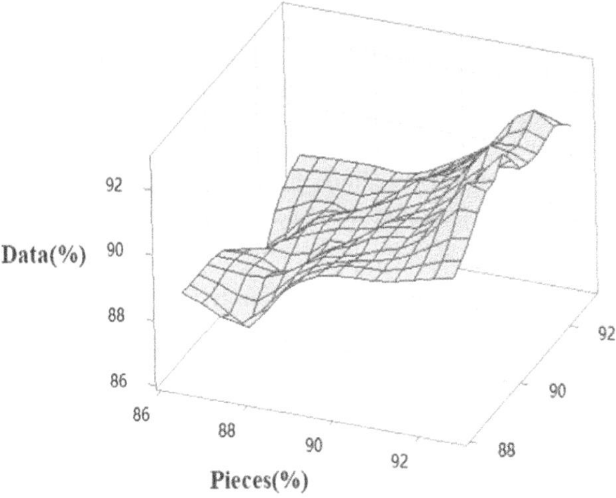

Fig. 3. Error detection and correction system of artificial neural networks

In comparison to the genetic algorithm, artificial neural networks have a much superior mistake detection and repair method (Fig. 3). Why? Because A.N.N.s raise the adjustment coefficient of the error detection and repair system and establish the threshold of Internet data to get rid of the scheme that doesn't measure up.

4.4 Rationality of Error Detection and Correction System

Figure 4 shows the error detection and correction system design, which incorporates the genetic algorithm for checking the accuracy of the artificial neural networks.

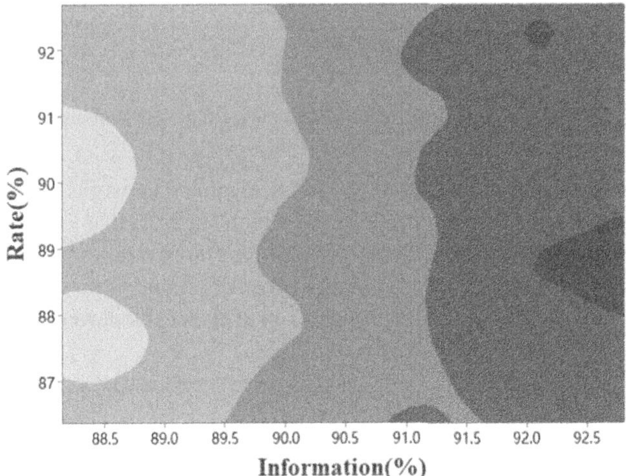

Fig. 4. Evaluation model of aging performance of different algorithms

You can see in Fig. 4 that the error detection and correction system using artificial neural networks is more rational than the one using a genetic algorithm. What's more, you can make it even more rational by making improvements to the current system. A decentralized data storage and administration platform may be built with the use of artificial neural networks, which will ensure that the results are securely saved and retained. The use of artificial neural networks allows for the generation of unique identifiers for each, as well as the storage of suitable data and schemes.

4.5 Validity of Error Detection and Correction System

In order to confirm the efficacy of the Artificial neural networks, the error detection and correction system scheme is integrated with the Genetic algorithm, and the error detection and correction system scheme is presented in Fig. 5 displayed.

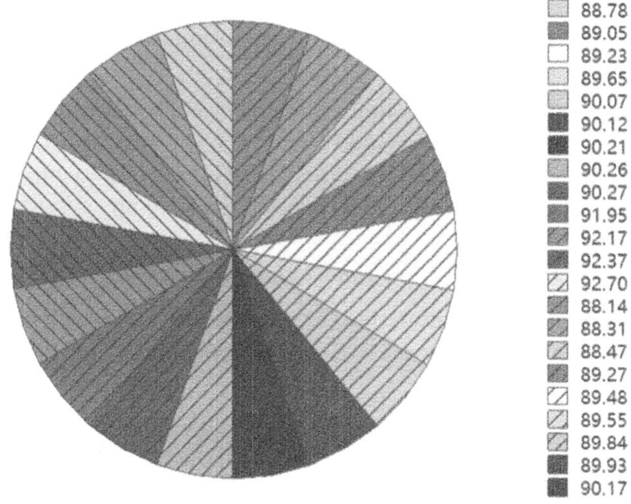

Fig. 5. ERROR detection and correction system of different algorithms

Compared to the Genetic algorithm, the Artificial neural networks have a more robust error detection and correction system (Fig. 5), which suggests that their performance is more consistent, as opposed to the Genetic algorithm's more erratic approach. Moreover, the error rate is lower for the Artificial neural networks. Table 4 shows the typical setup for the three approaches to error detection and repair systems that were already covered.

Table 4. compares the efficacy of several error detection and correction system.

Algorithm	Survey data	Error detection and correction system	Magnitude of change	Error
Artificial neural networks	84.97	85.08	88.65	89.08

(*continued*)

Table 4. (*continued*)

Algorithm	Survey data	Error detection and correction system	Magnitude of change	Error
Genetic algorithm	88.17	84.17	84.75	88.74
P	88.62	87.83	86.37	87.08

In terms of error detection and correction system accuracy, Table 4 reveals that the Genetic algorithm is flawed; furthermore, the error detection and correction system exhibits significant error rate variability. In comparison to the ant colony method, the error detection and correction system produced by artificial neural networks was superior. Simultaneously, the accuracy has hardly changed, and the error detection and repair system of artificial neural networks is above 90%. Artificial neural networks must be shown to be the best. The Artificial neural networks was normally investigated by many techniques to further validate the efficiency of the recommended strategy, as indicated in Fig. 6.

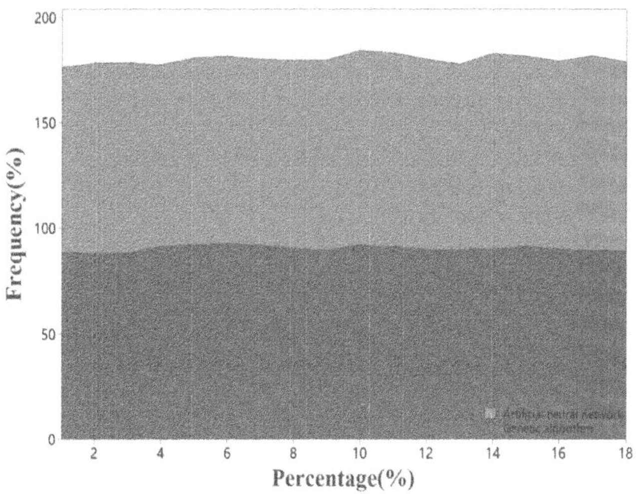

Fig. 6. Artificial neural networks error detection and correction system

As seen in Fig. 6, artificial neural networks outperform the genetic algorithm when it comes to mistake identification and repair. Why? Because A.N.N.s raise the adjustment coefficient of the error detection and repair system and establish the threshold of Internet data to get rid of the scheme that doesn't measure up.

5 Conclusion

This research aims to address the issue of an inefficient error detection and correction system by introducing an Artificial neural networks (ANN) that utilizes computer technology to improve the ANN. At the same time, it builds an Internet information collection system and examines the ANN's correctness and reliability. The results show that the ANN can improve the ANN's accuracy, and that the ANN can be used with the generic ANN. However, the ANN process places too much emphasis on ANN examination, leading to ingratiating.

References

1. Wu, Q., Sun, M., Wang, J.: Research on clustered pipeline leakage monitoring system based on artificial neural network multi-algorithm fusion. Inf. Syst. Eng. (3), 29–31 (2023)
2. Huang, X., Hu, Y., Huang, J., Yangpu: Research on dynamic growth simulation system of natural oak tree based on artificial neural network. (5) (2022)
3. Jiang, M., Qiu, S., Tong, S., Gan, H.: A detection method and system based on Vibe algorithm and artificial neural network. CN202210599662.X (2022)
4. Shao, X., Lei, G., Zeng, W., Huang, J.: Stomatic conductance simulation of Pinus eclipse and Cypress cherry nucleus based on classification gradient boosting algorithm and artificial neural network. China Rural Water Conserv. Hydropower. (2023)
5. Cui, J., Zhong, C., Jenny, H.: Research on zero bias compensation method for laser gyroscope based on artificial neural network. Autom. Instrument. (11), 5 (2022)
6. Zhou, H., Huang, W., Ben, H.Y., Yang, G.: A generalized artificial neural network unsupervised local learning method, system and application. CN202211165236.1 (2022)
7. Xie, M., Sun, Y., Tang, S., Cao, H.: Distribution network equipment state judgment model based on population optimization-probabilistic neural network. Adv. Technol. Electr. Eng. Energy. **42**(6), 79–87 (2023)
8. Jiang, X.: Design of robot assistance system for English spoken pronunciation based on deep learning. Autom. Instrument. (008) (2022)
9. Ma, X.: English grammar error detection based on bidirectional LSTM model. Inf. Technol. (009), 046 (2022)
10. Deng, B., Li, Y.: Research on tunnel blasting overmining prediction model based on artificial neural network and Artificial neural networks. Constr. Machin. (1), 94–100 (2023)
11. Xu, J., Huang, J., Pei, L., Bian, F.: Research on artificial unit price prediction of nuclear power engineering based on BP neural network. Shanxi Architect. (2023)
12. Bai, Y., Zhao, Y., Zhao, Y.: Vehicle-mounted recalibration method and cloud service system based on artificial neural network. CN202111245044.7 (2022)

English Network Independent Learning for College Students Based on ID3 Algorithm

Fang Lifeng[1] and Tong Yao[2](✉)

[1] Sichuan University Jinjiang College, Meishan City 620860, Sichuan, China
[2] Sichuan Tourism University, Chengdu 610100, Sichuan, China
yaotong2011tony@163.com

Abstract. Online English classes for college students rely heavily on students' capacity to study on their own, yet this poses a challenge. The issue of college students' inadequate capacity for self-learning in online English classes cannot be resolved by conventional methods of instruction, and the treatment of the matter is irrational. As a result, an ID3 algorithm for analysis that learns on its own is suggested in this work. Firstly, information theory is utilized to build and exploit learning resources, and indicators are split according to the needs of independent learning to eliminate independent learning the interfering element. After then, information theory builds a self-learning program out of several learning materials and combines the findings from these analyses. Under certain processing requirements, the ID3 algorithm makes adequate use of learning resources, according to data collected in MATLAB. Compared to more conventional forms of instruction, self-paced learning systems have several advantages.

Keywords: information theory · ID3 algorithm · Learning resource management · self-directed learning · Self-learning ability is not strong

1 Introduction

One of the core tenets of college-level English curricula is learner autonomy, which is crucial for the growth of independent learning [1]. On the other hand, learners face decision-making challenges due to the self-learning scheme's lack of comprehensiveness [2]. Some researchers have proposed using the ID3 algorithm to analyze data from self-learning resource management programs in order to optimize the scheme and determine the model's efficacy is shown in Fig. 1.

B. Brik and S. Nazir (Eds.): BigIoT-EDU 2024, LNICST 660, pp. 421–429, 2026.
https://doi.org/10.1007/978-3-032-18628-7_43

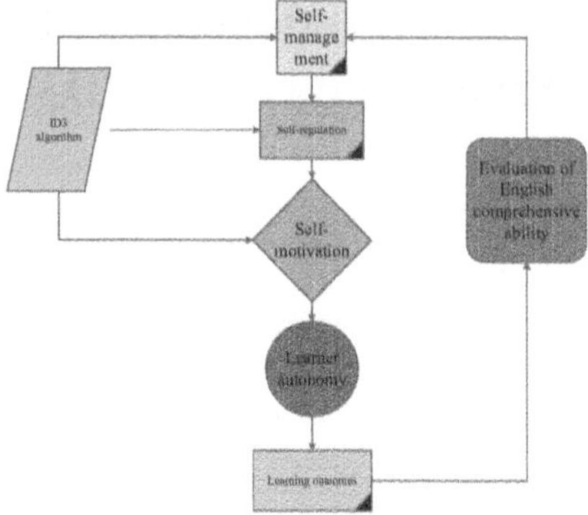

Fig. 1. Analysis process of learning resources

2 Related Works

A. **ID3 Algorithm**

Within its iterative process [3], the ID3 algorithm utilizes self-learning schemes with varying information feature levels to conduct a self-learning ability analysis. Once the analysis is finished, the ID3 algorithm compares the self-learning levels of various programs and records the best self-learning scheme [4]. The ID3 algorithm utilizes a learner autonomy strategy for learning resources and optimizes information parameters to achieve this goal [5]. The process of network autonomous learning is complicated, so it is necessary to combine the original analysis methods and contents [6, 7], as well as the existing knowledge structure and educational programs for analysis. Many factors need to work together [8].

B. **English Network Independent Learning**

The independent learning of college students' English network is comprehensively analyzed, and the ID3 algorithm's precision is guaranteed by setting the self-learning scheme's threshold and index weight. This learning tool necessitates an examination of one's capacity for autonomous learning since it is a test of self-learning solutions. Consistent with empirical evidence, the study of self-learning systems reveals that they exhibit a multi-dimensional distribution. The self-learning of the ID3 algorithm is higher than that of traditional teaching methods.

3 Optimization Strategies for Learning Resources

A. **Mathematical description of the ID3 algorithm**

The index parameters in the self-learning That which is being described is, and the integration function of the self-learning scheme is to finally judge the feasibility of self-learning, and the calculation is shown in Eq. (1).

$$set(x_i \cdot y_i) \leq \sum \cdot y_i \tag{1}$$

According to the results, it can be found that in the process of autonomous learning, the learning effect should meet the actual teaching requirements and meet the previous needs. The specific judgment process is shown in Formula (2).

$$mean(x_{ij}) = \left(x_{ij}^2 + 2\right) \succ \min(\sum x_{ij}) \tag{2}$$

In order to measure learning resources and enhance the quality of self-learning, the ID3 algorithm integrates the benefits of information theory. As shown in Eq. (3).

$$F(t_i) = \sum \cdot x_i \cdot \oint \cdot y_i \tag{3}$$

B. **Choice of self-directed learning options**

The learning process and learning content should also be compared and integrated to form effective political conditions as shown in Eq. (4).

$$h(x_i) = z_i \cdot \prod F - w_i \tag{4}$$

It is possible to derive the all-encompassing self-learning function in accordance with assumptions I and II, as shown in Eq. (5).

$$h(x_i) + F(t_i) \leq got(x_{ij}) \tag{5}$$

Carry out comprehensive comparison and conditional completion indicator comparison and indicator formation to achieve comprehensive analysis and. Comparison, and then evaluate and evaluate the self-learning situation. Test results indicated in Eq. (6).

$$h(x_i) + F(t_i) \leftrightarrow got(\sum x_{ij}) \tag{6}$$

C. **Analysis of self-directed learning programs**

Before the ID3 algorithm is run, conduct a comprehensive analysis of the self-learning approach, align the learning needs with the resource library, and filter out inadequate strategies. The anomaly review system can be framed as indicated by Eq. (6), with outcomes presented in Eq. (7).

$$So(x_i) = \frac{h(x_i) + F(t_i)}{got(\sum x_{ij})} \tag{7}$$

Among them, it is said that the plan must be put forward in order to avoid the need of integrating the plan, and the result is shown in Eq. (8).

$$ye(x_i) = \min[\sum h(x_i) + F(d_i)] \tag{8}$$

If the learning resource is its algorithm for self-learning will be impacted if it follows a non normal distribution, reducing the accuracy of the overall self-directed learning, and the calculation result is as shown in the formula (9) shown.

$$che(x_i) = \frac{\min[\sum h(x_i) + F(t_i)]}{\sum h(x_i) + F(t_i)} \times 100\% \quad (9)$$

This research is considered highly analytical since the learning resources are not directional, which indicates that the self-directed learning scheme is quite random. If the stochastic function of the learning resource is as formula (10).

$$che(x_i) = \frac{\min[\sum h(x_i) + F(t_i)]}{\sum h(x_i) + F(t_i)} \times \sum coor(x_i) \quad (10)$$

A high dynamic connection across the full self-learning scheme ensures that the learning resources satisfy typical needs; this is mostly due to the fact that information theory modifies the learning resources, eliminates redundant and unnecessary schemes, and augments the default scheme.

4 Results and Discussion

A. **Introduction to self-directed learning**

Based on self-learning in the teaching process. The learning content is mainly adult learning situation. The test time is twelve months. The test results are mainly through questionnaires, survey results and comprehensive comparison to form effective analysis data results and data contents, as well as comprehensive analysis as shown in Table 1.

Table 1. University self-directed learning requirements

Scope of application	Self-learning stage	The learn to investigate data integrity	Comprehensive outcome condition comparison of my study
Self-management	I	98.65	98.07
	II	94.28	94.65
Self-motivated	I	98.28	94.40
	II	98.87	95.10
Self-regulation	I	95.60	98.67
	II	98.82	92.79

The change of self-learning scheme in Fig. 1 shows that the ID3 algorithm has better [9] the self-learning scheme of ID3 algorithm has better speed and summation stability [10]. The obtained data results and data conditions meet the requirements, and there is no deficiency in the comprehensive comparison of data and the overall planning process of data. Realizing the overall planning of data, the integrity of data is reasonable, which can provide support for later analysis.

B. **Independent learning of English teaching to college students**

Comprehensive data comparison and comprehensive conditions can reflect the situation of self-learning, but it is still necessary to summarize the results of self-learning. This program includes self-learning content such as learning plans [11, 12], [13], online assignments, and unit tests for each unit. Following the pee-selection of the ID3 algorithm, The content of the test results is shown in Table 2.

Table 2. The overall picture of the self-paced learning programme

Category	Comprehensive comparison	Learning conditions	My academic performance
Personalized teaching model	94.87	98.80	97.57
Comprehensive English application ability	96.98	94.15	96.05
Schedule your own study time	94.05	94.51	94.16

C. **Accuracy and stability of self-directed learning**

That is, learning is a continuous process of volatility, and continuous observation is needed between fluctuations, and the self-learning scheme is presented in Fig. 2.

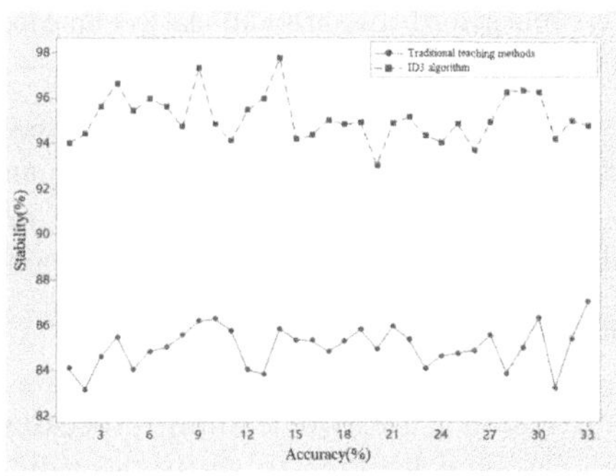

Fig. 2. Stability comparison of different self-learning algorithms

Figure 2 shows that compared to the traditional teaching method, ID3's self-learning is superior; its stability performance reaches 95%, suggesting that ID3's algorithm self-learning is relatively stable; in contrast, traditional teaching methods' self-learning is uneven and has not yet reached 90%. You can see the three algorithms' average self-learning schemes in Table 3.

Table 3. Comparison and integration of indicators for self-use learning.

Algorithm	Periodic academic performance	Professional academic performance	Comparison of indicator programs	Biases in autonomous learning
ID3 algorithm	97.87	98.80	97.57	1.69
Traditional teaching methods	87.81	85.27	87.39	4.93

In Table 3, it's evident that conventional teaching techniques lack autonomy and consistency in English instruction for college students, leading to notable changes and a high error rate. Conversely, the ID3 algorithm's self-learning surpasses 97%, maintaining consistent accuracy. For a deeper analysis of the ID3 algorithm's superiority, various methods are employed as demonstrated in Fig. 3.

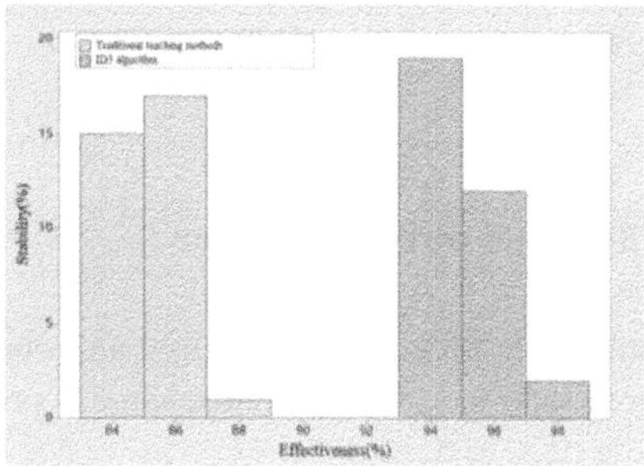

Fig. 3. Stability distribution comparison between traditional teaching methods and ID3 algorithm

According to Fig. 3, the ID3 algorithm significantly surpasses traditional methods in its self-learning capabilities, notably achieving between 95 and 98%. To discourage inappropriate self-study among students, the ID3 algorithm introduces an increased adjustment factor for college English courses and sets a data boundary. Scenario.

D. **The Effectiveness of self-directed learning**

Self-learning and general learning are two learning processes, but they should be analyzed with reference to general learning to verify the validity of all information. Therefore, the two are compared, and the comparison results are shown in Fig. 4.

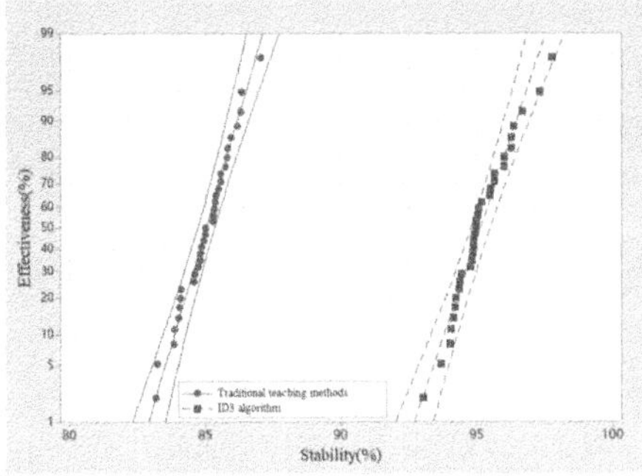

Fig. 4. Effectiveness and stability comparison of different self-learning algorithms

Figure 4 reveals that the self-learning of the ID3 algorithm surpasses that of the conventional teaching method, yet it boasts a reduced error rate, suggesting the ID3 algorithm's self-learning is more reliable than the traditional approach of student self-study. Table 4 presents the average self-learning strategies for the three algorithms.

Table 4. Comparison of the effectiveness of self-directed learning

Algorithm	The role of hobbies	The role of knowledge structure	Cognition of self theory	Improvement of academic performance
ID3 algorithm	72.59	54.96	73.47	2.44
Traditional teaching methods	27.81	60.27	37.39	5.11

As seen in Table 4 There are a lot of problems with the old ways of teaching English to college students, such as a lack of stability and independence in their learning and a high error rate due to the many changes that have taken place in the field. Overall, the ID3 algorithm outperforms more conventional forms of instruction and has better self-learning capabilities. While this is going on, the ID3 algorithm's self-learning rate is above 90% and the accuracy has hardly budged. In order to provide further evidence that the ID3 algorithm is better. Various approaches are used to investigate the ID3 algorithm in general, as illustrated in Fig. 5, in order to further validate the method described in this research.

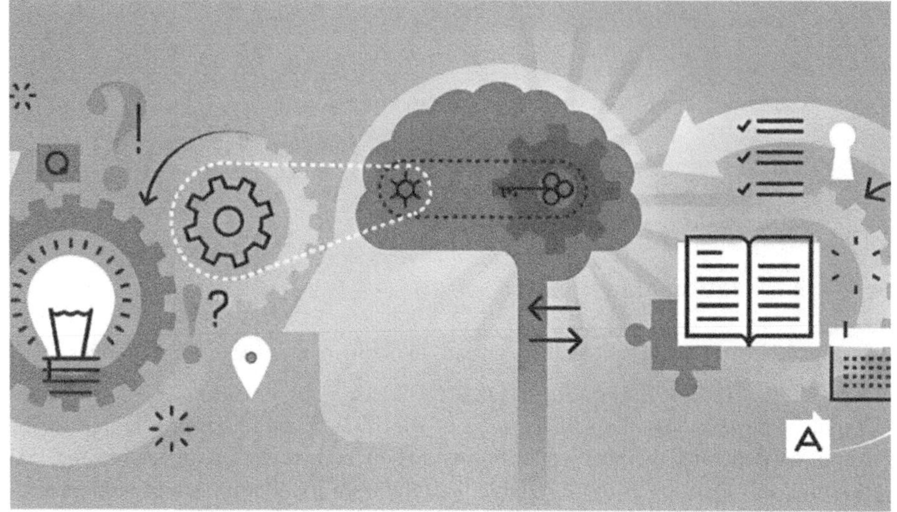

Fig. 5. Conceptual Diagram of ID3 Algorithm-Based Self-learning Framework

Based on Fig. 5 By increasing the adjustment of English teaching for college students' coefficients, setting thresholds for talents, and eliminating self-learning programs that do not meet the requirements, the ID3 algorithm's independent learning outperforms the traditional teaching method.

5 Conclusion

In response to the fact that college students' self-directed learning isn't perfect, this research presents the ID3 algorithm and uses information theory to examine how well college students can learn English on their own. Simultaneously, a meticulous exploration of both autonomous learning advancements and preliminary innovation is undertaken for the development of information gathering. Investigations reveal that the ID3 method can augment the precision and dependability of English self-study techniques for university attendees. While students typically engage in English learning individually, the ID3 approach's indicator selection appears misguided, as it excessively emphasizes self-directed study evaluation.

Acknowledgements. Research on emergency countermeasures for green and low-carbon tourism scenic spot management in case of natural disasters—Taking Jiuzhaigou Valley Scenic and Historic Interest Area scenic spot as an example (supported by Sichuan Tibet Smart Tourism Engineering Research Center of Sichuan Social Science Union, No. ZLGC2022B06).

References

1. Anzalone, L. et al.: Reinforced curriculum learning for autonomous driving in Carla. In: IEEE International Conference on Image Processing (ICIP). Electr Network (2021)

2. Arslan, N., et al.: Creative cognition, autonomous learning, and problem-solving: a mediation model. Hacettepe Universitesi Egitim Fakultesi Dergisi-Hacettepe Univ. J. Educ. **38**(3), 380–387 (2023)
3. Barbu, C., Mocanu, S.A.: On the development of autonomous agents using deep reinforcement learning. Univ. Politehnica Bucharest Sci. Bull. Ser. C-Elect. Eng. Comput. Sci. **83**(3), 97–116 (2021)
4. Choi, J. et al.: Modular reinforcement learning for autonomous UAV flight control. Drones **7**(7) (2023)
5. Flores, S.I., et al.: Processes employed to introduce autonomous learning. Stud. Self-Access Learn. J. **13**(4), 426–441 (2022)
6. Gil, A.D.M.: Strategies learning and autonomous learning. J. Learn. Styles **15**(30), 149–157 (2022)
7. Heide, N.F., Petereit, J.: Machine learning for the perception of autonomous construction machinery. At-Automatisierungstechnik **71**(3), 219–231 (2023)
8. Jebessa, E. et al.: Analysis of reinforcement learning in autonomous vehicles. In: IEEE 12th Annual Computing and Communication Workshop and Conference (CCWC). Electr Network (2022)
9. Kim, J. et al.: Continuous autonomous ship learning framework for human policies on simulation. Appl. Sci.-Basel **12**(3) (2022)
10. Lopez, V.G., et al.: Game-theoretic lane-changing decision making and payoff learning for autonomous vehicles. IEEE Trans. Veh. Technol. **71**(4), 3609–3620 (2022)
11. Narayan, N. et al.: Assuring learning-enabled increasingly autonomous systems. In: 17th Annual IEEE International Systems Conference (SysCon), Vancouver, Canada (2023)
12. Shukla, S. et al.: UBOL: user-behavior-aware one-shot learning for safe autonomous driving. In: 5th International Conference on Connected and Autonomous Driving (MetroCAD), Detroit, MI (2022)

Design and Implementation of Intelligent Platform for University Cybersquatting Training Based on Django Framework

Wu Chen(✉), Xue Lan, and Luo Qianqian

Jiangxi Vocational &Technical College of Information Application, Nanchang 330043, China
buhe3qu@163.com

Abstract. Network security education in higher education relies heavily on training intelligent platforms, however there is a misalignment in their posture that needs fixing. The design and implementation issues with college network security training cannot be solved by traditional genetic algorithms, and the results are less than optimal. In light of this need, this article both suggests and examines the architecture and execution. After that, the training intelligent platform's design and implementation are based on the MVC design theory, and the outcomes of both the design and execution are thoroughly examined. The results show that in the process of education and training, intelligent analysis method can promote the improvement, optimization and effect optimization rate of education level more than 6.7%, and promote the deepening of education level to reach more than 90%. Therefore, in the process of intelligent analysis, intelligent analysis methods can improve its overall effect.

Keywords: MVC design theory · Django framework · Train · Universities · Cybersquatting

1 Introduction

College and university network [1, 2] security training relies heavily on the design platform, which may expedite the achievement of precise [3] control. But there are some drawbacks to the design and implementation of the training intelligent platform due to the poor accuracy that occurs during the process of designing and implementing the platform [4, 5], which has certain negative effects on the design and implementation of the platform [6]. Experts in the field have speculated that the Django framework, when applied to the study of the training intelligent platform's design and implementation [7, 8], can yield useful insights into the platform's architecture and provide necessary assistance with its development and launch [9]. Based on this, this article suggests using the Django framework to improve the training intelligence platform's design and implementation scheme and to check the model's efficacy [10].The design and implementation of the training intelligence platform in Fig. 1.

B. Brik and S. Nazir (Eds.): BigIoT-EDU 2024, LNICST 660, pp. 430–440, 2026.
https://doi.org/10.1007/978-3-032-18628-7_44

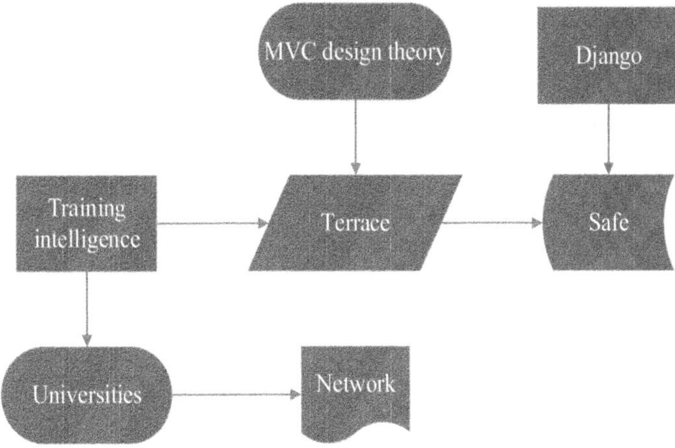

Fig. 1. Train for the design and implementation of intelligent platforms

2 Related Works

A. Intelligent Platform

Utilizing genetic algorithms, the Django framework's training intelligence platform is more closely modeled after the real thing in terms of both design and execution. Compared to the evolutionary algorithm [11], the Django framework is more logical and accurately designed and implemented for the AI training platform. Development and launch of an AI-powered training platform Training intelligence platform design and execution incorporates structural, the next steps are to obtain a preliminary design and implementation plan for the training intelligence platform, and then to analyze the design and implementation plan's feasibility [12]. A more precise verification of the training intelligent platform's design and implementation effect was achieved by selecting design and implementation levels corresponding to different stages of the platform [13].

B. Django Framework

The Django framework optimizes the design and execution of the training intelligence platform using a random optimization approach. To do this, it modifies the parameters of the Internet information scheme. The Django framework's design and implementation split the training intelligence platform's design and implementation into many layers, and various schemes are randomly selected. Iterative optimization and analysis of training intelligence platform design and execution at varying stages is what the procedure is all about. Once the optimization study is finished, we take a look at the various schemes' training intelligence platform designs and implementation levels, and we document the best one. With the Django framework, a decentralized platform for data storage and administration may be created, guaranteeing the safe recording and preservation of findings.

3 Train Optimization Strategies for the Design and Implementation of Intelligent Platforms

3.1 A Mathematical Description of the Django Framework

The goal of the Django framework is to optimize the training intelligent platform's design and implementation using computer technology. It does this by identifying the unqualified value parameters based on the various index parameters used in the platform's design and implementation, and integrate the design and implementation of the training intelligent platform as the function is, arriving to a conclusion on the training intelligent platform's practicability, calculated is a formula (1) shown.

$$\lim_{x \to \infty} (y_i \cdot t_{ij}) = y_{ij} \geq \max(t_{ij} \div 2) \tag{1}$$

With the help of framework analysis and comprehensive analysis, it can promote the improvement of its optimized structure is shown in Eq. (2).

$$mf(t_{ij}) = \partial\left(t_{ij}^{n} + yui \cdot t_{ij}\right) \succ mean\left(\sum t_{ij} + 4\right) mathfrakM \tag{2}$$

Django is a framework that integrates computer technology's benefits with quantification in training intelligence platform design and implementation; this may lead to more precise AI platform design and execution.

An intelligent platform for training has specific design and implementation needs, including as, the design and implementation of the training intelligent platform is, The training intelligent platform's design and execution have met with the pleasure of, and the judgment function of the design and implementation of the training intelligent platform is in Eq. (3).

$$fin(x_i) = mathbbR \prod \sum t_i \cap \xi \cdot \sqrt{ni} \to ointy_i \cdot pol \tag{3}$$

3.2 Selection of Training Intelligent Platform Design and Implementation Scheme

The second hypothesis is that the weight coefficient and the training intelligent platform's design and implementation function is, hence, an unqualified training intelligent platform must be designed and implemented in order for the training intelligent platform to be designed and implemented is shown in Eq. (4).

$$g(x) = \int_{1}^{n} \ddot{x} \prod F(d_i) \frac{dy}{dx} - w_i \tag{4}$$

Equation (5) shows the outcome, which state that a thorough the training intelligent platform's design and execution may be attained.

$$\lim_{x \to \infty} g(t_i) + F(d_i) \leq \cap \max(t_{ij}) \tag{5}$$

The standardization of all data is necessary to enhance the trustworthiness of the training intelligence platform's design and execution, as shown in Eq. (6).

$$g(t_i) + F(d_i) \leftrightarrow mean\left(\sum t_{ij} + 4\right) \tag{6}$$

3.3 Analysis of the Holistic Structure of Training of the Training Intelligent Platform

It is recommended to conduct a thorough analysis of the training intelligence platform's design and implementation prior to implementing the Django framework. After that, you should match the platform's design and implementation requirements to its library, and finally, you should get rid of any unqualified design and implementation schemes. Equation (6) allows us to suggest the anomaly assessment technique, and the results is shown in Eq. (7).

$$uo(t_i) = \frac{g(t_i) + F(d_i)}{mean\left(\sum t_{ij} + 4\right)} \sqrt{nk} \tag{7}$$

Throughout the process of matching analysis with training analysis, the data should be quantified as shown in Eq. (8).

$$h(t_i) = \cap Ai\sqrt{\left[\sum g(x) + k \cdot f(d_i)\right]} \tag{8}$$

After a thorough analysis of the training intelligence platform's design and implementation, the Django framework's correctness is guaranteed by setting the design and implementation's thresholds and index weights to thoroughly examine the design and execution of the training intelligent platform. If the design and implementation of the training intelligence platform is in a non normal distribution, the overall accuracy of the training intelligence platform's design and implementation will be reduced as a result of this impact on the platform's design and implementation is shown in Eq. (9).

$$accur(t_i) = \frac{\min[\sum g(t_i) + F(d_i)]}{\sum g(t_i) + F(d_i)} \times k\% \tag{9}$$

In accordance with the objective facts, the investigation into the design and implementation plan of the training intelligent platform reveals that it displays a multi-dimensional distribution. The training intelligent platform is considered a high-level analytical research because to its non-directional design and implementation, which suggests considerable unpredictability in the design and execution. If the random function of the design and implementation of the training intelligence platform is, the result of solving problem (9) may be given by formula (10).

$$accur(t_i) = \frac{\min[\sum g(t_i) + F(d_i)]}{\sum g(t_i) + F(d_i)} + randon(t_i) \tag{10}$$

Computer technology primarily modifies the training intelligent platform's design and implementation, gets rid of the redundant and unnecessary.

4 Results and Discussion

4.1 Introduction to the Design and Implementation of the Training Intelligent Platform

Taking the knowledge training of the first year of college as the research object, the training contents are mainly network technology and auxiliary technology training contents and training points. Based on the actual operation, the data test results are tested, and the specific analysis effect is evaluated for the questionnaire and the actual effect as shown in Table 1.

Table 1. Actual investigation effect analysis

Scope of application	Grade	Comprehensiveness of the test	Training of the design and implementation of intelligent platforms
College students	I	85.00	78.86
	II	81.97	78.45
University faculty	I	83.81	81.31
	II	83.34	78.19
Researchers	I	79.56	81.99
	II	79.10	80.11

It is clear that the Django framework is more accurate and reliable thanks to the improvements in the training intelligence platform's design and implementation shown in Table 1. It follows that the Django framework's training intelligence platform has superior design and implementation speed, accuracy, and stability in terms of summation.

4.2 Design and Implementation of Training Intelligent Platform

The effect needs to be fully displayed, so the display content will be summarized. The results during the summary process are shown in Table 2.

Table 2. Summary of testing of training effectiveness.

Category	Test the effect	Specific training content	Practical application of theory
College students	63.72	73.79	76.70
University faculty	65.49	82.52	74.76
Researchers	52.21	81.55	77.67

4.3 Time Tracking of Training Effectiveness

Figure 2 shows the design and execution of the training intelligent platform, which is constituted of the evolutionary algorithm, used to test the correctness of the Django framework.

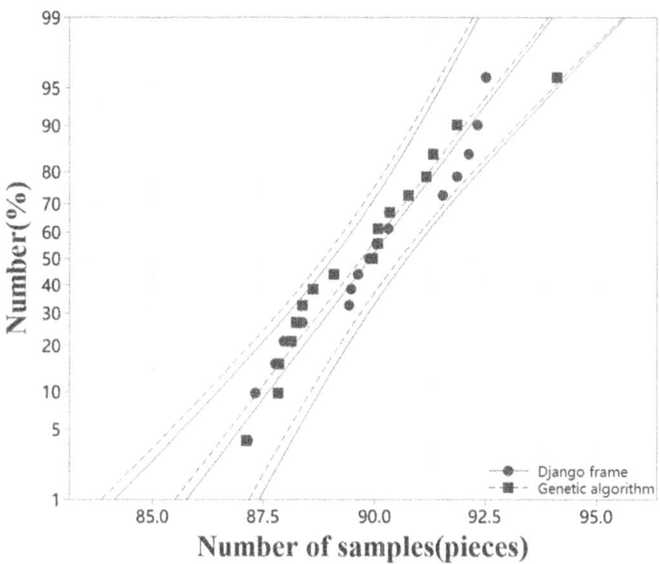

Fig. 2. Design and implementation of training intelligence platform with different algorithms

Figure 2 shows that the genetic algorithm's training intelligence platform is inherently unstable, in contrast to the Django framework's relatively stable design and implementation, which results in a lower error rate. This suggests that the Django framework's training intelligence platform is more stable overall. In Table 3, you can see the structure and methodology of the typical intelligent platform for training the aforementioned three algorithms.

Table 3. Comparison of the design and implementation accuracy of training intelligence platforms with different methods

Algorithm	Effects of training	Comprehensive knowledge integration	Understanding of relevant knowledge	Comprehensive judgment of trends
Django framework	39.82	58.41	75.73	72.82
Genetic algorithm	38.05	54.87	82.52	75.73
P	44.25	53.98	79.61	72.82

Table 3 shows that the genetic algorithm isn't perfect when it comes to training intelligent platform design and implementation accuracy; there have been major changes to the platform's design and implementation, and the error rate is quite high. When compared to genetic algorithms, the Django framework consistently produces better outcomes when it comes to the development and deployment of intelligence platforms for training. Also, the accuracy hasn't altered much, and the design and execution of the Django framework's training intelligence platform is above 90%. In order to prove that the Django framework is better. The efficiency of the technique suggested in this study is further validated by conducting a broad examination of the Django framework using various methodologies, as illustrated in Fig. 3.

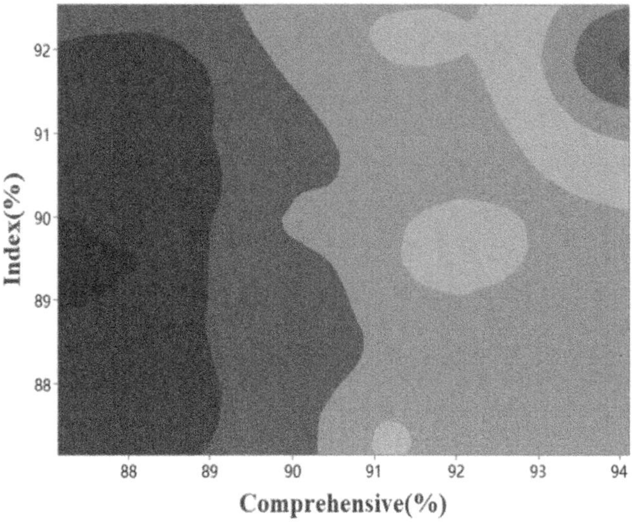

Fig. 3. Design and implementation of the Django framework's training intelligence platform

Figure 3 shows that compared to the genetic algorithm, the Django framework's training intelligence platform is far superior in terms of design and implementation. This is because the Django framework raises the adjustment coefficient for the platform's design and implementation, and it uses the threshold of online data to filter out any training intelligence platform schemes that don't match the requirements.

4.4 Rationality of Training the Design and Implementation of Intelligent Platforms

Using the evolutionary algorithm, the training intelligent platform was designed and implemented to evaluate the Django framework's correctness. Figure 4 shows the design and execution of this platform.

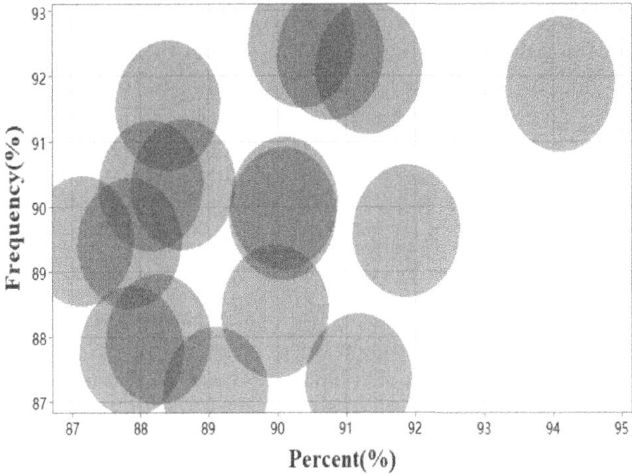

Fig. 4. Design and implementation of training intelligence platform with different algorithms

Figure 4 shows that compared to the genetic algorithm, the Django framework's training intelligence platform has better design and implementation rationality. This is because the Django framework allows for the improvement of the training intelligence platform's design and implementation, which in turn increases the platform's rationality. Each may have its own distinct identity made using the Django framework, which can also store all the essential data and plans.

4.5 Comparison of Training Results of Each Indicator

As shown in Fig. 5, the design and execution of the training intelligent platform include the evolutionary algorithm, which helps to test the efficacy of the Django framework.

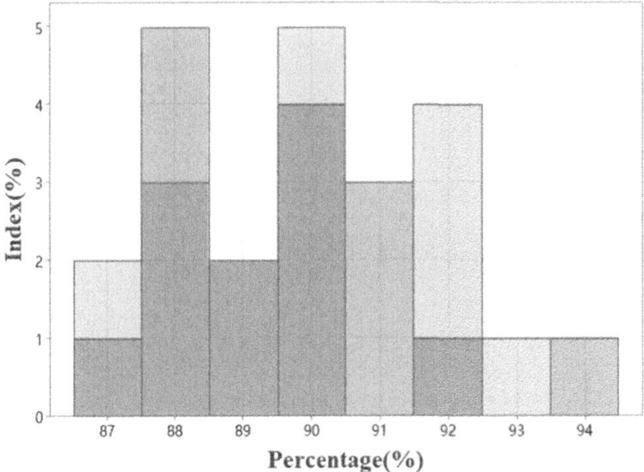

Fig. 5. Design and implementation of training intelligence platform with different algorithms

Figure 5 shows that compared to the genetic algorithm's training intelligence platform, the Django framework's is more stable in terms of design and implementation, with a lower error rate. In contrast, the genetic algorithm's training intelligence platform is more prone to design and implementation inconsistencies. In Table 4, you can see the overall plan for the three algorithms' average training intelligence platform's design and execution.

Table 4. The effect of contrast is persistent.

Algorithm	Improvement of ability	Expansion of application scope	Comprehensive training effect	The overall logic of the target
Django framework	56.64	53.98	77.67	76.70
Genetic algorithm	43.36	63.72	73.79	77.67
P	58.41	38.94	77.67	82.52

Table 4 shows that the genetic algorithm isn't perfect when it comes to training intelligent platform design and implementation accuracy; there have been major changes to the platform's design and implementation, and the error rate is quite high. When compared to genetic algorithms, the Django framework consistently produces better outcomes when it comes to the development and deployment of intelligence platforms for training. Also, the accuracy hasn't altered much, and the design and execution of the Django framework's training intelligence platform is above 90%. In order to prove that the Django framework is better. A broad study of the Django framework is conducted using several methodologies, as shown in Fig. 6, to further validate the efficiency of the method described in this research.

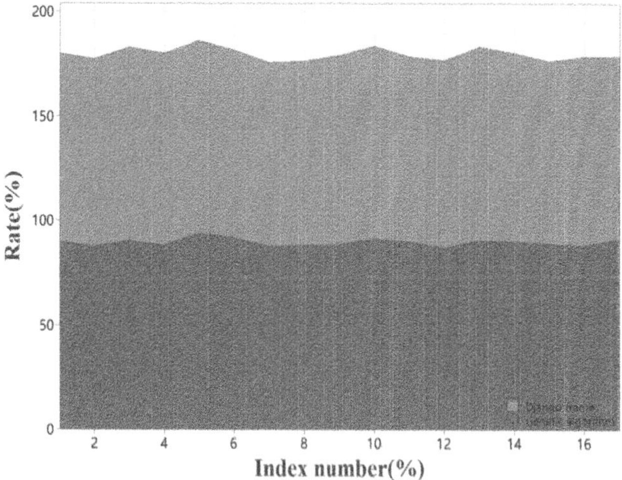

Fig. 6. The Django framework trains the design and implementation of intelligent platforms

Figure 6 shows that compared to the genetic algorithm, the Django framework's training intelligence platform is noticeably better in terms of design and implementation. This is because the Django framework raises the adjustment coefficient for the platform's design and implementation, and it uses the threshold of internet information to filter out any training intelligence platform schemes that don't meet the requirements.

5 Conclusion

This article presents the Django framework as a solution to the issue of the training intelligent platform's subpar design and execution, with the goal of optimizing both areas via the use of computer technology. Simultaneously, the Internet data collecting is built, and the correctness and reliability of the training intelligent platform's design and execution are examined thoroughly. According to the study's findings, the Django framework can make the training intelligence platform's design and execution more precise, as well as create and deploy a generic training intelligence platform. Unfortunately, the Django framework places an excessive amount of emphasis on the training intelligent platform's design and implementation, leading to illogical choices in the platform's design and implementation index.

Acknowledgment. Research on Effective Strategies of College Network Security Education in the Era of Mobile Internet, No:JC22213.

References

1. Li, S., Li, Q.: Design and research of cyberspace security offensive and defensive practice teaching platform for Django college students. J. Jilin Inst. Chem. Technol. **39**(7), 67–71 (2022)
2. Lin, B., Yang, B., Sun, F.: Design and implementation of college employment information visualization platform based on DjanGo framework. J. Liaoning Norm. Univ. (Nat. Sci. Ed.) (002), 045 (2022)
3. Guo, H.: Design and development of a file sharing platform based on Django framework. Inf. Rec. Mater. (003), 023 (2022)
4. Liu, Y., Tao, W., Shen, B., Yang, J., Da, P.: Design and implementation of construction data sharing platform based on Django. Mod. Comput. **28**(2), 4 (2022)
5. Wang, J.: Design and implementation of logistics inventory management system for colleges and universities based on Django. Comput. Age (007), 000 (2022)
6. Wu, L., Li, Q., Huang, X., Zhang, Z., Dong, G., Luo, F.: Design and implementation of film recommendation system based on DjanGo framework. Comput. Knowl. Technol.: Acad. Ed. **19**(4), 56–61 (2023)
7. Yang, H.: MVC framework design and implementation based on Django. Comput. Knowl. Technol.: Acad. Ed. **19**(4), 62–65 (2023)
8. Niu, H.: Design and implementation of online games based on Django and thrift frameworks. Software **43**(4), 177–180 (2022)
9. Sun, J., Zhang, T., Yang, J., Wang, J.: Design and development of android-based college canteen ordering system "pocket campus gang". Comput. Age (1), 78–81 (2023)

10. Yufen, W., Bye, h: Design and implementation of enterprise portal based on Django. Comput. Knowl. Technol.: Acad. Ed. **19**(4), 53–55 (2023)
11. Zheng, M., Chen, X., Zhong, Y., Liu, T.: Django-based work-study wage declaration system. Network Security Technology and Application (2023)
12. Zhang, T.: A project quality monitoring method based on Django framework. CN116257217A (2023)
13. Ye, D., Shen, J., Li, S., Zhan, C., Tu, X.: Design of ONT self-service installation software for Gigabit passive optical network based on Django. Automation Applications (2023)

Design and Development of College Students' English Network Self-Learning Based on Decision Tree Algorithm

Sirong Mu(✉)

The Open University of Jilin, Changchun 130022, China
13694303046@163.com

Abstract. College students' English networks rely on independent learning studies, but students often misjudge their own abilities. When applied to the English-speaking network of university students, the conventional ant colony algorithm fails miserably in its attempt to resolve the issue of network self-learning. As a result, this article reviews previous work on the topic and suggests future research directions for studying the English network self-learning of college students using the ID3 algorithm. To lower the interference factors in self-learning research, first we use information theory to find the influencing elements, and then we split the indicators according to the needs of self-learning research. Next, an independent learning study scheme of the ID3 algorithm is formed using information theory, the ID3 algorithm outperforms it under certain assessment criteria, including those pertaining to the speed and accuracy of self-learning research.

Keywords: information theory · ID3 algorithm · Self-directed study research · College students · Network · Autonomy

1 Introduction

College students' English networks rely heavily on autonomous learning research, which may expedite the process of exact control over such networks [1, 2]. Nevertheless, there are a number of drawbacks to independent learning research that arise from the self-learning research [3] scheme's issue of low accuracy [4]. Applying the ID3 algorithm [5] to the analysis of self-learning research schemes may successfully give equivalent assistance for self-learning research [6] according to certain experts. Based on this, this work suggests an ID3 method to evaluate the model's efficacy [7] and improve the self-learning research scheme [8, 9].

2 Related Works

2.1 E-learning Content in English

In order to maximize the self-learning research scheme, the ID3 algorithm makes use of computer technology. The method takes into account both the index parameters and the unqualified value parameters in the self-learning research is y_i found, along with the

B. Brik and S. Nazir (Eds.): BigIoT-EDU 2024, LNICST 660, pp. 441–449, 2026.
https://doi.org/10.1007/978-3-032-18628-7_45

self-learning research scheme's integration function is z_i to finally judge the feasibility of the self-learning research, which is calculated is $tol(y_i \cdot t_{ij})$ shown in Eq. (1).

$$\lim_{x \to \infty} \left(y_i \cdot t_{ij}\right) = \lim_{x \to \infty} y_{ij} \geq \max(t_{ij} \div 2) \tag{1}$$

Equation (2) shows the Network effect and self-directed learning.

$$mx(t_{ij}) = \partial\left(t_{ij}^2 + n \cdot t_{ij}\right) \succ y \cap st\left(\sum t_{ij} + rui\right) \tag{2}$$

Using self-learning research for quantification, the ID3 algorithm integrates the technology, which may enhance the accuracy of self-learning research.

The needs of research on self-directed learning is t_i, the self-learning research program is set_i, the satisfaction of the self-learning research program is y_i, and the self-learning program's judgment function is $F(t_i \approx 0)$ in Eq. (3).

$$\int F(x_i) = \cup lui \sum t_i \cap \xi \cdot \sqrt{n} \to \oint y_i \cdot ze \tag{3}$$

2.2 Choice of Self-Directed Learning Research Program

The role of self-learning in research is $g(t_i)$ and the weight coefficient is w_i. Consequently, as can be shown from Eq. (4), unqualified self-learning research is necessary for the self-learning study.

$$\sum g(t_i) = \int hi \cdot z_i \prod F(d_i) \frac{dy}{dx} - w_i \tag{4}$$

Equation (5) shows the outcome of obtaining the full function of self-learning research from assumptions I and II.

$$\lim_{x \to \infty} g(t_i) + F(d_i) \leq \cap \max(t_{ij}) \tag{5}$$

Equation (6) shows the effects of standardizing all data, which improves the efficacy and reliability of self-directed learning study.

$$g(x_i) + F(y_i) \leftrightarrow mean\left(\sum t_{ij} + 4\right) \tag{6}$$

2.3 Analysis of Self-Directed Learning Research Protocols

Prior to implementing the ID3 method, a thorough analysis of the self-learning research scheme should be conducted. The needs of the scheme should be matched with the resources available in the self-learning research library, and any unqualified schemes should be removed. The findings may be used to suggest the anomaly assessment system, as shown in Eq. (6) is $No(t_i)$ shown in Eq. (7).

$$top(t_i) = \frac{g(t_i) + F(d_i)}{mean\left(\sum t_{ij} + 4\right)} \frac{n!}{r!(n-r)!} \tag{7}$$

Among them, it is $\frac{g(t_i)+F(d_i)}{mean(\sum t_{ij}+4)} \leq 1$ said that in order for the strategy to be integrated, it must first be presented is $Zh(t_i)$ required, and the result is shown in Eq. (8).

$$trip(t_i) = n \cdot k \cdot \left[\sum g(t_i) + F(d_i)\right] \tag{8}$$

We established the threshold and index weights of the self-learning research scheme after a thorough analysis to guarantee that the ID3 method is accurate. In order to conduct thorough tests of self-learning research methods, precise analysis is essential in self-learning research. Is the study of self-learning is $unno(t_i)$ The precision of the overall self-learning study and the calculating result will be reduced due to the effects on its self-learning research plan in a manorial distribution is $accur(t_i)$ shown in Eq. (9).

$$rill(t_i) = \frac{\min[\sum g(t_i) + F(d_i)]}{\sum g(t_i) + F(d_i)} \times ri \tag{9}$$

A multidimensional distribution is consistent with objective facts, according to the study of self-learning research methods. This study is considered to be very analytical since the self-directed learning research is not oriented, which suggests that the self-learning research scheme is quite random. While conducting research on self-learning, if is $andon(t_i)$, then the calculation of Eq. (9) can be expressed as Eq. (10).

$$sy(t_i) = \frac{\min[\sum g(t_i) + F(d_i)]}{yill} \cdot \Phi \tag{10}$$

Computer technology enhances self-learning research by adjusting it, eliminating unnecessary and duplicate schemes, and supplementing the default scheme, resulting in a strong dynamic correlation throughout the entire self-learning research scheme. As a result, this type of research meets the usual requirements.

3 Optimization Strategies for Research

To optimize the scheme for self-learning research, the ID3 algorithm uses a random optimization method and tweaks the parameters of online information. At each stage of the ID3 algorithm's self-learning research process, it randomly chooses a new scheme [10]. Various self-learning research stages' optimization and analysis are carried out in the iterative procedure [11]. Following the completion of the optimization analysis, the best self-learning research is documented after combining the levels of self-learning research for various schemes [12].

4 Results and Discussion

4.1 Introduction to Self-Directed Learning Research

The self-learning research in difficult scenarios is the research object, and there are 12 pathways and 12 h for the exam. Table 1 shows the independent learning research plan of the unique self-learning research, which is meant to assist the research.

Table 1. Self-directed study research requirements

Scope of application	Grade	Content	Grammar
Education field	I	85.00	78.86
	II	81.97	78.45
Language teaching	I	83.81	81.31
	II	83.34	78.19
Educational technology	I	79.56	81.99
	II	79.10	80.11

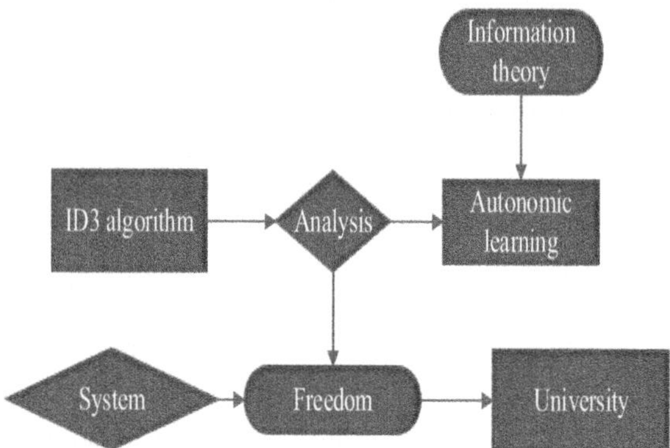

Fig. 1. Self-directed study of the analytical process of research

The self-directed learning research process in Table 1. Self-learning is a gradual process, so it is necessary to dig deeper with more knowledge, content and structure to form a flow chart, as shown in Fig. 1.

In Fig. 1 is the ID3 algorithm's self-learning research scheme, which uses logic of self-learning research. The ID3 method is more accurate and reliable, as shown by the adjustments to the self-learning research scheme in Fig. 2. Consequently, the ID3 algorithm produces superior results in terms of speed, accuracy, and stability of sums when used in self-learning research schemes.

4.2 Self-Directed Learning Research

There are three types of data used in self-directed learning research: unstructured, semi-structured, and structured. An initial plan for self-learning research was developed after the ore-selection of the ID3 method, and its practicability was thoroughly examined. For a more precise verification of the self-learning research impact, we used the self-learning research scheme provided in Table 2 and chose self-learning research with varying degrees of self-learning.

Table 2. The self-directed study research programme

Category	Learning ability	Condition	Comprehensive
Education field	38.94	74.76	78.64
Language teaching	61.06	80.58	73.79
Educational technology	41.59	79.61	76.70

4.3 Self-Directed Learning Research and Stability

Integrating the ant colony algorithm into the self-learning research scheme, as seen in Fig. 2, allows us to validate the ID3 method's correctness.

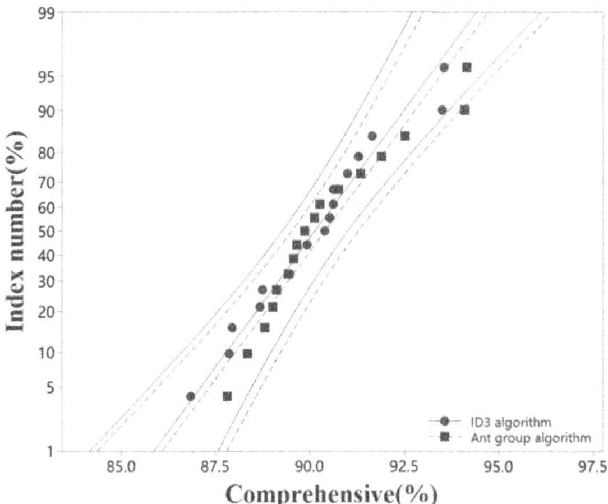

Fig. 2. Self-learning research of different algorithms

Figure 2 shows that the ID3 algorithm has more self-learning research but a lower error rate than the ant colony algorithm; this suggests that the ID3 algorithm's self-learning research is relatively stable, in contrast to the ant colony algorithm's self-learning research, which is uneven. Presented in Table 3 is the mean self-learning research method for the aforementioned three algorithms.

Table 3. Comparison of the accuracy of self-directed learning studies of different methods

Algorithm	Knowledge structure	Knowledge content	Voice skills	Writing
ID3 algorithm	77.67	79.61	75.73	81.55
Ant colony algorithm	73.79	81.55	80.58	81.55
P	81.55	72.82	79.61	77.67

According to Table 3, there are certain issues with the ant colony algorithm's accuracy in self-learning research. The method has undergone significant changes and has a high mistake rate. When compared to the ant colony method, the ID3 algorithm's self-learning research yields superior overall outcomes. Simultaneously, the ID3 algorithm's self-learning research has maintained an accuracy of above 90%. In order to provide further evidence that the ID3 algorithm is better. Various methodologies are used to assess the ID3 algorithm, as shown in Fig. 3, in order to further test the usefulness of the method provided in this research.

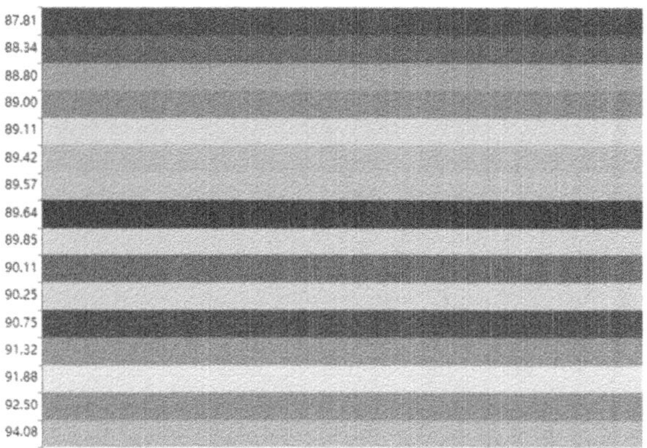

Fig. 3. Self-learning research on ID3 algorithm

As shown in Fig. 3, the ID3 algorithm's self-learning research outperforms the ant colony algorithm's. To establish an Internet information threshold, and discard any self-learning research scheme that falls short of the requirements.

4.4 Rationality of Self-Directed Learning Research

Figure 4 shows the self-learning research method that incorporates the ant colony algorithm to validate the ID3 algorithm.

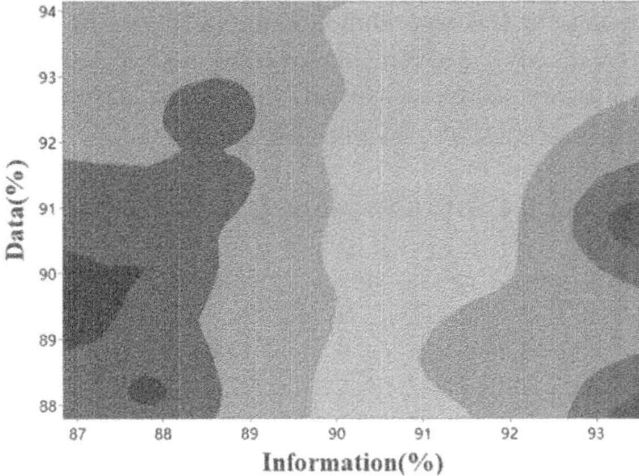

Fig. 4. Self-learning performance distribution of different algorithms under varying information and data completeness

Figure 4 shows that compared to the ant colony algorithm, the ID3 algorithm's self-learning research is more rational, and that further improvements to the ID3 algorithm may further raise the rationality of self-learning research. By using the ID3 algorithm, a decentralized platform for data storage and administration may be created, guaranteeing the safe recording and preservation of findings. An identification may be generated for each one using the ID3 technique, and the algorithm can save all the pertinent data and schemes.

4.5 Effectiveness of Self-Directed Learning Research

The process of testing students' pronunciation, words, expressions and use is shown in Fig. 5.

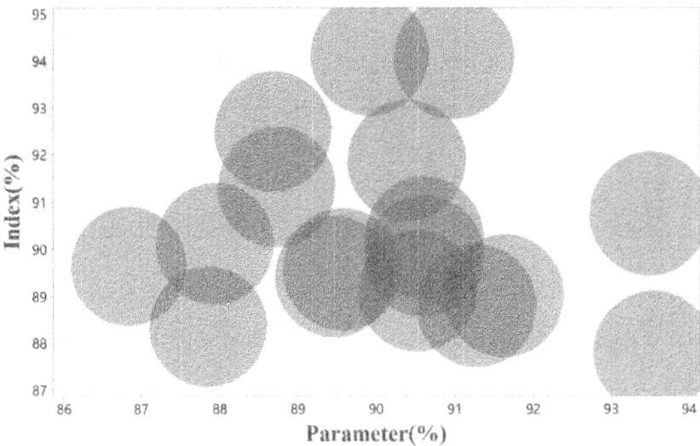

Fig. 5. Performance distribution of self-directed learning effectiveness across different parameter and index metrics

Figure 5 shows that the ID3 algorithm has more self-learning research but a lower error rate than the ant colony algorithm; this suggests to the ant colony algorithm's self-learning research, which is more inconsistent. Table 4 displays the mean self-learning research strategy of the aforementioned three algorithms.

Table 4. The effectiveness of self-directed learning studies

Algorithm	Word content	Application of knowledge points	Combined effect	Practical implementation
ID3 algorithm	75.73	75.73	72.82	73.79
Ant colony algorithm	82.52	82.52	74.76	81.55
P	79.61	82.52	75.73	81.55

From Table 4, we may deduce that the ant colony algorithm isn't very good at self-learning research, that it has changed a lot, and that it makes a lot of mistakes. When compared to the ant colony method, the ID3 algorithm's self-learning research yields superior overall outcomes. Simultaneously, the ID3 algorithm's self-learning research has maintained an accuracy of above 90%. In order to provide further evidence that the ID3 algorithm is better. The ID3 algorithm is often examined using several approaches to further confirm the efficacy of the suggested approach (Fig. 6).

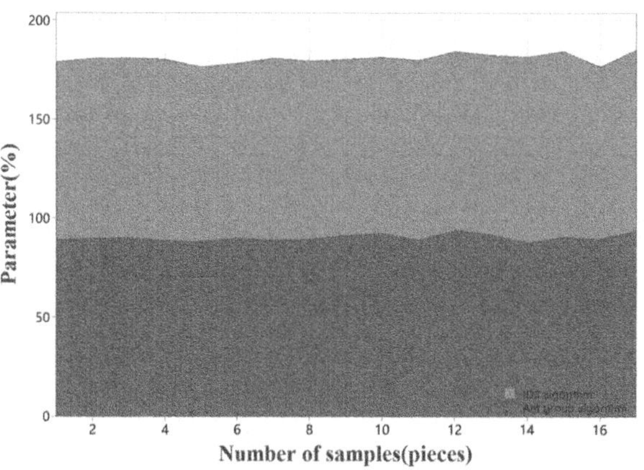

Fig. 6. Research on ID3 algorithm self-learning

The ID3 algorithm improves upon the ant colony algorithm in terms of self-learning research (as seen in Fig. 6), and this is due to the fact that it raises the adjustment coefficient of self-learning research, establishes the threshold for Internet information, and discards any self-learning research scheme that falls short of the demands.

5 Conclusion

The ID3 method and a combination of computer technologies are proposed in this work as solutions to the issue of suboptimal self-learning research. Concurrently, the reliability and correctness of self-learning studies are thoroughly examined, and the collection of Internet-based information is put together. The findings demonstrate that the ID3 algorithm is capable of performing generalized self-learning research on self-learning research and may enhance the precision of self-learning research. But the ID3 algorithm is so focused on self-learning research analysis that it picks signs for self-learning research irrationally.

References

1. Wang, L.: Research on college students' autonomous English learning based on the ID3 algorithm. Softwis Guid. (10), 3 (2010)
2. Yu, S.: Research on the predictive model of online teaching and learning effect based on ID3 algorithm. J. Gansu Univ. Technol. (Nat. Sci. Ed.) **035**(003), 110–114 (2021)
3. Zheng, Y.: Research on customer classification of business websites based on ID3 algorithm. Softwis Eng. **23**(3), 3 (2020)
4. Wang, Q., Liu, M.: Application of ID3 algorithm in the comprehensive quality evaluation of college students. Inf. Comput. (011), 034 (2022)
5. Yang, L.: Application of data mining technology in online learning. Doctoral dissertation, Guangxi Normal University (2014)
6. Bao, X., Zhong, L.: Research on fast classification method based on ID3 algorithm. Mod. Electron. Technol. **27**(7), 2 (2004)
7. Cao, A.: Research on data relevance of quality assurance system based on ID3 algorithm. Netw. Secur. Technol. Appl. (12), 3 (2018)
8. Yu, L.: Research on college students' autonomous English learning strategies based on learning style theory. J. Taiyuan Urban Vocat. Coll. (9), 2 (2014)
9. Wang, C.: Research on college students' autonomous English learning from a network perspective. High. Educ. Dev. (23), 2 (2013)
10. Zheng, P., Fu, X., Xu, J.: Data mining of English CET-4 conditional conclusion information based on ID3 algorithm. Inf. Commun. (002), 000 (2012)
11. Li, H., He, G.: Design of Deep Web Crawler Based on ID3 Classification Algorithm (2016)
12. Ma, X.: Research on College Students' Autonomous English Learning Based on Online Portfolio Website. Doctoral Dissertation, Hunan University (2019)

Construction of Chinese Graded Reading Resources Based on Network Corpus

Zhuang Bai(✉)

College of Foreign Languages, Bohai University, Jinzhou, Liaoning, China
baizhuang1984@163.com

Abstract. In Chinese graded reading, reading resource creation is crucial; yet, there is an issue with incorrect construction. The conventional rating assessment method cannot address the issue of resource development in Chinese graded reading, and the impact is not adequate. Hence, this research examines the creation of Chinese graded reading materials and suggests building them based on network corpus. First, the influencing elements are located using corpus language theory. Then, the indicators are split according to the needs of reading resource creation in order to decrease interference factors. Next, we use corpus language theory to build a network corpus reading resource creation scheme. Then, we investigate the outcomes of this scheme in detail. Based on the findings of the MATLAB simulations, the network corpus outperforms the conventional rating assessment system when it comes to the accuracy rate and time required to generate reading resources, according to certain evaluation criteria.

Keywords: Corpus language theory · Web corpus · Read resource building · Chinese · Assessments

1 Introduction

The creation of reading resources is a very significant aspect of Chinese graded reading [1], which may make the exact control of reading resource production quicker and faster [2]. Inadequate precision in the reading resource building plan [3, 4] is an issue that arises throughout the reading resource development process [5] and has an adverse effect on the reading resource construction [6]. According to certain researchers, the reading resource [7, 8] development plan can be better analyzed with the help of the network corpus, which in turn may give assistance for the reading resource [9] creation process. This research presents a network corpus as a means to optimize the technique for building reading resources and to test the model's efficacy [10]. The reading resource construction process in Table 1. Is shown in Fig. 1.

B. Brik and S. Nazir (Eds.): BigIoT-EDU 2024, LNICST 660, pp. 450–459, 2026.
https://doi.org/10.1007/978-3-032-18628-7_46

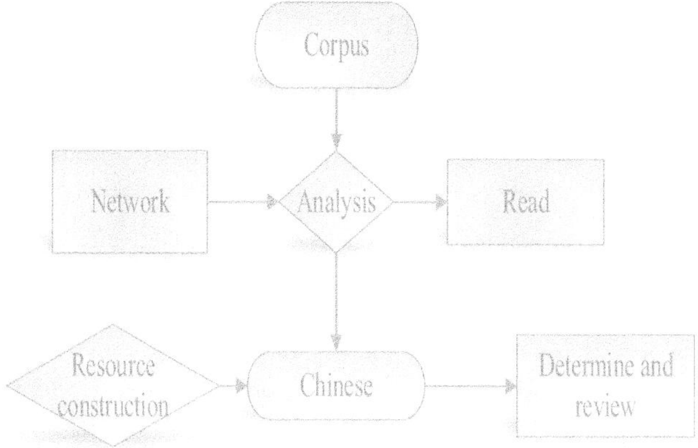

Fig. 1. Read the analysis process of resource building

2 Related Works

2.1 Construction of Chinese Graded Reading Resources

Utilizing computer technology, the network corpus optimizes the reading resource creation plan in accordance with the index parameters, it is discovered that the reading resource construction's unqualified value parameter is with the use of the network corpus, which integrates the benefits of computer technology, reading resource creation may be quantified, leading to more precise reading resource development. A thorough analysis of the reading resource construction is conducted, along with the reading resource construction scheme's threshold and index weight is set to ensure the accuracy of the network corpus. Reading resource construction is it is necessary to do a thorough evaluation of the reading resource building plan.

2.2 Network Corpus

In order to optimize the scheme of reading resource building, the network corpus makes adjustments to the Internet information parameters and uses a random optimization technique for reading resource development. Reading resource creation is divided into several tiers in the network corpus, and different techniques are randomly selected. In the iterative process, the reading resource construction tactics with various reading resource construction levels is optimized and analyzed. The best reading resource building is documented when the optimization study is finished, and several schemes' levels of reading resource construction are combined. he network corpus is now more accurate and reliable because to the adjustments made to the reading resource creation approach shown the network corpus's reading resource generation approach is superior in terms of speed, accuracy, and summation stability.

3 Read the Optimization Strategy of Resource Construction

3.1 Mathematical Description of the Web Corpus

The reading capacity creation plan is linked with the function to ultimately determine the feasibility of the reading resource development, which is calculated as shown in Eq. (1).

$$\lim_{x \to \infty} \left(y_i \cdot t_{ij}\right) = y_{ij} \geq \max(t_{ij} \div 2) \tag{1}$$

Language grading content as shown in Eq. (2).

$$totle(t_{ij}) = \partial\left(t_{ij}^2 \cdot t_{ij}\right) \succ mean\left(\sum t_{ij} + Ai\right) \tag{2}$$

The necessary reading materials for construction, the reading resource construction plan, the strategy for meeting the needs of resource development, and the evaluation mechanism for these plans are defined as shown in Eq. (3).

$$F(d_i) = \mathbb{R} \prod \sum t_i \cap \xi \cdot \sqrt{2} \rightarrow ointy_i \cdot 7 \tag{3}$$

3.2 Read the Selection of Resource Construction Plans

The role of building reading resources is, the weight coefficient is, Consequently, as can be shown from Eq. (4), unqualified reading resource development is inevitable when building reading resources.

$$im(t_i) = \int \ddot{x} + z_i \cdot \prod F(d_i) \frac{dy}{dx} - w_i \tag{4}$$

Equation (5) shows the outcome of constructing a reading resource function based on hypothesis I and II.

$$\underset{x \to \infty}{lim}\, g(t_i) + F(d_i) \leq \cap \max(t_{ij}) \tag{5}$$

Standardizing all data is essential for improving the efficacy of reading resource creation dependability; Eq. (6) shows the consequence.

$$g(t_i) + F(d_i) \leftrightarrow mean\left(\sum t_{ij} + 4ni\right) \tag{6}$$

3.3 Read the Analysis of the Resource Construction Plan

Prior to implementing the network corpus, a thorough evaluation of the reading resource building plan, a mapping of the requirements to the database, and the elimination of any unqualified plans must be completed. The findings may be used to suggest the anomaly assessment system is shown in Eq. (7).

$$No(t_i) = \frac{g(t_i) + F(d_i)}{mean\left(\sum t_{ij} + 4\right)} \cdot k \cdot \sqrt{b^2} \tag{7}$$

The plan must be put forth in order to avoid the need of integrating the plan is shown in Eq. (8).

$$hp(t_i) = \cap uo \cdot \left[\sum g(t_i) + F(d_i)\right] \tag{8}$$

Equation (9), which shows the calculation result, shows that if the reading resource construction follows a non-normal distribution, it will impact the reading resource development scheme and reduce the overall accuracy of the reading resource its construction.

$$ag(t_i) = ni \cdot \frac{\min[\sum g(t_i) + F(d_i)]}{\sum di} \tag{9}$$

According to the data collected from the reading resource building plans survey, these plans display a multi-dimensional distribution. It is considered a highly analytical research since the building of reading resources is not directed, suggesting that the building scheme of reading resources has substantial unpredictability. When building reading resources, if the function is random is, then the calculation of formula (9) can be expressed as formula (10).

$$Zp(t_i) = iint \frac{\min[\sum g(t_i) + F(d_i)]}{ti} + \int randon(t_i) \tag{10}$$

Computer technology enhances the default scheme, removes duplicate and irrelevant components, and makes adjustments to the reading resource construction process, ensuring that it meets normal requirements. This results in a strong dynamic correlation throughout the reading resource construction process.

4 Results and Discussion

4.1 Read the Resource Construction Briefing

This study aims to ease the process of building reading resources for use in complicated contexts.

Table 1. Read resource building requirements

Scope of application	Language classification	Language information	Read the material
Chinese language preparation	I	85.00	78.86
	II	81.97	78.45
Chinese language teacher	I	83.81	81.31
	II	83.34	78.19
Educational institutions	I	79.56	81.99
	II	79.10	80.11

The reading resource creation scheme of the online corpus is more in accordance with the real reading resource development needs, thanks to the rating assessment method. The network corpus outperforms the rating assessment method when it comes to the accuracy and rationale of reading resource development.

4.2 Read the Construction of Resources

Three types of information are included in the reading resource construction plan: structural, semi-structural, and non-structural. Following the network corpus pre-selection, we assessed the plan's viability and received the preliminary reading resource building plan. Table 2 shows the reading resource construction scheme, and picking reading resource construction with varying reading resource construction levels allows for more precise verification of the impact.

Table 2. Read the overall situation of the resource construction plan

Category	Pronounce	Word formation	Comprehensive
Chinese language preparation	85.32	85.90	83.95
Chinese language teacher	86.36	82.51	84.29
Educational institutions	84.16	84.92	83.68

4.3 Read Resource Construction and Stability

To check the correctness of the network corpus, the reading resource building scheme is integrated with the grade assessment system, and the reading resource construction scheme is presented in Fig. 2.

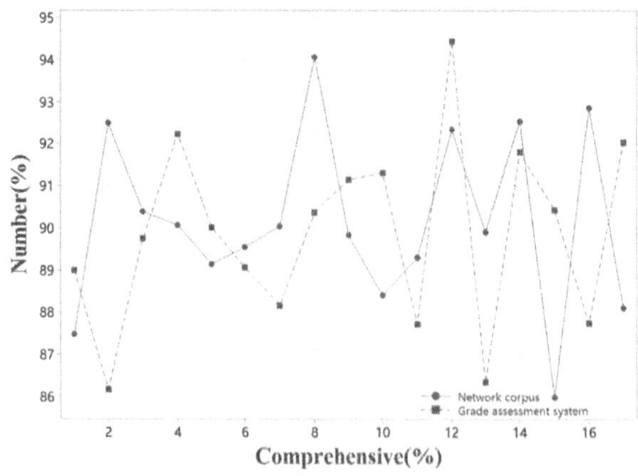

Fig. 2. Construction of reading resources for different algorithms

Figure 2 shows that the online corpus has more reading resources than the graded evaluation system, but with a lower error rate. This suggests that the online corpus's reading resources are more consistently built, in contrast to the graded evaluation system's uneven reading resources. The reading resource creation schemes of the three algorithms mentioned before are shown in Table 3.

Table 3. Comparison of the accuracy of reading resource construction by different methods

Algorithm	Overall effect	Comprehensive	Wield	Hierarchy
Web corpus	57.52	49.56	74.76	82.52
Rating system	41.59	61.95	75.73	74.76

Table 3 shows that there are problems with the rating assessment system's accuracy rate when it comes to building reading resources. There have been major changes in this area, and the mistake rate is rather high. When compared to the grade evaluation method, the overall outcome of using an online corpus to build reading materials is superior. Simultaneously, the network corpus reading resource creation is above 90%, and the accuracy has hardly budged. In order to provide further evidence that the network corpus is better. Figure 3 shows the results of several methodologies used to conduct a comprehensive study of the network corpus, which further demonstrates the efficacy of the suggested strategy.

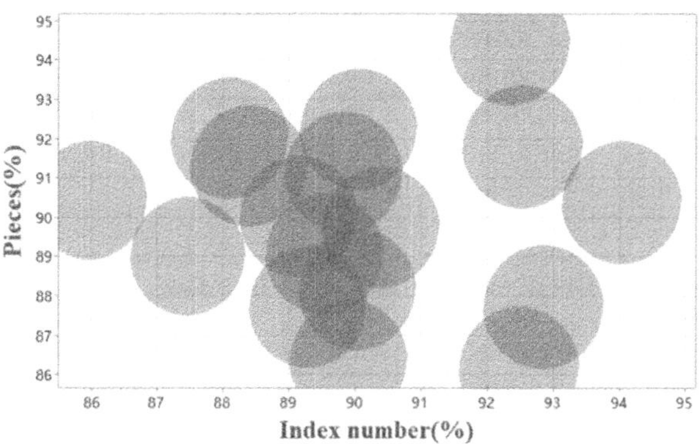

Fig. 3. Construction of reading resources for network corpus

Figure 3 shows that compared to the rating evaluation system, the network corpus produces far better reading resource construction. This is because the network corpus raises the adjustment coefficient, establishes the threshold for Internet information, and gets rid of the reading resource construction schemes that don't measure up.

4.4 Rationality of Reading Resource Construction

To verify the accuracy of the network corpus, the reading resource construction scheme is comprised with the grade evaluation system, and the reading resource construction scheme is shown in Fig. 4.

Fig. 4. Construction of reading resources for different algorithms

Figure 4 shows that comparing the online corpus to the grade assessment system improves the rationale of reading resource building, and that enhancing the development of reading resources utilizing network corpus further increases the rationality of reading resource construction. To guarantee the safe recording and preservation of findings, a web corpus might be introduced as a decentralized platform for data storage and administration. It is possible to assign a distinct identifier to each item and store all of the pertinent information and schemes in a web corpus.

4.5 Read About the Effectiveness of Resource Building

To evaluate the efficacy of the network corpus, the reading resource building scheme is integrated with the grade assessment system, and the reading resource construction scheme is illustrated in Fig. 5 presented.

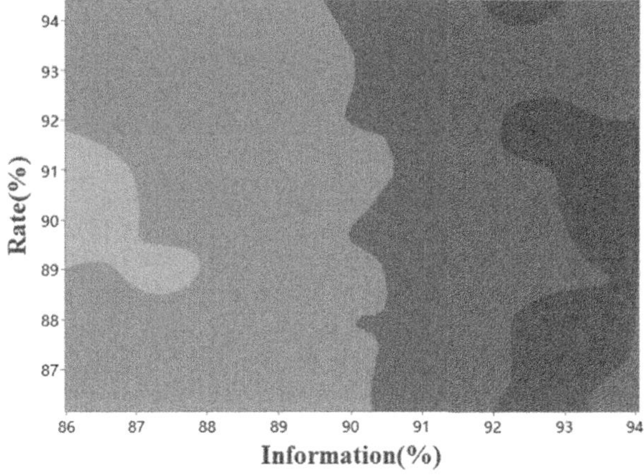

Fig. 5. Construction of reading resources with different algorithms

The online corpus has a higher structure for books to read than the graded evaluation system, but with a lower error rate (Fig. 5). This suggests that the network corpus's construction of reading resources is relatively stable, in contrast to the graded evaluation system's uneven construction. The average reading resource creation plan of the preceding three methods is provided in Table 4.

Table 4. Comparison of the effectiveness of reading resource construction by different methods

Algorithm	Stage effect	The end result	Learning effect	Satisfaction rate
Web corpus	60.18	81.55	79.61	75.73
Rating system	48.67	77.67	72.82	73.79

Table 4 shows that the rating evaluation system isn't perfect when it comes to reading resource construction accuracy; there have been significant changes in this area, and the error rate is high. In comparison, the online corpus has better overall results when it comes to reading resource construction accuracy, and it outperforms the grade evaluation system. Meanwhile, the network corpus has construction accuracy of reading resources greater than 90% and no significant changes in this area, further demonstrating its superiority. To further confirm the effectiveness of the proposed method, various methods were used to conduct a general analysis of the network corpus, as shown in Fig. 6.

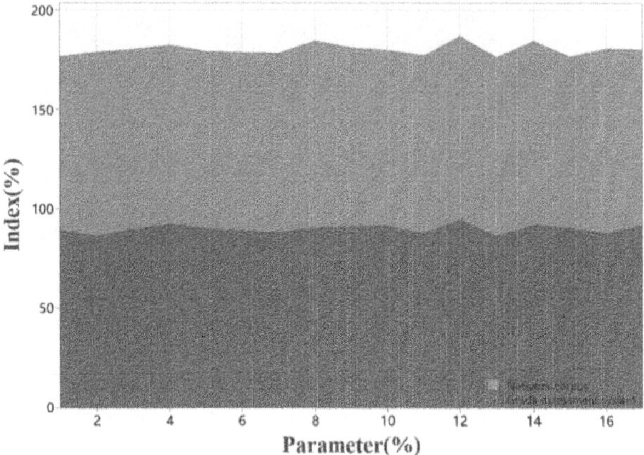

Fig. 6. Construction of network corpus reading resources

The construction of books in the network the is much superior to the rating evaluation system, as evidenced by Fig. 6. This is due to the fact that the network corpus increases the adjustment coefficient of reading resource construction and establishes the te reading resource construction.

5 Conclusion

Aiming at the issue that the creation of reading resources is not optimal, this research presents a network corpus and uses computer technology to optimize the development of reading resources. Concurrently, an online database is built, and the precision and dependability of reading resource construction are examined thoroughly. According to the findings, using a network corpus to build reading resources may increase their accuracy and make them more useful in general. Unfortunately, the network corpus approach places an excessive emphasis on reading resource building analysis, leading to illogical indicator selection for reading resource creation.

Acknowledgements. This work was financially supported by youth project of international Chinese education research project in 2021 (21YH83D): Research on the construction of Chinese-French bilingual teaching materials for Confucius institutes in Burundi under the background of 'the Belt an Road Initiative'.

References

1. Lu, W.: Construction of Chinese graded reading resources based on web corpora. World Chin. Lang. Teach. Assoc. (2010)
2. Guo, Y., Wang, J.: Research on dynamic grammar learning based on web corpus resources: taking "data-driven learning" as an example. China Sci. Technol Inform. **12**, 1 (2012)
3. Yang, J., Yang, J.: Construction concept of Chinese culture teaching resources based on corpora and the internet. Digit. Chin. Teach. (2012)

4. Liu, M., Jiang, Y., Li, Y., Li, H.: Research and application of Chinese readability formula based on primary Chinese textbooks. In: Abstracts of the 21st National Conference on Psychology (2018)
5. Wu, X., Du, Z.: Construction method of question-answering corpus based on neural network semantic analysis. CN108345640A (2018)
6. Li, Z.: Application of web-based corpora in foreign language teaching. China Sci. Technol. Inform. **4**, 2 (2011)
7. Gong, P.: An empirical study on college English pronunciation teaching based on web accent corpus. In: International Conference on Education & Educational Research (2013)
8. Chen, Z., Li, L.: Exploration of interpreting teaching strategies based on web and corpora. Foreign Lang. Electron. Teach. **1**, 5 (2009)
9. Li, L.: Research on the construction and sharing of high-quality teaching resources for ideological and political courses based on corpora and technologies. Res. Ideol. Polit. Courses **000** (003), 94–98 (2020)
10. Lin, J., Zhao, C., Ruichun, H., Wu, F., Wang, Z.: Development of Singapore Chinese teaching resource platform based on corpora. Chin. J. (2015)

Art Teaching Quality Evaluation System Based on Convolution Neural Network

Hashentuliguer Ha(✉) and Wu Yingga

Alxa Zuoqi Mongolian Experimental Primary School, The National University of Mongolia, Ulan Bator, Mongolia
ZM94781877@163.com

Abstract. In art education, the quality assessment system is crucial; nevertheless, the system's accuracy is an issue. The ineffectiveness and inadequacy of traditional mechanical learning methods make them unsuitable for use in art education. As a result, this study describes and evaluates a method for assessing the quality of art instruction that makes use of convolutional neural networks. As a first step in reducing interference elements in the quality assessment system, the indicators are split according to the needs of the system, and the influencing variables are located using neural theory. Then, using neuron theory as a basis, we construct the convolution neural network quality assessment system scheme and conduct a thorough analysis of the system's output. According to the findings of the MATLAB simulations, conventional machine learning is beaten out by convolution neural networks when it comes to the accuracy and speed of the quality assessment system's influencing elements under specific evaluation criteria.

Keywords: Neuron theory · Convolution neural networks · Quality evaluation system · Art · Teaching · System

1 Introduction

An important aspect of art education is the quality assessment system, which facilitates more rapid and exact control over the system [1]. Problems with accuracy [2] and the quality evaluation system scheme [3–5] arise throughout the process of the quality evaluation system, which has detrimental impacts on the quality evaluation system [6]. Using a convolutional neural network to examine the quality assessment system may help researchers better understand the system's architecture and identify areas for improvement, according to some researchers [7, 8]. Therefore, in the process of art painting, it is necessary to combine the space and color of art and painting. Quantify the indicators, transform them into sustainable analysis indicators, and substitute them into the formula, and finally output the best matching results, so as to provide corresponding support for painting and assist painting to complete its creation. The specific data collection process is shown in Fig. 1.

Through the data analysis in Fig. 1, it will be found that in the process of artistic creation and painting analysis, data collection and quantification of color indicators have

B. Brik and S. Nazir (Eds.): BigIoT-EDU 2024, LNICST 660, pp. 460–469, 2026.
https://doi.org/10.1007/978-3-032-18628-7_47

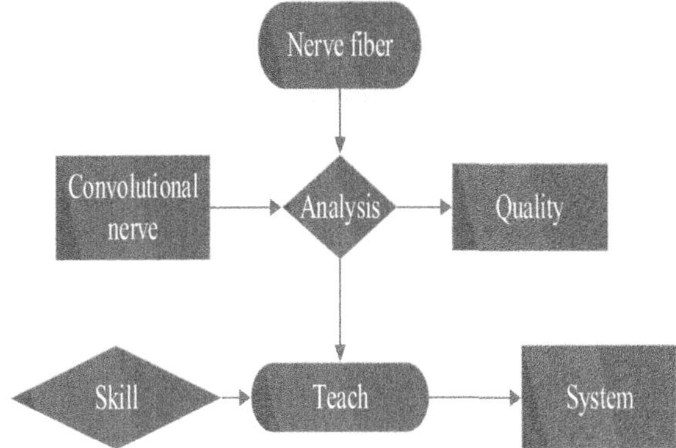

Fig. 1. The analytical process of the quality evaluation system

become the key to painting. Therefore, it is necessary to make in-depth judgment and analysis, and form effective analysis results to provide support for later creation.

2 Related Works

2.1 Art Teaching Quality Evaluation System

By combining the benefits of computer technology with quality assessment systems for quantification, convolutional neural networks may enhance the accuracy of quality evaluation systems. What if I were to do What is needed for the quality assessment procedure is, the quality evaluation system scheme is, meeting the requirements In order to optimize the quality assessment system's scheme, the convolutional neural network uses a random optimization technique and tweaks the parameters pertaining to online information [9]. The quality rating system is divided into several levels by the convolution neural network, which then randomly picks alternative methods. Various quality assessment system levels' techniques are improved and studied in the iterative process. Following the completion of the optimization study, many schemes' quality assessment system levels are combined, and the most effective system is documented [10, 11].

2.2 Convolution Neural Network

In agreement with the actual facts, the survey of the quality assessment system scheme reveals that the scheme exhibits a multi-dimensional distribution. High analytical study status is due to the quality assessment system's lack of directionality, which suggests a scheme with great unpredictability. If the quality assessment system's random function is Among these, the quality evaluation system satisfies typical standards; primarily, it is enhanced by computer technology, which modifies the system, eliminates unnecessary and redundant schemes, and augments the default scheme, resulting in a robust dynamic correlation throughout the entire system.

3 Optimization Strategy of Quality Evaluation System

3.1 Mathematical Description of Convolution Neural Networks

Convolutional neural networks is to use computer technology to improve the quality assessment system scheme, identify the unqualified value parameters in the system based on the different index parameters, and integrate the system's evaluation scheme is the procedure for determining the quality assessment system's practicability, computed is shown in formula (1).

$$\lim_{x \to \infty} \left(y_i \cdot t_{ij} \right) = y_{ij} \geq \max(t_{ij} \div 2) \tag{1}$$

$\lim_{x \to \infty} \left(y_i \cdot t_{ij} \right) = y_{ij}$ is the overall summary of colors and the overall structure require systematization, so as to show a more comprehensive. The painting results and effects are shown in Formula 2.

$$\max(t_{ij}) = \partial \left(t_{ij}^2 + 2 \cdot t_{ij} \right) \succ \frac{1}{2} \Phi \left(\sum t_{ij} + 4 \right) M \tag{2}$$

$\max(t_{ij})$ is the quality assessment plan being together with the judgment function of the quality assessment system and its scheme is as shown in Eq. (3).

$$F(d_i) = \mathbb{R}\sqrt{b^2 - 4ac} \sum t_i \cap \xi \cdot \sqrt{2} \to ointy_i \cdot 7 \tag{3}$$

$mathbbR\sqrt{b^2 - 4ac}$ is the comprehensive indicators and contents in the process of art painting, and the elements of art painting are reasonably analyzed.

3.2 Comparative Analysis of Various Artistic Points and Creative Points in the Process of Painting

Art painting. In the process, color, structure, space and other contents should be selected, so its integrity should be judged. While the display of color and space. Quantitative analysis can be carried out, and its spatial structure design can be carried out, including hollow design and distance design. In the process of education, the color effect of art is analyzed, and the specific results are shown in Formula 4.

$$L(t_i) = z_i \prod l(d_i) \frac{dy}{dx} - w_i \tag{4}$$

$L(t_i)$ is the color elements, color structures and lines in the process of art teaching evaluation are all divided into the key points in the evaluation. Indicators. The above indicators will all appear. Extreme maxima, so do a max analysis on it. The analysis results of the maximum values of colors, lines, etc. are shown in Formula 5.

$$\lim_{x \to \infty} g(t_i) + \lim_{x \to \infty} F(d_i) \leq \cap \max(t_{ij}) \tag{5}$$

$\lim_{x \to \infty} g(t_i)$ is the maximum value and $\max(t_{ij})$ is other indicators in Formula 5 are all carried out. A more comprehensive analysis, so it is necessary to summarize and form it as a whole. Indicator analysis. The judgment result is shown in Eq. 6.

$$g(t_i) + F(d_i) \leftrightarrow mean\left(\sum t_{ij} + 4\right) \tag{6}$$

$g(t_i) + F(d_i)$ is a comprehensive artistic display in fine art painting, with spatial and structural characteristics.

3.3 Analysis of the Quality Evaluation System Scheme

The findings may be used to suggest the anomaly assessment system, as shown in Eq. (7).

$$No(t_i) = \frac{g(t_i) + F(d_i)}{mean(\sum t_{ij} + 4)} \tag{7}$$

$No(t_i)$ is arts, paintings and comprehensive structural display features are a holistic expression, the result is shown in Eq. (8).

$$h(t_i) = \cap\left[\sum g(t_i) * F(d_i)\right] \tag{8}$$

$h(t_i)$ is to make sure the convolution neural network is accurate, the quality assessment system measures its performance and determines its threshold and index weight. An exact analysis is required of the quality assessment system because it is a solution to a system test. Given that the method for evaluating quality is When using a manorial distribution, the scheme of its quality assessment system will be impacted, which will lead to a decrease in the general accuracy of the system and the results of the calculations is shown in Eq. (9).

$$aur(t_i) = \mathrm{k}\frac{\min[\sum g(t_i) + F(d_i)]}{\sum g(t_i) + F(d_i)} \tag{9}$$

$\mathrm{aur}(\mathrm{t_i})$ as the final presentation of art painting, it should have visual effects. This index has a significant hint for painting art.

4 Results and Discussion

4.1 Introduction to the Quality Evaluation System

Table 1 shows the unique quality evaluation system scheme, which is designed to aid the quality evaluation system; the research aim is the quality evaluation system in difficult circumstances; the test period is 12 h; and there are 12 pathways.

The convolutional neural network quality assessment system plan, which incorporates machine learning, is more in line with the needs of the real quality evaluation system. Compared to machine learning, convolution neural networks provide a more reasonable and accurate quality rating approach. The convolution neural network now has improved accuracy and reliability thanks to the revised quality assessment system scheme shown in Fig. 2. This means that the convolution neural network's quality assessment system method is superior in terms of speed, accuracy, and summing stability.

Table 1. Quality evaluation system requirements

In the process of transformation, the way elements are transformed	The type of the element	Completeness of conversation data	Requirements for painting data output
Educational institutions	Basic indicators such as color	85.00	78.86
	Three-dimensional indicators such as spatial structure	81.97	78.45
Art examination	Basic indicators such as color	83.81	81.31
	Three-dimensional indicators such as spatial structure	83.34	78.19
Education policy	Basic indicators such as color	79.56	81.99
	Three-dimensional indicators such as spatial structure	79.10	80.11

4.2 Quality Evaluation System Situation

Information that is not structural nor semi-structural, as well as information that is structural, make up the quality assessment system's scheme. Following the ore-selection of the convolution neural network, the feasibility of the quality evaluation system scheme is examined, and the preliminary quality assessment system scheme is established. You may choose from a variety of quality assessment system levels to more precisely check the system's impact; Table 2 shows the strategy for these levels.

Table 2. In the process of painting artistic creation, the integration of its elements and key points is the result.

Category	Color structure	Spatial layout	Conversation content
Educational institutions	85.32	85.90	83.95
Art examination	86.36	82.51	84.29
Education policy	84.16	84.92	83.68

4.3 Quality Evaluation System and Stability

Figure 2 shows the quality assessment system scheme that the convolution neural network uses to ensure its correctness. This scheme is made of the quality evaluation system scheme of machine learning.

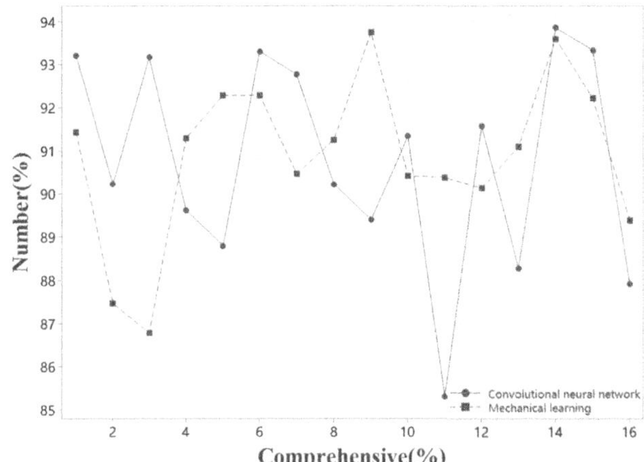

Fig. 2. Quality evaluation system for different algorithms

In Fig. 2, we can observe that the convolution neural network's quality evaluation system is more consistent and stable than the mechanical learning system, despite having a lower error rate. This suggests that the convolution neural network's evaluation system is superior overall. Presented in Table 3 is the average quality assessment system scheme for the aforementioned three methods.

Table 3. Determination of the final output result of the dialogue.

Algorithm	Space display	Color analysis	Connotation presentation	Artistic creation effect
Convolution neural networks	85.33	85.15	82.88	84.95
Machine learning	85.20	83.41	86.01	85.75

From Table 3, we can deduce that machine learning falls short when it comes to the quality assessment system's accuracy; furthermore, that the system has undergone significant changes, and the error rate is rather high. Convolution neural networks outperform machine learning in terms of the quality assessment method used for overall outcomes. Also, the convolution neural network's accuracy has remained relatively unchanged, and its quality assessment system is over 90%. In order to provide further evidence that convolution neural networks are better. Figure 3 shows the results of several approaches used for general convolutional neural network analysis, which helps to further confirm the efficacy of the suggested strategy.

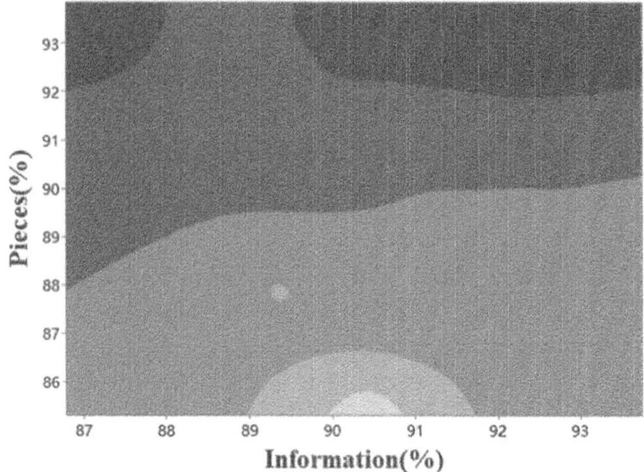

Fig. 3. Quality evaluation system for convolution neural networks

It can be analyzed from Fig. 3 that in the process of creation. A feature point appears on the left side, indicating that the painting process is highly innovative. With the support of various data such as element structure and spatial display, small-scale artistic creation can be carried out to reflect its creative connotation and characteristics.

4.4 The Rationality of the Quality Evaluation System

See Fig. 4 for a visual representation of the quality assessment system scheme that incorporates machine learning to confirm the convolution neural network's correctness.

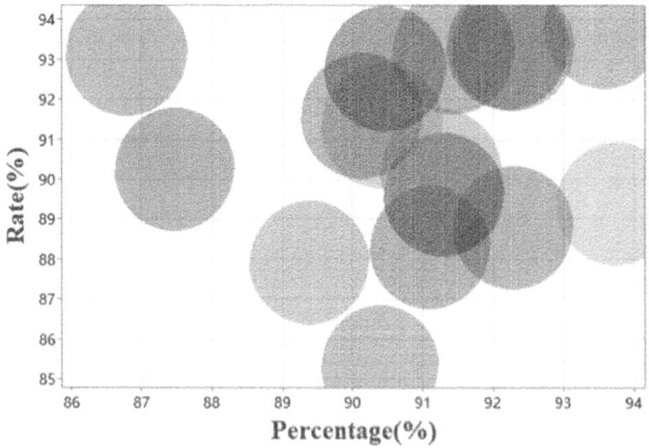

Fig. 4. Quality evaluation system for different algorithms

Figure 4 shows that compared to machine learning, convolution neural networks provide a more reasonable quality evaluation system, and that this system can be further improved by incorporating more convolutional neural network logic. With the help of convolution neural networks, a decentralized platform for data storage and administration may be set up, guaranteeing the safe recording and storage of findings. It is possible to assign a distinct identity to each using a convolution neural network, which can also store all of the pertinent information and plans.

4.5 Quality Measurement of the Effectiveness of the System

Figure 5 shows the quality evaluation system scheme that is used to test the convolution neural network's efficacy. This scheme is built of the quality evaluation system scheme of machine learning.

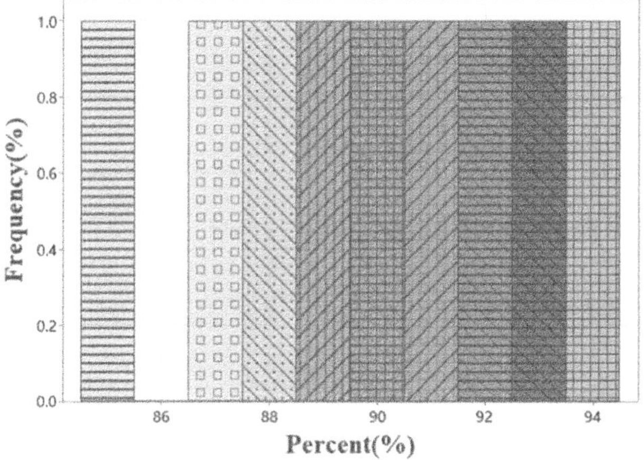

Fig. 5. Quality evaluation system for different algorithms

Figure 5 shows that compared to mechanical learning, convolution neural networks have a higher quality evaluation system with a lower error rate. This suggests that convolution neural networks have a more stable quality evaluation system overall, in contrast to mechanical learning, which has an uneven one. In Table 4, you can see the average quality assessment system scheme for all three of these methods.

Table 4. Connotation and external display in the process of artistic creation.

Algorithm	Showcase the vividness of things	The rationality of color matching	The location of the middle display	Overall feedback on artistic creation
Convolution neural networks	82.21	85.92	84.59	82.85
Machine learning	83.73	84.23	84.41	83.55

Table 4 shows that mechanical learning isn't 100% accurate when it comes to quality assessment systems; furthermore, these systems have undergone significant changes, and the mistake rate is rather large. Convolution neural networks outperform machine learning in terms of the quality assessment method used for overall outcomes. Also, the convolution neural network's accuracy has remained relatively unchanged, and its quality assessment system is over 90%. In order to provide further evidence that convolution neural networks are better. Figure 6 shows the results of several methodologies used to conduct general analyses of convolution neural networks, which further proves the efficacy of the suggested approach.

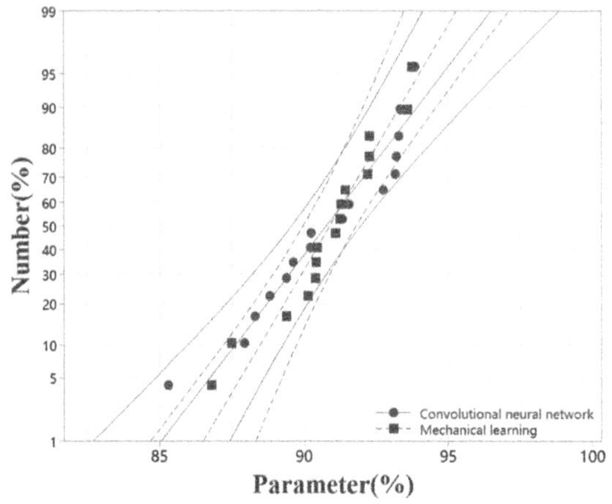

Fig. 6. Convolution neural network quality evaluation system

Figure 6 shows that compared to mechanical learning, the convolution neural network's quality evaluation system is far superior. This is because, among other things, it raises the quality evaluation system's adjustment coefficient and uses Internet information to eliminate schemes that don't meet the requirements.

5 Conclusion

In response to the fact that the current method for evaluating quality is far from perfect, the authors of this study suggest using a convolution neural network to streamline the review process. Concurrently, the Internet data collecting is built, and the quality assessment system's correctness and dependability are examined thoroughly. The findings demonstrate that the quality evaluation system may be implemented as a generic quality evaluation system and that the convolution neural network can enhance its accuracy. Nevertheless, the convolution neural network approach places an excessive emphasis on quality assessment system analysis, leading to illogical indicator selection.

Acknowledgements. Research on the practice of deep integration of information technology and discipline teaching to improve the efficiency of classroom teaching efficiency, Project approval number: ALSZQJYGHKT.

References

1. Jiang, Y., Lu, S., Liming, H.: Music art teaching quality evaluation system based on convolution neural network. J. Longyan Univ. **39**(5), 6 (2021)
2. Wu, X.: Singing voice recognition based on convolution neural network. (Doctoral dissertation, Southwest University of Science and Technology)
3. Liu, L., Sun, M.: Clothing aesthetic quality evaluation system based on deep convolution neural network. CN202111512629.0 (2022)
4. Liu, L., Sun, M.: Aesthetic quality evaluation system for clothing based on deep convolution neural network
5. Shao, X., He, R.: Music recommendation system and recommendation method based on convolution neural network. CN108595550A (2018)
6. Li Hui, W., Qiang, L.Z., Wendi, Z., Yuming, L.: Video conference content and quality detection system based on convolution neural network. Fujian Comput. **34**(5), 3 (2018)
7. He, R.: Music recommendation system based on convolution neural network. (Doctoral dissertation, Nanjing University of Posts and Telecommunications) (2020)
8. Wang, H., Xu, J., Zhu, Y., Zhang, C., Liu, Z., Bai, L., et al.: A method and system for detecting floating filaments in chemical fiber based on convolution neural network
9. Wei, W., Luo, H., Li, T., Chen, L., Lü, T.: Concrete quality detection method and system based on image and convolution neural network. CN111724358A (2020)
10. Zha, M., Zhang, X.: Product quality classification system based on convolution neural network. CN111582395A (2020)
11. Luo, J., Hu, J., Ren, J., Lan, L., Zhou, X., Yang, H.: Auxiliary diagnosis system for vocal cord leukoplakia based on convolution neural network model. CN112734749A (2021)

Research on the Application of Smart Education Platform in Classroom Teaching

Xianye Qi(✉) and Lina Jin

Lanzhou Resources and Environment Voc-Tech College, Lanzhou City, Gansu Province, China
{qxy210194,jinln}@lzre.edu.cn

Abstract. The education sector is undergoing a profound transformation. The education platform, as an important carrier of this transformation, has been widely applied on a global scale. These platforms make use of the Internet, big data, artificial intelligence and other advanced technologies to provide rich resources, tools and communication channels for the teaching process, break the space-time constraints of traditional education, and make knowledge acquisition and sharing more convenient. According to statistics, as of 2020, the global online education market has exceeded 200 billion US dollars, and is expected to reach 350 billion US dollars by 2025, demonstrating strong growth momentum. The results show that the smart education platform can have an impact on classroom education and classroom education level, with an improvement rate of more than 20%, and optimize the original teaching resources, with an optimization rate of more than 35%. Therefore, the smart platform can significantly optimize classroom education.

Keywords: Construction theory · Artificial intelligence technology · Classroom teaching · Applied research · Wisdom · Education platform

1 Introduction

Classroom teaching application research is a very important part of the intelligent education [1] platform, which can make the precise [2] control of classroom teaching application [3] research. Educational platforms can integrate resources [4], The effect has a significant impact [5] on application research scheme, which brings certain [6] negative effects to classroom teaching application research. Some scholars [7] claim Classroom education platform can integrate the application of listening, speaking, reading and writing resources and theoretical practice. The integration of [8] applied research analysis can effectively analyze classroom teaching application research programs, realize comprehensive analysis and optimization of classroom [9]. The educational platform integrates and analyzes information and data as a whole [10]. When the educational resources of the platform are integrated and the data is comprehensively utilized is shown in Fig. 1.

In addition, regular online testing and adaptive evaluation can comprehensively and accurately reflect students' learning outcomes, providing strong basis for teaching improvement.

B. Brik and S. Nazir (Eds.): BigIoT-EDU 2024, LNICST 660, pp. 470–479, 2026.
https://doi.org/10.1007/978-3-032-18628-7_48

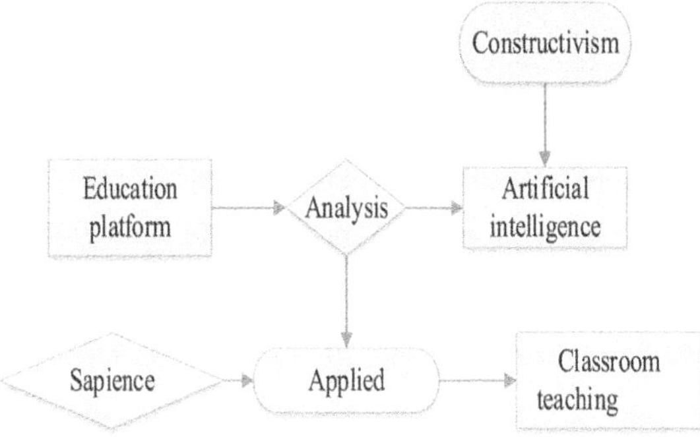

Fig. 1. The analytical process of applied research in classroom teaching

2 Related Works

2.1 Smart Platform

The role of smart education platforms in improving teaching quality is multifaceted. Through personalized learning, interactive teaching, and scientific evaluation, they create, interesting, and targeted teachers. With the continuous development of technology, these platforms will continue to be optimized, bringing greater changes to future education. The intelligent education platform for technical bottlenecks and security issues is facing a series of technical challenges while improving teaching efficiency and quality.

2.2 Teaching Content

Application of smart education platforms in classroom teaching, as well as their impact on teaching quality and student learning outcomes. By analyzing the characteristics and functions of educational platforms, we can understand how they promote personalized learning, enhance interaction between teachers and students, and provide data support for teaching decisions. In addition, this study will also focus on the challenges that educational platforms may encounter during implementation, such as technological adaptability, resource quality, and user privacy protection, and propose corresponding solutions. Teachers can view students' learning activities in real-time, intervene and guide them in a timely manner, and even design multi-modal teaching activities, such as simulation experiments, online discussions, project collaborations, etc., making the learning process more vivid and interesting.

3 Research Content and Methodology

3.1 Mathematical Description of Artificial Intelligence Technology

Meanwhile, more and more schools and educational institutions are exploring how to integrate educational platforms into daily teaching to improve teaching efficiency and learning experience as shown in formula (1).

$$\lim_{x \to \infty} \left(y_i \cdot t_{ij}\right) = y_{ij} \geq \max(t_{ij} \div 2) \tag{1}$$

Comprehensive analysis of educational resources and data. is shown in Eq. (2).

$$\max(t_{ij}) = \partial\left(t_{ij}^2 + 2 \cdot t_{ij}\right) \succ mean\left(\sum t_{ij} + 4\right)mathfrakM \tag{2}$$

The integration of educational resources, theoretical practice of data analysis and virtual simulation are the main aspects of educational optimization of military education platforms. y_i as shown in Eq. (3).

$$F(d_i) = mathbbR \prod \sum t_i \cap \xi \cdot \sqrt{2} \to ointy_i \cdot 7 \tag{3}$$

3.2 Selection of Applied Research Programs for Classroom Teaching

The smart education platform can build customized learning paths for each student through big data analysis and artificial intelligence technology as shown in Eq. (4).

$$g(t_i) = \ddot{x} \cdot z_i \prod F(d_i)\frac{dy}{dx} - w_i \tag{4}$$

These platforms can intelligently recommend suitable learning resources, such as video tutorials, online reading materials, interactive exercises, etc., based on multi-dimensional data such as student learning progress, understanding ability, and interest preferences is shown in Eq. (5).

$$\lim_{x \to \infty} g(t_i) + F(d_i) \le \cap \max(t_{ij}) \tag{5}$$

After the education platform is integrated, it is necessary to integrate the corresponding resources and contents, and the process of integration and comprehensive analysis. is shown in Eq. (6).

$$g(t_i) + F(d_i) \leftrightarrow mean\left(\sum t_{ij} + 4\right) \tag{6}$$

3.3 Analysis of Applied Research Programs in Classroom Teaching

This reduces ineffective and repetitive learning time. In addition, teachers can also obtain student learning data through the platform, providing more accurate guidance for individual tutoring and collective teaching. Shown in Eq. (7).

$$No(t_i) = \frac{g(t_i) + F(d_i)}{mean\left(\sum t_{ij} + 4\right)}\sqrt{b^2 - 4ac} \tag{7}$$

Innovation of Interactive Teaching Model Traditional classroom teaching models often center around teachers, while smart education platforms promote the transformation of teaching models, placing students in a more proactive position. Shown in Eq. (8).

$$Zh(t_i) = \cap\left[\sum g(t_i) + F(d_i)\right] \tag{8}$$

The online discussion area, collaboration tools, and real-time feedback system on the platform encourage is shown in Eq. (9).

$$accur(t_i) = \frac{\min[\sum g(t_i) + F(d_i)]}{\sum g(t_i) \widetilde{+} F(d_i)} \Gamma \tag{9}$$

Comprehensive integration and holistic analysis of data as Eq. (10).

$$accur(t_i) = \frac{\min[\sum g(t_i) + F(d_i)]}{\sum g(t_i) \widetilde{+} F(d_i)} \mathrm{B} \tag{10}$$

Evaluation and Feedback of Teaching Effectiveness: The smart education platform provides data support for the evaluation of teaching effectiveness. By tracking students' learning behavior, the platform can generate detailed learning reports, including indicators such as completion, understanding, and engagement.

4 Results and Discussion

4.1 Introduction to Applied Research in Classroom Teaching

Based on the teaching in colleges and universities, this paper makes a holistic analysis, and the survey objects are 120. Through the analysis of the platform of Android system, the construction of the platform, the data collected for the structure platform of B/S, and the test time was twelve months for 36 G. The test content includes educational content, educational indicators and experimental results. is shown in Table 1.

Table 1. Applied research requirements for classroom instruction

Scope of application	The main forms of education	Station data collector	Built income data indicators
Basic education	General education	85.00	78.86
	Targeted educational content	81.97	78.45
Vocational training	General education	83.81	81.31
	Targeted educational content	83.34	78.19
Distance education	General education	79.56	81.99
	Targeted educational content	79.10	80.11

4.2 Applied Research in Classroom Teaching

Firstly, data processing capabilities are the foundation of smart education platforms, but a large amount of teaching data requires efficient storage, analysis, and processing, which puts high demands on the platform's computing power and algorithm optimization as shown in Table 2.

Table 2. The overall picture of the applied research programme in the classroom

Category	Random data	Reliability	Analysis rate
Basic education	3.6	4.68	3.56
Vocational training	3.6	3.9	4.45
Distance education	2.4	4.68	4.45

4.3 Applied Research and Stability in Classroom Teaching

Secondly, real-time interactive functionality is a core feature of smart education, but network latency and stability issues may affect the teaching process, especially in large-scale online courses (MOOCs), which requires the platform to have strong concurrency processing capabilities. In addition, information security issues cannot be ignored. The protection of personal information and learning data of students is a regulatory requirement that education platforms must comply with. Data leakage or misuse may lead to serious trust crises as shown in Fig. 2.

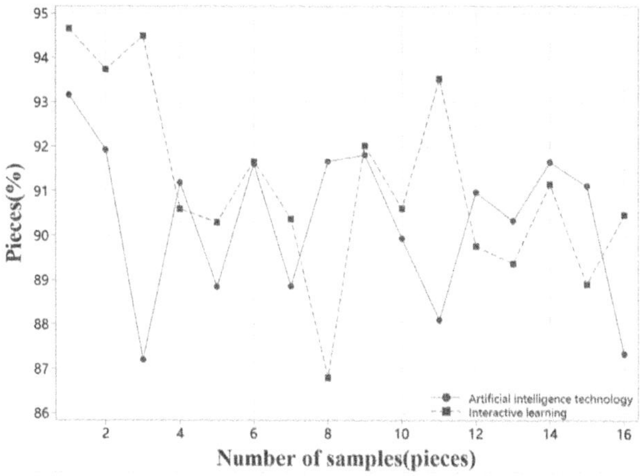

Fig. 2. The application of different algorithms in classroom teaching

The introduction of a smart education platform for teacher training and adaptability has put forward new demands for teachers' professional skills. Many teachers may not be familiar with new technologies and require specialized training to master the use of the platform is shown in Table 3.

Table 3. Comparison of the accuracy of applied research in classroom teaching

Algorithm	Theoretical education	Comprehensive education	Practical education	Relevance
Artificial intelligence technology	85.33	85.15	82.88	84.95
Interactive learning	85.20	83.41	86.01	85.75

At the same time, they need to adapt to the transition from traditional teaching models to digital teaching, and learn how to use platform resources to design and implement effective online courses. In addition, the role of teachers is also changing, shifting from being the transmitter of information to being the guide of learning and the manager of the learning process, which requires teachers to have higher educational technology and psychological knowledge, as in Fig. 3 shown.

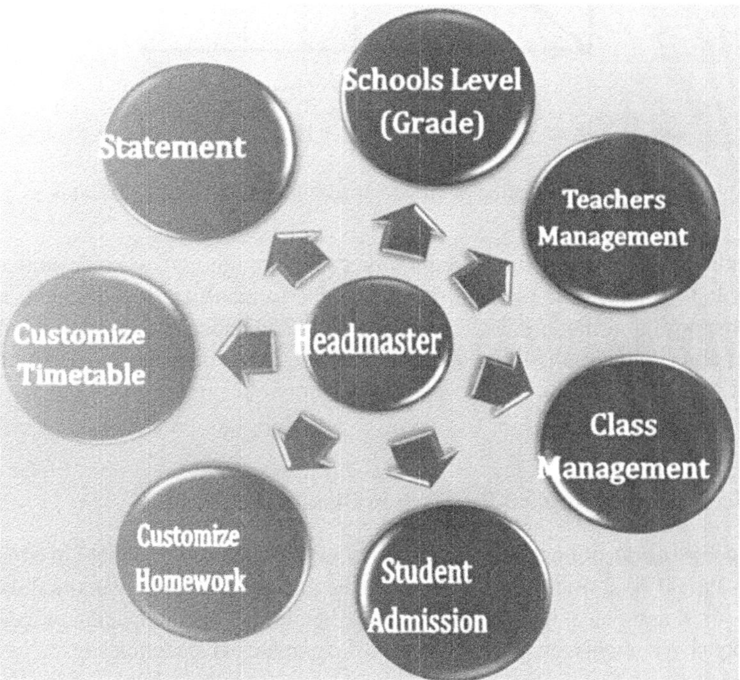

Fig. 3. The artificial intelligence technology in classroom teaching

As can be seen from Fig. 3, in the process of correlation analysis, it is necessary to find the main content and platform of data analysis and education, and use this as a framework to collect resources, build an association database of educational resources, and provide support for actual education and customer data.

4.4 Rationality of Applied Research in Classroom Teaching

When the learning and educational process is a gradual process, there are diversified changes between knowledge and needs. Therefore, the platform should be built according to the actual interest needs and knowledge. Specific build curve is shown in Fig. 4.

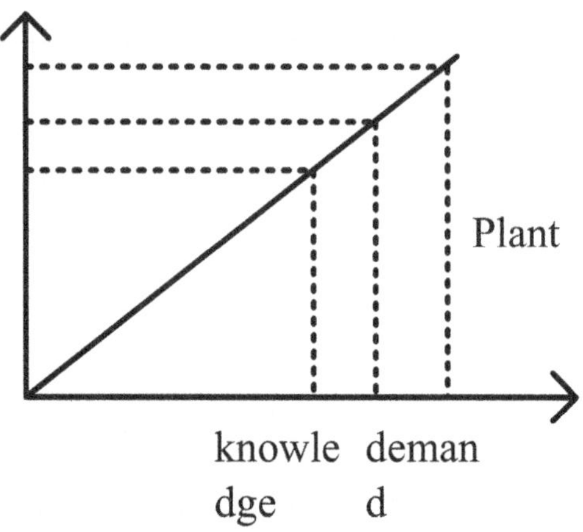

Fig. 4. The application of classroom teaching of different algorithms

In addition, the issue of the digital divide cannot be ignored, as some students may not be able to fully utilize platform resources due to insufficient equipment, network conditions, or digital literacy. Therefore, how to guide students to develop good online learning habits, improve their digital skills, and design platform interfaces and functions that attract and adapt to student needs are important issues in the development of smart education platforms.

4.5 Effectiveness of Applied Research in Classroom Teaching

In the process of educational platform analysis, a comprehensive database of educational platform should be formed. The contents in the database include diversified data such as video, files, and voice. Its content involves educational indicators, educational needs, comprehensive contents, etc. The display of the graphics is shown in Fig. 5.

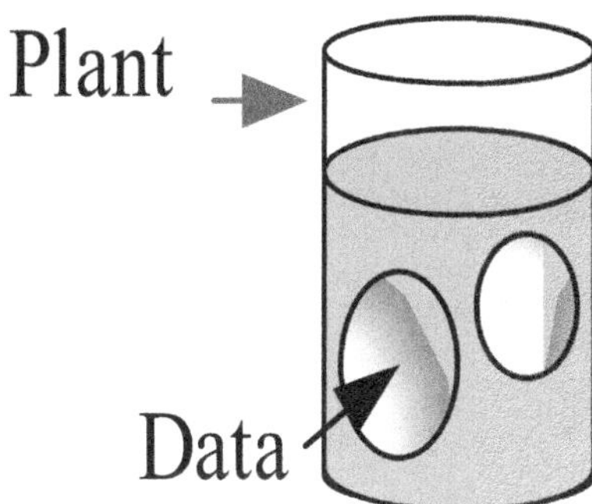

Fig. 5. Research on the application of classroom teaching of different algorithms

According to the analysis in the fog, the construction of educational platform should set a buffer area, expand the data based on the core data, and increase the compatibility of educational platform construction. Results of the overall construction of educational platform is shown in Table 4.

Table 4. Comparison of the effectiveness of applied research on classroom teaching of different methods

Algorithm	Comprehensive utilization of data platform	Utilization of development data	Build data applications	The association of data
Artificial intelligence technology	82.21	85.92	84.59	82.85
Interactive learning	83.73	84.23	84.41	83.55

Interdisciplinary integrated teaching: Explore how to use smart education platforms to break down disciplinary boundaries, promote interdisciplinary integrated teaching, and cultivate students' comprehensive abilities, as in Fig. 6 shown.

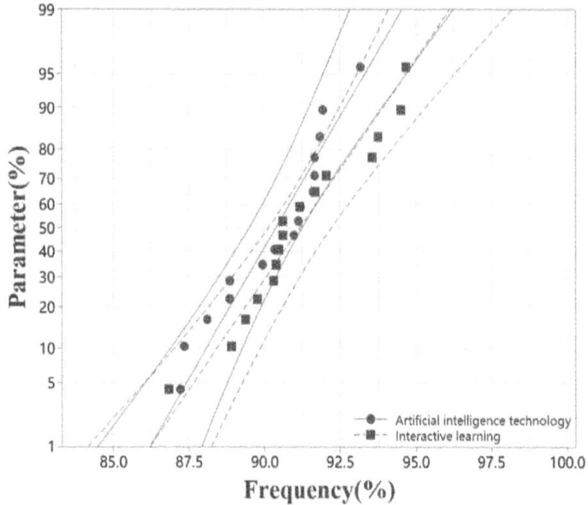

Fig. 6. Research on the application of artificial intelligence technology in classroom teaching

The transformation and training of teacher roles: Research how to support teachers to adapt to smart education platforms, provide professional development training, fully tap into the platform's potential, and improve teaching quality. Data security and privacy protection: Strengthen the platform's data security mechanism, protect student personal information, eliminate concerns from parents and teachers, and ensure the healthy development of smart education in a secure environment. Fairness and Accessibility: Ensure the accessibility of smart education platforms to all students, especially remote areas and vulnerable groups, narrow the digital divide, and promote educational equity.

5 Conclusion

This study delves into the application, revealing their important role in improving teaching quality, optimizing teaching processes, and addressing educational challenges. The smart education platform provides students with personalized learning paths by utilizing advanced data analysis and artificial intelligence technology, and making teaching more targeted and efficient. At the same time, the interactive function of the platform enhances communication between teachers and students, promotes student participation and learning motivation. In practical applications, smart education platforms not only provide rich teaching resources, making teaching adjustments more timely and accurate. In addition, through big data analysis, the platform can provide valuable insights for education managers to support the development and improvement of teaching strategies.

Acknowledgements. The 2023 Project of Gansu Province's Education Science "14th Five Year Plan"—Research on the Application of Smart Education Platform in Classroom Teaching—Taking the Vocational Undergraduate Course "Fundamentals of Mechanical Design" as an Example.

References

1. Wenfang, M., Guangmei, L.: Research on practical teaching practice of accounting smart classroom in applied undergraduate colleges under the background of "artificial intelligence + education." J. Changchun Inst. Technol.: Soc. Sci. Edition **23**(1), 91–95 (2022)
2. Lin, D.: Research on teaching strategies of elementary school mathematics classroom based on smart education. Educ. Inform. Forum **4**, 54–56 (2023)
3. Xiaoyun, L., Zheng, Z.: Construction and experimental research on teaching process of smart classroom: a case study of "modern educational technology and application" course. J. Gannan Normal Univ. **43**(6), 5 (2022)
4. Qian, L.: Application of moral and political education in the course of "computer programming" under the smart teaching mode. Ind. Technol. Forum **21**(1), 2 (2022)
5. Ran, C.: Research on the design of smart learning mode supported by Spoc. (10) (2022)
6. Bin, W.: Application research of smart classroom teaching mode based on internet of things technology: taking junior high school physics teaching as an example. Teacher's Expo: Bimonthly Issue **2**, 2 (2022)
7. Benxi, L.: Development of curriculum resources, grasp of teaching strategies, and cultivation of student literacy: achievements from the "Practice Research of Science and Humanities Literacy Education in Junior High School Classroom" (excerpt). Educ. Res. **5**(6), 99–101 (2022)
8. Zheng, Y.: Research on the application of game teaching method in elementary school English classroom (2022)
9. Kehong, L.: Experimental research on the teaching mode of smart classroom in adult higher education. Beijing Xuanwu Hongqi Amateur Univ. J. **1**, 5 (2022)
10. Lu, X.: Discussion on the application of educational cloud platform smart classrooms in junior high school mathematics teaching. Chin. Sci. Technol. J. Database (Full-text Version) Educ. Sci. (12), 4 (2022)

Design and Implementation of University English Self-learning Platform Based on Constructive Teaching Mode

Yanni Zhong(✉)

Wuhan Donghu University, Wuhan 430000, Hubei, China
rennezhong@163.com

Abstract. There is a problem with incorrect performance placement, but the concept and execution of the learning platform are crucial for independent college English study. When it comes to autonomously learning collegiate English, the usual particle swarm algorithm fails miserably because it does not account for the learning platform problem. Consequently, this paper presents an evaluation of the design and execution of a university English self-learning platform that is based on the Constructive Teaching Model. In order to diminish interference factors in the design and implementation of the learning platform, we first use construction learning theory to identify the influencing aspects. Then, we divide the indicators according to the demands of the learning platform's design and implementation. Next, a Constructive Teaching Model is developed and a Learning Platform Scheme is put into place using the principles of construction learning theory. The results of this process are then carefully evaluated. In terms of accuracy in learning platform design and execution as well as duration of influencing factors, the Constructive teaching model beats the conventional Particle swarm algorithm under certain assessment settings, according to the MATLAB simulation findings.

Keywords: Construction learning theory · Constructive teaching model · College English · Self-directed learning · Platform design

1 Introduction

An important aspect of college-level independent study of English is the development and deployment of learning platforms, which may facilitate the ever-increasing speed with which the assessment model for the exact regulation of aging performance [2] may be executed. On the other hand, there is a lack of accuracy in the design and implementation of the learning platform scheme [5], which has a negative influence on the design and implementation of the learning platform [6]. This is all part of the process of designing and implementing the learning platform [4]. Some studies have shown that it is possible to effectively examine the design and implementation of learning platforms [8], and that applying constructive teaching models [9] to the study of aging performance evaluation modes may help with the design and implementation of learning platforms. Based on this information, a Constructive teaching model is proposed [10] to optimize the design and execution of the learning platform scheme and prove the model's effectiveness.

B. Brik and S. Nazir (Eds.): BigIoT-EDU 2024, LNICST 660, pp. 480–489, 2026.
https://doi.org/10.1007/978-3-032-18628-7_49

2 Related Works

2.1 1The Constructive Teaching Model is Described Mathematically.

Using computer technology and index parameters, the Constructive Teaching Model will enhance the design and execution of learning platform schemes, it is y_i found that the unqualified value parameters in the design and implementation of learning platform is z_i, and the design and implementation of learning platform scheme is $tol(y_i \cdot t_{ij})$ connected with the function to ultimately assess the practicability of the learning platform's design and implementation, with the computation shown in Eq. (1).

$$\lim_{x \to \infty} (y_i \cdot t_{ij}) = \frac{n!}{\sqrt{2!}} y_{ij} \geq \max(t_{ij} \div 2) \tag{1}$$

The assessment of anomalies among them is shown by the equation.

$$\max(t_{ij}) = \partial \left(t_{ij}^2 + 2 \cdot t_{ij} \right) \succ \mathrm{A}Im \tag{2}$$

To improve the accuracy of the learning platform's design and execution, the Constructive Teaching Model integrates the advantages of computer technology and uses quantification.

Suppose I The requirements of the design and implementation of learning platform is t_i that the design and implementation of learning platform scheme is set_i, the technique for satisfying the design and implementation of learning platform is y_i, along with the evaluation role of the learning platform's development and launch the plan is $F(t_i \approx 0)$ as shown by Eq. (3).

$$F(d_i) = \coprod \sum t_i \cap \xi \cdot \sqrt{2} \rightarrow ointy_i \cdot 7 \tag{3}$$

2.2 Selection of Design and Implementation of Learning Platform Scheme

Hypothesis II The design and implementation of learning platform function is $g(t_i)$, The weighting factor is w_i, The design and execution of the learning platform necessitates the unqualified design and implementation, as shown in Eq. (4).

$$g(t_i) = \ddot{x} \cdot z_i \prod F(d_i) \frac{dy}{dx} \tag{4}$$

Equation (5) shows the outcomes of the design and execution of the learning platform under assumptions I and II, which allows for the complete functionality of the platform to be achieved.

$$\lim_{x \to \infty} g(t_i) + F(d_i) \leq mathbbF \max(t_{ij}) \tag{5}$$

Equation (6) shows the outcomes of standardizing all data, which is necessary to improve the effectiveness of the learning platform's design and execution.

$$g(t_i) + F(d_i) \leftrightarrow \sqrt{b^2 - 4ac} \left(\sum t_{ij} + 4 \right) \tag{6}$$

2.3 Analysis of Design and Implementation of Learning Platform Scheme

Before implementing the Constructive Teaching model, it is important to thoroughly examine the design and implementation of the learning platform. The requirements of the platform should be mapped to the library's design and implementation, and any unqualified design or implementation should be removed. Equation (6) may be used to produce the anomaly assessment system, and the outcomes is $No(t_i)$ shown in Eq. (7).

$$No(t_i) = \frac{g(t_i) + F(d_i)}{mean\left(\sum t_{ij} + 4\right)} \frac{n!}{r!(n-r)!} \tag{7}$$

Among them, it is $\frac{g(t_i)+F(d_i)}{mean(\sum t_{ij}+4)} \leq 1$ specified that the scheme must be $Zh(t_i)$ suggested; otherwise, the integration of the scheme is required; Eq. (8) shows the result.

$$Zh(t_i) = \lim_{x\to\infty}\left[\sum g(t_i) + F(d_i)\right]\lim_{x\to\infty} \tag{8}$$

The design and implementation of learning platform is $accur(t_i)$ thoroughly examined, The accuracy of the Constructive Teaching Model is ensured by establishing the threshold and index weight for the design and execution of the learning platform scheme. The design and implementation of learning platform is $unno(t_i)$ a systematic test design and implementation of learning platform scheme that must be thoroughly examined. According to Eq. (9), the overall accuracy of the learning platform is reduced if its design and execution are affected by a non-normal distribution, which in turn affects the learning platform scheme.

$$accur(t_i) = \frac{\min\left[\sum g(t_i) + F(d_i)\right]}{\sum g(t_i) + F(d_i)} \times 100\% \tag{9}$$

In line with empirical evidence, the study of the learning platform scheme's design and execution shows that the scheme exhibits a multi-dimensional distribution. The lack of direction in the learning platform's design and execution is indicative of the scheme's high degree of unpredictability, and hence it is $randon(t_i)$ considered as a high analytical research. Equation (10), which represents the calculation of Eq. (9) in this case, may be used in the design and implementation of a learning platform's stochastic function.

$$accur(t_i) = \frac{\min\left[\sum g(t_i) + F(d_i)\right]}{\frac{1}{2}\sum g(t_i) + F(d_i)} \mathrm{X} \tag{10}$$

The use of computer technology allows for adjustments to the learning platform's design and implementation, the removal of duplicate and irrelevant schemes, and the supplementation of the default scheme. This leads to a strong dynamic correlation of the entire learning platform scheme, ensuring that it meets standard requirements.

3 Design and Implementation of Learning Platform Optimization Approach

The Constructive Teaching Model optimizes the design and execution of learning platforms by modifying the characteristics of Internet information and using a random optimization approach. The learning platform's design and execution were broken down into numerous phases by the evolutionary algorithm, which then randomly selected alternate ways. During the iterative process, the design and implementation of learning platforms are evaluated and improved according to different design and implementation grades. After the optimization research is finished, the learning platform's design and implementation level is compared across several schemes, and the optimal one is documented.

4 Results and Discussion

4.1 1Introduction to the Design and Implementation of Learning Platform

The study aim is the design and implementation of a learning platform in difficult scenarios. There are 12 pathways and a 12-h test duration. Table 1 shows the particular design and implementation of the learning platform.

Table 1. Design and implementation of learning platform design and implementation of learning platform requirements

Scope of application	Grade	Accuracy	Design and implementation of learning platform
Incumbents	I	93.22	90.92
	II	91.51	93.90
University student	I	91.10	91.54
	II	91.48	92.65
Exchange student	I	94.17	91.75
	II	94.34	91.57

Table 2. The overall situation of the design and implementation of learning platform scheme

Category	Random data	Reliability	Analysis rate
Incumbents	91.18	92.85	88.82
University student	90.30	91.70	95.13
Exchange student	88.78	90.28	93.65
Mean	92.94	93.69	93.58
X6	92.41	93.66	96.41
	P =.258		

The design and implementation of learning platform process in Table 1 is shown in Fig. 1.

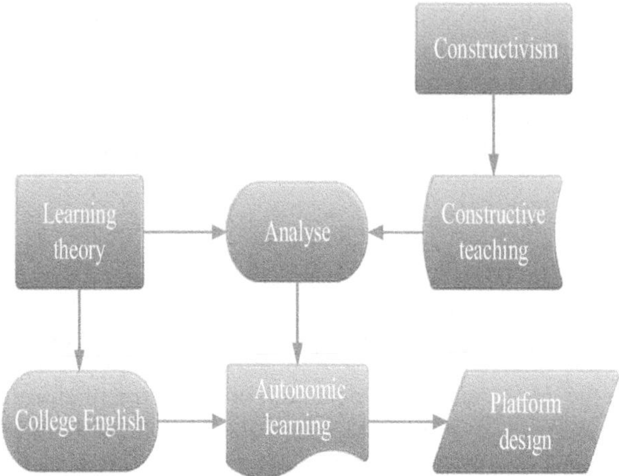

Fig. 1. Analysis process of design and implementation of learning platform

Closer to the actual requirements of learning platform design and execution is the Constructive teaching model's approach, which incorporates particle swarm arithmetic into its learning platform scheme. When comparing the two models, the Constructive Teaching Model is more logical and has a more accurate learning platform implementation than Particle Swarm Arithmetic. Figure 2 shows how modifying the design and execution of the learning platform scheme improves the accuracy and reliability of the Constructive teaching model. This led to faster, more accurate, and more stable summing thanks to the evolutionary algorithm's learning platform architecture.

5 2Design and Implementation of Learning Platform

Closer to the actual requirements of learning platform design and execution is the Constructive teaching model's approach, which incorporates particle swarm arithmetic into its learning platform scheme. When comparing the two models, the Constructive Teaching Model is more logical and has a more accurate learning platform implementation than Particle Swarm Arithmetic. Figure 2 shows how modifying the design and execution of the learning platform scheme improves the accuracy and reliability of the Constructive teaching model. This led to faster, more accurate, and more stable summing thanks to the evolutionary algorithm's learning platform architecture (Table 2).

5.1 Design and Implementation of Learning Platform and Stability

Figure 2 shows the design and execution of the learning platform scheme that incorporates particle swarm arithmetic in order to verify the validity of the Constructive teaching model.

While the error rate is lower in the Particle swarm arithmetic model, Fig. 2 shows that the Constructive teaching model has a more stable learning platform design and implementation than the Particle swarm arithmetic model, suggesting that the two models

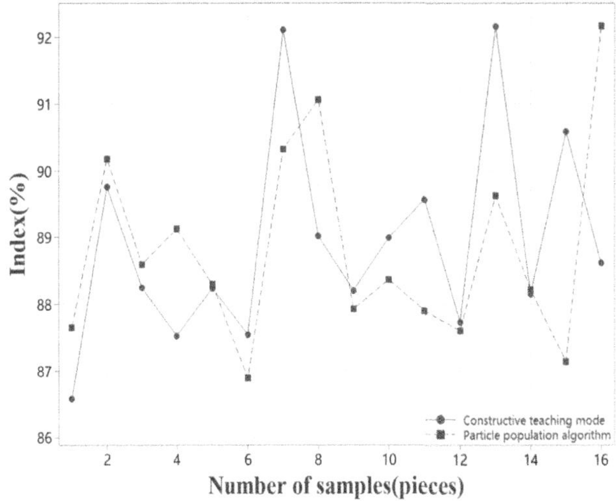

Fig. 2. Evaluation model of aging performance of different algorithms

are competing in terms of platform excellence. Table 3 shows the typical layout and execution of the learning platform concept for the three approaches mentioned before.

Table 3. Compares the accuracy of several design and implementation of learning platform.

Algorithm	Survey data	Design and implementation of learning platform	Magnitude of change	Error
Constructive teaching model	94.28	93.71	93.41	92.33
Particle swarm arithmetic	94.76	90.88	91.29	90.31
P	92.88	91.42	94.33	90.99

Table 3 reveals that there are issues with the precision of the learning platform's design and implementation in particle swarm arithmetic, and that there is a substantial error rate associated with the design and implementation of learning platforms. Compared to the ant colony method, the constructive teaching paradigm led to superior learning platform design and execution. Concurrently, the accuracy has hardly changed, and the design and execution of the learning platform according to the Constructive Teaching Model are above 90%. That is, to prove that models of constructive instruction are superior. The effectiveness of the proposed approach was further confirmed by conducting a comprehensive analysis of the Constructive Teaching Model utilizing a range of techniques, as seen in Fig. 3.

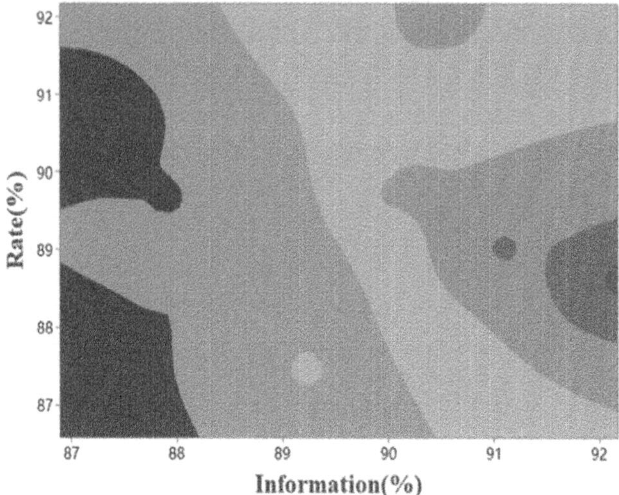

Fig. 3. Design and implementation of learning platform of Constructive teaching model

Figure 3 demonstrates that compared to particle swarm arithmetic, the Constructive teaching model's learning platform is much superior in terms of design and execution. This is due to the fact that the Constructive Teaching model raises the adjustment coefficient for learning platform design and execution and establishes the threshold for Internet information to ensure that no learning platform scheme fails to fulfill criteria.

5.2 Rationality of Design and Implementation of Learning Platform

See Fig. 4 for a visual representation of the learning platform scheme's design and execution. To ensure the Constructive teaching model is valid, it is combined with particle swarm arithmetic.

Figure 4 demonstrates that compared to particle swarm arithmetic, the Constructive teaching model's learning platform design and implementation is more rational, and that by enhancing this design and implementation, the rationality of the learning platform can be further enhanced. By incorporating Constructive teaching paradigms, a decentralized platform for data collection and administration may be established, ensuring the secure storage and preservation of discoveries. Constructive teaching models allow for the generation of unique identifiers for each, and the storage of suitable data and schemes.

5.3 Validity of Design and Implementation of Learning Platform

The success of the Constructive teaching model may be verified by including particle swarm arithmetic into the design and execution of the learning platform scheme. Figure 5 shows the result thereof.

Figure 5 demonstrates that the Constructive teaching model has a more stable learning platform design and implementation than the Particle swarm arithmetic model, while

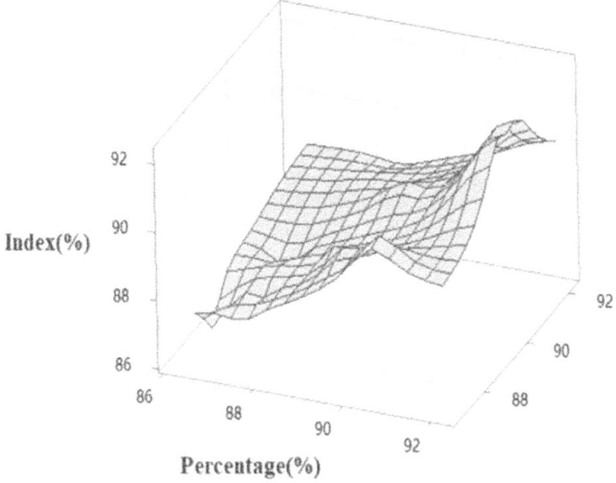

Fig. 4. Evaluation model of aging performance of different algorithms

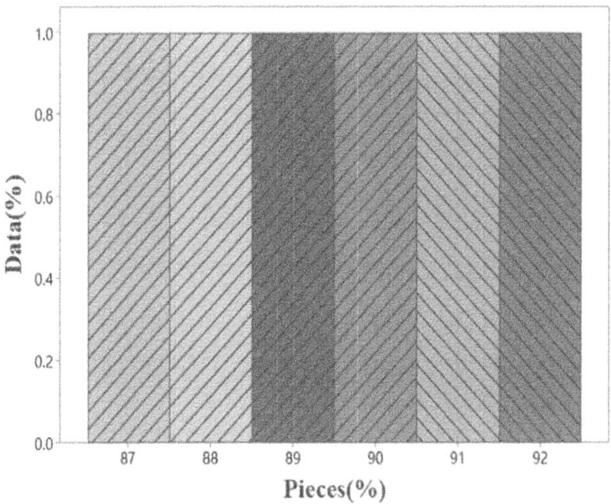

Fig. 5. Design and implementation of learning platform of different algorithms

the error rate is lower for the Constructive teaching model. This suggests that the Constructive teaching model's learning platform is higher in quality. Table 4 shows the typical layout and execution of the three approaches to the learning platform plan that were previously covered.

As can be seen from Table 4, there are certain issues with the accuracy of the learning platform's design and implementation in particle swarm arithmetic. Specifically, there is a significant error rate and noticeable variation in the design and execution of the learning platform. Compared to the ant colony method, the constructive teaching paradigm led to superior learning platform design and execution. Concurrently, the accuracy has

Table 4. Compares the efficacy of several design and implementation of learning platform.

Algorithm	Survey data	Design and implementation of learning platform	Magnitude of change	Error
Constructive teaching model	94.26	94.62	91.02	94.39
Particle swarm arithmetic	93.37	92.91	94.40	91.72
P	89.24	88.34	92.38	92.22

hardly changed, and the design and execution of the learning platform according to the Constructive Teaching Model are above 90%. That is, to prove that models of constructive instruction are superior. As shown in Fig. 6, the Constructive Teaching Model was usually subjected to a plethora of tests meant to confirm the method's effectiveness.

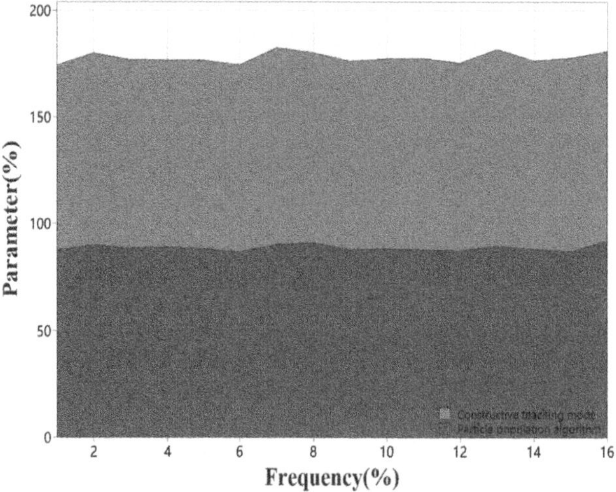

Fig. 6. Constructive teaching model design and implementation of learning platform

The Constructive teaching model's learning platform is much superior than Particle swarm arithmetic, as seen in Fig. 6. This is due to the fact that the Constructive Teaching model raises the adjustment coefficient for learning platform design and execution and establishes the threshold for Internet information to ensure that no learning platform scheme fails to fulfill criteria.

6 Conclusion

This study proposes a Constructive teaching model that enhances learning platform design and implementation via the use of computer technology. It aims to solve the problem of suboptimal design and execution. All the while, we're building the Internet data collection infrastructure and checking that the learning platform's design and execution are accurate and reliable. The results show that the general design and implementation of learning platforms may be used for the design and implementation of learning platforms, and that the Constructive teaching model can improve the accuracy of these processes. But the Constructive Teaching Model approach puts too much focus on learning platform design and implementation inspection, leading to illogical indicator selection for learning platform design and implementation.

References

1. Li T.: Analysis of autonomous learning primary school mathematics teaching model based on constructive theory chronicle star—primary school edition (22), 0028–0030 (2022)
2. Zhou Y.: Research on project-based teaching mode of applied college English based on blended online and offline teaching English Square: academic Research (19), 94–98 (2023)
3. Zhu W.: Research on the reform of business English blended teaching model based on SPOC education informatization forum **6**(11), 27–29 (2022)
4. Yin Y.: Analysis of the application of scaffolding teaching mode in middle school English writing teaching overseas English (12), 179–181 (2023)
5. Hong W.: Research on the reform and practice of college English teaching based on flipped classroom. J. Heilongjiang Teachers' Dev. Coll. **41**(7), 4 (2022)
6. Liu, X., Wang, Z., Liu, X., Sunday B.: The theoretical dimension and practical model of "student-centered"—taking the construction of online and offline hybrid courses in medicinal botany as an example. J. Hunan Univ. Tradit. Chin. Med. **43**(6), 1140–1143 (2023)
7. Zhang S.: Research on the teaching model of autonomous learning in primary school mathematics under the construction theory test questions and research (31), 3 (2022)
8. Zhang J.: The exploration of the teaching mode of returning to class in the teaching of test paper analysis (5), 3 (2022)
9. Zhang Y.: Research on the construction and implementation path of big data online case library teaching mode—taking jurisprudence course as an example research on legal education (2), 194 (2023)
10. Li G.: Exploration of autonomous learning teaching model based on constructive theory academic weekly (8), 2 (2022)
11. Liu, J.: Exploring the teaching model of primary school mathematics autonomous learning based on constructive theory mathematics learning and research (18), 66–68 (2022)

Research on the Application of New Media Technology in Japanese Language Teaching

Guangyu Zhou(✉)

College of Humanities & Information, Changchun University of Technology, Jilin 130122, China
34379275@qq.com

Abstract. WNew media technology refers to a new media form that realizes information collection, processing, dissemination and reception through digital technology, network technology, mobile communication technology and other means. It covers the Internet, mobile communications, social media, virtual reality (VR), augmented reality (AR), big data, cloud computing and many other fields. The remarkable features of new media technology include interactivity, immediacy, personalization, multi-media and globalization, which make information dissemination more convenient and efficient, and provide new possibilities for education. Compared with multimedia technology, new media technology can utilize digital technology to connect user terminals through computer networks, satellites, wireless communication networks, and other means to achieve teaching. The quality and effectiveness evaluation of Japanese language teaching are relatively ideal.

Keywords: Japanese language teaching · Teaching quality · New media technology · new media

1 Introduction

In the context of globalization, the teaching of Japanese has received extensive attention. However, the traditional Japanese teaching mode often focuses on the interpretation of grammar and vocabulary [1–7], ignoring the cultivation of practical language application ability, leading to students' deficiencies in oral communication and cultural understanding. In addition, due to the uneven geographical distribution of educational resources, students in some areas have no access to high-quality Japanese teaching resources, which further exacerbates the teaching problem. With the rapid development of technology, the introduction of new media technology becomes the key to solve these challenges. A virtual travel experience lets students read a destination introduction, or scan physical tags in an AR app to read relevant Japanese information in real time (Fig. 1).

Combined with the new media technology, the Japanese reading teaching has gradually formed a mixed, personalized and dynamic learning mode. Teachers can adjust the teaching content according to the students' learning progress and interests, and track the learning effect of the students through data analysis. For example, use an intelligent recommendation system to recommend reading materials for each student that are

B. Brik and S. Nazir (Eds.): BigIoT-EDU 2024, LNICST 660, pp. 490–499, 2026.
https://doi.org/10.1007/978-3-032-18628-7_50

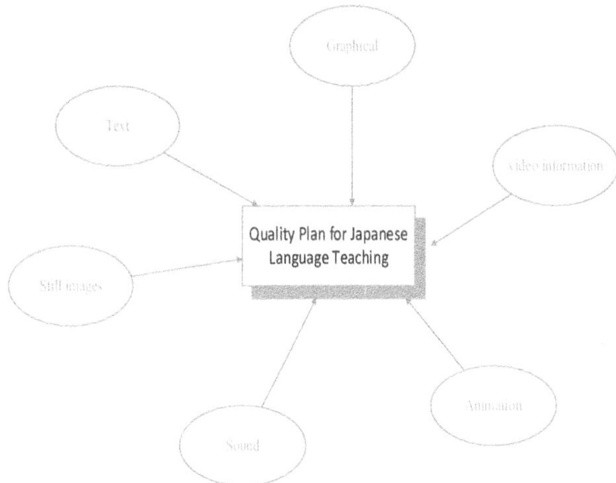

Fig. 1. Selection results of Japanese teaching quality plan

consistent with their level and related to their interests [8–11]. In addition, gamification learning is also a new attempt to design reading tasks into game levels to stimulate students' reading interest and motivation through the reward mechanism. At the same time, artificial intelligence (AI) speech recognition and natural language processing technologies can provide immediate feedback to help students improve their pronunciation and understanding. The application of new media technology not only enriches the teaching methods of reading, but also improves students' reading experience. Through diversified learning resources and interactive ways, students can improve their reading ability in a relaxed and pleasant atmosphere. At the same time, the real-time, interactive and personalized characteristics of new media technology have injected new vitality into the teaching of Japanese reading [12–18].

2 Related Works

A. *Development of educational technology and the integration of new media technology*

With the rapid development of information technology in the 21st century, educational technology has also ushered in unprecedented changes. Educational technology is no longer limited to the traditional blackboard and textbooks, but gradually turns to digital, network and intelligent. New media technologies, including social media, mobile devices, virtual reality, augmented reality, artificial intelligence, etc., have become new orites in education. The integration of these technologies has not only changed the teaching methods, but also greatly enriched the teaching resources, making the Japanese teaching no longer limited to the classroom, but extended to the students' daily life [19–22].

B. *The teaching theoretical basis of new media technology*

The application of new media technology in Japanese language teaching is mainly based on the following teaching theories: Constructivism theory: New media technology provides students with a platform to build their own knowledge, such as online discussion forums, interactive learning software, etc., to encourage students to learn in practice and deepen their understanding of Japanese through interaction and collaboration. Theory of multiple intelligences: New media technology meets the needs of different learning styles. For example, visual learners can understand Japanese through animation and video, auditory learners can learn pronunciation through audio materials, and interactive games are suitable for hands-on learners. Context learning theory: New media technology can simulate real context, such as Japanese dialogue practice in a virtual reality environment, so that learners can improve their language application ability in a near-real environment. Flipped classroom theory: New media technology enables teachers to preview the explanation content through video, and use class time for interaction and deepening understanding, so as to improve teaching efficiency.

To sum up, new media technology has a solid theoretical foundation in Japanese teaching and plays a significant role in teaching, which provides new possibilities for improving the quality of Japanese teaching.

C. *Traditional methods and limitations of oral English teaching*

Traditional methods of teaching spoken English usually include classroom simulation dialogue, role playing, group discussion, etc. Teachers usually design various situational dialogues based on the teaching materials to guide students to participate. However, there are some limitations to this teaching method. First, the limited class time fails to provide sufficient practice opportunities, so that students may lack coping ability in real-world scenarios. Secondly, the interaction patterns between students may be too fixed, limiting the diversity and flexibility of oral expression. Moreover, teachers 'one-to-one correction and feedback are difficult to cover all students, so that some students' problems can not be solved in time.

D. *Innovative application of new media technology in oral English teaching*

The application of new media technology has significantly improved the effect of oral English teaching. Through phonetic analysis, teachers can more accurately understand students' pronunciation weaknesses and provide targeted guidance. Interactive video teaching enables students to participate in interaction while watching, such as using, repeating, and answering questions, which enhances the engagement and depth of learning. Social media and online forums provide diverse platforms for students to communicate freely in an informal environment and develop natural and fluent oral habits. At the same time, the role of teachers is also changing. They are no longer just the transmitters of information, but become instructors and coordinators, guiding students to use new media resources to stimulate their interest in learning and promote independent learning. Through regular online discussions and project cooperation, teachers can monitor students' learning progress, provide timely feedback, and promote the continuous improvement of oral English skills. The integration of new media technology makes oral Japanese teaching more personalized and dynamic, which not only improves the teaching efficiency, but also enriches the learning experience, and opens up a new path for cultivating Japanese learners with practical communication skills.

3 Optimization Strategies for Japanese Language Teaching and Language Training Education in Universities

In the traditional Japanese writing teaching, teachers usually use classroom explanation, example analysis, homework correction and other ways to teach. Through imitation and practice, students gradually master the Japanese grammar structure, vocabulary collocation and expression skills. However, this model suffers from some limitations: Limited personalized guidance: it is difficult for teachers to provide personalized feedback and guidance according to each student's characteristics. Long feedback cycle: The correction of written assignments usually takes time, and students may have to wait a while to know the improvements. Lack of real-time interaction: traditional teaching methods are difficult to achieve immediate interaction and discussion, which limits students' immediate learning and improvement.

A. *Traditional methods and problems of reading teaching*

In the traditional teaching of Japanese reading, teachers usually rely on textbooks and paper materials to teach students through sentence-by-sentence translation, vocabulary interpretation, and article structure analysis. This approach, although well-grounded, has some limitations. First of all, the updating speed of paper data is limited, and it is difficult to keep up with the real-time changes of language. Secondly, a single teaching method may lead to students' lack of interest in reading, which may affect their enthusiasm for independent learning.

Moreover, the traditional teaching mode often ignores the communicative function of language, and students lack the opportunity to actually apply their reading skills in class.

$$f(x) = \omega^T \phi(x) + b \tag{1}$$

B. *Selection of Japanese Teaching Quality Plan*

The introduction of new media technology has brought about innovation to Japanese reading teaching. For example, digital textbooks and online reading platforms provide a rich variety of reading materials, including news, blogs, e-books and social media content, which are more relevant to real life and help students get exposed to vivid Japanese expressions. Using multimedia resources, teachers can design interactive reading tasks, such as video subtitle understanding, audio listening and reading, to enhance students' audio-visual perception.

$$G(x_i) = \sum_{i=1}^{I} \lambda_i(\omega T \phi(x_i) + b + e_i + y_i) \tag{2}$$

C. Exploration of the Evaluation Plan for Japanese Teaching Effectiveness

In addition, the learning management system (LMS) and online discussion forums can promote collaborative learning among peers and allow students to improve their reading comprehension during communication. The application of virtual reality (VR)

and augmented reality (AR) technology is also a new exploration direction. By simulating real scenes, students can read and understand Japanese content in an immersive environment to improve their practical application ability of the language.

4 Results and Discussion

A. *Introduction to the Evaluation of Japanese Teaching Effectiveness*

New media technology has brought innovations to the teaching of Japanese writing, including: Online writing platform: Using the online writing platform, the teachers can check the students' writing progress immediately, provide real-time feedback, and help the students to correct their mistakes in time. Virtual Writing Workshop: Through video conferencing software, teachers can organize virtual writing workshops, where students can share, discuss and modify their works in groups to improve their cooperative learning ability.

Table 1. Evaluation requirements for the effectiveness of Japanese language teaching in universities

Evaluation population	Language proficiency evaluation	Translation ability evaluation	Teaching quality evaluation
Freshman	65.8153	70.8917	79.2565
Sophomore	65.2675	73.1090	79.0479
Junior	65.3279	70.5151	81.1077

The evaluation process of Japanese language teaching effectiveness in Table 1 is shown in Fig. 2.

AI assistance: AI tools can automatically detect grammatical errors, spelling errors and providing students with preliminary suggestions for modification. Digital library: A rich online library, such as Japanese articles, news and literary works, provides students with rich writing materials and examples.

B. *The situation of Japanese language teaching and language training education in universities*

The application of new media technology has significantly improved the efficiency and effect of Japanese writing teaching: Improvement of writing skills: Students can quickly master writing skills and improve the accuracy and consistency of expression through multiple rounds of modification and immediate guidance from teachers. Enhanced learning autonomy: students can choose their own learning time and progress, and use multimedia resources to improve themselves. Higher student satisfaction: Student feedback showed that they preferred this interactive and timely feedback teaching style, which considered it was a significant help in improving their writing skills.

Through the application of new media technology, the teaching of Japanese writing has not only changed in form, but also promoted the improvement of students' writing

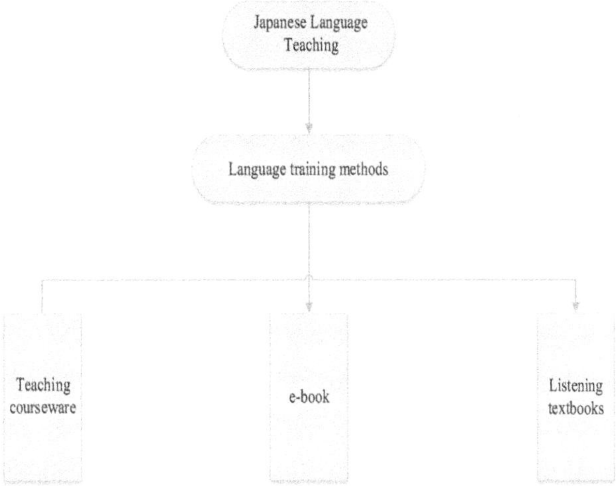

Fig. 2. Exploration process of Japanese language teaching and language training education in universities

ability in essence, and enhanced the interest and effectiveness of learning. In the future, with the continuous development of technology, the role of new media in the teaching of Japanese writing will be more significant (Table 2).

Table 2. Overall situation of Japanese language teaching quality plan

Teaching objects	Japanese speaking ability	Japanese translation ability
Freshman	64.1778	80.4502
Sophomore	64.8077	75.5750
Junior	64.1389	79.1358

C. *Oral and Translation Skills in Evaluating the Effectiveness of Japanese Teaching*

This study deeply discusses the application of new media technology in Japanese teaching, and finds that it plays a significant role in improving teaching efficiency, stimulating students' interest and enriching teaching methods. By introducing multimedia resources, such as animation, audio, video and interactive software, Japanese teaching has changed from a single textbook learning to a diversified and interactive learning experience (Fig. 3).

New media technology in oral teaching, such as the use of speech recognition software, enables students to practice in the simulated real dialogue environment, improving their oral expression ability. In reading teaching, digital textbooks and online reading platforms provide rich reading materials to help students expand their vocabulary and

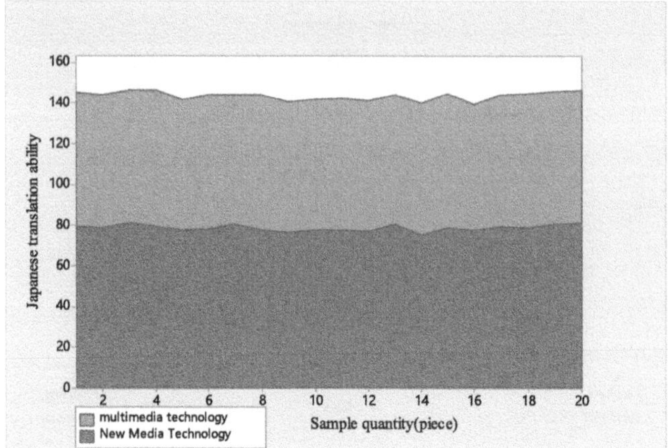

Fig. 3. The quality of Japanese teaching with different algorithms

enhance their understanding ability. In writing teaching, the use of collaborative editing tools and online writing platforms encourages students' creative thinking and critical thinking, while also facilitating real-time feedback and guidance from teachers (Table 3).

Table 3. Comparison of the evaluation of Japanese teaching effects by different methods

Algorithm	Interest	Simultaneous interpretation	Verbatim translation
New media technology	92.0111	90.4722	91.9644
Multimedia technology	79.1358	77.8976	80.4502

Despite the many positive effects of new media technology, there are also some problems and challenges in practice. First of all, the technology update and iteration speed, teachers need to constantly learn and adapt to new teaching tools, which constitutes a certain pressure in terms of time and resources. Secondly, although new media can attract students' attention, it may also lead students to rely too much on technology and ignore the basic listening, speaking, reading and writing exercises (Fig. 4).

Moreover, the instability of the network environment and information security problems may affect the teaching process. Moreover, for some remote areas or schools with limited resources, there are still obstacles to the access and application of new media technologies. Finally, the reform of the evaluation system needs to keep up to fully reflect the overall improvement of students' language ability in the new media environment.

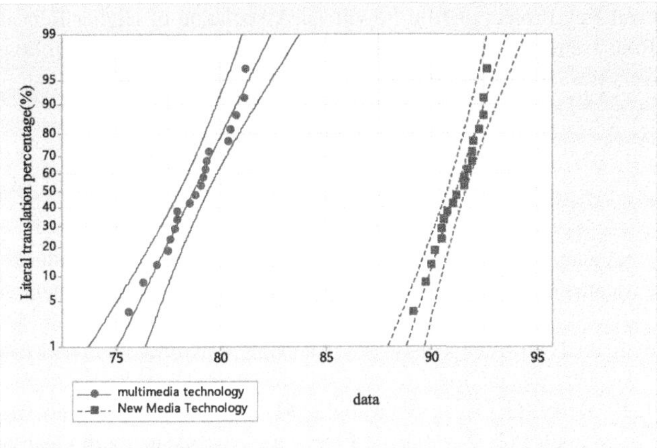

Fig. 4. The quality of Japanese language teaching in the evaluation of new media technology Japanese language teaching effectiveness

5 Conclusion

To sum up, the application of new media technology in Japanese teaching is a double-edged sword, which has both great potential and practical challenges. Future research should pay more attention to the in-depth integration of technology and teaching content, explore more personalized and intelligent teaching mode, and at the same time pay attention to the fairness and sustainability of technology application, so as to realize the overall progress of Japanese education.

In response to the issue of unsatisfactory teaching quality in Japanese language teaching and language training education in universities, this article proposes new media technology and combines it with new media theory to optimize Japanese language teaching and language training education in universities. At the same time, we will conduct in-depth exploration on the innovation of Japanese teaching effectiveness evaluation and threshold innovation, and construct a talent pool. Research has shown that new media technology can improve students' translation and oral abilities in Japanese language teaching and language training education in universities, and can evaluate the effectiveness of Japanese language teaching and language training education in universities. However, in the process of new media technology, excessive emphasis is placed on exploring the evaluation of Japanese language teaching effectiveness, resulting in unreasonable selection of evaluation indicators for Japanese language teaching effectiveness.

Acknowledgements. 1. 2022 Jilin Province Higher education research project "Research on Japanese Online Teaching in Universities in the COVID-19 Period" project number JGJX2022D665.

2. 2025 Annual Key Project of Jilin Provincial Association of Higher Education: Research on the Interdisciplinary Integration Path of "Foreign Language + Digital Literacy" in Applied Universities Driven by GAI Technology (JGJX25B48).

3. 2025 Annual Key Project of Jilin Provincial Association of Higher Education: Research on AI-Enabled Role Transformation and Digital Competence Development of Foreign Language Teachers in Universities (JGJX25B50).

References

1. Balaram, A., Kannan, K. N., Cepova, L., Kumar, M. K., Rani, B. S., Schindlerova, V.: Artificial intelligence for media ecological integration and knowledge management. Systems **11**(5) (2023)
2. Beck, T., Friedman, E.: Social technologies in and out of psychology. Theory Psychol. (2023)
3. Beckman, I. P., Berry, G., Ucak-Astarlioglu, M., Thornell, T. L., Cho, H., Riveros, G.: Stabilized Electrospun Polyacrylonitrile Fibers for advancements in clean air technology. Atmosphere **14**(3) (2023)
4. Bellido, J.: Patents in miniature: the effects of microfilm as an information technology, 1938–68. Technol. Cult. **64**(2), 407–433 (2023)
5. Cepeda, R. G.: Making a manual: the manual for the curation and display of interactive new media art. Artnodes (31), 7–8 (2023)
6. Dilleen, G., Claffey, E., Foley, A., Doolin, K.: Investigating knowledge dissemination and social media use in the farming network to build trust in smart farming technology adoption. J. Bus. Ind. Mark. **38**(8), 1754–1765 (2023)
7. Fan, H.: Research on innovation and application of 5G using artificial intelligence-based image and speech recognition technologies. J. King Saud Univ. Sci. **35**(4) (2023)
8. Han, S., Li, Z., Li, D., Ma, X.: Review of magnetic fluid rotary seal technology for liquid medium. Lubr. Eng. **48**(3), 1–9 (2023)
9. Hoetzlein, R. C.: Knowledge cultures in new media art. Artnodes (31), 1–9 (2023)
10. Hu, H., Cao, M., Song, P., Fu, M.: FEM-DEM coupling analysis on hexagonal convex ring 6063–T5 tube ultrasonic-assisted granular medium forming. Int. J. Adv. Manuf. Technol. **127**(5–6), 2505–2521 (2023)
11. Li, Z., Huang, Z., Su, Y.: New media environment, environmental regulation and corporate green technology innovation: evidence from China. Energy Econ. **119** (2023)
12. Lin, V.J., Ardoin, N.M.: Connecting technologies and nature: Impact and opportunities for digital media use in the context of at-home family environmental learning. J. Environ. Educ. **54**(1), 72–83 (2023)
13. Lyall, B., Nansen, B.: Redefining rest: a taxonomy of contemporary digital sleep technologies. Hist. Soc. Res.-Hist. Soz.Forschung **48**(2), 135–156 (2023)
14. McCall, M.W., Koufidis, S.F.: Broadband Bragg phenomenon in a uniform birefringent medium. Opt. Lett. **48**(5), 1096–1099 (2023)
15. Mialkovska, L., Zhvania, L., Yanovets, A., Tykha, L., Nykoliuk, T., Pimenova, O.: New media as modern communication technologies: the digital dimension. Khazar J. Hum. Soc. Sci. **26**(1), 79–91 (2023)
16. Pan, J., Zheng, Y., Chen, J., Li, Z.-Y.: Light transport through a magneto-optical medium: simple theory revealing fruitful phenomena. Opt. Express **31**(6), 9211–9223 (2023)
17. Park, J.: Virtual technology in Netflix k-drama: augmented reality, hologram, and artificial intelligence. Int. J. Commun. **17**, 130–148 (2023)
18. Peng, Y.: The meaning of space in new media art based on examples of new media artworks. Voprosy Istorii **1**(2), 132–137 (2023)
19. Petrova, S.: Food philosophy and identity. Filos.-Philos. **32**(1), 81–92 (2023)

20. Pringle, T.P.: The whole earth and apartheid: media, peer-production, segregation. New Media Soc. **25**(8), 1863–1887 (2023)
21. Sarda, T.: (2023) An onion with layers of hope and fear: a cross-case analysis of the media representation of Tor Network reflecting theoretical perspectives of new technologies. Secur. Priv. **6**(4)
22. Savut, E.: Metaverse as a futuristic public sphere alternative. J. Mehmet Akif Ersoy Univ. Econ. Adm. Sci. Fac. **10**(1), 509–529 (2023)

Design and Implementation of Online Dance Teaching System

Xianli Li(✉)

Yunnan College of Business Management, KunMing 650000, China
lixanli852022@163.com

Abstract. Low teaching quality is an issue, despite the critical role that good teachers play in dance education. When it comes to dance instruction, the standard model of education is inadequate and fails to meet expectations for excellent instruction. Consequently, this research suggests a method of evaluating instruction quality using online means. To begin, the instructional mode is used for content evaluation, and the indications are classified based on quality standards for instruction in order to mitigate the interfering component. Next, a teaching quality program is developed based on the impact of teaching mode on dance teaching quality, and the outcomes of this program are put into action. Thorough examination. According to MATLAB simulation, the online teaching method affects the quality of dance instruction and instruction quality to varying degrees depending on the assessment criteria. Compared to the standard instructional paradigm, the outcomes were superior.

Keywords: Teaching mode · Online teaching mode · Dance teaching

1 Introduction

One of the most significant developments in IT today is the rise of information management systems, which have revolutionized many different sectors and opened up exciting new possibilities for dance instruction. There are numerous moving parts in dance instruction, and an information management system may make coordinating resources and managing student data easier, faster, safer, and more efficient. In this post, we'll take a look at how information management systems have changed dance education and touch on a few typical use cases for these systems.

A. *Advantages of information management systems*

The benefits of information management systems, a relatively new kind of information technology, are as follows:

1. Effectiveness

Many problems, including sharing information and coordinating resources, plague the conventional information management approach [3]. By delivering scalable, distributed, and efficient information management services, the information management system may address the efficiency issue with information management.

B. Brik and S. Nazir (Eds.): BigIoT-EDU 2024, LNICST 660, pp. 500–507, 2026.
https://doi.org/10.1007/978-3-032-18628-7_51

2. Modularity

A variety of data types may be processed by the information management system, and users can access a wide range of applications, all tailored to their own requirements [4].

3. Data protection our information management system offers many layers of data protection, including backup, encryption, storage, and monitoring, to guarantee the safety of your data.
4. Ease of Use

So that users may manage information and resource coordination anytime, wherever, and increase work efficiency, the information management system can implement remote access and management over the network [5].

B. *Application of information management system in dance teaching*

Many different situations may benefit from information management system technology when used to dance instruction [6]. Here are just a few examples:

1. Administration of dance education materials

Information management systems provide intelligent dance teaching resource management services, which may increase the effectiveness and efficiency of dance teaching resource management—a fundamental business in dance instruction. Finding and fixing issues with resource management is as easy as mining and analyzing data from instructional resources. To illustrate the point, with the help of the information management system, important resources including dance instruction videos, music, lesson plans, and exam question banks may be updated in real-time and managed efficiently [8].

2. The administration of student records

An integral part of any dance education program's administration is the student information management system, which, via its services, allows for the intelligent administration and updating of student data. Ensuring the security and privacy of students' information is made possible with the assistance of an information management system, which allows for the real-time maintenance and updating of student data, including names, numbers, dates of birth, contact information, etc. [10].

3. Organizing and evaluating the course

The information management system's intelligent course management and assessment services may enhance the effectiveness and efficiency of dance curriculum management and evaluation, which is a crucial management link in the field. In order to increase the efficacy of instruction and the reliability of assessments, it is possible to manage and update critical information such as course progress, lesson material, homework assignments, and student feedback in real-time with the use of an information management system [11].

4. Collaboration and the sharing of knowledge

The teaching of dance often requires the cooperation and communication of several teaching teams [13]. By offering services for cross-team collaboration and communication, information management systems may facilitate team collaboration and teaching communication. Teams may collaborate more effectively with the help of an information management system, which allows for the rapid sharing of information [14], negotiation and decision-making in business, and the provision of real-time feedback and monitoring. For instance, with the help of an information management system, teaching teams may quickly communicate and share materials, which improves both the efficiency and quality of their work.

C. *The impact of information management systems on dance teaching*

The following are some of the most noticeable ways in which information management system technology has affected dance education:

1. Raise the bar for class effectiveness and efficiency

Improving the efficacy and quality of dance instruction is possible with the help of the information management system's intelligent teaching resource management, student information management, curriculum management, and assessment services.

2. Make workplace collaboration and information sharing a reality

Improving work productivity and the quality of information management is made possible with the help of the information management system, which allows various departments and teams to interact, exchange information rapidly, and accomplish business reporting.

3. Make data protection and security more robust

To guarantee the safety and dependability of data, the information management system may provide multi-level data security measures, such as data encryption, data storage, data backup, and data monitoring.

4. Enhance the student-teacher relationship and the quality of instruction

With the help of an information management system, it is possible to intelligently manage and update course materials and information in order to enhance both the learning impact and the teaching experience for students.

One of the most significant developments in IT today, information management system technology opens up a world of possibilities for growth and dance education. With the help of an information management system, dance classes may foster collaboration and information exchange, which in turn boosts the quality and efficiency of instruction, ensures the safety of student data, and enriches both the classroom experience and the students' ability to retain material. Problems with data privacy and security persist, nonetheless, as a result of implementing technology into information management systems. Thus, to guarantee the dependability and long-term growth of dance instruction, it is essential to thoroughly contemplate data privacy and security protections when using information management system technology. Technology in information management systems will continue to bolster and advance dance education as a result of ongoing study and development.

The effectiveness of listening to dance classes is greatly impacted by the teaching quality, which is an essential component of dance instruction. On the other hand, poor teaching levels are an issue with the teaching quality program, which impacts teaching outcomes. In order to properly assess the teaching quality scheme and provide matching assistance for the teaching quality, some academics think that the online teaching mode may be used to dance instruction analysis. So, to maximize the teaching quality scheme and test the model's efficacy, this research suggests an online teaching mode.

2 Related Works

A. *Mathematical description of the online teaching model*

To maximize the teaching quality program via the use of network information technology, identify the unqualified values in dance instruction, incorporate the program into the online learning environment, and then evaluate the program's efficacy is the goal of online teaching. Doing dancing classes is doable. Improving the quality of instruction is possible via the online teaching mode's combination of the benefits of network information technology with quantitative dance instruction.

First Hypothesis: The Need for High-Quality Instruction is q_i, the teaching quality program is set_i, ensuring that the program for teaching quality is met is o, and the evaluation measure for the program's instructional quality is $J(q_i \approx 0)$ As shown in Eq. (1).

$$J(q_i o) = \frac{o - 3q_i}{J} + \frac{1}{9} \Longleftrightarrow \iint_i o \tag{1}$$

B. *Selection of teaching quality programs*

Second Hypothesis: The Role of Dance Instruction is $k(q_i)$, and the weight coefficient is l_i, Unqualified dance instruction is necessary for high-quality instruction, as shown by Eq. (2).

$$k(q_i) = \left(\frac{k}{2} - l_i\right) \rightarrow \sum_{i=1}^{q} (2l_i - J)^2 \cdot \frac{i}{k} \tag{2}$$

C. *Analysis of teaching quality programs*

Prior to implementing the online teaching mode, a thorough evaluation of the teaching quality scheme across several dimensions must be carried out. The criteria for teaching quality must then be mapped to the dance teaching library, and any unqualified schemes must be eliminated. To begin, we do a thorough analysis of dance instruction, and then we establish the teaching quality plan's threshold and index weight to guarantee that our online teaching model can be implemented. Systematic testing of teaching quality schemes is necessary in dance instruction, and feasibility studies are necessary for this. The accuracy of dance instruction as a whole will suffer if its distribution is not normal; this will have an effect on the teaching quality system. Figure 1 shows the particular program selection that may be made to enhance the online teaching mode's accuracy and overall quality of instruction.

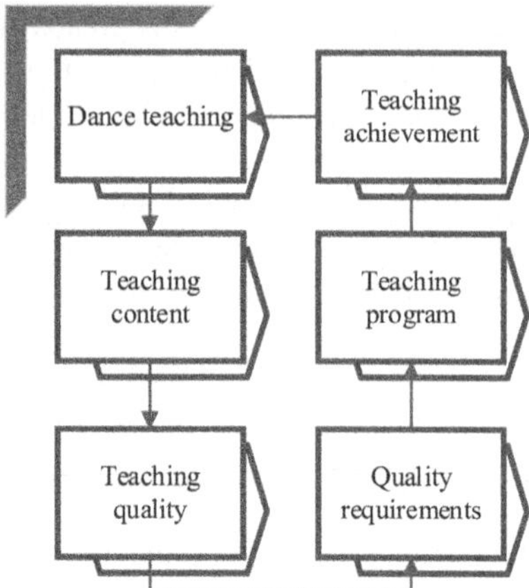

Fig. 1. The results of the selection of teaching quality programs

Consistent with empirical evidence, the teaching quality scheme survey reveals that it exhibits a multi-dimensional distribution. Due to the lack of direction in dance instruction, this research is considered to be highly analytical since it suggests that the teaching quality plan is quite random. The primary reason dance instruction is up to par is because network information technology fine-tunes it, gets rid of unnecessary and redundant plans, and augments the default plan, resulting in a robust dynamic correlation of the whole teaching quality scheme.

3 Optimization Strategies for Dance Instruction

In order to optimize dance instruction, the online learning mode uses a random optimization technique and tweaks the parameters of the lesson's content. Dance instruction in the online mode is organized into tiers of varying quality and schemes are chosen at random. Various teaching quality techniques are improved and evaluated in the iterative process. Following the completion of the optimization study, the best dance instruction is documented by comparing the quality levels of several programs.

4 Results and Discussion

A. *Introduction to the quality of teaching*

This work uses dance instruction in complicated circumstances as its research target, with a total of twelve pathways and twelve hours of testing time I shown.

The teaching quality process in Table 1 is shown in Fig. 2.

The teaching quality scheme of the online teaching mode is more in accordance with the real criteria for teaching quality as compared to the regular teaching mode. The internet teaching method outshines the traditional one when compared to listening efficiency and variety in dance instruction. Figure 2 shows how the teaching quality

Table 1. Teaching quality requirements

Scope of application	Grade	Listening efficiency	Quality of teaching
Classical dance	Standard	84.89	84.60
	Higher	84.56	84.96
Ballet	Standard	84.94	83.20
	Higher	87.05	84.35
Latin dance	Standard	85.32	86.55
	Higher	83.60	84.02

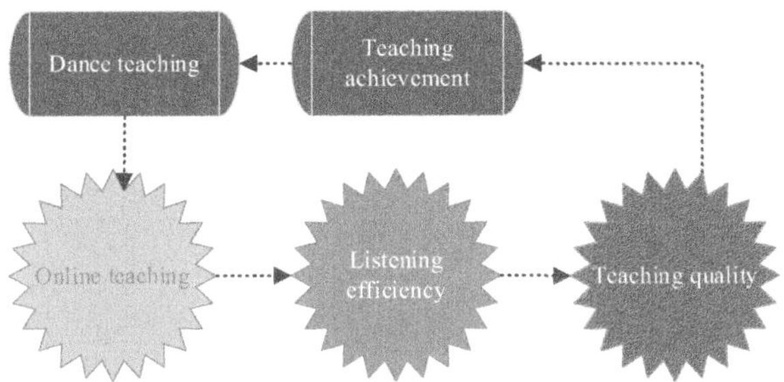

Fig. 2. The analytical process of dance teaching

scheme has changed, demonstrating how online learning is more efficient and quicker. Consequently, online education has superior program speed, program implementability, and summation stability in terms of teaching quality.

B. *Dance teaching*

There are three types of information included in the dance teaching quality program: non-structural, semi-structural, and structural. A dance education program with preliminary teaching quality is developed after the pre-selection of an online learning mode. Evaluate the practicability of instructing high-quality programs. Table 2 shows the teaching quality method that was used to choose dance lessons with varying degrees of difficulty so that the findings could be more precisely verified.

C. *Teaching quality: Teaching quality and stability*

The online teaching mode's correctness is checked by comparing the teaching quality scheme with the general teaching mode. Figure 3 shows the teaching quality scheme.

Figure 3 shows that as compared to the traditional classroom setting, online instruction provides better quality lessons with a lower error rate, suggesting that both settings maintain consistent levels of instruction. The level of instruction varies. Table 3 displays the mean strategy for teaching quality of the aforementioned three algorithms.

From Table 3, we can deduce that dance instruction has changed significantly and has a high mistake rate, and that the general teaching mode suffers from poor teaching

Table 2. Overall picture of the teaching quality programme

Category	Listening efficiency	Analysis rate
Classical dance	86.29	91.08
Ballet	90.23	89.15
Latin dance	88.71	87.20
Mean	88.30	87.70
X^6	87.66	87.92
P = 1.11		

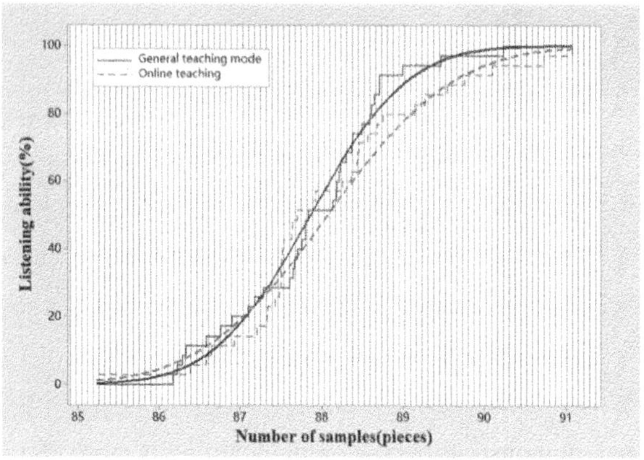

Fig. 3. Teaching quality of different algorithms

Table 3. Comparison of teaching quality and accuracy of different methods

Algorithm	Quality of teaching	Magnitude of change	Error
Online teaching mode	91.27	92.20	91.89
General teaching mode	90.27	90.43	88.96
P	87.80	87.49	89.71

quality and listening efficiency. Overall, the online teaching paradigm produces superior and more high-quality teaching outcomes compared to the traditional classroom model. Additionally, there has been no discernible change in the accuracy, and the online teaching mode boasts a teaching quality of above 91%. In order to provide more evidence that online education is better. The success of the suggested technique is further validated by conducting a broad study of the online teaching mode using various methodologies, as seen in Fig. 4.

Figure 4 shows that compared to the traditional classroom setting, online instruction yields far higher quality results. This is because, among other things, online instruction

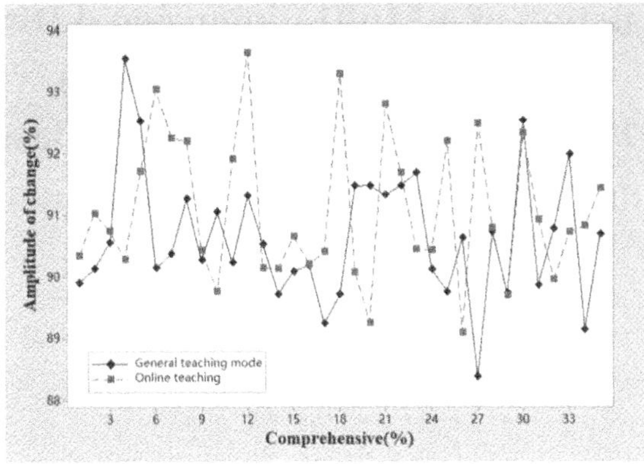

Fig. 4. Online teaching mode teaching quality teaching

raises the adjustment coefficient for dance instruction and establishes content thresholds to weed out low-quality programs.

5 Conclusion

This study presents an online teaching mode that optimizes dance instruction by merging network information technology, with the aim of addressing the issue of unacceptable quality of dance instruction. Concurrently, a library of instructional materials is built via thorough examination of optimizing teaching quality. Research has shown that dance education delivered via online platforms may enhance both the variety and overall quality of dance instruction. However, when using online learning as a style of instruction, there is an overemphasis on analyzing teaching quality, which leads to illogical indications of teaching quality.

References

1. Samala, A.D., Marta, R., Anori, S., Indarta, Y.: Online learning apps for students: opportunities and challenges. Educ. Adm.: Theory Pract. **28**(03), 1–12 (2022)
2. Siregar, E.S., Hasanuddin, S.S.D.: Predictor of multiple intelligence in educational practice. Educ. Adm.: Theory Pract. **28**(02), 49–56 (2022)
3. Harahap, S.H., Sunendar, D., Sumiyadi, Damayanti, V.S. Requirements analysis: drama education in high school. Educ. Adm.: Theory Pract. **28**(02), 66–73 (2022)
4. Supraja, P., Salameh, A.A.., Varadaraju, H.R., Anand, M., Priyadi, U.: An optimal routing protocol using a multiverse optimizer algorithm for wireless mesh network. Int. J. Commun. Netw. Inf. Secur. (IJCNIS) **14**(3), 36–46 (2022)
5. Paikaray, D., Chhabra, D., Sharma, S., Goswami, S., Shashikala, H.K. Jethava, G.: Energy efficiency based load balancing optimization routing protocol in 5G wireless communication networks. Int. J. Commun. Netw. Inf. Secur. (IJCNIS) **14**(3), 187–198 (2022)

Construction of a Multi-dimensional Dynamic College Students' Innovation and Entrepreneurship Platform Based on School-Enterprise Cooperation

Yang Jianhua(✉) and Miao Yu

Chongqing Three Gorges Vocational College, Wanzhou, Chongqing 404000, China
lonely-hua@163.com

Abstract. Single entrepreneurship and employment platform employment, single development and employment area play a significant role, but there are relatively many contents involved in the employment process, so it is necessary to make an overall judgment to improve the employment effect. This paper puts forward multi-dimensional dynamic analysis to make judgment, which can improve the employment efficiency of college students, and make students' employment intention and employment demand show a comparison, and the match between them reaches more than 80%. Moreover, it can find the danger of college students' future employment, optimize and judge it, and the recognition rate is greater than 80%. Therefore, a definite analysis can improve the employment effect of college students, make it more in line with the needs of the actual society, and improve the future employment environment of college students. Therefore, multi-dimensional analysis can have a significant effect on the employment platform and employment direction of college students.

Keywords: Natural Language Processing Theory · Multi-dimensional Dynamic Algorithms · Contemporary college students · Entrepreneurship platform construction

1 Introduction

The process of college students' entrepreneurship is a complicated process, and the integrity and comprehensive needs of college students' entrepreneurship. Social education is recognized by all aspects of the family [1, 2]. However, in the process of entrepreneurship, it is the combination of theory and practice, and it is also the sublimation of theory, which can verify its future development direction. In the process of starting a business, it is necessary to meet the actual needs of society, integrate with social conditions, form an effective comparison and analysis [3, 4], effectively identify the existing creative conditions and creative contents, and make a whole judgment on the indicators and contents, which has become the focus of research [5, 6]. In the process of

B. Brik and S. Nazir (Eds.): BigIoT-EDU 2024, LNICST 660, pp. 508–515, 2026.
https://doi.org/10.1007/978-3-032-18628-7_52

analysis, it is necessary to reflect multi-dimensionality. Multi-dimensionality includes social needs, practical factors, multi-factors and mystery, and will judge and integrate the actual satisfaction rate of response and birth, and combine the actual characteristics of college students, including daring to venture and do, integrating theory with practice, technological innovation and conduct in-depth analysis of various characteristics such as concept innovation [7, 8]. Diversity is an objective condition for comprehensive evaluation of college students' entrepreneurship, and it is also a condition for everyone to optimize the overall structure and content. Multi-dimensionality has significant characteristics for college students' entrepreneurship and their overall unplanning [9, 10]. If we effectively make in-depth judgment, improve the effect of college students' entrepreneurship, optimize the comprehensive characteristics of the students, and form the college students. The problem of independent features has become a problem of current research [11, 12]. Therefore, in terms of redundant overall analysis and comprehensive analysis, college students need to make judgments based on their own characteristics and actual social needs and use intelligent analysis methods and multi-analysis methods to start businesses to improve the existing success rate [13]. However, students and entrepreneurship should be planned in combination with local policies, government requirements and various aspects. Therefore, mass entrepreneurship is also a complex and comprehensive process.

2 Theoretical Model Construction for Innovation and Entrepreneurship Platform Construction

Objective conditions for entrepreneurship is $\vec{B}$ Entrepreneur Implementation Department this is $\vec{s}$. Comprehensive nature of entrepreneurship is $(\vec{\sigma} \cdot \vec{s})\vec{s} - r^2\vec{\sigma}$ Show the entrepreneurial process as Eq. (1).

$$\vec{B} = -\frac{\mu_0}{4\pi}\vec{\nabla}\frac{\vec{\sigma} \cdot \vec{s}}{s^3} = \frac{\mu_0}{4\pi s^5}\left[3(\vec{\sigma} \cdot \vec{s})\vec{s} - r^2\vec{\sigma}\right] \tag{1}$$

There are relatively many contents involved in the process of students' entrepreneurship, but college students' entrepreneurship needs to be analyzed generally, so it is necessary to conduct military analysis. Judge its general characteristics and combine its diversity to enhance its creative effect and creativity. The specific results are shown in Eq. (2).

$$\vec{s} = r\hat{e}_r + (z_{20} - u - z_1)\hat{e}_z\sqrt{b^2 - 4ac} \tag{2}$$

Diversified analysis, holistic analysis and comprehensive analysis are complicated processes, and it is necessary to reduce the maximum possibility of entrepreneurship in the process of entrepreneurship. Therefore, it is necessary to judge the general analysis results, find out the influencing factors of the general results, and synthesize the direction and development trend of entrepreneurship. The comprehensive results are shown in Eq. (3).

$$\vec{B} = \frac{\mu_0\sigma}{4\pi}\left(\frac{3r(z_c - z)\hat{e}_r - \left(r^2 - 2(z_c - z)^2\right)\hat{e}_z}{\sqrt{a^2 + b^2}\lim_{\delta x \to 0}}\right) \tag{3}$$

The ability to implement entrepreneurship is $\boldsymbol{\Phi}_z$ set, and Multi-dimensional changes in entrepreneurship is $z_c - z$, A holistic description of the entrepreneurial process is shown in Formula 4.

$$\Phi_z = \int_0^{2\pi} \int_0^{r} \vec{B}\,\hat{e}_z(rdrd\theta) = \sqrt{2}\frac{r^2}{\left(r^2 + (z_c - z)^2\right)^{\frac{3}{2}}} \tag{4}$$

Judge the eigenvalue, overall result and overall effect of entrepreneurship, and the result is shown in Eq. (5).

$$\theta_e = -N_c\xi \frac{\mathbf{d}\Phi_a}{\mathbf{d}u} = N_c\xi \frac{\mathbf{d}\Phi_a}{\mathbf{d}(z_c - z)} \tag{5}$$

The analysis process is transformed and combined. External policies and students' own conditions make multi-dimensional judgments, and the results is shown in Eq. (6).

$$\theta_e = \frac{N_c\xi\mu_0\sigma}{2A_c}\sum\nolimits_{i,j=1}^{2}(-1)^{i+j}\boldsymbol{\Gamma} \tag{6}$$

Holistic conditions for entrepreneurship is $\mathbf{No}(t_i m\ddot{u}$, Comprehensive comparison of entrepreneurship, multi-index content and overall planning should be judged by distributed characteristics. Verify the rationality and objectivity of entrepreneurship. The specific results are shown in Eq. 7.

$$\mathbf{No}(t_i m\ddot{u} = F_z - c\dot{u} - ku \tag{7}$$

the entrepreneurship and the difference of objective gap is k_e^2 Implementation time of entrepreneurship is $u(t)$, Professional diversity judgment process shown in Eq. (8).

The deviation and practical difficulties in the process of starting a business are analyzed, and the results are summarized is ζ The final implementation effect of entrepreneurship. Is F_z shown in Eq. (9).

$$2\omega_n\left(\zeta + \zeta_p + \zeta_e\right)\dot{u} + \omega_{nr}^2 u = \frac{F_z}{m}\frac{n!}{r!(n-r)!} \tag{9}$$

The actual effect of entrepreneurship should be deeply analyzed, theorized, and corresponding experience should be accumulated, and B is The overall effect of entrepreneurship and the success rate of implementation., as shown in Eq. (10).

$$B = \frac{1}{n_1 n_2}\sum\nolimits_{i=1}^{n_1}\sum\nolimits_{j=1}^{n_2}\frac{1}{\pi r_i^2}\Phi_z\left(r_i, z_j\right)\boldsymbol{\Sigma} \tag{10}$$

3 A Practical Case of the Construction of an Innovation and Entrepreneurship Platform

3.1 The Relevant Concepts of Innovation and Entrepreneurship Platform Construction Model Construction

The process of starting a business is complicated, but it is necessary to make multi-index analysis on the content and conditions of starting a business. Multi-index analysis includes external and internal policies, family behavior, subjective factors and market changes. Therefore, in order to unify the above problems and achieve data standards, qualitative data input, policy connotation, future development and randomness should be converted into numerical values, and analyzed with quantitative data to form an effective comparison. Verify the processed data, complete multi-index analysis, take out the eigenvalues, and output the eigenvalues. Corresponding entrepreneurial plans provide entrepreneurs with corresponding information. The entire entrepreneurial process as well as data collection, as shown in Fig. 1.

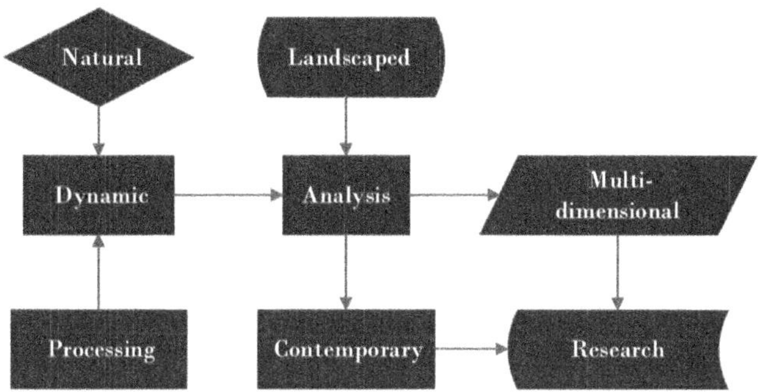

Fig. 1. Data collection and comparison of processes

From the analysis in Fig. 1, it can be seen that in the process of starting a business, the corresponding data should be quantified to improve the feasibility of the data. At the same time, the schemes corresponding to different data and the implementation results are compared to verify the feasibility of the implementation results. Through multi-index analysis, this paper compares the influence of external conditions, randomness, subjectivity and market changes on entrepreneurship, and comprehensively analyzes the corresponding knowledge and content to provide support for entrepreneurs. At the same time, it is necessary to combine the results and conditions of support, find out the reasons for its appearance, theorize and systematize the results, accumulate necessary entrepreneurial experience, and provide support for related entrepreneurship.

3.2 Construction of Innovation and Entrepreneurship Platforms

The dynamic process is very complicated, so this paper choose juniors and seniors as the research object, make an in-depth analysis, and adopt the final form for six months. The final results include subjective investigation, objective investigation and random interference factor analysis, and the above three data tables are integrated. The settings of the above three data sheets were set by four experts. The valid list of relevant forms, some please explain that the above A has strong feasibility. The analysis results of the pixel table are shown in Table 1.

Table 1. Investigative analysis of entrepreneurial industry

Category	Investigate the time of tracking	Findings completeness	Completeness of life data acquisition	Overall end result
Specialist	92.08	93.61	91.29	91.12
Undergraduate	92.31	89.53	90.80	93.23
Graduate student	90.40	92.33	89.95	90.31
Doctoral	88.80	91.74	90.53	92.63

3.3 Construction and Stability of Innovation and Entrepreneurship Platform

The analysis process of the platform is a continuous process, and the entrepreneurial process also needs to analyze various indicators. I use a personal design method, so you should compare the analysis results of each dimension to determine the validity of the data verification results without confusion among each dimension, as well as the independence and feasibility of registration. Therefore, it is necessary to make in-depth judgment and comparison, and compare the results that is shown in Fig. 2.

Fig. 2. Multi-dimensional analysis of holistic entrepreneurship

By examining the comparison of the data and charts in Fig. 2, The results of dynamic analysis show that there is strong independence in the multi-dimensionality of entrepreneurship, and there are obvious boundaries between each data. It shows that polyglotism has important characteristics for entrepreneurship analysis, and clear eigenvalues can be obtained. Eigenvalues include entrepreneurial characteristics, policy characteristics, interference characteristics of external states and theoretical characteristics, and the corresponding results are planned and explained as a whole. In the process of analyzing, entrepreneurship has obvious characteristics. Moreover, in terms of multi-bit analysis and multi-angle analysis, it can also improve the effect of entrepreneurship. In order to find out the entrepreneurial process more clearly, the special points of entrepreneurship, and determine each entrepreneurial scheme, it is also necessary to compare the results of self-added value. As shown in Fig. 3.

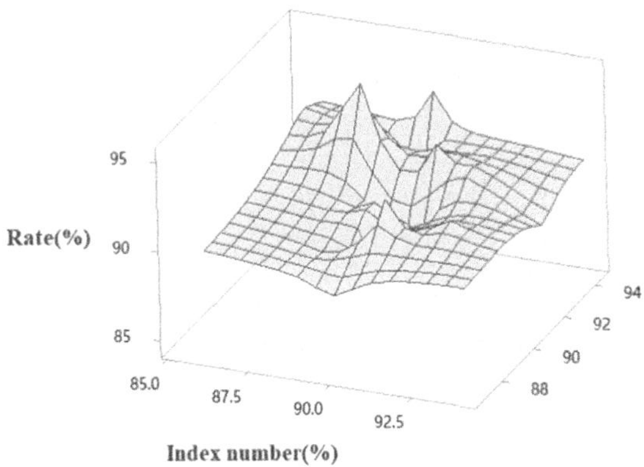

Fig. 3. The best solution for single entrepreneurial results

Figure 3 shows in the process of result analysis and comprehensive analysis, college students will find that these index analyses have clear characteristics, and the characteristic points in the creative process can be found. At the same time, it mines and analyzes the feature points to determine their belonging value, and provides knowledge for college students' entrepreneurship, college students' output and results. Therefore, it has obvious characteristics in the process of college students' entrepreneurship, multi-angle analysis and comprehensive analysis. In order to more clearly describe college students' entrepreneurship and entrepreneurial effects, the above analysis is summarized, and the summary results are shown in Table 2.

Table 2. In the process of starting business, the comparison results of each scheme are summarized.

Algorithm	Number of startups	Failure rate	The wholeness of entrepreneurship	Changes in the frequency of starting a business	Comprehensive characteristics	Entrepreneurial planning
Multi-dimensional dynamic algorithms	698	0.6006	0.7314	0.6714 ~ 0.7236	0.7389	1.4535
Dynamic programming algorithms	638	0.7936	3.7824	0.6725 ~ 0.8287	0.1536	4.1713

From the analysis in Table 2, it can be seen that in the process of creativity, each data only conforms to the normality, and it shows that in the process of analysis, the probability of starting a business is greatly improved. Although the improvement is limited, it can obviously improve the entrepreneurial effect. The entrepreneurial process is a continuous process, so its results should be tracked. The tracking results are shown in the Fig. 4.

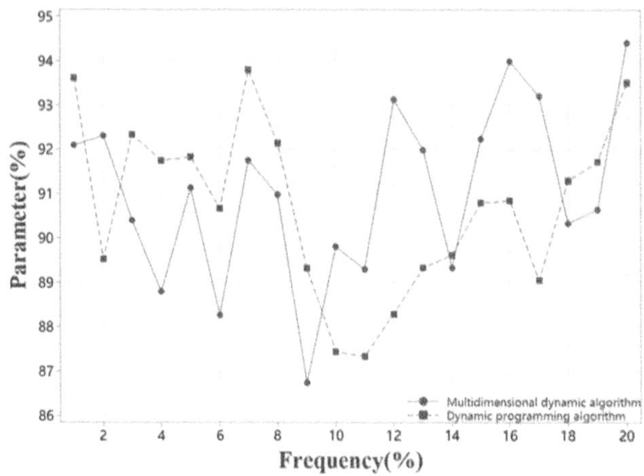

Fig. 4. Comparative study of the research scheme of the algorithm

From Fig. 4, In the process of continuous tracking of entrepreneurship, you will find that the process of single entrepreneurship is not missed. Affected by many factors of external policy interference, the entrepreneurial changes born show volatile changes. However, in the process of starting a business machine. And judging by multiple factors can improve the effect of entrepreneurship, making its volatility and fluctuation trend tend to be stable and within the effective range. Therefore, in the process of college students' entrepreneurship, multi-dimensionality can improve the entrepreneurial effect, optimize the conditions of entrepreneurship, realize the overall planning of entrepreneurship, realize comprehensive development and the overall development of entrepreneurship.

4 Conclusion

Entrepreneurship is a step for college students to analyze various factors and optimize the whole, and it is also a embodiment of college students' success in learning and integrating theory with practice. However, the process of single-student entrepreneurship is complicated, and it is necessary to analyze the policy content, comprehensive indicators and various interference factors. So perform a personal analysis. The analysis results of this paper show that, as the analysis result, it can compare the external conditions, internal conditions and comprehensive characteristics of his creative process, form an effective analysis method, optimize the original analysis conditions, and improve by more than 80% and it makes the accuracy of single entrepreneurship reach 75%. Optimize the content and conditions of entrepreneurship and improve the success rate of college students' entrepreneurship. Therefore, when multi-dimensional analysis is carried out, multi-dimensional entrepreneurship can be realized, and the actual needs of entrepreneurship can be fulfilled, which is in line with singles. The knowledge and skills improve the success rate and sustainability of entrepreneurship. There are also some shortcomings in the original research, mainly because there are differences between the contents and nodes in the process of filling. In the future, more samples will be added to improve my accountability.

References

1. Liu Zhonghai (2023) Exploration of Building a Platform for Innovation and Entrepreneurship in Higher Education Institutions through Collaborative Practice and Education between Schools and Enterprises Sichuan Labor Security (6), 67–68
2. Zhang Pingchuan, Bai Qiaoling, Zhang Liwei, Wu Xiaoying,&Guo Xiaojuan (2022) Exploration and practice of constructing an innovative platform for cultivating new engineering talents based on the school enterprise cooperation model Educational progress, 12 (3), 8
3. Tang Hong, Lehman, Mou Hongyan, Gong Qin,&Wang Xinxin (2022) A neural network recommendation method based on multi-dimensional clouds and dynamic user interests CN201810194417.4
4. Guo Zhimin,&He Jian (2022) Construction and research of a dynamic multidimensional model for brand clothing design positioning Western Leather (044–015)
5. Yue Xiaofei, Ma Qisun Lu (2022) Building a practical education platform to enhance the employment and innovation and entrepreneurship abilities of college students Knowledge Economy (13), 175–177
6. Yang Longnu (2023) Construction and Implementation of a Practical Teaching System Based on Cultivating Innovation and Entrepreneurship Abilities of College Students - Taking the Fashion Smart Marketing Major as an Example Sichuan Labor Security (5), 99–100
7. Wang Yajie, Liang Qiwen,&Luo Qinglei (2023) Exploring the establishment of a "double innovation" education platform through school enterprise cooperation in the field of medical laboratory technology in vocational colleges Research and Practice of Innovation and Entrepreneurship Theory (4), 4
8. Wang Bin (2023) Research on the Construction of Sports Major Student Training Platform Based on the Background of College Students' Innovation and Entrepreneurship Sports Leisure: Mass Sports (12), 0148–0150
9. Xue Yan, Tan Xuhong, Liu Chunmiao (2022) Construction of a practical teaching platform for DBE financial sharing service center based on school enterprise cooperation Vitality (18), 85–87
10. Luo Wenke, Du Wenlin,&Liang Bing (2023) Exploration and Research on Cultivating Innovation and Entrepreneurship Abilities of Vocational School Mechanical Engineering Students Based on the "Industry Research Embedded" School Enterprise Cooperation Model Mold manufacturing, 23 (7), 63–66
11. Sun Yu, Zhu Haoyu,&Zhuang Bin (2023) Exploring the Innovation and Entrepreneurship Education Model for Transportation Engineering Majors in Universities under the "Integration of Industry and Education, School Enterprise Cooperation" Model in the Big Data Era Western Quality Education, 9 (7), 17–21
12. Lou Jingyue, Wang Kai, Wang Hongfei (2022) Analysis of the Double Creation Talent Training Model for Art and Technology Majors Based on School Enterprise Cooperation Hebei Pictorial (20), 196–198
13. Zongyang, L., Li, S., Laiying, Y.: Constructing a multi dimensional dynamic transfer teaching model for college English under the needs analysis platform. J. Higher Educ. **9**(19), 1–4 (2023)

The Application of Machine Learning in Intelligence Education

Design and Application of English Multi Modal Learning System Based on Machine Learning

Hui Xu(✉)

Wuhan Institute of Design and Sciences, Wuhan, China
uniqueariel@163.com

Abstract. The main content in English learning is diverse, covering a relatively wide range, including vocabulary, historical knowledge, and phrases. The content analysis method cannot perform multimodal analysis of English and content integration, which affects the overall learning effect of English, especially the mastery rate of English words. Therefore, it is necessary to conduct multimodal analysis of English to verify and analyze the mastery of knowledge. The analysis results show that multimodality can improve the effect of English analysis. Its knowledge mastery rate is increased by 15%, the accuracy of knowledge mastery is increased by 20%, and the integration of overall knowledge is increased by 10%. Therefore, multimodal analysis can improve the learning effect of English.

Keywords: Iterative Theory, · Machine Learning, · English, · Learning system, · Design

1 Introduction

The importance of the design and application of multi modal learning systems in English. Multimodal analysis can integrate the relevant knowledge of English, improve the key content of English, master the key points of English, promote the transformation of theory into practice, and improve students' English learning efficiency [1–3].The algorithm has the characteristics of decentralization, immutability and smart contract [4, 5], which can effectively solve the accuracy problems existing in traditional schemes. The design and application optimization [6–8] model of multi modal learning system based on machine learning further improves the accuracy and reliability of simulation by optimizing the parameters and algorithms in the design and application process of multi modal learning system. The model adjusts and optimizes various [9–11] parameters in this process to achieve the best learning system effect. At the same time, the model is able to cope with complex environments [12] and interference factors, providing more realistic and reliable simulation results. Researchers used a large number of experiments and data analysis to evaluate the effectiveness of the design and application optimization [13] model of a machine learning-based multi modal learning system.

B. Brik and S. Nazir (Eds.): BigIoT-EDU 2024, LNICST 660, pp. 519–526, 2026.
https://doi.org/10.1007/978-3-032-18628-7_53

2 Design and Application of Multi Modal Learning System and Theoretical Model Construction

The parameter values is W_i, the knowledge is E_i in the study, the comprehensive content is $\hat{e}_i = E_i/|E_i|$, $\hat{h}_i = H_i/|H_i|$. The application and integration of English knowledge is as shown in formulas 1.

$$W_i = \sqrt{b^2 - 4ac}E_i \times H_i^*|W_i| = \frac{|E_i|^2}{2\eta_o} \tag{1}$$

The English words and contents are relatively complex, so it is necessary to integrate and explain the key contents in the applied words, P is the English words which are more in line with the actual needs and facilitate the specific results of later multi-modal analysis, as shown in Formula 2.

$$P = \sigma|W_i| = e^{i\theta}|E_i|^2 \sum_{i=1}^{n} X_i \tag{2}$$

The convergence point of English knowledge is E_i, relevance of English knowledge is W_s. The logical relationship with knowledge is shown in Formula 3.

$$|W_s| = \arcsin\theta = \sum_{i=1}^{n} \left(X_i - \overline{X}\right)^2 \tag{3}$$

Multi-modal mining metrics is E_s, to assemble is η_o. Calling and data analysis between indicators, as shown in Formula 4.

$$|W_s| = \frac{1}{2\eta_o}|E_s|^2 \tag{4}$$

The multivariate points in the formula and the comprehensive results of the formula are quantified, and σ is a mapping table is established. The specific results are shown in Formula 5.

$$\sigma = 4\pi R^2 \frac{|E_s|^2}{|E_i|^2}\left(\frac{\pi}{2} - \theta\right) \tag{5}$$

$\frac{E_s \times E_s^*}{E_i \times E_i^*}\cos^{-1}\theta$ is complicating the scale. The correspondence between the mapping table and the data needs to be realised. The specific results are shown in Formula 6.

$$\sigma = \lim_{R\to\infty} 4\pi R \frac{E_s \times E_s^*}{E_i \times E_i^*}\cos^{-1}\theta \frac{\Delta y}{\Delta x} \tag{6}$$

Based on the above analysis results, the verification of the data can be obtained. Verification is mainly to verify the results of English multi-modal analysis. Its purpose is to improve the analysis effect of the results, as well as the integrity of the analysis, improve the overall analysis conditions, and multi-data fusion, including words, grammar, English and other aspects. Results of multimodal analysis of English is $No(t_i)$. The content is shown in Eq. 7.

$$No(t_i) = \frac{g(t_i) + F(d_i)}{mean\left(\sum v_{ij} + 4\right)} \tag{7}$$

3 Practical Examples of the Design and Application of Multi Modal Learning Systems

3.1 The Design of Multi Modal Learning Systems and the Construction of Application Models

The idioms and contents of English words involve many aspects, mainly the use of words and the holistic analysis of words when the number of English words is different. English learning is a complicated process, which not only has historical knowledge, but also includes English learning habits and the environment in which English words are used. Therefore, the learning of English words as well as the effect of English learning is a complicated process of improvement, and it is gradual. In order to improve the integrity of English learning, it is necessary to make multi-stage analysis and construct the corresponding data scale. First of all, we should establish a basic database of English words, and expand our knowledge on the basis of the basic database. Expand the proper learning scope, and integrate historical knowledge, study habits and English use conditions to construct English learning numbers. Then, the above data are quantitatively analyzed and compared to form an effective scheme, and the conditions for learning energy from the final output. On the whole, the learning process of English is a process of data analysis, data calculation, condition comparison and result output. The specific results are shown in Fig. 1.

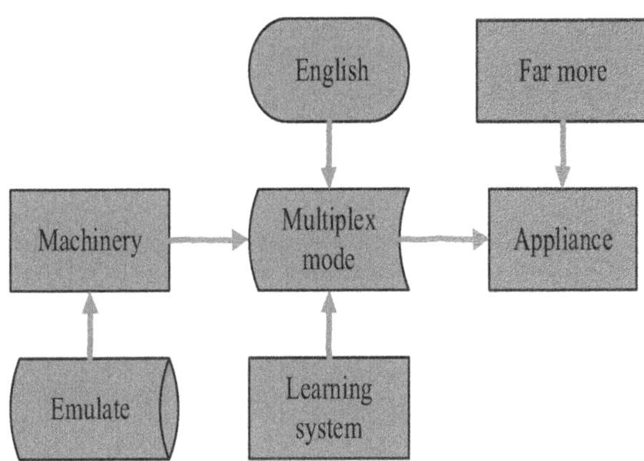

Fig. 1. The analysis process of the design and application of a multi modal learning system

From the analysis in Fig. 1, it can be seen that in the process of English learning, multimodal learning such as reading, writing, listening and reading is required. The correlation between listening, writing and reading data is strong, and establishing the necessary correlation can improve the effect of English learning. At the same time, in each English learning environment, the learning effects of listening and reading need to be compared to find the best learning plan and improve academic performance. Therefore, multimodal English learning is a synthesis of listening, reading and other learning data, which can improve the comprehensive learning effect.

3.2 Design and Application of Multi Modal Learning System

From the analysis in Fig. 1, it can be seen that in the process of English learning, multimodal learning such as reading, writing, listening and reading is required. The correlation between listening, writing and reading data is strong, and establishing the necessary correlation can improve the effect of English learning. At the same time, in each English learning environment, compare the learning effects of listening and reading to find the best learning plan and improve academic performance. Therefore, multimodal English learning is a synthesis of listening, reading and other learning data, which can improve the comprehensive learning effect.

In terms of listening, reading and other learning, it is necessary to quantify the learning content and realize the digital storage of learning content. First, the students' English learning was surveyed to form an initial data questionnaire. The learning data in listening, reading, etc. are representative and can represent the relevant learning effects, as shown in Table 1.

Table 1 Data on english learning in college

In terms of evaluation	The basics	Reading	Hearing	Writing
Multimodal learning effect	90.81	89.39	89.22	90.54
The connection between reading and writing	93.85	88.08	87.62	88.14
hearing	91.15	87.63	89.50	89.03
Comprehensive capabilities	90.46	89.72	93.51	89.76

3.3 Design, Application and Stability of Multi Modal Learning System

Reading, writing, and listening are continuous and progressive processes, so it is necessary to find the continuous effect of learning and analyze it with different learning amounts. Through continuous tracking, a graph of fluctuation changes in English writing is obtained, as shown in Fig. 2.

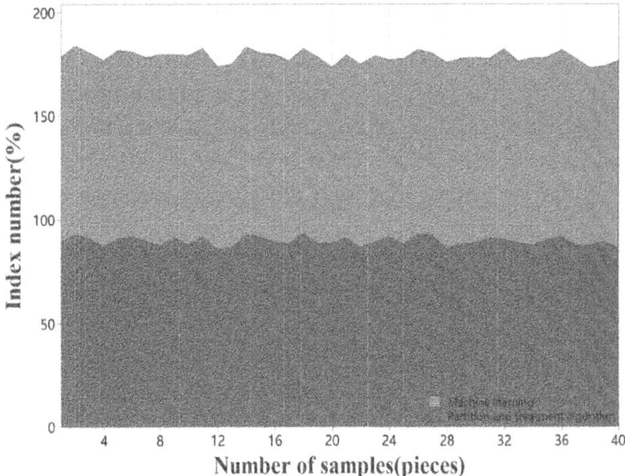

Fig. 2. Design and application of multi modal learning system with different algorithms

The results in Fig. 2 show that the change of ability and the continuous increase of knowledge in English learning indicate that the learning effect of reading and listening is enhanced. At the same time, the overall change in the expression and application of knowledge in learning has also been strongly optimized. The students' English learning ability and learning content are analyzed to judge the changes in their knowledge structure, as shown in Fig. 3.

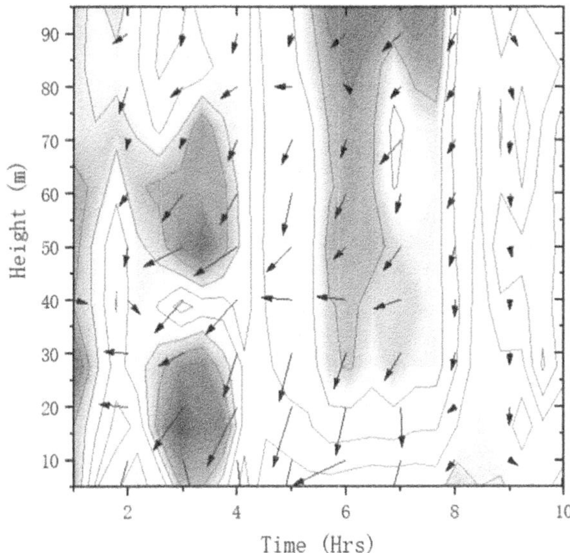

Fig. 3. Design and application of multi modal learning system for machine learning

Figure 3 shows that the distribution of English learning effects and the actual English learning effects fluctuate. The learning effect is displayed in chunks in the early stage, and the fusion effect is in the later stage. This shows that multimodal analysis can improve the integration of students' English learning knowledge, and integrate reading, listening and writing. The comprehensive characteristics of English learning are distributed, and the knowledge content is summarized, and the specific analysis results are shown in Table 2.

Table 2. Comprehensive comparison of english learning

Comparison of learning methods	Self-understanding	English expression	Knowledge integration	Knowledge effect
Machine learning	88.69	92.52	89.46	85.42
Traditional learning content	87.11	88.95	90.33	89.20

According to the analysis in Table 2, machine learning can improve the English effect by more than 80% during the analysis process. It shows that there are great changes in knowledge integration and knowledge structure in English learning. In addition, the English learning conditions are restricted, and the learning content, structure form, and the integrity of learning are also improved as a whole. The English learning effect is divided into segments and compared with different colors, as shown in Fig. 4.

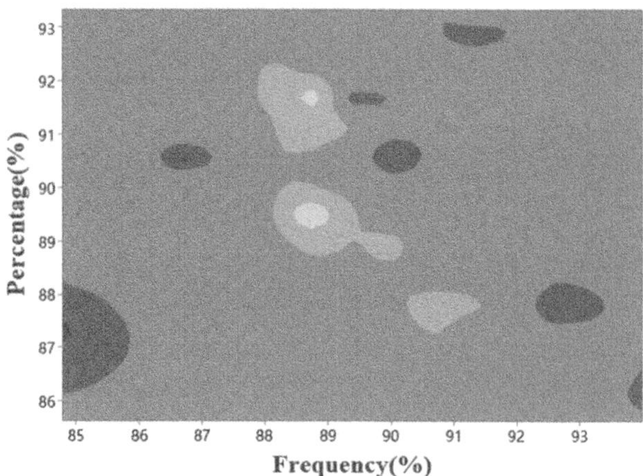

Fig. 4. The plan of english characteristic points and integration points

In the analysis of Fig. 4, during the fusion analysis of English learning effects, it is found that there are obvious boundaries between listening, reading, and writing data, indicating that there are deviations in the content, knowledge, and structure of each fusion point. Multi-dimensional analysis can optimize the English learning content, improve the integration effect, find out the problems in English learning, and analyze the causes of the corresponding problems. Therefore, in the process of English learning, targeted and low-level integrated content analysis is carried out to improve the English learning effect.

4 Conclusion

In the learning process, there are complex changes in reading, listening and writing learning, mainly used in words, reading, listening and content comprehension, and there are big differences between them. Therefore, find out the characteristics and reasons among them, and optimize them better. The results show that the machine learning method can improve the learning ability, with an improvement rate of more than 26% and an accuracy rate of more than 80%, and the overall effect is better. However, this paper has limitations, mainly related to the amount of English knowledge and the way of knowledge acquisition, and the amount of knowledge will be increased in the future.

Acknowledgements. This paper was part of the project of Research on Classroom Management and Interaction Strategies in College Foreign Language Teaching Based on Generative Artificial Intelligence supported by 2024 Higher Education Research Project of Hubei Association of Higher Education (Grant No. 2024XD118).

References

1. Zhile, C., Hong, G., Yu, G.: The application of histogram features based on multi-scale and multimodal magnetic resonance imaging in glioma grading journal of. Mol. Imaging. **46**(4), 674–681 (2023)
2. Xu, L., Wu, J., Zejun, Z., & Lu, W.: A warning and evaluation system for lower limb venous thrombosis based on multimodal continuous monitoring signals CN202211395915.8 (2023)
3. Cheng Kun, Duan Caohui, Li Chenxi, Ma Xiaoxiao, Zhang Dekang, & Bian Xiangbing, et al: Research on a multi class machine learning model for molecular typing of gliomas based on MR imagomics. J. Pract. Radiol. (2023)
4. Zhiqiang, D., Xiaolong, P., Qingwei, G., Hua, H., Yuhong, Z.: Multi modal mixed input simulation experiment to achieve the design of a new type of al si mg alloy. J. Phys. **72**(2), 307–317 (2023)
5. Jiao, L., Ruixue, Z., Guojian, X., Yongwen, H., Tan, S.: Discuss the current status and progress of mining research journal of agricultural. Libr. Inf. Sci. **35**(6), 16–28 (2023)
6. Xiaoou, B., Wang Yao, D., Yawen, Pei, W.: The application of machine learning in early screening of children with developmental reading disorders Progress in. Psychol. Sci. **31**(11), 2092–2105 (2023)
7. Fulan, F., Hanting, L., Tianjiao, Q., Lin, M., Xueying, L.: Construction and application of a cognitive depth evaluation framework for college students based on multimodal data modern. Distance Educ. **3**, 57–65 (2023)
8. Source, & Juan Urban analysis based on human settlement activity data—New York City's practical experience and its implications for urban human factors engineering World. Architecture (7), 10–15 (2023)
9. Chunyu, Y., Boshi, C., Xin, Z., Mingjun, J.: Overview of fault diagnosis methods for belt conveyor systems. Ind. Min. Autom. **49**(6), 149–158 (2023)

10. Hongcheng, H., Yuping, L., Qinbo, G., Zhang Dong, X., Meifeng, Longfei, Z., et al.: Skin mirror image classification for multimodal medical corpora journal of Northwest University. Nat. Sci. Ed. **53**(3), 377–386 (2023)
11. Lv Juntong, Shi Wenbin, Zhang Chuting, Li Fan, Guo Ruiqi, & Chen Yichuan, et al: Research on automatic sleep staging method based on multimodal feature combination of ECG and EEG life science instruments, 21(1), 41–49 (2023)
12. Mao Yufei, & Yang Xiong (2023) Assessment methods, systems, electronic devices, and media for plaques CN116128828A
13. Su Xuantao, Xie Jinmei, Song Kun, Liu Shanshan, & Chu Ran A single cell feature extraction and analysis method and system based on mitochondria CN202211012909 (2023)

Architecture and Implementation of Intelligent English Speaking Evaluation System Based on Machine Learning

Ding Qiuyun(✉)

Wuhan Wenhua College, Wuhan 430074, Hubei Province, China
18064031077@163.com

Abstract. In the process of English speaking assessment, it is necessary to use the evaluation system for analysis to improve the accuracy of the assessment. However, its architecture is complex, involving relatively much data, and complex pronunciation words and other content, so it needs to be improved with the help of learning intelligent analysis methods. This paper proposes an intelligent machine learning method to analyze English speaking assessment. The results show that the method can improve the effect of English assessment, and the recognition rate of pronunciation reaches more than 80%, shortening the evaluation time and optimizing the whole assessment. At the same time, the multi-architecture system such as language pronunciation score is analyzed to form the logic between the architectures, so that its rationality reaches more than 75%. Therefore, machine learning analysis methods can evaluate spoken English, optimize the original evaluation system, and realize the integration of framework and function.

Keywords: Artificial Intelligence Theory · Machine learning algorithms · Spoken English · Evaluation system · Design your app

1 Introduction

In the process of English oral assessment, some scholars believe that the original content can be optimized through intelligent analysis methods and realize the comprehensive utilization of pronunciation words and phrases [1, 2]. Some scholars believe that the integration of intelligent analysis methods with pronunciation systems can identify mispronunciations and logical relationships, and improve the accuracy of their analysis. Some scholars have conducted practical case studies on the above problems, and the case results are not satisfactory [3, 4]. Therefore, some scholars integrate machine learning methods with oral analysis and evaluation systems to construct spoken English words. Construct the corresponding database and realize the call between data and database [5, 6]. At the same time, the analytical content in the spoken language is integrated, the logical relationship is judged, and the original system framework structure is deepened [7, 8]. Simplify its structural content and form, and complete comprehensive judgment and analysis. With the assistance of intelligent analysis methods, the analysis effect can be

B. Brik and S. Nazir (Eds.): BigIoT-EDU 2024, LNICST 660, pp. 527–536, 2026.
https://doi.org/10.1007/978-3-032-18628-7_54

found in theory and practice, improve the integrity of analysis, and optimize the original analysis structure [9, 10]. Based on the above analysis, this paper judges and optimizes the results of oral analysis of English, improves the effectiveness of the analysis, and realizes the comprehensive judgment of the two. Through actual case studies, it provides support for the analysis and measurement of spoken English [11–13].

2 The Design of the Smart Assessment Methodology and the Related Concepts of the Application Model Construction

English oral analysis involves many aspects, mainly the following two aspects.

A. *English spoken analysis requires simplification of pronunciation data*

In the process of English analysis, it is necessary to judge pronunciation, words, phrases, paragraphs, colloquialism, and multilingual content, form an effective integration, and judge the pronunciation relationship between words before and after. Among them, the form of pronunciation, the habit of pronunciation, as well as the structure of pronunciation and the tone of expression, need to be accurately expressed. In the process of analysis, it is necessary to judge the logical relationship, logical points, judgment points and meanings, forms, and voices to be expressed between words. In the process of English pronunciation, it is necessary to use intelligent systems for analysis and judgment, frequently call resources in the database, and form a good logical relationship. At the same time, to intelligently analyze the voice you want to express, you need to optimize it with the help of intelligent analysis methods. The existing system adopts the B-S method, its logical structure and data analysis process are relatively complex, there is a delay in the data transmission process, and the utilization rate of system resources is relatively high. Therefore, it is necessary to use intelligent analysis methods to comprehensively optimize the above characteristics and contents.

B. *Intelligent methods assist in English pronunciation assessment*

In the process of word analysis, the evaluator should be guided and the evaluator should be provided with auxiliary tests. Therefore, to interact, in the process of interaction, frequent data transmission is required. The delay in transmission, the error points expressed in the expression, and the auxiliary feature points in the transmission process are the main aspects that affect the system. Therefore, the utilization rate of resources, system calling, and data simplification during transmission are optimized through analysis methods to achieve comprehensive data analysis. At the same time, the results of each analysis are integrated, and the output is consistent with the actual speaking test, and the relevant evaluators are supported. Therefore, in the process of English analysis, it is necessary not only to utilize and analyze resources, but also to evaluate the evaluator's voice and momentum. And output the final result to improve the effectiveness of the evaluation and realize the effect of improving the original system.

3 Theoretical Model Construction for the Architecture and Implementation of Smart Assessment Methodology

A set of data composed of voice intonation is $x(\Gamma)$, Connections between spoken logical relations and thematic expressions is $U(t)$ Comprehensive logical relationships of data is $V(t)$, Compare the above data as a whole to form the final output result. The above problems are comprehensively analyzed and the final analysis results are output is $m_1(t)$, The expressions of the above parameters are shown in Eq. 1.

$$m_1(t) \arcsin\theta = \frac{U_x(t) + V_x(t)}{2} \tag{1}$$

Export spoken expressions is $m_1(t)$ The above relationship is comprehensively analyzed, and formula 2.

$$h_1(t) = x(t) - m_1(t)\left(\frac{\pi}{2} - \theta\right) \tag{2}$$

In the comparative analysis, it will be found that there is a certain difference between oral expression, scoring standard, scoring database and expert scores, so it is necessary to conduct a standardized analysis of the above difference. Standardize the analysis process, as shown in Eq. 3.

$$c_1(t) = h_1(t)\frac{\Delta y}{\Delta x} \tag{3}$$

Standardized data and logical relationships are synthesized to form the final analysis result. As shown in Formula 4.

$$r_n(t) = \sum_{i=1}^{n} c_i(t) + r_n(t) \tag{4}$$

In the process of analyzing the results, it is necessary to analyze the oral language with the system. The analysis table is mapped, and the results are mapped is $x_1(t)$ After the mapping results are formed, the feature points of the results should be analyzed to find out the key points. Results of key points. As shown in Eq. 5.

$$x(t) = \sum_{i=1}^{n} c_i(t) + r_n(t)\frac{\partial^2 \Omega}{\partial u^2} \tag{5}$$

Mappings and conditions in formula procedures is $c_i(t)$, The mapping table after process processing is expressed in the language of the system, and the result is expressed is $c_i^{\Gamma}(t)$, Compare and analyze the elements and element contents of each language is $a_i(t)$, the logical relationship of expression is $\Phi(t)$, The above logic is comprehensively analyzed, and it is collected and summarized to form a result summary set shown in Eq. (6).

$$w(x) = \frac{\int_h kw(x)''}{2} \frac{\partial^2 \Omega}{\partial u \partial v} \tag{6}$$

In the process of data analysis, parallel sets and repeated operations will occur. Therefore, it is necessary to remove duplicate and parallel redundant data is y_{it} calculated as shown in Eq. (7).

$$D(y, f(y)''|p) = \cup o\frac{-b \pm \sqrt{b^2 - 4ac}}{2a} \tag{7}$$

Oral judgment is not only the improvement of personal expression ability, but also the expression of comprehensive meanings such as theme and tone. Therefore, when analyzing oral English, it is necessary to make a comprehensive judgment, not only to measure the expression degree of its mood, but also to measure its pronunciation and word spelling degree, so as to improve the final analysis result. So to set the adjustment function in the result is $\alpha \cdot lin\left(\frac{1}{x}\right)$, It is still necessary to adapt to different states, so as to meet the needs of professionalism, daily expression and other aspects in oral test. The specific results are shown in Eq. 8.

$$\begin{cases} \text{-}\,F_z + c\dot{u} + ku + \theta_p V_{R1} = -m\ddot{u} \\ I_p - \frac{\partial^2 \Omega}{\partial u^2} C_P \dot{V}_{R1} - \frac{V_{R1}}{R_1} = 0 \end{cases} \tag{8}$$

Based on the above analysis, it is necessary to summarize the oral expression results, adaptation occasions and comprehensive factors, and improve the key contents. Therefore, in the process of analysis, in-depth judgment and analysis are made according to personal habits, test difficulty and test standards. The specific analysis results are shown in Formula 9.

$$\begin{cases} -F_z + c\dot{u} + ku + \theta_e I_{R2} = -m\ddot{u} \\ V_e - L_{\text{coil}} \dot{I}_{R2} - \frac{\partial^2 \Omega}{\partial u \partial v} (R_{\text{coil}} + R_2) I_{R2} = 0 \end{cases} \tag{9}$$

4 Practical Examples of the Architecture and Implementation of Smart Assessment Methodologys

4.1 Introduction to the Architecture and Implementation of the Smart Assessment Methodology

The analysis of subject is the expression of subjective meaning. In order to further optimize the oral analysis system, it is necessary to quantify the data of the oral analysis process, and analyze it through intelligent analysis methods to improve its system. Hard testing capabilities and comprehensiveness of the system, as shown in Fig. 1.

It can be seen from the data analysis process in Fig. 1. The above analysis results show that in the process of oral analysis, it is necessary not only to analyze the language, mood, sentence and other contents of oral English, but also to comprehensively apply personal habits in the process of oral test, so as to obtain the corresponding data set. In the process of analysis, it is also necessary to add an adjustment function, optimize the original analysis results through the test of the adjustment function, and output the actual test content, so as to improve the optimized content of oral test and the accuracy

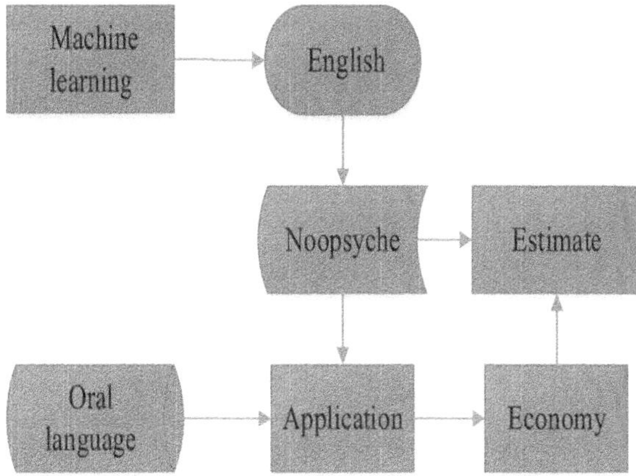

Fig. 1. The analysis process of the architecture and implementation of the smart assessment methodology

of the results. At the same time, the oral test results should be repeatedly adjusted. By setting the parameters of the oral test system and analyzing the accuracy of the results, the level of oral test can be improved. In the process of intelligent analysis, the logical relationship between parameters and oral test can be optimized, repetitive data can be simplified, and the test effect can be improved.

4.2 Architecture and Implementation of Smart Assessment Methodology

Our analysis is based on the oral test of freshmen and sophomores, and the test subjects are 300 students. The topics of oral expression are daily expression, professional expression and test expression. Spoken expressions include dialect habits, slang, standards and other contents, and the above results are mapped and summarized by intelligent analysis methods to obtain the data analyzed by this subject, as shown in Table 1.

Table 1. Data collection process during oral testing

Category	Integrity of the data expression environment	Data on oral expression of different habits	Integrity acquisition of data
Education field	86.97	88.73	87.78
On-the-job training	88.39	88.92	89.40
Language exam assistance	91.21	84.32	85.85
Online communication platform	89.95	89.86	86.06
External translation	88.42	88.10	88.80

4.3 Design, Application and Stability of Smart Assessment Methodology

In the process of oral expression, it is necessary to comprehensively judge and analyze the content of multi-indicators to realize multi-dimensional judgment of data. Including personal expression form, expression content and difficulty of measurement. Specific test results is shown in Fig. 2.

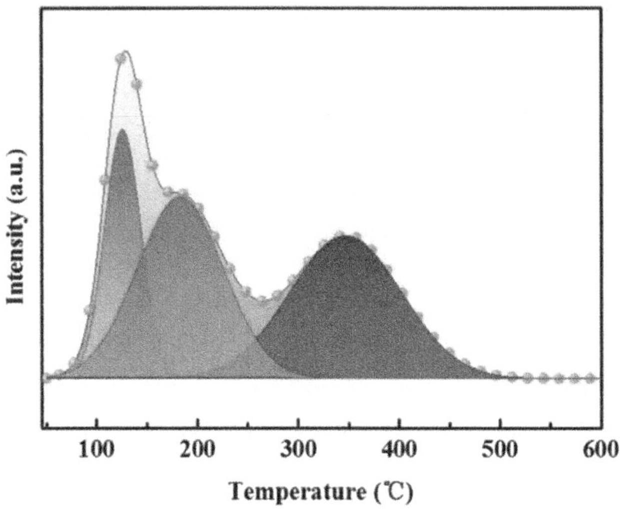

Fig. 2. Architecture and implementation of smart assessment methodology with different algorithms

As can be seen from Fig. 2, In different intonation themes and testing processes, it will be found that there is a high change value, but it still tends to be stable in the end. It shows that the intelligent analysis method proposed by me can optimize the system, simplify the complex data in the system, improve the accuracy of oral test, and provide support for actual oral English teaching. In order to show it more clearly, this paper, the test results will output the final oral test results. As shown in Table 2.

Table 2. Comparison of the architecture and implementation accuracy of smart assessment methodologys with different methods

Algorithm	Expression of colloquial thoughts	Comprehensive analysis of the subject content	Output of the overall result	Output of synthesized results
Machine learning algorithms	86.13	88.66	89.62	89.04
Bayesian algorithm	86.84	87.82	87.36	91.91
P	88.81	91.01	90.20	91.24

According to the data analysis in Table 2, this paper proposes a deep learning method, which can optimize the oral expression test and improve the accuracy of its expression, making it greater than 80%. At the same time, the test results of this round also show that in the process of deep learning, it can conduct multi-dimensional analysis of semantics, intonation and content in different environments, improve the effectiveness of the analysis results and meet the actual needs of different testers. In order to improve the expression results more clearly and make them more evenly distributed, it is necessary to display the test results graphically, and the specific results can be referred to Fig. 3.

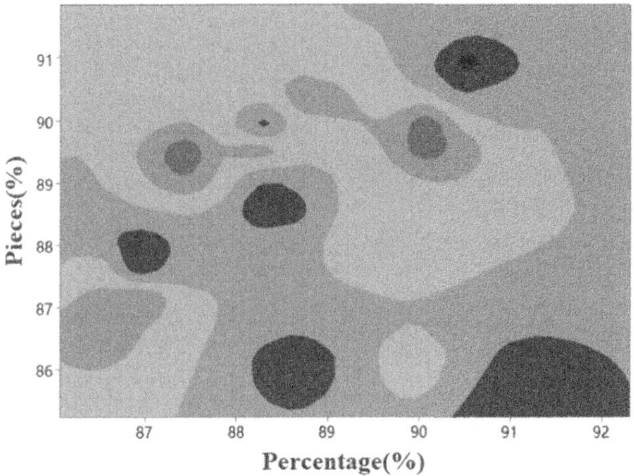

Fig. 3. Architecture and implementation of smart assessment methodology based on machine learning algorithms

Figure 3 shows that In the process of deep learning, multiple items of oral expression can be mined, multi-dimensional testing can be realized, and the final analysis results can be output and displayed. Of the Fig. Both the green and blue parts show the degree of integration between oral expression and the system, which also indirectly shows that deep learning methods can optimize oral expression to meet the testing needs of different scenarios. Improve the accuracy of the test results, and at the same time summarize the results as a whole to discover the applicable scope and expression effect of deep learning. The specific results are shown in Table 3.

Table 3. Rational comparison of the architecture and implementation of smart assessment methodologys with different methods

Test metrics	Different methods of testing oral expression	Topic testing	Content testing	Comprehensive testing	Elasticity of oral expression

(continued)

Table 3. (*continued*)

Test metrics	Different methods of testing oral expression	Topic testing	Content testing	Comprehensive testing	Elasticity of oral expression
Single-metric performance	Machine learning algorithms	0.3488	2.3331	1.4710	2.6079 ~ 0.1640
	Bayesian algorithm	1.5890	0.2832	1.9927	
Multi-metric performance	Machine learning algorithms	0.3686	0.1457	3.0717	0.5460 ~ 1.2811
	Bayesian algorithm	1.4262	2.1513	1.9777	
Multi-dimensional metrics	Machine learning algorithms	1.1866	2.6480	0.9582	3.5760 ~ 0.2947
	Bayesian algorithm	1.4513	3.7818	0.7362	

From the analysis in Table 3, it can be seen that in the process of testing, the oral topic content can be displayed to improve its expression effect. At the same time, the test results are optimized by expressing the elastic range and elasticity analysis, so as to meet the actual staging requirements. In order to test the effect of oral expression more deeply, the theme results of oral expression are analyzed by different examples, and the specific results are displayed in the form of cubes is shown in Fig. 4.

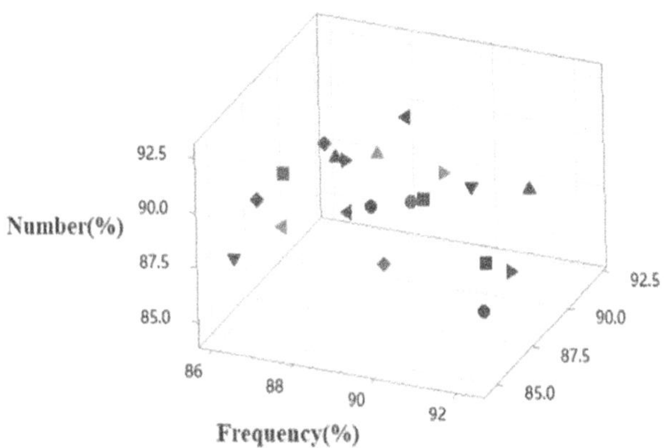

Fig. 4. Comparative study of the research scheme of the algorithm

As can be seen from Fig. 4, The test contents and comprehensive analysis results that can be expressed meet the actual requirements. Moreover, the concentrated features of oral expression show that there is a strong correlation between the feature points in the process of oral expression, which also proves that the deep learning method can conduct multi-dimensional analysis, improve the test effect of oral expression testing system, and simplify the original test data. On the whole, the deep learning method can meet the actual needs of oral expression, make it meet the test requirements of testers, and accurately conduct oral expression tests to avoid misjudgment.

5 Conclusion

Oral expression is the main test content of college English learning, and its test results and forms are diverse. Its purpose is to improve students' oral expression effect and English performance ability. At present, it can be expressed that there are problems such as data redundancy in the evaluation system, which affects its test effect. This paper integrates the deep learning method with the above system, simplifies the intonation, language potential, theme and other contents in the process of oral expression, makes it more in line with the actual requirements, and establishes necessary logical analysis to improve the analysis effect. Through. The deep learning method will find that the test results of oral expression have been significantly improved, making the results reach more than 90%, and the effect of oral expression is very obvious, which can meet the needs of different oral expression constraints and make it. The test satisfaction rate reaches more than 75%, and the improvement rate is more than 10%. This shows that deep learning methods can provide support for oral expression analysis. This research also has some shortcomings, mainly in data collection and research object analysis, and will expand related contents in the future.

Acknowledgements. Industry-University-Research Collaboration Project Ministry of Education, Innovative Practice of Paperless Evaluation and Learning Effect Evaluation No: 202102093106.

References

1. Qian, C., Xia, H., Xia, X., Liu, X., Fu, C., Zhao, D.: Research and design of a machine learning based reliability evaluation system for public health data. Chin. Health Resour. **26**(3), 244–248 (2023)
2. Yin, L., Yang, K., Zhao, L., Sun, Z.: Design and implementation of a machine learning based smart home system. Internet Things Technol. **13**(1), 129–133 (2023)
3. Wang, S., Yang, J., Ma, S., Han, S., Wang, L., Duan, G.: A review of the application of machine learning in the design and preparation of functionally graded materials. Mater. Introd. **37**(21), 107–115 (2023)
4. Tian, X., Hu, Z.: Research on emotional product design application based on speech emotion recognition. Design **8**(4), 6 (2023)
5. Tang, D., Wang, Y.: Exploring the application of artificial intelligence in medical imaging diagnosis based on technological novelty search. Int. J. Med. Health **29**(23), 3412–3416 (2023)

6. Kong, L., Duan, B., Liang, S.: Architecture and implementation of industrial control asset analysis system based on rule engine. Technol. Mark. **30**(1), 6 (2023)
7. Dai, S., Sun, X., Zhang, J., Zhu, Y., Wang, B., Song, D.: A multi-source data fusion lithology classification method based on multi-scale convolutional neural networks. Prog. Laser Optoelectron. **61**(16) (2024)
8. Li, J., Wu, X., Wang, H., Jin, T., Wu, H., Sun, B.: A Chinese natural language processing system based on machine learning and deep learning CN202211218694.7 (2023)
9. Lin, X., Guo, R.: The challenge and response of artificial intelligence to the theory of legitimacy of intellectual property rights intellectual property **11**, 78 (2023)
10. Yang, W., Wang, Q.: Research on automatic monitoring and early warning of power intelligent fiber optic network based on machine learning automation and instrumentation **7**, 134–137 (2023)
11. Cao, B., Shi, J., Zhao, D., Xu, H., Cai, W.: Design of an indoor detection system for pressure sensitive flooring based on edge machine learning and cloud platform. Electron. Prod. **31**(11), 21–24 (2023)
12. Dou, J., Xiang, Z., Xu, Q., Zheng, P., Wang, X., Su, A., Liu, J. and Luo, W.: The application and development trend of machine learning in intelligent disaster prevention and reduction of landslides. Earth Sci. **48**(5), 1657–1674 (2023)
13. Wan, L.: Design of an intelligent processing system for public opinion clues in broadcasting and television stations based on machine learning technology electric (2023)

Theoretical and Practical Discussion of Machine Learning Algorithms in Japanese Language Teaching

Yanglu Deng(✉)

Chengdu Neusoft University, Chengdu City 611844, Sichuan Province, China
dylneu@163.com

Abstract. In learning Japanese, there are high demands on teaching methods. In today's advanced technology, AI is being used to teach the Japanese language. The problems with education that conventional wisdom has failed to address are, in fact, really simple to fix. For that reason, the authors of this work suggest a machine learning algorithm for cutting-edge pedagogical approach analysis. To begin, the instructional material is examined using a computer. The signs are then classified according to the needs of the teaching technique in order to minimize the method's interference. After that, it creates a strategy for teaching the Japanese language, runs the outcomes of that strategy, and optimizes and innovates the approach. Thorough examination. Machine learning algorithms perform better in MATLAB simulations when subjected to certain assessment criteria. Innovate and teach Japanese teaching methods The rationality is superior to traditional pedagogy.

Keywords: Computer · machine learning algorithms · Japanese language teaching · Teaching methods

1 Introduction

As ML technology has progressed, more and more studies have investigated its potential use in English language instruction [1]. Through the use of machine learning, English language instructors may have a deeper understanding of their students' learning progress while simultaneously enhancing their students' learning and language proficiency [2]. The use of machine learning in ESL classrooms, along with the benefits and drawbacks of this approach, will be thoroughly examined in this article [3].

A. *The concept and characteristics of machine learning*

Machine learning refers to a method of applying artificial intelligence technology and algorithm models to let computers learn from data on their own and improve their judgment and decision-making ability. The characteristics of machine learning methods mainly include the following aspects:

B. Brik and S. Nazir (Eds.): BigIoT-EDU 2024, LNICST 660, pp. 537–546, 2026.
https://doi.org/10.1007/978-3-032-18628-7_55

1. Data-driven

The essence of machine learning is to train a model through data, thereby improving the judgment and decision-making ability of the model. Therefore, machine learning requires high data quality, large data scale, and clear data characteristics [4].

2. Algorithmic model

In order to learn and make predictions, machine learning techniques use mathematical models that extract characteristics from data. Every one of the three main categories of algorithm models—supervised learning, unsupervised learning, and reinforcement learning—has its own unique set of uses and potential outcomes in the real world [5].

3. Adaptability

Machine learning methods are adaptive, that is, based on the feedback from the data, constantly adjust and improve the model to better adapt to changes in data and predict changes in tasks [6].

B. *Application of machine learning in English teaching*

1. Speech recognition

Machine learning in the field of English speech recognition can be used to detect and correct students' pronunciation and intonation, thereby improving students' oral expression skills. Learning through data-driven methods and algorithmic models and then grading through speech discrimination software gives students a better grasp of spoken English skills [7].

2. Text Analytics

Machine learning can be used in the field of English text analysis to detect and correct students' grammar and vocabulary use. Learning through data-driven methods and algorithmic models can then be detected and corrected through natural language processing techniques to give students a better grasp of English grammar skills [8].

3. Personalized learning

Machine learning methods can adaptively adjust and improve the learning model according to students' learning behavior and feedback information to better adapt to students' learning needs and characteristics. Learning can be carried out through data-driven methods and algorithmic models, and then the model can be adjusted and improved according to students' learning behavior and feedback information to improve students' English learning effect [9].

C. *The effect and advantages of machine learning in English teaching*

1. Improve learning outcomes

Machine learning method in English teaching, through the learning of data-driven and algorithmic models, can better adapt to students' learning needs and characteristics, and improve students' learning effect [10].

2. Improve English language skills

Machine learning method in English teaching can aid in the development of pupils' English proficiency and their ability to listen, speak, read and write English through speech recognition, text analysis and other technologies [11].

3. Improve teaching efficiency

Through personalized learning and adaptive adjustment, machine learning can better adapt to students' learning needs and characteristics and improve teaching efficiency. At the same time, it can allow teachers to better understand the learning status of students, conduct targeted teaching, and improve teaching effectiveness [12].

4. Save teaching costs

Machine learning can realize automated teaching evaluation through algorithmic models and automatic grading systems, thereby saving teaching costs. In addition, manual error correction and grading can be reduced, and teaching efficiency can be improvedp [13].

D. *Issues that should be paid attention to in promoting machine learning*

1. Data scale

The effectiveness of machine learning is limited by the scale of the data, so when applying machine learning, you need to provide as much data as possible for better learning results [14].

2. Algorithm selection

Different English teaching tasks require different algorithm models, so it is necessary to select the appropriate algorithm for the specific task, and adjust and improve it.

3. Privacy Protection

In machine learning methods, data privacy protection is very important, and measures need to be taken to protect students' data privacy and avoid data leakage and abuse. Machine learning has several potential uses in the field of English language instruction, among which are the enhancement of students' learning outcomes and proficiency in the language and the improvement of instructors' insights about their students' progress. To fully use the application benefits of machine learning, it is important to pay attention to concerns like data size, algorithm selection, and privacy protection while promoting it.

One of the most critical parts of teaching Japanese is developing effective teaching strategies that facilitate student acquisition of the language [15]. Nevertheless, challenges to teaching Japanese arise from the process of insufficient logic in teaching approaches. Several researchers have hypothesized that by using machine learning algorithms to the study of Japanese education, we might better understand and support the country's pedagogical practices. A machine learning algorithm is suggested in this research to improve the teaching technique scheme and test the model's efficacy, based on this.

2 Related Works

A. *Mathematical description of a machine learning algorithm*

Based on the indications in the teaching method, the machine learning algorithm optimizes the teaching method scheme via computer simulation is y_i, finds the unqualified value in Japanese language teaching is z_i, and integrates the teaching method scheme is $tol(y_i \cdot s_{ij})$. Finally, the feasibility taught in Japanese classrooms is judged, and the calculation is shown in Eq. (1).

$$tol(y_i \cdot s_{ij}) = y_{ij} \geq \max(\frac{\Delta y}{\Delta s}\frac{\delta y}{\delta s} \cdot s_{ij}) \tag{1}$$

Equation (2) shows the evaluation of outliers among them.

$$\max(s_{ij}) = \left(s_{ij}^2 \times 3\right) \succ mean\left(\sum s_{ij} * \frac{\delta y}{\delta s}\frac{\partial^2 \Omega}{\partial u^2} dy \partial s\right) \tag{2}$$

Machine learning algorithms may enhance the practicability of teaching approaches by combining the benefits of computer simulation with Japanese language instruction and quantifying them.

I. The necessary pedagogical approach is s_i, the teaching method scheme is set_i, contentment with the instructional strategy is y_i, moreover, the evaluation function for the instructional strategy is $Q(s_i \approx 0)$, as shown by Eq. (3).

$$Q(r_i) = \sum s_i \cap \xi \to ointy_i \to \sum_{i=1}^{n} s_i Y_i \frac{1}{n} \sigma_s^2 \tag{3}$$

B. *Choice of teaching method and program*

Second Hypothesis: The Role of Education in Japan is $k(s_i)$, the weight coefficient is w_i, Consequently, as shown in Eq. (4), the approach to instruction necessitates the use of unqualified Japanese instruction.

$$k(s_i) = z_i \cdot \prod Q(r_i) - w_i \to \frac{s-\mu}{\sigma} \quad \int \lim_{s \to \infty} \frac{1}{n} \sigma_s^2 \mu_X \tag{4}$$

An all-encompassing function for teaching Japanese may be derived from assumptions I and II, as seen in Eq. (5).

$$k(s_i) + Q(r_i) \leq \max(s_{ij}) \tag{5}$$

Equation (6) shows the outcomes of standardizing all data, which is necessary to increase the efficacy of instructional techniques.

$$\widetilde{k(s_i) + Q(r_i)} \leftrightarrow mean\left(\sum s_{ij} * \frac{\delta y}{\delta s}\frac{\partial^2 \Omega}{\partial u^2} dy \partial s\right) \tag{6}$$

C. *Analysis of pedagogical schemes*

Prior to implementing the machine learning algorithm, a comprehensive analysis of the teaching method scheme should be conducted. The needs of the teaching method should be compared to the Japanese teaching library in order to weed out any unqualified ways is $No(s_i)$, Eq. (7) displays the outcomes, while Eq. (6) allows for the proposal of the anomaly assessment method.

$$No(s_i) = \frac{\widetilde{k(s_i) + Q(r_i)}}{mean\left(\sum s_{ij} * \frac{\delta y}{\delta s}\frac{\partial^2 \Omega}{\partial u^2} dy \partial s\right)} \tag{7}$$

Among them, $\frac{\widetilde{k(s_i)+Q(r_i)}}{mean\left(\sum s_{ij} * \frac{\delta y}{\delta s}\frac{\partial^2 \Omega}{\partial u^2} dy \partial s\right)} \leq 1$ It is said that in order for the strategy to be integrated, it must first be presented is $Zh(s_i)$, as shown by Eq. (8).

$$Zh(s_i) = \min[\sum \widetilde{k(s_i) + Q(r_i)}] \tag{8}$$

The accuracy of machine learning algorithms is ensured by conducting a complete analysis of Japanese teaching techniques and setting thresholds and indicator weights. Innovative analysis is necessary for the systematic testing of teaching approaches in Japanese language instruction. If the distribution of Japanese language instruction is nonnormal is $unno(s_i)$, The overall accuracy of the teaching method and the calculating result will be diminished as a consequence of this impact on its teaching method scheme is $accur(s_i)$, shown in Eq. (9).

$$accur(s_i) = \frac{\min[\sum \widetilde{k(s_i) + Q(r_i)}]}{\sum \widetilde{k(s_i) + Q(r_i)}} \times 100\% \tag{9}$$

A multidimensional distribution is shown by the teaching techniques and schemes in the survey, which is consistent with objective facts. The research is considered very analytical since the teaching technique plan is highly random, as the Japanese language is not taught in a directed fashion. When it comes to Japanese education, if is $randon(s_i)$, then the calculation of formula (9) can be expressed as formula (10).

$$accur(s_i) = \frac{\min[\sum \widetilde{k(s_i) + Q(r_i)}]}{\sum \widetilde{k(s_i) + Q(r_i)}} \times 100\% + randon(s_i) \tag{10}$$

In particular, the standardization of Japanese language instruction and its use of computer simulation operations to fine-tune that instruction, do away with superfluous and redundant plans, and augment the default plan ensure a robust dynamic correlation throughout the whole teaching method scheme.

3 Optimization Strategies for Japanese Language Teaching

In order to optimize the teaching of Japanese, the machine learning algorithm uses a random optimization technique and tweaks the parameters of the lesson's content. Algorithms trained by machine learning classify Japanese language instruction into many tiers, from which they randomly choose solutions. The iterative approach involves optimizing and analyzing the teaching method schemes at various stages of the technique. Once the optimization study is finished, the finest Japanese language education programs are determined by comparing their degree of teaching techniques.

4 Results and Discussion

A. *Introduction to teaching methods*

In this study, we examine the unique approach of teaching Japanese as a whole, with a focus on its application in complicated settings. We use a 12-h examination with 12 pathways to draw our conclusions. You may see the plan in Table 1.

Table 1. Teaching method requirements

Scope of application	grade	Viability	Teaching methods
Basic Japanese	Routine	85.56	83.38
	Higher	83.79	85.45
Japanese grammar	Routine	81.67	82.20
	Higher	82.02	87.18
Read in Japanese	Routine	83.90	84.17
	Higher	83.63	85.22

The teaching methodological process in Table 1 is shown in Fig. 1.

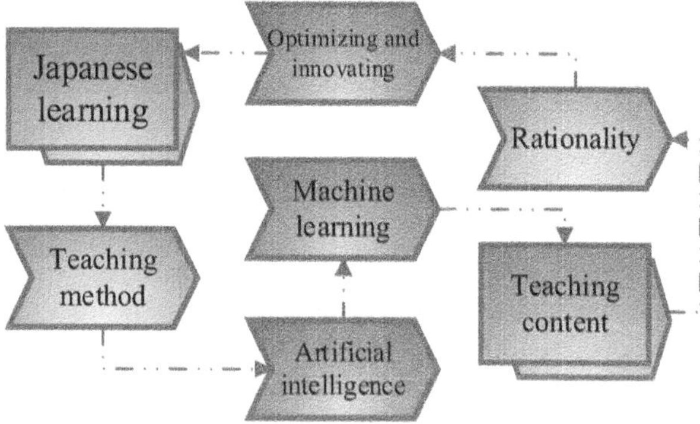

Fig. 1. The analytical process of Japanese language teaching

The requirements of machine learning algorithms for teaching techniques are more closely aligned with those of real methods of instruction than those of conventional methods. When compared to more conventional approaches, machine learning algorithms provide more innovative and sensible ways to teach Japanese. The improved reasoning and originality of the machine learning system are shown by the shifts in Fig. 2's instructional strategies. Consequently, machine learning algorithms have improved speed, rationality, and sum stability in their teaching approach schemes.

B. *Japanese language teaching*

Unstructured, semi-structured, and structural information are all part of the Japanese language instruction framework. Obtaining a preliminary lesson plan for teaching Japanese follows the pre-selection of machine learning algorithms, and the language instruction itself follows. Evaluate the practicability of educational remedies. As indicated in Table 2, a variety of Japanese language teaching techniques and methods for various levels of teaching ways were chosen to more precisely confirm the creative impact of these approaches.

Table 2. Overall picture of the pedagogical approach program

Category	Innovative	Analysis rate
Basic Japanese	88.68	87.55
Japanese grammar	83.47	85.93
Read in Japanese	81.74	88.01
Mean	84.95	83.35
X^6	84.98	86.29
P = 1.717		

C. *Teaching methods and stability of teaching methods*

In order to verify the accuracy of the machine learning algorithm, the teaching method scheme is compared with the traditional teaching method, which is shown in Fig. 2.

Figure 2 shows that compared to the traditional teaching method, the machine learning algorithm's method of instruction is more thorough and consistent, with a lower error rate. This suggests that the algorithm's method of instruction is more stable. Tabulated in Table 3 is the mean instructional approach for the aforementioned three algorithms.

Table 3 demonstrates that there are problems with the invention of teaching techniques in Japanese language instruction, that there have been substantial changes to the field, and that there is a high mistake rate when it comes to teaching the Japanese language. When compared to more conventional approaches, teaching with the overarching outcomes of machine learning algorithms yields superior results. Concurrently, the accuracy has remained relatively unchanged, and the way of teaching machine learning algorithms is above 92%. To provide further evidence that machine learning methods are better. It is common practice to examine the machine learning algorithm using many ways, as seen in Fig. 3, to further confirm the efficacy of the suggested approach.

Figure 3 shows that compared to the conventional approach, the machine learning algorithm's teaching method is vastly superior. This is because, among other things,

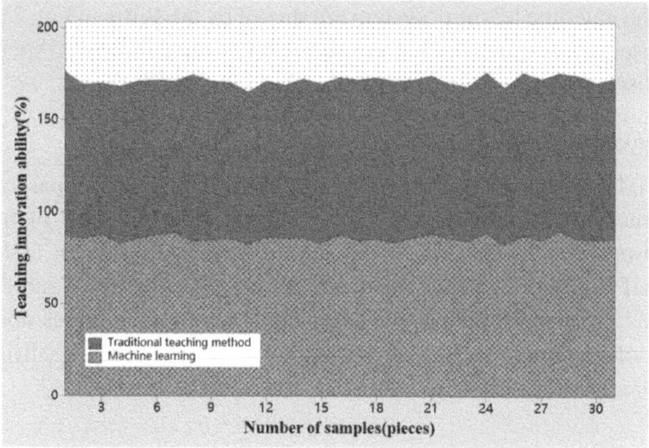

Fig. 2. Teaching methods of different algorithms

Table 3. Comparison of the accuracy of teaching methods of different methods

Algorithm	Teaching methods	Magnitude of change	Error
Machine learning algorithms	92.49	94.13	94.41
Traditional pedagogy	91.41	91.99	92.38
P	83.96	84.50	89.44

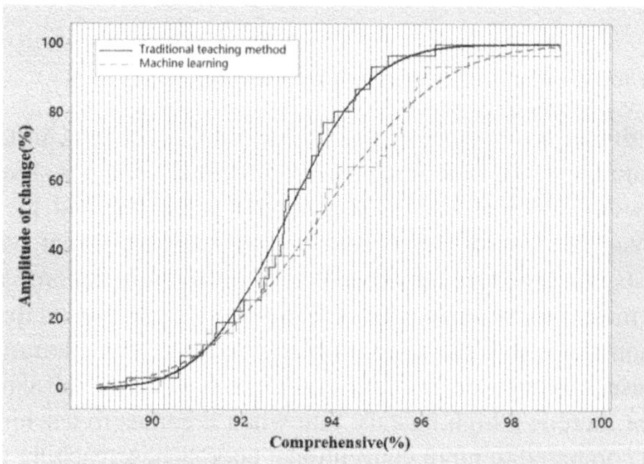

Fig. 3. Teaching methods of machine learning algorithm teaching methods

it raises the adjustment coefficient for Japanese instruction and establishes content thresholds for instruction, keeping out non-compliant instructional methods.

5 Conclusion

This study presents a machine learning algorithm that combines computer simulation operations to improve Japanese language education, aiming to address the issue of the current teaching method's inadequacy. Simultaneously, a body of instructional information is developed by conducting in-depth analyses of innovative teaching approaches. The application of machine learning algorithms in the classroom has the potential to make Japanese language instruction more logical and effective, according to research. The problem is that machine learning algorithms focus too much on analyzing instructional techniques, which leads to illogical indications being chosen for those approaches.

References

1. Anghelua, P.S., Dobrea, C.R., Cretu, F.R., Ganea, O., Breaz, T.O., Popescu, N.L.: Educational fields of higher education graduates in European Union. Front. Environ. Sci. **11** (2023)
2. Chan, P., Gulbaram, K., Schuetze, T.: Assessing urban sustainability and the potential to improve the quality of education and gender equality in Phnom Penh, Cambodia. Sustainability **15**(11) (2023)
3. Chang, C.-C., Tsai, L.-T., Meliana, D.: The concept of ocean sustainability in high school: measuring the ocean literacy of vocational high school students in Indonesia. Sustainability **15**(2) (2023)
4. Chen, M., Zimmer, C., Huang, S., Tian, R., Yang, B., Li, M.: The effectiveness of an online sexuality education module in promoting sexual knowledge and attitude change: a cluster randomized controlled trial. Health Educ. Res. **38**(2), 119–138 (2023)
5. Chen, W., Fan, X., Dai, F., Chen, T.: Student behavior identification during practice and training based on video image. Traitement Du Signal **40**(1), 249–256 (2023)
6. Chen, Y., He, H., Yang, Y.: Effects of social support on professional identity of secondary vocational students major in preschool nursery teacher program: a chain mediating model of psychological adjustment and school belonging. Sustainability **15**(6) (2023c)
7. Chen, Y., Jiang, Y., Zheng, A., Yue, Y., Hu, Z.-H.: What research should vocational education colleges conduct? An empirical study using data envelopment analysis. Sustainability **15**(12) (2023d)
8. Chinedu, C.C., Saleem, A., Muda, W.H.N.W.: Teaching and learning approaches: curriculum framework for sustainability literacy for technical and vocational teacher training programmes in Malaysia. Sustainability **15**(3) (2023)
9. Cook, J.A., et al.: Outcomes of peer-provided individual placement and support services in a mental health peer-run vocational program. Psychiatr. Serv. **74**(5), 480–487 (2023)
10. Doerr, K., Salisbury, S.K., HogenEsch, H., San Miguel, S.F., Reed, W.M.: Purdue's legacy of leading in graduating career-ready veterinarians. Javma-J. Am. Vet. Med. Assoc. **261**(3), 415 (2023)
11. Fan, J.-Y.: Professional literacy that Taiwan's bag manufacturing industry talents should possess: analyzing from a practical perspective. Front. Psychol. **13**, 1032763 (2022)
12. Ha, S.C., Lee, D.K., Choi, Y., Kang, W.S., Ahn, J.H., Chung, J.W., Park, H.J.: Long-term educational and occupational status of prelingually deaf children who have received a cochlear implant. Otolaryngol.-Head Neck Surg. (2023)
13. Han, Y., Yan, R., Gou, C.: An integrated multiple attribute decision making methodology for quality evaluation of innovation and entrepreneurship education with interval-valued intuitionistic fuzzy information. J. Intell. Fuzzy Syst. **44**(2), 2231–2249 (2023)

14. He, Y., Zeng, Q., Zhang, M.: The mediating roles of future work self and hope on the association between perceived social support and depressive symptoms among Chinese vocational school students: a cross-sectional study. Psychol. Res. Behav. Manag. **16**, 2125–2136 (2023)

Teaching Research and Analysis of Intelligent Robot CNC Technology in Mechanical Manufacturing

Li Guan-nan(✉)

Liaoning Vocational University of Technology, 121007, Fuxin, China
fuyanyu2023@163.com

Abstract. Numerical control (Numerical Control, NC) technology originated in the 1940s, is a computer program to control the mechanical equipment for automatic processing technology. This technology through the pre-programmed instructions, can accurately control the movement of the machine tool, to realize the efficient and accurate processing of the workpiece. With the rapid development of computer technology, the numerical control technology has gradually evolved into the modern computer numerical control (Computer Numerical Control, CNC), which further improves the machining accuracy and efficiency. The importance of CNC technology in the field of mechanical manufacturing is self-evident. It not only improves the production efficiency, reduces the error of manual operation, but also realizes the processing of complex shaped parts, which greatly expands the possibility of mechanical manufacturing. In mass production, numerical control technology enables enterprises to quickly respond to market changes, reduce production costs, and enhance competitiveness. In addition, with the transformation of manufacturing industry to intelligence and automation, numerical control technology has become one of the key technologies to realize industry 4.0 and intelligent manufacturing.ABB simulation shows that in the case of certain evaluation criteria, intelligent robot numerical control technology has a positive impact on intelligent robots The accuracy of CNC technology and the time of CNC technology are better than the MDI method.

Keywords: Numerical control theory · Intelligent robot numerical control technology · Mechanical engineering

1 Introduction

Intelligent robots, as an important part of advanced manufacturing technology, integrate various high technologies such as artificial intelligence, machine learning, sensor technology and robotics. In mechanical manufacturing, they can perform tasks with high reproducibility, high labor intensity or high precision requirements, such as welding, assembly, handling, and detection, etc. The numerical control technology process in Table 1 is shown in Fig. 1.

B. Brik and S. Nazir (Eds.): BigIoT-EDU 2024, LNICST 660, pp. 547–556, 2026.
https://doi.org/10.1007/978-3-032-18628-7_56

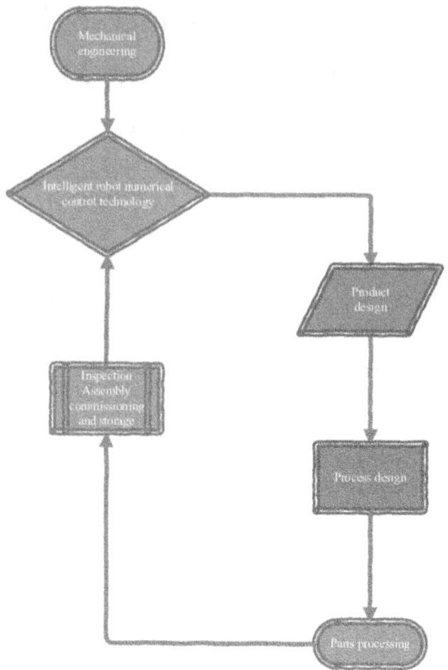

Fig. 1. Analysis process of mechanical manufacturing

Through project practice and simulation, students use the knowledge they have learned in practice to improve their ability to solve practical problems. Regular skill tests and project assessments, such as programming competitions and robot operation drills, can feedback students' skill levels in real time to timely adjust teaching methods and progress.

2 Related Concepts

A. *Principle and classification of CNC technology*

Numerical control technology, full name digital control (Numerical Control, NC), is a computer program to control mechanical equipment for automatic operation technology. Its basic principle is to transform the process, movement trajectory and operation instructions into digital information, input to the computer through the data input equipment, and then processed by the computer control system, and finally drive the machine tool or other mechanical equipment through the servo system to perform the predetermined movement.

CNC control technology is divided into many types, including point control, contour control and continuous control. Point control focuses on precisely moving the device from one position to another, regardless of the path. The contour control focuses on the continuous movement of the device along the predetermined path to ensure the shape accuracy of the artifact. Continuous control is between point control and contour control, allowing the device to move continuously within a given speed range.

B. *Robotics foundation and intelligent control theory*

Robotics is the science of studies on the design, manufacture, and application of robots. Basic concepts include mechanical structure, kinematics, dynamics, and sensor technology, as well as control strategies. Among them, kinematics focuses on the motion description of robots, while dynamics studies the mechanical behavior of robots. Intelligent control theory is a key part of robotics, which combines technologies such as artificial intelligence, machine learning, fuzzy logic and neural networks. These theories enable robots to make autonomous decisions, adapt to environmental changes, and handle uncertainties. For example, adaptive control allows the robot to adjust its behavior to different conditions, while fuzzy logic and neural networks provide the ability to deal with nonlinear problems and complex decisions.

C. *The combination point of numerical control technology and robotics*

FThe combination of intelligent robot numerical control technology is an important progress of modern manufacturing technology. In traditional CNC systems, the trajectory of the robot is usually controlled by pre-programmed instructions. However, combined with the intelligent control of robotics, the system is able to analyze the working environment in real time and adjust the processing strategies to improve the efficiency and precision. For example, a robot can use visual sensors to identify the position and attitude of the artifact, and then adjust its motion path using an adaptive control algorithm. At the same time, prediction models based on machine learning can predict tool wear, so as to dynamically adjust cutting parameters and ensure processing quality. In addition, by integrating artificial intelligence, the robot can achieve fault diagnosis and self-repair, reducing downtime and maintenance costs. This combination not only improves the level of automation of the manufacturing process, but also enhances the flexibility and intelligence of the system, so that the robot can adapt to the complex and changeable production tasks, and further promotes the digital and intelligent transformation of the manufacturing industry.

In modern machinery manufacturing, the application of intelligent robots has become a key component of the automated production line. Through accurate CNC systems, these robots can perform repetitive and accurate operations, such as material handling, assembly, and welding. Intelligent robots are equipped with vision systems and sensors that enable them to identify and locate parts, ensuring efficient collaboration on the production line. In addition, with advanced machine learning algorithms, the robot is able to continuously optimize its workflow, reduce downtime and production errors, and significantly improve production efficiency and product quality.

D. *CNC robotics technology in precision machining*

In the field of precision machining, the application of intelligent robot numerical control technology shows extremely high accuracy and flexibility. The robot arm can perform complex three-dimensional motion, accurately control the tool path, and achieve micron-level machining accuracy. For example, in the aerospace and medical device industries, robots are used to manufacture high-precision components, such as turbine blades and precision instruments. By integrating with the CAD / CAM system, the robot can automatically program and perform complex processing tasks, greatly reducing human error and processing time. At the same time, the real-time monitoring and feedback system ensures the stability of the processing process and avoids excessive cutting or workpiece damage.

In the quality control, intelligent robots also play an important role. Using integrated optical, acoustic, and force-sensing sensors, robots can perform nondestructive testing, such as detecting surface defects, dimensional precision, and material strength. Through the AI-driven image processing technology, the robot can automatically identify and classify the detection results, and quickly screen out the unqualified products, greatly improving the detection speed and accuracy of the detection. In addition, the robot can perform high-precision measurement tasks, such as coordinate measurement, to ensure that the product meets strict tolerance requirements. Through automatic testing, enterprises can timely find and correct the problems in the production process, reduce the rejection rate, and ensure the stability of product quality. The practical application of intelligent robot numerical control technology not only improves the production efficiency of mechanical manufacturing, but also reduces the labor cost, and ensures the reliability of product quality. With the continuous development of technology, intelligent robots will be integrated into machinery manufacturing in more links and deeper levels in the future, and promote the digital and intelligent transformation of the industry.

E. *The impact of robot numerical control technology on mechanical manufacturing*

Assessment of students' skill mastery In the process of learning intelligent robot numerical control technology, the degree of skills is an important indicator to measure the teaching effect. Through the teaching method combining theory and practice, students need to not only understand the working principle of CNC system, but also need to master programming languages, such as the writing of G code and M code, as well as robot path planning and control strategies. Through project practice and simulation, students use the knowledge they have learned in practice to improve their ability to solve practical problems. Regular skill tests and project assessments, such as programming competitions and robot operation drills, can feedback students' skill levels in real time to timely adjust teaching methods and progress. The connection between teaching effect and industry needs The educational goal of intelligent robot CNC technology should be closely connected with the needs of the industry. In machinery manufacturing, there is a growing demand for graduates with the technology to quickly adapt to the production line for efficient robot programming and troubleshooting. Therefore, the course design should focus on cultivating students' engineering practice ability and innovation ability, including the integration of robot systems, commissioning of automated production lines, and fault diagnosis and maintenance. Through the cooperation with enterprises, such as internship, practical training programs and the course design of industry-university-research combination, the teaching content can ensure the synchronization with the actual working environment, and the employment competitiveness of students can be improved.

3 Optimization Strategies for Mechanical Manufacturing

The practical application of intelligent robot numerical control technology not only improves the production efficiency of mechanical manufacturing, but also reduces the labor cost, and ensures the reliability of product quality. With the continuous development of technology, intelligent robots will be integrated into machinery manufacturing in more links and deeper levels in the future, and promote the digital and intelligent transformation of the industry.

A. *Mathematical description of numerical control technology of intelligent robots*

The combination of intelligent robot numerical control technology is an important progress of modern manufacturing technology. In traditional CNC systems, the trajectory of the robot is usually controlled by pre-programmed instructions. However, combined with the intelligent control of robotics, the system is able to analyze the working environment in real time and adjust the processing strategies to improve efficiency and precision.

$$hio\left(y_i \cdot x_{ij}\right) = y_{ij} \geq \max\left(x_{ij} - \bigcap_{i=1}^{n} X_i\right) \tag{1}$$

For example, a robot can use visual sensors to identify the position and attitude of the artifact, and then adjust its motion path using an adaptive control algorithm.

$$\max(x_{ij}) = \left(x_{ij}^2 + \sum_{i=1}^{n} X_i Y_i\right) \succ mean\left(\sum x_{ij}\right) \tag{2}$$

At the same time, prediction models based on machine learning can predict tool wear, so as to dynamically adjust cutting parameters and ensure processing quality. In addition, by integrating artificial intelligence, the robot can achieve fault diagnosis and self-repair, reducing downtime and maintenance costs.

This combination not only improves the level of automation of the manufacturing process, but also enhances the flexibility and intelligence of the system, so that the robot is able to adapt to the complex and changeable production tasks, and further promotes the digital and intelligent transformation of the manufacturing industry.

$$F(a_i) = \sum a_i \lim_{x \to \infty} \sqrt{a^2 + b^2} \to \oint b_i \tag{3}$$

B. *Intelligent robot applications on the automated production lines*

In modern machinery manufacturing, the application of intelligent robots has become a key component of the automated production line. Through accurate CNC systems, these robots can perform repetitive and accurate operations, such as material handling, assembly, and welding.

$$g(x_i) = z_i \cdot \sum_{i=1}^{n} (X_i - \overline{X})^2 - w_i \tag{4}$$

$$Bg(a_i) + F(d_i) \leq \max(a_{ij}) \cdot \frac{x - \mu}{\sigma} \tag{5}$$

Intelligent robots are equipped with vision systems and sensors that enable them to identify and locate parts, ensuring efficient collaboration on the production line. In addition, with advanced machine learning algorithms, the robot is able to continuously optimize its workflow, reduce downtime and production errors, and significantly improve production efficiency and product quality.

$$g(a_i) + f\left(d_i \cdot \frac{1}{n}\right) \leftrightarrow mean\left(\sum a_{ij}\right) \cdot \sum_{i=1}^{n} X_i \tag{6}$$

C. *CNC robotics technology in precision machining*

In the field of precision machining, the application of intelligent robot numerical control technology shows extremely high accuracy and flexibility. The robot arm can perform complex three-dimensional motion, accurately control the tool path, and achieve micron-level machining accuracy.

$$No(x_i) = \frac{g(x_i) + F(d_i)}{mean\left(\sum_{i=1}^{n} X_i Y_i\right)} \cdot \bigcup_{i=1}^{n} X_i \tag{7}$$

For example, in the aerospace and medical device industries, robots are used to manufacture high-precision components, such as turbine blades and precision instruments.

$$Zh(x_i) = \min\left[\sum f\left(x_i \cdot \frac{1}{n}\right) + f(d_i)\right] \cdot \begin{pmatrix} 1 & 0 \\ 0 & 1 \end{pmatrix} \tag{8}$$

By integrating with the CAD / CAM system, the robot can automatically program and perform complex processing tasks, greatly reducing human error and processing time. At the same time, the real-time monitoring and feedback system ensures the stability of the processing process and avoids excessive cutting or workpiece damage.

$$accur(x_i) = \frac{\min\left[\sum g\left(x_i \cdot \frac{dy}{dx}\right) + f(d_i)\right]}{\widetilde{\sum g(x_i) + F\left(d_i \cdot \frac{\delta y}{\delta x}\right)}} \times 100\% \tag{9}$$

In the quality control link, intelligent robots also play an important role. Using integrated optical, acoustic, and force-sensing sensors, robots can perform nondestructive testing, such as detecting surface defects, dimensional precision, and material strength. Through the AI-driven image processing technology, the robot can automatically identify and classify the detection results, and quickly screen out the unqualified products, greatly improving the detection speed and accuracy of the detection.

$$accur(x_i) = \frac{\min\left[\sum g\left(x_i \cdot \frac{dy}{dx}\right) + f(d_i)\right]}{\widetilde{\sum g(x_i) + F\left(d_i \cdot \frac{\delta y}{\delta x}\right)}} \times 100\% + randon(x_i) \tag{10}$$

In addition, the robot can perform high-precision measurement tasks, such as coordinate measurement, to ensure that the product meets strict tolerance requirements. Through automatic testing, enterprises can timely find and correct the problems in the production process, reduce the rejection rate, and ensure the stability of product quality.

4 Results and Discussion

A. *Assessment of students' skill mastery*

In the process of learning intelligent robot numerical control technology, the degree of skills is an important indicator to measure the teaching effect. Through the teaching method combining theory and practice, students need not only understand the working principle of CNC system, but also need to master programming languages, such as G code and M code, as well as robot path planning and control strategies.

Table 1. CNC technical requirements

Scope of application	Grade	Reform effect	CNC technology
Sample one	I	35.00	32.70
	II	36.03	34.09
Sample two	I	33.53	35.13
	II	34.27	38.76
Sample three	I	34.07	33.66
	II	35.07	38.09

B. *Assessment of students' skill mastery*

The educational goal of intelligent robot CNC technology should be closely connected with the needs of the industry. In machinery manufacturing, there is a growing demand for graduates with the technology to quickly adapt to the production line for efficient robot programming and troubleshooting. Therefore, the course design should focus on cultivating students' engineering practice ability and innovation ability, including the integration of robot systems, commissioning of automated production lines, and fault diagnosis and maintenance (Table 2).

C. *The connection between teaching effect and industry demand*

The educational goal of intelligent robot CNC technology should be closely connected with the needs of the industry. In machinery manufacturing, there is a growing demand for graduates with the technology to quickly adapt to the production line for efficient robot programming and troubleshooting (Fig. 2).

Therefore, the course design should focus on cultivating students' engineering practice ability and innovation ability, including the integration of robot systems, commissioning of automated production lines, and fault diagnosis and maintenance. Through

Table 2. The overall situation of the CNC technical solution

Category	Satisfaction	Analysis rate
Product design	83.24	85.42
Process design	83.28	86.13
Parts processing	84.92	90.04
Inspection	86.93	86.48
Assembly debugging	87.28	87.19
Storage	86.05	82.74
Mean	88.62	85.96
X6	35.01	34.25
P = 3.256		

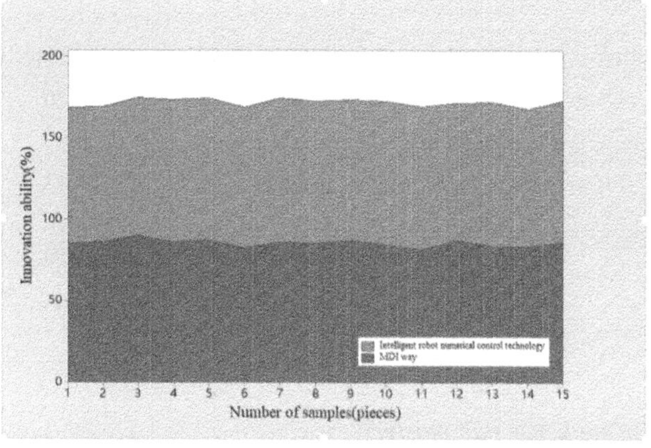

Fig. 2. CNC technology for different algorithms

the cooperation with enterprises, such as internship, practical training programs and the course design of industry-university-research combination, the teaching content can ensure the synchronization with the actual working environment, and the employment competitiveness of students can be improved (Table 3).

In the teaching process, the problems often encountered include the disconnection between theory and practice, the limitation of teaching resources, and the maintenance of students' interest and motivation. In order to solve these problems, teachers can use case teaching, integrate the real work scenes into the classroom, and enhance the relevance of learning (Fig. 3).

Use virtual simulation software to make up for the shortage of actual equipment and provide a safe and diverse practice environment. In addition, project-driven and competition mechanisms are introduced to stimulate students' enthusiasm for learning and develop teamwork and problem-solving skills. At the same time, regularly collect

Table 3. Comparison of the accuracy of CNC technology of different methods

Algorithm	CNC technology	Magnitude of change	Error
Intelligent robot numerical control technology	86.26	86.50	82.87
MDI way	86.12	86.40	83.63
P	33.758	34.216	32.879

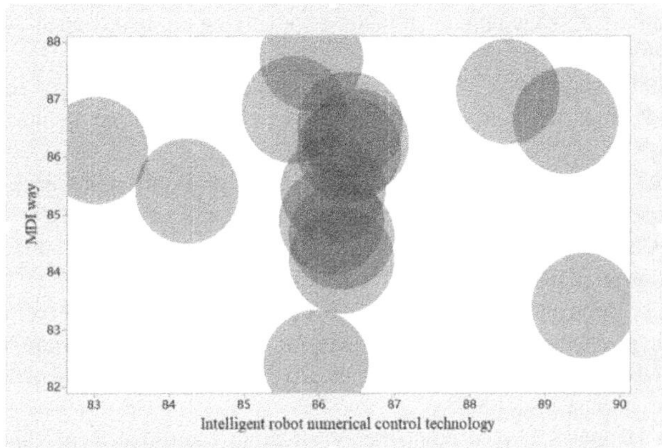

Fig. 3. Intelligent robot numerical control technology

student feedback, adjust the teaching methods and content, to ensure the pertinacity and effectiveness of teaching.

5 Conclusion

In the teaching of intelligent robot numerical control technology, the role of teachers should also need to be changed to guide and mentor, encourage students to study and explore independently, in order to adapt to the rapid development of scientific and technological environment. Through continuous teaching reform and innovation, we can cultivate future mechanical engineers with advanced skills and adaptability to meet the industry's demand for talents in the field of intelligent manufacturing.This study deeply explores the teaching and application of intelligent robot CNC technology in mechanical manufacturing, and reveals the importance and innovation potential of this field. We found that intelligent robot technology not only improves the accuracy and efficiency of CNC systems, but also plays the role of an innovator in teaching, helping students to better understand and master the complex manufacturing process.

Aiming at the problem that the numerical control technology of machinery manufacturing is not ideal; this paper proposes the numerical control technology of intelligent robots and combines the numerical control theory to optimize the mechanical manufacturing. At the same time, the reform of numerical control technology and threshold innovation are analyzed in depth to build an intelligent robot collection. Research shows that intelligent robot numerical control technology can improve the accuracy and stability of mechanical manufacturing and can carry out general numerical control technology for mechanical manufacturing. However, in the process of intelligent robot numerical control technology, too much attention is paid to the analysis of numerical control technology, resulting in unreasonable selection of numerical control technical indicators.

References

1. Abidi, S., Satouri, J.: New numerical method for solving optimal control. Aims Math. **8**(9), 21484–21500 (2023)
2. Al-Shaher, O.I., Mahmoudi, M., Mechee, M.S.: Numerical method for solving fractional order optimal control problems with free and non-free terminal time. Symmetry-Basel, **15**(3) (2023)
3. Andersson, K., Andersson, A., Oosterlee, C.W.: Convergence of a robust deep FBSDE method for stochastic control. SIAM J. Sci. Comput. **45**(1), A226–A255 (2023)
4. Andres, F., Castano, D., Munoz, J.: Minimization of the compliance under a nonlocal p-Laplacian constraint. Mathematics, **11**(7) (2023)
5. Aronna, M.S., Bonnans, J.F., San Goh, B.: Well-posedness of the shooting algorithm for control-affine problems with a scalar state constraint. Comput. Appl. Math. **42**(5) (2023)
6. Arora, C., Yadav, S.: Optimal control strategies to cope with unemployment during the Covid-19 pandemic. Iranian J Sci (2023)
7. Azmi, F.M., Haque, S.: Fixed point theory on triple controlled metric-like spaces with a numerical iteration. Symmetry-Basel **15**(7) (2023)
8. Burman E, Feizmohammadi A, Munch, A., Oksanen, L.: Spacetime finite element methods for control problems subject to the wave equation. ESAIM-Control. Optim. Calc. Var. **29** (2023)
9. Chen, X., Jin, T.: Optimal control for a multistage uncertain random system. IEEE Access **11**, 2105–2117 (2023)
10. Choquet, C., Diedhiou, M.M., El Dine, H.N., Saint-Jean, C.: A numerical scheme for the optimal control of groundwater pollution. Numer. Methods Partial Differ. Equ. **39**(4), 3037–3063 (2023)
11. Chukwu, C.W., Nyabadza, F., Asamoah, J.K.K.: A mathematical model and optimal control for Listeriosis disease from ready-to-eat food products. Int. J. Comput. Sci. Math. **17**(1), 39–49 (2023)
12. Fan, P.R., Li, S.J., Mao, L.: Seismic control performance and experimental study of multiple pounding tuned rolling mass damper. Earthq. Struct. **24**(4), 247–258 (2023)

Research on Early Warning of Comprehensive Quality Assessment of College Students Based on Machine Learning

Chao Wei(✉)

Shaanxi Technical College of Finance & Economics, Shaanxi 712000, China
wchao0132@126.com

Abstract. In today's society, the goal of higher education has shifted from simple knowledge teaching to cultivating the comprehensive quality of college students. The comprehensive quality of college students not only includes academic ability, but also covers moral quality, teamwork, innovative thinking, social practice and other aspects. However, due to the limited university educational resources and the individual differences of students, the traditional evaluation methods are often difficult to comprehensively and accurately reflect the comprehensive quality of college students. Therefore, the establishment of a scientific and objective evaluation system, as well as an early warning system combined with modern technology, has far-reaching significance for the timely detection of potential problems in students, optimizing the allocation of educational resources and improving the quality of education MATLAB simulation shows that under certain evaluation criteria, machine learning has the accuracy of comprehensive quality assessment of college students' comprehensive education The time required for comprehensive quality assessment is better than that of traditional assessment methods.

Keywords: Computer · Machine learning · Comprehensive education for university students · Comprehensive quality assessment

1 Introduction

In recent years, with the rapid development of big data and machine learning technologies, they are increasingly widely used in the field of education. Through the machine learning algorithm, students 'behavior data can be mined to predict students' learning performance and future development trend [1, 2], so as to realize the accurate evaluation and early warning of students' comprehensive quality. Such an early warning system can help educators to identify students who may face difficulties in advance, provide personalized support and intervention, and promote the comprehensive development of college students. After the system is launched, the early warning effect will be continuously monitored, and the model will be timely updated and adjusted according to the new data feedback to maintain its prediction capability [3, 4] (Fig. 1).

B. Brik and S. Nazir (Eds.): BigIoT-EDU 2024, LNICST 660, pp. 557–565, 2026.
https://doi.org/10.1007/978-3-032-18628-7_57

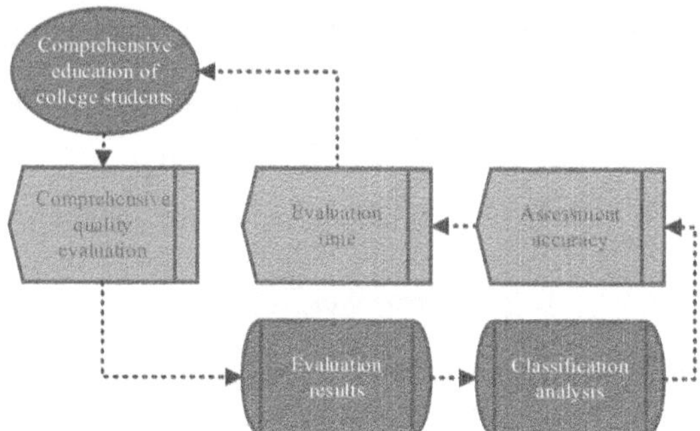

Fig. 1. The selection results of the comprehensive quality assessment program

Through the above steps, the machine learning model can effectively play a role in the comprehensive quality assessment and early warning system of college students, identify possible academic problems, psychological problems or other factors affecting the development of students in advance, and provide timely intervention basis for educators [5, 6].

2 Related Works

A. *Application of machine learning in college students' comprehensive quality assessment*

The main goal of this study is to construct a machine learning-based early warning system for comprehensive quality assessment of college students, which aims to predict students' performance in academic [7, 8], psychological, social and other aspects by collecting and analyzing their multidimensional data, so as to take timely intervention measures. The specific objectives of the study will include: A set of comprehensive quality evaluation framework covering multi-dimensional indicators is designed to comprehensively reflect the academic quality, ability, psychology and other aspects of college students. Select and apply suitable machine learning algorithms to build early warning models to predict the potential problems and needs of students. Collect and process the multi-source data of college students, including academic performance, behavioral records, social network data, etc., to provide data support for the model training. To evaluate the prediction performance of the early warning model, optimize the model parameters, and improve the accuracy and timeliness of the early warning. Realize the early warning system platform, integrate the prediction model, and provide real-time early warning information and decision support for educational managers. The research methods mainly include literature review, theoretical model construction, data collection and processing, machine learning model training and validation, and system development and application. We will use statistical analysis and machine learning technology, combined with pedagogy, psychology and other related theories, to conduct a scientific evaluation of the comprehensive quality of college students, and realize the intelligent education management through the early warning system[9, 10].

B. *The practical application of machine learning in the comprehensive quality assessment of college students*

Comprehensive quality assessment is based on the theoretical basis of pedagogy, psychology, and sociology. Guided by the theory of multiple intelligences, it emphasizes the comprehensive development of individuals in different fields, including intelligence, emotion, social interaction, moral quality, and physical health. At the same time, influenced by the concept of humanistic education, it emphasizes individual differences and potential development, aiming to promote students' all-round development and lifelong learning ability. Moreover, the theories of behaviorism and cognititism also provide an empirical basis to assess their quality level by observing and analyzing their behavioral performance. To construct the comprehensive quality evaluation index system, we need to fully consider the educational objectives, students' development needs and social requirements for talents. These indicators are usually divided into the following main categories: Knowledge and skills: including subject knowledge mastery degree, problem solving ability, critical thinking, innovation ability, etc. Emotion and attitude: such as learning interest, self-confidence, cooperative spirit, sense of responsibility, civic consciousness, etc. Social interaction: teamwork ability, communication skills, leadership, cross-cultural understanding, etc.

C. *The future development of machine learning in the comprehensive quality assessment of college students*

When choosing the evaluation method, it is necessary to take the qualitative and quantitative methods into account to evaluate the comprehensive quality of students comprehensively and accurately. Common methods include: Observation method: through the daily observation and records of teachers, peers and parents, to capture the students' classroom performance, activity participation, interpersonal communication and other behaviors. Portfolio: Collect students' learning results, such as research reports, art works, project design, and demonstrate their knowledge application and innovation ability. Self-evaluation and mutual evaluation: encourage students to reflect on themselves, and promote their self-understanding and social communication ability through peer evaluation.

As a new type of data analysis and prediction method, machine learning has been widely used in the comprehensive quality assessment of college students, improving the accuracy and efficiency of prediction and evaluation through the analysis and learning of a large amount of data. In the future, with the continuous development of information technology and artificial intelligence technology, the application of machine learning in the comprehensive quality assessment of college students will become more and more extensive and deep, providing more opportunities and challenges for the development of students.

The selection of evaluation methods should be conducted according to the evaluation objectives, the age of students and the actual situation of educational resources to ensure the fair, fair and effective evaluation process.

3 Optimization Strategies for Comprehensive Education for College Students

In the construction of the comprehensive quality evaluation and early warning system based on machine learning, data is the basis of model training and prediction. The data mainly comes from the following aspects: Academic performance: including subject grades, grade point average (GPA), course completion, etc., which are usually provided directly by the school's educational administration system. Extracurricular activities: including club activities, volunteer services, competition awards, etc., these information can be obtained from the student organization's records and the school activity database. Behavior performance: such as attendance rate, violation records, dormitory life performance, etc., these data can be obtained from the student management department. Mental health: students' emotional status, stress level and other information were collected through records from the psychological counseling center or anonymous questionnaires.

A. *Mathematical description of machine learning*

Machine learning plays a core role in the early warning system, which can learn patterns from a large amount of data to predict and identify potential problems. Common machine learning algorithms are: Decision tree: Build a series of rules to make predictions that are easy to understand and interpret. Random forest: It consists of multiple decision trees to improve the accuracy and stability of prediction through integrated learning. Support vector machine (SVM): Classification by constructing the maximum margin overplane, especially in small samples and high-dimensional space. Neural network: It simulates the working principle of human brain neurons and performs complex pattern recognition through multiple layers of nonlinear transformation. Deep learning: a large neural network containing multilayer nonlinear processing units, especially suitable for the processing of image, speech and text data.

$$E(k_i a) = \left(\frac{a}{2} - E\right) \cdot \sum_{I} a + k_1 + \frac{3}{E} \tag{1}$$

B. *Selection of comprehensive quality assessment schemes*

The early warning model is constructed in the following steps: Data preparation: collect multi-dimensional data of college students, such as academic performance, participation in extracurricular activities, social behavior, etc. Feature engineering: clean, transform and select the original data to extract the features related to the early warning target. Model selection: Select the appropriate machine learning algorithm according to the characteristics and data characteristics of the problem. Model training: Use the training data to adjust the model parameters, so that they can learn the rules in the data. Model validation: To evaluate the performance of the model on unseen data through cross-validation.

$$p(k_i) = \sum_{i=1}^{a} (k_i + P)^2 \cdot \sqrt[i]{P} + \iint_{i} a \tag{2}$$

C. *Analysis of comprehensive quality assessment program*

Optimization and evaluation are the key to ensuring the performance of the early warning model: Model optimization: it may involve parameter tuning, feature selection optimization, and integrated learning strategies, such as using grid search, random search, or gradient lifting methods. Evaluation indicators: evaluate the performance of the model using methods such as accuracy, recall, F1 score, AUC-ROC curve, especially focusing on the sensitivity and specificity of the model, to ensure accurate warning of abnormal situations. Model validation: Use the validation sets for model validation to avoid overfitting or underfitting. Model testing: Finally, the generalization ability of the model is evaluated on an independent test set to ensure that it can work stably in practical applications. Continuous monitoring and update.

4 Results and Discussion

A. *Introduction to comprehensive quality assessment*

Data preprocessing is a crucial step in machine learning, aiming to improve data quality, reduce noise and outliers, as well as transform the data into a format suitable for model training. Missing value processing: populate or delete missing values by interpolation, mean replacement, using specific flags, etc.

Table 1. Comprehensive quality assessment requirements

Scope of application	Grade	Accuracy	Comprehensive quality assessment
Moral character	Standard	87.69	89.51
	Higher	85.05	86.83
Ability to learn	Standard	86.72	85.39
	Higher	86.81	85.93
Civic literacy	Standard	85.93	88.54
	Higher	86.73	88.10

The comprehensive quality assessment process in Table 1 is shown in Fig. 2.

Outlier detection: statistical methods (such as Z-score, IQR) are used to identify and handle outliers to avoid their impact on model training. Data cleaning: Remove irrelevant information, such as stop words in unstructured text, and features unrelated to the target variable. Data normalization and normalization: Features at different scales are ensured at the same level by z-score, min-max scaling, etc. Data coding: the classified data (such as gender, community activities, etc.) are independently coded and converted into numerical form. Time series processing: For data with time series features, you need to consider the time window, such as using a sliding window to extract features.

B. *Comprehensive education of college students*

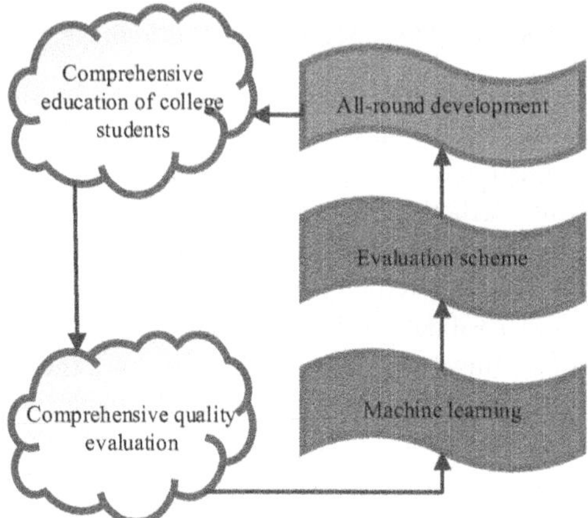

Fig. 2. The analytical process of comprehensive education for college students

Feature extraction and selection is the key to improve the model performance, which involves extracting the most predictive features of the target variable from the original data (Table 2).

Table 2. The overall situation of the comprehensive quality assessment program

Category	Viability	Analysis rate
Moral character	88.89	90.30
Ability to learn	91.52	89.78
Civic literacy	86.71	90.82
mean	88.37	89.27
X^6	89.13	87.94
P = 1.71		

C. *Comprehensive quality assessment and stability of comprehensive quality assessment*

Feature engineering: including the creation of new features (e.g., average score, activity participation frequency), aggregate features (e.g., semester average score), feature interaction (such as the product of grades and attendance), etc.

Social adaptability: including interpersonal communication, teamwork ability, etc., can be obtained through questionnaire survey or teacher evaluation. Personal traits: such as personality tests, hobbies and hobbies, which can be obtained through psychological assessment tools and self-reports (Fig. 3 and Table 3).

Standardized tests: mastery of knowledge and skills can be assessed using standardized tests to quantify. Growth record: record students' learning process and progress, and

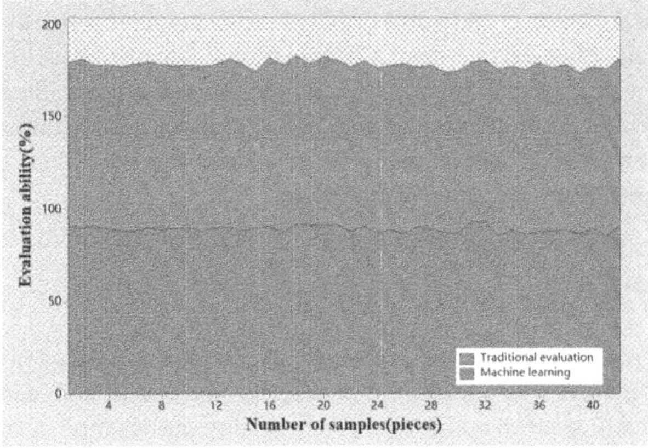

Fig. 3. Comprehensive quality evaluation of different algorithms

Table 3. Comparison of the accuracy of comprehensive quality assessment of different methods

Algorithm	Comprehensive quality assessment	Magnitude of change	Error
machine learning	92.68	92.27	90.51
Traditional assessment methods	90.39	85.33	87.74
P	88.79	85.77	90.26

reflect their long-term development. Scenario simulation: By simulating the real situation, the students' problem-solving and decision-making ability in a specific environment is investigated (Fig. 4).

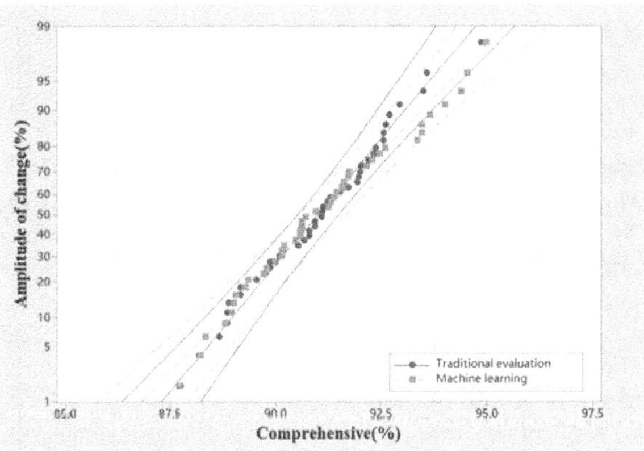

Fig. 4. Comprehensive quality assessment of machine learning comprehensive quality assessment

Moral character: honesty and trustworthiness, respect for others, justice and fairness, self-discipline, etc. Physical and mental health: physical quality, psychological quality, life skills, self-management ability, etc. Each index should set specific and operational evaluation criteria to ensure the fairness and objectivity of the evaluation. At the same time, the indicators should remain relatively independent and complement each other to reflect the comprehensive quality of individuals.

5 Conclusion

Aiming at the problem that the comprehensive quality assessment of college students' comprehensive education is not ideal, this paper proposes machine learning and combines artificial intelligence to optimize the comprehensive education of college students. At the same time, the accuracy of comprehensive quality assessment is analyzed in depth to construct a comprehensive quality set. Research shows that machine learning can improve the rationality and implementability of comprehensive education of college students, and can generally carry out comprehensive education for college students Comprehensive quality assessment. However, in the process of machine learning, too much attention is paid to the analysis of comprehensive quality assessment, resulting in irrationality in the selection of comprehensive quality assessment indicators.

Acknowledgements. Early warning research on the evaluation of college students' comprehensive quality based on machine learning (this project is supported by the 2022 general special scientific research plan of Shaanxi Provincial Department of Education, Project No.: 22JK0258).

References

1. Elsotohy, A.M., Soliman, A.M.A., Adail, A.S., Eisa, A.A., Othman, E.A.: Comprehensive power quality performance assessment for electrical system of a nuclear research reactor. Sci. Rep. **13**(1) (2023)
2. Fernandez, N., Camacho, L.A.: Water quality modeling in headwater catchments: comprehensive data assessment, model development and simulation of scenarios. Water **15**(5) (2023)
3. Ghodsi, Z., Jazayeri, S.B., Pourrashidi, A., Sadeghi-Naeini, M., Azadmanjir, Z., Baigi, V., Maroufi, S.F., Azarhomayoun, A., Faghih-Jouybari, M., Amirjamshidi, A., Naghdi, K., Habibiarejan, R., Shabani, M., Sepahdoost, A., Dehghanbanadaki, H., Habibi, R., Mohammadzadeh, M., Bahreini, M., O'Reilly, G.M., Vaccaro, A.R., Harrop, J.S., Davies, B.M., Yi, L., Ghodsi, S.M., Rahimi-Movaghar, V.: Development of a comprehensive assessment tool to measure the quality of care for individuals with traumatic spinal cord injuries. Spinal Cord Ser. Cases **9**(1) (2023)
4. Jimenez-Oyola, S., et al.: Heavy metal(loid)s contamination in water and sediments in a mining area in Ecuador: a comprehensive assessment for drinking water quality and human health risk. Environ. Geochem. Health **45**(7), 4929–4949 (2023)
5. Morales-Vargas, A., Pedraza-Jimenez, R., Codina, L.: Website quality evaluation: a model for developing comprehensive assessment instruments based on key quality factors. J. Doc. **79**(7), 95–114 (2023)

6. Shen, L.Q., Yao, Y., Geng, X.Q., Fang, R.G., Wu, D.P.: A novel no-reference quality assessment metric for stereoscopic images with consideration of comprehensive 3D quality information. Sensors **23**(13) (2023)
7. Wang, Z.H., Wang, Y.: Groundwater quality assessment by multi-model comparison: a comprehensive study during dry and wet periods in semi-arid regions. Environ. Sci. Pollut. Res. **30**(18), 51571–51594 (2023)
8. Xu, L.J., Liu, Y.J., Zhang, X.Y.: Study on comprehensive assessment of air quality of energy consumption in industrial parks: take Nanjing HX industrial park in China as an example. Pol. J. Environ. Stud. **32**(1), 387–397 (2023)
9. Yang, H.T., Jia, C., Yang, F., Yang, X., Wei, R.: Water quality assessment of deep learning-improved comprehensive pollution index: a case study of Dagu River, Jiaozhou Bay, China. Environ. Sci. Pollut. Res. (2023)
10. Yin, J.X., Li, C., Zhang, J., Ding, H., Han, L. F., Yang, W.Z., Li, F.Y., Song, X.B., Bie, S.T., Yu, H.S., Li, Z.: Comprehensive multicomponent characterization and quality assessment of Shuang-Huang-Lian powder injection using ultra-high-performance liquid chromatography-quadrupole time-of-flight-mass spectrometry and ultra-high-performance liquid chromatography-quadrupole-Orbitrap-mass spectrometry. Rapid Commun. Mass Spectrom. **37**(7) (2023)
11. Zarekar, A., Salehi, E., Nohegar, A., Ashrafi, K.: Prioritizing urban sustainability practices through comprehensive quality assessment and scenario planning. Int. J. Environ. Res. **17**(3) (2023)
12. Zhang, J., Wang, C., Wang, J.W., Yang, Y., Han, K.N., Bakpa, E.P., Li, J., Lyu, J., Yu, J.H., Xie, J.M.: Comprehensive fruit quality assessment and identification of aroma-active compounds in green pepper (*Capsicum annuum* L.). Front. Nutr. **9** (2023)

Personalized Assessment Algorithm for Preschool Education Based on Machine Learning

Ming Chen(✉)

Wuhan Business and Trade Vocational Collece, Wuhan 430205, Hubei, China
406010695@qq.com

Abstract. Individual education is the main content and method in teaching students in accordance with their aptitude. However, in the process of individualized education analysis. It needs to involve interests, abilities and personal conditions. Therefore, it is necessary to make an overall plan for personalized education and improve the effectiveness of its educational analysis. Through the deep machine learning analysis method, the integration of personalized education can improve students' academic performance and new learning ability. The enhancement degree is greater than 40%, which can meet students' reality, and the satisfaction rate of teachers' needs is greater than 80%. Therefore, deep mechanical learning can promote the development of personalized education and optimize the original educational content and form.

Keywords: Iterative Accumulation Theory · Algorithms Xi machine learning · Pre-school education · Professionalization of education · Evaluation algorithms

1 Introduction

There is a certain correlation between personalized education and deep learning. The main reason is that personalized education not only involves students' learning content, but also involves students' learning interest [1, 2]. It is necessary to judge the original resources and students' synthesis and needs. Therefore, in the process of personalized education and comprehensive comparison, it involves the iteration of multiple indicators and contents [3, 4]. Therefore, in the aspect of machine learning and comprehensive learning, it is necessary to combine students' learning characteristics and feature points, integrate them as a whole, and optimize the overall development of personalized education [5, 6]. Therefore, in the process of analysis, deep learning and comprehensive development are used to improve the effect of personalized education and meet its actual teaching needs. At the same time, it is also optimized for the integrity of personalized education [7, 8]. On this basis, this paper optimizes and promotes individualized education and comprehensive analysis, and its analysis effect provides support for classroom teaching and college teaching [9, 10].

B. Brik and S. Nazir (Eds.): BigIoT-EDU 2024, LNICST 660, pp. 566–573, 2026.
https://doi.org/10.1007/978-3-032-18628-7_58

2 Theoretical Model Construction of Personalized Evaluation Algorithms

Machine Learning improves the personalized evaluation algorithm strategy through computer technology, and analyzes a series of key parameters involved in the system research to identify the parameter values is W_i that do not meet the standards in the study E_i. Subsequently, the algorithm integrates these parameter values into the personalized evaluation algorithm scheme is $\hat{e}_i = E_i/|E_i|, \hat{h}_i = H_i/|H_i|$, and then comprehensively evaluates the implementation possibility of the study. The calculation process can be referred to Eqs. (1) and (2).

$$W_i = \frac{1}{2}E_i \times H_i^* \sum \frac{|E_i|^2}{2\eta_o}\hat{e}_i \times \hat{h}_i^* \tag{1}$$

In the process of mechanical learning, it is necessary to deal with some achievements and P is multiple indicators in preschool education. Therefore, comprehensive analysis methods such as qualitative and quantitative should be summarized into the data set, as shown in Formula 2.

$$P = \sigma|W_i| = \int \frac{\sigma}{2\eta_o}|E_i|^2\frac{1}{n} \tag{2}$$

η_o is personalized preschool education is the basis of analysis and in-depth verification is W_s. In terms of individualized education and multi-analysis, it is necessary to improve the analysis conditions of individualized education [11–13]. The specific results are shown in Eq. 3.

$$|W_s| = \frac{\mathrm{P}}{4\pi \mathrm{R}^2} = \frac{\sigma|E_i|^2}{\sum \eta_o R^2 8\pi}X_1, \ldots, X_n \tag{3}$$

Students' overall personalized and comprehensive attributes is E_s set, personalized boost rates is η_o, the specific process is shown in Formula 4.

$$|W_s| = \sqrt{\frac{1}{2\eta_o}|E_s|^2\frac{x-\mu}{\sigma}} \tag{4}$$

$\sum\sigma$ is students' personalized adjustment mechanism, as shown in Formula 5.

$$\sum\sigma = 4\pi R^2\frac{|E_s|^2}{|E_i|^2}\sum_{i=1}^{n}\sum X_i \tag{5}$$

σ is the comprehensive and individualized needs of students and the changing conditions of holistic planning and needs are shown in Formula 6.

$$\sigma = \lim_{R\to\infty}\int 4\pi R\frac{E_s \times E_s^*}{E_i \times E_i^*}\frac{x-\mu}{\sigma} \tag{6}$$

Make comprehensive judgment, as well as multi-index and corresponding content analysis to improve students' personalized analysis and needs. The judgment conditions in which is $IO(t_i)$ This analysis process is shown in the formula 7.

$$IO(t_i) = \sum_{i=1}^{n}\left(X_i - \int \overline{X}\right)^2 \frac{g(t_i) + F(d_i)}{\text{mean}\left(\sum v_{ij} + 4\right)}\sqrt{ji} \tag{7}$$

3 A Real-World Example of a Personalized Evaluation Algorithm

3.1 The Relevant Concepts of Personalized Evaluation Algorithm Model Construction

Students' personalized learning is influenced by many factors, including students' actual needs, students' content, students' objective attributes and behavior intensity. Therefore, it is necessary to realize the comprehensive analysis of data in the process of analyzing students' achievements and judging and integrating multiple information. Among them, quantitative data is obtained by calculation to obtain qualitative data mainly through mapping table, mapping relationship and mapping logic judgment, which realizes multi-data type judgment of student information, and completes comprehensive attributes and comprehensive judgment requirements. Therefore, in the process of overall analysis and judgment, students' integrity and overall planning also have strong characteristics. Therefore, the registration of students' academic performance, students' content, students' personality and other data has become the focus of research, facing students' demands. Tencent carried out. The result of normalizing the judgment and data is shown in Fig. 1.

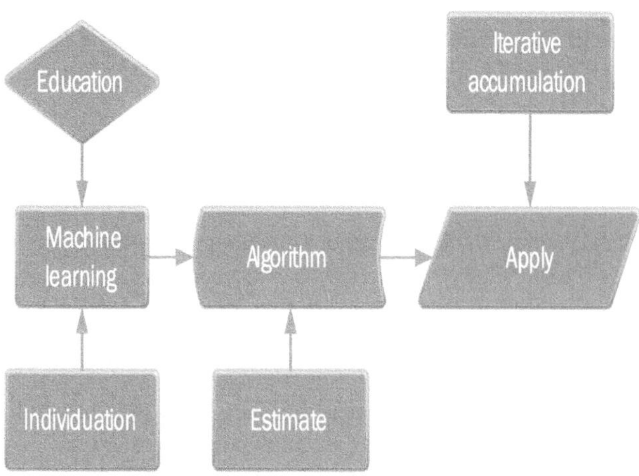

Fig. 1. The analysis process of the personalized evaluation algorithm

From the analysis in Fig. 1, in the process of students' personalized analysis and personalized attribute judgment, it is necessary to verify their educational situation, educational problems, analysis level and analysis structure first, so as to realize the integration of multiple data. At the same time, it is necessary to analyze the data content and data relationship and realize data integration and judgment by constructing intelligent analysis methods. It is the focus of research to fuse mapping charts, data types and data structures, fuse intelligent analysis and intelligent structures and output the final corresponding processing scheme.

3.2 Personalized Evaluation Algorithms

Based on the research content of preschool education, the students of your major are the survey objects, and the survey objects are 320 people, and the corresponding data are analyzed, including students' personalized training, personalized teaching plan, personalized content and achievements. The score is one and fifteen points for judgment. The summary results of the scores are shown in Table 1.

Table 1. Subject-related parameters of the study

Category	Individualized training program	Purify teaching content	Student's academic performance	Comprehensive judgment
Assessment of learning Xi ability	87.89	86.74	93.28	90.89
Cognitive ability assessment	87.57	88.74	89.57	88.54
Motor coordination assessment	88.08	90.29	90.43	91.83
Social-emotional assessment	86.84	90.59	91.59	89.36

From the in-depth analysis in Table 1, it can be seen that in the process of personalized training and personalized evaluation, the results are relatively reasonable and the results are relatively complete, which can be used for later functional analysis.

3.3 Personalized Evaluation Algorithm and Stability

Summarize the comprehensive indexes of personalized analysis and students' academic performance judgment to form an effective graphical comparison. The comparison results are shown in Fig. 2.

However, in the process of Fig. 2, it will be found that multi-dimensional analysis and judgment such as personalized learning, deep learning, and machine learning

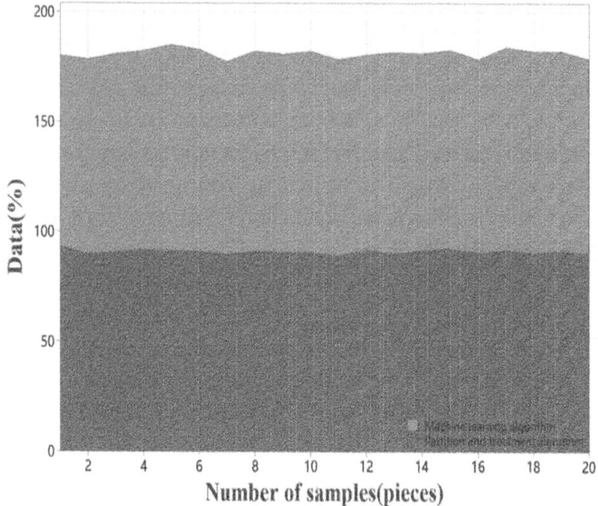

Fig. 2. Individualized evaluation algorithms for different algorithms

can improve students' personalized learning level and realize the synthesis of learning content. Moreover, it includes academic performance, learning content and multiple indicators to form a uniform distribution, and there is no significant impact. However, it is only a continuous analysis, and there is no relationship between the key points of external personalized learning, so it is necessary to judge the distribution map. The results of the distribution plot are shown in Fig. 3.

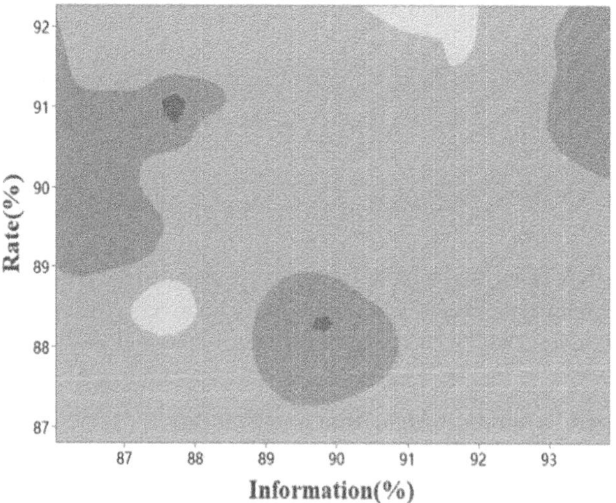

Fig. 3. Distribution feature identification of sexualization.

Do the analysis of the distribution map, and you can find the personalization of students in the form. Actual general analysis results are presented. Local and holistic changes. There are local individualized learning characteristics, but the overall distribution and color distribution, as well as students' learning situation, have no significant changes. Therefore, in the process of comprehensive analysis and personalized analysis, the intelligent method proposed in this paper is more effective, which can clarify the location and scope of personalization and optimize it. The analysis results are summarized and summarized as shown in Table 2.

Table 2. Rationalization and comparison of personalized evaluation algorithms of different methods

Algorithm	Learning situation	Students' integrity and learning	A comprehensive judgment of life	Rational planning
Machine learning methods	88.16	87.65	89.54	90.56
Divide and conquer algorithm	90.94	91.30	90.80	86.81

Judge students' interest points and find students' personalized content. In Table 2, it can be found that students' personalized characteristics, personalized points, learning environment and rationalization all show distributed characteristics greater than 80%, indicating that in the process of mechanical learning, there are obvious correlations between each feature point, and the feature points and generality are also very prominent. However, in order to explore the logic between students' personalized points and feature points, it is necessary to analyze the correlation of each point. The correlation analysis process is shown in Fig. 4.

According to the analysis results in Fig. 4, when the correlation analysis, diversification analysis and holistic analysis are carried out, each point is more than 80% to 90%, and the distribution characteristics of logical intersection are present among the correlation points, correlation contents and key points. It is further explained that with the assistance of machine deep learning. Students' personalized learning, personalized learning content and academic achievements are independent and related. Relevance means that there is good logic among achievements, and it can promote the improvement of academic achievements. The distribution of each point is relatively obvious, mainly due to the individualized characteristics of each point. The relative independence of holistic characteristics proves that mechanical learning has a significant promotion effect on preschool education.

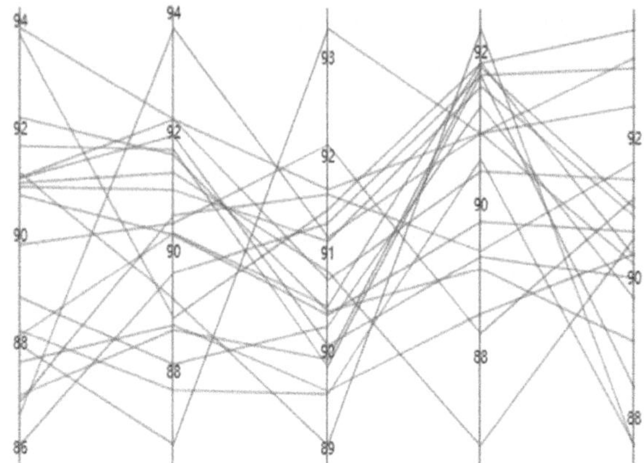

Fig. 4. Comparative study of the research scheme of the algorithm

4 Conclusion

Education is an important discipline for learning and comprehensive judgment, and it is also a main content of learning and analysis in universities. However, the analysis of preschool education and whether the analysis situation is consistent, as well as the integrity of the analysis situation, need further judgment and identification. Therefore, this paper proposes an intelligent analysis method for universities. Preschool education has in-depth analysis and influence, including students' personalized image, personalized content, personalized characteristics, and students' academic performance. The results show that machine learning can promote personalized optimization, improve its learning effect by more than 20%, and make the overall learning level reach more than 75%. Therefore, stimulating learning can promote the development of individualized learning. However, the research in this paper also has some limitations, mainly because machine learning also has shortcomings in the whole analysis process. Therefore, more samples will be expanded in the future to improve the effectiveness of this research.

References

1. Li, S., Zhang, F., Lin, H.: Research on forest fire risk assessment based on machine learning algorithms. J. Nanjing For. Univ. (Nat. Sci. Ed.) (005), 047
2. Xing, T., Zhou, C., Liu, S.: (2022) Service evaluation method and system based on federated machine learning algorithm CN202210192934.4
3. Chen, Y., Li, H.: A method for evaluating the effectiveness of Chinese speech recognition based on machine learning algorithms. Inf. Rec. Mater. (008) 023
4. Xing, T., Shi, K., Zhou, C.: A composite service evaluation method and system based on federated machine learning algorithms and cloud feedback CN112884163B
5. Mao, J., Shi, H., Cui, X., Cai, Y., Song, M.: Research on audit risk assessment based on stacking ensemble machine learning algorithm computer knowledge and technology: academic exchange (018-004) (2022)
6. Wei, Q., Wei Q., Xu, J., Bai, Y., Li, X., He, M., et al.: ET based on machine learning algorithms_ (0). Predict. Res. Water Sav. Irrig. **11**(9) (2022)

7. Peng, P., Wu, M., Li, C.: A method for establishing a prediction model for mental brain diseases based on machine learning algorithms CN202211220974.1 (2023)
8. Hu, X., Yin, L., Yang, Q., Wang, L.: Research on plastic classification based on near-infrared hyperspectral imaging technology. Prog. Laser Optoelectron. **61**(02) (2024)
9. Zhao, Z., Wang, Z., Yu, J., Xu, J., Bai, Y., Wang, X.: A rice safety risk assessment method based on the fusion of multiple machine learning algorithms CN202210306564.2 (2022)
10. Li, X., Hu, B., Bai, W.: Research progress on the application of machine learning algorithms based on ultrasound images in carotid artery plaque risk assessment. Chin. J. Med. Ultrasound: Electron. Ed. **19**(10), 4 (2022)
11. Li, B., Li, B., Ji, S., Xing, L., Zheng, L., Huang, P.: Topsis model based on combinatorial weighting and machine learning algorithm for water quality evaluation and analysis in a certain area of Shandong water conservancy technology and economy **28**(4), 5 (2022)
12. Peng, S., Guoni, L., Yuanyuan, L., Li, H., Donghua, C., Yufeng, L.: Dynamic assessment of agricultural drought risk in Anhui Province based on machine learning algorithms. Water Resour. Hydropower Technol. (Chinese and English) **53**(5), 14 (2022)
13. Tong, X., Chun, Y., Qinggang, M.: Construction of the risk assessment model of diabetes nephropathy based on multi label machine learning. Chinese General Practice Medicine **20**(2), 6 (2022)

Analysis of College Students' Mental Health Education Based on Machine Learning

Huimin Wangwan[1], L. I. Zou[2](✉), and Zhaoziyi Luo[2]

[1] College of Finance, Taxation and Finance, Yunnan College of Finance and Economics, Kunming, China

[2] Yunnan College of Finance and Economics, Kunming, China

1132425032@qq.com

Abstract. Students' mental health is an important part in the process of college education, but you are a college student, and it is difficult to identify problems in mental health. For this reason, we propose a braking method to conduct an in-depth analysis of the mental health of treatment to explore its impact on the overall situation of mental health, and analyze the key contents and indicator documents. The results show that when continuing to study, college students' mental health is effectively improved, with the improvement rate between 15% and 16%, and they can dig deep into the problems existing in mental health. Therefore, temporary health problems have not been effectively improved with the assistance of treatment methods. Strengthening the research of single-day health and improving its effectiveness is the key technology of my research.

Keywords: statistical theory · Machine learning algorithm · College students · Mental health · Analysis

1 Introduction

The mental health analysis plays a significant role in its analysis process [1], which enables the rapid and precise control of the aging performance evaluation model [2]. Nonetheless, during the health analysis, it is crucial that the scheme plays a key role [3, 4], but this suffers from a lack of accuracy, adversely affecting its effectiveness [5, 6]. According to some researchers [7], the scheme can be successfully analyzed if the health analysis is supported by employing Machine learning algorithms for studying the aging performance assessment mode [8]. To enhance the health analysis scheme and validate the model's efficiency, implementing a machine learning algorithm is proposed based on this information [9–11].

2 Related Concepts

2.1 The Machine Learning Algorithm Is Described Mathematically

The testing of mental health requires corresponding list analysis by China Construction Bank, otherwise it is difficult to achieve effective improvement. Therefore, it is necessary to regulate and constrain the scales in mental health., it is y_i found that the unqualified

B. Brik and S. Nazir (Eds.): BigIoT-EDU 2024, LNICST 660, pp. 574–584, 2026.
https://doi.org/10.1007/978-3-032-18628-7_59

value parameters in the health analysis plays a crucial role is z_i, and the health analysis plays a crucial role scheme is $tol(y_i \cdot t_{ij})$ integrated with the function to finally judge the feasibility of the health analysis plays a crucial role, and the calculation is shown in Eq. (1).

$$\lim_{x \to \infty} \left(y_i \cdot t_{ij}\right) = \sqrt{K} y_{ij} \geq \max\left(t_{ij} \div 2\right) \tag{1}$$

In fact, their overall situation and quantitative analysis need to be improved on the basis of effective in-depth and intelligent analysis. Equation illustrates the evaluation of outliers among them Eq. (2).

$$\max\left(t_{ij}\right) = \partial\left(t_{ij}{}^2 + 2 \cdot t_{ij}\right) \succ \frac{1}{2} \frac{n!}{r!(n-r)!} \tag{2}$$

The focus on health is to enhance the rationality and effectiveness of its analysis, better grasp students' thinking and overall analysis situation, and also test the psychological problems in Sect. 8 and Sect. 7.

Suppose I The requirements of the health analysis plays a crucial role is t_i that the health analysis plays a crucial role scheme is set_i, Psychological health is not a simple data analysis that requires the integration of scales and individual characteristics. Is y_i, and the judgment function of the health analysis plays a crucial role the scheme is $F(t_i \approx 0)$ as shown by Eq. (3).

$$F(d_i) = \prod 2 \sum t_i \bigcap \xi \cdot \sqrt{2} \to \oint y_i \cdot 7 \tag{3}$$

2.2 Selection of Health Analysis Plays a Crucial Role Scheme

Hypothesis II It is also necessary to make certain judgments about health, otherwise it is difficult to effectively explore, and it is still necessary to have one's own theory. Is $g(t_i)$, Health plays an important role in the life process of college students, and the content and conditions of mental health are also crucial in this regard. The health analysis plays a crucial role. Eq. (4).

$$g(t_i) = \ddot{x} \cdot z_i \prod F(d_i) \frac{dy}{dx} - w_i \Phi \tag{4}$$

Strengthening research on mental health, delving deeper into issues related to mental health, can be applied to health problems of different social classes and strata. is shown in Eq. (5).

$$\lim_{x \to \infty} g(t_i) + F(d_i) \leq \frac{n!}{r!(n-r)!} \max\left(t_{ij}\right) \tag{5}$$

Health is improved on the basis of social environment, personal and comprehensive environment are presented in Eq. (6).

$$g(t_i) \tilde{+} F(d_i) \leftrightarrow \sqrt{b^2 - 4ac}\left(\sum t_{ij} + 4\right) \tag{6}$$

2.3 Analysis of Health Analysis Plays a Crucial Role Scheme

In the research process of health, it is necessary to use scales, actual interviews, and relevant case studies as support, otherwise it is difficult to improve the effectiveness and rationality of its analysis given using Eq. (6), and the outcomes is $No(t_i)$ shown in Eq. (7).

$$No(t_i) = \frac{g(t_i) \tilde{+} F(d_i)}{mean(\sum t_{ij} + 4)} \tag{7}$$

Among them, it is $\frac{g(t_i) \tilde{+} F(d_i)}{mean(\sum t_{ij}+4)} \leq 1$ specified that the scheme must be $Zh(t_i)$ suggested; otherwise, the scheme integration is necessary; the outcome is illustrated in Eq. (8).

$$Zh(t_i) = \lim_{x \to \infty} \left[\sum g(t_i) \tilde{+} F(d_i) \right] \lim_{x \to \infty} \tag{8}$$

The health analysis plays a crucial role is $accur(t_i)$ thoroughly examined, Meaning is a personal issue that requires comprehensive analysis to determine whether it meets the requirements. Therefore, creating a new model is a complex and comprehensive analysis process is $unno(t_i)$ a systematic testPsychological health issues should be judged based on one's own situation, external conditions, and comprehensive content, and then the organization of psychological health research should be studied plays a crucial role's accuracy, as stated in Eq. (9).

$$accur(t_i) = \frac{\min \left[\sum g(t_i) \tilde{+} F(d_i) \right]}{\sum g(t_i) \tilde{+} F(d_i)} \frac{-b \pm \sqrt{b^2 - 4ac}}{2a} \tag{9}$$

The wire factory needs to analyze multiple aspects, and in the process of further analysis, it is necessary to consider the overall nature of current laws and the effectiveness of the dean's mental health., and hence it is $randon(t_i)$ considered as a high analytical research. The analysis results of opinions require more auxiliary support, otherwise it will be difficult to effectively utilize them as Eq. (10).

$$accur(t_i) = \frac{o\sqrt{2}\chi}{\frac{1}{2} \sum g(t_i) \tilde{+} F(d_i)} + randon(t_i) \tag{10}$$

The event is not a single issue, and confidence plays an important role in the entire analysis process. Therefore, based on this table and data syndrome, it is necessary to integrate the sexual aspect.

3 Health Analysis Plays a Crucial Role Optimization Approach

The role of health analysis is vital in the optimization of schemes; it utilizes a random optimization method through machine learning algorithms and modifies internet information parameters. The evolutionary algorithm divides the essential health analysis into several stages and then randomly selects alternative methods. The scheme for health analysis at different levels is refined and assessed throughout an iterative process. Once the optimization study concludes, the health analysis level across various schemes is compiled, and the optimal health analysis is documented.

4 Practical Examples of Health Analysis Plays a Crucial Role

4.1 Introduction to the Health Analysis Plays a Crucial Role

Conduct a psychological test on students and analyze the key points and survey questionnaire in the test results. The test lasts for 16 years, covering psychological and daily habits, and is judged on a scale of 1–5 is shown in Table 1.

Table 1. Health analysis plays a crucial role requirements

Scope of application	Grade	Accuracy	Health analysis plays a crucial role
Post-secondary students	I	89.08	91.58
	II	87.56	89.49
Undergraduate students	I	88.88	90.18
	II	89.52	86.50
Graduate students	I	89.86	87.97
	II	89.15	88.65

The health analysis plays a crucial role process in Table 1 is shown in Fig. 1.

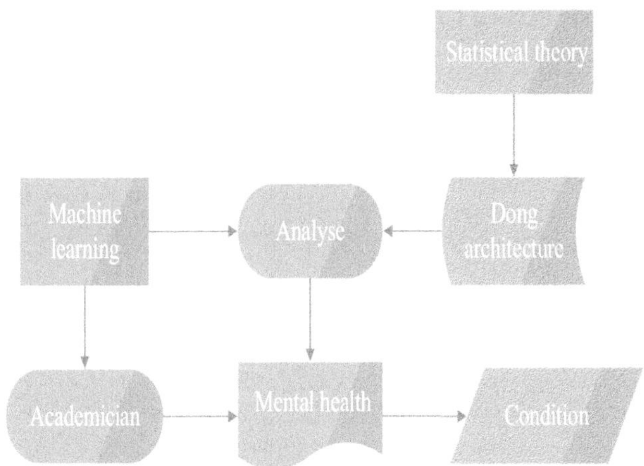

Fig. 1. Analysis process of health analysis plays a crucial role

In the process of conducting psychological testing, the results of the testing process should be based on actual situations, user analysis, and comprehensive needs, providing support for later opinions and digital comprehensive analysis. Therefore, in the process of conducting testing analysis, comprehensive judgments should be made based on specific situations to enhance the effectiveness of each city.

4.2 Health Analysis Plays a Crucial Role

Psychological health is also a purpose for the human body to engage in normal activities, and its health status is consistent with the duration of health. Therefore, psychological health is also an issue that cannot be ignored. How to effectively judge the existing health situation needs to be analyzed in conjunction with the overall situation. As a result, the evolutionary algorithm's health analysis plays a crucial role scheme has improved in terms of speed, accuracy, and summation stability (Table 2).

Table 2. The overall situation of the health analysis plays a crucial role scheme

Category	Random data	Reliability	Analysis rate
Post-secondary students	86.50	88.23	86.42
Undergraduate students	90.43	89.92	88.22
Graduate students	89.65	87.41	88.91
Mean	87.32	88.51	89.88
X6	91.65	92.53	90.56
	P = 1.273		

4.3 Health Analysis Plays a Crucial Role and Stability

The situation has also been discovered, and the key issues in mental health are currently the main research content. Therefore, it is necessary to comprehensively judge and verify whether the information changes in mental health checks meet the corresponding work needs a crucial role scheme is shown in Fig. 2.

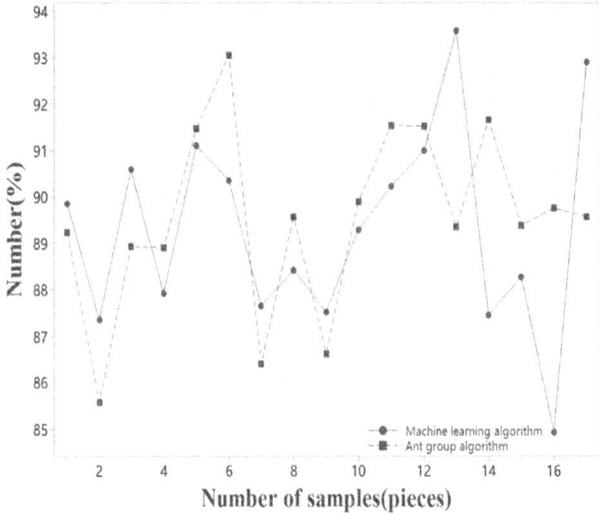

Fig. 2. Evaluation model of aging performance of different algorithms

Figure 2 shows that This competition activity is not only an important content, but also tests the key indicators of adapting to health, how to better judge mental health, and the key content of mental health. It is only about analyzing the overall health and comparing the results of mental health in shown Table. 3.

Table 3. Compares the accuracy of several health analysis plays a crucial role.

Algorithm	Survey data	Health analysis plays a crucial role	Magnitude of change	Error
Machine learning algorithm	85.33	85.15	82.88	84.95
Ant colony algorithm	87.10	88.28	88.30	87.11
P	85.08	89.28	92.26	90.23

Table 3 shows that Deep learning methods can make overall judgments on mental health, discover conceptual outliers in mental health, analyze and identify the latest role in mental health activities and the overall nature of mental health, and are currently the focus of research. The price of credit cards is now closely related to it, becoming a hot research topic., as shown in Figure 3.

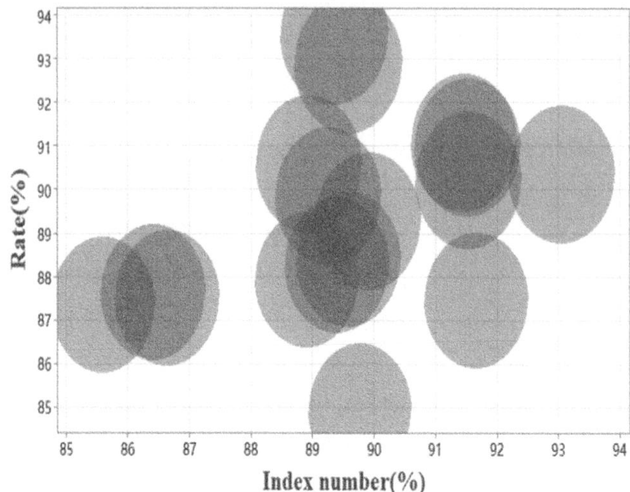

Fig. 3. Health analysis plays a crucial role of Machine learning algorithm

Figure 3 shows that the health analysis plays a crucial role of the Machine learning algorithm is significantly better than the ant colony algorithm. This is because the Machine learning algorithm increases the health analysis plays a crucial role's adjustment coefficient and sets the threshold of Internet information to eliminate the health analysis plays a crucial role scheme that does not meet the requirements.

4.4 Rationality of Health Analysis Plays a Crucial Role

The health analysis plays a crucial role scheme is integrated with the ant colony algorithm to check the correctness of the Machine learning algorithm, and the health analysis plays a crucial role scheme is depicted in Fig. 4.

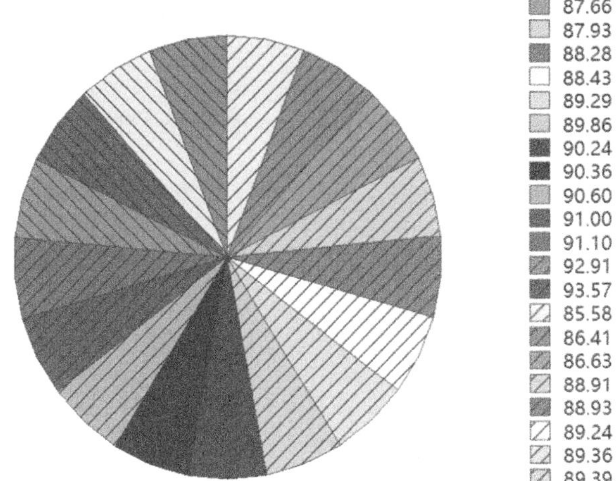

Fig. 4. Evaluation model of aging performance of different algorithms

Figure 4 shows that during the process of conducting surveys and analysis, should we combine various indicators to establish analysis standards for the first four words of sexual health activities? The average value of the indicators is between 80% and 90%, and there is a significant correlation between 18% of the analysis process and analysis content, indicating that the results can meet the actual requirements during the analysis process, and there is more correlation without treatment. This is a new challenge, love you.

4.5 Validity of Health Analysis Plays a Crucial Role

When establishing a key role and key application center in the fight against the epidemic, it is also necessary to make judgments on the main conditions and analysis of information health. How to analyze whether their current main activities involve people's mental health and whether they can improve the corresponding results. As long as six people provide support and clear commitments, they should have some in-depth management of themselves is shown in Fig. 5.

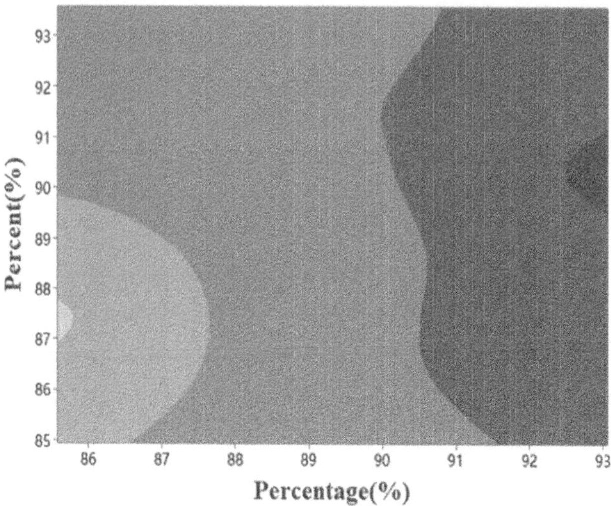

Fig. 5. Health analysis plays a crucial role of different algorithms

Figure 5 shows that tPsychological health activities are not a simple issue, and it is necessary to continuously explore the indicators of today's healthy exercise, determine the key annualized factors recommended by traditional Chinese medicine, and improve the results of the project. There were two specific discomforts.

Table 4. Compares the efficacy of several health analysis plays a crucial role.

Algorithm	Survey data	Health analysis plays a crucial role	Magnitude of change	Error
Machine learning algorithm	91.77	89.34	89.00	90.43
Ant colony algorithm	87.46	89.15	89.90	89.70
P	91.05	86.23	90.70	92.36

Table 4 shows that during the process of comprehensive observation in China, I know that through the current activities and problem testing conducted by the dean, I can download the link information to identify and judge. The happiest thing is the current concept of single news as illustrated in Fig. 6.

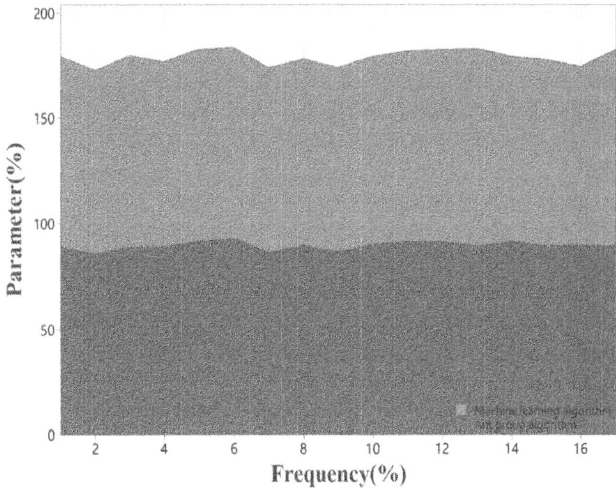

Fig. 6. Machine learning algorithm health analysis plays a crucial role

Figure 6 shows that now they and I still have different natures and certain differences. We can understand that sexual health can be effectively improved through targeted maintenance and judgment.

5 Conclusion

The function of health examination is crucial for the refinement of strategies; it applies a stochastic optimization technique via machine learning algorithms and adjusts internet data parameters. The evolutionary algorithm breaks down the critical health examination into multiple phases and then picks different approaches at random. The plan for conducting health examinations at various tiers goes through an iterative process of enhancement and evaluation. After the completion of the optimization research, the health examination levels across diverse plans are collated, and the most favorable health examination is recorded.

References

1. Ma, X.: Analysis of psychological health of college students based on hybrid clustering algorithm. Electron. Des. Eng. (010), 030 (2022)
2. Ma, X., Wang, Z., Zhao, J., Zhu, Y., Jiang, P., Wu, H.: Research on the psychological health status and model of nursing personnel under sudden public health incidents. Gen. Nurs. **21**(16), 2263–2267 (2023)
3. Wang, J., Yang, S.: Research on Algorithm for Analyzing Psychological Health Factors of College Students Based on Big Data Matching. Electron. Des. Eng., 030–009 (2022)
4. Chen, Y.: Construction of detection models, detection methods, and related devices for physical and mental state detection CN202111595271.2 (2022)
5. Lv, H., Yue C., Chen J., Xu W., Chai Q., Lu M., et al. Visualization analysis of research hotspots in pressure damage risk prediction based on machine learning algorithms. Tianjin Nurs. **31**(4), 432–437 (2023)

6. Zhang, Y., Fu, F.: A survey on the mental health status of minority college students based on a national sample (5) (2022)
7. Lai, S.: Exploration of Artificial Intelligence and Big Data in Psychological Health Education for College Students. Comput. Knowl. Technol. (018–006) (2022)
8. Wang, Y., Chen, L., Di, X.: A Study on the Psychological Health Status of Freshmen: An Empirical Analysis Based on Questionnaire Data from a University in Hebei Province. J. Handan Univ. **33**(1), 100–106 (2023)
9. Guan, Z., Li, F.: Prediction and response analysis of college graduation destinations based on machine learning SVM algorithm - Based on the Framework of Human Capital and Social Capital Special Zone Economy (8), 6 (2022)
10. Yan, C., Mao, T., Li, R., Wang, J., Chen, Y.: Analysis of mental health status and influencing factors of college students during closed management of COVID-19. School Health in China. **43**(7), 6 (2022)
11. Wang, Z., Peng, Q., Chen, Y., Guo, Z.: Analysis of the influencing factors of college students' mental health under the COVID-19 epidemic based on the random forest model. China Health Administration. (003), 039 (2022)

Research on English Speech Recognition Technology Based on Intelligent Learning System

Linbo Zhang(✉)

School of Languages and Cultural Communication, Xi'an Mingde Institute of Technology, Xi'an, China
zhanglb@mdit.edu.cn

Abstract. In order to improve the visual effect, we can use the intelligent analysis method to carry out deep active learning, verify the effectiveness of the research results, show the deep learning method, can judge the intonation and timbre in speech recognition, complete the comprehensive analysis, and improve the overall analysis effect. The recognition accuracy rate reaches between 80 and 90%, and the simplification rate of English speech recognition is simplified, with a simplification rate of 23%, so the deep machine learning method can improve the speech recognition effect and promote its application range.

Keywords: gradient descent theory · deep machine learning · Research · English · Speech recognition

1 Introduction

In order to improve the content and effectiveness of speech recognition, it is necessary to conduct a comprehensive analysis of speech recognition [1, 2]. Some scholars believe that the application of intelligent methods to speech recognition, the integration of accurate recognition and fuzzy recognition of speech can improve the speech recognition rate, simplify the recognition complexity of speech, and improve its recognition efficiency [3, 4]. Some scholars believe that the integration of this analysis method with language recognition may increase the difficulty of speech recognition, but it can be used as an auxiliary means to judge the effectiveness of speech pronunciation structure [5, 6]. Intelligent recognition of multiple recognition methods, which is used to gradually adjust the recognition database and optimize the recognition process [7–13]. Therefore, on the basis of the above analysis, this paper makes an overall judgment on speech recognition, optimizes the previous speech recognition effect, and makes a comprehensive judgment on it, so as to find the integration point of speech recognition and intelligent methods.

B. Brik and S. Nazir (Eds.): BigIoT-EDU 2024, LNICST 660, pp. 585–595, 2026.
https://doi.org/10.1007/978-3-032-18628-7_60

2 Related Concepts

2.1 The Deep Machine Learning Is Described Mathematically

The key of speech recognition is to decompose the speech content, form multi-party analysis effect, and optimize the speech structure. Deepening the analysis process of speech is y_i, the unqualified value parameters in the speech recognition research is z_i, and the speech recognition research scheme is $tol(y_i \cdot t_{ij})$ integrated with the function to finally judge the feasibility of the speech recognition research, and the calculation is shown in Eq. (1).

$$\lim_{x \to \infty} \left(y_i \cdot t_{ij} \right) = \sum_{i=1}^{n} X_i y_{ij} \geq \max \left(t_{ij} \div 2 \right) \tag{1}$$

After the speech recognition process is completed, it is necessary to judge the characteristics and features of speech, establish the logic of speech recognition, and reconstruct multiple elements such as pronunciation and intonation of speech Eq. (2).

$$\max \left(t_{ij} \right) = \partial \left(t_{ij}{}^{2} + 2 \cdot t_{ij} \right) \succ \sum_{i=1}^{n} X_i^2 \tag{2}$$

The built speech content should establish corresponding databases, deeply mine the speech information and apply it to different databases to improve it. At the same time, it is necessary to judge the integrity and content of speech, and establish a fuzzy analysis database to provide support for the later speech logic reorganization is set_i, the technique for satisfying the speech recognition research is y_i, and the judgment function of the speech recognition research the scheme is $F(t_i \approx 0)$ as shown by Eq. (3).

$$F(d_i) = \prod \sum t_i \cap \xi \cdot \sqrt{2} \to \oint y_i \cdot 7 \tag{3}$$

2.2 Selection of Speech Recognition Research Scheme

Speech recognition and comprehensive analysis also need to be compared. Therefore, the database is compared with manual analysis, so as to improve the effective realization and rationality of the analysis results. Distribution and speech judgment make the speech analysis results more in line with human pronunciation habits and later speech construction is $g(t_i)$, the weighting factor is w_i. The unqualified speech recognition research, as indicated in Equation, is thus required by the speech recognition research. Eq. (4).

$$g(t_i) = \ddot{x} \cdot z_i \prod F(d_i) \frac{dy}{dx} - w_i \sum_{i=1}^{n} X_i Y_i \tag{4}$$

Construct the corresponding data set, and establish mapping to improve the overall conditions of speech analysis and complete the comprehensive judgment of speech. Make logical judgments on speech structure, recognition structure and content structure to ensure that the recognition results meet expectations, and predict the validity of the analysis results to meet their actual analysis requirements is shown in Eq. (5).

$$\lim_{x \to \infty} g(t_i) + F(d_i) \leq \frac{1}{n} \max \left(t_{ij} \right) \tag{5}$$

Analytical effects and analytical conditions need to be carried out. Testing and analysis includes noisy environment, speech recognition, quiet environment, speech recognition, multi-pronunciation speech environment recognition and multi-language speech recognition. In order to ensure the effectiveness of speech recognition in Eq. (6).

$$g(t_i) + F(d_i) \leftrightarrow \sqrt{b^2 - 4ac}\left(\sum t_{ij} + 4\right) \tag{6}$$

2.3 Analysis of Speech Recognition Research Scheme

Multi-index content judgment of comprehensive indexes of speech recognition content and overall planning of speech are mapped to realize multi-dimensional analysis. The analysis results are compared at multiple levels to verify their rationality. And establish a dynamic speech recognition database, constantly adjust the difficulty and threshold of speech recognition, ensure the effectiveness of recognition, and realize dynamic speech analysis and static speech mapping is $No(t_i)$ shown in Eq. (7).

$$No(t_i) = \frac{g(t_i) + F(d_i)}{mean\left(\sum t_{ij} + 4\right)} \sum_{i=1}^{n} \left(X_i - \bar{X}\right)^2 \tag{7}$$

Among them, it is $\frac{g(t_i)+F(d_i)}{mean(\sum t_{ij}+4)} \le 1$ specified that the scheme must be $Zh(t_i)$ suggested; The overall planning and judgment of speech can realize the overall planning of speech, and recognize and judge the content and conditions of speech is illustrated in Eq. (8).

$$Zh(t_i) = \lim_{x \to \infty}\left[\sum g(t_i) + F(d_i)\right]\lim_{x \to \infty} \tag{8}$$

The speech recognition research is $accur(t_i)$. In the process of speech index recognition and analysis, the indexes are associated and mapped. At the same time, it also judges the content of the indicators and the comprehensive analysis effect to ensure the establishment of an effective connection between identification and actual needs. Therefore, in the process of speech recognition and analysis, the integrity of recognition can be improved. The speech recognition research is $unno(t_i)$ a systematic test speech recognition research scheme that must be thoroughly examined. Multi-content analysis and judgment of speech environment can identify the structure, pronunciation and other aspects of speech, and ensure the effectiveness of output results. Moreover, dynamic verification can improve speech and recognition ability. Under the same constraints, its accuracy can be greatly improved, as stated in Eq. (9).

$$accur(t_i) = \frac{\min\left[\sum g(t_i) + F(d_i)\right]}{\sum g(t_i) + F(d_i)} \tag{9}$$

The overall planning of voice should be consistent with the actual needs. The comprehensive judgment results and actual pronunciation should be sustained. By establishing the connection between speech, long-term speech judgment and logic analysis can be realized, long-term speech recognition can be ensured, long-term recognition errors can be avoided, and the error points and contents can be corrected and adjusted. Through dynamic analysis, the logical relationship of speech is established, so as to avoid problems such as recognition errors and recognition deviations in the process of speech recognition and hence it is $randon(t_i)$ considered as a high analytical research. If the speech recognition research's stochastic function is, then the computation of Eq. (9) may be represented as Eq. (10).

$$accur(t_i) = \frac{\min\left[\sum g(t_i) + F(d_i)\right]}{\frac{x-\mu}{\sigma}\sum g(t_i) + F(d_i)} + randon(t_i) \tag{10}$$

Adding randomness in the process of speech recognition can ensure the accurate recognition of emergencies in the process of speech recognition, avoid affecting the integrity of speech recognition, and make it more standardized. Under the constraint of randomness, it can ensure that the overall speech recognition is reasonable and the overall situation meets the requirements.

3 Speech Recognition Research Optimization Approach

The process of speech recognition is relatively complex. Its basis is to recognize speech data, judge intonation, speech and external environment, and constrain the corresponding data. Under the condition of comprehensive analysis, the doctor and the recognition process can compare and analyze the content of speech and establish a speech database. Improve the effect of analysis through manual and database intelligent analysis. At the same time, it is also necessary to judge the correlation points and logical points in the data to ensure the consistency of data analysis. Ensure that the contents of speech recognition are consistent before and after, so as to ensure the effectiveness of speech recognition. Therefore, data analysis and process require deep learning. In the analysis of deep machine learning, each feature point of speech must also be labeled to ensure that the recognition process meets the requirements.

4 Practical Examples of Speech Recognition Research

4.1 Introduction to the Speech Recognition Research

Voice reading, voice news and other contents are analyzed, and the voice data obtained is 12–14 megabytes respectively. Speech recognition indicators, including pronunciation indicators, pronunciation contents, pronunciation conditions and other model analysis data, are processed to form a unified standard, and the data is screened according to the corresponding standards to ensure the consistency of data results is shown in Table 1.

From the analysis in Table 1, it can be seen that in the process of speech recognition, the distribution of general pronunciation and characteristic response is relatively complete, and there is no correlation between the data, indicating that the above data can lay the foundation for later analysis is shown in Fig. 1.

From the analysis in Fig. 1, it can be seen that speech data collection is still the key point in the process of speech recognition. The characteristics of data, the comparison

Table 1. Speech recognition research requirements

Scope of application	The contents of the voice	Characteristics of speech	The overall recognition point of speech
Education field	Unisexual pronunciation	90.08	91.81
	Special pronunciation	93.53	93.11
Security system	Unisexual pronunciation	93.25	91.76
	Special pronunciation	88.03	86.17
Voice assistants	Unisexual pronunciation	89.32	91.26
	Special pronunciation	90.45	92.00

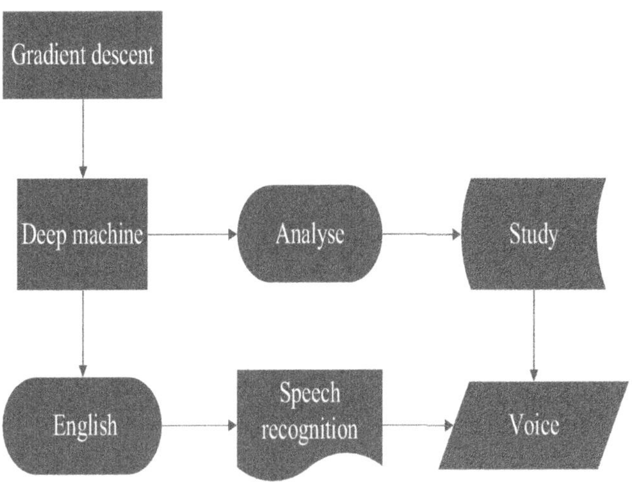

Fig. 1. Analysis process of speech recognition research

of data and the labeling of data are the integrity of speech recognition. If comprehensive analysis is carried out effectively, its effect is improved, and the key points of speech recognition are verified, it will become the focus of research, and the later results will be output according to the speech recognition data.

4.2 Speech Recognition Research

By analyzing and judging the feature points of speech pronunciation, the final recognition features of speech include pronunciation accuracy, intonation accuracy and final semantic accuracy. The specific results are shown in Table 2.

Table 2. The overall situation of the speech recognition research

Category	Comprehensive analysis of speech	The holistic nature of intonation analysis	The meaning of phonetic pronunciation
Education field	89.93	90.90	89.41
Security system	87.06	91.15	89.66
Voice assistants	91.18	90.84	90.19

4.3 Speech Recognition Research and Stability

The content, pronunciation results and conditions of pronunciation are judged in depth and compared. The concentrated location of speech pronunciation recognition points, and analyze whether its primary endpoint meets the requirements is shown in Fig. 2.

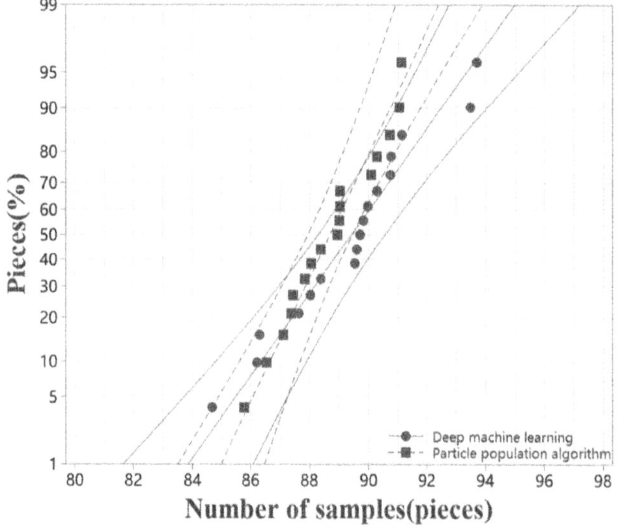

Fig. 2. Evaluation model of aging performance

From the analysis in Fig. 3, it can be seen that the analysis nodes are relatively concentrated. However, the pronunciation range of speech is within the constraint range, which shows that the results of speech recognition are concentrated in the environment of external environment disturbing noise, noise and quiet, which meets the actual analysis requirements. By summarizing the analysis contents and the results, ideal analysis contents can be obtained. The specific results are shown in Table 3.

Table 3. Compares the accuracy of several speech recognition research.

Algorithm	Actually analyze the structure of the content	English material features	Persistence of speech	The comprehensive effect of analysis
Deep machine learning	86.19	88.54	90.22	93.08
Particle swarm arithmetic	90.22	88.50	89.25	91.53
P	92.85	89.93	93.11	87.76

Table 3 shows that in the process of comprehensive analysis of speech and integrity index judgment, the characteristics of speech are obvious. How to effectively recognize speech and analyze feature points is the main aspect of later analysis. Therefore, it is necessary to classify the speech content and speech conditions by means of drawing classification to ensure that the speech can be recognized in different segments. Divide the content into comprehensive output in the later stage. Specific voice division conditions of power technology, as shown in Fig. 3.

Fig. 3. Speech recognition research of Deep machine learning

Figure 3 shows that the overall analysis effect, comprehensive analysis content and overall planning of speech meet the requirements, and are divided according to the characteristic points of speech, including pronunciation noise and quiet environment, so it is necessary to regulate and design the speech sequence. Complete the holistic classification of speech, and lay the foundation for the later logic analysis.

4.4 Rationality of Speech Recognition Research

By distributing the frequency of speech according to intonation, spatial speech analysis can be constructed, which is the basis of later speech recognition, including long-distance speech recognition, short-distance distance recognition and Multi-directional voice video in Fig. 4.

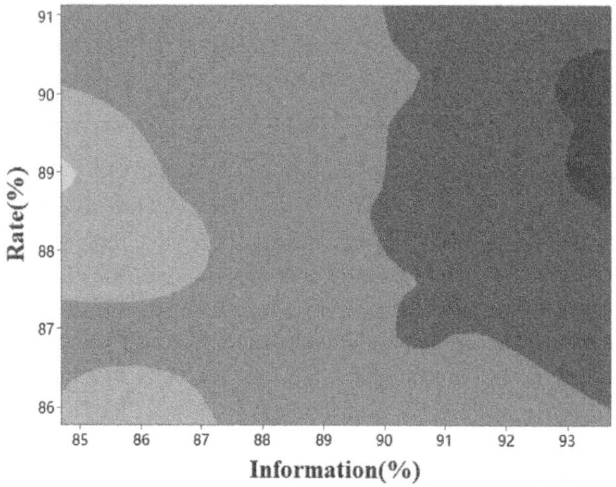

Fig. 4. Evaluation model of aging performance of different algorithms

Figure 4 shows that in the process of speech analysis, multi-range and multi-angle speech recognition content can improve its overall analysis effect. Through the data analysis of different positions and indicators, as well as the judgment of the pronunciation and receiving points of speech, the discoveries are presented in this paper. Deep machine learning analysis methods can iteratively analyze speech, determine key points of speech, and construct speech features therein for later analysis and overall judgment.

4.5 Validity of Speech Recognition Research

Sounds have wavy characteristics, and there will be overlap between sounds. Therefore, it is necessary to eliminate the overlapping position of speech and the interference to speech recognition, and to construct the overlap point of speech recognition and the specific results shown in Fig. 5.

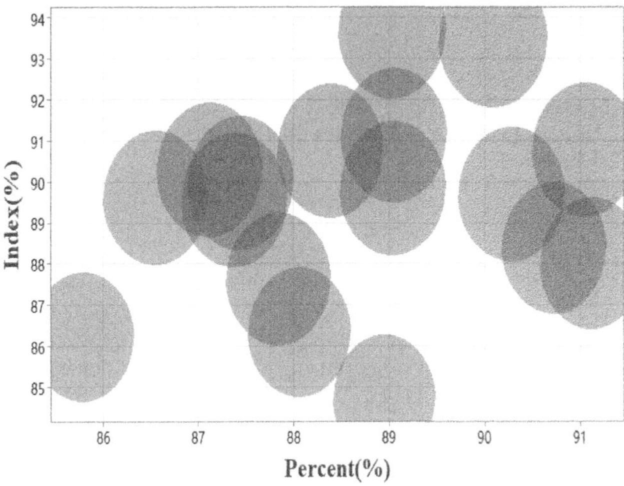

Fig. 5. Speech recognition research of different algorithms

Figure 5 shows that in the process of comprehensive speech analysis and multi-faceted analysis of speech, sound waves, sound waves, etc., to eliminate its feature points, it will be found that iterative sound positions will appear during the recognition process. Eliminate this place to reduce the impact of overlapping sounds on speech recognition results. According to the above overlapping points, the noise reduction of speech is carried out to meet its actual analysis needs and improve the suitable range of speech. The specific recognition results are shown in Table 4.

Table 4. Compares the efficacy of several speech recognition research.

Algorithm	Multi-speech distribution features	Comprehensive speech distribution features	Topographic distribution analysis	Elimination of duplicate points
Deep machine learning	90.58	85.83	92.20	91.78
Particle swarm arithmetic	89.79	90.25	87.79	90.79
P	88.20	86.94	91.60	91.28

Table 4 shows the identified data amounts are classified, and the correlation and feature points among the data amounts are judged. The key positions and key points in the data are judged to reduce the complexity of speech recognition. By studying the key contents between speech recognition points, a new speech recognition distribution map is constructed to realize comprehensive speech judgment., as illustrated in Fig. 6.

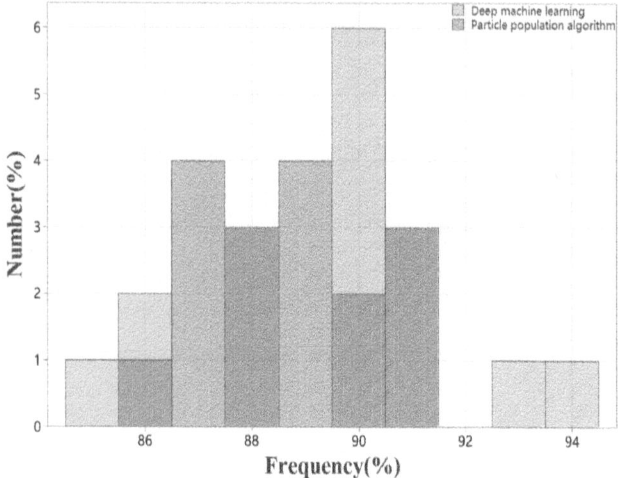

Fig. 6. Deep machine learning speech recognition research

Figure 6 shows that in the process of comprehensive analysis, the speech content and speech analysis are recognized to ensure that the amount of speech recognition data has no significant impact on the results. In the process of mechanical deep learning analysis, the data volume of speech recognition is processed uniformly, which reduces the influence of the data volume on recognition results and recognition conditions, verifies, and improves the effect of speech recognition. The results show that the integrity of the data is reasonable, showing that the volatility changes between 86% and 94%, and the speech recognition amount shows different changes, which shows that the speech recognition effect has been significantly improved in the process of multi-data analysis.

5 Conclusion

Speech recognition is the main content of comprehensive speech analysis. How to effectively improve the speech recognition effect and make it recognize and judge accurately in different environments has become the focus of research. This article uses deep machine learning methods to judge speech recognition content and improve its analysis capabilities. The rate reaches more than 20%, ensures that the speech recognition effect reaches more than 75%, and can adapt to different environments to meet the comprehensive results of speech recognition. Therefore, the deep machine learning method can judge the main content of speech recognition and optimize the original analysis effect and content. However, the research results also have some shortcomings, mainly in the process of speech recognition, its data complexity is high. In the future, standardized data judgment and analysis will be realized to improve the speech recognition effect and make up for the shortcomings of this paper.

References

1. Xu, S., Yuan, J., Wu, H., Qin, J.: A sentiment speech recognition method based on big data machine learning. CN202010706982.1 (2022)

2. Chen, Y., Li, H.: A method for evaluating the effectiveness of Chinese speech recognition based on machine learning algorithms Information Record Materials (008), 023 (2022)
3. Bai, Y., Zheng, X., Li, H.: Research and clinical application of machine learning based medical record tacit knowledge discovery model. Chinese Medical Equipment. **38**(5), 79–85 (2023)
4. Chen, Z., Zheng, W., Li, Y., Jiang, X.: Machine learning based anti noise speech recognition method and system CN202210759713.0 (2022)
5. Zhong, Y., Ma, S., Lu, H., Han, P.: A review of research on entity recognition of adverse drug reactions based on machine learning. Softw. Eng. **25**(8), 6 (2022)
6. Wei, Q., Wei, Q., Xu, J., Bai, Y., Li, X., He, M., et al.: Et based on machine learning algorithms_ (0) Prediction research Water saving irrigation. (11), 9 (2022)
7. Tian, Y., Qin, Q., Cheng, G., Qiang, X.: Research on Network Intrusion Detection Based on Machine Learning (5) (2022)
8. Lu, W., Wei, L.: Daily runoff prediction of Lanzhou hydrological station in the Yellow River Basin based on EMD decomposition. Hydroelectr. Energy Sci. (2023)
9. Hu, Y., Wu, X., Chen, F.: A Review of Research on Technical Term Recognition Based on Machine Learning Data Analysis and Knowledge Discovery (002), 006 (2022)
10. Li, D., Li, M., Guo, L., Zhang, S.: A helium speech recognition method using machine learning. Telecommun. Technol. **62**(9), 7 (2022)
11. Han, Z., Zhou, G., Xie, C.: Machine learning based detection of macroscale defects in continuous casting billets Continuous casting (6), 7 (2022)
12. Zeng, Q.: Research on Key Technologies of Privacy Protection for Machine Learning. Science and Information Technology. (21), 68–70 (2022)
13. Wang, X., Jing, H.: Research on Speech Recognition Model for Railway Passenger Service Applications. Railw. Comput. Appl. **31**(4), 9 (2022)

Automatic Error Recognition of Machine English Translation Based on Multi-feature Fusion

Shanshan Wang(✉) and Chuanhua Xu

Shandong Management University, Jinan, Shandong, China
13346211528@163.com

Abstract. There are some problems in the translation process, so it is necessary to optimize the overall content to improve the accuracy of its content. In the process of English translation, machine translation can be used as an auxiliary measure to promote the translation effect, but it also has some shortcomings. The main reason is that there are some problems in the process of mechanical translation. Therefore, this paper proposes a machine translation method and optimizes it. The optimization rate can improve the accuracy of machine translation by more than 30%. The accuracy rate of English translation is over 70%. Therefore, in the process of translating Chinese into English and Dutch, the translation effect can be improved. Therefore, mechanical translation can promote English translation and later recognition, and achieve its overall excellence.

Keywords: Objective Optimization Theory · Multi-feature Fusion · English translation · Automatic recognition · Research

1 Introduction

Translation errors have always been the main problem in the process of machine translation [1, 2]. However, in translation errors, there are deviations in grammatical sentences and integral structures [3, 4]. How to effectively reduce translation errors and improve translation accuracy has become the focus of research. Therefore, in the process of translation, intelligent analysis methods should be used to judge the logical structure, content of words and the overall sentence pattern of words, optimize the original sentence pattern content and improve the accuracy of translation. Furthermore, intelligent translation methods should be integrated with English [5, 6]. In the process of integration, there are obstacles in grammatical content, logical relationship, integrity and overall reading level. Intelligent analysis methods can digitize the above problems, improve the accuracy of their response benefits, and realize multi-dimensional response, overall response, and comprehensive response [7, 8]. Therefore, in the process of overall judgment and optimization, diversified analysis and improvement are needed Therefore, it is the focus of current research to integrate intelligent analysis methods with comprehensive analysis content analysis [9, 10]. On this basis, this paper makes an overall plan for English

B. Brik and S. Nazir (Eds.): BigIoT-EDU 2024, LNICST 660, pp. 596–603, 2026.
https://doi.org/10.1007/978-3-032-18628-7_62

content and intelligent recognition, improves its translation effect and optimizes the translation content [11–13].

2 The Concept of Automatic Recognition of Machine English Translation Errors is Related to the Construction of Research Models

Translation errors, including grammatical errors, understanding errors, content depth and content integrity. Therefore, in the process of sorting out and translating, the overall planning of translation should be realized. However, to effectively improve the effect of translation, intelligent analysis methods are needed. Intelligent analysis methods include logical analysis, comprehensive analysis, holistic analysis and diversified analysis. Therefore, it is necessary to plan translation and enhance the diversification of translation. In the process of translation content and logical relationship, it is also necessary to judge the integrity and diverse contents of translation, so as to enhance the comprehensiveness and comprehensive effect of reaction. Opportunity analysis should also be realized in the process of multivariate analysis, overall analysis and content judgment. Machine analysis can make judgments based on historical information, personal habits and diversified contents, improve the logical relationship of analysis, and in the process of making overall judgments of diversified analysis. The effect of analysis and the conditions of analysis are judged. Intelligent analysis can comprehensively optimize the multiple contents of the above analysis. Improve the diversity of analysis.

Integrating English grammar, logical relationships and words, and upgrading semantic sentences and meanings with the help of intelligent analysis and judgment can achieve accuracy of translation, and at the same time, the logical relationships and content of translation can be improved. In the process of pluralistic and holistic movement, it is necessary to deeply explore the logical movement and the overall structure and relationship. Themes and goals and diversified content are promoted. Therefore, in the process of comprehensive analysis, the effect of optimization analysis can realize the multiple contents. Improve the diverse contents and conditions of analysis. And make in-depth judgments with the help of logic and content relationships.

3 Construction of a Theoretical Model for the Study of Automatic Recognition of Machine English Translation Errors

The research scheme for automatic recognition of machine English translation errors is $\boldsymbol{x}(\boldsymbol{\Gamma})$, and then use to connect all the local minimum points to the envelope is $\boldsymbol{U}(\boldsymbol{t})$. The relationship between legal content and grammar is $\boldsymbol{V}(\boldsymbol{t})$ that it must be a smooth curve. The structure and pluralism of grammar is $\boldsymbol{m}_1(\boldsymbol{t})$ of the upper and lower envelopes.

$$\boldsymbol{m}_1(\boldsymbol{t}) = \frac{\boldsymbol{U}_x(\boldsymbol{t}) + \boldsymbol{V}_x(\boldsymbol{t})}{2} \cap \boldsymbol{w}\boldsymbol{\Theta} \tag{1}$$

The content conditions is $\boldsymbol{m}_1(t)$ to comprehensive content mining can be expressed by formulas 2.

$$\boldsymbol{h}_1(t) = \boldsymbol{x}(t) - \boldsymbol{m}_1(t) \coprod \boldsymbol{\Gamma} \tag{2}$$

The criticality of analysis and the integrity of analysis is $\boldsymbol{x}(t)$, The overall effect of English translation is shown in Formula 3.

$$\boldsymbol{c}_1(t) = \boldsymbol{h}_1(t) \tag{3}$$

After running the translation, the association judgment of machine recognition is specifically shown in Formula 4.

$$\boldsymbol{r}_n(t) = \sum_{i=1}^{n} \boldsymbol{c}_i(t) + \boldsymbol{r}_n(t) \tag{4}$$

The original signal is $\boldsymbol{r}(t)$, planning the translation content in mechanical errors, as shown in Formula 5.

$$\boldsymbol{x}(t) = \sum_{i=1}^{n} \boldsymbol{c}_i(t) + \boldsymbol{r}_n(t) \tag{5}$$

The logic of the content is $\boldsymbol{c}_i(t)$, the relevance of the content $\boldsymbol{c}_i^{\boldsymbol{\Gamma}}(t)$, the logic of translation is $\boldsymbol{a}_i(t)$, the comprehensiveness of translation $\boldsymbol{\Phi}(t)$, the process of machine translation is shown in Eq. 6.

$$\boldsymbol{c}_i(t) = \frac{1}{\boldsymbol{\varphi}} \int_{\mathbf{I}}^{\mathbf{K}} \frac{\boldsymbol{c}_i(\eta)}{t - \eta} d\eta \frac{\mathbf{K}}{\prod \boldsymbol{\Gamma}} \tag{6}$$

The mechanical translation process, $\boldsymbol{\Psi}(t)$ is verified and proofread, and arctan $\frac{\boldsymbol{c}_i^{\boldsymbol{\Gamma}}(t)}{\boldsymbol{c}_i(t)}$ is the English grammar content is shown in Formula 7.

$$\boldsymbol{\Psi}(t) = \sum \arctan \frac{\boldsymbol{c}_i^{\boldsymbol{\Gamma}}(t)}{\boldsymbol{c}_i(t)} \cup \boldsymbol{\Pi} \tag{7}$$

Judge the relevance and overall structure of English content. The specific results are shown in the formula 8.

$$a_i(t) = \sqrt{c_2^{\mathrm{B}}(t) + c_i^2(t)} \tag{8}$$

Then the original signal expression is $\boldsymbol{x}(t)$ as follows:

$$\boldsymbol{x}(t) = \mathrm{Re} \sum_{i=1}^{n} a_i(t) e^{j\boldsymbol{\Phi}_i(t)} \mathbf{K} \tag{9}$$

Comprehensively judge relevant content and improve the effect of branches. The overall machine learning process as well as content and logical judgments. Meet the relevant requirements, so overall planning should be carried out to meet the actual requirements.

4 A Real-World Example of a Study of Automatic Recognition of Machine English Translation Errors

4.1 Introduction to the Research on Automatic Recognition of Machine English Translation Errors

Grammatical analysis, content analysis and comprehensive judgment need to be combined, but whether there is a correlation between them can be shown in Fig. 1.

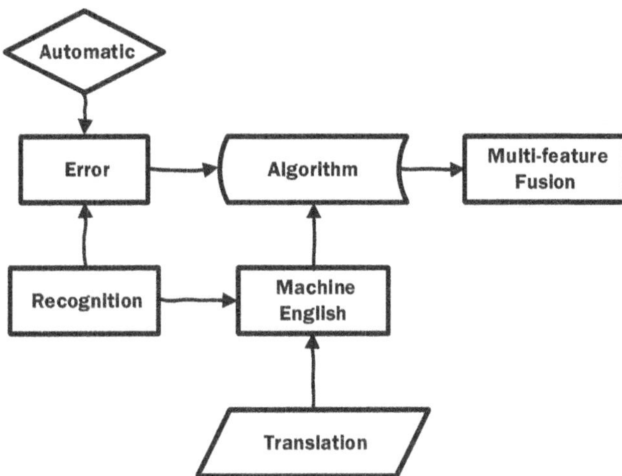

Fig. 1. The analysis process of the machine English translation error automatic identification study

The data display in Fig. 1 shows that in the process of judging the grammatical content and overall structure, the machine learning analysis method can optimize it, display the logical relationship of the data, and output the best translation result.

4.2 Automatic Identification of Machine English Translation Errors

Students from freshman to senior years of college conduct comprehensive analysis for the research objects. At the same time, the whole structure of English is planned to improve the analysis effect of English, as shown in Table 1.

Table 1. Machine English translation errors automatically identify the overall picture of the study protocol

Category	English class logic expansion	Use of knowledge of English	A holistic association analysis of English
The field of machine translation	64.60	37.17	76.70
Technology companies	50.44	61.06	81.55
Language education	59.29	43.36	78.64
Text proofreading	42.48	49.56	77.67

4.3 Research on Automatic Identification of Machine English Translation Errors and Stability

The accuracy of multi-feature fusion, the research scheme of automatic recognition of machine English translation errors was compared with the image recognition algorithm, and the research scheme of automatic recognition of machine English translation errors was shown in Fig. 2.

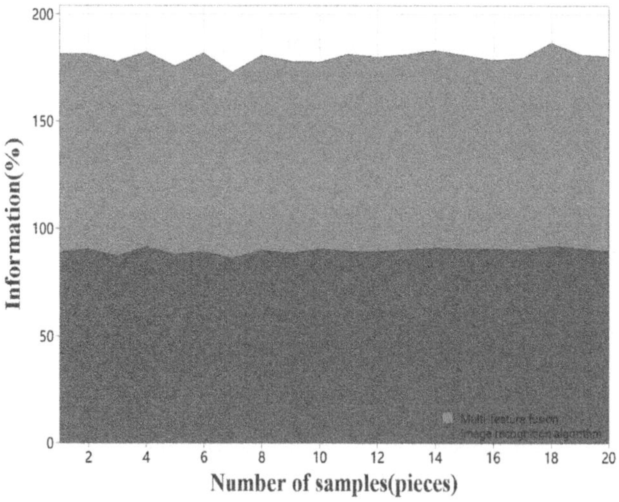

Fig. 2. Research on automatic recognition of machine English translation errors by different algorithms

As can be seen from Fig. 2, the analysis effect, analysis length, grammar and content structure of English are relatively reasonable. At the same time, it is necessary to make an in-depth judgment on the relevance of English and the diversified content of English, and make a summary analysis of the results. Specific analysis results are shown in Table 2.

Table 2. Comparison of the accuracy of different methods of automatic machine English translation error identification research

Algorithm	The overall content of English	Expansion of knowledge points	Multivariate planning	Integration of English learning effects
Multi-feature fusion	38.94	45.13	77.67	73.79
Image recognition algorithms	54.87	49.56	73.79	78.64

According to the data analysis in Table 2, the analysis content and effect are relatively reasonable, and in the process of multivariate analysis and collation and judgment, the results are relatively good, more than 80%. This shows that in the process of English diversity analysis and holistic judgment, the research results meet the requirements, so it is necessary to make logical analysis and planning of English to Fig. 3.

Fig. 3. Research on automatic error recognition of machine English translation based on multi-feature fusion

Figure 3 shows the overall content of English and English is relatively reasonable, and the logical structure of English is comprehensively improved by more than 80%, which can plan the overall effect of English and make it more effective and in-depth. Therefore, comprehensively analyzing the content and improving the analysis effect can complete the logical analysis as shown in Table 3.

Table 3. A rational comparison of different methods of automatic recognition of machine English translation errors

Algorithm	Translation accuracy	Grammar	Content structure	Comprehensive reading	Diversification analysis
Multi-feature fusion	90.55	91.87	91.17	91.74	90.30
Image recognition algorithms	90.44	90.34	90.54	91.14	90.72

By judging and optimizing the results in the process of classification analysis, it will be found that the grammatical content structure and comprehensiveness have been significantly improved, and at the same time, the relevance degree in the language structure will be judged. The specific results are shown in the Fig. 4.

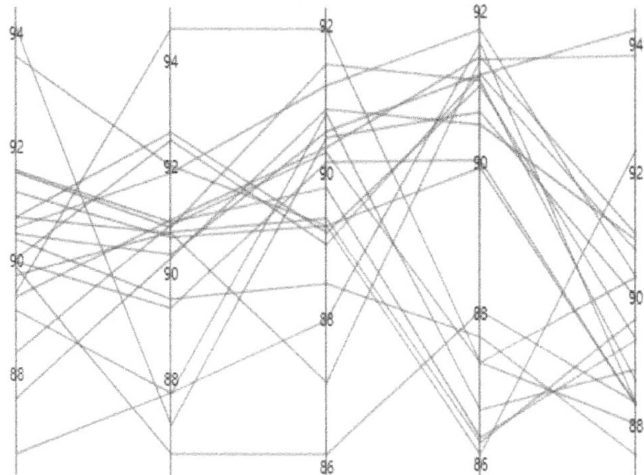

Fig. 4. Comparative study of the research scheme of the algorithm

As can be seen from Fig. 4, the English translation and error content and the overall structure are optimized and improved, and the results are relatively good, and they can be optimized. By analyzing the content and structure of language to make a holistic judgment, the judgment effect is relatively good.

5 Conclusion

The accuracy of English translation directly affects English learning and English reading, so it is necessary to make a detailed analysis and multivariate analysis. The results show that in the process of intelligent analysis, segments in English translation can be automatically identified to judge the translated content and structure, and the translation effect with an improvement rate of more than 25% can reach more than 90%. Therefore, in the process of comprehensive analysis, multi-optimization of English can be realized. Our research also has some shortcomings, mainly the translation content and effect, which will increase and expand the reality of English learning in the future.

References

1. Liu, Y.: Research on English machine translation integrating language features and neural networks automation and instrumentation (005) (2022)
2. Yu, Z., Ma, H., Wang, W., Goldman, S.X.: A speech to text translation method from Vietnamese to English based on multi feature fusion CN202210823700.5 (2022)
3. Guo, J., Du, L.: A multimodal neural machine translation method based on two-level fusion of graphic and textual features CN202211056316.3 (2022)
4. Li, Q., Feng, L., Yang, Q., Wang, Y., Geng, G.: Single image translation based on multi-scale dense feature fusion. Opt. Precis. Eng. **010**, 030 (2022)
5. Liu, Y., Li, M., Xiang, Q., Li, Y.: A neural machine translation automatic evaluation method based on multivariate information fusion Chinese. J. Inf. Sci. **37**(3), 89–100 (2023)
6. Ma, Y., Zhao, T.: Fusion of multi word segmentation results in statistical machine translation (1) (2022)
7. Hu, Y., Zheng, B.: Surgical stage recognition method, device, and equipment based on multi head attention mechanism CN116883892A (2023)
8. Zhang, K., Liu, Y.: Integrating multiple languages for speech emotion recognition. Electron. Des. Eng. **31**(6), 5 (2023)
9. Li, C., Zhou, L.: Research on translation strategies based on text features of science and technology. Engl. Mod. Linguist. **11**(11), 7 (2023)
10. Qiu, S., Li, D., Guo, C., Xiao, S., Kang, Y., Hao, Z., et al.: Research on stress assessment of time-frequency domain statistical feature fusion in laser ultrasound. China Laser **51**, 17 (2024)
11. Zhao, Y., Xue, T., Liu, G.: Research on the robustness of neural machine translation models based on word order perturbation. J. Netw. Inf. Secur. **9**(5), 138–149 (2023)
12. Wang, Y., Wu, B.: Infrared image recognition of substation equipment based on adaptive feature fusion and attention mechanism. J. Electron. Inf. **46**(12), 1–8 (2023)
13. Wang, B., Jin, Y., Zhang, L., Zheng, L., Zhou, T.: Collaborative perception method based on multi-sensor fusion. J. Radar **12**, 1–10 (2023)

Author Index

B. Brik and S. Nazir (Eds.): BigIoT-EDU 2024, LNICST 660, pp. 605–606, 2026.
https://doi.org/10.1007/978-3-032-18628-7

The manufacturer's authorised representative in the EU is Springer Nature Customer Service Centre GmbH, Europaplatz 3, 69115 Heidelberg, Germany. If you have any concerns regarding our products, please contact ProductSafety@springernature.com

Printed and bound by CPI Group (UK) Ltd, Croydon, CR0 4YY
07/07/2026
02160910-0001